Zondervan Illustrated Bible Backgrounds Commentary

ABOUT THE AUTHORS

General editor and commentary on Acts:

Clinton E. Arnold (Ph.D., University of Aberdeen), professor and chairman, department of New Testament, Talbot School of Theology, Biola University, Los Angeles, California

Gospel of John:

Andreas J. Köstenberger (Ph.D., Trinity Evangelical Divinity School; Dr. rer. soc. oec., Vienna University of Economics), professor of New Testament and Greek, director of Ph.D./Th.M. studies, Southeastern Baptist Theological Seminary, Wake Forest, North Carolina

Volume **2**

John, Acts

Zondervan Illustrated Bible Backgrounds Commentary

Clinton E. Arnold

GENERAL EDITOR

ZONDERVAN™

GRAND RAPIDS, MICHIGAN 49530

ZONDERVAN™

Zondervan Illustrated Bible Backgrounds Commentary: Volume 2, *John, Acts*
  John—Copyright © 2002 by Andreas J. Köstenberger
  Acts—Copyright © 2002 by Clinton E. Arnold

Requests for information should be addressed to:

Zondervan, *Grand Rapids, Michigan 49530*

Library of Congress Cataloging-in-Publication Data
  Zondervan illustrated Bible backgrounds commentary / Clinton E. Arnold, general editor.
    p.cm.
  Includes bibliographical references.
  Contents: v. 1. Matthew, Mark, Luke—v. 2. John, Acts—v. 3. Romans to Philemon—
v. 4. Hebrews to Revelation.
  ISBN 0–310–21806–3 (v. 1)—ISBN 0–310–21807–1 (v. 2)—ISBN 0–310–21808-X (v. 3)—
ISBN 0–310–21809–8 (v. 4)
  1. Bible. N.T.—Commentaries.   I. Arnold, Clinton E.
  BS2341.52.Z66 2001
  225.7—dc21   2001046801
                                                                      CIP

This edition printed on acid-free paper.

Printed in China

Interior design by Sherri L. Hoffman

02 03 04 05 06 07 08 /❖ HK/ 10 9 8 7 6 5 4 3 2 1

CONTENTS

INTRODUCTION

All readers of the Bible have a tendency to view what it says it through their own culture and life circumstances. This can happen almost subconsiously as we read the pages of the text.

When most people in the church read about the thief on the cross, for instance, they immediately think of a burglar that held up a store or broke into a home. They may be rather shocked to find out that the guy was actually a Jewish revolutionary figure who was part of a growing movement in Palestine eager to throw off Roman rule.

It also comes as something of a surprise to contemporary Christians that "cursing" in the New Testament era had little or nothing to do with cussing somebody out. It had far more to do with the invocation of spirits to cause someone harm.

No doubt there is a need in the church for learning more about the world of the New Testament to avoid erroneous interpretations of the text of Scripture. But relevant historical and cultural insights also provide an added dimension of perspective to the words of the Bible. This kind of information often functions in the same way as watching a movie in color rather than in black and white. Finding out, for instance, how Paul compared Christ's victory on the cross to a joyous celebration parade in honor of a Roman general after winning an extraordinary battle brings does indeed magnify the profundity and implications of Jesus' work on the cross. Discovering that the factions at Corinth ("I follow Paul . . .

I follow Apollos . . .") had plenty of precedent in the local cults ("I follow Aphrodite; I follow Apollo . . .") helps us understand the "why" of a particular problem. Learning about the water supply from the springs of Hierapolis that flowed into Laodicea as "lukewarm" water enables us to appreciate the relevance of the metaphor Jesus used when he addressed the spiritual laxity of this church.

My sense is that most Christians are eager to learn more about the real life setting of the New Testament. In the preaching and teaching of the Bible in the church, congregants are always grateful when they learn something of the background and historical context of the text. It not only helps them understand the text more accurately, but often enables them to identify with the people and circumstances of the Bible. I have been asked on countless occasions by Christians, "Where can I get access to good historical background information about this passage?" Earnest Christians are hungry for information that makes their Bibles come alive.

The stimulus for this commentary came from the church and the aim is to serve the church. The contributors to this series have sought to provide illuminating and interesting historical/cultural background information. The intent was to draw upon relevant papyri, inscriptions, archaeological discoveries, and the numerous studies of Judaism, Roman culture, Hellenism, and other features of the world of the New Testament and to make the results accessible to people in the church. We recognize that some readers of the commentary will want to go further, and so the sources of the information have been carefully documented in endnotes.

The written information has been supplemented with hundreds of photographs, maps, charts, artwork, and other graphics that help the reader better understand the world of the New Testament. Each of the writers was given an opportunity to dream up a "wish list" of illustrations that he thought would help to illustrate the passages in the New Testament book for which he was writing commentary. Although we were not able to obtain everything they were looking for, we came close.

The team of commentators are writing for the benefit of the broad array of Christians who simply want to better understand their Bibles from the vantage point of the historical context. This is an installment in a new genre of "Bible background" commentaries that was kicked off by Craig Keener's fine volume. Consequently, this is not an "exegetical" commentary that provides linguistic insight and background into Greek constructions and verb tenses. Neither is this work an "expository" commentary that provides a verse-by-verse exposition of the text; for in-depth philo-

logical or theological insight, readers will need to have other more specialized or comprehensive commentaries available. Nor is this an "historical-critical" commentary, although the contributors are all scholars and have already made substantial academic contributions on the New Testament books they are writing on for this set. The team intentionally does not engage all of the issues that are discussed in the scholarly guild.

Rather, our goal is to offer a reading and interpretation of the text informed by what we regard as the most relevant historical information. For many in the church, this commentary will serve as an important entry point into the interpretation and appreciation of the text. For other more serious students of the Word, these volumes will provide an important supplement to many of the fine exegetical, expository, and critical available.

The contributors represent a group of scholars who embrace the Bible as the Word of God and believe that the message of its pages has life-changing relevance for faith and practice today. Accordingly, we offer "Reflections" on the relevance of the Scripture to life for every chapter of the New Testament.

I pray that this commentary brings you both delight and insight in digging deeper into the Word of God.

Clinton E. Arnold
General Editor

LIST OF SIDEBARS

John

Acts

LIST OF CHARTS

INDEX OF PHOTOS
AND MAPS

ABBREVIATIONS

1. Books of the Bible and Apocrypha

1 Chron.	1 Chronicles
2 Chron.	2 Chronicles
1 Cor.	1 Corinthians
2 Cor.	2 Corinthians
1 Esd.	1 Esdras
2 Esd.	2 Esdras
1 John	1 John
2 John	2 John
3 John	3 John
1 Kings	1 Kings
2 Kings	2 Kings
1 Macc.	1 Maccabees
2 Macc.	2 Maccabees
1 Peter	1 Peter
2 Peter	2 Peter
1 Sam.	1 Samuel
2 Sam.	2 Samuel
1 Thess.	1 Thessalonians
2 Thess.	2 Thessalonians
1 Tim.	1 Timothy
2 Tim.	2 Timothy
Acts	Acts
Amos	Amos
Bar.	Baruch
Bel	Bel and the Dragon
Col.	Colossians
Dan.	Daniel
Deut.	Deuteronomy
Eccl.	Ecclesiastes
Ep. Jer.	Epistle of Jeremiah
Eph.	Ephesians
Est.	Esther
Ezek.	Ezekiel
Ex.	Exodus
Ezra	Ezra
Gal.	Galatians
Gen.	Genesis
Hab.	Habakkuk
Hag.	Haggai
Heb.	Hebrews
Hos.	Hosea
Isa.	Isaiah
James	James
Jer.	Jeremiah
Job	Job
Joel	Joel
John	John
Jonah	Jonah
Josh.	Joshua
Jude	Jude
Judg.	Judges
Judith	Judith
Lam.	Lamentations
Lev.	Leviticus
Luke	Luke
Mal.	Malachi
Mark	Mark
Matt.	Matthew
Mic.	Micah
Nah.	Nahum
Neh.	Nehemiah
Num.	Numbers
Obad.	Obadiah
Phil.	Philippians
Philem.	Philemon
Pr. Man.	Prayer of Manassah
Prov.	Proverbs
Ps.	Psalm
Rest. of Est.	The Rest of Esther
Rev.	Revelation
Rom.	Romans
Ruth	Ruth
S. of III Ch.	The Song of the Three Holy Children
Sir.	Sirach/Ecclesiasticus
Song	Song of Songs

Sus.	Susanna
Titus	Titus
Tobit	Tobit
Wisd. Sol.	The Wisdom of Solomon
Zech.	Zechariah
Zeph.	Zephaniah

2. Old and New Testament Pseudepigrapha and Rabbinic Literature

Individual tractates of rabbinic literature follow the abbreviations of the *SBL Handbook of Style*, pp. 79–80. Qumran documents follow standard Dead Sea Scroll conventions.

2 Bar.	2 Baruch
3 Bar.	3 Baruch
4 Bar.	4 Baruch
1 En.	1 Enoch
2 En.	2 Enoch
3 En.	3 Enoch
4 Ezra	4 Ezra
3 Macc.	3 Maccabees
4 Macc.	4 Maccabees
5 Macc.	5 Maccabees
Acts Phil.	Acts of Philip
Acts Pet.	Acts of Peter and the 12 Apostles
Apoc. Elijah	Apocalypse of Elijah
As. Mos.	Assumption of Moses
b.	Babylonian Talmud (+ tractate)
Gos. Thom.	Gospel of Thomas
Jos. Asen.	Joseph and Aseneth
Jub.	Jubilees
Let. Aris.	Letter of Aristeas
m.	Mishnah (+ tractate)
Mek.	Mekilta
Midr.	Midrash I (+ biblical book)
Odes Sol.	Odes of Solomon
Pesiq. Rab.	Pesiqta Rabbati
Pirqe. R. El.	Pirqe Rabbi Eliezer
Pss. Sol.	Psalms of Solomon
Rab.	Rabbah (+biblical book); (e.g., Gen. Rab.=Genesis Rabbah)

S. ʿOlam Rab.	Seder ʿOlam Rabbah
Sem.	Semahot
Sib. Or.	Sibylline Oracles
T. Ab.	Testament of Abraham
T. Adam	Testament of Adam
T. Ash.	Testament of Asher
T. Benj.	Testament of Benjamin
T. Dan	Testament of Dan
T. Gad	Testament of Gad
T. Hez.	Testament of Hezekiah
T. Isaac	Testament of Isaac
T. Iss.	Testament of Issachar
T. Jac.	Testament of Jacob
T. Job	Testament of Job
T. Jos.	Testament of Joseph
T. Jud.	Testament of Judah
T. Levi	Testament of Levi
T. Mos.	Testament of Moses
T. Naph.	Testament of Naphtali
T. Reu.	Testament of Reuben
T. Sim.	Testament of Simeon
T. Sol.	Testament of Solomon
T. Zeb.	Testament of Zebulum
Tanh.	Tanhuma
Tg. Isa.	Targum of Isaiah
Tg. Lam.	Targum of Lamentations
Tg. Neof.	Targum Neofiti
Tg. Onq.	Targum Onqelos
Tg. Ps.-J	Targum Pseudo-Jonathan
y.	Jerusalem Talmud (+ tractate)

3. Classical Historians

For an extended list of classical historians and church fathers, see *SBL Handbook of Style*, pp. 84–87. For many works of classical antiquity, the abbreviations have been subjected to the author's discretion; the names of these works should be obvious upon consulting entries of the classical writers in classical dictionaries or encyclopedias.

Eusebius

Eccl. Hist.	Ecclesiastical History

Josephus

Ag. Ap.	*Against Apion*
Ant.	*Jewish Antiquities*
J.W.	*Jewish War*
Life	*The Life*

Philo

Abraham	On the Life of Abraham
Agriculture	On Agriculture
Alleg. Interp	Allegorical Interpretation
Animals	Whether Animals Have Reason
Cherubim	On the Cherubim
Confusion	On the Confusion of Thomas
Contempl. Life	On the Contemplative Life
Creation	On the Creation of the World
Curses	On Curses
Decalogue	On the Decalogue
Dreams	On Dreams
Drunkenness	On Drunkenness
Embassy	On the Embassy to Gaius
Eternity	On the Eternity of the World
Flaccus	Against Flaccus
Flight	On Flight and Finding
Giants	On Giants
God	On God
Heir	Who Is the Heir?
Hypothetica	Hypothetica
Joseph	On the Life of Joseph
Migration	On the Migration of Abraham
Moses	On the Life of Moses
Names	On the Change of Names
Person	That Every Good Person Is Free
Planting	On Planting
Posterity	On the Posterity of Cain
Prelim. Studies	On the Preliminary Studies
Providence	On Providence
QE	Questions and Answers on Exodus
QG	Questions and Answers on Genesis
Rewards	On Rewards and Punishments
Sacrifices	On the Sacrifices of Cain and Abel
Sobriety	On Sobriety
Spec. Laws	On the Special Laws
Unchangeable	That God Is Unchangeable
Virtues	On the Virtues
Worse	That the Worse Attacks the Better

Apostolic Fathers

1 Clem.	*First Letter of Clement*
Barn.	*Epistle of Barnabas*
Clem. Hom.	*Ancient Homily of Clement* (also called *2 Clement*)
Did.	*Didache*
Herm. Vis.; Sim.	*Shepherd of Hermas, Visions; Similitudes*
Ignatius	*Epistles of Ignatius* (followed by the letter's name)
Mart. Pol.	*Martyrdom of Polycarp*

4. Modern Abbreviations

AASOR	Annual of the American Schools of Oriental Research
AB	Anchor Bible
ABD	*Anchor Bible Dictionary*
ABRL	Anchor Bible Reference Library
AGJU	Arbeiten zur Geschichte des antiken Judentums und des Urchristentums
AH	*Agricultural History*
ALGHJ	Arbeiten zur Literatur und Geschichte des Hellenistischen Judentums
AnBib	Analecta biblica
ANRW	*Aufstieg und Niedergang der römischen Welt*

ANTC	Abingdon New Testament Commentaries	BSV	Biblical Social Values
		BT	*The Bible Translator*
BAGD	Bauer, W., W. F. Arndt, F. W. Gingrich, and F. W. Danker. *Greek-English Lexicon of the New Testament and Other Early Christina Literature* (2d. ed.)	BTB	*Biblical Theology Bulletin*
		BZ	*Biblische Zeitschrift*
		CBQ	*Catholic Biblical Quarterly*
		CBTJ	*Calvary Baptist Theological Journal*
		CGTC	Cambridge Greek Testament Commentary
BA	*Biblical Archaeologist*	CH	*Church History*
BAFCS	Book of Acts in Its First Century Setting	CIL	*Corpus inscriptionum latinarum*
BAR	*Biblical Archaeology Review*	CPJ	*Corpus papyrorum judaicorum*
BASOR	*Bulletin of the American Schools of Oriental Research*	CRINT	*Compendia rerum iudaicarum ad Novum Testamentum*
BBC	*Bible Background Commentary*	CTJ	*Calvin Theological Journal*
		CTM	*Concordia Theological Monthly*
BBR	*Bulletin for Biblical Research*	CTT	Contours of Christian Theology
BDB	Brown, F., S. R. Driver, and C. A. Briggs. *A Hebrew and English Lexicon of the Old Testament*	DBI	*Dictionary of Biblical Imagery*
		DCM	*Dictionary of Classical Mythology.*
BDF	Blass, F., A. Debrunner, and R. W. Funk. *A Greek Grammar of the New Testament and Other Early Christian Literature*	DDD	*Dictionary of Deities and Demons in the Bible*
		DJBP	*Dictionary of Judaism in the Biblical Period*
		DJG	*Dictionary of Jesus and the Gospels*
BECNT	Baker Exegetical Commentary on the New Testament	DLNT	*Dictionary of the Later New Testament and Its Developments*
BI	*Biblical Illustrator*	DNTB	*Dictionary of New Testament Background*
Bib	*Biblica*		
BibSac	*Bibliotheca Sacra*		
BLT	Brethren Life and Thought	DPL	*Dictionary of Paul and His Letters*
BNTC	Black's New Testament Commentary	EBC	*Expositor's Bible Commentary*
BRev	*Bible Review*	EDBT	*Evangelical Dictionary of Biblical Theology*
BSHJ	Baltimore Studies in the History of Judaism		
		EDNT	*Exegetical Dictionary of the New Testament*
BST	The Bible Speaks Today		

EJR	*Encyclopedia of the Jewish Religion*	*JAC*	*Jahrbuch fur Antike und Christentum*
EPRO	Études préliminaires aux religions orientales dans l'empire romain	*JBL*	*Journal of Biblical Literature*
EvQ	*Evangelical Quarterly*	*JETS*	*Journal of the Evangelical Theological Society*
ExpTim	*Expository Times*	*JHS*	*Journal of Hellenic Studies*
FRLANT	Forsuchungen zur Religion und Literatur des Alten und Neuen Testament	*JJS*	*Journal of Jewish Studies*
		JOAIW	*Jahreshefte des Osterreeichischen Archaologischen Instites in Wien*
GNC	Good News Commentary		
GNS	Good News Studies	*JSJ*	*Journal for the Study of Judaism in the Persian, Hellenistic, and Roman Periods*
HCNT	*Hellenistic Commentary to the New Testament*		
HDB	*Hastings Dictionary of the Bible*		
HJP	*History of the Jewish People in the Age of Jesus Christ, by E. Schürer*	*JRS*	*Journal of Roman Studies*
		JSNT	*Journal for the Study of the New Testament*
HTR	*Harvard Theological Review*	JSNTSup	Journal for the Study of the New Testament: Supplement Series
HTS	Harvard Theological Studies		
HUCA	*Hebrew Union College Annual*	*JSOT*	*Journal for the Study of the Old Testament*
IBD	*Illustrated Bible Dictionary*	JSOTSup	Journal for the Study of the Old Testament: Supplement Series
IBS	*Irish Biblical Studies*		
ICC	International Critical Commentary	*JTS*	*Journal of Theological Studies*
IDB	*The Interpreter's Dictionary of the Bible*	*KTR*	*Kings Theological Review*
		LCL	Loeb Classical Library
IEJ	*Israel Exploration Journal*	LEC	Library of Early Christianity
IG	*Inscriptiones graecae*	LSJ	Liddell, H. G., R. Scott, H. S. Jones. *A Greek-English Lexicon*
IGRR	*Inscriptiones graecae ad res romanas pertinentes*		
ILS	*Inscriptiones Latinae Selectae*	MM	Moulton, J. H., and G. Milligan. *The Vocabulary of the Greek Testament*
Imm	*Immanuel*		
ISBE	*International Standard Bible Encyclopedia*	MNTC	Moffatt New Testament Commentary
Int	*Interpretation*	*NBD*	*New Bible Dictionary*
IvE	*Inschriften von Ephesos*	NC	Narrative Commentaries
IVPNTC	InterVarsity Press New Testament Commentary	NCBC	New Century Bible Commentary Eerdmans

NEAE	New Encyclopedia of Archaeological Excavations in the Holy Land	OTP	Old Testament Pseudepigrapha, ed. by J. H. Charlesworth
NEASB	Near East Archaeological Society Bulletin	PEQ	Palestine Exploration Quarterly
New Docs	New Documents Illustrating Early Christianity	PG	Patrologia graeca
		PGM	Papyri graecae magicae: Die griechischen Zauberpapyri
NIBC	New International Biblical Commentary		
NICNT	New International Commentary on the New Testament	PL	Patrologia latina
		PNTC	Pelican New Testament Commentaries
		Rb	Revista biblica
NIDNTT	New International Dictionary of New Testament Theology	RB	Revue biblique
		RivB	Rivista biblica italiana
		RTR	Reformed Theological Review
NIGTC	New International Greek Testament Commentary		
		SB	Sources bibliques
NIVAC	NIV Application Commentary	SBL	Society of Biblical Literature
NorTT	Norsk Teologisk Tidsskrift	SBLDS	Society of Biblical Literature Dissertation Series
NoT	Notes on Translation		
NovT	Novum Testamentum		
NovTSup	Novum Testamentum Supplements	SBLMS	Society of Biblical Literature Monograph Series
NTAbh	Neutestamentliche Abhandlungen		
		SBLSP	Society of Biblical Literature Seminar Papers
NTS	New Testament Studies		
NTT	New Testament Theology	SBS	Stuttgarter Bibelstudien
NTTS	New Testament Tools and Studies	SBT	Studies in Biblical Theology
OAG	Oxford Archaeological Guides	SCJ	Stone-Campbell Journal
		Scr	Scripture
OCCC	Oxford Companion to Classical Civilization	SE	Studia Evangelica
		SEG	Supplementum epigraphicum graecum
OCD	Oxford Classical Dictionary		
		SJLA	Studies in Judaism in Late Antiquity
ODCC	The Oxford Dictionary of the Christian Church		
		SJT	Scottish Journal of Theology
OGIS	Orientis graeci inscriptiones selectae	SNTSMS	Society for New Testament Studies Monograph Series
OHCW	The Oxford History of the Classical World		
		SSC	Social Science Commentary
OHRW	Oxford History of the Roman World		

SSCSSG	Social-Science Commentary on the Synoptic Gospels
Str-B	Strack, H. L., and P. Billerbeck. *Kommentar zum Neuen Testament aus Talmud und Midrasch*
TC	Thornapple Commentaries
TDNT	*Theological Dictionary of the New Testament*
TDOT	*Theological Dictionary of the Old Testament*
TLNT	*Theological Lexicon of the New Testament*
TLZ	*Theologische Literaturzeitung*
TNTC	Tyndale New Testament Commentary
TrinJ	*Trinity Journal*
TS	*Theological Studies*
TSAJ	Texte und Studien zum antiken Judentum
TWNT	*Theologische Wörterbuch zum Neuen Testament*
TynBul	*Tyndale Bulletin*
WBC	Word Biblical Commentary Waco: Word, 1982
WMANT	Wissenschaftliche Monographien zum Alten und Neuen Testament
WUNT	Wissenschaftliche Untersuchungen zum Neuen Testament
YJS	Yale Judaica Series
ZNW	*Zeitschrift fur die neutestamentliche Wissenschaft und die Junde der alteren Kirche*
ZPE	*Zeischrift der Papyrolgie und Epigraphkik*
ZPEB	*Zondervan Pictorial Encyclopedia of the Bible*

5. General Abbreviations

ad. loc.	in the place cited
b.	born
c., ca.	circa
cf.	compare
d.	died
ed(s).	editors(s), edited by
e.g.	for example
ET	English translation
frg.	fragment
i.e.	that is
ibid.	in the same place
idem	the same (author)
lit.	literally
l(l)	line(s)
MSS	manuscripts
n.d.	no date
NS	New Series
par.	parallel
passim	here and there
repr.	reprint
ser.	series
s.v.	*sub verbo*, under the word
trans.	translator, translated by; transitive

Zondervan
Illustrated
Bible
Backgrounds
Commentary

JOHN

by Andreas J. Köstenberger

Who Wrote the Gospel?

The Gospel itself claims to have been written by a member of Jesus' inner circle, an apostle, one of the Twelve. Since the apostolic office was foundational and unrepeatable in the history of the church (Acts 2:42; Eph. 2:20), their message, the gospel, has special authority. As an apostle (i.e., one specially commissioned by Jesus Christ), John was given a mission to testify to what he had seen and heard

(John 15:27; 1 John 1:1–4). In fact, being an eyewitness of Jesus' ministry was an indispensable requirement for apostleship (Acts 1:21–22; cf. John 1:14).

Implicit in John is also the claim of having been written by the disciple who was closest to Jesus during his earthly ministry. All the Gospel writers concur that John's relationship with Jesus was particularly close. In the present Gospel, the apostle conceals himself behind the

THE SEA OF
GALILEE

▶ John
IMPORTANT FACTS:

- **AUTHOR:** The apostle John, the son of Zebedee.
- **DATE:** A.D. 80–90.
- **OCCASION AND PURPOSE:**
  - To demonstrate that Jesus is the Messiah, the Son of God, by presenting and commenting on seven selected messianic signs.
  - To show that the Christian faith is universal, applying to Jews and non-Jews alike, and the only way to God.
  - To equip believers for mission.
  - To evangelize unbelievers by equipping believers to share the good news.
- **KEY THEMES:**
  1. Jesus as the preexistent, incarnate Word, the fully divine and human Messiah, the crucified and risen Savior of the world.
  2. The Jewish rejection of Jesus the Messiah and the universal offer of salvation to everyone who believes.
  3. Believers' need to follow Jesus through obedient, committed, and faithful discipleship, realized through love and unity in the Christian community and dependence on the Holy Spirit.

expression "the disciple whom Jesus loved" (13:23; 19:26; 20:2; 21:20). As an apostolic eyewitness, John is uniquely qualified to write an authoritative account of Jesus' life: "The man who saw it has given testimony, and his testimony is true" (19:35; cf. 21:24).

Where and Why Was the Gospel Written?

John's purpose is bound up with believing in Jesus and having life in his name (20:30–31). By presenting certain startling events in Jesus' ministry as evidence that Jesus is the long-awaited Messiah, John seeks to lead his readers to place their faith in Jesus. In the aftermath of the destruction of Jerusalem and the temple in A.D. 70, John shows Jesus to be the fulfillment of Jewish as well as universal human aspirations.

While ancient tradition places the writing of John's Gospel at Ephesus (Irenaeus, *Haer.* 3.1.2), the work ultimately transcends any one historical setting and applies to the entire church of John's as well as our day. Some of the material incorporated in this Gospel probably grew over years of preaching and teaching. John's awareness of the contents of the other canonical gospels may also have influenced his final selection of material.

Together with Rome, Corinth, Antioch, and Alexandria, Ephesus ranked among the most important urban centers of the Roman empire. Located at the intersection of major trade routes, Ephesus was the largest and most well-known city of Asia Minor (modern Turkey).

In an important development, Emperor Augustus declared Ephesus as capital of the province of Asia in place of Pergamum. The Ephesian temple of Artemis was one of the seven wonders of the ancient world, and its theater could seat 25,000 people. Ephesus acquired its first imperial temple (attaining to the status of *neokoros*, "temple warden") during the latter years of Domitian's reign (A.D. 81–96).

A Gospel of Decision

John's Gospel has rightly been called "a Gospel of decision." Every person must choose between light or darkness, faith or unbelief, life or death. Light, life, and salvation, in turn, can be attained only by faith in the crucified and risen Messiah, Jesus.

RUINS AT EPHESUS

(left) The town council building (the *prytaneion*).

(right) Columns of the mercantile agora.

▼

The Word's Eternal Preexistence (1:1–2)

Like the other evangelists, John gives an account of the life and ministry of Jesus. But he does so differently from the start. Matthew and Luke begin their Gospels with Jesus' family tree and an account of his birth. Mark jumps immediately to the ministry of John the Baptist, Jesus' forerunner. But John begins his account by showing Jesus embarking on a journey—not from Galilee to Jerusalem, but from existing eternally with God to becoming a human being like us. Thus we start in 1:1 in eternity past and arrive in 1:6 around A.D. 29 in the land of Palestine. Jesus' ministry is about to begin.

In the beginning (1:1). When hearing the phrase "in the beginning," any person in John's day familiar with the Scriptures would immediately think of the opening verse of Genesis: "In the beginning God created the heavens and the earth." John reaches back even farther into eternity past. His point is that in the beginning, even prior to creation, someone already existed along with the Father: the Word (cf. 1 John 1:1).

Was the Word (1:1). Echoes of the creation account continue here with allusion to the powerful and effective word of God ("And God said, 'Let there be light,' and there was light"; Gen. 1:3). The psalmists and prophets alike portray God's word (*logos*) in almost personal terms (e.g., Ps. 33:6; 107:20; 147:15, 18; Isa. 55:10–11). Isaiah, for instance, describes God's "word" as coming down from heaven and returning to him after achieving the purpose for which it was sent (Isa. 55:10–11). John takes the prophetic depiction of God's word in the Old Testament one decisive step further. No longer is God's word merely spoken of in personal terms; it now has appeared as a real person, the Lord Jesus Christ (cf. 1 John 1:1; Rev. 19:13).

While the primary source of John's depiction of Jesus as the Word is the Old Testament, his opening lines would resonate with his Greek-speaking audience. In Stoic philosophy, for instance, *logos* was used to refer to the impersonal principle of Reason, which was thought to govern the universe. It is a mark of John's considerable theological genius that he is able to find a term ("the Word") that is at the same time thoroughly biblical—that is, rooted in Old Testament teaching—and highly relevant for his present audience.[1]

The Word was with God (1:1). The term "God" (*theos*) is familiar to John's readers since it refers to the God revealed in the Old Testament. This word occurs in Genesis 1:1 (LXX) with reference to the Creator. The same expression is also used for "god" in the Greco-Roman world whose pantheon was made up of dozens of deities. In contrast, the Jews believed in only one God (Deut. 6:4).

The Word was God (1:1). Having distinguished the Word (i.e., Jesus) from God, John now shows what both have in common: They are God.[2] From the patristic era (Arius) to the present (Jehovah's Witnesses), it has been argued that this verse merely identifies Jesus as *a* god rather than as God, because there is no definite article in front of the word *theos*. But John, as a monotheistic Jew, would hardly have referred to another person as "a god." Also, if he had placed a definite article before *theos*, this would have so equated God and the Word that the distinction established between the two persons in the previous clause ("the Word was *with* God") would have been all but obliterated. Clearly calling Jesus God stretched the boundaries of first-century Jewish monotheism.[3]

Moreover, in Greek syntax it is common for a definite nominative predicate noun preceding the verb *einai* (to be) not to have the article,[4] so that it is illegitimate to infer indefiniteness from the lack of the article in the present passage. If, in fact, John had merely wanted to affirm that Jesus was divine, there was a perfectly proper Greek word for that concept (the adjective *theios*).

The Word's Involvement in Creation (1:3–5)

Through him all things were made (1:3). The affirmation that all things were made through *wisdom* or through God's *Word* is thoroughly in keeping with Jewish belief. John's contention, however, that everything came into being through "him"—that is, *Jesus*, God-become-flesh—is startling indeed. Nevertheless, this notion is in no way unique to John; it pervades much of the New Testament. Paul speaks of Jesus as the image of the invisible God, through whom and for whom all things were created (Col. 1:16). Jesus is the "one Lord . . . through whom all things came and through

whom we live" (1 Cor. 8:6). Hebrews refers to Jesus as God's Son through whom he made the universe (Heb. 1:2). The Aramaic Targum refers to the "word" (*memra*) of the Lord as an agent of creation.[5] Greco-Roman parallels likewise portray various intermediaries as instrumental in creation (e.g., Lucretius, *Rer. Nat.* 1:4–5, 21–23 [first cent. B.C.]), as does Philo, the Hellenistic Jewish philosopher, who identifies wisdom and the Word (*Alleg. Interp.* 1.65; *Heir* 191; *Dreams* 2.242–45) and portrays the latter as the instrument through which the universe was created (*Cherubim* 127).[6]

Life . . . light (1:4). Both "life" and "light" are universal religious terms,[7] but John's teaching is deeply rooted in the Old Testament. At creation, calling forth "light" was God's first creative act (Gen. 1:3–5). Later, God placed lights in the sky to separate between light and darkness (1:14–18). Light, in turn, makes it possible for "life" to exist. Thus on the fifth and sixth days of creation, God makes animate life to populate both the waters and dry land, culminating in his creation of humankind (1:20–31; 2:7; 3:20).

Now, according to John, life was "in him," Jesus. Jesus is the source of life, including both physical and spiritual ("eternal") life. He also is the source of

▶ The Stoic Understanding of "the Word"

In Stoic thought, which drew on ideas attributed to the pre-Socratic philosopher Heraclitus (c. 500 B.C.), Logos was Reason, the impersonal rational principle governing the universe. Zeno, the founder of this school of thought (c. 336–263 B.C.), believed that "the General Law, which is Right Reason, pervading everything, is the same as Zeus, the Supreme Head of the government of the universe" (*Fragm.* 162).

People were to live in keeping with Reason, whose spark was thought to reside within them, or at least with the wisest and best of them. Stoic teaching on the Logos may have constituted common ground between John and some of his readers but hardly represents the major source of John's teaching regarding "the Word."

light, since only those who possess spiritual, eternal life have within themselves the capacity to "walk in the light," that is, to make moral decisions that are in accordance with the revealed will of God.

This again shows John's knack for contextualization. While drawing on solidly Old Testament concepts, he employs these universal terms to engage adherents of other religions and worldviews. For some, light was wisdom (or wisdom was even superior to light; cf. Wisd. Sol. 7:26–30); for others, light was given by the Mosaic law (*2 Bar.* 59:2) or Scripture (Ps. 19:8; 119:105, 130; Prov. 6:23); still others looked for enlightenment in philosophy, morality, or a simple lifestyle. Into this religious pluralism of his day, John proclaims Jesus as the supreme Light, who is both eternal and universal and yet personal.

Light . . . darkness (1:5). Beneath this contrast between light and darkness lies a significant cluster of Old Testament passages. Most interesting in this regard are several instances in Isaiah that depict the coming Messiah as a light entering the darkness. In Isaiah 9:2, we read that "the people walking in darkness have seen a great light; on those living in the land of the shadow of death a light has dawned." In Isaiah 60:1–5, a time is envisioned when the nations will walk in God's light and the glory of the Lord will shine brightly.[8]

Some believe John is here alluding to the Greek dualism between light and darkness. Rather than affirming belief in a personal God who is sovereign, all-powerful, and good, the Greeks viewed reality in terms of polar opposites, such as light and darkness or good and evil. John, however, refutes this kind of thinking in his first letter, where he states emphatically, "God is light; in him there

◄

MENORAH

The seven-branched Jewish candelabrum.

is no darkness at all" (1 John 1:5). Another kind of light/darkness dualism is found in the Dead Sea Scrolls, particularly in the so-called "War Scroll" (1QM) depicting the battle between the "sons of light" and the "sons of darkness." But because of the sectarian nature of the Qumran community, light is never offered to those who live in darkness (cf. 1QS 3:21; 4:9–14).[9]

In John, however, Jesus urges his listeners to "put your trust in the light while you have it, so that you may become sons of light" (John 12:36; cf. 8:12; 9:5). Light and darkness are no equally matched duality, but in the titanic battle between Jesus and Satan, Jesus, "the light," emerges as the overwhelming victor. Regarding this final outcome, John's readers are never left in suspense. Rather, the evangelist announces at the outset that the darkness has not overcome the light (1:5).[10] To be sure, at the cross, the forces of evil appear to have gained the upper hand; but this is followed by the resurrection.

John the Witness to the Light (1:6–8)

A man . . . sent from God (1:6). The evangelist now moves on to anchor Jesus' ministry firmly in salvation history. This phrase is reminiscent of the Old Testament description of a prophet whose role was to function as a spokesman for God (e.g., Ezek. 2:3).

His name was John (1:6). The name "John," a common name in the Hellenistic world of that day, occurred frequently among the members of the Jewish priesthood, which included John's father Zechariah (Luke 1:5).[11] "John" in this Gospel always means "John the Baptist." The "other John" known from Matthew, Mark, and Luke—that is, John the apostle, the son of Zebedee—is not referred to by name in this Gospel. It is likely that he, as the author of the present gospel, conceals himself behind the phrase "the disciple whom Jesus loved" (first used in 13:23; see comments there).

All . . . might believe (1:7). The desired (though not actual) result of John's ministry is that "all might believe" in Jesus (cf. comments on 1:9). The expression "believe" is found frequently in the Old Testament to describe the trust God desires from his people. Abraham "believed the LORD" and thus became the father, not just of the Jewish nation, but of all believers (Gen. 15:6).[12] Israel as a nation, on the other hand, is known

in the Old Testament not so much for her faith in God as for her unbelief (John 12:38; cf. Isa. 53:1). While John is not averse to "believing" as the affirmation of certain religious truths, he is much more concerned about active, relational trust in Jesus Christ.

The World's Rejection of the Light (1:9–11)

The true light (1:9). The coming of the Messiah is frequently depicted in the Old Testament in terms of light.[13] An important oracle, picked up also by Qumran, envisions the coming of "a star" out of Jacob (Num. 24:17). Isaiah, too, describes the coming of the Messiah as "a light" shining in darkness (Isa. 9:2; cf. 42:6–7; see comments on John 1:5). Malachi announces that "the sun of righteousness will rise with healing in its wings" (Mal. 4:2). Echoing these words, Zechariah (father of John the Baptist) says about Jesus that "the rising sun will come to us from heaven to shine on those living in darkness" (Luke 1:78–79). By affirming that Jesus is the "true light"—just as he is the "true bread from heaven" (John 6:32) and the "true vine" (15:1)—John indicates that Jesus is the fulfillment of Old Testament hopes and expectations.

Some have suggested that John is here engaging the Greek dualism between shadow and reality, contending that the expression "true light" is better rendered "*real* light" (in distinction to a mere resemblance). Perhaps some of John's Greek-speaking readers took it that way. But the primary contrast seems to be, not between real over against ideal in the Greek sense, but between earlier manifestations of God in Old Testament times through the law or various prophets and God's final, definitive revelation through Jesus Christ (cf. 1:17; 5:39; 12:38; cf. Heb.

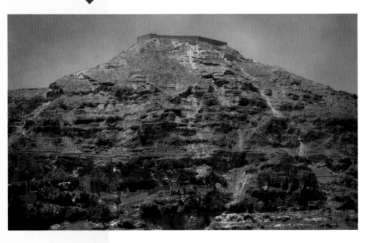

JUDEAN WILDERNESS

Jebel Quruntul, a mountain in the desert near Jericho associated with the temptation of Jesus.

1:1–3). In that sense, previous manifestations of God were merely "foreshadowing" the coming of the fulfillment, Jesus, who is the very essence to which the entire Old Testament symbolism points (see also John's portrayal of certain of Jesus' acts as "signs").

The true light . . . was coming into the world (1:9). This is a subtle way to convey the Christian gospel to Hellenistic ears. There also may be an implied contrast with Hellenistic religions that offered false "light."

Believing in His Name (1:12–13)

Received him . . . believed in his name (1:12). On one level, believing in "the name" of Jesus is nothing other than to believe in Jesus (3:18). Yet the phrase "believe *in the name* of Jesus" places particular emphasis on the fact that in order to believe in Jesus one must believe that he bears the divine name, the name of God. In the early church, the name of Jesus could simply be called "the Name" (Acts 5:40–41; 3 John 7).

Gave the right to become children of God (1:12). The expression translated "right" (*exousia*; cf. 5:27; 10:18; 17:2; 19:10) refers to the authorization or legitimate claim of becoming God's children, which has now been made available to all who believe in Jesus as Messiah. This assumes that in one sense sinful people are not God's children (even though they are created by God) unless and until they believe in Jesus Christ. John is careful to distinguish believers as children (*tekna*) of God from Jesus, who is the unique Son (*huios*) of God. In the Old Testament, the Hebrews are called God's children (Deut. 14:1), even God's son and firstborn (Ex. 4:22). Yet Old Testament saints did not

call God "Father" or "Abba"; this constitutes a later development.

Not of natural descent, nor of human decision or a husband's will (1:13). "Natural descent" renders the phrase *ex haimatōn* (lit., "out of bloods"); it denotes a blood relationship, on the basis of the belief that natural procreation entails the intermingling of bloods (cf. Ezek. 16:6; Wisd. Sol. 7:1–2). Descent from the patriarchs was vital in the Jews' understanding of their divine sonship (cf. esp. John 8:31–41). The phrase "a husband's will" implies the Old Testament concept of male headship.

But born of God (1:13). In the Old Testament, God is said to have given birth to his people Israel (Deut. 32:18). See comments on John 3.

The Incarnation of the Word (1:14)

The Word became flesh (1:14). Rather than using the term "(hu)man (being)" (*anthrōpos*) or "body" (*sōma*), John here employs the almost crude term "flesh" (*sarx*; cf. Rom. 8:3). The affirmation that "the Word became flesh" takes the opening statement ("in the beginning was the Word") one step further: That same Word has now taken on human nature. While John does not elaborate on the precise way in which Jesus did so, his contention that deity assumed human nature in Jesus would have been anathema for Greeks, who held to a spirit-matter dualism and could hardly have imagined immaterial Reason becoming a physical being. The idea of gods appearing in human form in itself was not uncommon to the ancients. But John makes clear that the Word did not merely manifest itself as an apparition—as was alleged by the Docetists (from *dokeō*, "seem")—but that it literally became flesh.[14]

And made his dwelling among us (1:14). The Greek word for "made his dwelling" (*skēnoō*) literally means "to tabernacle" (from the word for "tent"). This rare term, which is used elsewhere in the New Testament only in the book of Revelation (Rev. 7:15; 12:12; 13:6; 21:3), suggests that in Jesus, God has come to take up residence among his people once again, in a way even more intimate than when he dwelt in the midst of Israel in the tabernacle (Ex. 40:34–35; see further the chart below). Jesus' "making his dwelling among us" is here related to the Incarnation, that is, his assumption of human flesh. In a slightly different application, both Paul and Peter refer to the human body as a "tent" (cf. 2 Cor. 5:1, 4; 2 Peter 1:13–14). The Matthean equivalent is Jesus as Isaiah's Immanuel, "God with us" (Matt. 1:23; cf. Isa. 7:14; 8:8, 10; Matt. 18:20; 28:20).

His glory (1:14). In the Old Testament, God's glory was said to dwell first in the tabernacle and later in the temple.[15] The intertestamental period was marked by the absence of God's revelation in light of Israel's apostasy. Now, in Jesus, God's glory has taken up residence in the midst of his people once again.

The One and Only (1:14). In Genesis 22:2, Isaac is called Abraham's "only" son, even though the patriarch had earlier fathered Ishmael. "Only" son therefore means "unique" son (in Isaac's case, son of promise). In both the Old Testament and intertestamental literature, the Son of David as well as Israel are called God's "firstborn" or even "only" son (cf. Ps. 89:27; *4 Ezra* 6:58; *Pss. Sol.* 18:4). In a decisive step, John applies the designation "One and Only" (*monogenēs*) to God's unique Son par excellence, Jesus (cf. 1:18; 3:16, 18; 1 John 4:9).

The Father (1:14). The word "Father" is more personal than the term "God" (*theos*; see comments on 1:1). It is Jesus' favorite way of referring to God in John. While Jesus taught his disciples to call God "Father" as well (Matt. 6:9 par.), his divine sonship remains unique. Thus, shortly after his resurrection, Jesus tells Mary to tell his disciples, "I am returning to *my* Father and *your* Father, to *my* God and *your* God" (John 20:17). The relationship Christians are able to enjoy with God their "Father" is unique among the world's religions, many of which portray God as remote, stern, impersonal, or mystical. The special fatherhood of God for believers is already implied in the reference to the "children of God" who are "born of God" (see 1:12–13 above).

Full of grace and truth (1:14). "Grace" occurs in John's Gospel only in 1:14–17 in the phrase "grace and truth." In distinction from the Pauline writings (where it denotes God's unmerited favor; see Eph. 2:8–9), "grace" in this

THE TABERNACLE

A model of the courtyard and structure.

▼

Gospel, in conjunction with "truth," alludes to the Old Testament phrase "lovingkindness and truth" (cf. Ps. 25:10; 26:3; 40:10; Prov. 16:6; see also Ps. 83:12 LXX = Ps. 84:11). The word "truth" refers to God's covenant faithfulness to his people Israel. According to John, this faithfulness found ultimate expression in God's sending of Jesus, his unique Son.

John's Witness (1:15–16)

He . . . has surpassed me because he was before me (1:15). John the Baptist was six months older than Jesus (Luke 1:24, 26) and began his ministry before Jesus did (3:1–20). The Old Testament generally (though not without exception) supports the notion that rank and honor are directly tied to one's age (Gen. 49:3; Prov. 16:31). Thus priority in time (such as being the firstborn) implied preeminence (Deut. 21:17; Isa. 61:7). In the context of John's openings words (where Jesus is portrayed as having existed with God from eternity), the Baptist's personal confession also points to Jesus' eternal origin (John 1:14; cf. 8:58; 12:41) and thus his preeminence.

Fullness of his grace (1:16). The term "fullness" occupied an important place in Gnosticism, the first major Christian heresy, which began to germinate in the second half of the first century (1 Tim. 6:21). For John, fullness can be found in one thing only: the grace of God displayed in Jesus, whose purpose was to bring "life . . . to the full" (10:10). When John attributes "fullness of grace" to Jesus, he evokes parallels with similar descriptions of God in the Old Testament.[16]

The Superior Revelation Brought by Jesus (1:17–18)

The law was given through Moses; grace and truth came through Jesus Christ (1:17). The law is seen as the gracious gift of God, albeit a gift that has now been superseded by God's gracious giving of his Son.[17] Note that what is referred to here is the event of the giving of the law, not later abuses (including legalism) by the Jews (cf. Paul).

No one has ever seen God (1:18). In the Old Testament, God had stated clearly that no one could see his face and live (Ex. 33:20). Moses received a glimpse of God's "back" (33:23), as did Hagar (metaphorically; Gen. 16:13). Old Testament saints were usually terrified of seeing God (Ex. 3:6b; Judg. 13:21–22;

Parallels between John 1:14–18 and Exodus 33–40 [A-1]	
John 1:14–18	**Exodus 33–34**
The Word "tented" among the disciples (1:14)	God gloriously dwelt in a tent (33:7; 40:34–35)
The disciples saw the Word's glory (1:14)	God's glory passes by Moses (33:18–23; 34:6–7)
Jesus is full of grace and truth (1:14, 17)	God abounds in lovingkindness and truth (34:6)
Disciples receive (lit.) "grace instead of grace" (1:16)	Israel finds grace in God's sight (33:14)
The law was given through Moses (1:17)	Moses was given the law (34:27–28)
Jesus is mediator between God and humanity (1:17–18)	Moses is mediator between God and Israel (34:32–35)
No one has ever seen God (1:18)	No one can see God's face and live (33:20)

| \multicolumn{3}{c}{Chronology of Jesus' Ministry in John's Gospel[A-2]} |

TIME	LOCATION/EVENT	PASSAGE IN JOHN
Origin (1:1–18)		
Eternity Past	The Word was with God	1:1–18
Initial ministry (1:19–2:12; A.D. 29–30)		
Summer/fall 29	John the Baptist near the Jordan	1:19–34
Subsequently	Jesus' calling of his first disciples	1:35–51
Winter/spring 30	The wedding at Cana of Galilee	2:1–12
First Passover and first full year of ministry (2:13–4:54; A.D. 30–31)		
April 7, 30	Jesus' first Passover (Jerusalem)	2:13–3:21
Spring/summer 30	John the Baptist near the Jordan	3:22–36
Dec./Jan./Feb. 30/31?	Jesus' ministry in Samaria	4:1–45
Subsequently	The healing at Cana of Galilee	4:46–54
Second year of ministry (ch. 5; A.D. 31–32)		
March 27, 31	Passover not recorded in John	Matt. 12:1 par.?
Oct. 21–28, 31?	The Sabbath controversy (Jerusalem)	5:1–47
Second Passover recorded in John and third year of ministry (6:1–11:54; A.D. 32–33)		
April 13 or 14, 32	Jesus' second Passover recorded in John (Galilee)	6:1–21
Subsequently	Jesus' teaching in the synagogue of Capernaum	6:22–71
Sept. 10–17, 32	Jesus at the Feast of Tabernacles (Jerusalem)	7:1–52; 8:12–59
Oct./Nov. 32?	Healing of blind man, good shepherd discourse	9:1–10:21
Dec. 18–25, 32	Jesus at the Feast of Dedication (Jerusalem)	10:22–39
Jan./Feb. 33?	Jesus' withdrawal to the area near the Jordan	10:40–42
March 33?	The raising of Lazarus (Bethany near Jerusalem)	11:1–53
March 33?	Jesus' withdrawal to Ephraim	11:54
Third Passover in John, passion week, resurrection appearances (11:55–21:25; A.D. 33)		
Friday, March 27, 33	Jesus arrives at Bethany	11:55–12:1
Saturday, March 28, 33	Dinner with Lazarus and his sisters	12:2–11
Sunday, March 29, 33	"Triumphal entry" into Jerusalem	12:12–50
Monday–Wednesday, March 30–April 1, 33	Cursing of fig tree, temple cleansing, temple controversy, Olivet discourse	Synoptics
Thursday, April 2, 33	Jesus' third Passover recorded in John (Jerusalem), betrayal, arrest	13:1–18:11
Friday, April 3, 33	Jewish and Roman trials, crucifixion, burial	18:12–19:42
Sunday, April 5, 33	The empty tomb, first resurrection appearance	20:1–25
Sunday, April 12, 33	Second resurrection appearance recorded in John	20:26–31
Prior to May 14, 33	Third resurrection appearance recorded in John	21[A-3]

Job 13:11; Isa. 6:5). The reason for humanity's inability to see God is twofold: (1) God is spirit (John 4:24); (2) mankind fell into sin and was expelled from God's presence (Gen. 3; Isa. 59:2). Jesus surmounted both obstacles: (1) He who is himself God became a human being so that others could see God in him (John 14:9–10); (2) he who was without sin died for us sinners, so that our sinfulness no longer keeps us from entering into fellowship with God (Rom. 5:1–2, 6–11).

But God the One and Only (1:18). The phrase "God the One and Only," which John here uses with reference to Jesus, is both striking and unusual (though note the equally clear ascriptions of deity to Jesus in 1:1 and 20:28). Some manuscripts, apparently in an effort to soften this statement, read "one and only Son" in keeping with 3:16, 18. If "God the One and Only" is what John actually wrote, this would identify Jesus even more closely as God than the phrase "one and only Son." Judaism believed that there is only one God (Deut. 6:4). As John shows later in his Gospel, Jesus' claims of deity bring him into increasing conflict with the Jewish authorities. In the end, the primary charge leading to his crucifixion is blasphemy (John 19:7; cf. 10:33).

At the Father's side (1:18). Literally, John here says that Jesus is "in the Father's lap," an idiom for greatest possible intimacy. This is the way the term is used in the Old Testament, where it portrays the devoted care of a mother for her children (Num. 11:12; Ruth 4:16; Lam. 2:12). The most pertinent New Testament instance of the expression is the reference to "Abraham's side" in Luke 16:22. These parallels show just how intimate John considered Jesus' relationship

with the Father to be. Access to divine revelation was also prized in the pagan mystery religions and Jewish apocalypticism and mysticism. But John here claims that Jesus' access to God far exceeds that claimed by other religions.

John's Witness to the Priests and Levites (1:19–28)

John the Baptist is at this time baptizing at the Jordan (see 1:28). Luke (Luke 3:1) informs us that it was the fifteenth year of the reign of Tiberius Caesar (A.D. 14–37), which brings us up to A.D. 29.[18] Pontius Pilate (A.D. 26–36) is governor of Judea, Herod Antipas tetrarch of Galilee (4 B.C.–A.D. 39), and Herod Philip II tetrarch of Iturea and Traconitis (4 B.C.–A.D. 34). In light of the information provided by Luke that Jesus is "about thirty years old" when he starts his ministry (3:23; about thirty-three years to be precise; see introduction

JUDEA, SAMARIA, AND GALILEE

The region of Batanea is east of the Sea of Galilee.

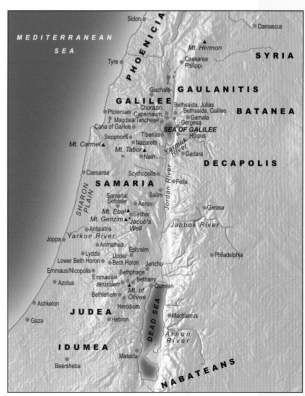

to John 1:35–42 below), John the Baptist, six months Jesus' elder (Luke 1:26), is about thirty-three and a half years old at this time.

The Jews of Jerusalem sent priests and Levites (1:19). Ministering mainly in and around the temple area in Jerusalem, these priests and Levites are specialists in ritual purification, an important issue in John the Baptist's and other baptizers' ministries (see 3:25). According to Luke, crowds come to John from all different walks of life (Luke 3:7–14). Matthew refers to both Pharisees and Sadducees (3:7); Pharisees lived scattered all over Palestine as local interpreters of the law while Sadducees were mainly stationed near the temple. It seems that everyone in that day wants to see what John the Baptist is up to.

I am not the Christ (1:20). As in 1:15, John the Baptist disavows being the expected deliverer/Messiah. Rather, he professes to be the voice of one calling in the desert, "Make straight the way for the Lord" (1:23 citing Isa. 40:3; cf. Matt. 3:1 par.). Messianic hopes were at a fever pitch in early first-century Palestine.[19] Many Jews waited for the coming greater Son of David predicted in the Old Testament (cf. 2 Sam. 7:11b–16; Hos. 3:5; cf. Matt. 1:1, 6, 17; Luke 3:31; Rom. 1:3). This does not mean, however, that these Jews are united in their expectations of what the Messiah will be, nor does it mean that their expectations are necessarily in accordance with scriptural predictions. John gathers many of the messianic expectations of Jesus' day in John 7.

"Are you Elijah?" He said, "I am not" (1:21). See also comments on 5:35. In addition to the Messiah, first-century

Jews were looking for Elijah.[20] Elijah, who never died (2 Kings 2:11), was to come "before that great and dreadful day of the LORD" (Mal. 4:5). Some expected him to settle rabbinic disputes, others thought he would perform great miracles or introduce the Messiah (e.g., *4 Ezra* 6:26–27). In any case, he would "restore all things" (Matt. 17:11), turning the hearts of the fathers to their children and vice versa (Mal. 4:6; cf. Luke 1:17; Sir. 48:10).

John denies literally being the returning prophet Elijah. Nevertheless, Jesus clearly states that John the Baptist was Elijah (Matt. 11:14; 17:12; Mark 9:13), since his ministry constituted the typological fulfillment of the prophecy of Malachi 4:5 (cf. Luke 1:17). As the Synoptic Gospels make clear, the Baptist indeed resembled Elijah in his rugged lifestyle (Matt. 3:4; cf. 2 Kings 1:8) and powerful message of judgment (cf. Matt. 3:7–12; Luke 3:7–17). Even before the Baptist's birth, an angel prophesied to his father Zechariah that John would "go on before the Lord *in the spirit and power of Elijah*" (Luke 1:17, italics added).[21]

Are you the Prophet? (1:21). "The Prophet" was yet a third end-time figure expected by the Jews (cf. 6:14; 7:40). The coming of this individual was predicted by Moses in Deuteronomy 18:15, 18.[22] Samaritans had a similar expectation.[23] The Qumran community likewise was committed to waiting "until the prophet comes, and the Messiahs of Aaron and Israel" (1QS 9:11; see also the collection of messianic passages in 4QTest 5–8, citing Deut. 18:18–19). According to *4 Ezra* 2:18, God would also send his servants Isaiah and Jeremiah (cf. 2 Macc. 15:13–16; Matt. 16:14). Again, John denies being this expected end-time figure.

I am the voice of one calling in the desert (1:23). By applying the words of Isaiah 40:3 to himself, John presents himself as "the herald of a new exodus, announcing that God is about to redeem his people from captivity, as he had in the days of Moses."[24] The desert had been the place of God's gathering and deliverance of his people from slavery in Egypt. Many leaders in the history of Israel, from Moses to Paul, were equipped for their divinely appointed task in the desert. The Baptist's statement makes clear that, rather than being a messianic figure himself, his ministry is preparatory, yet in keeping with Old Testament prophecy. Interestingly, the Qumran community applied the same passage from Isaiah to itself (1QS 8:12–14).[25]

Some Pharisees (1:24). see comments on 3:1.

Why then do you baptize? . . . I baptize with water (1:25–26). There is no clear indication in the Hebrew Scriptures that the coming of the Messiah to Israel would be preceded by a baptism of repentance for the Jews. Hence the questioning of the Jewish delegation seems legitimate. However, the Old Testament does use water as a symbol for cleansing and renewal (Ps. 51:2, 7; Ezek. 36:25–26; Zech. 13:1; cf. 1QS 4:20–21).

Various forms of baptism and ritual purification were practiced in the first century—most notably proselyte baptism, which marked a Gentile's conversion to Judaism. Yet John is baptizing not *Gentiles*, but *fellow Jews*. Some Jewish communities practiced *self-immersion*, citing Ezekial 36:25; John is baptizing *other Jews*, for which we have no other evidence. At times Jews might *rebaptize* themselves as they felt the need to be cleansed; John's baptism is *once-and-for-all*. Only a figure such as the Christ, Elijah, or the Prophet (who John the Baptist denies being) can, in the religious leaders' minds, assume such authority.

JORDAN RIVER

This location is just south of the Sea of Galilee.

He is the one who comes after me (1:27). See the Baptist's explanation at 1:15; see also 8:56–58.

The thongs of whose sandals I am not worthy to untie (1:27). R. Joshua b. Levi (A.D. 250) taught that "all manner of service that a slave must render to his master, the pupil must render to his teacher—except that of taking off his shoe" (b. Ketub. 96a). But the Baptist acknowledged that he is unworthy to untie Jesus' shoelaces, a task judged too menial even for a disciple![26] This is a telling statement of just how great the Baptist considers Jesus to be.

Bethany on the other side of the Jordan (1:28). John takes care to distinguish this "Bethany beyond the Jordan" (cf. 10:40) from "Bethany near Jerusalem," the village where Lazarus was raised from the dead (11:1, 18). The "Bethany" mentioned in the present passage, one of the places where John baptizes (note the later mention of Aenon near Salim in 3:23), is probably not a village but the region of Batanea in the northeast (called Bashan in the Old Testament). This is suggested by the fact that Jesus is said to leave from Bethany for Galilee in 1:43

and apparently calls Philip to follow him on the same day.

Hence Bethany must have been within a day's journey and thus closer to Galilee than to Judea.[27] If this reconstruction is correct, "Bethany" is a variant spelling of "Batanea," chosen by the evangelist to underscore that Jesus' ministry begins and ends in "Bethany." At Bethany in the (Galilean) north, John the Baptist confesses Jesus as "the Lamb of God"; at Bethany in the (Judean) south, Jesus nears his crucifixion. The mention of all four major regions of the Promised Land—Judea, Samaria, Galilee, and the Transjordan (of which Batanea was a part)—indicates that the sending of Jesus is for the whole of Israel.

John's Witness at Christ's Baptism (1:29–34)

The Lamb of God (1:29). John says Jesus is "the," not just "a" lamb (amnos), of God; he is the Lamb par excellence. And he is the Lamb of God, that is, the lamb especially provided by God for the sins of the world.[28] As is common in John's Gospel (e.g., 11:49–52), the Baptist here speaks better than he knows. For he himself, it appears, merely thinks of the lamb referred to in Isaiah 53:7 (LXX amnos; cf. Acts 8:32; 1 Peter 2:21–25), which Judaism interpreted not in terms of a dying Messiah, but as substitutionary suffering for sin that fell short of actual death (cf. Matt. 11:2–3; Luke 7:18–20).[29]

The evangelist, however, places the Baptist's declaration into the wider context of his passion narrative, where Jesus is shown to be the ultimate fulfillment of the yearly Passover lamb (see Ex. 12) whose bones must not be broken (John 19:36; cf. 19:14). Paul makes the same point when he writes, "For Christ, our Passover lamb, has been sacrificed"

LEATHER SANDALS

These well-preserved sandals were found at Masada and date to the first-century A.D.

▼

(1 Cor. 5:7). The expression "Lamb of God" would have acquainted a Hellenistic audience with the Jewish roots of Christianity. Yet the added phrase "who takes away the sin *of the world*" immediately points to the universal implications of the lamb's sacrifice.

Who takes away the sin of the world (1:29). The Lamb of God will *take away sin.* How? By means of a sacrificial, substitutionary death. According to the pattern set by the Old Testament sacrificial system, the shed blood of the substitute animal covers the sins of others and appeases the divine wrath by way of atonement (cf. 1 John 2:2; 4:10). As the book of Hebrews makes clear, however, the entire Old Testament sacrificial system was merely provisional until the coming of Christ. The idea that the Messiah would suffer for the sins of *the world* (rather than merely for Israel) was foreign to Jewish first-century ears. John makes clear that Jesus came to save the entire world (John 3:17) and that he is the Savior of the world, not just Israel (4:42).

I myself did not know him (1:31). John here acknowledges that he did not know that Jesus *was the Messiah* until he saw the sign referred to in 1:32–33.

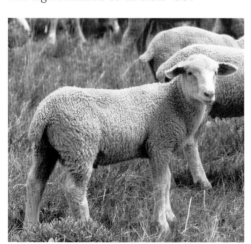

I saw the Spirit come down from heaven as a dove and remain on him (1:32). The Spirit does not merely *descend* on Jesus but *remains* on him, a sign of his divine anointing. For while in Old Testament times the Holy Spirit came on certain individuals for a temporary enablement to a particular task,[30] Isaiah prophesied that the Messiah will be full of the Spirit at all times (Isa. 11:2; 61:1; cf. Luke 4:18).[31] Thus, the Baptist testifies later in John's Gospel that "God gives the Spirit without limit" (John 3:34).

Will baptize with the Holy Spirit (1:33). The Messiah's "baptism with the Holy Spirit" is in keeping with the Old Testament prediction that God will pour out his Spirit on all people in the last days.[32]

Son of God (1:34). While some early manuscripts read "Son of God" (NIV), others, including a recently published papyrus (P[106]), have "the Chosen One of God." If "Chosen One of God" is what John wrote, this closely parallels the wording of Isaiah 42:1, where God promises to pour out his Spirit on his "chosen one." While Old Testament Israel was called God's "chosen people," and Jesus' disciples, too, are said to be "chosen" (e.g., John 6:70; 13:18; 15:16, 19), Jesus is "the Chosen One" par excellence. The expression "chosen one of God" also occurs in Qumran texts (4Q534), but its messianic nature is disputed.[33]

Andrew, Another Disciple, and Then Peter Follow Jesus (1:35–42)

Stepping out of the shadow of the Baptist, Jesus begins his own ministry by calling his first disciples. According to Luke 3:23, Jesus is "about thirty years old" at this time. If Jesus was born in 5 or 4 B.C.

▶ **Translations of Aramaic Terms in John's Gospel**

1. Rabbi (which means Teacher; 1:38; 20:16)
2. The Messiah (that is, the Christ; 1:41; 4:25)
3. Cephas (which, when translated, is Peter; 1:42)

4. Siloam (this word meant Sent; 9:7)
5. Thomas (called Didymus [twin]; 11:16; 20:24; 21:2)
6. The place of the Skull (which in Aramaic is called Golgotha; 19:17)

(as is commonly held to be the most likely date for his birth) and if (as has been argued, see introduction to 1:19–28) the Baptist's ministry started in A.D. 29, Jesus would be about thirty-three years old at this point.[34] The events recorded in 1:35–4:42 apparently belong to the period between Jesus' baptism and temptation and the beginning of his Galilean ministry (see Mark 1:14–15).

When the two disciples heard him say this, they followed Jesus (1:37). Disciples in that day literally "followed" or walked behind the one they had chosen as their teacher (e.g., *y. Ḥag.* 2:1).[35] In John's Gospel, however, the term gradually moves from this literal to a more figurative sense to denote a "following" of Jesus' teaching (8:12; 10:4–5, 27; 12:26).

Rabbi (which means Teacher) (1:38). The Semitic term "rabbi" (lit., "my great one") was a common term of honor used by disciples to address their teacher. For the benefit of John's Greek-speaking readers, he here translates the term into Greek (*didaskalos*; cf. 20:16). By the end of the first century A.D., the expression had become a technical term for "ordained" teachers who had satisfied certain formal requirements of rabbinic training. At this point, however, the term is used more generally to refer to a respected Jewish religious teacher, such

as Nicodemus (3:10), Jesus (1:38, 49; 3:2; 4:31; 6:25; 9:2; 11:8; 20:16), and even John the Baptist (3:26).

It was about the tenth hour (1:39). Starting to count, as was customary, from sunrise at around six A.M., "tenth hour" would mean about 4 P.M. Because daylight was going to run out before too long, people refrained from engaging in major outdoor activities past that hour and began to make preparations for lodging if necessary. This was not confined to the Jewish world: "Caesar, for two reasons, would not fight that day; partly because he had no soldiers in the ships, and *partly because it was after the tenth hour of the day.*"[36] Since the main meal was usually taken in the late afternoon, "tenth hour" may also indicate that Jesus extended table fellowship to these two disciples of John the Baptist.[37]

right ▶

LARGE ROCK (CEPHAS)

A huge rock outcropping at Timnah.

Andrew, Simon Peter's brother (1:40). This statement seems to presuppose the readers' knowledge of Synoptic tradition (written or oral), since Simon Peter is not mentioned until the following verse. See also 3:24; 4:44; 6:67; 11:1–2. Andrew is mentioned elsewhere in this gospel only in 1:44; 6:8; 12:22.

Andrew . . . was one of the two (1:40). The name of the other disciple is not mentioned. This unusual omission can best be explained if the disciple is John the evangelist, since he never refers to himself by name in this Gospel (see comments on 1:6).

The Messiah (that is, the Christ) (1:41). The term "Messiah" is a transliteration of the Aramaic/Hebrew word meaning "the Anointed One" (see "Translations of Aramaic Terms in John's Gospel").[38] In the Old Testament, the term variously refers to the king of Israel (1 Sam. 16:6), the high priest (Lev. 4:3), or others set apart for a particular office.[39] Since John's readers are not necessarily expected to know Aramaic, the predominant language of first-century Palestine, John translates the term into the equivalent Greek expression (*Christos* also means "the Anointed One"). The term "Messiah" is also found in Jewish writings preceding or roughly contemporary with the New Testament, such as the Qumran scrolls[40] or other literature.[41]

Simon son of John (1:42). Last names as we use them today were not in existence in biblical times. Instead, a person would be known by who his father was (e.g., Simon, son of John) and/or by his origin (e.g., Jesus of Nazareth; Simon of Cyrene).

Cephas (1:42). Cephas is an Aramaic word meaning "rock" (cf. Matt. 16:16–18). In Old Testament times, God frequently changed people's names to indicate their special calling (e.g., Abraham, Israel). Rabbis in Jesus' day likewise occasionally gave characteristic names to their disciples. Jesus' "renaming" of Simon Peter is therefore in keeping with both biblical and rabbinic precedents.

(Which, when translated, is Peter) (1:42). "Peter" does not appear to have been a proper name in ancient times. It may have been used by Jesus as a nickname.[42]

▶ References to Time in John's Gospel

Generally, people in the first century A.D. counted time from sunrise to sunset (c. 6 A.M.–6 P.M.). As Jesus himself says, "Are there not twelve hours of daylight?" (11:9). Thus "the fourth hour," for instance, would mean "about 10 A.M." In addition, the day was divided into three-hour intervals, and in this day before wristwatches, people often approximated the estimated time to the next full three-hour segment. "The sixth hour," then, may mean "roughly at 12 noon," which may span anywhere from 10:30 or 11 A.M. to 1 or 1:30 P.M.

John's Gospel contains the following four references to time:

1. *"about the tenth hour"* (1:39): Jesus' first followers opt to stay with him at about 4 P.M.
2. *"about the sixth hour"* (4:6): Jesus meets the Samaritan woman at the well at around noon.
3. *"yesterday at the seventh hour"* (4:52): Jesus healed the royal official's son at about 1 P.M.
4. *"about the sixth hour"* (19:14): Jesus' trial before Pilate ended at around noon.

Philip and Nathanael Follow Christ (1:43–51)

Finding Philip, he said to him, "Follow me" (1:43). Jesus' practice of calling his followers went counter to contemporary practice, where disciples opted to attach themselves to a rabbi of their choice (cf. 15:16).

Philip, like Andrew and Peter, was from the town of Bethsaida (1:44). Mark seems to indicate that Andrew and Peter were from Capernaum (Mark 1:29; cf. 1:21); here they are said to be from Bethsaida. Most likely, Andrew and Peter grew up in Bethsaida and subsequently moved to Capernaum (which is only a few miles directly west of Bethsaida). This is similar to Jesus, who is regularly said to be from Nazareth (John 1:45) although he had moved to Capernaum (Matt. 4:13).

Bethsaida (meaning "place of the fishery") is probably to be identified with the mound called et-Tell, located east of the Jordan River about one and a half miles before it enters the north shore of the Sea of Galilee. After Jerusalem and Capernaum, Bethsaida is the most frequently mentioned city in the Gospels (cf. Matt. 11:21 par.; Mark 6:45; 8:22; Luke 9:10;

John 12:21).[43] Mark records that a blind man was healed in this city, and the feeding of the four thousand took place in a deserted place nearby. Tragically, the city was cursed by Jesus along with Chorazin and Capernaum because of its unbelief.

Philip found Nathanael (1:45). Nathanael is also mentioned in 21:2 as one of the seven disciples to whom Jesus appears on the shore of the Sea of Galilee. There we learn that Nathanael came from Cana of Galilee, the site of two of Jesus' signs (cf. 2:1–11; 4:46–54). Since the name Nathanael is not mentioned in the Synoptic Gospels, it is likely that this is the personal name of Bartholomew (Bar-Tholomaios = son of

REFLECTIONS

IT IS STRIKING HOW JESUS' FIRST followers do not merely attach themselves to Jesus but immediately seek to bring others to him as well. The first thing Andrew did was to find his brother Simon, while Philip recruited Nathanael. This is where Old Testament Israel had gone astray: Rather than fulfilling her role as a channel of blessing to other nations, God's "chosen people" construed their election as ethnic privilege. Where they should have shared their joy and faith in God with those outside, their pride and presumption led the Jews jealously to guard their blessings and to keep them for themselves. It must be different with members of the new covenant community: Those who are called by Jesus must be willing to share the good news of salvation in Christ with others, what is more, to be driven by a passionate desire to see unbelievers come to faith.

RUINS AT BETHSAIDA

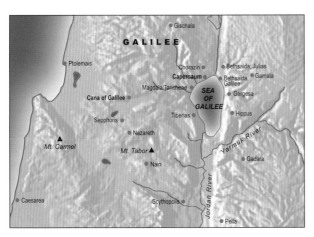

GALILEE

Nazarenes probably had relations with their more cosmopolitan neighbors and more than likely also came into contact with the Greek-speaking Gentile traders who passed through Sepphoris in the north or the Esdraelon Valley in the south.

◀ *left*

GALILEE

Nazareth was located west of the Sea of Galilee near Sepphoris.

Tholomaios), who is linked with Philip in all three Synoptic apostolic lists (Matt. 10:3; Mark 3:18; Luke 6:14).

The one Moses wrote about in the Law, and about whom the prophets also wrote (1:45). "The Law and the Prophets" was a common Jewish designation for the Hebrew Scriptures in their entirety. Philip has come to believe that Jesus is the Messiah foretold in the Scriptures, both in the Law (cf. Deut. 18:15, 18; see comments on "the Prophet" at John 1:21) and in the Prophets (e.g., Isa. 9:1–7; 11:1–5, 10–12; 52:13–53:12).

Jesus of Nazareth, the son of Joseph (1:45). While born in Bethlehem, Jesus grew up in Nazareth, so that he could properly be said to be "from Nazareth."

Nazareth! Can anything good come from there? (1:46). It is ironic that Nathanael, himself from the small village of Cana in Galilee (21:2; cf. 2:1–11), here displays prejudice against the relatively insignificant Galilean town of Nazareth (cf. later 7:41, 52). Mentioned neither in the Old Testament nor in Josephus, Nazareth was a small town of no more than two thousand people, located about three and a half miles southeast of the regional capital Sepphoris. The

True Israelite, in whom there is nothing false (1:47). The rendering "true Israelite" (NIV) is incorrect. Rather, Jesus says, "truly" here is an Israelite in whom there is nothing false (lit., "no deceit"; *dolos*). In this Nathanael differs from the original "Israel" (i.e., Jacob), who was deceitful (*dolos*; cf. Gen. 27:35–36 LXX). Nathanael is free from such duplicity of heart (cf. Ps. 32:2) and thus prepared to consider whether or not the claims regarding Jesus are true.[44] This attitude stands in sharp contrast not only with Jacob of old, but also with the hypocrisy of the Pharisees (Matt. 26:4 = Mark 14:1: *dolos*).

I saw you while you were still under the fig tree (1:48). In the Greco-Roman world, such knowledge was regularly

MODERN NAZARETH

▼

attributed to magic or some other mysterious link to the gods. The Jews, however, considered access to divine revelation to be the mark of a true prophet. Yet Jesus was more than a prophet: he was the unique Son of God, whose place "at the Father's side" (1:18) provides him with an unlimited supply of divine insight. Nevertheless, Jesus does not display his supernatural knowledge to impress others but to identify himself as Messiah (1:49–51).

Fig tree (1:48). The fig tree is sometimes used in the Old Testament as a figure for home or prosperity, at times in an end-time or messianic context (1 Kings 4:25; Isa. 36:16; Mic. 4:4; Zech. 3:10). In rabbinic literature it is a place for meditation on the Scriptures and prayer (e.g., *Midr. Qoh.* 5:11 §2).

Rabbi (1:49). See comments on 1:38.

Son of God . . . King of Israel (1:49). By calling Jesus "Son of God," Nathanael identifies him as the Messiah predicted in the Old Testament (cf. 2 Sam. 7:14; Ps. 2:7; see John 20:31 below). The term "Son [of God]" was also a current messianic title in Jesus' day.[45] "King of Israel," too, is a common designation for the Messiah (cf. 12:13; note also the phrase

"king of the Jews" in chs. 18–19). Because of the expression's political overtones, however, Jesus is reluctant to identify himself in such terms (6:15), for his kingdom is "not of this world" (18:36).

I tell you the truth (1:51). This phrase renders the Greek transliteration of the Hebrew term *amēn* ("it is firm"). While the Synoptics feature a single *amēn*, John always uses the double expression *amēn, amēn*, perhaps in order to stress the authoritative nature of Jesus' pronouncements. In the Old Testament, the term confirms the truthfulness of someone else's statement. Jesus, by contrast, uses the expression to assert the veracity of *his own* sayings.[46]

Heaven open, and the angels of God ascending and descending (1:51). The imagery is drawn from Jacob's vision of the ladder "resting on the earth, with its top reaching to heaven, and *the angels of God* were *ascending and descending* on it [or: him, that is, Jacob, italics added]" (Gen. 28:12).[47] As the angels ascended and descended on Jacob (who was later renamed "Israel")—a sign of God's revelation—so the disciples are promised further divine confirmation of Jesus' messianic identity.

Son of Man (1:51). Apart from functioning (as in the Synoptics) as Jesus' favorite self-reference (6:27; 9:35; cf. Ezek.), the expression is fused in Johannine theology to denote both Jesus' heavenly origin and destination (John 1:51; 3:13; 6:62; cf. Dan. 7:13) and his "lifting up" (substitutionary sacrifice) on the cross (John 3:14; 6:53; 8:28; 12:23, 34; 13:31). The Son of Man is also presented as the end-time judge (5:27). Notably, the term is always found on Jesus' lips in John's Gospel (12:34 is no real exception).

The Wedding at Cana (2:1–11)

After calling his first disciples, Jesus takes them along to a wedding in Cana of Galilee, not far from his hometown, Nazareth. Jesus here performs the first of his startling signs, providing his followers with an initial glimpse of his messianic identity. In anticipation of that great messianic banquet at the end of time, Jesus is here shown to fill up the emptiness of Judaism. John's Ephesian audience may also have read the present account in light of the myth of Dionysius, the Greek god of wine and the most popular deity in the Hellenistic world.[48]

The Setting (2:1–2)

On the third day (2:1). "The third day" is to be counted from the last event narrated, Jesus' encounter with Nathanael. Including the first day in one's calculation, this means two days later. In conjunction with John's initial testimony to Jesus in 1:19–28 and the three references to "the next day" in 1:29, 35, and 43, this completes an entire week of activity.

Day 1: John the Baptist testifies concerning Jesus (1:19–28).

Day 2: John the Baptist's encounter with Jesus (1:29–34; "the next day").

Day 3: John the Baptist refers two of his disciples to Jesus (1:35–39; "the next day").

Day 4: Andrew introduces his brother Peter to Jesus (1:40–42).

Day 5: Philip and Nathanael follow Jesus (1:43–51; "the next day").

Day 6: No information is given (Sabbath?).

Day 7: Jesus attends the wedding at Cana (2:1–11; "on the third day").[49]

If no information is given regarding Day 6 because it was a Sabbath, the Cana wedding—or at least the day on which Jesus and his friends joined the wedding party—would have fallen on a Sunday. This may not have been the first day of the wedding, since weddings lasted for a whole week (cf. Judg. 14:12) and it is unlikely that wine ran out immediately.

A wedding (2:1). Jewish weddings were important and joyful occasions in the lives of the bride and the groom and their extended families, and the entire community joined in the celebration (see "Jewish Weddings"). Cana was not far

Jesus' Signs in John's Gospel		
Event	Reference in John	Date
1. Changing water into wine	2:1–11	Winter/Spring, A.D. 30
2. Temple cleansing	2:13–22[A-4]	Spring, A.D. 30
3. Healing of nobleman's son	4:46–54	Spring, A.D. 31
4. Healing of lame man	5:1–15	Fall, A.D. 31
5. Feeding of multitude	6:1–15	Spring, A.D. 32
6. Healing of blind man	9:1–41	Fall, A.D. 32
7. Raising of Lazarus	11:1–44	Spring, A.D. 33

from Nazareth (less than ten miles), and the fact that the guest list includes Jesus and his disciples as well as his mother may indicate the wedding of a close family friend or relative. This may also explain why Jesus' mother feels responsible to help when the hosts run out of wine.

At Cana in Galilee (2:1). Despite its insignificance, Cana becomes the site of Jesus' first and third signs (cf. 4:54: the second sign *in Cana*). Several sites have been proposed for ancient Cana ("place of reeds"). Some older commentators suggest Kafr Kennamm, some four miles northeast of Nazareth on the road to Tiberias, but this is rendered unlikely by the doubling of the letter "n" in "Kafr Kennam."[50] The probable location is Khirbet Qânam in the Plain of Asochis, about eight miles northeast of Nazareth (cf. Josephus, *Life* 16, 41 §§86, 207).[51] Fittingly, Khirbet Qânam overlooks a marshy plain featuring plenty of reeds. To date, the site has not been excavated, but cisterns and the remains of buildings are visible and nearby tombs are cut into the rocks. Some first-century coins have also been found on the site. The plain where Cana was located was apparently part of the royal domain of the Herodians and was cultivated by their tenants under the supervision of royal officials (cf. 4:46).[52] John's mention of "Cana in Galilee" seems to presuppose another Cana (not in Galilee), perhaps in Lebanon (referred to in Josh. 19:28; cf. 16:8; 17:9).[53]

Jesus' mother . . . Jesus and his disciples . . . invited to the wedding (2:1–2). Mary may have been a friend of the family, helping behind the scenes.[54] Jesus may

▶ **Jewish weddings**[A-5]

Marriage was the norm in Jewish life on the basis of Genesis 1:28. People generally married young (*b. Sanh.* 76b; cf. Tobit 4:13; Josephus, *Ag. Ap.* 2.25 §199–203), men between the ages of eighteen and twenty-four (*m. ʾAbot* 5:21), women as early as age thirteen or fourteen. Generally, it was considered important that bridegroom and bride come from similar social backgrounds, that the age difference between them not be too considerable, and that the bride be free from physical defects. Family background was also judged to be important; even compatibility in height is occasionally mentioned.

On the eve of the wedding day, the bride was brought from her father's home to that of her husband in joyful procession. Veiled by a bridal veil and surrounded by her bridesmaids, she was led by "the friends of the bridegroom" (often not found in Galilee) and the "children of the bridechamber." Upon arrival, the bride was led to her husband, and the couple was crowned with garlands. This was followed by the signing of the marriage contract (*ketubah*). After the marriage supper, which could last up to a full day, the "friends of the bridegroom" led the pair to the bridal chamber.

▶ Jesus' Natural Family [A-6]

Jesus was miraculously conceived in the womb of his mother Mary by the Holy Spirit (Matt. 1:18–23; Luke 1:35). Mary's husband Joseph apparently died in Jesus' youth, for he is never mentioned in Scripture past the account of the twelve-year-old Jesus in the temple (Luke 2:41–52). The names of Jesus' brothers are given in Matthew 13:55 and Mark 6:3 as James, Joseph, Judas, and Simon. [A-7] No names are supplied for Jesus' sisters; the best attested names in post-canonical tradition are Salome and Mary.

Jesus is called "the carpenter's son" in Matthew 13:55 and "the carpenter" in Mark 6:3, indicating that he took up his father's trade, as was customary in Judaism (though *tektōn* probably means "craftsman, artisan, builder"—that is, someone who works in wood, stone, and metal). He met strong opposition within his own household (Mark 3:21, 31–34 par.). His own brothers did not believe in him as late as midway through his earthly ministry (John 7:1–9). Later, Jesus' mother and brothers are among those praying in the upper room prior to Pentecost (Acts 1:14). According to Paul, the risen Christ appeared to one of his brothers, James (1 Cor. 15:7).

have been invited because of a childhood association, because he was one of the distinguished people in the neighborhood, or both. The group of Jesus' disciples presumably included the five mentioned in 1:35–51.

Jesus Turns Water into Wine (2:3–11)

In Jewish thought, wine is a symbol of joy and celebration: "There is no rejoicing save with wine" (*b. Pesah.* 109a). In John, running out of wine at the Cana wedding may be symbolic of the barrenness of Judaism. Prophetic expectation cast the messianic age as a time when wine would flow freely.[55] At a cultural level, running out of wine was considered to be a major social faux pas, since the host was responsible to provide the wedding guests with wine for seven days.

Jesus' mother said to him, "They have no more wine" (2:3). If women's quarters at ancient Jewish weddings were indeed near the place where the wine was stored, Mary may have learned of the shortage of wine before word reached Jesus and the other men.[56] In what may have constituted a breach of etiquette, Mary informs Jesus, in the process disturbing the male guests.

Dear woman (2:4). Jesus' address of his mother as "woman" sounds brusque; at the very least, it establishes polite distance.[57] Yet the expression, while not particularly endearing, need not be harsh.[58] The unusual nature of Jesus' use of this address for his own mother is underscored by the fact that this practice is without parallel in ancient Jewish or Greco-Roman literature.[59] Jesus' making provision for his mother at the foot of the cross indicates that this address does not show absence of filial affection (19:25–27).

Why do you involve me? (2:4). The underlying thrust of this phrase is: "What do you and I have in common (as far as the matter at hand is concerned)?" The implied answer: "Nothing." As Old Testament parallels make clear, the phrase always distances two parties and frequently carries a reproachful connotation.[60] Jesus is here issuing a fairly sharp rebuke to Mary (cf. Matt. 12:46–50), similar to his rebuke of Peter when he fails to understand the nature of Jesus' calling (cf. 16:23). Alternatively, Jesus may be advising his mother that he has already decided to help and that he will do so when he chooses to rather than in response to her prompting (cf. 2 Kings 3:13).[61]

Do whatever he tells you (2:5). The fact that she is able to give instructions to the servants may indicate that Mary is help-

ing the bridegroom's mother with the preparation of dishes. The wording of Mary's instructions to the servants perhaps alludes to Pharaoh's words to the Egyptians to go to Joseph and to "do what he tells you" (Gen. 41:55).

Nearby stood six stone water jars (2:6). The jars stood *nearby*—probably not in the dining room itself, but more likely in a passage near the courtyard near the well. There are *six* jars: In light of the significance the number seven has for John, the number six may connote imperfection as falling one short of the perfect number seven. The jars are made of *stone*, because stone was not itself considered to contract uncleanness.

The kind used by the Jews for ceremonial washing (2:6). This practice may have involved the washing of certain utensils used at the wedding and the washing of the guests' hands (cf. Mark 7:2–5; more broadly, John 3:25).

Each holding from twenty to thirty gallons (2:6). The original text reads "two to three *metrētēs*"; one *metrētēs* equals roughly ten gallons.[62] This adds up to a

▶

WATER JARS

Large storage jars found in Ekron.

▶ # Wine[A-8]

Scripture portrays wine both as a blessing, commended even by the example of Christ,[A-9] and as an emblem of violence, corruption, or wickedness incurring divine wrath.[A-10] In the Greco-Roman world, and presumably in the Palestine of Jesus' day, three kinds of wine were in use: fermented wines, which were usually mixed in the proportion of two or three parts of water to one of wine; new wine, made of grape juice (similar to cider, not fermented); and wines in which, by boiling the unfermented grape juice, the process of fermentation had been stopped and the formation of alcohol prevented.

Passages such as Matthew 11:19 clearly suggest that Jesus drank fermented wine; Mark 14:25 implies the same. Moreover, the latter passage intimates that wine will be drunk in heaven. Thus, neither Christ's teaching nor his example can be adduced in favor of advocating total abstinence from alcohol. Rather, proper use of wine must be distinguished from excessive consumption. Some may judge total abstinence to be expedient for personal or local reasons (cf. Rom. 14:21; 1 Cor. 6:12), but should not insist that this is the only biblical option.

REFLECTIONS

REFLECTIONS

WE ALL HAVE HEARD STORIES OF now famous conductors or performers who, as virtual unknowns, were thrust into the limelight unexpectedly when the regular cast had to be replaced on short notice. It was their opportunity to prove themselves, and they seized it. Jesus, too, has such an experience when called on to help with the shortage of wine at the wedding of Cana—and he makes the most of it, revealing his glory to his disciples, who believe in him. He wants us likewise to stand ready to be used in case a sudden need arises. May we be alert and available whenever he needs us.

total of one hundred and twenty to one hundred and eighty gallons for all six jars combined. A large number of wedding guests must be accommodated for the course of an entire week of festivities.

The servants (2:7). "The fact that there were servants, and more than one, indicates that the family was in at least comfortable if not opulent circumstances."[63]

The master of the banquet (2:8). The role of "master of the banquet" (*architriklinos*; lit. "ruler of the table") is a position of honor, with one of the master's primary duties being the regulation of the distribution of wine. Sirach 32:1–2 (c. 180 B.C.) counsels, "If they make you master of the feast [*hēgoumenos*], do not exalt yourself; be among them as one of their number. Take care of them first and then sit down; when you have fulfilled all your duties, take your place, so that you may be merry along with them and receive a wreath for your excellent lead-

ership." The position may represent an adaptation of the Greco-Roman "ruler of the feast" (called a *symposiarch*), even though differences may apply. Apparently, the "master of the banquet" did not join the wedding party at the table but, as a head waiter in charge of catering, supervised the serving of food and drink, with several servants under him carrying out his orders. He may also have served as "master of ceremonies."[64]

Return to Capernaum (2:12)

Went down (2:12). Jesus goes "down" from Cana to Capernaum, since Cana is located in the hill country while Capernaum is situated directly at the Sea of Galilee at a lower elevation (the site has been excavated: Tel-Hûm).

Capernaum (2:12). Capernaum, located on the northwest corner of the Sea of Galilee, is about sixteen miles to the northeast of Cana; it can easily be reached in a day's journey (about six to eight hours).[65] After the imprisonment of John the Baptist and after encountering strong opposition in his hometown of Nazareth, Jesus permanently moves to Capernaum (cf. Matt. 4:12–13; Luke 4:28–31). Matthew ties Jesus' taking up of residence

CAPERNAUM

An aerial view of the remains of the synagogue.

in Capernaum to the fulfillment of Old Testament prophecy, calling it "his own town," owing to the length and variety of his activities there (Matt. 9:1).

The Cleansing of the Temple (2:13–25)

Cleansing was an important part of Passover observance. Even today, observant Jews search their house prior to Passover in order to remove any vestiges of leavened bread. The "Feast of Unleavened Bread" began with the Passover meal and continued for seven days (14–21 Nisan; cf. Ex. 12:18–19; Mark 14:12). The major point of the temple cleansing in John is the fact that Jesus is presented as the replacement of the temple in the life of the messianic community. According to John, Jesus' mission is to cleanse the community of God from defilement and to restore the proper worship of God (this echoes Old Testament prophetic concerns: cf. Zech. 14:21; Mal. 3:1, 3). Ultimately, true cleansing is provided only by Christ's death on the cross on our behalf (cf. John 13:10–11; 15:3).[66]

Jewish Passover (2:13). The Passover was the most important Jewish feast, com-

memorating God's dramatic deliverance of the Jews from Egypt on the night of the Exodus, when the death angel "passed over" the firstborn in homes whose doorposts had been marked with blood (cf. Ex. 12, esp. vv. 14–16). It was celebrated on the fourteenth day of the lunar month Nisan (full moon at the end of March or the beginning of April), which marked the beginning of the festive calendar. The Passover was one of the three annual pilgrim feasts that all Jewish men were to celebrate in Jerusalem (cf. Deut. 16:16).[67] Large numbers of worshipers from the outlying provinces of Palestine (Luke 2:41–42) and the

right ▶

GALILEE, SAMARIA, AND JUDEA

This map shows the routes from Capernaum to Jerusalem.

Jewish Festivals in John's Gospel[A-11]		
Name of Feast	**Reference in John**	**Time Celebrated**
Passover	2:13, 23	April 7, A.D. 30
"A feast of the Jews"	5:1	October 21–28, A.D. 31?
Passover	6:4	April 13/14, A.D. 32
Tabernacles (Booths)	7:2	September 10–17, A.D. 32
Dedication (Hanukkah)	10:22	December 18–25, A.D. 32
Passover	11:55; 12:1	April 3, A.D. 33

Diaspora (Acts 2:5) filled the capital city (cf. Josephus, *J.W.* 2.1.3 §10). The present Passover, the first during Jesus' public ministry, probably took place on April 7 in A.D. 30.[68]

Went up (2:13). People went "up" to Jerusalem because it was situated at a higher elevation than Galilee and because it was the capital city.

Temple courts (2:14). "Temple courts" (*hieron*), in distinction to the temple building proper (*naos*; see comments on 2:20 below), generally denotes the area surrounding the temple. In the present instance, this probably refers to the outermost court, the Court of the Gentiles. Gentiles were barred from entry into the inner court of the temple. A complete Greek inscription to this effect was discovered in 1870:

> *No foreigner shall enter within the*
> *balustrade of the temple,*
> *or within the precinct,*
> *and whosoever shall be caught shall*
> *be responsible for (his) death*
> *that will follow in consequence (of his*
> *trespassing).*[69]

Men selling cattle, sheep and doves, and others sitting at tables exchanging money (2:14). The sale of sacrificial animals rendered a valuable service to those who travelled to the Passover from afar, enabling them to buy the animals on site rather than having to carry them for long distances. *Cattle* and *sheep* were needed for various kinds of offerings (e.g., Ex. 20:24; 22:30; 24:5; Lev. 1:3–9; 4:2–21; 8:2; 22:21). *Doves* were required for the purification of women (Lev. 12:6; Luke 2:22–24), especially if they were poor (Lev. 12:8), the cleansing of people with certain kinds of skin diseases (14:22), and other purposes (15:14, 29).

The *money-changers* likewise rendered a service: Visitors to Jerusalem needed their money changed into the local currency because the temple tax, paid by

WARNING INSCRIPTION

A first-century inscription from the balustrade around the temple building warning Gentiles not to enter.

TEMPLE MOUNT

Leen Ritmeyer's classic drawing of the Jerusalem temple mount.

JERUSALEM
THE TEMPLE MOUNT
DURING THE SECOND TEMPLE PERIOD
A RECONSTRUCTION BASED ON ARCHAEOLOGICAL AND HISTORICAL EVIDENCE

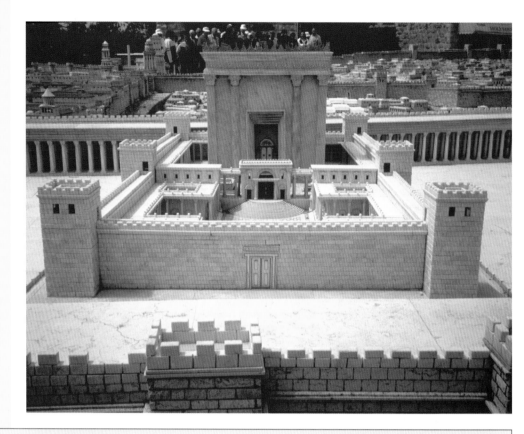

▶

THE JERUSALEM TEMPLE

The model shows the temple proper and the courts.

▶ The Jerusalem Temple

The Jerusalem temple was a symbol of Jewish national and religious identity. The original temple was built by Solomon. It was destroyed by the Babylonians in the sixth century B.C. and rebuilt by Zerubbabel (Ezra 3; Hag. 1–2; Zech. 4). Later renovated by Herod, the edifice was renowned for its magnificence. Josephus raved that "the exterior of the building wanted nothing that could astound either mind or eye. For, being covered on all sides with massive plates of gold, the sun was no sooner up than it radiated so fiery a flash that persons straining to look at it were compelled to avert their eyes, as from the solar rays. To approaching strangers it appeared from a distance like a snow-clad mountain; for all that was overlaid with gold was of purest white" (*J.W.* 5.5.6 §§222–24). Even the rabbis, who were no friends of Herod, had to admit that "he who has not seen the Temple of Herod has never seen a beautiful building" (*b. B. Bat.* 4a).

Surrounded by porticoes, the temple consisted of an Outer Court (the Court of the Gentiles) and an Inner Temple, made up of the Court of Women on the east and the Inner Court on the west. Behind these rose the temple itself, a huge edifice 300 feet wide, long, and high. In Jesus' day, the temple, once the glorious symbol of God's dwelling with his people, had degenerated into a place of commerce and perfunctory ritual (John 2:14–16). It was razed in A.D. 70 by the Romans, shortly after the restoration of the entire temple area had been completed. This destruction had been predicted by Jesus, who saw in it God's judgment of Israel on account of its rejection of the Messiah (Matt. 24:1–2 par.). John's Gospel, most likely written within a decade or two after the destruction of the temple, presents Jesus as the replacement of the temple and as people's new proper focus of worship (John 2:19–21; cf. 4:19–24).A-12

Begun in 20 B.C., Herod's new structure towered 15 stories high, following the floor dimensions of the former temples in the Holy Place and the Most Holy Place. The high sanctuary shown here in a cutaway view was built on the site of the former temples of Solomon and Zerubbabel, and was completed in just 18 months.

CUBITS

FEET

Drawn to scale, the height of a 6 ft. man equals 4 cubits.

Most Holy Place

Holy Place

60 cubits

Side rooms within walls

Golden vine

Veil

Incense Altar

20

40 cubits

100 cubits high and 100 cubits wide

"The Great Gate"

The outer courts surrounding the temple mount were not completed until A.D. 64. The entire structure was demolished by the Romans in A.D. 70

Dimensions of rooms, steps, doorways, cornices, and exterior measurements are mentioned in history (Josephus and the Mishnah) but are subject to interpretation, and all drawings vary.

Basin

Altar

N

◄

THE JERUSALEM TEMPLE

This cutaway reconstruction is based on testimony from Josephus and the Mishnah.

slanted tunnel within walls ascends to upper levels

Most Holy Place

Holy Place

Portico

TOP VIEW

SIDE ELEVATION

Was the Ark still present during the Roman period? Josephus describes the Most Holy Place as having "nothing at all" which was accurate on the day he wrote it. Yet the Mishnah hints that the Ark was hidden (*Shekalim 6:12*).

Fearing Roman intervention, it could have been secretly moved into the Temple interior for use only on the Day of Atonement. It may be hidden underground to this day.

every conscientious Jewish male of twenty years or over, had to be paid in that currency. The coinage of choice was Tyrian, owing to its high silver content (*m. Bek.* 8:7).[70] The annual half-shekel equalled half a Tyrian stater or tetradrachma, so that two Jews often joined together to pay the tax in one coin (cf. Matt. 17:27). The temple tax was collected in Jerusalem from 25 Adar on, the lunar month preceding Nisan.[71]

The merchants' primary offense was that of disrupting Gentile worship.[72] The temple establishment had amassed excessive wealth in Jesus' day, which made the merchants and money-changers part of a system that exploited the poor for the alleged purpose of beautifying and administering the affairs of the temple.[73] The sale of sacrificial animals and money exchange should have been facilitated near the temple rather than within its walls. This, incidentally, is exactly what had been the case earlier in Israel's history when the animal merchants had set up shop across the Kidron Valley on the slopes of the Mount of Olives.

Zeal ... will consume me (2:17). Jesus' cleansing of the temple stirs in his disciples the memory of the righteous sufferer of Psalm 69:9 (cf. John 2:16: "my Father's *house*" with Ps. 69:9: "zeal for your *house*"). While God's people were warned against "zeal without knowledge" (Prov. 19:2; cf.

Rom. 10:2), religious zeal was an important part of Jewish piety. In the Old Testament, Phinehas is promised a covenant of a lasting priesthood, "because he was zealous for the honor of his God" (Num. 25:13). In fact, God himself is shown to be zealous for his holy name (Isa. 59:17; Ezek. 39:25).

First-century Palestine was rife with religious as well as nationalistic zeal.[74] The Pharisees were concerned for the religious state of Judaism, while the Zealots played an important part in the rebellion against Rome in A.D. 66–70. Particularly notorious were the Sicarii (from Latin *sicae*, "dagger"), religious terrorists who murdered people in broad daylight in an effort to destabilize the political situation in Roman-occupied Palestine.[75] Jesus' zeal, righteous rather than blindly nationalistic, was so great it would "consume" him. This refers to his death, which brings life to the world (cf. John 6:51).

The Jews (2:18). See "'The Jews' in John's Gospel" at 5:10.

REFLECTIONS

WE ALL KNOW THE CLICHÉ OF "gentle Jesus, meek and mild." But when he cleanses the temple, Jesus, in truly prophetic style, does something highly courageous and startling. Sure enough, his authority is promptly challenged. But Jesus does not back down. He displays spiritual authority and confidence and is not afraid to take bold action where necessary. Of course, as the rest of this Gospel amply makes clear, Jesus' confidence is rooted in humility and dependence on God. In this, too, we must follow his example.

It has taken forty-six years to build this temple (2:20). The NIV rendering suggests, almost certainly incorrectly, that the temple building was still under reconstruction at the time of the temple cleansing. However, historical records indicate that Herod the Great (37–4 B.C.) began the project of restoring the temple building proper (*naos*, the term used here) in the eighteenth year of his reign, i.e., 20/19 B.C. (Josephus, *Ant.* 15.11.1 §380) with completion a year and a half later in 18/17 B.C. (*Ant.* 15.11.6 §421). Forty-six years later is A.D. 29/30, which places Jesus' first Passover in the spring of A.D. 30.[76] The restoration of the entire temple area (*hieron*, see comments on 2:14) was not completed until A.D. 63/64 under Herod Agrippa II and governor Albinus (*Ant.* 20.9.7 §219), shortly before its destruction by the Roman army in the Jewish war of A.D. 66–70.[77]

The Scripture and the words that Jesus had spoken (2:22). The Scripture may be Psalm 69:9 as in 2:17; "Jesus' word" probably refers to the saying in 2:19.

He knew all men (2:24). According to Jewish belief, God knows people's hearts and judges their motivations.[78] The present statement implies that Jesus is God or at least possesses a divine attribute. Jesus' knowledge of people's hearts is displayed in his encounters with Nicodemus and the Samaritan woman in the following two chapters.[79]

Jesus' Conversation with Nicodemus (3:1–21)

While still in Jerusalem, Jesus is paid a nightly visit by Nicodemus, a high-ranking Jewish rabbi. Later, on his way back from Judea to his native Galilee, Jesus encounters a Samaritan woman at a well. The contrast between these two individuals could hardly be more extreme. Nicodemus, the esteemed "teacher of Israel," is a wealthy member of the Sanhedrin, the Jewish ruling council, who comes to Jesus at night in order to avoid the crowds. The Samaritan is a nameless, immoral woman who meets Jesus in the heat of day, probably because she is too ashamed to draw water when other people are at the well. In both instances, Jesus directs the conversation to what he perceives to be the central issue: in Nicodemus's case, his need to be "born again," in the case of the Samaritan woman, her need to repent from her sinful lifestyle and to trust Jesus the Messiah.

Nicodemus (3:1). The name Nicodemus was common in first-century Palestine. The fact that a wealthy philanthropic Jew by the same name was living in Jerusalem around A.D. 70 adds historical plausibility to John's account (*b. Git.* 56a; *b. Ketub.* 66b).[80] Apparently, Nicodemus represents a more open element among the Pharisees (cf. 12:42; Acts 5:34–39).

A member of the Jewish ruling council (3:1). "Jewish ruling council" (lit., "ruler," cf. 7:26, 48; 12:42) refers to the Sanhedrin (from *synedrion*, "gathering, assembly"), the highest national body in charge of Jewish affairs.[81] Headquartered in Jerusalem, it was composed of Pharisees and Sadducees. When Judea became a Roman province in A.D. 6, the Sanhedrin became even more autonomous in handling internal Jewish matters. As John's Gospel progresses, the Sanhedrin turns out to be the driving force in the plot against Jesus.

At night (3:2). First-century Judaism encouraged the study of Torah at night with reference to passages such as Joshua

1:8 or Psalm 42:8 (cf. 1QS 6:7). Nicodemus may have come to Jesus at night in order to avoid the crowds rather than out of fear. John later shows Nicodemus to be outspoken in his support of Jesus (John 7:50–52) and refers to his coming to Jesus at night without a hint of disparagement (19:39).

Rabbi (3:2). See comments on 1:38. It is remarkable that this highly respected Jewish teacher would honor the about thirty-year-old Jesus as a fellow rabbi, especially since Jesus was known to lack formal rabbinic training (7:15).

We know you are a teacher who has come from God (3:2). While doubtlessly intended as a compliment (contrast the categorical denial of Jesus' divine commission by other Pharisees in 7:15), Nicodemus still falls far short in understanding Jesus' true nature—for he is the heaven-sent Son of Man (3:13).

For no one could perform the miraculous signs you are doing (3:2). It was commonly held in Judaism that miracles attested to God's presence. References to "signs" in the Old Testament cluster around two major periods: the "signs and wonders" performed by Moses at the Exodus (Ex. 4:1–9; etc.); and the signs—with attendant symbolism, but not necessarily miraculous—performed by various Old Testament prophets (e.g., Isa. 20:3).[82] While Jesus discourages dependence on "signs and wonders" (cf. John 4:48), he does perform various signs, both miraculous (e.g., 2:1–11) and nonmiraculous (2:14–22). These signs show him to be not only a divine prophet (6:14; 7:40) but the God-sent Messiah (7:31; 20:30–31). The present statement probably refers primarily to Jesus' Jerusalem signs (cf. 2:23) rather than to his first sign in Cana of Galilee (2:11). For a similar acknowledgment, see 11:47.

If God were not with him (3:2). This is a common Jewish expression, used by Jesus himself (8:29; 16:32) and frequently found in the Old Testament (e.g., Gen. 21:20; 26:24; 28:15; 31:3; Deut.

▶ The Pharisees

The roots of this Jewish party can be traced to the Hasidim, a group of pious Jews in the second century B.C. The Pharisees, "a distinctive group of ostentatious religious pietists" (cf. Josephus, *J.W.* 1.5.2 §110), emphasized preserving the traditions of the fathers, which included both oral and written tradition in further development of the Old Testament Scriptures (Josephus, *Ant.* 13.10.6 §298, 13.16.2 §408; 17.2.4 §41; Hippolytus, *Haer.* 9.28.3).[A-13] Unlike the Sadducees (who only accepted the Pentateuch), the Pharisees believed in the resurrection (Josephus, *J.W.* 2.8.14 §§162–63; *Ant.* 18.1.3 §§12–14). They were a close-knit group (*J.W.* 2.8.14 §166) and avoided luxury (*Ant.* 18.1.3 §12). [A-14]

The Gospels portray the Pharisees as generally antagonistic toward Jesus (though there are exceptions such as Nicodemus or Joseph of Arimathea). Jesus, in turn, charged them with hypocrisy (e.g., Matt. 23:23–26; Luke 18:9–12). According to Josephus, the Pharisees had "the masses as their ally" (*Ant.* 13.10.6 §298), and their interpretation of Scripture had a reputation for accuracy (*Ant.* 17.2.4 §41; *J.W.* 1.5.2 §110; 2.8.14 §162; *Life* 38 §191) and set the standard for Jewish liturgy and ritual (*Ant.* 18.1.3 §15). In John's Gospel, the Pharisees are shown to mastermind the plot against Jesus in conjunction with the Sadducee-dominated high priests, who in turn controlled the Jewish supreme council, the Sanhedrin (John 7:32, 45; 11:47, 57; 12:42; 18:3).

31:23; Josh. 1:5; Jer. 1:19). Through his polite yet cautious introductory statement, Nicodemus tacitly inquires as to what new doctrine Jesus is propagating. John thus presents Nicodemus's conversation with Jesus as a typical encounter between a person interested primarily in orthodox doctrine and the One who has come to bring life itself.

Kingdom of God (3:3). The exact expression "kingdom of God" is, surprisingly, not found in the Old Testament. Yet Nicodemus has no difficulty understanding its meaning. The Hebrew Scriptures make clear that "the LORD is king" and that his sovereign reign extends to every creature (e.g., Ex. 15:18; Ps. 93:1; 103:19). Moreover, the Jews expected a future kingdom ruled by the Son of David (Isa. 9:1–7; 11:1–5, 10–11; Ezek. 34:23–24; Zech. 9:9–10), the Lord's Servant (Isa. 42:1–7; 49:1–7), indeed, the Lord himself (Ezek. 34:11–16; 36:22–32; Zech. 14:9). While not everyone was to be included in this kingdom, Jews in Jesus' day generally believed that all Israelites would have a share in the world to come, with the exception of those guilty of apostasy or some other blatant sin (m. Sanh. 10:1).

Born again (3:3). The notion of a new beginning and a decisive inner transformation of a person's life is also found in certain Old Testament prophetic passages (e.g., Jer. 31:33–34; Ezek. 11:19–20; 36:25–27; see comments on John 3:5). This concept of a new spiritual birth is similar to that of a "new creation" (cf. 2 Cor. 5:17; Gal. 6:15). The term *anōthen*, translated "again" in the NIV, can mean either "from above" (be it fig. [John 3:7, 31; 19:11; James 1:17; 3:15, 17] or lit. ["from top to bottom": Matt. 27:51 =

Mark 15:38; John 19:23]) or "from the beginning" (Luke 1:3; Acts 26:5: "for a long time"; Gal. 4:9: "all over again" [with *palin*, "again"]). This potential ambiguity opens up the possibility of misunderstanding.

Born of water and the Spirit (3:5). The fact that "born of water and the Spirit" further develops "born again" in 3:3 suggests that one birth is in view rather than two. The closest Old Testament parallel is Ezekiel 36:25–27 which predicts God's cleansing of human hearts with water and their inner transformation by his Spirit (see also Isa. 44:3–5; *Jub.* 1:23–25).[83] The terminology may also be reminiscent of first-century proselyte baptism, where the Gentile convert to Judaism was compared to a newborn child. Thus R. Yose ben Ḥalafta (c. A.D. 130–160) said, "One who has become a proselyte is like a child newly born" (b. *Yebam.* 48b; cf. 22a; 62a; 97b; b. *Bek.* 47a).

Flesh gives birth to flesh, but the Spirit gives birth to spirit (3:6). Although the Old Testament does not literally refer to God's Spirit "giving birth" to spirit (cf. 6:63), it does hold out the vision that God, who is spirit (4:24), will "put a new spirit" in his people (Ezek. 36:26; cf. 37:5, 14).

You must be born again (3:7). "You" is in the plural, which shows that this requirement does not extend solely to Nicodemus but to the entire group he represents (cf. "anyone" in 3:3, 5; "we" in 3:2, 11). This includes the Pharisees and the Sanhedrin—and thus the entire Jewish religious leadership—but ultimately the entire nation.

The wind blows wherever it pleases . . . born of the Spirit (3:8). "Wind" and

"Spirit" translate the same Greek and Hebrew words (Gk. *pneuma*; Heb. *ruaḥ*). Both the Old Testament and Jewish literature contain numerous references to the mystery of the wind's origin (cf. Eccl. 8:8; 11:5; *1 En.* 41:3; 60:12; *2 Bar.* 48:3–4). In the present instance, the point of Jesus' analogy is that both wind and spiritual birth are mysterious in origin. Nevertheless, while they themselves are invisible, their effects can be observed. Despite its inscrutability, spiritual birth is nonetheless real, as real as the mysterious movements of the wind. Moreover, just as the wind blows "where it pleases," so the Spirit's operation is not subject to human control, eluding all efforts at manipulation.

You are Israel's teacher (3:10). Jesus may be returning Nicodemus's compliment in 3:2, where that rabbi had called Jesus "a teacher come from God" (cf. 3:11). The definite article before "teacher" in the original suggests that Nicodemus was an established, recognized teacher.[84]

Earthly ... heavenly (3:12). "Earthly things" may refer to the elementary teaching on the necessity of a spiritual birth. If "Israel's teacher" stumbles over such a foundational truth, how can Jesus enlighten him on "heavenly things," such as the more advanced teachings of the kingdom? A similar sentiment is expressed in the Wisdom of Solomon (first century B.C.): "We can hardly guess at what is on the earth . . . but who has traced out what is in the heavens?" (Wisd. Sol. 9:16; cf. Judith 8:14).

The Talmud tells the story of Rabban Gamaliel (c. A.D. 90) conversing with the Roman emperor Nerva (A.D. 96–98) or Domitian (A.D. 81–96) at the occasion of a visit to Rome. When the emperor claims to know what Gamaliel's God is doing and where he is seated, the rabbi becomes distressed and, when asked for the reason, tells the emperor, "I have a son in one of the cities of the sea, and I yearn for him. Please tell me about him." When the emperor protests that he has no way of knowing where he is, Gamaliel replies, "You do not know what is on earth, and yet [claim to] know what is in heaven!" (*b. Sanh.* 39a).

No one has ever gone into heaven except the one who came from heaven—the Son of Man (3:13). The Old Testament identifies heaven as the place where God dwells.[85] John's Gospel refers several times to a descent *from* heaven, be it of the Spirit (1:32–33), angels (1:51), the Son of Man (3:13), or the "bread of life" (6:33, 38, 41, 42, 50, 51, 58). However, this is one of only three instances where it speaks of an ascent *into* heaven (angels: 1:51; the Son of Man: 3:13; the risen Lord: 20:17). Jesus here contrasts himself, the "Son of Man" (cf. Dan. 7:13), with other human figures who allegedly entered heaven, such as Enoch (Gen. 5:24; cf. Heb. 11:5), Elijah (2 Kings 2:1–12; cf. 2 Chron. 21:12–15), Moses (Ex. 24:9–11; 34:29–30), Isaiah (Isa. 6:1–3), or Ezekiel (Ezek. 1; 10). A whole cottage industry of intertestamental literature

---

R E F L E C T I O N S

WE MUST CONSCIOUSLY CULTIVATE AN OPENNESS to new spiritual insights from God, even if this involves a radical change of life. Nicodemus, the revered "teacher of Israel," was confronted with his need to be "born from above." Would he be open to acknowledge his spiritual need and humble himself before God? Would he be receptive to that new revelation? The older we get, the harder it may be to retain such openness, but without it we will either suffer spiritual death altogether (if we are unbelievers) or cease to grow as a Christian.

revolved around such figures and their heavenly exploits (e.g., *1 En.*).[86] While believers can expect to join Christ in heaven one day (cf. John 14:1–3; 17:24), only Jesus came down from heaven as well as ascended back up to heaven (cf. Luke 24:51; Acts 1:9; though note the similar ascent-descent pattern by angels in John 1:51).

Just as Moses lifted up the snake in the desert (3:14). The allusion is plainly to Numbers 21:8–9, where God is shown to send poisonous snakes to judge rebellious Israel. When Moses intercedes for his people, God provides a way of salvation in the form of a raised bronze serpent, so that "when anyone was bitten by a snake and looked at the bronze snake, he lived" (Num. 21:9). But the primary analogy established in the present passage is not that of the raised bronze serpent and the lifted-up Son of Man. Rather, Jesus likens the restoration of people's physical lives as a result of looking at the bronze serpent with people's reception of eternal life as a result of "looking" in faith at the Son of Man (cf. John 3:15–18). Yet as in the case of desert Israel, it is ultimately not a person's faith but the God in whom the faith is placed who is the source of salvation: "[They] received a symbol of deliverance to remind them of your law's command. For the one who turned toward it was saved, not by the thing that was beheld, but by you, the Savior of all" (Wisd. Sol. 16:6–7).

Everyone who believes in him (3:15). This phrase strikes a markedly universal note. While looking at the bronze serpent in the desert restored life to believing Israelites, there are no such ethnic restrictions on believing in Jesus. *Everyone* who believes will receive eternal life (cf. 3:16–18 and comments on 1:4, 9, 12). God

sent Jesus to save not just Israel, but the entire world (3:17).

Its insistence on the universality of the Christian message marks John's Gospel off from sects such as the Qumran community or the large number of mystery religions, all of which saw salvation limited to a select few. At the same time, however, John's Gospel does not teach universal*ism*, that is, the notion that all will eventually be saved. Rather, salvation is made contingent on *believing in him*, that is, Jesus (cf. 20:30–31).

Eternal life (3:15). See comments on "life" at 1:4.

For God so loved the world (3:16). The Old Testament makes abundantly clear that God loves all that he has made, especially his people (e.g., Ex. 34:6–7; Deut. 7:7–8; Hos. 11:1–4, 8–11). In the Mishnah, R. Aqiba (c. A.D. 135) is quoted as saying, "Beloved is man for he was created in the image [of God]. . . . Beloved are Israel for they were called children of God" (*m. ʾAbot* 3:15). In these last days, God has demonstrated his love for the world through the gift of his one and only Son. Significantly, God's love extends not merely to Israel but to "the world," that is, sinful humanity.[87] Just as God's love encompasses the entire world, so Jesus made atonement for the sins of the whole world (1 John 2:2).

That he gave his one and only Son (3:16). On the phrase "one and only," see comments on 1:14, 18. The next verse says that God *sent* his Son; here the term used is "he gave." This draws attention to the sacrifice involved for God the Father in sending his Son to save the world. Surely to see his son die in such a cruel fashion would break any father's heart, much more that of our heavenly Father.

In a similar Old Testament passage, Abraham was asked to give up his "only son," Isaac (Gen. 22). Unlike Jesus, however, Isaac was not offered up but spared when God provided a substitute. Note also the parallel wording in the messianic prophecy of Isaiah 9:6, that "to us a *son* is *given.*"

Perish . . . eternal life (3:16). Already in the Old Testament, blessings for obedience correspond to curses for disobedience (Deut. 28–30). In John, likewise, there is no middle ground. Believing in the Son (with the result of eternal life) or refusing to believe (which results in destruction) are the only options. Since "perish" is contrasted with "*eternal* life," it stands to reason that perishing is eternal as well. Yet "perishing" does not mean annihilation in the sense of total destruction but spending eternity apart from God and from Jesus Christ, in whom alone is life (John 1:4).

God did not send his Son into the world to condemn the world, but to save the world through him (3:17). The Old Testament makes clear that God would rather save than judge (e.g., Ezek. 18:23). The Jews, however, believed that the coming Messiah would save Israel but judge the Gentiles. "In no time at all, with the coming of harvest, the straw is disposed of in the water, the chaff in the wind, and the weeds in flame, but the wheat is brought in for safe-keeping. . . . Likewise, the peoples of the earth . . . in the time-to-come, when the day of judgment arrives, will be dragged into the Valley of Hinnom. . . . Only Israel will remain in the time-to-come" (*Midr. Ps.* 2:14).

Isaiah's words "Morning is coming, but also the night" (Isa. 21:12) were taken to mean that when the Messiah, the Son of David, comes, "there will be morning for the righteous, and night for the wicked, morning for Israel, and night for idolaters [i.e., the nations]" (*y. Ta'an.* 1:1; cf. *Num. Rab.* 16:23). The Qumran sect maintained that only its own members would be saved while the rest of the world would perish: "There will follow a time of salvation for the people of God and a period of rule for all the men of his lot [i.e., the Qumran covenanters], and of everlasting destruction for all the lot of Belial" (1QM 1:5). The adherents of mystery religions likewise believed that only they were the initiated. Contrary to these expectations, John affirms that the Messiah's coming manifested God's saving will for all, not just Jews.

Light . . . darkness (3:19). For general remarks, see comments on 1:4–5. In the present passage, "light" and "darkness" have clear moral connotations, grounding the world's rejection of Jesus in human depravity, which is the result of the Fall (Gen. 3; Rom. 1:18–32). In the ultimate analysis, sin (including people's failure to recognize God's Messiah) is irrational and self-destructive. Notably, and contrary to Jewish self-perception, the Jews are not exempt from this pattern; they are shown to be in bondage to sin and spiritual blindness, refusing to face their guilt and preferring to suppress the truth instead (John 8:31–59; 9:39–41; cf. Matt. 21:33–46 par.; Acts 7).

In the Hellenistic world, Plato's well-known "Allegory of the Cave" (*Republic* 7.1–11; c. 390 B.C.), provided a partial analogy to John 3:19–21. According to this myth, human beings live from birth in a cave, a world of shadows. Only those who dare step out of this dark existence can experience the light, but many prefer to stay in the darkness. However, in

Plato's allegory, the person who has seen the light is the philosopher who is cognizant of the world of ideas and thus is able better to explain reality; in Jesus' teaching, the light is himself (cf. 1:4–5; 8:12; 9:5), and people's main problem is not ignorance but sin.[88]

For fear that his deeds will be exposed (3:20). The verb "exposed" points further to the shame that comes through such exposure (cf. 16:8). An interesting parallel is found in the *Damascus Document* of the Qumran sect: "And so is the judgment of everyone who enters the congregation of the men of perfect holiness and is slack in the fulfillment of the instructions of the upright. . . . When *his deeds are evident*, he shall be expelled from the congregation" (CD 20:1–3).

Lives by the truth (3:21). Similar is 5:29: "those who have done good." "Lives by the truth" contrasts with "does evil" in the preceding verse. The literal rendering of the phrase is "does the truth," a typical Jewish expression meaning "acts faithfully." It is found in the Old Testament (Neh. 9:33 LXX; Isa. 26:10 LXX), apocryphal literature (Tobit 4:6; 13:6), and the Qumran scrolls (1QS 1:5; 5:3).

Done through God (3:21). This unique phrase literally means "accomplished *in* God" (cf. Mark 14:6), that is, through God rather than by one's own strength. This excludes human pride (see Jer. 9:23–24). For not just salvation, but also subsequent works are, properly understood, works "done through God."

John the Baptist's Witness Concerning Christ (3:22–36)

Judean countryside (3:22). The Greek word *gē* usually means "land" or "region."

However, this rendering seems to be excluded here, for Jesus has been in *the land of* Judea ever since attending the Passover (i.e., from 2:23–3:21). Thus, the word likely means "countryside" (cf. Mark 1:5: *chōra*) here. If so, Jesus leaves the vicinity of Jerusalem and heads north. The next verse places him with John the Baptist at Aenon near Salim (see comments on John 3:23), while 4:3 indicates that Jesus leaves Judea altogether, returning to Galilee (cf. 2:12) via Samaria.

Spent some time (3:22). As in 11:54, this refers to an indefinite period of time Jesus spends with his disciples. In Acts, the only other place where this word (*diatribō*) occurs in the New Testament, the stay may be longer but need not extend for more than "seven days" (Acts 20:6) or "eight or ten days" (25:6).

Aenon near Salim, because there was plenty of water (3:23). "Aenon" is a Semitic term meaning "springs"—hence the mention of "plenty of water" (lit., "many waters," i.e., springs), an ideal site for John's (and Jesus') baptismal preaching. "Salim" comes from the Hebrew word for "peace." The location of this place is disputed. The two primary sites

39

John

◄

JUDEA AND SAMARIA

that have been suggested both lie in Samaria: One possibility is the Salim eight miles southeast of Beth Shean (Scythopolis), the other the Salim four miles southeast of Shechem further south.[89] The presence of a town (known from early times) called Sâlim in the latter location and of modern ʿAinûn eight miles to the northeast favors the second site. Also, the latter location, being further south, seems to cohere better with the geographical markers of 3:22 and 4:3. In either case, if we assume the reconstruction of "Bethany near the Jordan" in 1:28 is correct (see comments), John has moved south.

Ceremonial washing (3:25). The issue of ritual purification, while of significant interest to first-century Jews (see also the Dead Sea Scrolls), is clearly peripheral to the ministries of Jesus and John the Baptist. Hence no further explanation is provided (see also 2:6; 11:55; 18:28; 19:31).

Rabbi (3:26). See comments on 1:38. This is the only place in John's Gospel where the Baptist is called "Rabbi." While the Baptist, who engaged predominantly in a prophetic-style ministry, may not fit the stereotype of a Jewish rabbi, the term was at that time still sufficiently wide to subsume the Baptist. Later, the term came to be used only for those who had undergone formal rabbinic training.

On the other side of the Jordan (3:26). Salim must be located on the west side of the Jordan (cf. 1:28: "Bethany on the other side of the Jordan," that is, east of the Jordan).

A man can receive only what is given him from heaven (3:27). In keeping with contemporary practice, John uses the word "heaven" to circumscribe the name of God (similarly, Jesus in 19:11: "from above"). John here tells his disciples that he must not exceed the calling he

TEL SALIM
▼

received from God or compare himself with others (cf. 21:20–22).

Sent ahead of him (3:28). The phrase is used in the Old Testament for messengers sent ahead of a given person (e.g., Gen. 24:7; 32:3; 45:5; 46:28; cf. Ps. 105:17).

The bride belongs to the bridegroom. The friend who attends the bridegroom (3:29). John likens himself to the best man at a wedding who stands ready to do the bridegroom's bidding (e.g. *m. Sanh.* 3:5; *m. B. Bat.* 9:4).[90] He thus makes clear that the purpose of his ministry was to elevate Jesus, so that there was no rivalry between the two men. Jesus calls himself "the bridegroom" in Matthew 9:15 par.

Joy (3:29). Joy was the overriding theme at Jewish weddings.

Has certified (3:33). The word translated "has certified" (*sphragizō*) literally means "to seal" in the sense of confirming or authenticating something to be true.[91] The term is derived from the practice of signing important documents by pressing one's distinctive mark, which was engraved on one's signet ring, onto hot wax. Here the expression indicates that everyone who accepts Christ's testimony about himself agrees ("seals") that God is truthful. In 6:27, it is said that God has put his "seal of approval" upon the Son of Man.

For God gives the Spirit without limit (3:34). Literally, the text reads: "for he." Later Jewish rabbis were convinced that God gave his Spirit to the prophets in measured amounts: "Even the Holy Spirit resting on the prophets does so by weight [i.e., appointed measure], one prophet speaking one book of prophecy and another speaking two books. . . . Even the words of the Torah which were given from above were given by measure, namely Scripture, Mishnah, Talmud, *Halachah* [legal portions], and *Haggadah* [narrative portions]. One man becomes versed in Scripture, another in Mishnah, etc." (*Lev. Rab.* 15:2 on Lev. 13:2; attributed to R. Aḥa [c. A.D. 320]). Jesus, by contrast, is the One on whom the Spirit has come to rest in all his fullness, as the Baptist has previously testified (cf. John 1:32–33). In keeping with this notion, the Apocalypse portrays Jesus as the One who holds the seven spirits of God (Rev. 3:1) and as the Lamb who has seven horns and seven eyes, which are the seven spirits of God (5:6).

Has eternal life (3:36). The present tense "has" indicates that eternal life is not merely a future expectation but already a present experience. This exceeds Old Testament hopes and claims made by other world religions.

Will not see life (3:36). Similar to "see/enter the kingdom" and "do the truth," "see life" is a Jewish expression meaning "experiencing or enjoying life." The corresponding expression "see death" occurs in 8:51.[92]

Christ Witnesses to the Woman at the Well (4:1–26)

After an eventful stay in Jerusalem for the Passover and an extended baptizing ministry in the Judean countryside (2:13–3:36), Jesus journeys back north to Galilee. His trip leads him through Samaritan territory. But rather than rushing on in order to avoid religious defilement through an encounter with this despised race, Jesus takes the time to talk with a Samaritan woman at a well, which results in her entire village being evangelized. In the process, Jesus identifies himself as Messiah and is recognized by his converts as the Savior of the world.

The Pharisees heard that Jesus was gaining and baptizing more disciples than John (4:1). There were others baptizing in Judea during this period, but Jesus and John are distinctive in that they use baptism as an initiatory rite for Jews. The Pharisees have investigated John's credentials (1:19, 24); now they are looking into those of Jesus.

Had to go (4:4). "Had to" may indicate divine necessity: That is, Jesus' going through Samaria is according to the plan and will of God (cf. 9:4; 10:16; 12:34; 20:9).

Through Samaria (4:4). This was the usual trek taken by travellers from Judea to Galilee. As Josephus writes, "It was the custom of the Galileans at the time of a festival to pass through the Samaritan territory on their way to the Holy City" (*Ant.* 20.6.1 §118; cf. idem., *J.W.* 2.12.3 §232). Again, Josephus comments, "I further wrote to my friends in Samaria to provide for their safe convoy through that district; for Samaria was now under Roman rule and, for rapid travel, it was

essential to take that route, by which Jerusalem may be reached in three days from Galilee" (*Life* 52 §269). Strict Jews, however, sought to bypass Samaria by opting for a longer, less direct route, which involved crossing the Jordan and traveling on the east side.

Sychar (4:5). The small village of Sychar was probably located at the site of modern ʿAskar about two miles east of Nablus, centrally situated just east of Mount Gerizim and Mount Ebal.[93] ʿAskar may also be the *ʾên Sokder* mentioned in the Mishnah (*m. Menah.* 10:2).[94] An identification of Sychar with biblical Shechem (about a mile from ʿAskar) is unlikely, since Shechem was probably destroyed in 128 B.C. (or at least prior to 107 B.C.) by the Hasmonean high priest John Hyrcanus I (Josephus, *J.W.* 1.2.6 §63; *Ant.* 13.9.1 §§255–56). Subsequent to the conquest of Jerusalem by the Roman general Pompey (63 B.C.), Sychar apparently became the most important Samaritan city in place of Shechem. John is the first ancient author to mention Sychar/ʿAskar.[95]

Near the plot of ground Jacob had given to his son Joseph (4:5). It was deduced from Genesis 48:21–22 and Joshua 24:32 that Jacob gave his son Joseph the land at Shechem which he had bought from the sons of Hamor (Gen. 33:18–19) and which later served as Joseph's burial place (Ex. 13:19; Josh. 24:32).[96]

Jacob's well was there (4:6). The reference to Jacob's well and the later mention of Mount Gerizim (4:20) places Jesus' encounter with the Samaritan woman within the framework of "holy geography," which Jesus is shown to transcend. Holy sites were—and still are—of great importance in Jewish and Samari-

SAMARIA

▼

tan life, as they are in all major world religions. Apparently, Jacob's well was a convenient stop for pilgrims travelling from Galilee to Jerusalem or vice versa.[97]

The site of Jacob's well is reasonably certain, although the Old Testament nowhere mentions Jacob digging a well here (or anywhere). The current well is about one hundred feet deep. Such a deep well is unusual in an area where there are many springs. ʿAskar is nearly a mile to the north and has its own well, but perhaps it did not two thousand years ago. Shechem, on the other hand, is only 250 feet from Jacob's well, which suggests to some that Shechem and not ʿAskar is the true Sychar (see comments on 4:5).

Tired as he was from the journey (4:6). Since it was about noon when Jesus sat down at the well (see below), he and his disciples would have been traveling for about six hours up to that point if they had started their journey at daybreak.

Sat down by the well (4:6). Wells were usually carved out from solid limestone rock, with a small curb remaining to guard against accident (cf. Ex. 21:33). This is probably where Jesus sat down to rest.[98]

About the sixth hour (4:6). This probably means around twelve noon (see comments on 1:39).

Samaritan woman came to draw water (4:7). Apparently, the woman is from the district, not the town, of Samaria (the town of Samaria is located several miles north of Sychar). If Sychar is ʿAskar, it is surprising that the woman does not go to the well there (Ain ʿAskar). Perhaps that well did not always flow or the woman lives closer to the well of Jacob. Women were more likely to come in groups to fetch water (Gen. 24:11; Ex. 2:16) and to do so either early in the morning or later in the day when the heat of the sun was not so fierce (Gen. 24:11: "toward evening"). By contrast, this Samaritan woman comes alone, and she comes in the heat of the midday sun. Both observations suggest that this woman is looked down upon in her community on account of her low reputation (see 4:16–18).

Will you give me a drink? (4:7). By asking a woman who has come to the well alone for a drink, Jesus, himself being alone (4:8), breaks all rules of Jewish piety (see comments on 4:9). His taking the initiative is open to the charge of acting in a

THE SITE OF
JACOB'S WELL

The structure is a Byzantine-era church rebuilt by the Crusaders and, later, the Orthodox church.

flirtatious manner. Also, the fact that Isaac and Jacob met their prospective wives at wells (Gen. 24:17; 29:10) creates the sort of precedent that would further have cautioned devout Jews.

His disciples had gone into the town to buy food (4:8). Apparently, Jesus and his disciples carry little or nothing to eat on their journeys (Matt. 12:1 par.; 16:6–7 par.; cf. 10:9–10 par.). Rather, they bring with them the necessary money to buy what they need on the way (cf. John 12:6; 13:29). Purchasing food, together with the preparation and cooking of food and waiting on tables, were common tasks of disciples.[99] That Jesus and his disciples are willing to purchase food from Samaritans indicates a certain freedom from the self-imposed regulations of the stricter Jews, who would have been unwilling to eat food handled by Samaritans. As Rabbi Eliezer (c. A.D. 90–130) used to say, "He that eats the bread of the Samaritans is like to one that eats the flesh of swine" (*m. Šeb.* 8:10). Moreover, with certain dry foods, there was no conveyance of defilement.

You are a Jew and I am a Samaritan woman. How can you ask me for a drink? (For Jews do not associate with Samaritans.) (4:9). Generally, Jews avoided contact with Samaritans, especially Samaritan women, although there would have been a certain spectrum depending on locale, class, education, and other factors.[100] Some Jews were willing to eat with Samaritans (*m. Ber.* 7:1; 8:8), but many were not because of ritual defilement. Samaritans were thought to convey uncleanness by what they lay, sat, or rode on, as well as by their saliva or urine. Samaritan women, like Gentiles, were considered to be in a continual state of ritual uncleanness: "The daughters of

the Samaritans are [deemed unclean as] menstruants from their cradle" (*m. Nid.* 4:1).[101] Apart from these ethnic sensibilities, men would generally not want to discuss theological issues with women. Hence the woman's surprise: Did Jesus not know that even her water jar was considered unclean by his fellow-Jews?

The gift of God . . . living water (4:10). On a literal level, the expression "living water" refers to the much sought-after fresh spring water, as opposed to stagnant water (Gen. 26:19; Lev. 14:6; Jer. 2:13). Ultimately, God is known to be the source and giver of life. In Numbers 20:8–11, an incident to which Jesus may allude in the present passage, water gushes out of the rock, supplying the Israelites with much-needed refreshment. In Jeremiah 2:13, God laments that his people have forsaken him, "the spring of living water." In Isaiah 12:3, the prophet envisions the joy with which people "will draw water from the wells of salvation" in the last days.

For the ancient Jews, the greatest "gift of God" was the Torah (the law). Other "gifts of God," apart from the lights in the sky and rain, were considered to include peace, salvation, the land of Israel, and divine mercy (*Gen. Rab.* 6:5; attributed to Yoḥanan ben Zakkai [c. A.D. 70] and other rabbis). Rabbinic thought associated the provision of water with the coming of the Messiah: "As the former redeemer made a well to rise [cf. Num. 21:17–18], so will the latter Redeemer bring up water" (*Eccl. Rab.* 1:9; see comments on 6:31).

In John, Jesus is identified explicitly with God the Creator and Life-giver (John 5:26) and shown to dispense the gift of "living water," later unveiled as the Holy Spirit (7:37–39). This end-time blessing, bestowed after Jesus' exaltation, transcends John's water baptism (1:26, 33), Jewish ceremonial purification (2:6; 3:25), proselyte baptism (cf. 3:5), and the torch-lighting and water-pouring symbolism of the Feast of Tabernacles (chs. 7–8). It also supersedes nurturing or healing waters such as Jacob's well (ch. 4) or the pools of Bethesda and Siloam (chs. 5 and 9). In fulfillment of the Old Testament prophetic vision (Ezek. 47:9; Zech. 14:8), Jesus has inaugurated the age of God's abundance.

Sir (4:11). The word translated "sir" is *kyrios*, which can also mean "Lord." Here, however, it is merely a respectful address of Jesus without further Christological implications.[102]

Nothing to draw with and the well is deep (4:11). The well is still over one hundred feet deep and was probably deeper at that time. In fact, Jacob's well may have been the deepest well in all of Palestine.[103] John's use of a different

▶ The Samaritans[A-15]

The Samaritans occupied a curious middle position between Jews and Gentiles. Their origins went back to the intermarriage of Israelites left behind during the Assyrian exile of the northern kingdom with Gentiles (2 Kings 17:24). The Samaritans themselves, however, claimed descent from Joseph by way of the tribes of Manasseh and Ephraim (Josephus, *Ant.* 9.14.3 §291; 11.8.6 §§341, 344). In contrast, at least some Jews preferred to trace the Samaritans' ancestry back to Shechem, the rapist of Dinah, the sister of Jacob's twelve sons (Gen. 34). Because they occupied territory that according to the Jews belonged to the two above-mentioned tribes (which had not yet returned from exile), they saw the Samaritans as an obstacle to the fulfillment of God's end-time promises to the Jews (cf. Sir. 50:26: "the foolish people that live in Shechem"; *T. Levi* 5–6).

In Jesus' day, relations between Jews and Samaritans were generally characterized by bitter hostility (e.g., *T. Levi* 7:2, which calls Shechem "City of the Senseless"). In an apparent attempt to ease the tension, Herod the Great married a Samaritan woman named Malthace, who bore him both Antipas and Archelaus (Josephus, *J.W.* 1.28.4 §562; *Ant.* 17.1.3 §20), but to little avail. On the whole, Samaritans were considered to be irremediably impure.

Despite their recognition of the five books of Moses, they were suspected of being an idolatrous cult on the basis of their veneration of Mount Gerizim as a holy mountain (cf. *m. Ḥul.* 2:8). The Jewish historian Josephus portrays the Shechemites as a refuge for Jewish religious apostates (*Ant.* 11.11.7 §§346–47). He also records an occasion (between A.D. 6–9) when some Samaritans tried to desecrate the Jerusalem temple on the eve of the Passover (*Ant.* 18.2.2 §§29–30) and another instance (in A.D. 52) when they attacked Jewish pilgrims on their way to Jerusalem (*Ant.* 20.6.1–3 §§118–36).

To call someone—especially a fellow-Jew—a "Samaritan" was a gross insult (cf. *b. Soṭah* 22a)[A-16] and may have been tantamount to accusing him of religious apostasy (cf. 8:48; Josephus, *Ant.* 11.8.6 §340). When Jesus sent out the Twelve, he explicitly instructed them not to enter any town of the Samaritans, thus upholding an ethnic (as well as salvation-historical) distinction between these people and the Jews (Matt. 10:5). At a later time, Jesus' disciples were indignant when they were not welcome in a Samaritan village because Jesus was headed for Jerusalem (Luke 9:51–56; cf. Josephus, *Ant.* 20.1.1 §6). Jesus himself broke with his Jewish contemporaries' hostility toward Samaritans (see Luke 10:33; 17:16). His coming had created a level playing field where ethnic distinctions gave way to spiritual considerations bound up with obedience to God and acceptance of Jesus as Messiah (cf. esp. John 4:23–24).

Greek word for "well" in the present passage (*phrear*; cf. 4:6: *pēgē*) may indicate that the cistern (*phrear*) is fed by an underground spring (*pēgē*). Travellers usually carried a skin bucket (*antlēma*) for drawing water, which they could let down the well with a rope. In the present instance, Jesus' disciples are probably carrying it with them, but they have gone to buy food, presumably taking it along (4:8); in any case Jesus could not get "living" water out of the well (see comments on 4:10).

Are you greater than our father Jacob (4:12). Jesus' significance surpasses that of all the major previous figures in the history of God's people, be it Abraham (8:53), Moses (1:17), Jonah, or Solomon (Matt. 12:41–42).

According to Josephus, the Samaritans claimed descent from Joseph through Ephraim and Manasseh (*Ant.* 11.8.6 §341). The Jews sharply disagreed (see "The Samaritans" at 4:9). Jesus himself seems to side with his fellow Jews when he refers to a Samaritan leper as a "foreigner" (Luke 17:18). Yet in the present passage, Jesus refuses to get sidetracked by this (for him) peripheral point (cf. John 4:19–20).

Who gave us the well and drank from it himself (4:12). This is sheer tradition. The book of Genesis does not record Jacob ever digging a well, much less drinking from it himself or giving it to any of his sons. Mention is merely made of Jacob's buying and giving Shechem to Joseph (Gen. 33:19; 48:22), in the vicinity of which Jacob's well is located (see comments on John 4:5–6).[104]

Will become in him a spring of water welling up to eternal life (4:14). Isaiah envisioned a time in the last days when people would joyfully "draw water from the wells of salvation" (Isa. 12:3).[105] In a dry, hot climate such as that of Palestine, people were particularly aware of their need for water and the blessing it represents. Similar terminology is found in the *Targum Neofiti* of Genesis 28:10: "When *our father Jacob* raised the stone from above the mouth of the well [at Haran], the well *overflowed* and came up to its mouth, and was *overflowing* for twenty years."[106] A Samaritan liturgy for the Day of Atonement says of the Taheb, the Samaritan Restorer, that "water will flow from his buckets" (cf. Num. 24:7).[107]

I have no husband (4:17). While technically truthful, the woman's statement is potentially misleading. On the face of it, it can be taken to imply that she is unattached and thus available (see comments on 4:7).[108] Jesus, with fine irony, quickly removes all doubt.

You have had five husbands, and the man you now have is not your husband (4:18). If the NIV rendering is correct, the woman is in conflict with Jewish law, since rabbis generally disapproved of more than three legal marriages in a lifetime, even in case of the death of previous husbands (*b. Yebam.* 64b; cf. *b. Nid.* 64a). However, it is perhaps more likely that this is another instance of a wordplay, here involving the word *anēr*, which can mean either "man" or "husband." Jesus may tell the woman that she had five "men" (with whom she lived in fornication) and that the one she is now living with is not her "man," that is, husband (though he may be that of another woman, note the emphatic position of "your" in the Greek). In other words, the woman is a serial fornicator.[109] Some argue that "five men or husbands" alludes to a tradition cited in Josephus, according to which the Samaritans had five gods (*Ant.* 9.14.3 §288; cf. 2 Kings 17:24, 30–31), just as "five colonnades" in 5:2 are taken to refer to the Jewish Pentateuch.[110]

You are a prophet (4:19). The woman acknowledges that Jesus knows her life circumstances without apparently having been told by anyone—hence he must be "a prophet" (cf. Luke 7:39).

Our fathers worshiped on this mountain (4:20). "Our fathers" refers back to Abraham (Gen. 12:7) and Jacob (33:20), who built altars in this region. Mount Gerizim was the site where the Israelites were blessed by Moses (Deut. 11:29; 27:12). The Samaritans held that many other significant events during the patriarchal period were associated with this mountain.[111] It is unclear precisely when the Samaritans built a temple at that location. Samaritan tradition places construction in the fifth century B.C., while Josephus claims that the temple was built in 332 B.C.[112] Since the names mentioned by Josephus coincide strikingly with those of Nehemiah 13:28, Samaritan tradition may be closer to the truth than Josephus.[113] In Hellenistic times, Antiochus IV Epiphanes converted the Samaritan sanctuary into a temple of Zeus Horkios ("the Guardian of Oaths"), while the Samaritans continued their worship at an altar erected on another peak of the mountain.[114] In 129 B.C., it was razed by John Hyrcanus and the Jews (*Ant.* 13.9.1 §§254–56).

The Jewish-Samaritan dispute regarding the proper place of worship had thus been raging for centuries when the Samaritan woman broached the subject with Jesus. Josephus tells of an argument between Egyptian Jews and Samaritans before Ptolemy Philometor in around 150 B.C. as to whether the sanctuary was to be on Mount Gerizim or Mount Zion (*Ant.* 13.3.4 §74; cf. 12.10).

That Samaritan beliefs regarding the sanctity of Mount Gerizim continued unabated is illustrated by an incident in A.D. 36 (recounted in *Ant.* 18.4.1 §§85–87) involving a Samaritan troublemaker put down by Pilate. "Although bereft of a sanctuary, the Samaritan high priest and priesthood continued to sacrifice on Mount Gerizim in the first century."[115] During Jesus' conversation with the Samaritan woman, Mount Gerizim would have been in full view. From Jacob's well, they may have even been able to see the temple's ruins, perhaps turning to look at them when the woman mentioned the place.

You Jews claim . . . Jerusalem (4:20). *Midr. Ps.* 91:7, commenting on Genesis 28:17, says that "when a man prays in Jerusalem, it is as though he prays before the throne of glory, for the gate of heaven is in Jerusalem, and a door is always open for the hearing of prayer." The Pentateuch, however, does not specifically identify

MT. GERIZIM

Jerusalem as the proper place of worship—though other portions of Scripture do (see 2 Chron. 6:6; 7:12; Ps. 78:68)—which led the Samaritans to establish their own sanctuary on Mount Gerizim. The Samaritans accepted only the Pentateuch as Scripture (see comments on 4:22).

A time is coming when you will worship the Father neither on this mountain nor in Jerusalem (4:21). The woman has just acknowledged Jesus as a prophet (4:19). Now he uses prophetic language: "a time is coming" (cf. 1 Sam. 2:31; 2 Kings 20:17; Jer. 31:31). Jesus' prophecy was literally fulfilled through the events of A.D. 66–70, when the Romans under Titus razed Jerusalem, including the temple (cf. Luke 21:20, 24). Spiritually speaking, the crucified and resurrected Christ would serve as a substitute for the Jerusalem temple as the new center of worship for God's people (John 2:19–22).

You Samaritans worship what you do not know (4:22). The Samaritans had greatly truncated their knowledge of God by restricting their canon to the Pentateuch. Jesus says "what" (neuter) rather than "whom" (masculine) you do not know, perhaps pointing to the less than personal character of Samaritan worship.

Salvation is from the Jews (4:22). See "The Jews" at 5:10. In Psalm 76:1, the psalmist exclaims, "In Judah God is known; his name is great in Israel." Jesus here acknowledges that the Jewish people are the instrument by which God's redemption is mediated to others. This contrasts with Samaritan religious ignorance (see previous comment). Nevertheless, while Jesus freely acknowledges Jewish salvation-historical preeminence, he does not allow it to become a barrier to keep others from benefiting from divine

salvation blessings.[116] It was precisely the fact that the Jews wanted to keep God's gifts to themselves that drew God's judgment.

God is spirit . . . worship in spirit and in truth (4:24). "God is spirit" does not refer to the Holy Spirit but identifies God as a spiritual rather than material being. The spiritual nature of God is taught clearly in the Old Testament.[117] Because God is spirit, the Israelites were not to make idols "in the form of anything" as did the surrounding nations (Ex. 20:4).

Messiah (called Christ) is coming (4:25). See comments on 1:41. Although the Samaritan woman refers to a coming "Messiah," the Samaritans did not regularly use this expression until the sixteenth century,[118] preferring terms such as "Taheb" (meaning "the Restorer"). The figure of the Taheb apparently originated independently of Deuteronomy 18:15–18 and was only later identified with the "prophet like Moses."[119]

He will explain everything to us (4:25). Rather than looking for a royal Messiah from the house of David (as did the Jews), Samaritans apparently expected a "teaching" Messiah.[120]

The Disciples Rejoin Jesus (4:27–38)

Disciples . . . were surprised to find him talking with a woman (4:27). Some rabbis (such as Yose ben Yoḥanan, a very early rabbi) held that to talk too much to a woman, even one's own wife, was a waste of time, diverting one's attention from the study of the Torah. Potentially, this habit could grow to be a great evil leading even to hell (*m. ʾAbot* 1:5). Consequently, some rabbis taught that it was as inappropriate to provide one's daughter with a knowledge of the Torah as it was to sell them into prostitution (*m. Soṭah* 3:4; attributed to R. Eliezer [c. A.D. 90–130]).[121] As in other encounters with women, Jesus broke with this prejudice (cf. 7:53–8:11; 11:17–40; also Luke 7:36–50; 8:2–3; 10:38–42).

But no one asked, "What do you want?" or "Why are you talking with her?" (4:27). On other occasions, the disciples were not so bashful (e.g., Matt. 19:13 par.).[122] Perhaps the reason why they refrain from questioning Jesus here is that the woman is still there, so that an open challenge would have created an awkward situation. Generally, it was certainly considered appropriate in first-century Judaism for disciples to question their rabbi's actions, as long as this was done respectfully and appropriately.[123]

Leaving her water jar (4:28). The water jar was probably a large earthenware pitcher carried either on the shoulder or the hip.[124] The woman here abandons her original purpose for coming to the well (to draw water) in order to tell her townspeople about Jesus. "Leaving her water jar" may therefore have symbolic overtones.

Come, see a man who told me everything I ever did. Could this be the Christ? (4:29). Regarding the Samaritan Taheb as prophet-revealer, see comments on 4:25. "Who told me everything I ever did" is an obvious exaggeration, understandable in light of the woman's excitement. Rabbinic literature is somewhat ambivalent regarding the validity of a Samaritan's testimony. One relevant passage states, "No writ is valid which has a Samaritan as witness excepting a writ of divorce or a writ of emancipation" (*m. Giṭ.* 1:5). Yet the document proceeds,

"They once brought a bill of divorce before Rabban Gamaliel . . . and its witnesses were Samaritans; and he pronounced it valid."

The witness of Samaritan *women*, especially those of low repute, may have been subject to further limitations. Regarding women witnesses in general, Josephus writes, "From women let no evidence be accepted, because of the levity [lightness, triviality] and temerity [overboldness, rashness] of their sex" (*Ant.* 4.8.15 §219). Yet the present instance represents not a formal courtroom scene, but an informal situation where a Samaritan woman goes back to her village and tells her fellow townspeople about a remarkable encounter she has had. Perhaps precisely *because* of the woman's reputation for immorality, her compatriots are curious to see for themselves what created such a remarkable change in the woman's disposition.

Rabbi, eat something (4:31). See comments on 1:38. Disciples regularly cared for the physical well-being of their master, a concern that extended from buying food to tending to him when he was sick and burying him after he had died.[125]

I have food to eat that you know nothing about. . . . My food . . . is to do the will of him who sent me (4:32–34). Jesus here asserts that fulfilling his mission is

BREAD

more important to him than physical food (cf. Matt. 6:25; Mark 3:20–21). The present statement may echo Deut. 8:3: "Man does not live on bread alone but on every word that comes from the mouth of the LORD" (cf. Matt. 4:4; Luke 4:4). The Old Testament prophet Jeremiah testified, "When your words came, I ate them; they were my joy and my heart's delight" (Jer. 15:16).

To finish his work (4:34). In one sense, God was considered to have finished his work (Gen. 2:2). In another sense, it was recognized that God continues to sustain his creation (cf. John 5:17). In the present passage, Jesus affirms his commitment to complete the task God has given him to do, that is, his redemptive work on the cross (12:23–24; 17:4; 19:30).

Do you not say, "Four months more and then the harvest"? (4:35). Apparently, the saying quoted here by Jesus is a common proverb (cf. Matt. 16:2–3), though there is no independent evidence for its existence. Jesus' statement can be taken to imply that four months remain until the harvest. If so, the present event occurred some time in December or January, since the time of harvest extended from March until May (barley was harvested in March, wheat from mid-April until the end of May).

Alternatively, the proverb as commonly used may simply indicate the need for patience, similar to the saying, "Rome was not built in a day."[126] Jesus' point may be that while sowing and reaping are separated by (a minimum of) four months, his coming has ushered in the end-time harvest, so that sowing and harvest paradoxically coincide. Then again, the saying may have been a general proverb *and* have been uttered by Jesus about four months prior to harvest time, so that there is no need to choose between the above alternatives. See further the following comment.

Look at the fields! They are ripe for harvest (4:35). If the proverb quoted in the previous verse is to be taken literally, the fields are not actually ripe for harvest. Rather, Jesus' statement may be metaphorical rather than literal, pointing his disciples to the approaching mass of white-clothed Samaritans.[127] Elsewhere Jesus uses similar imagery (Matt. 9:37–38; Luke 10:2).

Even now the reaper draws his wages (4:36). Payment was usually made only for work completed. Thus, the disciples must not delay getting to work when others are already receiving wages.[128] R. Tarfon (c. A.D. 130) used to say, "The day is short and the task is great and the laborers are idle and the wage is abundant and the master of the house is urgent" (m. ʾAbot 2:15).

The sower and the reaper may be glad together (4:36). The joy of reaping a harvest is universally known. The Old Testament refers to it both literally (Deut.

WHEAT
▼

16:13–14) and metaphorically (Ps. 126:5–6; Isa. 9:3). Sowing, on the other hand, was often laborious (Ps. 126:5). In the present instance, however, it is not just the reaper who is able to rejoice but also the sower. Jesus here conjures up images of a glorious, restored Edenic prosperity (cf. Amos 9:13: "The days are coming . . . when the reaper will be overtaken by the plowman"), a time when streams of blessing will flow from God's presence (cf. Ps. 36:8; 46:4; 87:7; Ezek. 47:1–12).

The saying "One sows and another reaps" is true (4:37). Usually, the saying points to the sad inequality of life: One sows without enjoying the benefits of the resulting crop, while another, who has not sown, reaps the fruit of that person's labor at a later time. In the case of the end-time spiritual harvest referred to by Jesus, however, the intervening time is collapsed, so that sower and reaper rejoice together (4:36). Nevertheless, as Jesus points out in the present verse, this does not mean that the distinction between sower and reaper is obliterated.[129]

Many Samaritans Believe (4:39–42)

Many of the Samaritans . . . believed in him because of the woman's testimony (4:39). Apart from this instance, there is no precrucifixion evidence for a large contingent of Samaritan disciples; Acts 8:4–25 treats the evangelization of the Samaritans as a fresh venture. Historically, Jesus' Samaritan mission may have been preparatory for the early church's effort at evangelizing this group. Theologically, John may be seeking to show that the Samaritan mission of the early church was based on precedent in Jesus' own ministry (cf. Acts 1:8; 8:4–25). Jesus' pattern of ministry in John coincides with that of the mission of the early church (Acts 1:8): first Judea (Nicodemus, John 3), then Samaria (John 4), then the Gentiles (10:16; 11:52; 12:20–32).

That town (4:39). The village referred to is Sychar (cf. 4:5).

They urged him to stay with them, and he stayed two days (4:40). The Jews' concern regarding ritual purity, which caused them to refrain from association with Samaritans, was clearly not a major concern for Jesus (cf. 4:9).

Savior of the world (4:42). Interestingly, the Old Testament never calls the Messiah "Savior," and the expression was not a messianic title in first-century Judaism. The

REFLECTIONS

RATHER THAN BEING RUGGED

Christian individualists—a contradiction of terms—we stand in a rich tradition of faith. We must seek to be ever more conscious of our place in salvation history and see ourselves as part of the historic Christian movement. North American Christians in particular at times operate as if they were the first Christians—but they are not. We can benefit from insights into Scripture gained by previous interpreters—patristic, medieval, or more recent. We can draw strength from the unswerving faith displayed by a succession of Christian martyrs in ages past. And we can be assured that when we get to heaven, we will be greeted by others in that "great cloud of witnesses" who have gone before us.

Samaritans likewise did not view their Taheb as a redeemer. Philo calls God "Savior of the world" (*Spec. Laws* 2.198). The title "Savior" was also applied to many Greek gods and even Roman emperors, including Nero (A.D. 54–68).[130] By identifying Jesus as "Savior of the world," John thus challenges his surrounding culture (cf. Rev. 13:18; see also comments on John 20:28). In the present context, Jesus' large-scale harvest among the Samaritans is considered the first sign of the universal scope of his saving mission.

Return Trip to Galilee (4:43–45)

He left for Galilee (4:43). We are not told how long it takes Jesus to travel to Galilee or where in Galilee he goes prior to his return visit to Cana (4:46). But from Sychar to Cana is about forty miles, a trip that could be accomplished in two or three days.

A prophet has no honor in his own country (4:44). (Cf. 4:19.) This comment seeks to qualify the sense in which Jesus is "welcomed" at his return to Galilee. John may be assuming his readers' familiarity with Synoptic tradition, according to which Jesus is rejected in his native Galilee, including Nazareth.[131] The saying is also found in the *Gospel of Thomas* (Logion 31) and a papyrus document (P. Oxy. 1).

Jesus Heals the Royal Official's Son: His Second Sign in Cana (4:46–54)

A certain royal official (4:46). The term "royal official" (*basilikos*) usually refers to someone in the service of a king;[132] the official may also have been a centurion.[133] Perhaps he was "a wealthy aristocrat, probably much influenced by Greco-Roman culture and not very religious by general Palestinian Jewish standards."[134]

Whose son lay sick (4:46). The sickness of the royal official's son involves some kind of fever (4:52) and is apparently terminal (4:47, 49).

Capernaum (4:46). See comments on 2:12 and the following verse.

He went to him (4:47). To travel from Capernaum to Cana involves a day's journey of about fourteen miles. The trip is mostly uphill, since Cana lies in the Galilean hill country while Capernaum is several hundred feet below sea level. If the royal official leaves Capernaum at sunrise, he can reach Cana at noon, and at the seventh hour (i.e., 1 P.M.) hear Jesus' comforting words that his son will live (4:50). On the way back, however, he can complete only half of his journey on the same day, so that his servants meet him at the plain of Gennesaret on the following day (4:51–52).[135]

To come (4:47). Literally, "come down," for Capernaum is lower in elevation than Cana (see previous comment).

Miraculous signs and wonders (4:48). The expression probably harks back to the "signs and wonders" performed by Moses at the Exodus.[136]

Come down. . . . You may go. Your son will live (4:49–50). This is a rare instance of a long-distance miracle (on the unusual nature of Jesus' signs selected by John, see comments on 2:10). Another similar remarkable incident (that of the healing of the centurion's servant in Capernaum) is narrated in Matthew 8:5–13 (Luke 7:1–10 par.). See also the activities by the first-century Jewish miracle worker and faith healer Ḥanina ben Dosa. According to rabbinic tradition, when Rabban Gamaliel's son fell ill, he sent two disciples to this healer and asked him to pray for his son's healing. When Ḥanina ben Dosa had finished praying, he said to the messengers, "Go, the fever has left him." They wrote down the hour, and when they came back to R. Gamaliel, he said to them, "You have not been a moment too soon or too late, but so it happened: at that very moment the fever left him and he asked for water to drink" (*b. Ber.* 34b).[137]

Your son will live (4:50). This may be an allusion to Elijah and the woman of Zarephath in 1 Kings 17:23. If so, Jesus' messianic activity is here placed within the compass of the miraculous healing ministry of Elijah in the Old Testament (cf. Luke 4:23–27).

Seventh hour (4:52). The healing takes place around 1 P.M. (see "References to Time in John's Gospel" at 1:39).

Second miraculous sign . . . having come from Judea to Galilee (4:54). This is the second sign Jesus performs after having come from Judea to Galilee. In the interim, other signs have been performed in Jerusalem and the vicinity (2:23; 3:2; 4:45). Thus John closes the cycle of Jesus' first ministry circuit, starting and ending in Cana of Galilee.

The Healing at the Pool of Bethesda (5:1–15)

A little while after completing his first "ministry circuit," Jesus travels to Jerusalem in order to attend an unspecified feast; this is the second of three trips by Jesus to the Jewish capital recorded in this Gospel (the time may be October, A.D. 31). Passing by the pool of Bethesda, Jesus takes pity on a lame man and heals him (the fourth sign in this Gospel). Healers were much sought after in the ancient world, both in Judaism and in Greco-Roman society. Rabbinic literature speaks of Ḥanina ben Dosa, who operated as a miracle worker and faith healer in first-century Galilee. In the Hellenistic world, shrines were dedicated to Asclepius and other gods of healing.[138] John must consider this event to be very important, since it is the only event he selects from Jesus' second year of ministry.

Some time later (5:1). This expression marks the passing of an indefinite period of time. Up to a year and a half may have passed since the last feast recorded, the Jewish Passover, at which Jesus had cleansed the temple and met with Nicodemus.

Went up to Jerusalem (5:1). It was customary for Jews at any place and any elevation in Palestine to use the expression going "up" to Jerusalem.

REFLECTIONS

"THE MAN TOOK JESUS AT HIS word and departed." This is the essence of faith: taking Jesus at his word and acting on the basis that Jesus' word is true. Jesus was a man of his word. Am I? Can others take me at my word? Can my daughter count on me coming to her ballet recital when I have told her that I would be there? Can my wife count on me being home after work when I told her I would be? In the official's case, he was called to believe that Jesus could do something as difficult as healing at a long distance. His faith still challenges us today.

A feast of the Jews (5:1). This is the only unnamed festival in John. This feast was most likely one of the several festivals taking place in Jerusalem in September/October, perhaps the Feast of Tabernacles (which, if the year was A.D. 31, fell on October 21–28).[139] This is suggested by the fact that some manuscripts (such as Codex Sinaiticus) have "the" feast of the Jews, which was the conventional name for the Feast of Tabernacles.[140]

In Jerusalem near the Sheep Gate a pool (5:2).[141] A "Sheep Gate" is mentioned in the book of Nehemiah (3:1, 32; 12:39). In Jesus' day, this was apparently a small opening in the north wall of the temple. The sheep would have been washed in the pool before being taken to the sanctuary. This is also the place where invalids would lie in hopes of being healed. The upper class and those wishing to be ritually pure would avoid this area, but not Jesus.

Surrounded by five covered colonnades (5:2). The five colonnades may have been erected by Herod the Great.[142] Four covered colonnades enclose two separate pools (viewed as a unity)[143] in a rough trapezoid, with a fifth one separating them.[144] There the sick can lie and be partially protected from the weather. Some argue that "five" colonnades is also symbolic of the five books of Moses, the Pentateuch (see comments on 4:18).[145]

Which in Aramaic is called Bethesda (5:2). For John's translation of Aramaic or Hebrew terms, see the chart at 1:38. "Bethesda"[146] may mean "house of (divine) mercy"—which would be a fitting term, given the desperate state of the people lying there in hope of miraculous healing—or "house of the two springs," or the name may be derived from the root "pour out" or "slope."[147]

Here a great number of disabled people used to lie (5:3). Official Judaism almost certainly did not approve of the superstition associated with the alleged healing powers of the pool of Bethesda. After all, healing shrines were characteristic of pagan cults, such as the one surrounding the Greek god of healing, Asclepius. Apparently, however, the Jewish authorities looked the other way, tolerating this expression of popular religion. See comments on 5:7.

An invalid (5:5). Though the man's illness is not detailed, 5:7 suggests that he

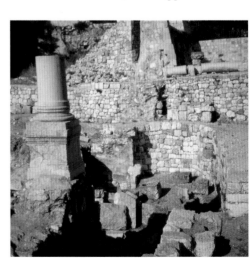

is paralyzed, lame, or extremely weak (the Gk. word used is the general expression for "disabled"). We do not know the invalid's age or exactly how long he has been lying there. A similar healing is recorded in Matthew 9:1–8 par.

For thirty-eight years (5:5). This man has been an invalid longer than many people in antiquity lived (average life expectancy for men barely exceeding forty years of age), roughly as long as Israel's wanderings in the desert (Deut. 2:14).[148] For all that time, nothing has cured him (cf. Mark 5:25–26; cf. Luke 8:43). The length of the man's plight is also in keeping with John's selection of "difficult" miracles performed by Jesus (see comments on John 2:10).

Jesus saw him . . . and learned that he had been in this condition for a long time (5:6). The Greek term rendered "learned" can just as well refer to supernatural knowledge rather than to knowledge gained through diligent inquiry (cf. 1:47–48; 4:17–18). Possibly Jesus' conversation with the invalid is occasioned by the man's request for alms (cf. Acts 3:1–5).

I have no one to help me (5:7). Contrast this with the paralytic in Mark 2:1–12, whose four friends carry him to Jesus by lowering his mat through a roof.

When the water is stirred (5:7). The stirring of the waters may have been created by intermittent springs or spring water. Superstition attributed the movement of the water to an angel of the Lord coming down from time to time and stirring up the waters. Some later manuscripts add: "from time to time an angel of the Lord would come down and stir up the waters."

Your mat (5:8). A mat (*krabattos*) was the poor man's bedding. The term is used in distinction from "bed" (*klinarion*; Acts 5:15). Normally made of straw, it was

THE BETHESDA POOLS

POOL OF BETHESDA

An artistic reconstruction.

Major Archaeological Finds Relating to John's Gospel		
Site or Artifact	Location	Passage in John
Inscription barring Gentiles from entry into inner temple	Jerusalem	2:14–17
Herod's temple	Jerusalem	2:20
Jacob's well	Nablus	4:5–6
Pool of Bethesda	Jerusalem	5:2
Ancient fishing boat	Galilee	6:22–24; 21:8
Early synagogue	Capernaum	6:59
Pool of Siloam	Jerusalem	9:7
Siloam inscription	Jerusalem	9:7
Tomb of Lazarus	Bethany	11:38
Caiaphas tomb/inscription	Jerusalem	11:49; 18:13–14
Pilate inscription	Caesarea	18:29
Stone pavement	Jerusalem	19:13
Skeletal remains of crucified man	Jerusalem	19:18
Garden tomb[A-17]	Jerusalem	19:41–42

light and could be rolled up and carried about by any healthy person.

It is the Sabbath; the law forbids you to carry your mat (5:10). Although the Jews may have thought of Old Testament passages such as Exodus 31:12–17, Jeremiah 17:21–27, or Nehemiah 13:15, 19, the man is not actually breaking any biblical Sabbath regulations. According to Jewish tradition, however, the man is violating a code that forbids the carrying of an object "from one domain into another" (*m. Šabb.* 7:2; in the present instance, his mat). Apparently, it was permissible to carry a bed with a person lying on it, but not one that was empty (*m. Šabb.* 10:5). At this point, Jesus is accused, not of violating the law himself, but of enticing someone else to sin by issuing a command that will cause that person to break the law. "To forbid this man from carrying his bed was like forbidding a modern man to move a chair or a campstool. Either he must have left his bed at the pool, to be stolen, or he must have stayed there to watch it, or he must have been allowed to take it home with him."[149]

At the temple (5:14). The pool of Bethesda is located just north of the temple area. Jesus meets the man again just a short distance from where the original healing has taken place.

REFLECTIONS

IT IS NEVER TOO LATE TO TRUST JESUS. HERE IS A man who has been through an almost endless cycle of futility and frustration. For thirty-eight years he has been an invalid, and all his hopes for healing have been dashed time and time again. Then comes Jesus. Rather than rely on friends or superstition, the man must rely on Jesus. Jesus speaks the word, and the man gets well. The man born blind later has a similar experience. Many of us can gratefully testify that Jesus has redeemed us from a life of purposelessness and futility. Let's now live for him.

Stop sinning or something worse may happen to you (5:14). The comment seems to imply that at least sometimes—including in the case of the invalid?—sickness may be a result of sin (e.g., 1 Kings 13:4; 2 Kings 1:4; 2 Chron. 16:12). Jesus' Jewish contemporaries generally held that suffering was a direct result of sin (cf. John 9:2). Given expression already by the "miserable counselors" in the book of Job, rabbinic literature states the principle succinctly: "There is no death without sin, and there is no suffering without iniquity" (*b. Šabb.* 55a with reference to Ezek. 18:20; attributed to R. Ammi [c. A.D. 300]). However, the Old Testament features several instances where suffering is transparently not a result of sin (e.g., 2 Sam. 4:4; 1 Kings 14:4; 2 Kings 13:14). Jesus himself, likewise, rejects simple cause-and-effect explanations (cf. Luke 13:1–5; John 9:3). Nevertheless, Jesus acknowledges that sin may well lead to suffering. In the present instance, the "something worse" he threatens probably does not refer to a worse physical condition but rather to eternal judgment for sin (cf. 5:22–30).

Jesus' Defense (5:16–30)

The Jews charge Jesus not only with breaking the Sabbath but with blasphemy. In response, he declares that he has come, not to detract attention away from the Father, but to lead people to him. The Jews resist him out of personal ambition. Jesus himself claims to be the life-giver and judge, terms reserved in the Old Testament exclusively for God.

My Father (5:17). It would be highly unusual for a Jew of that day to address God simply as his "Father" without some qualifying phrase like "in heaven" in order to avoid undue familiarity.[150] The Jews' response in verse 18 confirms the perceived inappropriateness of Jesus' terminology.

Is always at his work to this very day (5:17). According to Genesis 2:2–3, God rested on the seventh day of creation. But if God observes the Sabbath, who sustains the universe? The consensus among Jewish rabbis at the end of the first century

---

▶ "The Jews" in John's Gospel

In recent years, scholars have been troubled by the negative portrayal of "the Jews" in John's Gospel.[A-18] This has been taken by some as evidence that John is guilty of anti-Semitism. However, this charge is clearly unjustified. John's primary concern is not ethnic but salvation-historical. Acknowledging that "salvation is from the Jews" (4:22), John points to the fact that the Jewish nation, represented by its religious leadership, has rejected Jesus as Messiah. Note, of course, that all the members of Jesus' inner circle, the Twelve, are Jews, as are most of his first followers. Nevertheless, the Jews, *as a nation*, have joined the world in its sinful rebellion against God and his Sent One. Thus, Jesus must set up a new messianic community that will be able to carry on his work once he returns to God the Father. Jews are welcome in this community if they believe that Jesus is the Messiah. In fact, many believe that one of John's major purposes for writing is to reach out to unbelieving Jews.

A.D. was that God does indeed work constantly, but that this does not amount to his breaking the Sabbath. For the entire universe is his domain, so that he cannot be charged with transporting an object from one domain to another; and God lifts nothing to a greater height than himself (cf. *Gen. Rab.* 11:10; *Ex. Rab.* 30:9 citing Isa. 6:3; Jer. 23:24). The Letter of Aristeas (second century B.C.) says of God that he "is continually at work in everything" (210). Eusebius later wrote, "It is plainly said by our legislation that God rested on the seventh day. This does not mean, as some interpret, that God no longer does anything. It means that, after he had finished ordering all things, he so orders them for all time" (Frag. 5 in Eusebius, *Praep. Ev.* 13.12.11).[151]

And I, too, am working (5:17). Jesus could have objected to the—inaccurate—Jewish interpretation of the Old Testament Sabbath command that prohibited work normally done on the other six days of the week. These regulations (which refer to regular work) hardly apply to the man's picking up his mat after a miracle cure! But rather than taking this approach, Jesus places his own activity on the Sabbath plainly on the same level as that of God the Creator. If God is above Sabbath regulations, so is Jesus (cf. Matt. 12:1–14 par.).

Calling God his own Father (5:18). See 5:17. Just as Jesus is uniquely God's "own" Son (Rom. 8:32), God is uniquely "his own" Father (cf. John 10:29–30). The designation "my Father" for God was extremely rare in the Old Testament (but see Jer. 3:4; cf. Ps. 89:26).

Making himself equal with God (5:18). The Jews of the first century were committed monotheists, believing in only one God.[152] This became an important distinguishing characteristic of Jewish religion in a polytheistic environment. Thus the Roman historian Tacitus writes, "The Jews conceive of one God only" (*Hist.* 5.5).[153] Jesus' claim of a unique relationship with God seemed to compromise this belief by elevating him to the same level as the Creator, as if he were a second God.

The Son can do nothing by himself (5:19). Similarly, Moses affirms in the Old Testament, "This is how you will know that the LORD has sent me to do all these things and that it was not my idea" (Num. 16:28). Just like the Son, so believers can do nothing of eternal significance without Christ (John 15:5).

Just as the Father raises the dead and gives them life, even so the Son gives life to whom he is pleased to give it (5:21). Old Testament and intertestamental Jewish literature concur that raising the dead and giving life are the sole prerogatives of God.[154] Jesus' contemporaries therefore do not believe that the Messiah will be given authority to raise the dead. Rabbi Yoḥanan (c. A.D. 70), for instance, cites three prerogatives of God not delegated to others: the key of rain (cf. Deut. 28:12), the key of childbirth (cf. Gen. 30:22), and the key of raising the dead (cf. Ezek. 37:13; *b. Taʿan.* 2a).

The *Shemoneh ʿEsreh*, an ancient Jewish prayer dating to around A.D. 70–100,[155] likewise affirms:

> *You are mighty forever, O Lord;*
> *you restore life to the dead . . .*
> *who sustains the living out of grace,*
> *makes the dead alive out of great*
> *mercy. . . .*
> *Who is like you, O King,*
> *who makes dead and alive again. . . ?*

▶ Sabbath and Sunday Observance

In the early church, a transition took place from the Jewish Sabbath to the Christian Sunday. This day was called "the Lord's Day" (Rev. 1:10), for on it Jesus had risen from the dead. It was considered to be "the first day of the week" (John 20:1 and Synoptic parallels) and was the day on which the early church met for worship (Acts 20:7; 1 Cor. 16:2). The first Christians did not think of Sunday as a mere substitute for the Sabbath. In fact, nowhere is the Old Testament command to "keep the Sabbath holy" repeated in the New Testament. Rightly understood, the fulfillment of the Sabbath is to be found in the salvation rest provided for believers by Jesus (Heb. 4:3, 9–11), ultimately pointing to heaven itself (6:20; 12:2).

In this life, Sunday (the name "Sunday" is not biblical but, like other names of days of the week, derives from Roman terminology) is to be a day celebrating Jesus' resurrection, a day not of legalistic preoccupation but of joyful liberty. That was already true for the intention underlying the Sabbath: "The Sabbath was made for man, not man for the Sabbath" (Mark 2:27). Communal worship, recreation, time spent with one's family and with God's people, and works of helpfulness, love, and necessity all have their place in using "the Lord's Day" in a way pleasing to the Lord.

> And you are faithful to raise the
>   dead.
> Blessed are you, O Lord, who restores
>   the dead.

This background renders Jesus' claim of being able to raise the dead and to give them life at will all the more startling. To be sure, Elijah was sometimes considered to constitute an exception because he was used by God to raise the dead. Yet Jesus' claim is much bolder than that of Elijah. For Jesus is not merely God's instrument in raising other people but he chooses to give life *to whom he is pleased to give it.*

The Father judges no one, but has entrusted all judgment to the Son (5:22). Genesis 18:25 states that God is "the Judge of all the earth" (cf. Judg. 11:27). In Psalm 2:2, "the LORD" is associated with "his Anointed One" in rule and judgment. The final judgment will take place after the resurrection on the last day (Rev. 20:11–15). According to the rabbis, God alone will judge the world. There is no passage in rabbinic literature that unambiguously places the judgment of the world in the hands of the Messiah. Apart from carrying out God's judgment on his enemies in keeping with Jewish nationalistic expectations (e.g., *Pss. Sol.* 17:21–27), the Messiah remains very much in the background as far as judgment is concerned, even in the Apocrypha. The singular exception is the Son of Man (or "Chosen One") in the Similitudes of Enoch.[156] See also the following comment.

He who does not honor the Son does not honor the Father, who sent him (5:23). In the Old Testament, Moses and the prophets were considered to be God's agents and mouthpieces who acted and spoke on God's behalf. The Jewish fundamental affirmation regarding a messenger (*šaliaḥ*) is that "a man's agent is like the man himself" (e.g., *m. Ber.* 5:5).[157] This is true of any messenger, particularly a trusted servant, and even more so of a man's son, especially his first-born.[158] Thus, anyone who fails to acknowledge the authority of Jesus (the sent Son) in fact rejects his Sender, that is, the Father. Authorized representatives were not unique to Judaism. The Roman *legatus*, for instance, fulfilled a similar role. To this day, the failure to honor an ambassador is a failure to honor the government he or she represents.

The dead will hear the voice of the Son of God and those who hear will live (5:25). This statement is reminiscent of Ezekiel's vision of the valley of dry bones (Ezek. 37). There are no similar texts in intertestamental Jewish literature.

For as the Father has life in himself, so he has granted the Son to have life in himself (5:26). The Old Testament states repeatedly that God grants life to others.[159] But here Jesus claims that God has granted him life *in himself*, a divine attribute.

Because he is the Son of Man (5:27). Literally, the phrase reads, "he is Son of Man"—the only instance of this phrase without articles before both "Son" and "Man" in the entire New Testament. This may be accounted for in part by Colwell's rule (see comments on "The Word was God" at 1:1); it may also indicate an allusion to Dan. 7:13 (LXX), where the phrase "son of man" likewise does not feature any article (cf. Rev. 1:13; 14:14).[160]

All who are in their graves will hear his voice and come out—those who have done good will rise to live, and those who have done evil will rise to be condemned (5:28–29). In the first century, there was

no consensus as to whether all would be raised or just the righteous (though see Dan. 12:2). Sheol was thought of as containing chambers where the dead are kept until the great day of judgment.[161]

By myself I can do nothing . . . I seek not to please myself but him who sent me (5:30). See comments on 5:19 and 23. The Mishnah cites a saying attributed to Rabban Gamaliel III, son of R. Yehudah the Patriarch (c. A.D. 200): "Do his will as if it was your will that he may do your will as if it was his will. Make your will of no effect before his will that he may make the will of others of no effect before your will" (*m. ʾAbot* 2:4).

Testimony Regarding Jesus (5:31–47)

If I testify about myself, my testimony is not valid (5:31). The interrogation of witnesses was central to Jewish legal procedure.[162] The need for multiple witnesses, already taught in the Hebrew Scriptures (Deut. 17:6; 19:15), is reiterated by Jewish tradition. According to the Mishnah, "None may be believed when he testifies of himself" (*m. Ketub.* 2:9), "for no individual can be deemed trustworthy in himself" (*m. Roš Haš.* 3:1). Josephus writes, "Put not trust in a single witness, but let there be three or at the least two, whose evidence shall be accredited by their past lives" (*Ant.* 4.9.4 §219).

There is another (5:32). The Jews may think of John the Baptist (cf. 5:33–35), but Jesus is referring to God the Father (5:37; see comments), in common Jewish fashion avoiding the name of God.

He has testified to the truth (5:33). Similarly, 18:37 (cf. 3 John 3, 12). The Qumran community considered itself as "founded on truth . . . true witnesses for the judgment" (1QS 8:5–6).

John was a lamp that burned and gave light (5:35). See 1:7–9. The verb "was" (past tense) may indicate that John is now dead or at least in prison (cf. 3:24). "A lamp" is more accurately rendered "the lamp" (note the Gk. article), pointing to a known person or phenomenon. Most likely, Psalm 132:17 is in view, where it is said that God will "set up a lamp" (*lychnos*) for his "anointed one." The book of Sirach portrays Elijah as having arisen "like fire [*pyr*], and his word burned like a torch [*lampas*]" (Sir. 48:1). While the Baptist earlier denies being Elijah (John 1:21), Jesus here identifies him as that "lamp" set up by God to cast its light on the coming Messiah. Inherent in the designation of the Baptist as a "lamp" is the recognition that his witness is small (though important) and of a temporary nature.

You chose . . . to enjoy his light (5:35). The word for "enjoy" also occurs in Psalm 132:16 (LXX; see previous comment), where it is said that the saints "will ever sing for joy." Josephus wrote that people "were aroused [*or* overjoyed] to the highest degree" by the Baptist's message (*Ant.* 18.5.2 §118).

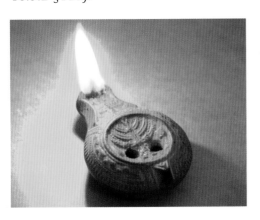

The Father . . . has himself testified concerning me (5:37). Jesus may here refer to the voice at his baptism (Matt. 3:17 par.), an event not explicitly mentioned in John, though the primary reference is probably to God's witness in Scripture.[163] In mishnaic teaching, God is also cast as a witness: "God . . . is the Judge, he is the Witness, he is the Complainant, and it is he that shall judge [i.e., render the ultimate judgment]" (*m. ʾAbot* 4:22).[164]

You have never heard his voice nor seen his form (5:37). Old Testament figures who heard the voice of God include Noah (Gen. 7:1–4), Abraham (12:1–3), Moses (Ex. 3:4–4:17; 19:3–6, 9–13; 33:11), Samuel (1 Sam. 3:4, 6, 8, 11–14), and Elijah (1 Kings 19:13, 15–18). Abraham (Gen. 18:1–2), Jacob (32:24–30), Moses (Ex. 33:11), and Isaiah (Isa. 6:1–5) all "saw" the Lord in one sense or another. While not seeing God directly, Israel received the Law at Mount Sinai and accepted it from God's servant Moses. Now the Jews are rejecting greater revelation from an even greater messenger (cf. John 1:17–18; 8:56–58; 12:41; Heb. 1:1–3; 2:1–3; 3:1–6).

Nor does his word dwell in you (5:38). The Old Testament depiction of a God-fearing individual is that of someone who has the Word of God living in his heart (Josh. 1:8–9; Ps. 119:11).

You diligently study the Scriptures (5:39). Jewish scribes "numbered the verses, words and letters of every book. They calculated the middle word and the middle letter of each. They enumerated verses which contained all the letters of the alphabet, or a certain number of them."[165] When copying the Scriptures, scribes were not to write more than one

◀ *left*

AN OIL LAMP

letter before looking at the original again (*b. Meg.* 18b).[166]

Because you think that by them you possess eternal life (5:39). The famous first-century Jewish rabbi Hillel used to say, "The more study of the Law the more life. . . . If a man . . . has gained for himself words of the Law he has gained for himself life in the world to come" (*m. ᾿Abot* 2:7). Similarly, the apocryphal work Baruch states: "She is the book of the commandments of God, the law that endures for ever. All who hold her fast will live, and those who forsake her will die" (4:1).

These are the Scriptures that testify about me (5:39). For John, it is not merely that individual sayings of Scripture are fulfilled in Jesus,[167] but Scripture in its entirety is oriented toward him.[168] See comments on 5:46–47.

I have come in my Father's name, and you do not accept me; but if someone else comes in his own name, you will accept him (5:43). Deuteronomy 18:19 says regarding the "prophet like Moses": "If anyone does not listen to my words that the prophet speaks in my name, I myself will call him to account." The false prophet Shemaiah is charged by the true prophet Jeremiah with speaking in his own name.[169] Jesus himself predicted the proliferation of false Christs as a sign of the end times (Matt. 24:5 par.), and Josephus reports a string of messianic pretenders in the years prior to A.D. 70.[170] The delegation sent to investigate John the Baptist (1:19–22) is no doubt aware of such stirrings.

You accept praise from one another (5:44). In the rabbinical schools, "Scripture study had become a world in which men sought fame by showing their intellectual prowess. One big authority was set over against another, and the result was barren logomachy [verbal disputes], where men sought *honour one of another*."[171]

Your accuser is Moses, on whom your hopes are set (5:45). See 9:28–29. With regard to Old Testament Israel, Moses frequently served as intercessor.[172] According to the first-century work *Assumption of Moses*, Moses, "in every hour both day and night, had his knees fixed to the earth, praying and looking steadfastly toward him who governs the whole earth with mercy and justice, reminding the Lord of the ancestral covenant" (11:17; cf. 12:6; *Jub.* 1:19–21). Yet both the "Song of Moses" and the Book of the Law are said to function as a witness against Israel (Deut. 31:19, 21, 26; cf. Rom. 3:19).

In Jesus' day, many Jews, in keeping with the Old Testament and intertestamental portrayal of Moses, saw the latter's role primarily as that of continuing mediator and advocate, who prayed for them in heaven as he had interceded for the Israelites on earth.[173] The Samaritans, too, increasingly regarded Moses as their intercessor in heaven.[174] Even many pagans knew Moses as Israel's lawgiver (e.g., Diodorus Siculus, *Bib. Hist.* 1.94.2.8; 34/35.1.3.9; first cent. B.C.). Jesus sharply rebukes this reliance on Moses' intercession; to him, Moses is not the Jews' advocate but their accuser.

Moses . . . wrote about me (5:46). See comments on 5:39. The reference may be to the first five books of the Old Testament, which are attributed to Moses, or to the prediction of a "prophet like [Moses]" in Deut. 18:15, or to both.

But since you do not believe what he wrote, how are you going to believe what I say? (5:47). This refers to the Jews' failure to grasp the true essence of Scripture, including its prophetic orientation toward Jesus (cf. Matt. 5:17). The argument is from the lesser to the greater, a customary rabbinic device used frequently by Jesus (3:12; 6:27; 7:23; 10:34–36), Paul (Rom. 5:15, 17; 2 Cor. 3:9, 11), and other New Testament writers (Heb. 9:14; 12:9, 25). Jesus' words in Luke 16:31 are similar: "If they do not listen to Moses and the Prophets, they will not be convinced even if someone rises from the dead." The same reasoning is found in an ancient Jewish commentary: "If . . . they believed in Moses, is it not implied by *Kal vaḥomer* [i.e., an argument from the lesser to the greater] that they believed in God?" (*Mek. Ex.* 14:31; 2d cent. A.D.).

Jesus Feeds the Five Thousand (6:1–15)

After defending himself against the charge of breaking the Sabbath, Jesus once again leaves Jerusalem. He returns to Galilee and is found on the east side of the Sea of Galilee, shortly before another Passover (April, A.D. 32). There Jesus performs another one of his startling messianic signs, feeding a large multitude. In keeping with Jewish expectation, Jesus reveals himself as the antitype to Moses, not only providing bread for his people (as Moses did the manna), but also revealing himself as the life-giving "bread" who will give his flesh for the world.

Some time after this (6:1). As much as half a year may have passed since the previous event recorded in John.

The far shore of the Sea of Galilee (that is, the Sea of Tiberias) (6:1). The "far shore" of the Sea of Galilee was normally considered to be the east side, since most Jewish activity occurred on the west side. In Old Testament times, the Sea of Galilee was referred to as Kinnereth because it was shaped like a lyre.[175] Around A.D. 17–18, Herod Antipas founded a city called Tiberias (cf. 5:23) on the west side of the lake in honor of his patron, the reigning Roman emperor Tiberius (A.D. 14–37; see Josephus, *Ant.* 18.2.3 §36). Tiberias is one of the few cities in the Holy Land that has kept its Roman name, probably because it was founded in Roman times and entirely supplanted the previously existing village of Rakkath (Josh. 19:35). Gradually, the name of the city was transferred to the lake. On a popular level, this transfer probably did not take place until late in the first century (around the time when John was writing his Gospel), hence his choice to provide both names (cf. 21:1). The name "Sea of Tiberias" is attested in first-century literature (*Sib. Or.* 12.104). It is also preserved in Jewish tradition (*Yamma shel Tiberya; t. Sukkah* 3:9) and by the Arabs, who call the lake *Bahr Tabariyeh.*[176]

THE SEA OF GALILEE

Mountainside (6:3). "Mountainside" need not designate any specific mountain or hill but may refer simply to "the hill country" or "the high ground" east of the lake, known today as the Golan Heights.

Sat down (6:3). Like other rabbis, Jesus usually sat down to teach (Matt. 5:1; Mark 4:1; 9:35; Luke 4:20), although here teaching is not mentioned explicitly.

Jewish Passover feast was near (6:4). This is the second of three Passovers mentioned by John, and the only one Jesus spends in Galilee (in A.D. 32, Passover fell on April 13/14). In the life of the Jewish nation, Passover was a time of intense nationalistic zeal. The nearness of this feast provides the framework for the ensuing feeding of the multitude and Jesus' claim of being the "bread of life."

A great crowd coming toward him (6:5). People have apparently walked the several miles around the (shorter) north side of the lake and caught up with Jesus and the disciples.

Philip (6:5). Philip would be the natural choice, since, like Andrew (cf. 6:8) and Peter, he is a native of nearby Bethsaida (1:44).

Where shall we buy bread for these people to eat? (6:5). In the desert, Moses asked God a similar question: "Where can I get meat for all these people?" (Num. 11:13). There are several other parallels between John 6 and Numbers 11: the grumbling of the people (Num. 11:1; John 6:41, 43); the description of the manna (Num. 11:7–9; John 6:31); the reference to the eating of meat (Jesus' flesh) (Num. 11:13; John 6:51); and the striking disproportion between the existing need and the available resources (Num. 11:22; John 6:7–9).

Eight months' wages would not buy enough bread for each one to have a bite! (6:7). "Eight months' wages" renders the phrase "two hundred denarii." One denarius was approximately one day's pay (Matt. 20:2; cf. John 12:5). Philip quickly estimates that it would take over half a year's income to feed the entire crowd (no pay on Sabbaths or other holy days).

A boy (6:9). This "boy" may be a teenager or even someone in his early twenties, though he may have been younger as well. The same word is used to refer to young Joseph in Genesis 37:30 (LXX); Daniel and his friends in Daniel 1 (LXX); and Tobit's son who is at a marriageable age in Tobit 6.

Five small barley loaves and two small fish (6:9). The common word for bread, *artos*, usually designates wheat bread; here it refers to bread made of barley. Barley was common food for the poor, its "lower gluten content, low extraction rate, less desirable taste, and indigestibility" rendering it "the staple of the poor in Roman times."[177] Philo writes that barley products are "suited for irrational animals and people in unhappy circumstances" (*Spec. Laws* 3.57). The more well-to-do preferred wheat bread (Philo, *Spec. Laws* 2.175), which was traded at twice or even three times the value of barley (2 Kings 7:1, 16, 18; Rev. 6:6; *m. Ketub.* 5:8). The fish were probably dried or preserved, perhaps pickled. The word used for "fish" here is the rare term *opsarion*

(cf. 21:9–13), a diminutive form of *opson*, which originally meant cooked food and then came to refer to any relish taken with food.

Have the people sit down ... the men sat down, about five thousand of them (6:10). In addition to the men, there were women and children (cf. Matt. 14:21). The total may have been as many as twenty thousand people.

There was plenty of grass in that place (6:10). Mark 6:39–40 mentions that the grass was green, which points to spring (near the Passover), before the summer heat would turn it brown.

Jesus ... gave thanks (6:11). If Jesus used the common Jewish form of thanksgiving, he would have uttered a prayer such as the following: "Blessed are you, O Lord our God, King of the universe, who brings forth bread from the earth."[178]

Gather the pieces that are left over. Let nothing be wasted (6:12). Similarly, it is said of Ruth, "She ate all she wanted and had some left over" (2:14).[179] It was customary at Jewish meals to collect what was left over. Pieces of bread were not to be thrown around (*b. Ber.* 50b), and food the size of an olive or larger must be picked up (*b. Ber.* 52b).[180] The expression "that nothing may be lost" is also documented in rabbinic literature with reference to food: "Let the poor come and eat the food, so that it not go to waste" (*y. Sanh.* 6:6; *y. Ḥag.* 2:2). Jesus applies the same care to preserving all the Father has given him (John 10:28–29; 17:11–12, 15).

They gathered them and filled twelve baskets with the pieces of the five barley loaves left over (6:13). The baskets used

◀ *left*

DENARIUS

A Tyrian silver denarius with the image of Alexander the Great.

to gather the leftovers were probably made of stiff material, perhaps wicker. "Twelve" baskets may allude to Jesus' restoration of Israel (the twelve tribes) by calling twelve disciples to form the core of his new messianic community.

Miraculous sign (6:14). See comments on 2:11.

The Prophet who is to come into the world (6:14). See 1:21; 6:31; 7:40. The underlying passage is doubtless Deuteronomy 18:15–18, which also featured significantly in the messianic expectations of the Qumran community (cf. 4QTest 5–8; 1QS 9:11). Jesus' multiplication of barley loaves is reminiscent of the miracle performed by Elijah's follower, Elisha (2 Kings 4:42–44). In 1 Kings 19, a parallel between Elijah and Moses is obvious (cf. Ex. 24:18; 34:28). The popular expectation expressed in John 6:14 may represent an amalgamation of the two figures.[181] In Jesus' day, the notion of the "Prophet" was apparently merged with that of "king" (John 6:15). Indeed, "the step from a prophet like Moses (6:14), the first Redeemer and worker of miracles, to a messianic deliverer was a short one for enthusiasts in contemporary Israel to make."[182] This fig-

ure also figured prominently in early Christian preaching (Acts 3:23; 7:57).

They intended to come and make him king by force (6:15). The present incident is reminiscent of the Zealots, a militant movement that found in Galilee fertile soil for its nationalistic brand of Judaism.

Withdrew again to a mountain by himself (6:15). Earlier Jesus had withdrawn to this mountainous area with his disciples (6:1–3). Now he goes by himself farther up what is known today as the Golan Heights (cf. Matt. 14:23; Mark 6:46).

Jesus Walks on the Water (6:16–24)

From the mountaintop of participating in the feeding of the multitudes, the disciples descend to the valley of experiencing a violent storm as they try to cross the

REFLECTIONS

PEOPLE IN JESUS' DAY STILL recounted Israel's wanderings in the desert and God's provision of manna, the heavenly bread, for his people through Moses. So caught up were they in their religious observances and remembrances that they were blind to the "new thing" God was doing in their midst that very day, even though God had plainly predicted it through the prophets. Jesus' "substitute presence," the Holy Spirit, is in our midst today, ready to do his work. Let us not get so caught up in the past that we miss God's will for us in the present.

Sea of Galilee. Many of them are fishermen and well acquainted with the lake. Nevertheless, they are gripped with fear and need to be rescued by Jesus. This is all the more remarkable since a similar incident has taken place earlier (Matt. 8:23–27 par.).

When evening came, his disciples went down to the lake, where they got into a boat and set off across the lake for Capernaum (6:16–17). Perhaps it is late afternoon, because only in the next verse has darkness set in. The disciples are on the east side of the lake and attempt to row the six or seven miles back to Capernaum on the northwest side.

By now it was dark. . . . A strong wind was blowing and the waters grew rough (6:17–18). "The Sea of Galilee lies about six hundred feet below sea level. Cool air from the south-eastern tablelands can rush in to displace the warm moist air over the lake, churning up the water in a violent squall."[183] Even today, power boats are to remain docked as the winds buffet the water. How much more could violent storms have wreaked havoc to the wooden boats used in Jesus' time.

Rowed three or three and a half miles (6:19). "Three or three and a half miles" translates "twenty-five or thirty stadia." A *stadion* was equivalent to 606.75 feet. The lake was about 61 stadia at its greatest width. If the multiplication of the loaves took place at the eastern shore of the Sea of Galilee, the shortest distance to Capernaum would be five to six miles. After rowing for about three and a half miles, the disciples were driven off course and found themselves halfway towards Magdala, where the lake was the widest.

The next day . . . in search of Jesus (6:22–24). Apparently, the crowd, which has been fed on "the far shore" (6:1), has remained there during the events of 6:16–24. Next, "some boats from Tiberias" end up where the crowd is (presumably east across the lake from Tiberias). Finally, the multitude and the people in the boats decide to head back to Capernaum across the northern quarter of the lake.

Boats from Tiberias (6:23). Tiberias is (even today) the chief city on the west side of the lake (see comments on 6:1). Whereas Capernaum is located on the northwest edge of the lake, Tiberias is several miles to the south, just about at the midpoint of the western shore.

Jesus the Bread of Life (6:25–59)

Jewish literature celebrated God's provision of manna for Israel in the desert. People expected the Messiah to perform a similar feat. The age of the Messiah would be an age of abundance, when God's blessings would be poured out on Israel. In the following discourse, Jesus presents himself as the fulfillment of these expectations. In contrast to popular belief, however, God's provision of life through his Messiah entails substitutionary suffering. Jesus will have to "give his flesh for the life of the world," and only those who "eat his flesh" and "drink his blood" will partake of God's salvation blessings.

On the other side of the lake (6:25). This refers to the area in or around Capernaum (see 6:24, 59).

Do not work for food that spoils, but for food that endures to eternal life (6:27).

As essential for human existence, bread and water are universal symbols of life. This symbolism may be applied to salvation, the law, the Scriptures, or wisdom. In Judaism, the Torah (law) was commonly called "bread." *Gen. Rab.* 54:1, for instance, interprets Proverbs 25:21 in terms of the "bread and water of the Torah" (see also *Gen. Rab.* 70:5; *Song Rab.* 1.2 §3). In Gnosticism, the imagery referred to knowledge (*gnōsis*), in the mystery religions to the sacramental meal.[184]

The Son of Man (6:27). See comments on 1:51.

God the Father has placed his seal of approval (6:27). See comments on 3:33.

To do the works God requires (6:28). Literally, "to work the works of God." "To work works" is a common Semitic expression.[185] The phrase "works of God," which may reflect Zealot parlance, refers in Jewish literature normally to works *done by God*, not those *required by him* (cf. 3:21; 9:3–4). Similar terminology is found in the Qumran scrolls: "I shall open your eyes so that you can see and understand the deeds of God" (CD 2:14).[186] The ensuing conversation is just the type that will have occurred in the synagogue (see comments on 6:59).

The work of God is this: to believe in the one he has sent (6:29). In light of the Jewish emphasis on "works of the law,"[187] Jesus' answer is nothing less than stunning: God's requirement is summed up as believing in "the one he has sent," that is, the Messiah.

What miraculous sign then will you give that we may see it and believe you? (6:30). "Jews demand miraculous signs" (1 Cor. 1:22). In Judaism, a "sign from heaven" was considered to be the highest form of legitimation. In *Ex. Rab.* 9:1, the rainbow provided by God for Noah after the flood is called a wonder or sign.

Our forefathers ate the manna in the desert (6:31). The psalmist celebrated the memory of God's provision of manna in the desert: "He gave a command to the skies above and opened the doors of the heavens; he rained down manna for the people to eat, he gave them the grain of heaven. Men ate the bread of angels; he sent them all the food they could eat" (Ps. 78:23–25). The *Sibylline Oracles* state that "those who honor the true eternal God inherit life . . . feasting on sweet bread from starry heaven" (*Frag.* 3:49; 2d cent. B.C.?). A first-century Jewish work expresses the expectation of an end-time recurrence of God's provision of manna: "And it will happen at that time that the treasury of manna will come down again from on high, and they will eat of it in those years because these are they who will have arrived at the consummation of time" (*2 Bar.* 29:8; cf. Rev. 2:17).

The same expectation is also found in later rabbinic tradition. Thus R. Berechiah

ANCIENT SEALS

Hebrew-inscribed clay bullae dating from the seventh century B.C.

▼

(c. A.D. 340) said in the name of R. Isaac (c. A.D. 300): "As the first Redeemer was, so shall the latter Redeemer be. . . . As the former Redeemer [i.e., Moses] caused manna to descend [citing Ex. 16:4], so will the latter Redeemer cause manna to descend" (*Eccl. Rab.* 1:9). Similarly, "R. Eleazar Ḥisma [c. A.D. 120] says: You will not find it [the manna] in this world but you will find it in the world to come" (*Mek. Ex.* 16:25).

As it is written: "He gave them bread from heaven to eat" (6:31). The divine provision of manna for Israel in the desert (Ex. 16:4, 15) is celebrated in both Old Testament and intertestamental literature.[188] Philo interprets the manna as referring to the Word of God (the divine Logos) or wisdom.[189]

It is not Moses . . . but it is my Father who gives you the true bread from heaven . . . the bread of God (6:32–33). The Old Testament passages cited on 6:31 indicate that the Jews likewise regarded God as the giver of the manna, with Moses as his mediator. In Jewish thought, "bread [of God]" was taken to refer to the Torah or the bread of the Presence (*Gen. Rab.* 70:5), in keeping with Old Testament usage.[190]

Gives life to the world (6:33). In rabbinic teaching, the giving of the law at Sinai was described thus: "The earth trembled when he gave life to the world" (*Ex. Rab.* 29:9). In the present passage, the same function is fulfilled by Jesus (cf. 5:39).

He who comes to me will never go hungry, and he who believes in me will never be thirsty (6:35). Jesus plainly claims to fulfill Old Testament messianic expectations. One of the closest parallels is Isaiah 55:1: "Come, all you who are thirsty, come to the waters; and you who have no money, come, buy and eat!" (cf. Isa. 49:10, cited in Rev. 7:16).

The Jews began to grumble about him (6:41). There are obvious parallels between Jesus' Jewish opponents and Israel in the desert (cf. Ex. 16:2, 8–9; Num. 11:4–23). Just as the Israelites grumbled about the first giver of bread, Moses, they grumble about the second giver, Jesus.

Is this not Jesus, the son of Joseph, whose father and mother we know? (6:42). Even the Jews in Jesus' own part of Palestine are ignorant of his virgin conception. Note 4:44, where the evangelist refers to Jesus' saying that a prophet is not without honor except in his own country. The Jews here object, not to the notion that a man (like Jesus) can receive a divine calling, or even that someone like Elijah might appear on earth and live among human beings, but to Jesus' claim of descent from heaven in face of his obvious (or so it seemed) human origin.[191] See further 8:31–59 below, esp. v. 41.

SEAT OF MOSES

The "seat of Moses" from the synagogue at Chorazim in lower Galilee.

▼

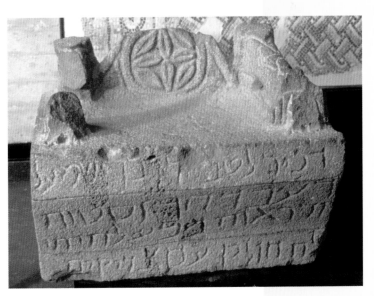

▶ Capernaum and its Synagogue

Jesus' headquarters, Capernaum ("village of Nahum"), located on the northwest shore of the Sea of Galilee, was a reasonably prosperous town apparently populated by both Jews and Gentiles in Jesus' day. It is probable that no more than a thousand people lived there in the first half of the first century A.D. After having been uninhabited for almost a thousand years, Capernaum, known as Tel-Hûm, was rediscovered by the American scholar Edward Robinson, who also recognized the remains of a synagogue. In 1866, Charles Wilson identified Tel-Hûm with Capernaum.

In subsequent years, several important structures have been found, including a fourth-century A.D. synagogue (with initial construction in the third century) and a fifth-century octagonal church built on top of a first-century house believed by some to have been the house of Simon Peter. According to Luke 7:5, the synagogue visited by Jesus in Capernaum was built by a Roman centurion. It is possible that the floor of basalt stones from the beginning of the first century A.D., discovered under the fourth-century synagogue, belonged to this building.[A-19]

No one can come to me unless the Father who sent me draws him (6:44). Rabbinic sources use the expression "to bring near to the Torah" with reference to conversion. Thus the first-century rabbi Hillel urged his followers to be those "loving peace and pursuing peace, loving mankind and bringing them near to the Law" (*m. ᵓAbot* 1:12; see also Jer. 31:3; Hos. 11:4; comments on John 12:32).

It is written in the Prophets: "They will all be taught by God" (6:45). The expression "the Prophets" may refer to the general tenor of Old Testament prophetic teaching or to "the Prophets" as a division of the Old Testament. "They will all be taught by God" paraphrases Isaiah 54:13 (cf. Jer. 31:34). In Judaism, to learn the Torah was to be taught by God himself. The expression "disciples of God" (i.e., the ones taught by God) is also found in the Qumran writings (CD 20:4; 1QH 10:39; 15:10, 14). See also the messianic parallel in *Psalms of Solomon* 17:32: "And he will be a righteous king over them, taught by God . . . and their king shall be the Lord Messiah" (prior to A.D. 70).

He who believes has everlasting life (6:47). There is a certain affinity between John's teaching on predestination and the Qumran doctrine of the "two spirits" (1QS 3:14–4:6). The rabbinic view is summed up by the saying attributed to Rabbi Akiba (c. A.D. 135): "All is foreseen, but freedom of choice is given" (*m. ᵓAbot* 3:16).

Unless you eat the flesh of the Son of Man and drink his blood, you have no life in you (6:53). For "Son of Man," see comments on 1:51. Old Testament teaching, in particular the Mosaic law, proscribed the drinking of blood as well as the eating of meat containing blood.[192] A midrash on Ecclesiates 2:24 reads, "All the references to eating and drinking in this book signify Torah and good deeds" (see a similar comment on Eccl. 8:15). The Hebrew idiom "flesh and blood" refers to the whole person. Later rabbinic theology speaks of "eating the Messiah" (*b. Sanh.* 99a).[193]

He said this while teaching in the synagogue in Capernaum (6:59). There is evidence that some synagogue services allowed the kind of exchange found in the present passage.[194] The discourse is particularly appropriate if the lectionary readings for that time of year were Exodus 16 and Isaiah 54.[195]

Many Disciples Desert Jesus (6:60–72)

Jesus' teaching on the "bread of life" is impossible to tolerate even for many of his disciples. The ensuing large-scale defection marks a watershed in John's Gospel. Chapter 6 thus ends on a note of failure (as ch. 12 does later). This does not mean that Jesus' ministry itself has failed. Rather, John shows how the scope of Jesus' followers is narrowed, so that in the end it is only a believing remnant (constituting the core group of the new messianic community) that is gathered to be instructed by the Messiah (chs. 13–16).

The Spirit gives life (6:63). The Old Testament depicts the Spirit as life-giving (Gen. 1:2; Ezek. 37:1–14; cf. *Midr. Mek. Ex.* 15:2b: "The words of the law which I have given you are life for you").[196] The rabbis said: "Great is the Law, for it gives life to those who practice it both in this world and in the world to come, as it is written (Prov. 4:22)" (*m. ʾAbot* 6:7).

The flesh counts for nothing (6:63). At Qumran, the dualism is between two spirits. Here and in 3:6, it is between flesh and spirit.

The words I have spoken to you are spirit and they are life (6:63). Life came into being through God's word (Gen. 1). Later, the Israelites were told, "Man does not live on bread alone but on every word that comes from the mouth of the LORD" (Deut. 8:3). The Old Testament viewed God's word as efficacious in and of itself (Isa. 55:11; Jer. 23:29), as did the New Testament writers (e.g., Heb. 4:12). The emphasis in the present passage lies on the fact that it is *Jesus'* words that are spirit and life (cf. John 5:40, 46–47). The Jews, however, believed that life was to

SYNAGOGUE REMAINS AT CAPERNAUM

be found in the words of the law: "The words of the Torah which I have given you are life unto you" (*Mek. Ex.* 15:26, citing Prov. 4:22; cf. John 5:39).

Lord (6:68). Since the term *kyrios* here introduces a confession of Jesus as the "Holy One of God" (6:69), it does not merely (as in earlier passages, e.g., 6:34) address Jesus as "sir" but rather acknowledges him as Lord, which at least means "Master" and may allude to the name used for God in the LXX.

To whom shall we go? You have the words of eternal life (6:68). "To whom shall we go?" may refer to the possibility of transferring allegiance to a better Rabbi (cf. 1:35–37).

Holy One of God (6:69). See especially 1:34, "the Chosen One of God" (see comments). While there is no evidence that the expression "the Holy One of God" functioned as a messianic title in Judaism,[197] it clearly does so here. The term is also seldom used in the Old Testament, occasionally occurring with regard to people consecrated to God. The expression "the Holy One of Israel" is used with reference to God (Ps. 71:22; Isa. 43:3; 54:5), who is "the Holy One" par excellence.[198]

In John, the holy God is identified with Jesus (note the definite article "*the* Holy One"). The closest parallel in the present Gospel is probably 10:36, where Jesus refers to himself as "the one whom the Father set apart as his very own and sent into the world" (cf. John 17:17–19). This makes clear that holiness does not merely (or even primarily) refer to moral perfection but foremost of all to a setting apart for mission, in Jesus' case the revelation of God and the redemption of humanity.

Have I not chosen you, the Twelve? (6:70). In the Old Testament, the Israelites were God's "chosen people" (Deut. 10:15; 1 Sam. 12:22). In the New Testament, this designation is transferred to the community of believers in Jesus (e.g., Eph. 1:4, 11; 1 Peter 1:1–2; 2:9).

(He meant Judas, the son of Simon Iscariot) (6:71). At least six interpretations of "Iscariot" have been advanced, the most likely being "man of Kerioth."[199] It was common in that day for father and son to have the same last name, especially if "Kerioth" refers to their hometown. "Kerioth" may refer to the Kerioth Hezron in Judea (i.e., Hazor), mentioned in Joshua 15:25, or to the Kerioth in Moab referred to in Jeremiah 48:24. This means that Judas is the only non-Galilean among the Twelve.

Jesus Goes to the Feast of Tabernacles (7:1–13)

As much as an entire year may have passed since Jesus' last major clash with the Jerusalem authorities. In what may be the following year's Feast of Tabernacles (A.D. 32), Jesus braces himself once again for intense opposition. This is now the third (and, as it turns out, final) trip of Jesus to the Jewish capital, which finds Jesus spending two months in Jerusalem from Tabernacles to the Feast of Dedication (10:22). At this stage of Jesus' ministry, he is increasingly viewed within the matrix of messianic expectations. Was the Coming One to emerge from secret, mysterious beginnings or a known figure of Davidic descent? Did Jesus' miracles identify him as Messiah?

The Jews there were waiting to take his life (7:1). On "the Jews," see "'The Jews' in John's Gospel" at 5:10. Because

Galilee and Judea are under different jurisdictions (Herod Antipas and the Roman prefect, respectively), it affords a certain amount of protection for Jesus to stay away from Judea, where the Jews are "waiting" ("seeking" is more accurate) to take his life (but see Luke 13:31).

The Jewish Feast of Tabernacles was near (7:2). Almost half a year has passed since the Passover mentioned in 6:4.[200] The Feast of Tabernacles was celebrated from 15–21 Tishri, which fell in September or October (Lev. 23:34; in A.D. 32, it was celebrated September 10–17), after the grape harvest and exactly two months prior to the Feast of Dedication (see 10:22 below). Josephus calls it "the greatest and holiest feast of the Jews" (*Ant.* 8.4.1 §100). The mishnaic tractate called *Sukkah* ("The Feast of Tabernacles") provides some helpful information regarding the large crowds and festivities at this most popular of Jewish feasts (cf. esp. *m. Sukkah* 5:2–4). The Feast of Tabernacles is called the "Feast of Booths" in some translations, because the people lived in booths to commemorate God's faithfulness to the Israelites during their desert wanderings (Lev. 23:42–43; cf. Matt. 17:4 par.).

Jesus' brothers (7:3). The most natural understanding is that "brothers" refers to other naturally born sons of Mary—younger, of course, than Jesus.

The right time for me has not yet come; for you any time is right (7:6). "To the Jews it was a self-evident truth that every man had his time."[201] As the wise preacher had said, "There is a time for everything, and a season for every activity under heaven" (Eccl. 3:1; cf. *Eccl. Rab.* 3:1). Later rabbis concurred: "He [Simeon ben Azzai; c. A.D. 120–140]

used to say: Despise no man and deem nothing impossible, for there is not a man that has not his hour and there is not a thing that has not its place" (*m. ʾAbot* 4:3). The Qumran community held similar views.[202] Jesus' statement that his brothers have no particular "time" but that their "time" is always present is therefore striking, even novel.

Not publicly, but in secret (7:10). Jesus does not make the journey to Jerusalem with the pilgrim caravan. Rather than traveling in public, Jesus goes later by himself. This he judges necessary in order not to hasten the time of his execution in light of mounting opposition. Moreover, the fact that he does not travel with his extended family (as was customary) points to Jesus' increasing isolation even among his flesh and blood relations. How large the company of travelers might be can be seen from the incident recounted in Luke 2:44, where Joseph and Mary traveled for an entire day thinking Jesus was in their company among their relatives and friends when in fact he was not.

No, he deceives the people (7:12). Matthew records a similar charge (27:63:

REFLECTIONS

AS JOHN REMINDED HIS READERS EARLIER, "JESUS himself had pointed out that a prophet has no honor in his own country" (4:44)—to which may now be added, "or even in his own family"! This underscores the extent to which Jesus' true identity remained a mystery even to those closest to him. Similarly, we may often find it most difficult to be God's witnesses in our natural families. But we must not relinquish this serious responsibility. In Jesus' case, both his mother and his brothers are found later among the circle of believers (Acts 1:12). With the necessary perseverance, and if this is God's sovereign will, we, too, may in due course reap a spiritual harvest in our own family.

73 John

"that deceiver"). Josephus names several first-century messianic pretenders or deceivers: Theudas, who in A.D. 45 or 46, claiming to be a prophet, promised to part the Jordan, and misled many (*Ant.* 20.5.1 §§97–98; cf. Acts 5:36); "the Egyptian," who also claimed to be a prophet and sought to reenact the conquest of Jericho, led the masses astray (*Ant.* 20.8.5 §§169–72; cf. *J.W.* 2.13, 5–6 §§261–65; Acts 21:38); an unnamed impostor (c. A.D. 61) who led his followers into the desert promised them salvation and deliverance (*Ant.* 20.8.10 §188); later (after A.D. 70) a certain Jonathan lured crowds into the desert and raised hopes of signs (*J.W.* 7.11.1 §§437–40).[203]

Jesus himself is called a deceiver in later Jewish literature. The Babylonian Talmud preserves a tradition to the effect that Jesus was executed on Passover Eve because he was a deceiver who practiced sorcery and led Israel astray (*b. Sanh.* 43a; cf. *b. Soṭah* 47a). According to Jewish law, the punishment for leading the people astray was stoning, further distinguishing between one who misleads an individual and one who leads an entire town astray (*m. Sanh.* 7:4, 10). Deuteronomy 13:1–11 stipulates that a false prophet must die "because he preached rebellion against the LORD your God . . . [and] has tried to turn you from the way the LORD your God commanded you to follow" (Deut. 7:5).

For fear of the Jews (7:13). "The Jews" here refers to the Jerusalem authorities, represented by the Sanhedrin.

Jesus Teaches at the Feast (7:14–24)

Halfway through the Feast (7:14). "Halfway" is a vague expression that may refer to the exact middle of the Feast (i.e., the fourth day) or merely to a time other than the first or the last day (7:37).

Go up to the temple courts and begin to teach (7:14). The main temple building (*naos*; cf. 2:19–21) was surrounded by several courts (*hieron*, here translated "temple courts"), including the Court of Women, the Court of (Israelite) Men, and the Court of the Gentiles. Jesus is probably teaching here in one of the outer porticoes.

The Jews (7:15). This probably refers to the Judean crowds as well as to the Jewish authorities.

How did this man get such learning without having studied? (7:15). A similar question is raised regarding Jesus' followers in Acts 4:13. It was common for Jewish males in Jesus' day to be able both to read and to have a basic understanding of the Scriptures. What is unusual, however, is Jesus' ability to carry on a sustained discourse in the manner of the rabbis, including frequent references to Scripture. Moreover, while the rabbis of Jesus' day teach by frequent appeal to other authorities, Jesus regularly prefaces his teachings by asserting unique authority: "You have heard that it was said . . . but I tell you" (cf. Matt. 5:21ff.); "I tell you the truth."[204]

Increasingly, however, it was not enough for a Jew to master the written Scriptures or even the oral law; formal rabbinic training became the norm, so that in the post-Jamnia period (after c. A.D. 90) the term "rabbi" came to refer exclusively to those who had undergone formal rabbinic training. According to one passage from the Babylonian Talmud, "If one has learnt Scripture and Mishnah but did not attend upon Rabbinical scholars, R. Eleazar (A.D. 80–120) says he is an '*am* ha-ʾareṣ; R. Samuel b. Naḥmani (c. A.D. 300) says he is a boor; R. Jannai (c. A.D. 240) says he is a Samaritan; R. Aḥab. Jacob (c. A.D. 300) says he is a magician [i.e., one who deceives the people]" (b. Soṭah 22a). See also 7:49 below.

My teaching is not my own (7:16). The age in which Jesus lived did not prize originality. If Jesus had acknowledged that he was self-taught or had originated his own message, he would have been immediately discredited for arrogance. In the Judaism of his day, there was only one way to teach and learn the word and will of God: through Scripture and its interpretation. There was no access to God other than through the Torah. In appealing to someone other than himself as the authority for his teaching, Jesus is not unlike other rabbis of his day. The rabbis referred back to the earlier rabbis; Jesus appeals to the Father, claiming direct knowledge from God (8:28).

He who speaks . . . there is nothing false about him (7:18). This verse is composed of maxims. The central contrast seems to be between a false prophet, who deserves to be executed (Deut. 18:9–22), and Jesus as the Son of God, who must be followed. The portrayal of Jesus concurs with the Palestinian Targum, where the dutiful son is one who is "concerned with the honor of his father" (Tg. Ps.–J. on Gen. 32:7 [8], 11 [12]).[205]

Has not Moses given you the law? (7:19). It was cause for great pride among the Jews that they were the recipients of the law (Rom. 2:17; 9:4). The Pharisees saw themselves as disciples of Moses (John 9:28).

Not one of you keeps the law (7:19). "Keeps the law" (lit., "does the law") is a

rabbinic expression meaning to act in such a way that the law is done. Thus it is said of Abraham that he "kept [lit., did] the entire Torah even before it had come" (t. Qidd. 5:21).[206]

You are demon-possessed (7:20). Literally, "you have a demon" (cf. 8:48; 10:20; Matt. 12:24 par.). The same charge was levelled against John the Baptist (Matt. 11:18). Josephus (Ant. 6.13.7 §§300–309) recalls an incident at the Feast of Tabernacles several decades later (c. A.D. 62) where one Jesus, son of Ananias, prophesied Jerusalem's destruction under "some supernatural impulse" but was scourged severely and "pronounced a maniac" by Albinus the procurator.

Accusations Leveled Against Jesus by His Opponents in John's Gospel	
Galilean, Nazarene	1:46; 7:41, 52; 18:5, 7; 19:19
Breaking the Sabbath	5:16, 18; 9:16
Blaspheming	5:18; 8:59; 10:31, 33, 39; 19:7 (cf. Lev. 24:16)
Deceiving the people	7:12, 47
Demon-possessed	7:20; 8:48–52; 10:20–21
Illegitimate birth	8:41
Samaritan (apostate?)	8:48
A sinner	9:16, 24–25, 31
Madness	10:20
A criminal	18:30
Royal pretender, political threat	19:12; cf. 19:15, 21

I did one miracle (7:21). Here Jesus is probably referring to the healing of the invalid in 5:1–15.

Yet, because Moses gave you circumcision (though actually it did not come from Moses, but from the patriarchs) (7:22). As Jesus (John?) parenthetically points out, the Sabbath was actually instituted before Moses with Abraham (Gen. 17:9–14) in the time of the Patriarchs.

You circumcise a child on the Sabbath. Now if a child can be circumcised on the Sabbath so that the law of Moses may not be broken, why are you angry with me for healing the whole man on the Sabbath? (7:22–23). Jesus here uses the common rabbinic argument "from the lesser to the greater" (see comments on 5:47). The difficulty Jesus raises is that two commandments of God apparently conflict with one another. The Jews are to circumcise their males on the eighth day after birth (Lev. 12:3); yet no regular work is to be performed on the Sabbath. What should be done when the eighth day falls on a Sabbath? The Jews always concluded that it was permissible to go ahead and circumcise on the eighth day regardless of whether it fell on a Sabbath. Thus R. Yose b. Ḥalafta (c. A.D. 140–165) said, "Great is circumcision which overrides even the rigor of the Sabbath" (m. Ned. 3:11).[207]

So much for the "lesser" issue. What about the "greater" one of "healing the whole man"? Again, later rabbinic teaching generally concurs that, granted the lesser premise that circumcision (which "perfects" but one member of the human body) supersedes the Sabbath commandment, the saving of the entire body transcends it all the more. A saying attributed to R. Eliezer (c. A.D. 90) reads: "Now if on account of a single limb of a person, they override the prohibitions of the Sabbath, is it not logical that one should override the prohibitions of the Sabbath on account of [the saving of] the whole of him?" (t. Šabb. 15:16). R. Eleazar b. Azariah (c. A.D. 100) judged similarly: "If circumcision, which affects but one only of the two hundred and forty-eight members of the human body, suspends the Sabbath, how much more shall [the saving of] the whole body suspend the Sabbath!" (b. Yoma 85b; cf. Mek. Ex. 31:13).

Stop judging by mere appearances, and make a right judgment (7:24). This challenge has many formal Old Testament parallels.[208]

Is Jesus the Christ? (7:25–44)

Isn't this the man they are trying to kill? . . . they are not saying a word to him. Have the authorities really concluded that he is the Christ? (7:25–26). "They are not saying a word to him" is a rabbinic expression reflecting tacit approval (t. Sukkah 1:1). "The authorities" probably refers to the Sanhedrin (cf. 7:48; 12:42).

When the Christ comes, no one will know where he is from (7:27). According to rabbinic teaching, some believed the Messiah would be born of flesh and blood, yet be wholly unknown until he set to procure Israel's redemption. Others in Judaism were sure about at least the geographic origin of the Messiah (Matt. 2:1–6); still, the Jewish leaders could tell Herod little else about the Messiah's family or circumstances. Some in the crowd were also convinced that the geographic origin of the Messiah was known (John 7:42). In a civilization without family names, the place of origin is equivalent to an identifying name, such as Joseph "of Arimathea" or Jesus "of Nazareth" (cf. Gen. 29:4; Judg. 13:6).

When the Christ comes, will he do more miraculous signs than this man? (7:31). While there is little direct evidence in the Old Testament that miracles were expected of the Messiah, this may be implied from the fact that Jews expected a prophet like Moses (Deut. 18:15, 18), and Moses performed miraculous signs at the Exodus (Ex. 7–11). Yet even if Jews in Jesus' day were not expecting a miracle-working Messiah, it would be natural for them to wonder, after witnessing Jesus' miracles, whether he might be the Messiah (see Mark 13:22; cf. Deut. 13:1–3).[209]

Then the chief priests and the Pharisees sent temple guards to arrest him (7:32). While there was technically only one "*chief*" priest at a given time (cf. 11:49, 51; 18:13), others who had formerly held this office apparently retained the title. The designation may also have extended to other members of the chief priestly families. Annas in particular, the patriarch of his family, skillfully controlled matters through his relations. Alternately, "chief priests" may not refer to present and past high priests but to principal priests, that is, higher temple officials including, besides the high priest himself, the captain of the temple, the temple overseer, and the treasurers.[210]

The *Pharisees* belonged to the Sanhedrin not as a party but as members of a group of men who knew the Scriptures. Josephus points to the Pharisees' influence among the people (*Ant.* 13.10.5 §288; 18.1.4 §17). Almost all the chief priests were Sadducees (cf. Acts 5:17; Josephus, *Ant.* 20.9.1 §199). The Sadducees and Pharisees made strange bedfellows. Faced with a common threat in the person of Jesus, they band together (John 7:32, 45; 11:47, 57; 18:3). Technically, only the chief priests have authority to arrest Jesus, but presumably the chief priests seek to arrest Jesus with Pharisaic support, perhaps even at Pharisaic urging.

The primary responsibility of the *temple guards*, who were drawn from the Levites, was maintaining order in the temple precincts as a kind of temple police force. Moreover, since the Romans granted the Jews a significant degree of autonomy in managing their own affairs, the Sanhedrin was able to deploy the temple guards also in matters removed from the actual sanctuary. If Jesus was still teaching in the vicinity of the temple, they would not have had to go far. The guards were commanded by "the captain of the temple," who was also drawn from one of the priestly families and whose authority in practical matters was second only to that of the high priest.

I am with you for only a short time (7:33). This is September/October (A.D. 32). Half a year later (March/April of A.D. 33) Jesus is crucified.

The Jews said to one another, "Where does this man intend to go that we cannot find him? Will he go where our people live scattered among the Greeks, and teach the Greeks?" (7:35). "The Jews" may refer to the authorities or the crowd in general. Old Testament parallels to the phrase "Where does this man intend to go that we cannot find him" may include Isaiah 55:6; Hosea 5:6; Amos 8:12. The expression "where our people live scattered" is a technical term referring to the Diaspora (Gk. "scattered"), that is, the large number of Jews living outside of Palestine in various parts of the empire and beyond.

The Greek word *diaspora* occurs about ten times in the LXX and regularly refers to the Jews' dispersion among the Gentiles.[211] A rabbinic source (*b. Sanh.* 11b) has Rabban Gamaliel (II, c. A.D. 90) address a letter "to our brethren the Exiles in Babylon and to those in Media, and to all the other exiled [sons] of Israel." Jews lived outside Palestine ever since the Babylonian exile. When they were allowed to return from exile, some went back but many did not. In later years, many cities boasted a considerable Jewish population, including Antioch, Alexandria, and Rome.

"Greeks" (cf. also 12:20) is regularly used in the New Testament in contrast with "Jews."[212] This suggests that the expression simply means "Gentile," whether literally Greek or of some other non-Jewish background. The phrase seems to have functioned as an umbrella term for Gentiles, owing to the dominance of Greek culture and language in the Greco-Roman world at large.[213] Interestingly, Jesus' Jewish interrogators do not think that Jesus will teach Diaspora Jews but Gentiles, presumably because it was assumed that only the latter need instruction in the Scriptures.

On the last and greatest day of the Feast (7:37). Every day during the Feast of Tabernacles, priests marched in solemn procession from the Pool of Siloam to the temple to pour out water at the base of the altar. The seventh day of the Feast of Tabernacles, the last day proper of the festival (Lev. 23:34, 41–42), was marked by a special water-pouring rite and lights ceremony (*m. Sukkah* 4:1, 9–10). This water rite, though not prescribed in the Old Testament, was firmly in place well before the first century A.D.[214] This rite was followed by a sacred assembly on the eighth day.[215] Hence, by the first century, many Jews had come to think of the Feast as an eight-day event.[216] The eighth day of the Feast of Tabernacles was set apart for sacrifices, the joyful dismantling of the booths, and repeated singing of the *Hallel* (Pss. 113–118).

Whether Jesus' words in John 7:37–38 and 8:12 are spoken on the climactic seventh day with its water-pouring and torch-lighting ceremonies or on the eighth day of joyful assembly and celebration, they would have a tremendous impact on the pilgrims who assemble for the Feast. Just when the events of the Feast and their attendant symbolism are

beginning to sink into people's memories, Jesus' words promise a continuous supply of water and light, perhaps also alluding to the supply of water from the rock in the desert. If these words are spoken on the eighth day—when no water pourings were performed—Jesus' offer of spiritual water is particularly striking (cf. *m. Sukk.* 4:9; 5:1). The eighth day of this feast is also the last festival day in the Jewish year. Philo speaks of it as "a sort of complement (*plērōma*) and conclusion of all the feasts in the year" (*Spec. Laws* 2.213).

If anyone is thirsty, let him come to me and drink (7:37). The Feast of Tabernacles was associated with adequate rainfall (see Zech. 14:16–17, a passage read on the first day of the feast, according to the liturgy in *b. Meg.* 31a). Another Old Testament passage associated with this feast is Isaiah 12:3: "With joy you will draw water from the wells of salvation." The festival seems to speak of the joyful restoration of Israel and the ingathering of the nations. Here Jesus presents himself as God's agent to make these end-time events a reality.

As the Scripture has said, streams of living water will flow from within him (7:38). Possible scriptural allusions include those promising spiritual blessings,[217] including the blessing of the Spirit,[218] in line with the feast itself.[219] "From within him" probably refers to the one who believes in Jesus the Messiah. Jewish parallels abound. In a mishnaic passage, R. Eleazar b. Arak (c. A.D. 90–130) is called "an ever-flowing spring" (*m. ᵓAbot* 2:8). A saying attributed to R. Meir (c. A.D. 140–165) affirms, "He that occupies himself in the study of the Law for its own sake merits many things . . . he is made like a never-failing spring and like

◄

"STREAMS OF LIVING WATER WILL FLOW"

The Hazbani River in northern Galilee, one of the tributaries of the Jordan River.

a river that flows ever more mightily" (*m. ʾAbot* 6:1).

Also, according to certain traditions,[220] Jerusalem was situated in the *navel* of the earth, so that John may be using *koilia* (lit., "belly"; NIV simply translates as "him") as a synonym for Jerusalem.[221] "Said R. Joshua b. Levi [c. A.D. 250], 'Why is it [the court of women] called *place of drawing [water]?* For from there they draw the Holy Spirit, in line with the following verse of Scripture, 'With joy you will draw water from the wells of salvation' (Isa. 12:3)" (*y. Sukkah* 5:1).[222] In connection with the water from the rock, the Targum on Psalm 78:16 reads: "He made streams of water come from the rock and caused them to come down like rivers of flowing water." The idea of water flowing from the new Jerusalem (Ezek. 47:1–12) and from the rock are related in *t. Sukkah* 3:3–18.

By this he meant the Spirit (7:39). Occasionally in the Old Testament, water is used as a symbol for the Holy Spirit (cf.

Isa. 44:3; Ezek. 36:25–27; Joel 2:28). Rabbinic parallels include *y. Sukkah* 5:1 (see previous comment); *Gen. Rab.* 70:8, where the "three flocks of sheep" in Genesis 29:1 are interpreted (among other things) as "the three festivals" (i.e., Passover, Pentecost, and Tabernacles) and "the well out of which they watered the flocks" as "the divine Spirit"; and *Ruth Rab.* 4:8: "'And drink of that which the young men have drawn' refers to the Festival of Water-Drawing. And why is it called 'Drawing'? For from there they drew the inspiration of the Holy Spirit, as it is said, 'Therefore with joy shall ye draw water out of the wells of salvation (Isa. 12:3).'" The most pertinent Qumran parallel is 1QS 4:20–21 (but there water is for cleansing rather than giving life).

Surely this man is the Prophet. . . . He is the Christ (7:40–41). "The Prophet" refers to "the prophet like Moses" (Deut. 18:15–18; see comments on John 6:14). In first-century thinking, the Prophet and the Christ were often viewed as two separate personages (cf. 1:21). The Qumran community looked forward to the coming of the Prophet and the Anointed Ones of Aaron and Israel (1QS 9:11), whereby the Prophet was held to be different from the priestly and royal Messiahs. Concerning the eschatological successor to Moses, we read in *Eccl. Rab.* 1:9, "As the former redeemer made a well to rise (Num. 21:17–18), so will the latter Redeemer bring up water (Joel 4:18)" (*Eccl. Rab.* 1:9).

How can the Christ come from Galilee? Does not the Scripture say that the Christ will come from David's family and from Bethlehem, the town where David lived? (7:41–42). There is ample scriptural support for people's contention that the Messiah would come from David's family and from Bethlehem, a village located south of Jerusalem in the heart of Judea.[223] Matthew 2:5–6 confirms that at least by the beginning of the first century A.D., Jewish scholars generally expected the Messiah to be born in Bethlehem (cf. Luke 2:1–2a).[224] No comparable evidence exists for a Galilean origin (cf. 7:52).

The Unbelief of the Jewish Leaders (7:45–52)

The temple guards . . . the chief priests and Pharisees (7:45). See comments on 7:32.

"No one ever spoke the way this man does," the guards declared (7:46). These guards were chosen from the Levites and were religiously trained. They were not, therefore, merely "brutal thugs." In the fulfillment of their duties, they would have heard many teach in the temple courts; even as biblical nonexperts, they recognize Jesus' teaching as unique.

This mob that knows nothing of the law—there is a curse on them (7:49). The disparaging designation "people of the land" (Heb. ʿammê ha-ʾareṣ; NIV: "this mob") is the way the unschooled masses were typically viewed by the rabbis. Originally, the whole nation was known by this expression (Ezek. 22:29); later, the term came to refer to the common folk as compared with the leaders (Jer. 1:18); finally, it came to represent the mixed population that settled in Samaria and Judea during the Exile, in distinction from the returning Jews (Ezra 10:2, 11).[225] Rabbi Hillel, living a generation before Jesus, said, "A brutish man dreads not sin, and an ignorant man (Heb. ʿammê ha-ʾareṣ) cannot be saintly" (m. ʾAbot 2:6). R. Dosa b. Harkinas (c. A.D. 90) commented, "Morning sleep and midday wine and children's talk and sitting in the meeting-houses of the ignorant people (Heb. ʿammê ha-ʾareṣ) put a man out of the world" (m. ʾAbot 3:11).

Nicodemus, who had gone to Jesus earlier and was one of their number (7:50). See 3:1–15.

Does our law condemn anyone without first hearing him to find out what he is doing? (7:51). See Acts 5:34–39, where, perhaps only two years later, Gamaliel, another rabbi, acts much like Nicodemus here. Old Testament law charges judges to investigate accusations against a person fairly (Deut. 1:16) and thoroughly (17:4; 19:18). In light of the fact that many of the Sanhedrin members have just expressed contempt toward the ignorant masses, John surely sees irony in Nicodemus's calling them to task on a point of simple Jewish—indeed, universal—legal procedure (cf. m. Sanh. 5:4). Consider the Roman Governor Festus's statement to King Agrippa: "It is not the Roman custom to hand over any man before he has faced his accusers and has had an opportunity to defend himself against their charges"[226] (Acts 25:16). Later rabbinic rulings concur: "Unless a mortal hears the pleas that a man can put forward, he is not able to give judgment."[227]

Are you from Galilee, too? Look into it, and you will find that a prophet does not come out of Galilee (7:52). The text may say "a prophet" or "the prophet" because of the manuscript tradition. Prophets had indeed come out of Galilee in the past, including Jonah (2 Kings 14:25) and possibly Elijah (1 Kings 17:1) and Nahum (Nah. 1:1). Rabbi Eliezer (c. A.D. 90), speaking in Upper Galilee, said, "There was not a tribe of Israel from which there did not come prophets" (b. Sukkah 27b). Similarly, Seder ʿOlam Rabbah 21: "You have no city in the land of Israel in which there has not been a prophet." Regarding contemporary attitudes of contempt for Galilee, see esp. y. Šabb. 16:8, where R. Ulla (c. A.D. 280) says of R. Yoḥanan ben Zakkai (d. c. A.D. 80) that he had lived for eighteen years in Galilee and had only been given two cases to decide. Hence he said, "O Galilee, Galilee, you have hated the Torah. You will end up working for tax farmers."

[Jesus and the Adulterous Woman (7:53–8:11)]

Both internal and external evidence indicate that the story of Jesus and the adulterous woman is not a part of the original Gospel but has been inserted at its present location by a later scribe. As far as external evidence is concerned, all the early papyri and the best major uncial manuscripts omit the account. Also, none of the early church fathers show awareness of this narrative, passing in their comments immediately from 7:52 to 8:12. The instability of the tradition is also apparent in that the text is inserted at various places in the Gospels, be it after 7:36, 7:44, or 21:25, or even in the Gospel of Luke after 21:38.

Internally, the insertion of John 7:53–8:11 clearly disrupts the unity and coherence of 7:1–52 and 8:12–59. Moreover, the account differs sharply in language and style from the rest of John. In fact, the pericope features a total of 14 unique words not elsewhere found in this Gospel, two and a half times as many as the next closest passage. For these reasons it is best not to treat the story as part of the Gospel and to consider it as a—possibly authentic—pericope that initially circulated separately in oral tradition and was eventually attached between 7:52 and 8:12.[228]

The Validity of Jesus' Testimony (8:12–30)

Still on the temple grounds, Jesus gets embroiled in renewed conflict with his Jewish opponents. After the Pharisees challenge the legitimacy of his witness, controversy centers in particular around the person of Abraham.

I am the light of the world (8:12). In the Old Testament, God himself (Ps. 27:1; 36:9) as well as his word (or "law"; Ps. 119:105; Prov. 6:23) are called a "light." Light imagery is also applied to the end-time servant of the Lord (Isa. 49:6; cf. 42:6) and to the Lord's own presence in the midst of his people in the last days.[229] Contemporary Judaism applied the

phrase "light of the world" not only to God but also to Israel, Jerusalem, the patriarchs, the Messiah, famous rabbis (e.g., Yohanan ben Zakkai), the Torah, the temple, and even Adam.[230] The universality of "light" symbolism in religious language issues in numerous non-Jewish parallels.[231]

Here "light" terminology is applied to the symbolism of the Feast of Tabernacles. As part of the festivities, four golden lamps were put in place, and an abundance of oil was poured into large golden bowls. The lamps rose over the outside walls of the temple and were said to illumine the entire city of Jerusalem. In the ensuing joyous celebration, the pious danced with torches and spoke words of praise. Levites played their musical instruments, standing on the steps that led from the Court of the Israelites to the Court of Women. The dancing and singing lasted all night until dawn. Notably, the main candelabrum was left until the last night to remind the Israelites that they still awaited their full salvation in the future—but now, Jesus declares himself to be "the light of the world."[232] The celebration ended with two priests with trumpets slowly descending the steps, affirming people's loyalty to Yahweh (cf. *m. Sukkah* 5:2–4).

Whoever follows me will never walk in darkness (8:12). On the contrast between light and darkness in John, see comments on 1:5. Similar language is also found in the Dead Sea Scrolls[233] and Jewish intertestamental literature. In *Joseph and Asenath*, God is said to call people "from darkness to light, and from error to truth, and from death to life" (8:9).

Will have the light of life (8:12). The phrase "light of life" is found in the Old Testament as well as in other Jewish literature. Consider Psalm 36:9: "For with you is the fountain of life; in your light we see light." Psalm 56:13 reads, "that I may walk before God in the light of life" (cf. Job 33:30). Also, *Psalms of Solomon* 3:12: "Those who fear the Lord shall rise up to eternal life, and their life shall be in the Lord's light, and it shall never end" (cf. *4 Bar.* 9:3). In the Qumran scrolls it is said that man's "sins are atoned so that he can look at the light of life" (1QS 3:7). Similarly, apocalyptic literature: "The righteous ones shall be in the light of the sun and the elect ones in the light of eternal life" (*1 En.* 58:3; cf. 58:4–6; 92:4).

Here you are, appearing as your own witness; your testimony is not valid (8:13). Jesus himself earlier affirmed this: "If I testify about myself, my testimony is not valid" (5:31). Old Testament law required multiple witnesses in capital cases and other crimes (Num. 35:30; Deut. 17:6; 19:15). Later Jewish legislation adopted the principle and applied it to other legal situations: "None may be believed when he testifies of himself. . . . None may testify of himself" (*m. Ketub.* 2:9; cf. *m. Roš Haš.* 3:1).

Because I am not alone (8:16). Similarly, 16:32: "I am not alone, for my Father is with me." See also *m. ʾAbot* 4:8: "He [R. Ishmael, late second century A.D.] used to say: 'Judge not alone, for none may judge alone save One.'"

I stand with the Father, who sent me (8:16). Literally, "but I and he who sent me." According to later Jewish tradition (attributed to R. Yehudah, c. A.D. 150), when the priests marched in procession around the altar at the Feast of Tabernacles, singing the Hosanna of Psalm 118:25, they did not sing "O Lord" but rather "I and he" in order to avoid using the name of God (*m. Sukkah* 4:5; cf. *m. Yoma* 6:2), whereby "I and he" lent expression to the fellowship between Israel and Yahweh. Jesus' words "I and he who sent me" may correspondingly indicate that Christ had now taken the place of Israel in relation to God (cf. John 15:1).

In your own Law (8:17). By calling the Law "your own Law," Jesus distances himself from his Jewish opponents (cf. 10:34; see also 6:49: "your forefathers"; 7:56: "your father Abraham"; 15:25: "their Law").[234] Apparently, this is also how Gentiles referred to the Law when in dialogue with Jews.[235]

It is written that the testimony of two men is valid (8:17). See comments on 7:13. Apparently, "the Jews took this [the requirement of at least two witnesses] so seriously that they interpreted Scripture to mean 'two witnesses' wherever a witness is mentioned unless it is specifically laid down that only one is required."[236]

I am one who testifies for myself; my other witness is the Father, who sent me (8:18). Jesus here states plainly that he and his Father are the two witnesses that attest to his truthfulness.[237] There may be a hint of deity in Jesus' "I am" statement, recalling passages such as Isaiah 43:10. In Jewish tradition, the combined witness of father and son was not acceptable, at least for certain purposes (*m. Roš Haš.* 1:7). In the present instance, the Jews expect witnesses whose statements can be heard and compared with each other, so that it can be determined whether or not they agree. In John 5:31–39, Jesus had listed a whole series of witnesses, including the Father, John the Baptist, Jesus' own works, and the Scriptures.

Where is your father? (8:19). In the ancient Near East, "to question a man's paternity is a definite slur on his legitimacy."[238] See also 14:8: "Lord, show us the Father and that will be enough for us."

You do not know me or my Father. . . . If you knew me, you would know my Father also (8:19). "Like father, like son"—as well as the equivalent, "Like mother, like daughter" (Ezek. 16:44)—was a truism in the ancient Near East as much as it is in many parts of the world today. This family resemblance pertains both to external physical features and to character traits.

The temple area near the place where the offerings were put (8:20). The treasury stood in the Women's Court (cf. Mark 12:41–44 par.), not far from the hall where Sanhedrin meetings were held. The Court of Women also was the place where the celebration of lights took place during the Feast of Tabernacles (see comments on John 8:12). Each of the thirteen trumpet-shaped receptacles had inscriptions regarding the intended use of the respective offerings: "gold for the mercy seat," "frankincense," "bird offerings," "wood," "freewill offerings," etc. (cf. *m. Šeqal.* 6:5). There may actually have been several treasuries (cf. Josephus, *J.W.* 5.5.2 §200), the treasury so-called being the place where the alms boxes were set up. A number of chambers were also used to store valuable items, both temple and private property (cf. *J.W.* 6.5.2 §282; *Ant.* 19.6.1 §294).

I am going away . . . and you will die in your sin. Where I go, you cannot come (8:21). Dying in one's sins, with one's sins unrepented and unatoned for, renders one subject to the wrath and judgment of the holy God. How much better to repent, confess one's sins, believe, and live (Deut. 24:16; cf. Ezek. 3:16–21; 18).

Will he kill himself? (8:22). This misunderstanding reveals the contempt (or at least low moral esteem) in which the Jews held Jesus (for a list of accusations leveled against Jesus, see comments on 7:20). Exceptional cases—such as Samson (Judg. 16:30) or the holdouts against the Romans committing mass suicide at Masada (A.D. 73)—were viewed favorably, but generally Jewish people shuddered at the thought of someone's taking his or her own life (e.g. Judas: Matt. 27:3–10; Acts 1:18–19). The corpse of such a person was left unburied until sunset (Josephus, *J.W.* 3.8.5 §377), and there was no public mourning.

Moreover, it was believed that suicide excluded one from the future age. According to the rabbis, the person who committed suicide could not pay with his life for the shedding of his blood (cf. Gen. 9:5), so that he must spend the afterlife in a state of damnation. Josephus writes, "But as for those who have laid mad hands upon themselves, the darker regions of the nether world receive their souls, and God, their father, visits upon their posterity the outrageous acts of the parents" (*J.W.* 3.8.5 §375; cf. 7.8.6 §320–401). In contrast to this negative view, contemporary pagan philosophers frequently considered suicide as an "honorable death."[239]

You are from below; I am from above. You are of this world; I am not of this world (8:23). The contrast between an "upper" heavenly and a "lower" earthly realm was recognized in Judaism, yet these two spheres were considered to be related through the concept of creation. The realm of the dead was imagined as under the earth, and this underworld, the "darkness of the depths" (*Jub.* 7:29; cf. 5:14), was also regarded as the place of judgment (*Jub.* 22:22; prior to 100 B.C.). A mishnaic tractate affirms the mystery attached to the division between what is above and what is below: "Whosoever gives his mind to four things it were better for him if he had not come into the world—what is above? what is beneath? what was beforetime? and what will be hereafter?" (*m. Ḥag.* 2:1). For John, however, the "lower" realm entails a moral dimension.[240]

If you do not believe that I am [the one I claim to be] (8:24). The proper Old Testament background of this "I am" statement (also in 8:28 and 58) appears to be Exodus 3:13–14 as further developed in Isaiah 40–55.[241] Thus Isaiah 43:10 says, "'You are my witnesses,' declares the LORD, 'and my servant whom I have chosen, so that you may know and believe me and understand that I am he.'" In context, the phrase "I am he" in this passage means "I am (forever) the same," and perhaps even "I am Yahweh," alluding to Exodus 3:14. Anyone other than God who applied this designation to himself was guilty of blasphemy and subject to God's wrath (Isa. 47:8–9; Zeph. 2:15).

Lifted up the Son of Man (8:28). The phrase "lifted up" (*hypsoō*) probably harks back to the Suffering Servant of Isaiah, who "will be raised and lifted up and highly exalted" (Isa. 52:13).

I do nothing on my own but speak just what the Father has taught me (8:28). Jesus, as the sent Son, again affirms his dependence on the Father, in keeping with the Jewish maxim that "a man's agent (*shaliaḥ*) is like the man himself" (e.g., *m. Ber.* 5:5).

I always do what pleases him (8:29). David was "a man after God's own heart"[242]—yet he was guilty of adultery and murder. In Isaiah 38:3, Hezekiah prays, "I have walked before you faithfully and with wholehearted devotion and have done what is good in your eyes"; yet Hezekiah was hardly perfect. In all of human history, only Jesus can legitimately claim that he always does what pleases God.

The Jews' and Jesus' Relationship to Abraham (8:31–59)

Hold to my teaching (8:31). The measure of any disciple is whether or not one holds to the master's teaching (cf. 2 John 9). The perfect follower of a Jewish rabbi was one who had "fully absorbed his master's teaching" and "was drawing on it to spread it abroad" (*b. Yoma* 28a; see also *T. Jos.* 1:3: "I have not gone astray: I continued in the truth of the Lord"; *Gospel of Thomas* 19: "If you become my disciples and listen to my words . . .").

Then you will know the truth, and the truth will set you free (8:32). Judaism held that what made people free was the study of the law. "R. Nehunya b. Ha-Kanah [c. A.D. 70–130] said: 'He that takes upon himself the yoke of the Law, from him shall be taken away the yoke of the kingdom and the yoke of worldly care; but he that throws off the yoke of the Law, upon him shall be laid the yoke of the kingdom and the yoke of worldly care" (*m. ʾAbot* 3:5; cf. 6:2; 1QS 4:20–21).

In Greek philosophy, both freedom and truth constituted virtues along with self-restraint, justice, and courage.[243] Philo wrote an entire essay on the Stoic notion that only the wise man is free. The Stoics believed that freedom was acquired by living in accordance with

Reason. The Stoic philosopher Epictetus (c. A.D. 50–120), son of a slave woman and for many years a slave himself, devoted his entire life to a passionate quest for freedom and independence. He contended that "freedom by the truth" (to be understood in terms of intellectual emancipation against the background of Epictetus's own slave background) is found by following some great philosopher.[244] Jesus' words would surely have resonated in the minds of John's Greek-speaking audience: One greater than Plato and Aristotle was here.

REFLECTIONS

FREEDOM IS ONE OF HUMANITY'S most prized possessions. Yet freedom is more than being able to do whatever a person would like to do. Freedom must be founded on truth, including the truth of human sinfulness. Only the one who has faced his or her own sinfulness and acknowledged a need for a Savior—Jesus—can experience true freedom. Sin enslaves even those who deem themselves "free" merely because they enjoy a certain degree of personal or political independence. But those who have trusted in the "Lamb of God, who takes away the sin of the world" have been set free from their bondage to sin.

We are Abraham's descendants (8:33). Several Old Testament passages extol the blessings of descent from Abraham: "O descendants of Abraham his servant, O sons of Jacob, his chosen ones" (Ps. 105:6); "But you, O Israel, my servant, Jacob, whom I have chosen, you descendants of Abraham my friend" (Isa. 41:8). However, even then, physical descent from Abraham was considered insufficient by itself.[245] While both Ishmael and Esau were Abraham's offspring, they were not sons of promise.[246] Thus Paul concluded, "For not all who are descended from Israel are Israel. Nor because they are his descendants are they all Abraham's children" (Rom. 9:6–7).

Descent from Abraham was the Jews' pride and a major source of confidence regarding their salvation (cf. esp. Matt. 3:9 par., including John the Baptist's exhortation).[247] The Jews considered Abraham to be the founder of the worship of God; he recognized the Creator and served him faithfully.[248] Apart from descent from Abraham, it was God's deliverance of the Israelites from slavery in Egypt that was seen to ensure the Jews' freedom: "God brought Israel out of captivity . . . from darkness and the shadow of death . . . from a yoke of iron to the yoke of the Torah . . . from slavery to freedom . . . from servitude to redemption" (*Ex. Rab.* 15:11).

And have never been slaves of anyone (8:33). Freedom was considered the birthright of every Jew. God's law laid down that no Jew, however poor, must ever descend to the level of slave: "If one of your countrymen becomes poor among you and sells himself to you, do not make him work as a slave. . . . Because the Israelites are my servants, whom I brought out of Egypt, they must not be sold as slaves" (Lev. 25:39–42). According to the Talmud, R. Simeon b. Gamaliel, R. Simeon, R. Ishmael, and R. Akiba held that "all Israel are royal children" (*b. Šabb.* 128a; cf. Matt. 8:12: "subjects of the kingdom").

Everyone who sins is a slave to sin (8:34). Jewish ethics viewed human existence as conflict between the evil and good impulses (*yeṣer*; e.g., *m. Ber.* 9:5). The law served to restrain the evil impulse and to help the good impulse prevail.[249] The idea that serious offenses subject humankind to the power of sin is attested in both Jewish intertestamental and rabbinic literature. The second-century B.C. work *Testaments of the Twelve Patriarchs* features the following: "The prince of error blinded me, and I was ignorant—as a human being, as flesh, in my corrupt sins—until I learned of my own weakness after supposing myself to be invincible" (*T. Jud.* 19:4); "Flee from the evil tendency, destroying the devil by your good works. For those who are two-faced are not of God, but they are enslaved to their evil desires, so that they might be pleasing to Beliar and to persons like themselves" (*T. Ash.* 3:2).

Rabbinic Judaism concurred. "Happy is he who is [master] over his transgressions, but his transgressions are not [master] over him."[250] R. Akiba (d. c. A.D. 135) said, "At first it [the evil impulse] is like a spider's web, but eventually it becomes like a ship's rope" (*Gen. Rab.* 22:6). The reality of sin was also acknowledged by the Qumran community (CD 1:8–9: "And they realized their sin and knew that they were guilty men").[251] Greek philosophy, on the other hand, prized wisdom, self-control, and other virtues. According to the Stoics, only the wise are free; the fool is a slave. Socrates denied that an individual can be called free who is controlled by passions. In the present instance, Yom Kippur, the Day of Atonement, which had just passed, should have served as a reminder that the Jews, too, were sinners.[252]

A slave has no permanent place in the family, but a son belongs to it forever (8:35). Compare the reference to Genesis 21:10 in Galatians 4:30: "The slave woman's son will never share in the inheritance with the free woman's son." In both Palestine and the Hellenistic world, households included slaves as well as sons. For Jewish slaves, this dependent relationship lasted only six years; in the seventh year they must be set free. In the Greco-Roman world, too, slaves were occasionally granted freedom, though this was not formally mandated.

The notion of a "son" being set over God's house "forever" is found in an important messianic text: "I will be his father, and he will be my son. . . . I will set him over my house and my kingdom forever; his throne will be established forever" (1 Chron. 17:13–14). The special status of sons even with regard to taxation by earthly kings is affirmed by Jesus in Matthew 17:25–26. In Hebrews 3:5–6, Moses and Christ are contrasted in terms of the temporary status of servant and the permanent position of son.

If you were Abraham's children . . . then you would do the things Abraham did (8:39). In Genesis 18:1–8, Abraham welcomed divine messengers with eager hospitality. In 12:1–9; 15:1–6; 22:1–19, he displayed obedience to God (though the book of Genesis records less noble instances in Abraham's life as well). The rabbis frequently upheld Abraham as a moral example to be emulated by the Jews: "He in whom are these three things is of the disciples of Abraham our father. . . . A good eye and a humble spirit and a lowly soul—[they in whom are these] are of the disciples of Abraham our father" (*m. ʾAbot* 5:19); "Whoever is merciful to his fellow-men is certainly of the children of our father Abraham, and whosoever is not merciful to his fellow-men is certainly not of the children of our father Abraham" (*b. Beṣa* 32b).[253] In rabbinic literature, a distinction is made between people who act like Abraham and those who act like Balaam (m. ʾAbot 5:19). Generally, Abraham was believed to have fulfilled the whole Torah even before the law was given.

"You are doing the things your own father does." "We are not illegitimate children" (8:41). "Illegitimate children" translates the literal "have been born of sexual immorality" (*porneia*). The prophets had compared Yahweh's covenant with Israel to a marriage relationship: idolatry amounted to spiritual adultery.[254] The Jews' rebuttal may imply that they considered Jesus' birth illegitimate.[255] The earliest attestation of the Jewish belief that Jesus was born out of *porneia* may be *m. Yeb.* 4:13: "I found a family register in Jerusalem and in it was written, 'Such-a-one is a bastard through [a transgression of the law of] thy neighbour's wife (Lev. 18:20),' confirming the words of R. Joshua."[256]

The only Father we have is God himself (8:41). In 8:39, the Jews had said that Abraham is their father (cf. 8:33, 37). Now they say they have only one father, God. This is entirely in keeping with Old Testament teaching (though not necessarily Jewish practice): "This is what the LORD says: Israel is my firstborn son" (Ex. 4:22). "Is . . . the LORD . . . not your Father, your Creator, who made you and formed you?" (Deut. 32:6). "But you are our Father, though Abraham does not know us or Israel acknowledge us; you, O LORD, are our Father, our Redeemer from of old" (Isa. 63:16). "Yet, O LORD, you are our Father. We are the clay, you are the potter; we are all the work of your hand" (Isa. 64:8). "I am Israel's father, and Ephraim is my firstborn son" (Jer. 31:9). "Have we not all one Father? Did not one God create us?" (Mal. 2:10).

I came from God (8:42). In pagan religions, the term "come" (*hēkō*) was commonly used for the saving appearance of deity.[257] In Jesus' case, it refers to his divine origin. This is part of John's portrayal of Jesus as coming from God and returning to him (metaphorically depicted in terms of descent and ascent; cf. 16:28).[258]

You belong to your father, the devil. . . . He was a murderer from the beginning (8:44). The plot to kill Jesus (cf. 8:37, 40) is ultimately inspired by Satan himself (13:2, 27). The phrase "murderer from the beginning" primarily refers to the fall narrative in Genesis 3 rather than the first murder in Genesis 4. It was commonly recognized in Jewish intertestamental literature that death was the result of Satan's initiative: "God created us for incorruption, and made us in the image of his own eternity, but through the devil's envy death entered the world, and those who belong to his company experience it" (Wisd. Sol. 2:23–24; cf. Sir. 25:24; Rom. 5:12).

Still, a reference to Cain, the murderer of Abel, may be secondarily in view (cf. 1 John 3:15). If so, Jesus' comment may imply that the devil is the father of "the Jews" because they want to kill Jesus, their fellow-Jew, just as Cain killed his brother Abel.[259] Other Jewish intertestamental texts refer to those outside the community as "children of destruction" (*Jub.* 15:26), "sons of Beliar" (15:33), or "sons of darkness" (1QS 1:10; 1QM passim). Finally, Antiochus Epiphanes IV, who erected the "abomination of desolation" in the Jewish temple in 167 B.C. and who serves as a type of the Antichrist in biblical literature,[260] is called "murderer and blasphemer" in 2 Macc. 9:28 (see comments on John 10:38).

Not holding to the truth, for there is no truth in him (8:44). "Not holding to the truth" may refer to the fall of Satan (Isa. 14:12?), which preceded the fall narrative in Genesis 3. Parallels are found at Qumran: "The Community council shall be founded on truth . . . true witnesses for the judgment and chosen by the will (of God)" (1QS 8:5–6); "they look for you with a double heart, and are not firmly based in your truth" (1QH 12:14).

He is a liar and the father of lies (8:44). See Genesis 2:17; 3:4; and previous comment. In the Scrolls, the opponent of the Teacher of Righteousness is called the "Man of Lies" (1QpHab 2:1–2; 5:11; CD 20:15). The Teacher himself says of the people who want to divert him from his path, "They are sowers of deceit and seers of fraud, they have plotted evil against me . . . and are not firmly based in your truth" (1QH 12:9–10, 14).

Can any of you prove me guilty of sin? (8:46). In Isaiah 53:9, it is said regarding the Suffering Servant that there was no "deceit in his mouth." Alluding to this passage, *Testament of Judah* 24:1 speaks of the Star from Jacob, who will arise like the Sun of righteousness, "and in him will be found no sin" (this may be a Christian interpolation). Christ's sinlessness is affirmed by the unanimous testimony of the early church.[261] See also *Gospel of Thomas* 104: "What is the sin that I have committed, or wherein have I been defeated?"

You are a Samaritan and demon-possessed (8:48). The Jews' riposte challenges Jesus' *paternity* in return: If he says the Jews are of their "father the devil" (8:44), he will be charged with having been birthed by a Samaritan! The label

Samaritan may also imply the charge of apostasy. Like the Samaritans, Jesus calls into question the legitimacy of the Jews' worship. Finally, "Samaritan" may intimate that Jesus' *miracles are due to demonic influence or magic*.[262] In the Babylonian Talmud, a person who learned Scripture and the Mishnah but did not study with a rabbi is described by one teacher as belonging to "the people of the land," by another as a Samaritan, and by a third as a magician.[263]

I honor my Father and you dishonor me (8:49). Christ's calm, non-retaliatory response evokes reminiscences of Isaiah's Suffering Servant (cf. 1 Peter 2:23 alluding to Isa. 53:7). According to Jewish law, rejection of someone's messenger was tantamount to rejection of the sender himself. In many non-Western societies, honor and shame are of utmost importance.[264] Dishonoring of a person is regarded as inexcusable.

Will never see death (8:51). The phrase is a common Jewish expression.[265] It serves as "a graphic expression of the hard and painful reality of dying," stressing the bitter fate awaiting all human beings.[266] However, exceptions such as Enoch or Elijah showed that the power of death was not absolute.

Abraham died and so did the prophets (8:52). The Old Testament Scriptures, Jewish tradition, and Greco-Roman beliefs agree that death is the common lot of humanity. "What man can live and not see death, or save himself from the power of the grave?" writes the psalmist (Ps. 89:48). "Where are your forefathers now? And the prophets, do they live forever?" declares the prophet (Zech. 1:5). Even people the Jews believed to have been exceptionally close to God were not exempt from death. A later rabbinic passage narrates God's response to Moses when the latter expresses reluctance to die: "Behold Abraham, who honored my name in the world and died" (*Tanḥ.* 6:11). Greco-Roman culture concurs. The great classical Greek poet Homer queries, "Now, friend, do you too die? Why do you lament thus?" (*Iliad* 21.107). Lucretius, a first-century B.C. writer, echoes these sentiments: "And the Master . . . Epicurus himself died. . . . And will *you* kick and protest against your sentence?" (*De Rer. Nat.* 3.1037–50).

You do not know him (8:55). The Jews do not "know" God, because they fail to "acknowledge" him. A similar charge was leveled against the Jews by some of the Old Testament prophets (e.g., Hos. 4:1; 6:6). Several later prophetic passages predict a time when people *would* know God (e.g., Isa. 11:9; Jer. 31:31–34; Hab. 2:14). But even the prophets could not claim to be free from sin or to know God the way Jesus claimed for himself.

Your father Abraham rejoiced at the thought of seeing my day; he saw it and was glad (8:56). "To say that Abraham saw the Messiah was neither new nor offensive to Jewish teachers; it was its application to Jesus that was unbelievable."[267] Appealing to Genesis 15:17–21, R. Akiba (d. c. A.D. 135) taught that God revealed to Abraham the mysteries of the coming age (*Gen. Rab.* 44:22; *4 Ezra* 3:14; *2 Bar.* 4:4; *Apoc. Abr.* 31). Abraham's "rejoicing" was taken by Jewish tradition to refer to his laughter at the prospect (or actual birth) of his son Isaac. This interpretation was based partly on Genesis 17:17 (interpreted as joy, not scorn, as in Philo, *Names* 154–69) and partly on Genesis 21:6 (cf. *Jub.* 15:17;

16:19–29; see also *Tg. Onq.*). It has been suggested that the reference here may be to Abraham's rejoicing when he announced to Isaac on the way to the sacrifice, "God himself will provide the lamb for the burnt offering, my son" (Gen. 22:8). In *Testament of Levi* 18:2, 6, Levi predicts the coming of a "new priest" for whom "the heavens will be opened, and from the temple of glory sanctification will come upon him, with a fatherly voice, as from Abraham to Isaac."

My day (8:56). The "day of the Lord" here has become *Jesus'* "day." While this expression usually refers to the final judgment, here it probably denotes his incarnation.

You are not yet fifty years old (8:57). According to Luke 3:23, Jesus was about thirty years old when he began his ministry. If this is the fall of A.D. 32, Jesus would be about thirty-five (perhaps almost thirty-six) years old. The age of fifty was commonly considered to mark the end of a man's working life and his attainment of full maturity (cf. Num. 4:3, 39; 8:24–25; *m. ʾAbot* 5:21: "at fifty for counsel").[268] Jesus, the Jews may be saying, has not even reached full maturity, and he makes claims such as having seen Abraham. Also, the book of *Jubilees* uses "fifty years" to measure the eras since the creation.[269] Note also the interesting reference in *Pesiq. Rab.* 21:12: "The letter *nun*, whose numerical value is fifty, signifies that Abraham was fifty years old when he recognized his Maker."

Before Abraham was born, I am (8:58). Jesus' language here echoes God's self-identification to Moses in Exodus 3:14 (cf. Isa. 43:10, 13). Thus Jesus does not merely claim preexistence—or he could have said, "before Abraham was born, I was"—but deity (see the people's reaction in 8:59). Note also *Gospel of Thomas* 19: "Jesus said, 'Blessed is he who came into being before he came into being.'"

At this, they picked up stones to stone him (8:59). Stoning was the prescribed punishment for blasphemy (Lev. 24:16; cf. Deut. 13:6–11; *m. Sanh.* 7:4). However, such punishment was to be the result of righteous judgment, not mob violence (Deut. 17:2–7).[270] Already in Old Testament times, people considered stoning righteous men such as Moses (Ex. 17:4), Joshua and Caleb (Num. 14:10), or David (1 Sam. 30:6). Stephen, the church's first martyr, was stoned on account of alleged blasphemy (Acts 7:57–60). Paul, too, was stoned repeatedly, although he escaped with his life (Acts 14:19; 2 Cor. 11:25), as were other Christian saints (Heb. 11:37). The availability of stones in the temple area points to the fact that the temple was still being renovated (cf. John 2:20; Josephus, *Ant.* 17.9.3 §216; *J.W.* 2.1.3 §§11–12).

Jesus Heals a Man Born Blind (9:1–12)

Healings of blind men by Jesus are also featured in the other canonical Gospels.[271] In John, this is the sixth sign and the third healing selected by the evangelist. Restoring sight to the blind is considered to be a messianic activity in the Old Testament (Isa. 29:18; 35:5; 42:7). The healing probably took place anywhere between October and mid-December (A.D. 32).

As he went along (9:1). The scene probably took place in the area south of the temple at one of the two southern gates, Jesus recently having left the temple grounds (8:59).[272]

A man blind from birth (9:1). The man's blindness from birth raises the ante for the ensuing miracle and makes it all the more striking (see comments on 2:10). In ancient Palestine, blind people were cast wholly on the mercy of others. They would frequently position themselves near sanctuaries on the assumption that passersby would be in a charitable mood. In the present instance, Jesus and his disciples would notice the begging man as they leave the temple grounds (8:59).

Rabbi (9:2). See comments on 1:38.

Who sinned, this man or his parents, that he was born blind? (9:2). Jewish rabbis generally believed in a direct cause-and-effect relationship between suffering and sin (cf. the book of Job). R. Ammi (c. A.D. 300) said, "There is no death without sin, and there is no suffering without iniquity" (*b. Šabb.* 55a). Jesus, however, while acknowledging the possibility that suffering may be the direct result of sin (cf. 5:14), denies that such is invariably the case (cf. Luke 13:2–3a). Underlying the disciples' statement is the concern not to charge God with perpetrating evil on innocent people (cf. Ex. 20:5; Num. 14:18; Deut. 5:9). Regarding the possibility that the man's blindness from birth may be the result of prenatal sin, one may note Jewish speculation surrounding the struggle of Jacob and Esau in their mother Rebecca's womb.[273]

There are also several parallels regarding the possibility that the man's blindness was the result of his parents' sin prior to his birth. Some texts refer to a mother worshiping in a pagan temple during her pregnancy, with the fetus's "participation" in the pagan rite (*Song Rab.* 1.6.3; *Ruth Rab.* 6:4). An Aramaic Targum tells of parents who brought a rebellious boy to the elders saying, "We have transgressed the decree of the Memra [word] of the Lord: because of this, this son of ours, born to us, is stubborn and rebellious; a glutton with meat and a drunkard with wine" (*Tg. Ps.-J.* on Deut. 21:20). Other sayings speak of children being born epileptic or leprous on account of the sins of their parents. However, several Old Testament and intertestamental passages strongly challenge the notion that children suffer for their parents' sin (e.g., Jer. 31:29–30; Ezek. 18; cf. Tobit 3:3).

This happened so that the work of God might be displayed in his life (9:3). (Cf. 11:4.) "Work of God" is literally "works of God."[274] The thought here is that even evil ultimately contributes to the greater glory of God. An instance of this is the pharaoh of the Exodus.[275]

As long as it is day, we must do the work of him who sent me (9:4). Compare the statement attributed to R. Tarfon (c. A.D. 130): "The day is short and the task is great and the laborers are idle and the wage is abundant and the master of the house is urgent" (*m. ʾAbot* 2:15). Note also the statement attributed to R. Simeon ben Eleazar (c. A.D. 190): "Work so long as you can and it is possible for you and it is still within your power" (*b. Šabb.* 151b).

Night is coming, when no one can work (9:4). This statement has the ring of common sense, if not a proverbial saying (cf., e.g., Rom. 13:12: "The night is nearly over; the day is almost here. So let us put aside the deeds of darkness and put on the armor of light"). Another proverb that takes the night symbolism in a different direction is found in Menander: "The night refreshes, the day brings forth work."[276] Apart from rare exceptions

(such as shepherds, night watchmen, or special messengers), no one works in the dark. Here, of course, "night" also connotes the world's spiritual darkness apart from Jesus (cf. John 9:5).

While I am in the world (9:5). Jesus' announcement to his disciples that his earthly role will be limited in time is contrary to the popular notion that the Messiah and the messianic age will last forever (cf. 12:34).

I am the light of the world (9:5). See comments on 8:12.

He spit on the ground, made some mud with the saliva, and put it on the man's eyes (9:6). Jesus' use of saliva is reminiscent of the healing of the deaf and mute man in the Decapolis (Mark 7:33) and of the blind man in Bethsaida (8:23). According to some Jewish rabbis, the saliva of a firstborn has healing properties.[277] In the surrounding pagan culture, however, saliva was frequently associated with magical practices—most frequently cited is the healing of the blind soldier, Valerius Aper, apparently by Asclepius, in which an eye-salve was used[278]—so that many rabbis seem to have condemned the use of saliva.[279] John may here wish to stress Jesus' superiority over pagan healers such as the well-known god Asclepius.

Similar to people in other cultures, Palestinian Jews apparently believed that human excreta (including saliva) were forms of dirt rendering a person ceremonially unclean. Under certain conditions, however, that very "dirt" could become an instrument of blessing in the hands of authorized individuals. Thus blood and saliva generally pollute, but in certain contexts blood cleanses and saliva cures. In the Old Testament, saliva may convey ceremonial uncleanness (Lev. 15:8). If the reversal of this taboo also applies, then by using saliva to cure a man, Jesus claims to possess unusual spiritual authority (cf. Matt. 8:1–4).[280]

Wash in the Pool of Siloam (this word means Sent) (9:7). A connection with the previous chapters is established by the fact that the water for the water-pouring rites of the Feast of Tabernacles was drawn from the pool of Siloam (cf. *m. Sukkah* 4:9–10). In the Old Testament, Elisha does not heal Naaman immediately but sends him to wash in the Jordan (2 Kings 5:10–13).

Regarding the Pool of Siloam itself, Isaiah speaks of "the gently flowing waters of Shiloah" (Isa. 8:6; cf. Neh. 3:15). The existence of a "basin of the latrines of Siloam" is attested by a reference in the Copper Scroll of Qumran (3Q15 10:16). Josephus frequently refers to the Pool of Siloam.[281] A part of the major water system built by King Hezekiah, this rock-cut pool was located southwest of the City of David (excavated in 1880).[282] Its water was "sent" (hence its name) via Hezekiah's tunnel from the Gihon spring in the Kidron valley (cf. 2 Chron. 32:30). There is some debate as to whether it is to be identified with the "Lower" or "Old Pool" (Isa. 22:9, 11), the "Upper Pool" (cf. 2 Kings 18:17; Isa. 7:3; 36:2), or some other pool.[283]

As in other places, John translates Semitic words: Siloam "means Sent" (see comments on 1:38). The underlying Old Testament reference may be Genesis 49:10, which was interpreted messianically by both Jewish and Christian interpreters: "The scepter will not depart from Judah until Shiloh comes."[284] Rabbinic sources mention the pool as a place of purification.

Isn't this the same man who used to sit and beg? (9:8). Begging as a way of life was a common feature in first-century Palestine.[285] It was about the only way a blind person could make a living in that day. Beggars were "the truly poor," whose "hand-to-mouth existence was considered hardly worth living" (on the poor, see *m. Pe'ah* 8).[286] In Judaism, the giving of alms was considered to be of greater significance than all the commandments (*b. B. Bat.* 9a,b), constituting, together

POOL OF SILOAM

(left) The remains of the pool in Jerusalem.

(right) An artistic reconstruction of the first-century appearance of the pool.

▼

with the law and obedience, one of three pillars of the world (*m. ʾAbot* 1:2). Charitable deeds were viewed as a way to gain merit with God (*b. Šabb.* 151b; cf. Sir. 3:3–4; 35:1–2) and as protection against the devil (*Ex. Rab.* 31:1).

The Pharisees' First Interrogation of the Formerly Blind Man (9:13–17)

The day . . . was a Sabbath. . . . Some of the Pharisees said, "This man is not from God, for he does not keep the Sabbath" (9:14–16). According to the Pharisees, Jesus may have "broken" the Sabbath in the following ways: (1) Since he was not dealing with a life-or-death situation, Jesus should have waited until the next day to heal the man; (2) Jesus had kneaded the clay with his saliva to make mud, and kneading (dough, and by analogy clay) was included among the thirty-nine classes of work forbidden on the Sabbath (*m. Šabb.* 7:2; cf. 8:1; 24:3); (3) later Jewish tradition stipulated that it was not permitted to anoint eyes on the Sabbath, although opinion seems to have been divided. R. Yehudah (d. A.D. 299) said it was permissible to do so; R. Samuel declared it was not, but when his own eyes gave him trouble he asked the former if it was allowable, and Yehudah said it was so for others, but not for *him* (*b. ʿAbod. Zar.* 28b)!

Some of the Pharisees said, "This man is not from God, for he does not keep the Sabbath." But others asked, "How can a sinner do such miraculous signs?" So they were divided (9:16). The division apparent in this verse roughly follows the differing ways of reasoning followed by the schools of Shammai and Hillel. The former based its argument on foundational theological principles ("anyone who breaks the law is a sinner") while the latter argued from the established facts of the case ("Jesus has performed a good work").[287] Already in Old Testament times, the Israelites were warned against the appearance of a prophet or dreamer who would perform "a miraculous sign or wonder" to lead people astray (Deut. 13:1–5).

He is a prophet (9:17). The only notable miracle-working prophets were Elijah and Elisha (cf. 2 Kings 5:10–14). Another possible antecedent figure is Moses (Deut. 18:15, 18; 34:10–12).

The Pharisees' Interrogation of the Man's Parents (9:18–23)

The Jews . . . sent for the man's parents (9:18). On "the Jews," see "The 'Jews' in John's Gospel" at 5:10. The man's parents would be able to confirm whether or not he was actually born blind. It is possible that the man is staying under his parents' roof and spends his days begging in the temple courts.

Ask him. He is of age; he will speak for himself (9:21). "He is of age" probably means he is old enough to give legal testimony about himself, that is, at least thirteen. Beyond this, the man's age is not known. Alternatively, the phrase may indicate that the man is old enough to reason and answer the Pharisees' questions for himself.

His parents said this because they were afraid of the Jews, for already the Jews had decided that anyone who acknowledged that Jesus was the Christ would be put out of the synagogue (9:22). Confession of Jesus as Christ was the mark of the early Christians.[288] Expulsion from the assembly of the exiles is reported already in Ezra 10:8. Since the synagogue was the center not only of Jewish religious, but also of communal life, expulsion from it represented a severe form of social ostracism (as well as effectively barring a person from worshiping God in the company of his people).

The reference to expulsion from the synagogue is often considered to be anachronism, that is, a later practice (roughly sixty years later) being attributed back to this time. The discussion revolves around the liturgical Eighteen Benedictions, which were recited by all pious Jews three times a day.[289] The twelfth of these benedictions is believed to have been rewritten by Samuel the Lesser, a rabbi at the school at Jamnia (c. A.D. 85–90), in response to a request by R. Gamaliel II, leader of the school (cf. *b. Ber.* 28b). This revision, ironically called "the benediction of the heretics" (*birkat ha-minîm*), was supposedly prepared for the Sanhedrin that was reconstituted after the fall of Jerusalem in A.D. 70, in order to exclude Christian Jews from the synagogue by including in the liturgy a phrase no Christian could utter:

> For the apostates let there be no hope,
> and let the arrogant government
> be speedily uprooted in our days.
> Let the Nazarenes [noṣrim = Christians?] and the Minim [heretics]
> be destroyed in a moment,
> and let them be blotted out of the book of life
> and not be inscribed together with the righteous.

However, there are several questions regarding this reconstruction: (1) It is uncertain whether the twelfth benediction contained the term *noṣrim*.[290] (2) If it did, it is unclear whether this term meant "Christians." (3) Even if (1) and (2) are answered in the affirmative, this does not mean that a church-synagogue conflict around A.D. 90 was the exclusive or even primary factor behind John's references to synagogue expulsion. The historical background at the time of writing was considerably more complex, including the destruction of Jerusalem and the temple, rising Roman emperor worship, persecution of Christians, the threat of proto-Gnosticism, and other factors. (4) Even if John uses such terminology in order to reflect contemporary frictions, this does not mean that these references are anachronistic.[291]

The Pharisees' Second Interrogation of the Formerly Blind Man (9:24–34)

Give glory to God (9:24). This phrase constitutes a solemn exhortation to tell the truth and to make a confession, with the implication that the person so exhorted has done wrong.[292]

This man is a sinner (9:24). Especially the stricter rabbinic school of Shammai would infer that anyone who broke the Sabbath (and thus broke the law) was a sinner (see comments on 9:16).

"What did he do to you? How did he open your eyes?" . . . "I have told you already" (9:26–27). In Jewish jurisprudence, diligent cross-examination was considered vital in assessing the evidence: "The more a judge tests the evidence the more is he deserving of praise" (*m. Sanh.* 5:2).

Hurled insults (9:28). Pouring sarcasm was a common way of dealing with people of perceived lower status, which conveyed the notion that they were unworthy of receiving a direct answer.

We are disciples of Moses (9:28). There is some debate as to how common this self-designation was among the Jews of Jesus' day (cf., e.g., Matt. 23:2).[293] In *b. Yoma* 4a, it is applied to Pharisees as opposed to Sadducees. In *m. ʾAbot* 5:19, Jews are referred to as "the disciples of Abraham" while Christians are dismissed as "the disciples of Balaam the wicked" (i.e., Jesus!). The Pharisees indicate that they regard Moses, through whom God gave the law to Israel, as the paradigmatic teacher (often called "our teacher" by the rabbinate). "Those who call themselves his disciples consciously regard themselves as links in the chain which stretches back to Moses and at the beginning of which is the clear and unequivocal revelation to the will of God for the people through him."[294]

We know that God spoke to Moses (9:29). "The LORD would speak to Moses face to face, as a man speaks with his friend" (Ex. 33:11; cf. Num. 12:2–8). The Pharisees' comment harks back to the establishment of Israel as a nation through the giving of the Mosaic covenant at Sinai. However, according to the rabbis, this law consisted not merely of the written word (the Pentateuch) but also oral tradition passed on from generation to generation. Thus *m. ʾAbot* 1:1 states, "Moses received the [Oral] Law from Sinai and committed it to Joshua, and Joshua to the elders, and the elders to the Prophets; and the Prophets committed it to the men of the Great Synagogue."[295]

We know that God does not listen to sinners (9:31). Scripture clearly establishes a link between a person's righteousness and God's responsiveness to that person's prayer.[296] Later rabbis shuddered at the thought of God's listening to sinners. R. Akiba (c. A.D. 135) said, "God forbid that the Almighty should cause the sun to stand still at the behest of those who transgressed his will" (*b. Sanh.* 90a). Another rabbinic passage poses the rhetorical question, "Does the All-Merciful perform miracles for liars?" (*b. Ber.* 58a).[297]

He listens to the godly man who does his will (9:31). There is ample Old Testament substantiation for the cured man's contention. "The eyes of the LORD are on the righteous and his ears are attentive to their cry" (Ps. 34:15). "He fulfills the desires of those who fear him; he hears their cry and saves them" (Ps. 145:19). "The LORD is far from the wicked but he hears the prayer of the righteous" (Prov. 15:29). There are also rabbinic parallels: "If one is filled with the fear of God his words are listened to" (*b. Ber.* 6b; attributed to R. Ḥelbo [c. A.D. 300] in the name of R. Huna). "He who fulfills the will of God and prays with true earnestness is heard both in this world and also in that to come" (*Ex. Rab.* 21:3; cf. Isa. 65:24). The term *theosebēs* ("godly man"; only here in the New Testament) is occasionally used in Greek writings to mean "religious" or "pious."[298] It is also found in Josephus—with reference to David (*Ant.* 7.7.1 §130; 7.7.3 §153) and others (*Ant.* 12.6.3 §284; 14.12.3 §308; 20.9.11 §195; *Ag. Ap.* 2.14 §140)—and in Philo (*Names* 197), who likewise uses the expression in a broad sense to refer to a "God-fearing" person.

Nobody has ever heard of opening the eyes of a man born blind (9:32). Opening of the eyes of the blind is limited to unusual circumstances in the Old Testament (e.g., 2 Kings 6:8–23). Instances of blind persons being healed in Jewish tradition are extremely rare (Tobit 11:10–14; cf. 2:10). But the healing of *a man* *born blind* is without parallel. The phrase "nobody has ever heard" literally reads "not heard from of old" (i.e., from the world's beginning), a common Jewish expression in both the Old Testament and rabbinic literature (e.g., Isa. 64:4).[299]

You were steeped in sin at birth (9:34). The common rabbinic view of human nature implicitly denied universal human sinfulness by implying that people could act on their good impulses (*yeṣer*) and resist evil ones. Yet the reality of human sin is clearly taught in the Old Testament: "Surely I was sinful at birth, sinful from the time my mother conceived me" (Ps. 51:5). The apostle Paul establishes the same truth in his letter to the Romans (cf. Rom. 1–3, esp. 3:23; cf. 6:23). Thus the Pharisees are unduly self-righteous in linking the man's sinfulness from birth with his physical defect of blindness while failing to include themselves under the rubric "sinful from birth."

And they threw him out (9:34). This refers to the man's expulsion from the synagogue. The way in which this is carried out suggests an impulsive, impromptu decision rather than the culmination of a formal investigation issuing in a solemn act of excommunication. The Pharisees' prejudiced procedure of interrogating the blind man and his parents violates their own laws, which stipulate that witnesses are to be examined fairly and without prejudice (see comments on 5:31 and 9:26–27).

The Pharisees' Spiritual Blindness (9:35–41)

The blind will see and those who see will become blind (9:39). Both giving sight to the blind[300] and the blinding of those who see[301] are common Old Testament themes. Elsewhere, Jesus calls the Pharisees "blind guides" (Matt. 23:16; cf. 15:14; 23:26). The phrase "blind ones in heart" is found in an ancient papyrus (P. Oxy. 1.20–21). For the blinding effect of wickedness, see Wisdom of Solomon 2:21. In rabbinic Judaism this metaphorical usage is rare,[302] while Philo, under the influence of Greek philosophy, uses it frequently (e.g., *Agriculture* 81; *Heir* 48; *Spe. Laws* 4.189).

R E F L E C T I O N S

FOR THE MAN BORN BLIND, THIS HEALING RESTORED his sight. "One thing I do know. I was blind but now I see!" But for John, the event also serves as a parable illustrating the condition of human blindness brought about by sin and spiritual pride. The Pharisees are quick to conclude that Jesus is a sinner because in their view he broke the Sabbath. But they are slow to find fault with themselves, haughtily claiming to be "disciples of Moses." "First take the plank out of your own eye," Jesus counseled, "and then you will see clearly to remove the speck from your brother's eye." If we fail to judge our own sin, we will see God do great things in the lives of those around us—but we ourselves will miss out.

The Shepherd and His Flock (10:1–21)

As winter (A.D. 32/33) approaches, the last winter prior to Jesus' crucifixion the following spring, Jesus talks about his relationship with his close followers. He portrays himself as the messianic shepherd and his disciples as "the sheep of his pasture" (Ps. 100:3; Ezek. 34:31). The Jewish leadership, on the other hand, proud claimants of Abrahamic heritage but spiritually blind, are not even among his "sheep."[303] Interestingly, a roughly contemporaneous passage, *2 Baruch* 77:11–16, portrays the law as a true shepherd (as well as light and water).

Thus, Jesus claims to fulfill the functions generally attributed to the law in his society.[304]

Enter the sheep pen by the gate (10:1). The sheep pen may have been a courtyard (cf. 18:15) near or bordering a house, surrounded by a stone wall and topped by briars, where one or several families kept their sheep. The gate, which probably could be locked, would have been guarded by a doorkeeper (cf. 10:3), who was hired to stand watch.[305]

Thief and a robber (10:1). The words "thief" and "robber" overlap in meaning and may reflect Semitic parallelism (cf. Obad. 5; Ep. Jer. 57), whereby "thief" may focus on the covert nature of entrance and "robber" on violence (cf. Luke 10:30, 36). Shepherds had to be on guard against either threat in order to avoid loss of sheep.

The man . . . is the shepherd of his sheep (10:2). The shepherd was the authorized caretaker of the flock. His task required dedication, courage, and vigilance. In Jesus' day, shepherds were regarded as vulgar and members of the lower class. This contrasts with the Old Testament designation of both God and his Messiah as shepherds.

The watchman opens the gate (10:3). On "the gate," see comments on 10:1. The watchman was an undershepherd who provided access to the flock. The existence of a watchman suggests that the pen in mind here is large enough to house several flocks and hence warrants the need of a doorkeeper.

The sheep listen to his voice (10:3). In the Old Testament, God communicated with his people preeminently through the Law (which spelled out God's moral expectations for his people) and the Prophets (who called people back to obedience to the law). People listened to God's voice by living in conformity with his revealed will. At the present time (from the perspective of the earthly Jesus), those who desire to follow God do so by listening to Jesus'

▶

SHEPHERD AND HIS SHEEP

This was taken near Jericho.

words and by obeying his commandments (e.g., 15:10). In the future, God the Father (and Jesus) will speak to his own through the Spirit (16:13–15).

He calls his own sheep by name (10:3). Apparently, Palestinian shepherds used to give nicknames to some of their sheep.[306] Analogously, God in the Old Testament called some of his closest servants, as well as Israel as a whole, "by name" (e.g., Ex. 33:12, 17; Isa. 43:1). The shepherd's calling out of his own suggests the presence of more than one flock in the pen (see comments on John 10:3).

And leads them out. When he has brought out all his own (10:3–4). The wording is reminiscent of Old Testament passages such as Numbers 27:15–17 or Ezekiel 34:13. Jesus frequently uses sheep to illustrate people's helplessness and need for guidance. The leading out of sheep is a delicate task. It involves pushing the flock from the fold, where many of them are crowded, through the gate.

He goes on ahead of them (10:4). Western shepherds usually drive their sheep, often using a sheep dog. Their Near Eastern counterparts, on the other hand, both now and in Jesus' day, lead their flocks by beckoning them on with their voice. Often there is a helper watching the tail end of the flock.[307] Israel's exodus from Egypt is occasionally portrayed in terms of a flock being led by its shepherd.[308] Old Testament prophetic literature holds out similar visions of end-time deliverance for God's people (Mic. 2:12–13).

They will never follow a stranger; in fact, they will run away from him because they do not recognize a stranger's voice (10:5). In ancient times as well as today, sheep, while helpless and in need of guid-

ance, are able to discern between their shepherd's voice and the call of strangers. This intimacy of a shepherd and his flock provides a beautiful illustration of the trust, familiarity, and bond existing between Jesus and his followers.

Jesus used this figure of speech, but they did not understand (10:6). The term "figure of speech" (*paroimia*) is roughly equivalent to the expression "parable" (*parabolē*). Both terms apparently render the broad Hebrew expression *mashal*. They occur side-by-side in several instances (e.g., Sir. 39:3; 47:17) and do not differ significantly in meaning.[309]

I am the gate for the sheep (10:7). The present verse begins to present an alternate scenario (continued through 10:18) to that portrayed in 10:1–5. "When the sheep were out on the hills in the warm season and did not return at night to the village at all, they were collected into sheep-folds on the hillside. These . . . were just open spaces enclosed by a wall. In them there was an opening by which the sheep came in and went out; but there was no door of any kind. What happened was that at night the shepherd himself lay down across the opening and no sheep could get out or in except over his body."[310] Jesus' words may hark back to messianic readings of passages such as Psalm 118:20, "This is the gate of the LORD through which the righteous may enter."

All who ever came before me were thieves and robbers (10:8). The Old Testament prophet Ezekiel refers to the "shepherds of Israel who only take care of themselves" but "do not take care of the flock" (Ezek. 34:2–4; see entire ch.). "All who ever came before me" hints at messianic pretenders who promise their followers freedom but instead lead them into armed conflict and doom. Jesus' statement also may have more overtly political overtones, evoking reminiscences of then-recent events in Jewish history, such as the Maccabean times when the high priests Jason and Menelaus betrayed their office and thus contributed to the desecration of the temple.

The spectrum of "thieves and robbers" may also encompass pseudo-prophets, such as the ones mentioned by Luke and Josephus (cf. Acts 5:36–37; 21:38; see comments on John 7:12), the Zealots, and even the high-priestly circles that controlled Judaism in Jesus' day. Sadducees in particular were known to use temple religion for their own profit, and elsewhere both the Pharisees (Luke 16:14) and the teachers of the law (Mark 12:40) are denounced for their greed. Perhaps the closest connection in the present context is with the Pharisees, whose attitude toward the man born blind exemplifies a blatant usurpation of religious authority and a perversion of godly leadership (cf. John 9).

I am the gate; whoever enters through me will be saved (10:9). As attested in

Greek literature since Homer, people in ancient times frequently thought of entering heaven by a gate. Jesus' claim to be "the door" resonates with this kind of thinking (cf. 1:51). The notion of a "gate to heaven" appears also in Jewish sources, both in the Old Testament and apocalyptic literature.[311] In the latter, the visionary receives a glimpse of the eternal truth of heaven, which is the source of final salvation (cf. Rev. 4:1). Apart from providing access to angels, the doors of heaven are the means by which knowledge and salvation are made known (e.g., *Odes Sol.* 17:6–11; 42:15–18; after A.D. 100). The Synoptics and Acts refer to "entering" God's kingdom as through a door or gate.[312]

He will come in and go out (10:9). Jesus' language (a Semitism) here echoes covenant terminology, especially Deuteronomic blessings for obedience (cf. Deut. 28:6; cf. Ps. 121:8). It is also reminiscent of Moses' description of Joshua (LXX: *Iēsous*, Jesus), who led Israel into the Promised Land: "May the LORD . . . appoint a man over this community to go out and come in before them, one who will lead them out and bring them in, so the LORD's people will not be like sheep without a shepherd" (Num. 27:16–17).

Find pasture (10:9). "Find pasture" is a common Old Testament expression (e.g., 1 Chron. 4:40). The psalmist basked in the assurance of God's provision (Ps. 23:2). The imagery is also found in Old Testament references to Israel's final restoration (Isa. 49:9–10) and deliverance from the nations (Ezek. 34:12–15).

Steal and kill and destroy (10:10). Threefold repetition of parallel expressions (positive or negative) is a device denoting emphasis in biblical literature (e.g., Matt. 7:7). The word for "kill" (*thyō*) is not the common term and may connote the abuse of the sacrificial system by the priestly authorities.

Have life, and have it to the full (10:10). On "life," see comments on 1:4. "Have life" means "to have eternal life," that is, "to be saved." But this does not merely entail participation in the age to come (as was the general view among Jews). According to John, Jesus gives a full life already in the here and now (which does not imply the absence of persecution, cf. 15:18–25). In the Old Testament, it is especially the prophet Ezekiel who envisions pasture and abundant life for God's people (cf. 34:12–15, 25–31).

I am the good shepherd (10:11). God is portrayed as the shepherd of his flock in numerous Old Testament passages.[313] The people of Israel, in turn, are described as "the sheep of his pasture."[314] God as the true shepherd is also contrasted with unfaithful shepherds, who are subject to divine judgment.[315] David (or the Davidic Messiah) is spoken of frequently as a (good) shepherd.[316] Moses, likewise, is portrayed as the "shepherd of his flock."[317] Philo speaks of a "good [*agathos*] shepherd" (*Agriculture* 44, 49) and applies shepherd terminology not only to kings and wise men but also to both God and his firstborn Son or Word (*Agriculture* 50–54; *Posterity* 67–68). In non-Jewish circles, too, gods and great men were described as shepherds.[318]

The good shepherd lays down his life for the sheep (10:11). Young David, first shepherd, then king, literally risked his life for his sheep (1 Sam. 17:34–37; cf. Sir. 47:3). Several Old Testament passages hint at the Messiah's self-sacrifice (Isa. 53:12; Zech. 12:10; 13:7–9).

The hired hand is not the shepherd . . . when he sees the wolf coming, he abandons the sheep and runs away. Then the wolf attacks the flock and scatters it. The man runs away because he is a hired hand and cares nothing for the sheep (10:12–13). Both Old Testament and later Jewish literature are replete with references to leaders who fail to perform their God-given responsibilities and as a result render their charge vulnerable to attack.[319] Shockingly, the shepherds themselves have turned into wolves (Ezek. 22:27). The "hired hands" of Israel (whose function is temporary) are contrasted with those who hold a permanent shepherding office: God and his Messiah, whose role is patterned after God's "good shepherd" par excellence, David (1 Sam. 17:34–36). The figure of the hired hand who abandons his sheep in times of adversity was well known in Jesus' day. As one intertestamental passage (c. A.D. 100) reads, "Do not forsake us, like a shepherd who leaves his flock in the power of savage wolves" (*4 Ezra* 5:18).

According to Old Testament legislation, the hired hand was not required to make restitution for an animal torn to pieces by a wild beast (Ex. 22:13). Later mishnaic law stipulated that if one wolf attacked the flock, the hireling must protect it. However, if two wolves threatened the sheep, no blame was attached to the hired man for any damage caused to the sheep (*m. B. Meṣiʿa* 7:8–9).[320] In Jesus' illustration, the "hired hand" is contrasted with "thieves and robbers" (John 10:1, 8, 10). While the latter are thoroughly wicked, the "hired hand" merely proves to be more committed to his own safety than to the sheep entrusted to his care. Under normal circumstances, he is willing to shepherd the flock for pay. In the face of danger, however, he puts self-interest first. Later in the Gospel, Jesus predicts that his disciples will be scattered (16:32). Elsewhere, Jesus sends his disciples out "as sheep among wolves" (Matt. 10:16; Luke 10:3). Paul likewise predicts that "savage wolves" will attack the Ephesian flock soon after his departure (Acts 20:29).

I know my sheep and my sheep know me . . . the Father knows me and I know the Father (10:14–15). Jesus' relationship with his followers ("know") is portrayed as an intimate, trusting relationship, in which Jesus, the good shepherd, cares deeply for those in his charge. This relationship is patterned after God's relationship with Old Testament Israel.[321] The saying "I know my sheep and my sheep know me" has a proverbial ring to it. Boring cites a Greek parallel, "I know Simon and Simon knows me."[322]

I have other sheep that are not of this sheep pen. I must bring them also (10:16). In light of Old Testament expectations of the incorporation of the Gentiles among God's people, the "other sheep that are not of this sheep pen" are probably Gentiles (see esp. Isa. 56:8).

There shall be one flock and one shepherd (10:16). The notion of one flock being led by one shepherd as a metaphor for God's providential care for his united people is firmly rooted in Old Testament prophetic literature[323] and continued in later Jewish writings.[324] Yet while the Old Testament envisions primarily the gathering of the dispersed sheep of Israel, the present passage talks about the bringing together of Jews and Gentiles into one messianic community (cf. Eph. 2:11–22; 4:3–6).

In the Hellenistic world, likewise, leaders were prized who promoted unity. Thus Plutarch (A.D. 45–125) describes the primary principle underlying the philosophy of Zeno, founder of the Stoics, as follows: "that all the inhabitants of this world of ours should not live differentiated by their respective rules of justice into separate cities and communities, but that we should consider all men to be of one community and one polity, and that we should have a common life and an order common to us all, even as a herd that feeds together and shares the pasturage of a common field" (*De Alex.* 6).[325]

This command I received (10:18). Jesus here invokes covenantal language, relating his relationship with his disciples to the relationship between God and Israel in the Old Testament.[326]

Demon-possessed and raving mad (10:20). See 7:20; 8:48, 52. It appears that in ancient times insanity and demon-possession were frequently linked. See also a partial parallel in intertestamental literature, where the life of the righteous is considered madness (*mania*) by the unrighteous (Wisd. Sol. 5:4). The Sibyl likewise defends herself against the charge of madness: "Some will say that I am Sibylla born of Circe [a magic-working

REFLECTIONS

MANY, IF NOT MOST, HUMAN LEADERS LEAD OUT OF self-interest. They may project concern for those they lead, but when push comes to shove, it becomes clear that they only use others to accomplish their own ends. Tragically, this was the case with Israel's leaders for much of the nation's history. Even in Jesus' day, the Jewish religious leadership resembled "thieves and robbers" more than a "good shepherd." And what about church leaders today? Are our churches pastored by selfless, sacrificial servants or self-aggrandizing individuals who pursue their own agendas and ambitions under the guise of a religious office?

goddess] as mother and Gnostos as father, a crazy liar. But when everything comes to pass, then you will remember me and no longer will anyone say that I am crazy, I who am a prophetess of the great God" (*Sib. Or.* 3:814–18; c. 150 B.C.).

Can a demon open the eyes of the blind? (10:21). See John 9. The psalmist says that it is the Lord who gives sight to the blind (Ps. 146:8; cf. Ex. 4:11).

The Unbelief of the Jews (10:22–42)

Unlike Tabernacles and the other two major annual feasts celebrated in Jerusalem, the Feast of Dedication—with its festive lamps—was joyously commemorated in Jewish homes as well as in the temple. The feast fell near the time of the winter equinox (second half of December). A popular family celebration, it provided a stark contrast with the pagan Saturnalia, which were celebrated during the same period. Since there is no mention that Jesus went up to Jerusalem for the Feast of Dedication, it is possible that he spent the time from Tabernacles to Dedication (about two months) in Jerusalem. Alternatively, Jesus and his followers may have returned to Galilee subsequent to the Feast of Tabernacles only to embark on what turned out to be Jesus' final journey to Jerusalem (Matt. 19:1; Mark 10:1; Luke 9:51).[327]

The Feast of Dedication (10:22). This is the first reference to this feast by this name (*ta enkainia*) in Jewish literature.[328] The eight-day Feast of Dedication (also called *Ḥanukkah* or the Feast of Lights, *phōta*) celebrated the rededication of the temple in December, 164 B.C. The temple had been desecrated in 167 B.C. when the Seleucid ruler Antiochus IV Epiphanes offered a sacrifice to Zeus on a pagan altar (called "the abomination of desolation"[329]). A revolt started by the Jewish priest Mattathias issued in the miraculous defeat of Antiochus's troops through Mattathias's son Judas in 164 B.C. (1 Macc. 2:1–4:35), inaugurating a period of Jewish independence that lasted until 63 B.C., when the Roman general Pompey conquered Palestine. Judas immediately tore down "the abomination of desolation" and refurbished the temple (1 Macc. 4:36–51; cf. 2 Macc. 10:1–4). The temple was rededicated on the 25th of Chislev (Dec. 14), 164 B.C., three years after its desecration.[330]

There are similarities between the accounts of the Feast of Dedication, called "the festival of booths in the month of Chislev" (2 Macc. 1:9 [c. 124 B.C.]; cf. 10:6), and the Feast of Tabernacles (Lev. 23:42–43). Its association with the biblical Feast of Tabernacles lent Dedication a certain amount of scriptural legitimacy. Both festivals celebrated God's protection of Israel during her wanderings in the desert. Beyond this, the Feast of Dedication also commemorated God's intervention in the restoration of the temple, the apostasy among the Jews that had led to the temple's desecration, and the Jews' regaining of their religious (and national) freedom. As Josephus writes, "And from that time to the present we observe this festival, which we call the festival of Lights, giving this name to it, I think, from the fact that the right to worship appeared to us at a time when we hardly dared hope for it" (*Ant.* 12.7.7 §325; cf. 12.7.6–7 §§316–24).[331]

It was winter, and Jesus was in the temple area walking in Solomon's Colonnade (10:22–23). Probably owing to the cold winter weather (in A.D. 32, the Feast of Dedication fell on December 18), Jesus taught not in an open court but in the temple area called Solomon's Colonnade which, being about two hundred yards long,[332] offered protection from the raw east wind and was located on the east side of the temple (Josephus, *J.W.* 5.5.1 §§184–85; *Ant.* 15.11.3 §§396–401; 20.10.7 §§220–21). Solomon's Colonnade, which was commonly (but erroneously) thought to date back to Solomon's time and which in fact derived from the pre-Herodian Hasmonean period, formed part of a magnificent covered structure that surrounded the outermost court of the temple on all sides. It later became the gathering place for the early Jerusalem church (cf. Acts 3:11; 5:12).

If you are the Christ, tell us plainly (10:24). Owing to the political connotations of the term "Messiah" in first-century Palestine, Jesus avoided using the expression with reference to himself (cf. 6:14–15; 11:48). Similarly, Luke 22:67: "If you are the Christ, tell us."

No one can snatch them out of my hand (10:28). "Snatch" connotes the use of force (see comments on "robbers" in 10:1 and 8, above). The present assertion contrasts with the figure of the hireling, who abandons the flock in the face of danger (cf. 10:12–13). See also the references to the "hands" of the prophet and of God in Ezekiel 37:15–19, and the following note.

My Father . . . is greater than all; no one can snatch them out of my Father's hand (10:29). Jesus' reference to the Father's sovereign power recalls statements in both Old Testament and Jewish intertestamental literature that no one can deliver out of God's hand (Isa. 43:13) and that the souls of the righteous are in his hand (Wisd. Sol. 3:1).

I and the Father are one (10:30). This echoes the basic confession of Judaism: "Hear, O Israel: The LORD our God, the LORD is one" (Deut. 6:4). For Jesus to be one with the Father yet distinct from him amounts to a claim to deity (cf. John 1:1–2). This challenged narrow Jewish notions of monotheism, even though there are already hints in the Old Testament of a plurality within the Godhead.

The Jews picked up stones to stone him (10:31). See 5:18; 8:59. Stoning was to be carried out on the basis of a judicial sentence rather than as impulsive act of mob violence. But because the Roman authorities retained sole jurisdiction over capital punishment (cf. 18:31), and because large crowds could quickly turn volatile, especially in an oppressed nation replete with nationalistic fervor and religious fanaticism, lynching always remained a possible outcome (cf. Acts 7:54–60). In certain cases, Jewish law actually seems to have encouraged such a procedure (*m. Mak.* 3:2). In light of the relationship between the Feast of Dedication and the consecration of the temple and John's portrayal of Jesus as the temple's replacement (John 2:19–21), the Jews' attempt to stone Jesus for blasphemy is in fact presented by the evangelist as an effort on the Jews' part to blaspheme the "holy sanctuary of God," Jesus—and that at the Feast commemorating the rededication of the temple!333

But for blasphemy, because you, a mere man, claim to be God (10:33). Later Jewish law limited blasphemy to pronouncing the name of God, the tetragrammaton ("Yahweh"): "'The blasphemer' is not culpable unless he pronounces the Name itself" (*m. Sanh.* 7:5; cf. 6:4); this Jesus is never recorded as doing. However, it is unlikely that the Sadducees—who controlled legal proceedings in the Sanhedrin, the highest Jewish court—ever adopted so narrow a definition of blasphemy in Jesus' day. Rather, a broader interpretation of blasphemy prevailed, based on passages such as Numbers

15:30–31 ("anyone who sins defiantly . . . blasphemes the LORD") or Deuteronomy 21:22 ("guilty of a capital offense"). See also Mark 14:61–64.334

Is it not written in your Law, "I have said you are gods"? If he called them "gods," to whom the word of God came . . . (10:34–35). The passage quoted is Psalm 82:6.335 In the Old Testament, the phrase "to whom the word of God came" is often used with reference to those who speak or act in God's name. The phrase "the word of the LORD that came" is found at the opening of the prophetic books of Hosea, Joel, Micah, and Zephaniah (see also Luke 3:2). In the original context, the expression may have referred to: (1) Israel's corrupt judges, who were called "gods" because the administration of justice was a divine prerogative delegated to a few select individuals (Deut. 1:17; cf. Ps. 82:1–4); (2) angelic powers who abused the authority God had given to them over the nations (unlikely in light of the scarcity of references to angels in John); (3) Israel at the time of the giving of the law.336 Arguing, in typical rabbinic fashion, from the lesser to the greater (see comments on John 5:47), Jesus' point here is that if Israel can in some sense be called "god" in the Scriptures, how much more is this designation appropriate for him who truly is the Son of God.337

The Scripture cannot be broken (10:35). Jesus' statement is evidence for his belief in the inviolability of God's written word (in the present instance, the Hebrew Scriptures). Elsewhere, Jesus contends that "until heaven and earth disappear, not the smallest letter, not the least stroke of a pen, will by any means disappear from the Law until everything is accomplished"

(Matt. 5:18). Paul and Peter concurred (2 Tim. 3:16; 2 Peter 1:20–21).

The one whom the Father set apart as his very own and sent into the world (10:36). In the Old Testament and intertestamental literature, the term "set apart" was used for those appointed to fulfill an important task or office, be it Moses the lawgiver (Sir. 45:4), Jeremiah the prophet (Jer. 1:5), or the Aaronic priests.[338] In the LXX, variants of the term *ta egkainia* ("Dedication," 10:22) refer to the dedication of the tabernacle altar (Num. 7:10–11), Solomon's temple (1 Kings 8:63), and the second temple (Ezra 6:16–17). Just as Jesus replaces the Sabbath (John 5, 9), the manna (ch. 6), and the light and water at the Feast of Tabernacles (chs. 7–9), so his reference to his own setting apart recalls the event behind the celebration of the Feast of Dedication: the consecration of the altar that replaced "the abomination of desolation" erected by Antiochus IV Epiphanes.

Believe the miracles (10:38). Old Testament figures recognized for performing unusual works were Elisha (who was given the key to the womb and enabled a barren woman to conceive), Elijah (who was given the key to the rain in answer to prayer), and both prophets together with Ezekiel (who were given the key to the graves and who raised the dead), all three works usually being reserved for God's direct intervention (*Midr. Ps.* 78 §5).[339]

The Father is in me, and I in the Father (10:38). Some have seen a parallel to Jesus' assertion of oneness with God in Antiochus Epiphanes's boast that he was "God Manifest" (the meaning of the Greek epithet "Epiphanes"). This claim

made by Antiochus may also lie behind the Jews' charge that Jesus (like the Seleucid ruler, see 2 Macc. 9:28) was a blasphemer (cf. John 10:33, 36).[340]

Jesus went back across the Jordan to the place where John had been baptizing in the early days (10:40). See comments on 1:28. This probably refers to the region of Batanea in the tetrarchy of Philip in the northeast, a safe distance from the jurisdiction of the Jerusalem leaders. Notably, Jesus does not return to Galilee, his ministry there having come to a close (as far as the fourth evangelist is concerned) with the events of chapter 6.

John never performed a miraculous sign (10:41). Jewish sources do not praise putatively great men unless some miracle is attributed to them.[341] The Synoptic writers likewise never attribute miracles to John the Baptist, though Herod reportedly thought Jesus—who *did* perform miracles—was John the Baptist come back to life (Mark 6:14).

Jesus Learns of Lazarus's Death (11:1–16)

With the Feast of Dedication past (the year is now A.D. 33) and the threat to Jesus' life in Jerusalem and vicinity becoming increasingly severe, Jesus withdraws to the place where John had baptized in the early days of his ministry. (John had long been cast into prison and subsequently been killed.) One more great climactic miracle is about to follow, the seventh and final Johannine sign, which anticipates Jesus' own resurrection.

Now a man named Lazarus (11:1). "Now a [certain] man . . . was" recalls the similar introduction in 5:5 (cf. 1 Sam.

He was from Bethany, the village (11:1). The present Bethany (not previously mentioned in John's Gospel) must be distinguished from the Bethany featured in 1:28 and 10:40–42.[342] The village referred to here was situated east of the Mount of Olives, less than two miles from Jerusalem on the road to Jericho. This Bethany is mentioned elsewhere (together with Bethphage) as the place where Jesus stayed when visiting Jerusalem (Matt. 21:17; 26:6 par.). It is probably to be identified with the village of Ananyah mentioned in Nehemiah 11:32.[343] Today the town is called El-'Azariyeh in commemoration of Lazarus. The term "village" (*kōmē*) is elsewhere in John applied only to Bethlehem (John 7:42).

◀ left

JUDEA

Bethany was a village two miles east of Jerusalem.

1:1; Job 1:1). Lazarus is a shortened form of Eleazar (Heb. *El'azar*, "whom God helps," "whose help is God"). This was the name of the third son and successor of Aaron, whose descendants were the high priests of the house of Zadok. Ossuary inscriptions show that the name Eleazar was common in New Testament times.

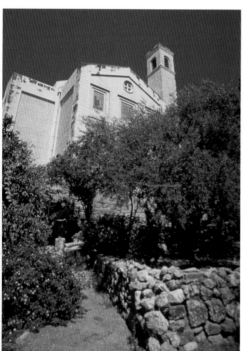

Mary and her sister Martha (11:1). Apparently, Martha was the older of the two sisters, since she acts as the hostess in the Lukan passage (cf. 12:2). Note also that she is named first in 11:5 below ("Martha and her sister"). The names Mary, Martha, and Lazarus were discovered in ossuary inscriptions in a tomb near Bethany in 1873.[344] Mary was a common name, the Greek form of the Hebrew Miriam. Martha was an Aramaic name, meaning "lady," feminine of *mar*, "Lord." The fact that of the three names in this family, one is Hebrew (Lazarus), one Aramaic (Martha), and one Greek (Mary), is typical of the end of the second temple period and attests to the way in which cultures interpenetrated each other. See comments on Luke 10:38–42.

He stayed where he was two more days (11:6). If the place where Jesus is staying

◀ left

BETHANY

The site of the village of ancient Bethany.

when the news of Lazarus's illness reaches him is the region of Batanea, located approximately a hundred miles to the north-east of Jerusalem (see comments on 1:28; cf. 10:40–42), the following reconstruction of the events surrounding the raising of Lazarus best fits the evidence. Apparently, Lazarus is still alive when the initial news regarding his illness reaches Jesus (11:4). Two days later, Jesus, presumably by means of supernatural insight, announces to his followers that Lazarus has died, taking this as the divine signal to depart for Bethany.[345] If a person traveled an average of twenty to thirty miles a day on foot, it would take four days for Jesus to get to the scene (11:17).

Are there not twelve hours of daylight? (11:9). Similarly, *b. Sanh.* 38b: "R. Yohanan [Aha] b. Hanina (c. A.D. 300) said: 'The day consisted of twelve hours.'" Both Romans and Jews divided the day into twelve "hour" periods. Since the length of daylight extended, according to season, from ten to fourteen hours a day, the twelve "hours" of daylight varied accordingly. Most people did their work as long as there was daylight; once darkness came, it was time to stop working.

He has no light (11:10). The Greek adds the phrase "in him" (not represented in the NIV). This indicates a shift from the realm of nature (daylight) to symbolic language ("light" inside a person; cf. Matt. 6:23; par. Luke 11:35). In Semitic thought, the eye was regarded as light in a person's body. From there it is only a small step to the notion that a person is connected with the divine world of light. The shift in the image from *walking in* the light to light *being in a person* is also attested in the Qumran texts: "through your glory, my light becomes visible, for

from darkness you make my light shine" (1QH 17:26–27). A similar statement appears in the *Gospel of Thomas*: "There is light within a man of light, and he lights up the whole world. If he does not shine, he is darkness" (*Gos. Thom.* 24). A possible Old Testament parallel is Jeremiah 13:16.

Lazarus has fallen asleep (11:11). The equivalent Old Testament phrase (esp. in the books of Kings and Chronicles) is he or she "slept with his [or her] fathers" (i.e., the person died), suggesting falling into an irrevocable sleep (cf. Job 14:11–12). Occasionally death is considered to be a sleep from which people will one day be awakened (Dan. 12:2; cf. *4 Ezra* 7:31–32).[346]

Thomas (called Didymus) (11:16). The name Thomas (both Heb. *tōm* and Aram. *tōmam* mean "twin") is not attested in literature prior to John's Gospel. However, the Greek term *didymos* (which also means "twin") is known also to have served as a proper name. It is therefore likely that Thomas was a genuine Greek name patterned after its Hebrew or Aramaic equivalents.[347]

Jesus Comforts Lazarus's Sisters (11:17–37)

By coming to console Martha and Mary after their brother's death, Jesus fulfills one of the most essential obligations in the Jewish culture of his day. The presence of a well-known teacher who has traveled a long distance would be particularly comforting to Lazarus's sisters. Yet, ultimately, Jesus has much greater things in mind (cf. 11:4, 15).

Lazarus had already been in the tomb for four days (11:17). Later Jewish sources attest the rabbinic belief that death was irrevocable three days after a person had died. "R. Abba b. R. Pappai and R. Joshua of Siknin said in the name of R. Levi (after A.D. 250): 'For three days [after death] the soul hovers over the body, intending to re-enter it, but as soon as it sees its appearance change, it departs' . . . Bar Kdappara said: 'The full force of mourning lasts for three days. Why? Because [for that length of time] the shape of the face is recognizable'" (*Lev. Rab.* 18:1 on Lev. 15:1; cf. *Eccl. Rab.* 12:6).

Burial usually followed shortly after death, as in the case of Ananias and Sapphira (Acts 5:6, 10). This is presupposed by the mishnaic stipulation that "evidence [of the identity of a corpse] may be given only during the first three days [after death]" (*m. Yebam.* 16:3) and the belief that one should visit a burial place of one newly buried for three days to ensure that the person was really dead. In the classic rabbinic text on death and mourning we read, "We go out to the cemetery and examine the dead within three days. . . . It once happened that [a man who was buried] was examined [and found to be living], and he lived for twenty-five years and then died. Another [so examined lived and] begat five children before he died" (*Sem.* 8 Rule 1).[348]

Bethany was less than two miles from Jerusalem, and many Jews had come . . . to comfort them (11:18–19). The original wording specifies that Bethany was fifteen *stadia* from Jerusalem. Since one *stadion* was approximately 200 yards, fifteen *stadia* equal about 3000 yards or just over 1.7 miles. It may be inferred that the "many Jews" who came to comfort Martha and Mary were from Jerusalem. If so, the family enjoyed considerable social standing, for although comforting the bereaved was generally regarded as a religious duty, not every villager would have been consoled by "many Jews" from a nearby city.[349]

Since burial in ancient Palestine took place on the day of death, mourning for the passing of a loved one followed burial. In Jesus' time, men and women walked separately in the funeral procession, and after the burial the women returned from the grave alone to begin a thirty-day mourning period. This included frequent expressions of loud wailing and other dramatic displays of grief.[350] The Talmud prescribes seven days of deep and thirty days of light

TOMB OF LAZARUS
▼

mourning: "Three days for weeping and seven for lamenting and thirty [to refrain] from cutting the hair and [donning] pressed clothes" (*b. Mo'ed Qaṭ.* 27b).

Mary stayed at home (11:20). The Greek reads, "she was seated in the house." It was customary for those mourning the loss of a loved one to be seated when receiving the condolences of their friends (Job 2:8, 13; Ezek. 8:14; cf. *Ruth Rab.* 2:14). A sitting posture was also common for mourners in ancient Rome, being adopted, for example, by Cato when learning of the defeat at Pharsalus (Plutarch, *Cato Minor* 56.4). John's characterization of Mary and Martha agrees with Luke's Gospel, where Mary sits at Jesus' feet while Martha is busy with her household duties (cf. Luke 7:38–42).[351]

"Your brother will rise again." . . . "I know he will rise again in the resurrection at the last day" (11:23–24). Martha's affirmation of end-time resurrection is in keeping with Jesus' own teaching (cf. 6:39–44, 54), which in turn coheres with Pharisaic beliefs (cf. Acts 23:8; Josephus, *J.W.* 2.8.14 §163) and those of the majority of first-century Jews.[352] The Sadducees (as well as the Samaritans), flatly denied such a view.[353]

The resurrection of the dead was the subject of lively debate between the Pharisees and their opponents: "Sectarians [*minim*] asked Rabban Gamaliel [II; c. A.D. 90]: Whence do we know that the Holy One, blessed be He, will resurrect the dead? He answered them from the Torah, the Prophets, and the Hagiographa [i.e., the Writings], yet they did not accept it" (*b. Sanh.* 90b, referring to Deut. 31:16; Isa. 26:19; Song 7:9). Other mishnaic passages likewise denounce those who refuse to affirm the resurrection of the dead: "And these are they that have no share in the world to come: he that says there is no resurrection of the dead prescribed in the Law . . ." (*m. Sanh.* 10:1; cf. *m. Ber.* 9:5).

Belief in the resurrection is also evident from the second of the Eighteen Benedictions: "Lord, you are almighty forever, who makes the dead alive. . . . Blessed are you, Lord, who makes the dead alive" (cf. *m. Ber.* 5:2; *m. Soṭah* 9:15).[354] The old idea of Jewish corporate personality, where one continued to exist only in the lives of one's descendants, hardly provided satisfactory hope for many pious Jews in Jesus' day.[355]

The Christ, the Son of God, who was to come into the world (11:27). For "the Christ," see comments on 1:41. For "Son of God," see comments on 1:34 and 1:49. "[He] who was to come into the world" takes up the messianic expression derived from Psalm 118:26, which is applied to Jesus by others in the Gospels (see esp. Matt. 11:3 par.; John 12:13 par.).

The Teacher (11:28). "The teacher" was a natural way of referring to Jesus for any disciple in the pre-resurrection period. The fact that this term is here used by a woman (talking to another woman) is significant. While contemporary rabbis regularly refused to instruct women, Jesus took a radically different approach.

Supposing she was going to the tomb to mourn there (11:31). Literally, "to weep." In keeping with Jewish custom, Mary is expected to give way to her grief and weep at the tomb.[356]

The Jews who had come along with her also weeping (11:33). According to Jewish funeral custom, even a poor family was expected to hire at least two flute players and a professional wailing woman (*m. Ketub.* 4:4; attributed to R. Judah, c. A.D. 150), and Mary and Martha's family was anything but poor (cf. 12:1–3). The present heart-breaking scene would have been preceded by a formal funeral procession including burial, in which wailing women and flute-players as well as shouts of grief from the men in the procession punctuated laments sung in the house of death, on the way to the tomb, and during the burial itself (cf. Matt. 9:23 par.).[357]

Deeply moved in spirit and troubled (11:33). "Deeply moved" (NIV) hardly does justice to the underlying Greek word *embrimaomai*, which has the connotation of anger and snorting (in animals). The term occurs twice in the LXX (as verb or noun), both in the context of the venting of fierce anger (Dan. 11:30; Lam. 2:6). Thus, Jesus is shown here not merely to express empathy and grief but to be positively upset, even angry, in the face of the human suffering resulting from death (cf. John 12:27; 13:21). "Troubled" (*tarassō*) has connotations of being agitated and stirred up inside (cf. Est. 4:4: "in great distress"), like the waters of Bethesda (John 5:7) or the waves and breakers of a waterfall (Ps. 42:5–7). Being in anguish is an experience frequently described by David in his psalms.[358]

Jesus wept (11:35). The expression *dakryō* (only here in the New Testament) occurs occasionally in the LXX.[359] Owing to the force of the verb tense in the Greek original (an ingressive aorist), "Jesus burst into tears" would be a better translation. This is suggested by comparison with instances of *dakryō* in the same grammatical form in Greco-Roman and Hellenistic Jewish literature, where the term is regularly rendered this way.[360]

THE RAISING OF LAZARUS

A Roman catacomb fresco depicting the raising of Lazarus.

The Raising of Lazarus (11:38–44)

Old Testament instances of raisings of the dead include Elijah's raising of the widow's son (1 Kings 17:17–24), Elisha's raising of the son of the Shunammite woman (2 Kings 4:32–37), Elisha's "posthumous" raising of a dead man (2 Kings 13:21), and the witch of Endor's illicit bringing of Samuel out of the grave at King Saul's request (1 Sam. 28; see also Ezekiel's vision of the valley of dry bones in Ezek. 37:1–14). Raisings of the dead were generally viewed in light of the final resurrection and as an expression of God's power to bring it about.

The tomb. It was a cave with a stone laid across the entrance (11:38). "Archaeological surveys in the vicinity of Jerusalem have given us a clear idea of a well-to-do family tomb from the time of Jesus. Scores of such tombs have been found in the slopes of the valleys to the east and south of Jerusalem. . . . As the making of a tomb-cave required a vertical rock-face for the entrance, the sites chosen were often disused quarries. . . . The cave cut out of the rock usually consisted of a main hall, with a smaller vestibule. The bodies of the deceased were laid in a pit in the hall for the first year, till only the bones remained. Afterwards these were collected and placed in small stone boxes, the ossuaries. These miniature coffins were then placed in *loculi* (horizontal niches cut into the rock). The caves were closed by a stone door; for additional security a rolling stone was sometimes provided."[361]

Though the shaft of the cave could have been vertical or horizontal, from the way Lazarus came out as well as from archaeological evidence and mishnaic regulations, it would appear that the cave was horizontal. The burial place was outside the village in order for the living not to contract ritual impurity from contact with the corpse. There is ample Jewish evidence for the use of natural caves for burial, which were further prepared by artificial means (*m. B. Bat.* 6:8).[362] Jesus' own body would later be put in a similar tomb (Mark 15:46, par.).

There is a bad odor, for he has been in there four days (11:39). While the Jews used spices at burials (though not embalming as the Egyptians did), this did not prevent decomposition.[363]

Jesus looked up and said (11:41). An Old Testament antecedent to Jesus' prayer here is that of Elijah: "Answer me, O LORD, answer me, so these people will know that you, O LORD, are God" (1 Kings 18:37; cf. Ps. 118:21; 121:1; 123:1; cf. Matt. 11:25; John 6:11).[364] The gesture of looking up is rarely attested for the later period (cf. 1 Esd. 4:58; Josephus, *Ant.* 11.5.6 §162). The Jews generally believed that extraordinary things can be accomplished through the power of almighty God as a result of the prayer of his righteous servants (though magical practices made their way into Judaism as well).[365] Greco-Roman culture, by contrast, attributed superhuman powers to "divine men." Jesus' contemporaries frequently viewed him as a miracle-worker who was able to perform extraordinary feats by virtue of his supernatural power. Jesus' prayer counters this perception. It shows that he has no authority apart from the Father and that he is neither a magician nor a "divine man" by Greco-Roman standards.

Father (11:41). "Father" is the customary address for God used by Jesus in prayer, occasionally adorned by a divine attribute such as "Holy Father" (17:11) or "Righteous Father" (17:25).[366] At times, the address is "Our Father in heaven" (Matt. 6:9) or "Father, Lord of heaven and earth" (Matt. 11:25). The address "Father" is also found in Qumran scrolls (4Q372, frag. 1, 16).

Jesus called in a loud voice, "Lazarus, come out!" (11:43). "Wizards muttered their incantations and spells (cf. Isa. 8:19). Not so the Son of God."[367]

His hands and feet wrapped with strips of linen (11:44). "The corpse was customarily laid on a sheet of linen, wide enough to envelop the body completely and more than twice the length of the corpse. The body was so placed on the sheet that the feet were at one end, and then the sheet was drawn over the head and back down to the feet. The feet were bound at the ankles, and the arms were tied to the body with linen strips. . . . Jesus' body was apparently prepared for burial in the same way (cf. 19:40; 20:5, 7)."[368] The custom of wrapping the *hands and feet* of a dead person in linen cloths is not attested elsewhere in Jewish texts. Frequently, deceased loved ones were dressed in flowing and valuable garments, a practice later abolished by Rabbi Gamaliel II.[369] Yet contrary to pagan custom the Jews did not bind up their dead to prevent them from returning to life.

The word for "strips of linen" (*keiriai*) is used several times in fragments of medical papyri suggesting narrow strips tied around the body. "Fine linen" is frequently mentioned as an Egyptian export and is associated with the wealthy in the Old Testament.[370] In rabbinic times, it was thought that at the final resurrection the dead would rise in their clothes. "R.

Hiyya b. Joseph [c. A.D. 260] further stated: The just in the time to come will rise [apparelled] in their own clothes" (*b. Ketub.* 111b). "R. Eliezer [c. A.D. 90] said: All the dead will arise at the resurrection of the dead, dressed in their shrouds . . . and the people who descend into the earth dressed (with their garments), will they not rise up dressed (with their garments)? . . . Learn from Samuel, the prophet, who came up clothed with his robe . . . (1 Sam. 28:14)" (*Pirqe R. El.* 33).

And a cloth around his face (11:44). The face was bound up with another cloth, called *soudarion* (a loan word from the Latin *sudarium*, "sweat-cloth"), which in life was often worn around the neck (cf. *b. Moʾed Qaṭ.* 27a).

The Plot to Kill Jesus (11:45–57)

Come to visit Mary (11:45). This may indicate that it is Mary rather than Martha who has an extensive circle of friends.

Chief priests and Pharisees (11:47). See comments on 7:32.

Called a meeting of the Sanhedrin (11:47). The term *synedrion* ("Sanhedrin") in the sense of "council meeting" is rare in the New Testament, yet frequent in secular Greek (e.g., Diodorus Siculus, *B.H.* 13.111.1), in the LXX (e.g., Prov. 31:23; 2 Macc. 14:5), and in Hellenistic Jewish literature.[371] Most large Jewish centers had a sanhedrin or local court, but the Supreme or Great Sanhedrin was located in Jerusalem. The Sanhedrin was the Jewish judicial, legislative, and executive body, which, under Roman overall jurisdiction, managed the nation's internal affairs. In Jesus' day, the Council's members were controlled by the chief priests, drawn from the extended family of the high priest who presided over the Sanhedrin. The vast majority of these priests were Sadducees, with Pharisees (most of whom were scribes or teachers of the law) constituting an influential minority.[372]

The calling of an official Sanhedrin meeting was legally the responsibility of the high priest. The wording of the NIV suggests an official meeting of the Sanhedrin, though a more informal gathering is equally plausible (in which case the word rendered "Sanhedrin" in the NIV may simply mean "gathering" or "assembly"). The latter alternative would explain why Caiaphas is called "one of them" (11:49), even though in a formal Sanhedrin meeting he would have presided over the proceedings of the Council. The casual way in which Caiaphas is introduced and the bluntness of his language also may indicate that this is not an official gathering of the Sanhedrin with the high priest presiding (contrast Matt. 26:57–66 par.).[373] From this point on, the Pharisees are only referred to infrequently in John's Gospel; control of proceedings against Jesus has now been seized by the chief priests.

If we let him go on like this, . . . the Romans will come and take away both our place and our nation (11:48). In Jewish literature, "the place" (Heb. *maqom*)

Jewish High Priests from 200 B.C. to the Time of Jesus (Selective List)[A-20]	
1. *Pre-Maccabean:*	
Simon the Righteous (after 200 B.C.)	Jason (175–172 B.C.)
Onias II (to 175 B.C.)	Menelaus (172–162 B.C.)
2. *Maccabean:*	
Jonathan (152–143/2 B.C.)	Aristobulus I (104–103 B.C.)
Simon (142/1–134 B.C.)	Alexander Jannaeus (103–76 B.C.)
John Hyrcanus I (134–104 B.C.)	Hyrcanus II (76–67 and 63–40 B.C.)
3. *Post-Maccabean:*	
Annas (A.D. 6–15)	Simon, son of Kamithos (A.D. 17–18)
Ishmael b. Phiabi I (c. A.D. 15–16)	Joseph Caiaphas (c. A.D. 18–36/7)
Eleazar, son of Annas (c. A.D. 16–17)	

place, but *the place* for the sake of *the nation*. Therefore *the place* itself shared in the misfortunes that befell *the nation* and afterward participated in its benefits; and what was forsaken in the wrath of the Almighty was restored again in all its glory when the great Lord became reconciled" (2 Macc. 5:19).

It appears, therefore, that the Jews' repeated, traumatic (albeit temporary) loss of land and temple elicited fear (at least on the part of its leaders) that God would once again visit the nation in judgment and allow them to be exiled and the temple to be destroyed if Israel was disobedient to God. This preoccupation, here expressed in relation to Jesus, surfaces again in a later Sanhedrin meeting, when false witnesses testify that Stephen "never stops speaking against *this holy place*," predicting that Jesus would "destroy *this place*" (Acts 6:13–14). Still later, Paul is likewise charged with teaching "all men everywhere against our people and our law and *this place*" as well as with defiling "*this holy place*" by bringing Greeks into the inner temple area (Acts 21:28).

"Take away our nation" (*ethnos*) refers to the feared removal of the Jews' semi-autonomous status by the Romans (cf. 2 Macc. 5:19; see comments on John 11:47). The Roman overlords were concerned to preserve public order. The Pharisees had strained to be free from domination, be it by Hasmoneans, Pompey, or Herodians, ever since their party had come into existence, in order to devote themselves fully to the practice of the law. Jewish sources indicate that the authorites had been nervous for some time prior to the Jewish War (A.D. 66–74). With this comports also the Pharisees' initial opposition to the armed

◀ *left*

JUDEA

Ephraim was located about 20 miles north of Jerusalem.

may refer metaphorically to the Lord (e.g. *Gen. Rab.* 68:9; *b. ʿAbod. Zar.* 40b), the Promised Land (2 Macc. 1:29), Jerusalem (*m. Bik.* 2:2), or the temple. Of these, the temple is the most concrete and climactic referent, since it is located in Jerusalem, the capital city of the Promised Land, and the place where God himself dwells. Importantly, the temple assumes a central role in God's judgment of Israel. Thus God announced the Babylonian exile through the prophet, "What I did to Shiloh I will now do to the house that bears my Name, the temple you trust in, *the place* I gave to you and your fathers. I will thrust you from my presence" (Jer. 7:14; cf. Neh. 4:7).

The next major instance of God's judgment on his people Israel involving the temple is the desecration of the temple by the Seleucid ruler Antiochus IV Epiphanes (see comments on John 10:22). In an important apocryphal passage, the fortunes of "the place" (i.e., the temple) and the Jewish "nation" are said to be closely linked. After recording the pillaging of the temple by Antiochus, the author writes, "But the Lord did not choose the nation for the sake of *the holy* revolt against Rome, which led to the destruction of the temple in A.D. 70 (cf. Josephus, *J.W.* 2.17.3–5 §§411–24). Josephus reports several portents of the end taking place in Jerusalem (*J.W.* 6.5.3–4 §§288–315; cf. *Ant.* 14.163–84).

Again, the irony would be all too apparent to John's readers (esp. after A.D. 70): What the Jewish leadership strenuously seeks to avoid, namely, for history to repeat itself and for God's judgment to fall on Israel's nation as typified by the temple, is precisely what ensues in the wake of Jesus' crucifixion (cf. 2:13–22).[374]

Who was high priest that year (11:49). "That year" need not imply that the high priestly office rotated annually but may simply indicate that Caiaphas happened to be high priest in that fateful year when Jesus was tried and crucified. In fact, Caiaphas held on to his office for a remarkably long time (eighteen years; A.D. 18–36), longer than any other high priest in the first century. But John's remark may also convey the notion that the high priest's term generally lasted for a year and that considerable uncertainty attached to the high priestly office in that day. In fact, if a single one of his actions displeased the Roman governor, the high priest was subject to removal. Valerius Gratus, Pilate's predecessor, repeatedly deposed high priests after a short length of office. Thus the three high priests prior to Caiaphas (A.D. 15–18) as well as his immediate successor (A.D. 36) all held their office only approximately one year (cf. also the three high priests under Agrippa [A.D. 41–44] and the majority of high priests from A.D. 44–66).[375]

▶ Joseph Caiaphas

Caiaphas's full name was Joseph Kayyafa, *Kaiaph* being the family name. He was made high priest by the Roman prefect Valerius Gratus (A.D. 15–26) in A.D. 18 (cf. Josephus, *Ant.* 18.2.2 §35) and held his position until A.D. 36, when he and Pontius Pilate were both removed from office by Vitellius, proconsul of Syria (cf. Josephus, *Ant.* 18.4.3 §95). The fates of Caiaphas and Pilate were closely linked, and it is possible that the former occupied his office through a financial arrangement with the latter. Throughout Caiaphas's tenure, his father-in-law Annas, who had been high priest for several years himself (A.D. 6–15), continued to exercise considerable influence (see 18:13 and comments on 11:47).

Caiaphas himself must have been a "genius of balance, diplomatically adept toward the prefect and the Herodian rulers, conscious of his powerful position yet not so hated by his Jewish contemporaries that he elicited prolonged protests."[A-21] Thus he managed to retain his office during the rule of two procurators, both of which must be judged difficult: Gratus, who in his first three years of office had changed high priests as many as four times, whereby Annas himself, Caiaphas's father-in-law had been his first victim (A.D. 15–18; cf. Josephus, *Ant.* 18.2.2 §§33–35), and Pilate (see comments on 18:29). Caiaphas is mentioned by name in connection with Jesus' death only in John and Matthew (26:57; but see Luke 3:2; Acts 4:6); he is named in Mark. Recent excavations in Jerusalem may have unearthed Caiaphas's tomb.[A-22]

◀

CAIAPHAS OSSUARY

Spoke up, "You know nothing at all!" (11:49). Caiaphas's opening words display a rudeness that was allegedly characteristic of Sadducees. Josephus (who, being a Pharisee, is hardly unbiased in this regard) states, "The Sadducees . . . are, even among themselves, rather boorish in their behavior, and in their intercourse with their peers are as rude as to aliens" (*J.W.* 2.8.14 §166).

It is better for you that one man die for the people than that the whole nation perish (11:50). Dying "for the people" invokes the memory of the Maccabean martyrs (2 Macc. 7:37–38). The question of whether Israelites should turn other Israelites over to the government was also discussed in rabbinic Judaism. Some argued that if there is good reason to turn over one person in particular, this was permissible. Others disagreed. One such passage takes its point of departure from 2 Samuel 20, where Sheba is slain while the city of Abel is spared. "It was taught: If a company of people are threatened by heathens, 'Surrender one of you and we will kill him, and if not we will kill all of you,' they should all be killed and not surrender one soul of Israel. But if they specified a particular person, as in the case of Sheba the son of Bichri [2 Sam. 20:1], they should surrender him and should not all be killed" (*Gen. Rab.* 94:9; cf. *t. Ter.* 7:20).

The same case is taken up in the Jerusalem Talmud, where Rabbi Yoḥanan (d. A.D. 279) appears to have prevailed over against R. Simeon b. Laqish with the view that even an innocent Israelite should be sacrificed for the rest: "[It applies] even if he is not subject to execution, as was Sheba the son of Bichri" (*y. Ter.* 8:10). Another incident involved Ulla the son of Kdosher who was wanted by the government. He fled to R. Joshua b.

Levi, pursued by officers dispatched to arrest him. The rabbi's advice was for him to surrender: "Better that you should be executed rather than that the whole community should be punished on account of you" (*Gen. Rab.* 94:9). Yet another later rabbinic passage states categorically: "Better one life should be risked than all should be certain [to die]" (*Gen. Rab.* 91:10 on Gen. 48:10).[376] Caiaphas's ruling is thus firmly rooted within Jewish thought.

He did not say this on his own, but as high priest that year he prophesied (11:51). In the Old Testament, prophecy was occasionally associated with the high priest (Num. 27:21). Zadok the priest is called a "seer" (2 Sam. 15:27), and at one time the high priest sought to determine God's will by way of the Urim and Thummim (perhaps lots). Josephus recounts how Saul ordered the high priest to don his high priestly garments and to prophesy whether or not an attack on the Philistines would be successful. The high priest predicted victory, which did in fact ensue (*Ant.* 6.6.3 §§115–16; cf. 1 Sam. 14:15–23). As another instance where the high priest functioned as a prophet Josephus cites the high priest Jaddua's prediction that Alexander the Great would spare Jerusalem (*Ant.* 11.8.4 §327).[377]

The same Jewish historian also points to the prophetic gift of the Hasmonean ruler John Hyrcanus (135–104 B.C.), who is said to unite in himself the offices of king, priest, and prophet.[378] Apparently, in the vacuum of prophetic voices in the intertestamental period, the priestly class claimed the gift of prophecy for itself. Philo claims that "the true priest is necessarily a prophet" (*Spec. Laws* 4.192). The view that utterances could on occasion have a deeper prophetic meaning is found elsewhere in Judaism, though not with particular reference to the high priest, and prophecy was often considered to be unwitting (cf. Philo, *Moses* 1.274, 277, 283, 286). "R. Eleazar [c. A.D. 270] taught in the name of R. Jose ben Zimra [c. A.D. 220]: None of the Prophets, as they uttered their prophecies, knew that they were prophesying, except Moses and Isaiah who did know" (*Midr. Ps.* 90 §4).

The scattered children of God (11:52). Israel's end-time hopes were tied to the expectation that the "scattered children of God" (i.e., Jews in the dispersion) would be regathered in the Promised Land by the Messiah (or messiahs, cf. 1QS 9:11) to share in God's kingdom.[379] Yet at the same time, Old Testament prophetic literature frequently depicts the Gentiles as streaming toward the mountain of the Lord (Isa. 2:2–3; 56:6–8; 60:6; Zech. 14:16; cf. 1 Peter 1:1), and the Jerusalem temple is characterized as "a house of prayer for all nations" (Isa. 56:7; cited in Mark 11:17). In the present context ("for the Jewish nation, and not only for that nation . . ."), clearly "the scattered children of God" refers to the Gentiles (cf. esp. John 10:16; see also 12:20–21, 32). A similar thought appears in the *Odes of Solomon* 10:5–6: "And the Gentiles who had been scattered were gathered together . . . and they became my people for ever and ever" (after A.D. 100).[380]

He withdrew to a region near the desert, to a village called Ephraim (11:54). The reference is probably to Old Testament Ophrah (Josh. 18:23) or Ephron (2 Chron. 13:19), site of the modern village of Et-Taiyibeh, four miles northeast of Bethel (cf. Josephus, *J.W.* 4.9.9 §551) and less than twenty miles north of Jerusalem.[381]

The Jewish Passover, many went up from the country to Jerusalem (11:55). Passover is one of the three pilgrim feasts for which Jewish men were required to travel to Jerusalem. This is the third and final Passover mentioned by John. If the first Passover took place in A.D. 30 (see comments on 2:20), the year of Jesus' passion is A.D. 33.[382] Regarding the "many," recent scholarship estimates that the population of Jerusalem swelled from about 100,000 inhabitants to around a million during each of the three festivals.[383]

For their ceremonial cleansing before the Passover (11:55). Ceremonial uncleanness prevented a person from celebrating the Passover.[384] Need for purification arose particularly for those who lived in contact with Gentiles, since the latter frequently buried their dead near their houses, which would make their Jewish neighbors subject to the purification commanded by the law (Num. 19:11–12). Old Testament law stipulated the need for ceremonial cleansing before the Passover for anyone who had defiled himself, such as by touching a corpse (9:6–14). The appropriate purification rites might last as long as a week (19:12), so that many traveled to Jerusalem early, especially in light of the large numbers involved (Josephus, *J.W.* 1.11.6 §229; *m. Pesaḥ.* 9:1).

The chief priests and Pharisees had given orders that if anyone found out where Jesus was, he should report it so that they might arrest him (11:57). Both Old Testament and mishnaic legislation make provision for the kind of search ordered here by the chief priests and Pharisees. The Mosaic law obliged any Jew who heard a curse spoken aloud to report this to the authorities (Lev. 5:1).

The Mishnah stipulates a procedure for covertly capturing a person who leads people into idolatry (*m. Sanh.* 7:10).

Jesus Anointed at Bethany (12:1–11)

On the Friday evening before Passion week, Jesus arrives in Bethany, where a dinner is celebrated in his honor (it is now March, A.D. 33). The next day, "Palm Sunday," Jesus sets out for Jerusalem and is given a hero's welcome. The Pharisees are increasingly exasperated, while Jesus' appeal is shown to extend even to some Greeks who want to see Jesus.

Six days before the Passover (12:1). If John, as is likely, thinks of Passover as beginning Thursday evening (as do the Synoptics), "six days before the Passover" refers to the preceding Saturday, which began Friday evening.

A dinner was given in Jesus' honor (12:2). If Jesus arrives Friday evening, the festivity recounted here probably takes place on Saturday. "Dinner" (*deipnon*) refers to the main meal of the day. It was usually held toward evening but could commence as early as mid-afternoon, so

that there is no perfect correspondence to our terms "lunch" and "dinner" today. Nevertheless, Jesus' words in Luke 14:12, "when you give a luncheon [*ariston*] or dinner [*deipnon*]," show that the midday and the evening meal were distinct. Moreover, "dinner" may refer to a regular meal or to a festive banquet (cf. Matt. 23:6 par.; Mark 6:21). Elsewhere in John's Gospel, the term is used of the Last Supper (13:2, 4; 21:20). In first-century Palestine, banquets usually started in the later hours of the afternoon and quite often went on until midnight. Banquets celebrating the Sabbath could begin as early as midday.

Martha served, while Lazarus was among those reclining at the table with him (12:2). Martha's serving at the table may indicate that by this time Sabbath has come to an end. Possibly, the meal is connected with the *Habdalah* service, which marked the end of a Sabbath (*m. Ber.* 8:5). It is probable that Lazarus, Mary, and Martha provide the meal, though a large dinner in this small village, celebrated in honor of a noted guest, may well have drawn in several other families to help with the work. "Reclining at the table" may indicate a banquet rather than a regular meal (see 13:2–5, 23).[385]

Jesus' Final Week (John 12–21; March 27–April 3, A.D. 33)		
Time	**Location/Event**	**Passage in John**
Friday, March 27, 33	Jesus arrives at Bethany	11:55–12:1
Saturday, March 28, 33	Dinner with Lazarus and his sisters	12:2–11
Sunday, March 29, 33	"Triumphal entry" into Jerusalem	12:12–50
Monday-Wednesday, March 30–April 1, 33	Cursing of fig tree, temple cleansing, temple controversy, Olivet discourse	Synoptics
Thursday, April 2, 33	Third Passover in John; betrayal, arrest	13:1–18:11
Friday, April 3, 33	Jewish and Roman trials, crucifixion, burial	18:12–19:42

Then Mary took about a pint (12:3). A *litra* (a measurement of weight equivalent to the Latin *libra*) amounted to about eleven ounces or a little less than three-quarters of a pound (half a liter). Then, as today, this is a large amount of perfume.[386]

Pure nard, an expensive perfume (12:3). See Song 1:12; 4:13–16 (LXX). Nard, also known as spikenard, is a fragrant oil derived from the root and spike (hair stem) of the nard plant, which grows in the mountains of northern India.[387] This "Indian spike," used by the Romans for anointing the head, was "a rich rose red and very sweetly scented."[388] The Semitic expression is found in several papyri, including one from the early first century (P. Oxy. 8.1088.49). The rare term "pure" (*pistikēs*) may mean "genuine" (derived from *pistis*, "true, genuine") in contrast to diluted, since nard apparently was adulterated on occasion. "Perfume" (*myron*) is used here probably in the generic sense of "fragrant substance" (cf. Mark 14:3). The Synoptic parallels indicate that the perfume was kept in an "alabaster jar" (Matt. 26:7; Mark 14:3).[389] For "expensive," see comments on 12:5.

She poured it on Jesus' feet (12:3). "Poured" translates the Greek word *aleiphō*, which literally means "anoint." Anointing the head was common enough

(Ps. 23:5; Luke 7:46), but anointing the feet was unusual (usually simply water was provided), even more so during a meal, which was definitely improper in Jewish eyes. Somewhat similar was the Babylonian custom for women to drip consecrated oil onto the heads of rabbis present at the wedding of a virgin, and for slave girls to bathe the hands and feet of a guest in oil.

The Greek poet Aristophanes cites an instance where a daughter is washing, anointing (*aleiphō*), and kissing her father's feet (*Vespae* 608). In the present instance, it is hard not to see royal overtones in Mary's anointing of Jesus, especially in light of the fact that the event is immediately followed by Jesus' triumphal entry into Jerusalem, where he is hailed as the king of Israel who comes in the name of the Lord (12:13, 15). Attending to the feet was servant's work (see comments on 1:27; 13:5), so Mary's action shows humility as well as devotion.

Wiped his feet with her hair (12:3). The use of hair rather than a towel for wiping Jesus' feet indicates unusual devotion. The act is all the more striking since Jewish women (esp. married ones) never unbound their hair in public, which would have been considered a sign of loose morals (cf. Num. 5:18; *b. Soṭah* 8a).[390] The fact that Mary (who was probably single, since no husband is mentioned) here acts in such a way toward Jesus, a well-known (yet unattached) rabbi, is sure to raise some eyebrows (see comments on 4:7). Also unusual is the wiping off of the oil.

Worth a year's wages (12:5). "A year's wages" translates "three hundred denarii." One denarius was the daily remuneration of a common laborer (cf. Matt. 20:2; see

▶
ROMAN ERA GLASS
CONTAINERS

comments on John 6:7). Three hundred denarii is therefore roughly equivalent to a year's wages, since no money was earned on Sabbaths and other holy days. This perfume is outrageously expensive owing to its being imported all the way from northern India. Its great value may indicate that Mary and her family are very wealthy. Alternatively, this may have been a family heirloom that has been passed down to Mary.

Money bag (12:6). The expression originally denoted any kind of box to hold the reeds of musical instruments. Later, the term was used for a coffer into which money is cast (2 Chron. 24:8, 10). In the present instance, what may be in mind is therefore not a "bag" (NIV) but a box made of wood or some other rigid material (cf. Plutarch, *Galba* 16.1; Josephus, *Ant.* 6.1.2 §11). The money kept in this container probably helps meet the needs of Jesus and his disciples as well as provide alms for the poor. The funds would be replenished by followers of Jesus such as the women mentioned in Luke 8:2–3, who supported his ministry.

It was intended that she should save this perfume for the day of my burial (12:7). While it was not uncommon for people in first-century Palestine to spend considerable amounts in funeral-related expenses, it is unusual that Mary here lavishly pours out perfume on Jesus while he is still alive. The word for burial (*entaphiasmos*) refers not so much to the event itself as to the laying out of the corpse in preparation for burial (cf. 19:40).

You will always have the poor among you, but you will not always have me (12:8). The allusion is probably to Deuteronomy 15:11: "There will always be poor people in the land." Jewish sources indicate that care of the dead was to take precedence over almsgiving. *b. Sukkah* 49b praises *gemilut ḥasadim* ("the practice of kindness") above charity, among other reasons because it can be done both to the living and the dead (by attending their funeral; cf. *t. Peʾah* 4:19).

The Triumphal Entry (12:12–19)[391]

The next day (12:12). This is probably Sunday of Passion week, called "Palm Sunday" in Christian tradition.

The great crowd (12:12). With Jerusalem's population at that time being about 100,000 and the amount of pilgrims amounting to several times the population of Jerusalem, the "great crowd" gathered at the Jewish capital at the occasion of the Passover may have numbered up to a million people. Many of these pilgrims were probably Galileans, who were well acquainted with Jesus' ministry.

The Feast (12:12). Passover (see 12:1 above and comments on 2:13).

Palm branches (12:13). Date palm trees did grow in the vicinity of Jerusalem, especially Jericho, the "City of Palms" (Deut. 34:3; 2 Chron. 28:15).[392] The palm tree served as a symbol of righteousness: "The righteous will flourish like a palm tree" (Ps. 92:12). In the Old Testament, palm branches are associated not with Passover but with the Feast of Tabernacles (Lev. 23:40). However, by the time of Jesus palm branches had already become a national (if not nationalistic) Jewish symbol (Josephus, *Ant.* 3.10.4 §245; 13.13.5 §372; cf. *Jub.* 16:31). Palm branches were a prominent feature at the rededication of the temple in Maccabean times (2 Macc. 10:7; 164 B.C.) and were also used to celebrate Simon's victory over the Syrians (cf. 1 Macc. 13:51; 141 B.C.). Later, palms appear on the coins minted by the insurrectionists during the Jewish wars against Rome (A.D. 66–70 and 132–135) and even on Roman coins themselves. Apoc-alyptic end-time visions likewise feature date palms (Rev. 7:9; *T. Naph.* 5:4).

In the present instance, people's waving of palm branches may signal nationalistic hopes that in Jesus a messianic liberator had arrived (cf. 6:14–15).[393] A later rabbinic source reads, "It is the one who takes the palm branch in his hand who we know to be the victor" (*Lev. Rab.* 30:2). The Greco-Roman world knew palm branches as symbols of victory (e.g., Suetonius, *Caligula* 32: "ran about with a palm branch, as victors do").

Went out to meet him, shouting, "Hosanna!" (12:13). See Psalm 118:25. The phrase "went out to meet him" (rare in biblical literature) was regularly used in Greek culture, where such a joyful reception was customary when Hellenistic sovereigns entered a city. An instance of this is recorded by Josephus when Antioch came out to meet Titus (*J.W.* 7.5.2 §§100–101). The term "Hosanna," originally a transliteration of the identical Hebrew expression,[394] had become a general expression of acclamation or praise. Most familiar was the term's occurrence in the Hallel (Pss. 113–18; see esp. 118:25), a psalm sung each morning by the temple choir during various Jewish festivals (cf. *m. Pesaḥ.* 5:7; 9:3; 10:7). At such occasions, every man and boy would wave their *lulab* (a bouquet of willow, myrtle, and palm branches; *b. Sukkah* 37b; cf. Josephus, *Ant.* 3.10.4 §245) when the choir reached the "Hosanna!" in Psalm 118:25 (*m. Sukkah* 3:9).

Blessed is he who comes in the name of the Lord! (12:13). See Psalm 118:26. In its original context, Psalm 118 conferred a blessing on the pilgrim headed for Jerusalem, with possible reference to the

PALM BRANCHES

(right) A date palm in the Sinai region.

(bottom) A palm tree is depicted on a coin minted during the Bar Cochba revolt against Rome (c. A.D. 132).

Davidic king. Later rabbinic commentary interpreted this psalm messianically (*Midr. Pss.* on Ps. 118:24). Note also the interesting connection between a donkey and the "ruler from Judah" in Genesis 49:11.

Blessed is the King of Israel! (12:13) For the title "King of Israel," see comments on 1:49.

Jesus found a young donkey and sat upon it (12:14). For a fuller description of how Jesus "found" the donkey, see Matthew 21:1–3 par. Two associations with the donkey were dominant in first-century Palestine: humility (see comments on 13:1–20) and peace (see comments on 14:27). In contrast to the war horse (cf. Zech. 9:10), the donkey was a lowly beast of burden: "Fodder and a stick and burdens for a donkey" (Sir. 33:25; cf. Prov. 26:3). Donkeys were also known as animals ridden on in pursuit of peace, be it by ordinary folk, priests, merchants, or persons of importance (Judg. 5:10; 2 Sam. 16:2). Jesus' choice of a donkey invokes prophetic imagery of a

king coming in peace (Zech. 9:9; cf. 12:10: "He will proclaim peace to the nations"), which contrasts sharply with notions of a political warrior messiah (cf. 1 Kings 4:26; Isa. 31:1–3). The early Christians were often mocked as worshiping a donkey, a man in form of a donkey, or a donkey's head, such as in the famous graffito of a crucified slave with the head of a donkey and of another slave worshiping with the inscription "Alexamenos worships God" (early 3d cent. A.D.?).[395]

Do not be afraid, O Daughter of Zion; see, your king is coming, seated on a donkey's colt (12:15). See Zechariah 9:9. The phrase "Do not be afraid" does not occur in the Hebrew or other versions of Zechariah 9:9, replacing the expression "Rejoice greatly." It may be taken from Isaiah 40:9, where it is addressed to the one who brings good tidings to Zion (cf. Isa. 44:2; Zeph. 3:16).[396] "Daughter of Zion" is a common way of referring to Jerusalem and its inhabitants, especially in their lowly state as the oppressed people of God.

left

A YOUNG DONKEY IN MODERN JERUSALEM

right

A PALM SUNDAY PROCESSIONAL ON A JERUSALEM STREET

▼

An early messianic prophecy speaks of a ruler from Judah who will command the obedience of the nations and who rides on a donkey (Gen. 49:10–11). Yet the rabbis had difficulty reconciling this notion of a humble Messiah with that of the Danielic Son of Man "coming on the clouds of heaven" (*b. Sanh.* 98a; c. A.D. 250). However, riding on a donkey does appear as one of the three signs of the Messiah in *Eccles. Rab.* 1:9 (c. A.D. 300), where the latter redeemer in Zechariah 9:9 is featured as the counterpart to Moses in Exodus 4:20. Note too 1 Kings 1:38, where Solomon (whose name means "peaceable") rode into Jerusalem for his coronation on King David's mule.

The whole world has gone after him! (12:19). "The whole world" constitutes a common Jewish hyperbolic phrase. So it is said that "all the world" followed the high priest (*b. Yoma* 71b); that Hezekiah taught the Torah to "the whole world" (*b. Sanh.* 101b); that "the people [lit., the world] were flocking to David" (*b. B. Meṣi'a* 85a; cf. 2 Sam. 15:13); and that "all the people [lit., world] came and gathered around" a certain rabbi (*b. 'Abod. Zar.* 19b). The early Christians were said to "have caused trouble all over the world" (Acts 17:6).

Jesus Predicts His Death (12:20–36)

There were some Greeks among those who went up to worship at the Feast (12:20). As elsewhere in the New Testament, the term "Greeks" refers not to people literally hailing from Greece, but to Gentiles from any part of the Greek-speaking world, including Greek cities in the Decapolis (see comments on 7:35). Most likely, these "Greeks" were God-fearers who had come up to Jerusalem to worship at the Feast (cf. Acts 17:4: "God-fearing Greeks"). Like the Roman Cornelius (Acts 10) or the centurion who had a synagogue built (Luke 7:5), such God-fearers were attracted to the Jewish way of life without formally converting to Judaism. They were admitted to the court of the Gentiles in the temple but forbidden entrance into the inner courts on the warning of death.

They came to Philip, who was from Bethsaida in Galilee (12:21). See 1:44. It is possible that the "Greeks" singled out Philip—and Andrew—because of their Greek names; although they were both Jews, they were the only two members of the Twelve with Greek names (with the possible exception of Thomas, see comments on 11:16). If these "Greeks" were from the Decapolis or from the territories north or east of the Sea of Galilee (such as Batanea, Gaulanitis, or Trachonitis), they may have known (or found out) who among Jesus' disciples it was who came from the nearest town—Philip, who hailed from Bethsaida (located in Gaulanitis). Galilee, in fact, was more Hellenized than much of the rest of Palestine and bordered on pagan areas (cf. Matt. 4:15). Moreover, Philip, because of his origin, would have been able to speak Greek.

Philip went to tell Andrew; Andrew and Philip in turn told Jesus (12:22). Philip is mentioned along with Andrew in 1:44 and 6:7–8 (cf. Mark 3:18).

For the Son of Man to be glorified (12:23). See comments on 1:51. The reference to the glorification of the Son of Man may well hark back to Isaiah 52:13, where it is said that the Servant of the Lord "will be raised and lifted up and highly exalted" (LXX: *doxasthēsetai*). In pre-Christian usage, the glory of the Son of Man and his function of uniting heaven and earth are conceived in primarily apocalyptic terms (Dan. 7:13; cf. *1 En.* 45–57, esp. 46 and 48; first century A.D.?).

Unless a kernel of wheat falls to the ground and dies, it remains only a single seed. But if it dies, it produces many seeds (12:24). The principle of life through death is here illustrated by an agricultural example. In rabbinic literature, the kernel of wheat is repeatedly used as a symbol of the eschatological resurrection of the dead. By an argument "from the lesser to the greater," "if the grain of wheat, which is buried naked, sprouts forth in many robes, how much more so the righteous, who are buried in their raiment" (*b. Sanh.* 90b).[397]

The man who loves his life will lose it, while the man who hates his life in this world will keep it for eternal life (12:25). The love/hate contrast reflects Semitic idiom, pointing to preference rather than actual hatred.[398] The present statement is couched in Hebrew parallelism, taking the form of a *mashal* with two antithetical lines. Such wisdom sayings use paradox or hyperbole to teach a given truth in as sharp terms as possible (cf. *b. Taʿan.* 22a).

The paradox enunciated here has particular applicability if judged as Christ's verdict on Greco-Roman ideals of life. For the Greeks, the goal of human existence was bound up with self-fulfillment and the attainment of personal maturity. Following Christ, however, involves sacrifice of oneself and one's own interests, a truth seen supremely in Jesus' cross.

Whoever serves me must follow me; and where I am, my servant also will be (12:26). This teaching coheres closely with teacher-disciple relationships in first-century Palestine. "Being a disciple required personal attachment to the teacher, because the disciple learned not merely from his teacher's words but much more from his practical observance of the Law. Thus the phrase 'to come after someone' is tantamount to 'being someone's disciple.'"[399] What is more, the truth enunciated here extends beyond a disciple's earthly life to his eternal destiny (7:34, 36; 14:3; 17:24).

Father, glorify your name! (12:28). The glory of God as the ultimate goal of his salvific actions is a theme pervading the Old Testament.[400]

A voice came from heaven (12:28). This is one of only three instances during

left

HEADS OF WHEAT IN A FIELD

right

KERNELS OF WHEAT

Jesus' earthly ministry when a heavenly voice attests to his identity.[401] The rabbis called this voice *bat qol* (lit., "daughter of a voice"). Since it was commonly believed that the prophetic office had ceased and would not be renewed until the onset of the messianic age, the *bat qol* was the most that could be expected in the interim: "Since the death of the last prophets, Haggai, Zechariah and Malachi, the Holy Spirit [of prophetic inspiration] departed from Israel; yet they were still able to avail themselves of the *bat qol*" (*b. Sanh.* 11a; cf. *t. Soṭah* 13:3).[402]

A later rabbinic passage illustrates this belief: "One would hear not the sound which proceeded from heaven, but another sound proceeded from this sound; as when a man strikes a powerful blow and a second sound is heard, which proceeds from it in the distance. Such a sound would one hear; hence it was called 'Daughter of the voice'" (*Tosafot* on *b. Sanh.* 11a).[403] The all-important difference between the New Testament instances of the heavenly voice and the rabbinic notion of the *bat qol* is that while the rabbis thought of the divine voice as a mere echo, the heavenly voice attesting Jesus is the voice of God himself.

It had thundered (12:29). Thunder was considered to speak of the power and awesomeness of God (1 Sam. 12:18; 2 Sam. 22:14; Job 37:5). It was part of the theophany at Mount Sinai (Ex. 19:16, 19). God's intervention on behalf of his people is portrayed like a fierce thunderstorm sweeping down on his enemies (Ps. 18:7–15). In such instances, the power of the Creator is tied to that of Israel's Redeemer (Ex. 9:28; 1 Sam. 7:10; Ps. 29:3; cf. Sir. 46:16–17). The manifestations of God's power also highlight the contrast between his omnipotence and the idols' powerlessness (Jer. 10:13 = 51:16).

In New Testament times, light and sound accompanied the manifestation of the risen Christ to Saul (Acts 9:7; 22:9). In the Apocalypse, peals of thunder are shown to emanate from God's throne (Rev. 4:5; 8:5; 11:19; 16:18; cf. 2 Esd. 6:17). The *Sibylline Oracles* speak of a "heavenly crash of thunder, the voice of God" (*Sib. Or.* 5:344–45). The notion of heaven answering human speech in thunder is also found in the ancient Greek world. Thus in Homer's classic work, Odysseus's prayer is followed by divine thunder: "So he spoke in prayer, and Zeus the counselor heard him. Straightway he thundered from gleaming Olympus" (*Odyssey* 20.97–104).[404]

Others said an angel had spoken to him (12:29). In Old Testament times, angels (or the angel of the Lord) spoke to Hagar (Gen. 21:17), Abraham (22:11), Moses (cf. Acts 7:38), and Daniel (Dan. 10:4–11). In the New Testament, angels are said to minister to Jesus (Matt. 4:11; Luke 22:43; cf. Matt. 26:53), and at one point it was surmised that Paul, too, may have heard an angelic voice (Acts 23:9). Angelic voices are commonplace in the book of Revelation (Rev. 4:1; 5:2; 6:1; etc.).

Now the prince of this world will be driven out (12:31). "Prince" is literally "ruler" (*archōn*). Similar terminology is also found in Paul's writings (2 Cor. 4:4; 6:15; Eph. 2:2; 6:12). There are several Jewish (though no rabbinic) parallels to the phrase "prince of the world" with reference to Satan.[405] The title "prince of this world" occurs in relation to Beliar in the *Ascension of Isaiah* (1:3; 10:29; cf. 2:4). In *Jubilees*, "Mastema" is called "chief of the spirits" or simply "prince"

(10:8; 11:5, 11; etc.). More generally, the Qumran texts contain the notion that the "dominion of Belial" extends to his entire "lot."[406] However, unlike extensive intertestamental speculation regarding the demonic supernatural, John is much more restrained, limiting his treatment of Satan exclusively to his role in the plot against Jesus leading to the latter's crucifixion. See comments also on John 14:30; 16:11; also Luke 10:18.

Will draw all men to myself (12:32). "All men" is generic, "all people." This does not imply universalism (the ultimate salvation of all; see comments on 1:9). Rather, the approach of Gentiles prompts Jesus' statement that after his glorification he will draw "all kinds of people," even Gentiles, to himself (cf. 10:16; 11:52).

The Law (12:34). "The Law" may refer to the Hebrew Scriptures in their entirety rather than merely to the five books of Moses (cf. 10:34; 15:25).

The Christ will remain forever (12:34). Palestinian Judaism in Jesus' day generally thought of the Messiah as triumphant, and frequently also as eternal. Such expectations were rooted in the Son of David, of whom it was said that God would "establish the throne of his kingdom forever" (2 Sam. 7:13; cf. John 12:16). This prospect was nurtured both in the Psalms (e.g., Ps. 61:6–7; 89:3–4, 35–37) and prophetic literature (Isa. 9:7; Ezek. 37:25; cf. Dan. 7:13–14). It was also affirmed in intertestamental Jewish writings (*Pss. Sol.* 17:4; *Sib. Or.* 3:49–50; *1 En.* 62:14) and at the outset of Luke's Gospel (Luke 1:33).

Perhaps the closest parallel to the present passage is Psalm 89:37, where David's seed is said to "remain forever" (LXX: *menei eis ton aiōna*). Notably, this psalm is interpreted messianically both in the New Testament (Acts 13:22; Rev. 1:5) and rabbinic sources (*Gen. Rab.* 97, linking Gen. 49:10; 2 Sam. 7:16; Ps. 89:29). But probably Jesus refers not so much to any one passage but to the general thrust of Old Testament messianic teaching. Elsewhere in John, people express the expectation of a Davidic Messiah born at Bethlehem (John 7:42) and of a hidden Messiah to be revealed at the proper time (7:27; cf. 1:26).

The Christ . . . the Son of Man (12:34). It is unclear whether Palestinian Jews in Jesus' day, whose concept of Messiah was bound up largely with the expectation of the Davidic king, also linked the Coming One with the apocalyptic figure of the Son of Man (cf. Dan. 7:13–14).[407]

Walk while you have the light, before darkness overtakes you. The man who walks in the dark does not know where he is going. Put your trust in the light (12:35–36). The term "walk" (*peripateō*) frequently occurs in John's Gospel in a figurative sense in conjunction with light and darkness.[408] Similar terminology can be found in the Qumran literature: "the sons of justice . . . walk on paths of light,"

ROMAN CROSS

A model of a typical Roman cross with a nameplate on the top and two wooden beams for the arms and legs.

while "the sons of deceit . . . walk on paths of darkness" (1QS 3:20–21; cf. 4:11). The notion of "walking in the light" or "in darkness" in John resembles the thought in the Scrolls that there are two ways in which people may walk, light and darkness. Both John and the Scrolls hark back independently to Old Testament terminology, especially Isaiah: "Let him who walks in the dark, who has no light, trust in the name of the LORD" (Isa. 50:10); "the people walking in darkness have seen a great light" (9:2, quoted in Matt. 4:16). The important difference between John and the Scrolls is that the former calls people to "put their trust in the light," while the latter assume that the members of the community are already "sons of light."

Sons of light (12:36). "Son of . . ." reflects Hebrew idiom; the expression "sons of light," however, is not attested in rabbinic literature. A "son of light" displays the moral qualities of "light" and has become a follower of the "light" (cf. Luke 16:8; 1 Thess. 5:5; Eph. 5:8). The phrase is also common in the Dead Sea Scrolls, where it designates members of the Qumran community.[409] "Born of light" occurs in *1 Enoch* (108:11; cf. also *T. Naph.* 2:10: "so you are unable to perform the works of light while you are in darkness").

The Jews Continue in their Unbelief (12:37–50)

Even after Jesus had done all these miraculous signs in their presence, they still would not believe in him (12:37). The Jews' failure to believe in Jesus' day is reminiscent of the unbelief of the desert generation, which had witnessed God's mighty acts of power (displayed through Moses) at the Exodus (Deut. 29:2–4). No greater sign than the raising of Lazarus—the seventh, climactic sign in John—could be given.

This was to fulfill the word of Isaiah the prophet (12:38). This leads off a whole series of fulfillment quotations in John's Gospel, stressing the fulfillment of Old Testament prophecy in the events of Jesus' life, especially the events surrounding his crucifixion.[410]

Lord, who has believed our message and to whom has the arm of the Lord been revealed? (12:38). The reference cited is Isaiah 53:1 (LXX; cf. Rom. 10:16). In the original context, Isaiah' message pertains to the Servant of the Lord, who was rejected by the people but exalted by God (cf. Isa.52:13–15). In John's Gospel, the passage is applied to Jesus the Messiah, who is that promised Servant, and to the rejection of his message and his miraculous signs ("arm of the Lord") by the Jewish people. Thus Jewish rejection of God's words is nothing new; as Isaiah's

MENORAH

Fragments of plaster found in a Herodian-era house discovered in Jerusalem. This is the earliest depiction of the candelabrum, which stood in the temple.

message had been rejected, so is Jesus'. The phrase "arm of the LORD" serves in the Old Testament frequently as a figurative expression for God's power.[411]

He has blinded their eyes and deadened their hearts, so they can neither see with their eyes, nor understand with their hearts, nor turn—and I would heal them (12:40). The reference cited is Isaiah 6:10 (here closer to the Hebrew than to the LXX). The Hebrew original moves from heart to ears to eyes and then back from sight to hearing to understanding. John does not refer to hearing but focuses instead on sight, probably owing to his mention of Jesus' miraculous signs in John 12:37. The Jews considered the heart to be the seat of mental as well as physical life (cf. Mark 8:17–21 par.).

Isaiah . . . saw Jesus' glory (12:41). In light of the preceding quotation of Isaiah 6:10, the background to the present statement is probably the call narrative in Isaiah 6. This is confirmed by the Targums (Aramaic paraphrases of the Old Testament). One Targum of Isaiah 6:1 changes "I saw the LORD" to "I saw *the glory* of the LORD," and changes "the King, the LORD Almighty" in Isaiah 6:5 to *"the glory of the shekinah of the eternal* King, the LORD of hosts" (*Tg. Ps.-J.,* 1st cent. B.C.–3d cent. A.D.). The notion of a preexistent Christ who was present and active in the history of Israel appears elsewhere in the New Testament (cf. 1 Cor. 10:4; see also Philo, *Dreams* 1.229–30). Later interpreters speculated that the prophet looked into the future and saw the life and glory of Jesus (*Ascen. Isa.* [2d cent. A.D.]).

But because of the Pharisees . . . for fear they would be put out of the synagogue (12:42). See comments on 9:22.

He does not believe in me only, but in the one who sent me (12:44). See comments on 5:23. The entire closing section (12:44–50) presupposes Jewish teaching on representation, according to which the emissary represents the one who sends him (cf. *m. Ber.* 5:5).[412]

That very word which I spoke will condemn him at the last day (12:48). Verses 48–50 echo the book of Deuteronomy (cf. 18:19; 31:19, 26).[413] There it is God who takes vengeance on the man who refuses to hear; in the Targums, it is God's *memra* or word. "And the man who does not listen to his words which he [the future prophet] will speak in the name *of my memra, I in my memra will be avenged of him"* (*Tg. Neof.* on Deut. 18:19); "*my memra* will take revenge on him" (*Tg. Ps.-J.* on Deut. 18:19).

Sometimes in intertestamental Jewish literature, the Law seems to take a more active part in the process of judging: "And concerning all of those [the sinners], their end will put them to shame, and your Law which they transgressed will repay them on your day" (*2 Bar.* 48:47); "and he will destroy them without effort by the law (which was symbolized by the fire)" (*4 Ezra* 13:38). In Wisdom of Solomon 9:3, wisdom is described as an assessor with God in judgment (cf. Philo, *Moses* 2.53).

I know that his command leads to eternal life (12:50). According to the book of Deuteronomy, God's commandments provide the framework within which Israel is to fulfill her calling as a people set apart for God (e.g., Deut. 8:3; 32:46–47). Jews commonly saw the law of Moses as the source of life (32:45–47; cf. John 5:39). The problem, however, is that no one keeps the law perfectly or is able to do so.

Jesus Washes His Disciples' Feet (13:1–17)

In the face of Jewish hardening, Jesus now turns his attention to the Twelve. After one final memorable demonstration of his love and after exposing the betrayer, Jesus prepares his followers for the difficult times ahead.

It was just before the Passover Feast (13:1). According to the Synoptics (Mark 14:12; Luke 22:15), Jesus and his disciples celebrated the Passover during the early hours of Nisan 15 (Thursday evening, with days beginning at sundown), with preparations having been made earlier that day, Nisan 14, the day on which the paschal lambs were slaughtered at the temple (usually between 3 and 5 P.M.). Some believe that John places the Last Supper on Nisan 14, Wednesday evening, with Jesus' crucifixion occurring on Thursday afternoon, when the lambs are slaughtered at the temple in preparation for Passover.[414] A closer look at the relevant passages, however, shows that none of these actually conflicts with the Synoptic accounts.[415]

His own (13:1). "His own" are now the Twelve, the representatives of the new messianic community, no longer the old covenant community, which had rejected Jesus as Messiah (cf. 1:11).

The evening meal was being served (13:2). On the Greek word for "evening meal" (*deipnon*), see comments on 12:2 (see also 1 Cor. 11:20).

Took off his outer clothing, and wrapped a towel around his waist (13:4). Jesus here adopts the stance of a menial (even

▶ John's Gospel and Ancient Farewell Discourses[A-23]

Patterned after Moses' "farewell discourse" in Deuteronomy (31–33) and other similar Old Testament farewells,[A-24] the intertestamental period saw the production of an entire genre of such works.[A-25] Most of these testaments were written between the second century B.C. and the third century A.D. and include the following features:

1. Predictions of death and departure
2. Predictions of future challenges for the followers/sons of the dying man after his death
3. Arrangements regarding succession or continuation of family line
4. Exhortations to moral behavior
5. A final commission
6. An affirmation and renewal of God's covenant promises
7. A closing doxology

However, John's presentation of Jesus' "farewell discourse" (John 13:31–17:26) may not be consciously patterned after the intertestamental genre "testament" but merely build on the precedent of Moses' final words in Deuteronomy. In keeping with the genre's concern for proper succession, Jesus announces the coming of "another helping presence" (14:16; cf. 14:26; 15:26; 16:7), which would ensure continuation between his ministry and that of his disciples (see esp. 15:26–27; 16:8–11).

Yet important differences apply as well. Jesus' farewell is merely temporary—his followers will see him again "in a little while"—so that Jesus' final words focus on the future, while Jewish farewell discourses regularly consist of extended rehearsals of the past. Likewise, extensive detailed predictions regarding the future, common in intertestamental testaments, are almost entirely absent from Jesus' instructions to his followers. Also, the vine allegory in chapter 15 is without precedent in Jewish farewell discourses.

non-Jewish; cf. *Mek. Ex.* 21:2) slave, a position looked down on by both Jews and Gentiles. Other rabbis also stressed the virtue of humility, yet with certain limitations. R. Yehudah ha-Nasi (d. A.D. 217), for example, a highly respected Jewish teacher said to embody all the seven virtues listed by the sages for the righteous (*y. Sanh.* 11:3), "was said to be so humble that he would do anything for others except relinquish his superior position."[416] Jesus, for his part, knows no such boundaries.

The expression "wrap a towel around his waist" indicates that Jesus girds himself like a servant (Luke 12:37; 17:8). "Towel" (*lention*), which occurs in the New Testament only here and is not attested in earlier Greek literature, is a loanword from the Lat. *linteum* (similar to *soudarion*; see John 11:44).[417] It refers to a long towel fastened to the shoulder, which allowed Jesus to gird himself and still to use the end to dry the disciples' feet (cf. 1 Peter 5:5). Suetonius recalls an instance when the Roman emperor Caligula humiliated senators by having them wait on him in similar attire (*Caligula* 26.2).

He poured water into a basin and began to wash his disciples' feet (13:5). The Old Testament recounts several instances of footwashing as part of ancient hospitality.[418] Several intertestamental passages mention the washing of a guest's feet immediately prior to a meal.[419] The same custom was also common among the Greeks, as is illustrated by a reference to Odysseus having his feet washed after his return (*Odyssey* 19:386–88).[420] The disciples probably recline on mats around a low table, each leaning on his left arm, with the feet pointing outward (see comments on 13:23). In first-century Pales-

tine, where people walked long distances in sandals and where roads were dusty, hospitality demanded that the host arrange for water to be available for the washing of feet (done upon arrival, not during the meal). Rather than washing the feet in the basin itself, water was poured over the feet from one vessel and caught in another (cf. 2 Kings 3:11).[421]

To perform acts of service for one's teacher was considered a common duty of a disciple.[422] In fact, it was maintained that "the service of the Torah is greater than the study thereof" (*b. Ber.* 7b).[423] The washing of feet, however, was considered too demeaning for disciples (or even a Jewish slave) and thus was assigned to non-Jewish slaves. "All manner of service that a slave must render to his master a student must render to his teacher, except that of taking off his shoe";[424] "the sages said: A Hebrew slave must not wash the feet of his master, nor put his shoes on him."[425] Jesus' adoption of the stance of (a non-Jewish) slave would thus be shocking to his disciples and cries out for an explanation. For while there are occasional exceptions featuring people other than non-Jewish slaves washing the feet of others,[426] the washing of the feet of an inferior person by a superior is not attested elsewhere in Jewish or Greco-Roman sources.[427]

No part with me (13:8). (Cf. 14:1–3; 17:24). The notion of "having a part [*meros*] in something" occurs elsewhere in the New Testament with regard to inheritance (Luke 15:12). In Old Testament times, each of the twelve tribes of Israel (except Levi) was to have its "share" in the Promised Land (Num. 18:20; Deut. 12:12; 14:27). Later, the expression is used with reference to people's being assigned a place in God's eternal kingdom, both in terms of fellowship with God (Rev. 20:6; 21:8; 22:19) or separation from him (Matt. 24:51; Luke 12:46). In Acts 8:21 Peter rebukes Simon Magus using similar language.

A person who has had a bath needs only to wash his feet; his whole body is clean (13:10). See 15:3. Two terms for washing are contrasted here: "have a bath" (*louō*) and "wash" (*niptō*).[428] "Have a bath" may refer to Jewish ceremonial cleansing in preparation for Passover (11:55). Alternatively, Jesus may allude to the custom (at least in some quarters) "for guests at a meal to take a bath before leaving home, and on arrival at their host's house to have their feet, but only their feet washed."[429] Thus according to Plutarch (first cent. A.D.), both Cato the Younger and Pompey had a bath (*louō*) before supper (*deipnon*).[430] In any case, Jesus' disclaimer would caution his followers (and John's readers) against interpreting his actions as a mandate for ritual washings common in Judaism (*katharismos*; cf. 2:6; 3:25).

You call me "Teacher" and "Lord" (13:13). John's Gospel regularly portrays Jesus as being addressed as "Teacher" and "Lord" by his disciples or others. The designation "Rabbi" was in keeping with Jewish teacher-disciple relationships. "Lord," however, was a word commonly applied to God in the LXX (though it could also simply mean "sir"; see 4:11, 15, 49; 5:7).

You also should wash one another's feet (13:14). As can be seen from 1 Timothy 5:10, the phrase "washing the feet of the saints," in extension of its literal application here, had already become an accepted figurative expression for Christian service by the time of the writing of John's Gospel.

An example (13:15). The Greek word *hypodeigma* can denote both an "example," be it good[431] or bad,[432] and a "pattern" (Heb. 8:5; 9:23; cf. Acts 7:44). In several Jewish intertestamental texts, *hypodeigma* is associated with exemplary death[433] or other virtues such as repentance (Sir. 44:16). Greco-Roman writers likewise use the term to denote examples of various virtues. Diodorus of Sicily says that the Roman senate left "models and patterns" (*typous kai hypodeigmata*) for all who strive for the empire (*Bib. Hist.* 30.8). Plutarch comments that the Romans, while skillful in warfare, left no examples of civil virtues such as gentleness and humanity (*Marc.* 20.1). Thus the major difference between Jesus and the Greco-Roman world is not so much the concept of leaving an example itself as the nature of this example: While Greeks and Romans prized virtues such as courage or military prowess, Jesus exemplifies humility, self-sacrifice, and love.

Now that you know these things, you will be blessed if you do them (13:17). Similar statements are attested in Greco-Roman sources. Several centuries before Christ, the Greek writer Hesiod remarked, "Blessed and fortunate is he who knowingly does all these things" (*Opera et dies* 826–27). The Roman Seneca, banished by Caligula and later tutor of the young Nero, stated, "He is not happy who only knows them [the things learned], but he who does them" (*Ep.* 75.7).

But this is to fulfill the scripture: "He who shares my bread has lifted up his heel against me" (13:18). On fulfillment quotations, see comments on 12:38. The text cited is Psalm 41:9. By Jesus' day, David had become a "type" or model of David's "greater Son," the coming Messiah on the basis of passages such as 2 Samuel 7:12–16 or Psalm 2. Several major themes of David's life are given a messianic application in the New Testament, especially those focusing on his suffering, weakness, and betrayal.[434] In rabbinic interpretation, Psalm 41:9 was taken to refer to Ahithophel's conspiracy with Absalom against David.[435] In ancient Semitic cultures, eating bread at the table of a superior amounted to a pledge of loyalty (2 Sam. 9:7–13; 1 Kings 18:19; 2 Kings 25:29), and "to betray one with whom bread had been eaten . . . was a gross breach of the traditions of hospitality."[436]

The expression "lifted up his heel against me" is capable of several interpretations. Carson (citing Bruce) sees it as "has given me a great fall" or "has taken cruel advantage of me" or "has walked out on me." Morris and others think the imagery may be that of a horse preparing to kick. Brown notes that "to show the bottom of one's foot to someone in the Near East is a mark of contempt . . . some [though not Brown himself] would see here a reminiscence of Genesis 3:15: 'You shall bruise his heel.'" Barrett suggests "the action of one who 'shakes off the dust of his feet against' another" (cf. Luke 9:5; 10:11).[437] From Jacob (in whose case the heel connotes trickery) to Achilles (whose heel, suggesting weakness, may be the most famous of all), it appears that the heel is patient of a wide variety of symbolic applications.

I am telling you now before it happens, so that when it does happen you will believe that I am He (13:19). The phrase chosen

by Jesus echoes similar expressions referring to God in the Old Testament: "When this happens, you will know that I am the Sovereign LORD" (Ezek. 24:24); "'You are my witnesses,' declares the LORD, 'and my servant whom I have chosen, so that you may know and believe me and understand that I am he'" (Isa. 43:10; cf. 41:26; 48:3, 5–6).

Jesus was troubled in spirit (13:21). All three instances of Jesus' being troubled in spirit in this Gospel (cf. 11:33; 12:27) relate to the horror of human death (an effect of the work of Satan). This acknowledgment of inner turmoil on the part of Jesus contrasts sharply with the ideal of Greek philosophers to remain tranquil and unmoved in all circumstances, often on the basis of the view that one's fate had already been determined by the gods (cf. our expression "Stoic" today).[438]

The disciple whom Jesus loved (13:23). This expression probably refers to the historical figure of John the son of Zebedee as an oblique form of self-reference on part of the evangelist.[439] Since his recipients doubtless know him well, the author can dispense with his proper name.[440]

Reclining next to him (13:23). Reclining at meals was first introduced into Judaism from the Hellenistic world[441] and initially viewed as a sign of decadence (Amos 6:4–7). By New Testament times, however, reclining had become standard practice at banquets and feasts, including Passover celebrations. This leisurely way of observance—which symbolized freedom in contrast to Israel's bondage in Egypt[442]—stood in marked, self-conscious contrast with the haste that marked the first Passover on the night of the Exodus (Ex. 12:11).

The usual arrangement at a formal meal was to have a series of couches arranged in a U around the table. The guests reclined with their heads toward the table and their feet stretched out obliquely away from it. They leaned on the left elbow, which meant that the right hand was free to secure food. The host, or the most important person, reclined in the center of the chief couch, a couch for three, placed at the junction of the two arms of the U. The place of honor was to the left of, and thus slightly behind, the principal person. The second place was to his right, and the guest there would have his head on the breast of the host.[443] The place of the beloved disciple, [sic] was clearly on the principal couch where he could lean back on Jesus' breast.[444]

While "the disciple whom Jesus loved" reclined at Jesus' right (rather than left), this was nonetheless the place of a trusted friend. In an interesting parallel, Pliny recounts an incident where Nerva, the Roman emperor, dined one evening with a few select friends, and one Veiento

RECLINING AT THE TABLE

A model of a table, eating utensils, and terracotta pottery typical of the Roman period.

▼

"was placed next to the Emperor, and actually reclined upon his bosom" (*in sinu recumbebat; Ep.* 4.22.4).

The one to whom I will give this piece of bread when I have dipped it in the dish (13:26). The host at a feast (here Jesus) may well dip a tasty bit into a common bowl and pass it on to someone as a sign of honor or friendship. "Piece of bread" (*psōmion*) refers to a morsel, usually bread, though sometimes meat. Perhaps the scene takes place "at an early point of the paschal meal when bitter herbs were dipped into a bowl of fruit puree, the haroset sauce of dates, raisins and sour wine."[445] The fact that Jesus can pass the morsel to Judas Iscariot so easily suggests that he is close by, possibly on Jesus' left.

Satan entered into him (13:27). Two interesting parallels are found in first-century Jewish documents: "I determined inwardly to destroy him [Joseph], because the Prince of Error blinded my mind" (*T. Sim.* 2:7); "if the mind is disposed toward evil . . . it accepts the evil and is overmastered by Beliar" (*T. Ash.* 1:8). The Qumran scrolls reveal the belief, also found in John (e.g., 8:44), that the relation between the devil and evil human beings is like that of father to child (see comments on 12:36; cf. Wisd. Sol. 2:24). In Judaism in general, however, a person's will was considered decisive in determining which of two impulses, that toward good or that toward evil, prevailed (see comments on 8:34). See comments on Luke 22:3.

Charge of the money (13:29). See comments on 12:6.

Some thought Jesus was telling him to buy what was needed for the Feast (13:29). This being the night of the Passover (Nisan

15), the disciples think Judas is being dispatched to buy what is needed for the Feast—not the Passover, but the Feast of Unleavened Bread (the *hagigah*). This festival started that very night and went on for seven days. Since the next day (Friday, still Nisan 15) was a high feast day, and the following day a Sabbath, Jesus may have considered it expedient to make necessary purchases (such as more unleavened bread) that night. While there is some debate on the subject (cf. *m. Pesaḥ.* 4:5), the making of such purchases was probably both possible and lawful (though not necessarily convenient). A similar piece of legislation is found in one rabbinic passage, which says, "In Jerusalem on the eve of Passover when it falls on a Sabbath, a man may leave his cloak and take his Passover-lamb and make his reckoning with the seller after the close of the Festival-day" (*m. Šabb.* 23:1).

Or to give something to the poor (13:29). Almsgiving was an important part of Jewish piety. As the famous rabbi Hillel said, "The more charity, the more peace" (*m. ʾAbot* 2:7). For pilgrims to Jerusalem, it was customary to give alms to the poor (Josephus, *Ant.* 4.8.19 §227). On Passover night, the temple gates were left open from midnight on, allowing beggars to congregate (*Ant.* 18.2.2 §§29–30).[446] Almsgiving was regarded as particularly meritorious when done in Jerusalem[447] (see comments on 9:8; 12:4–8).

A Talmudic maxim reflects a much older principle: "Even a poor man who himself lives from alms, should give alms" (*b. Giṭ.* 7b).[448] While Jesus himself is poor,[449] this does not keep him from showing concern for others who are poor. "Sell your possessions and give to the poor" is his advice both to the disciples and to the rich young ruler (Luke 12:33;

18:22). The early church remembered an otherwise unrecorded saying of Jesus, "It is more blessed to give than to receive" (Acts 20:35).

It was night (13:30). The main meal was usually eaten in the late afternoon, but the Passover celebration took place at night.[450] The present reference may also convey the notion of spiritual darkness entered by the betrayer (cf. Luke 22:53, "this is your hour—when darkness reigns"; cf. the statements in Matt. 26:20 [Mark 14:17], "when evening came"; 1 Cor. 11:23, "on the night he was betrayed").

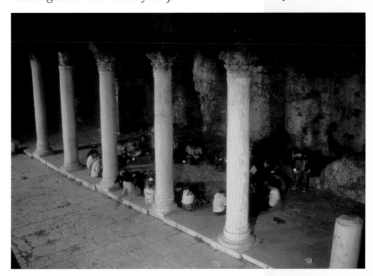

NIGHT IN JERUSALEM

A group of people sitting at the second-century Roman cardo in Jerusalem.

Jesus Predicts Peter's Denial (13:31–38)

God is glorified in him, God will glorify the Son in himself, and will glorify him at once (13:32). Once again, there are echoes of Isaiah (e.g., Isa. 49:3, where God says to the Servant of the Lord: "You are my servant, Israel, in whom I will display my splendor").

My children (13:33). Fulfilling the paschal role of head of the family, Jesus here addresses his followers as his "dear children." "The address is also very fitting if the Last Discourse is thought of as a farewell speech, for in this literary genre the scene is often that of a dying father instructing his children."[451]

A new command I give you: Love one another. As I have loved you, so you must love one another. By this all men will know that you are my disciples (13:34–35). The command to love one's neighbor as oneself was not new.[452] Love within the community was also highly regarded at Qumran (e.g., 1QS 1:10), and Josephus speaks similarly of the Essenes (*J.W.* 2.8.2 §119). Neighbor love is also emphasized by the famous first-century rabbi Hillel, who said, "Be of the disciples of Aaron, loving peace and pursuing peace, loving mankind and bringing them near to the Law" (*m. ʾAbot* 1:12). There are several parallels in other Jewish literature: "My children, beware of hatred . . . for hatred is not willing to hear the words of God's commandments concerning the love of one's neighbor" (*T. Gad* 4:1–2). "Now, my children, let each one of you love his brother . . . loving one another."[453] However, what is new is Jesus' commandment for his disciples to

love one another *as he has loved them*—laying down one's life for others (cf. 13:1; 15:13). That the early Christians did love one another is attested in the famous statement by the church father Tertullian, "See how they love one another" (*Apol.* 39). Regarding the Jews, the Roman Tacitus wrote, "the Jews are extremely loyal toward one another, and always ready to show compassion, but toward every other people they feel only hate and enmity" (*Hist.* 5.5; cf. Josephus, *J.W.* 2.8.14 §166).

Before the rooster crows (13:38). Apparently, roosters in Palestine frequently crowed in the late night hours, so that the Romans assigned the label "cockcrow" to the watch between midnight and 3 A.M. (cf. Mark 13:35; see also comments on John 18:27).

Jesus Comforts His Disciples (14:1–4)

In the last few quiet moments before his arrest, Jesus prepares his followers for the time subsequent to his return to the Father. As far as they are concerned, nothing can be worse than the departure of their beloved teacher. But according to Jesus, this will actually work out to their benefit. For he will send another "Counselor" (14:16), who will take up Jesus'—and the disciples'—case. From his exalted position with the Father, Jesus will be able to grant his followers' requests and enable them to accomplish even greater works than he has done during his earthly ministry.

Do not let your hearts be troubled (14:1). In keeping with Semitic anthropology, the expression "heart" denotes the seat of a person's will and emotions. On

---

R E F L E C T I O N S

"SEE HOW THEY LOVE ONE ANOTHER." CAN PEOPLE say that about Christians today? When doctors performing abortions are assassinated, when Christians are frequently belligerent, even hate-filled, how will the world know that we are Jesus' disciples? The answer is they will not. More important than being right or holding all the proper beliefs is that we are people of love. God so loved the world that he gave his Son. Will we who are saved be moved by his love and love fellow believers as well as those outside the faith? For this was—and still is—Jesus' burning desire: "that the world may know that you sent me."

"be troubled," see comments on 11:33; 12:27; 13:21. In the Old Testament, God's chosen servants as well as his people Israel were frequently told not to be afraid, whether the occasion was entering the Promised Land (Deut. 1:21, 29; 20:1, 3; Josh. 1:9) or threats from their enemies, such as the Babylonians (2 Kings 25:24) or the Assyrians (Isa. 10:24). Note too that in other farewell discourses, encouragement not to be afraid was common (*1 En.* 92:2; *T. Zeb.* 10:1–2; *Jub.* 22:23).

Trust in God; trust also in me (14:1). The Greek word *pisteuō*, elsewhere frequently translated "believe," denotes personal, relational trust in keeping with Old Testament usage (e.g., Isa. 28:16).

In my Father's house are many rooms (14:2). In Jesus' day, many dwelling units ("rooms")[454] were combined to form an extended household.[455] It was customary for sons to add to their father's house once married, so that the entire estate grew into a large compound (called *insula*) centered around a communal courtyard. The image used by Jesus may also have conjured up notions of luxurious Greco-Roman villas, replete with numerous terraces and buildings and situated among shady gardens with an abundance of trees and flowing water. Jesus' listeners may have been familiar with this kind of setting from the Herodian palaces in Jerusalem, Tiberias, and Jericho (cf. Josephus, *J.W.* 5.4.4 §§176–83).

Apocalyptic intertestamental literature provides extensive descriptions of heavenly dwelling places for the saints.[456] Philo regards heaven as a paternal house or city to which the soul returns after death: "So will you be able also to return to your father's house, and be quit of that long endless distress which besets you in a foreign land."[457] The rabbis believed that there were seven classes or departments, graded according to merit, in the heavenly Garden of Eden (*Midr. Ps.* 11 §6); the church fathers held similar views. John, however, is decidedly non-apocalyptic, and his treatment is much more restrained than Philo's existential allegorizing. The rabbinic notion of a compartmentalized heaven is likewise foreign to John.

Rather than elaborating on the characteristics of his Father's house, Jesus is content to stress that there is plenty of room and that the believers' future is bound up with a homecoming comparable to a son's return to his father's house (cf. Luke 15:11–32; note also Luke 2:49, where Jesus calls the temple "my Father's house"). In keeping with Jewish patriarchal culture, Jesus, the Son of the Father, establishes his followers "as members of the Father's household" and "makes his home accessible to them as a final place of residence."[458]

Prepare a place for you (14:2). Jesus' provision seems to be patterned after Deuteronomy, where God is said to have gone ahead and prepared a place for his people in the Promised Land (e.g., Deut. 1:29–33).[459] There may also be irony in the fact that the Jews fear that their "place" will be taken away from them by the Romans (11:48; a fear that materialized in A.D. 70), while Jesus' disciples can look forward to a "place" prepared for them by their master.[460]

I will come back and take you to be with me that you also may be where I am (14:3). This refers to the Second Coming (see 21:22–23; 1 Thess. 4:16–17).

Similar terminology is found in Song of Songs 8:2a, where the bride says she will bring her lover to her mother's house. Here Jesus, the messianic bridegroom (John 3:29), is said first to go to prepare a place for his own in his Father's house and then to come to take them home to be with him.

Jesus the Way to the Father (14:5–14)

As in the previous chapter, the farewell discourse is occasionally punctuated by questions from Jesus' disciples. The asking of clarification questions was an important aspect of the teacher-disciple relationship in first-century Judaism.[461]

I am the way and the truth and the life (14:6). In the Old Testament and intertestamental Jewish literature, "the way(s) of truth" is a life lived in conformity with God's law (e.g., Ps. 119:30; Tobit 1:3; Wisd. Sol. 5:6). In Psalm 86:11, "way" and "truth" occur in parallelism: "Teach me your way, O LORD, and I will walk in your truth." In 16:11, the notions of way, truth, and life are combined: "You have made known to me the path of life." A life devoted to walking in truth, in turn, will have eternal consequences: "The path of life leads upward for the wise to keep him from going down to the grave" (Prov. 15:24).

In the Dead Sea Scrolls, the ways of truth are contrasted with the ways of darkness and deceit.[462] The Qumran covenanters considered themselves to be "the Way" in absolute terms,[463] so that those who elected to join their ranks were said to have chosen "the Way" (1QS 9:17–18). At Qumran, "the Way" was understood to constitute strict legal observance as interpreted by the "Teacher of righteousness." The first Christians likewise

considered themselves to be followers of "the Way."[464] Jesus' claim to be "the way," then, may reflect this whole chain of usage of "way" imagery, from the Old Testament to the early church. Because he in his very essence is truth and life, Jesus is the one and only way of salvation.

No one comes to the Father except through me (14:6). In keeping with Jesus' claim, the early Christians maintained, "Salvation is found in no one else, for there is no other name under heaven given to men by which we must be saved" (Acts 4:12). In the Old Testament, people expressed their faith in God by keeping the law; now that Jesus has come, he is the way. In the Jewish and Greco-Roman world of the first century as well as in today's pluralistic climate, Jesus' message is plain: He does not merely claim to be "a" way or "a" truth or "a" life, but "the way and the truth and the life," the only way to salvation.

If you really knew me, you would know my Father as well. From now on, you do know him and have seen him (14:7). The verb "to know," in the sense of "acknowledge," was part of Near Eastern covenantal language.[465] In the Old Testament, people are frequently exhorted to know God (e.g., Ps. 46:10; 100:3), with knowledge of God generally being anticipated as a future blessing rather than claimed as a present possession.[466]

Lord, show us the Father (14:8). In the Old Testament, Moses asked and was given a limited vision of God's glory: "Now show me your glory" (Ex. 33:18). The prophet Isaiah was granted a vision of "the Lord seated on a throne, high and exalted" (Isa. 6:1). Later, the same prophet predicted that in the day of the

Messiah the glory of the Lord would be revealed (40:5). In Jesus' day, many Jews longed for a first-hand experience of God.

The words I say to you are not just my own. Rather, it is the Father, living in me, who is doing his work (14:10). In Deuteronomy 18:18, God said regarding the prophet like Moses, "I will put my words in his mouth, and he will tell them everything I command him." In 34:10–12, Moses is said to have been sent by the Lord to do signs and works.

Anyone who has faith in me . . . will do even greater things than these (14:12). "Greater things" has a primarily qualitative dimension, marking Jesus' "signs" as preliminary and his disciples' ministry as "greater" in the sense that it is based on Jesus' completed work on the cross (12:24; 15:13; 19:30) and belongs to a more advanced stage in God's economy of salvation (cf. Matt. 11:11). Jesus' followers are benefiting from others' labors, reaping what they have not sown, and will bear fruit that remains (John 4:31–38; 15:8, 16).

Thus, in keeping with motifs current in both Jewish life in general and farewell discourses in particular, the disciples are designated as Jesus' successors, taking their place in a long string of precedessors that range from the Old Testament prophets to John the Baptist and climax in Jesus.[467] In this sense, Jesus' followers—not just his original disciples, but "anyone who has faith in me"—will do greater things even than Jesus, aided by answered prayer in Jesus' name (14:13) and in close, spiritual union with their exalted Lord (ch. 15).

Whatever you ask in my name (14:13). Praying in Jesus' name does not involve magical incantations but rather expresses alignment of one's desires and purposes with God (1 John 5:14–15). Jews frequently recalled the patriarchs in their prayers, hoping that God would be moved to hear them on account of these holy men.

Jesus Promises the Holy Spirit (14:15–31)

If you love me, you will obey what I command (14:15). Jesus' words echo the demands of the Deuteronomic covenant.[468]

Another Counselor (14:16). In secular Greek, "Counselor" (*paraklētos*) refers primarily to a "legal assistant" or "advocate" (though the word never became a technical term such as its Lat. equivalent *advocatus*). In John's Gospel, legal overtones are most pronounced in 16:7–11. In later rabbinic writings, the role of advocate (*sanêgôr*) is associated with the Holy Spirit (*Lev. Rab.* 6:1 on Lev. 5:1). R. Eliezer ben Jacob made the well-known

---

REFLECTIONS

DO GREATER THINGS THAN JESUS did? This claim seems daring. The difficulty evaporates when one realizes that these "greater works" are still works of Jesus, now carried out from his exalted position with the Father through his commissioned, faithful followers. Because Jesus is now with the Father, we can expect to do greater works than even Jesus did: on the basis of his once-for-all death on the cross, and in answer to believing prayer for all that is necessary to accomplish the mission Jesus never relinquished.

statement, "He that performs one precept gets for himself one advocate (*pᵉraqlîṭ*); but he that commits one transgression gets for himself one accuser (*qaṭêgôr*)" (*m. ᵓAbot* 4:11). Also, both the noun *paraklē-sis* and the verb *parakaleō* are used in the Old Testament with regard to the "consoling" expected to occur during the messianic era (e.g., Isa. 40:1; cf. *b. Makk.* 5b).

The Spirit of truth (14:17). The expression "spirit of truth" was current in Judaism. One first-century Jewish document says, "Two spirits await an opportunity with humanity: the spirit of truth and the spirit of error. . . . And the spirit of truth testifies to all things and brings all accusations" (*T. Jud.* 20:1–5). Similarly, the Qumran literature affirms that God placed within a human being "two spirits so that he would walk with them until the moment of his visitation; they are the spirits of truth and of deceit" (1QS 3:18; cf. 4:23–26). Yet the above parallels are merely those of language, not thought. For while these expressions are part of an ethical dualism in intertestamental literature (including Qumran), John's Gospel does not feature a "spirit of error" corresponding to the Spirit of truth (but see 1 John 4:6, where "the Spirit [or spirit] of truth and the spirit of falsehood" occur together). Rather, the Spirit of truth is the other "Counselor," who takes the place of Jesus' "helping presence" while on earth with his disciples.

I will not leave you (14:18). Compare Moses' parting words to Israel: "The LORD . . . will never leave you nor forsake you" (Deut. 31:6; cf. Josh. 1:5; Heb. 13:5).

Orphans (14:18). In Old Testament times, orphans needed someone to plead their case. Here, the term "orphan" is used in a metaphorical sense in connection with Jesus' departure and the resulting loss that his disciples will experience. In secular Greek, "orphans" can denote both children bereft of only one parent and disciples left without their master.[469] Plato wrote regarding the followers of Socrates that, in the face of their teacher's imminent death, "they felt that he was like a father to us and that when bereft of him we should pass the rest of our lives as orphans."[470]

On that day (14:20). The phrase frequently has end-time connotations and is commonly found in Old Testament prophetic literature (e.g., Isa. 2:11; 3:7, 18; 4:1–2).

Show myself (14:21). The Greek verb used here (*emphanizō*), along with its cognates, sometimes refers in the LXX to theophanies, that is, manifestations of God (e.g., Ex. 33:18).

Judas (not Judas Iscariot) (14:22). This Judas is probably the "Judas of James" mentioned in Luke 6:16 and Acts 1:13, not Jude, the half-brother of Jesus (Matt. 13:55; Mark 6:3).

If anyone loves me, he will obey my teaching (14:23). "Teaching" here is *logos*, often translated "word." The synonymous use of "word" and "command" (14:21) harks back to the Old Testament, where the Ten Commandments are called "words" of God (Ex. 20:1; cf. Deut. 5:5, 22). The expressions "commands" and "word[s]" are used interchangeably in Psalm 119 (e.g., 119:10, 25, 28).

We will come to him and make our home with him (14:23). This is the only place in the New Testament where the Father and the Son are both said to indwell believers. Elsewhere, it is Christ (Gal. 2:20; Eph. 3:17) or the Spirit (Rom. 8:9, 11; 1 Cor. 3:16). In Old Testament times, God dwelt among his people, first in the tabernacle (Ex. 25:8; 29:45; Lev. 26:11–12), then in the temple (Acts 7:46–47). In the New Testament era, believers themselves are the temple of the living God (1 Cor. 6:19; 2 Cor. 6:16; cf. 1 Peter 2:5).

Two interesting parallels to the phrase "make our home" are found in Josephus, where Jonathan is said to have "taken up residence" in Jerusalem (*Ant.* 13.2.1 §41) and Elijah is shown to "make his dwelling" in a cave (*Ant.* 8.13.7 §350). Philo frequently speaks of God or the Word (*logos*) as dwelling in people. People long for spiritual intimacy with their Creator; only the Lord Jesus Christ can fulfill this craving of the human heart (cf. John 14:6).

All this I have spoken (14:25). Literally, "all these things." This expression will recur a total of six times in the second part of the Farewell Discourse (15:11; 16:1, 4, 6, 25, 33). Reiterated phrases also occur in prophetic writings (e.g., "I the LORD have spoken" in Ezek. 5:13, 15, 17; 17:21, 24).

The Counselor (14:26). See comments on 14:16.

The Holy Spirit (14:26). The term "Holy Spirit" occurs only infrequently in the Old Testament (Ps. 51:11; Isa. 63:9–10). There are several references to the "Holy Spirit" in intertestamental literature (e.g., Wisd. Sol. 9:17; *Odes Sol.* 8).

Will teach (14:26). See the parallel in 16:13. Both passages together echo Psalm 25:5: "Guide me in your truth and teach me" (cf. 25:9). See also Nehemiah 9:20: "You gave your good Spirit to instruct them." Teaching in the sense of authentic exposition of Scripture was a vital part of Judaism. In Qumran, the primary teaching office was occupied by the "teacher of righteousness," who interpreted the Hebrew Scriptures prophetically with reference to the Dead Sea community. However, one important difference between the Holy Spirit and the "teacher of righteousness" is that the former will guide people into truth definitively while the latter will be followed by another "teaching righteousness" at the end of time (CD 6:11).

Will remind you of everything I have said to you (14:26). This promise has important implications for the life of the church and for the writing of the New Testament. "Remembering" was also an important part of the Jewish testament tradition.[471] There are several parallels in intertestamental literature between the consoling, teaching presence of the Paraclete and the period after the death of a revered leader in the testaments. In one such work the people tell Baruch, "Everything which we can remember of the good things which the Mighty One has done to us we shall remember, and that which we do not remember he knows in his grace" (*2 Bar.* 77:11). A literary parallel is found in the intertestamental book of *Jubilees*, where God reassures Jacob, "I will cause you to remember everything" (*Jub.* 32:25).

Peace I leave with you (14:27). In the Greek world, peace (*eirēnē*) was essentially a negative concept, denoting the absence of war.[472] Though this is also part of the term's range of meaning in Hebrew thought (e.g., Judg. 3:11, 30;

5:31; 8:28; etc.), the expression peace (*shālôm*) usually had much richer connotations, conveying the notion of positive blessing, especially that of a right relationship with God.[473] This is evident in the blessing given by Moses and Aaron: "The LORD bless you and keep you; the LORD make his face shine upon you and be gracious to you; the LORD turn his face toward you and give you peace" (Num. 6:24–26; cf. Ps. 29:11; Hag. 2:9).

The Old Testament prophetic writings in particular look forward to a period of peace inaugurated by the coming of the Messiah. The "Prince of Peace" (Isa. 9:6) will "command peace to the nations" (Zech. 9:10; cf. 14:9), and there will be good tidings of peace and salvation (Isa. 52:7; cf. 54:13; 57:19; Acts 10:36). Through the royal Messiah, God will make an everlasting "covenant of peace" with his people (Ezek. 37:26). This accords also with intertestamental notions that "the souls of the righteous are in the hand of God, and no torment will ever touch them . . . they are at peace" (Wisd. Sol. 3:1, 3).

The present phrase, "Peace I leave with you," reflects the customary Jewish greeting and word of farewell, whereby "leave" (*aphiēmi*) probably has the sense of "bequeath" (cf. Ps. 17:14; Eccl. 2:18). Here (as in John 16:33) the context of greeting is farewell; after the resurrection, it is welcome (20:19, 21, 26). By invoking "that day" anticipated by the prophets (14:20), Jesus places this period squarely within the context of Old Testament expectation. On the merits of his substitutionary death, the departing Lord bequeaths to his followers the permanent end-time blessing of a right relationship with God (cf. Rom. 1:7; 5:1; 14:17).

My peace I give you. I do not give to you as the world gives (14:27). On peace in general, see previous comment. Apart from his peace, the departing Jesus also bestows on his followers his love (15:9, 10) and joy (15:11). This triad is also

▶

ARA PACIS **IN ROME**

Caesar Augustus built the "altar of peace" in Rome to celebrate his inauguration of the age of peace.

found in Paul's teaching on the fruit of the Spirit (Gal. 5:22). The *pax Romana* ("Roman peace"), secured by the first Roman emperor, Augustus (30 B.C.–A.D. 14), had been obtained and was maintained by military might. The famous *Ara Pacis* ("altar of peace"), erected by Augustus to celebrate his inauguration of the age of peace, still stands in Rome as a testimony to the world's empty messianic pretensions.[474] The peace given by Jesus, by contrast, was not afflicted with the burden of having been achieved by violence (cf. John 18:11). Philo, the Hellenistic Jew, calls peace "the highest of blessings . . . a gift no human being can bestow" (*Moses* 1.304), holding up as the loftiest ideal "a soul, in which there is no warring, whose sight is keen, which has set before it as its aim to live in contemplation and peace" (*Dreams* 2.250).[475]

Do not be afraid (14:27). Moses' parting counsel in his farewell discourse is likewise, "Do not be afraid" (Deut. 31:6, 8).

The prince of this world (14:30). Lit., "the world's ruler." See comments on 12:31.

He has no hold on me (14:30). This phrase constitutes an idiomatic rendering of a Hebrew expression frequently found in legal contexts with the sense "he has no claim on me."[476] The present phrase does not mean "he has no *power* over me" (cf. 19:11: *kata*, not *en*; though this is of course true as well), but "he has no *legal claim* or hold on me." The reason for this is Christ's sinlessness (cf. 8:46).

Come now; let us leave (14:31). This may indicate that Jesus and his followers now leave the Upper Room and embark on a nightly walk, perhaps passing vineyards on the way, which would provide

a fitting backdrop for Jesus' teaching on the vine and the branches (15:1–17). Some have suggested that Jesus' "vine" metaphor was occasioned by the golden vine overhanging the main entrance to the temple.[477] Alternatively, Jesus may have told his disciples it was time to go and then added some further instruction before finally getting underway (cf. 18:1).

The Vine and the Branches (15:1–17)

Vine imagery was common in the ancient world, as in the case of the cult of Dionysos, the Greek god of wine. The Old Testament frequently uses the vineyard or vine as a symbol for Israel, God's covenant people, especially in two "vineyard songs" found in Isaiah.[478] However, while the vine's purpose for existence is the bearing of fruit for its owner, references to Israel as God's vine regularly stress Israel's failure to produce good fruit, issuing in divine judgment.[479] In contrast to Israel's failure, Jesus claims to be the "*true* vine," bringing forth the fruit Israel has failed to produce. Thus Jesus, the Messiah and Son of God, fulfills Israel's destiny as the true vine of God (Ps. 80:14–17).[480] The intimate relationship between Jesus and his followers has already been depicted in terms of a shepherd and his flock (John 10). The

VINEYARD NEAR JERICHO

illustration of a vine and its branches, even more than that of a shepherd and his flock, focuses on the organic, vital connection between the branches and the vine.

I am the true vine (15:1). Joseph is called a "fruitful vine" in Genesis 49:22. The expression "true vine" is also found in Jeremiah 2:21 (LXX): "I had planted you like a choice *vine* of sound and *reliable* stock." Building on the Old Testament depiction of Israel as a vine, the vine in later years served as a symbol for wisdom (Sir. 24:17), the dominion of the Messiah (*2 Bar.* 39:7), and the Judaism of Jesus' day. The Jerusalem temple was adorned with a golden vine with large clusters of grapes (see comments on John 14:31). Coins of the first Jewish revolt (A.D. 66–70) feature a vine and branches as a symbol of Jerusalem, and the rabbinic school at Jamnia headed by R. Yoḥanan ben

Zakkai after the destruction of the temple was known as a "vineyard" (*m. Ketub.* 4:6). Philo, characteristically, interprets the reference to Israel as a vine in Isaiah 5:7 in terms of "that most holy vineyard," the virtuous soul (*Dreams* 2.172–73).

My Father is the gardener (15:1). The gardener (*geōrgos*) may merely be the one who tills the soil (the term is translated "farmer" in 2 Tim. 2:6 and James 5:7), which in Palestine was frequently all that was done for the vineyard. Yet the term can also refer more specifically to a vinedresser, as in the Synoptic parable of the tenants (Matt. 21:33–41 par.). Isaiah's first vineyard song, which constitutes the background of this parable, depicts God as spading, clearing, planting, and taking care of the vineyard, only to be rewarded with sour grapes (Isa. 5:1–7; cf. Ps. 80:8–9). The Roman writer Lucian portrays God as *geōrgos*, who acts without human collaboration (*Phal.* 2.8; second century A.D.).

He cuts . . . he prunes (15:2). The term "prune" (*kathairō*) is found frequently with reference to agricultural processes (though not necessarily pruning) in secular Greek (e.g., Xenophon, *Oecon.* 18.6; 20.11). The vinedresser does two things to ensure maximum fruit production. In the winter, he cuts off the dry and withered branches. This may involve pruning the vines to the extent that only the stalks remain. Later, when the vine has sprouted leaves, he removes the smaller shoots so that the main fruitbearing branches receive adequate nourishment.[481] Philo refers to "superfluous shoots . . . which are a great injury to the genuine shoots, and which the husbandmen cleanse and prune" (*Dreams* 2.9; 2.64; *Agriculture* 10).

The pruning activity of the divine vinedresser resembles that of every earthly *geōrgos*. [482] Since the term underlying "cut" (*airō*) can mean either "cut off" (negative purpose) or "lift up" (restorative), some have argued that the present reference should be understood in the latter sense. But this is almost certainly erroneous. More likely, the antithetical parallelism of the first part of each statement ("every branch in me that bears no fruit"/"every branch in me that does bear fruit") is matched by corresponding divine action, be it judgment (negative; see 15:6) or discipline (positive). [483] In the case of Jesus' followers, Judas was an example of the former, Peter of the latter.

Branch (15:2). The term "branch" (*klēma*) occurs in the LXX regularly for the "shoot" of a vine (e.g., Num. 13:23; Ezek. 17:6) as distinct from the "branch" (*klados*) of other trees. The expression is used particularly of vine tendrils, though it occasionally refers to heavier branches as well.

Bears no fruit . . . does bear fruit . . . even more fruitful (15:2). The bearing of fruit is God's creative (Gen. 1:11–12, 22, 28) and redemptive purpose (cf. 15:8, 16). The Old Testament prophets envisioned a time when Israel would "bud and blossom and fill all the world with fruit" (Isa. 27:6; cf. Hos. 14:4–8).

Clean (15:3). See 13:10–11. The adjective "clean" (*katharos*) is occasionally used in Greek literature in connection with the growth of vines (Xenophon, *Oecon.* 20.20).

Remain in me, and I will remain in you (15:4). "In" language harks back to Old Testament covenant theology, including

prophetic texts regarding a future new covenant. [484]

Like a branch that is thrown away and withers; such branches are picked up, thrown into the fire and burned (15:6). Verses 6 and 7 further develop the contrast of 15:2 (see comment). The present imagery may hark back to the parallel in Ezekiel, where a vine failing to produce fruit is said to be good for nothing but the fire (Ezek. 15:1–8; cf. 19:12). Fire is a common Jewish and biblical symbol for divine judgment. [485]

My joy may be in you and that your joy may be complete (15:11). See Psalm 19:8. In keeping with John's focus on believers' present experience of salvation blessings, he grounds their joy in Old Testament prophetic notions of end-time rejoicing. [486] John the Baptist epitomizes this salvation-historical fulfillment of joy (John 3:29; even already in his mother's womb: Luke 1:41, 44), as does Jesus' mother Mary (1:46–48). The early Christians likewise experienced this complete joy (Acts 13:52; Rom. 15:13; 2 Tim. 1:4).

As in the case of love, John's treatment of joy is remarkably restrained in comparison with other writings such as the *Odes of Solomon* (e.g., 15:1; 23:1; 31:3, 6; 40:4). In rabbinic thought, joy was imperfect in the present age, marred by the certain prospect of death and the worries of this life (*Gen. Rab.* 42:3; attributed to R. Samuel b. Naḥman, c. A.D. 260). Only the age to come, the messianic era, would see perfect joy. [487] Jesus' reference to "perfect joy" thus amounts to his claiming to be the Messiah.

Greater love has no one than this, that he lay down his life for his friends (15:13). Friendship was considered important in the Greco-Roman world. The supreme duty of friendship may involve self-sacrifice for one's friend even to the point of death. Aristotle wrote "that a virtuous man's conduct is often guided by the interests of his friends . . . and that he will if necessary lay down his life in their behalf" (*Eth. Nic.* IX.8.9).[488] Plato, writing on "love's peculiar power," commented, "Only such as are in love will consent to die for others" (*Symp.* 179B). Of the Epicurean Philonides it was said that "for the most beloved of his relatives or friends he was ready to offer his neck" (*Life Phil.* 22). The present statement would thus resonate particularly with John's Greco-Roman audience. Both the Old Testament and rabbinic literature recognize the sanctity of risking one's life for another, though this was not commanded but left up to the individual, and one's own life was often considered to take precedence over the life of another. Friendship was also the subject of extended reflection in intertestamental wisdom literature (esp. Sir. 6:5–17).[489]

You are my friends if you do what I command (15:14). In the Old Testament, only Abraham (2 Chron. 20:7; Isa. 41:8) and by implication Moses (Ex. 33:11) are called "friends of God." Other Jewish writings apply this designation, besides Abraham[490] and Moses,[491] to other Old Testament figures such as Isaac, Jacob, and Levi (*Jub.* 30:20; CD 3:3–4), or to the Israelites in general (e.g., *Jub.* 30:21), "holy souls" (Wisd. Sol. 7:27), and students of Torah (*m.* '*Abot* 6:1). Because of Abraham's and Moses's unusual degree of access to God, later Jews speculated what revelations other than the ones recorded in Scripture they might have received, which sparked the development of a body of pseudepigraphal literature around these two figures. Here Jesus extends the same privilege of friendship to all believers, predicated on their obedience to his commands.

I no longer call you servants . . . I have called you friends (15:15). The disciples' role as servants is intimated in 13:16 and implied in 13:13.[492] Philo wrote, "It is folly to imagine that the servants of God take precedence over his friends in receiving their portion in the land of virtue" (*Migration* 45). The distinction between servants (*douloi*) and friends (*philoi*) is also found in Gnosticism and mystery religions. As Clement of Alexandria writes, "Wherefore also all men are His; some through knowledge, and others not yet so; and some as friends, some as faithful servants, some as servants merely" (*Strom.* 7.2). On friends, see comments on John 15:13–14.

You did not choose me, but I chose you (15:16). Election is hardly ever mentioned in the case of the Old Testament "friends of God" (Abraham and Moses). Only once is it said of Abraham (Neh. 9:7) and Moses (Ps. 106:23) that they were "chosen" by God. The Old Testament concept of election is primarily related to the king and people of Israel, God's "chosen people" (see comments on John 6:70).[493] In terms of teacher-pupil

---

R E F L E C T I O N S

FRIENDSHIP IS A MUCH-TREASURED, THOUGH OFTEN elusive, prize. Hardly has there ever been a more unequal friendship than the one between Jesus and his followers: he the eternal, incarnate Word, they sinners in desperate need of redemption. Nevertheless, Jesus extended his friendship to believers. We can continue this cycle by befriending those who are unlike us or may seem unable to repay us for our friendship, especially those outside the faith.

relationships, Jesus here breaks with contemporary custom, for it was common in first-century Palestine for disciples to attach themselves to a particular rabbi, not vice versa, as is summed up by the well-known dictum of R. Joshua b. Perahyah (c. 100 B.C.): "Provide yourself with a teacher" (*m. ʾAbot* 1:6).

Appointed you (15:16). The same or a similar expression is used in the Old Testament for God's appointment of Abraham as father of many nations (Gen. 17:5; cf. Rom. 4:17), the ordination of Levites (Num. 8:10), and Moses' commissioning of Joshua (27:18). In the New Testament, the word used here (*tithēmi*) refers to being "set apart" for a particular ministry, such as Paul's apostolic work or a great number of other callings in the church; in Hebrews 1:2, the phrase even refers to Jesus' being made heir.

The World's Hatred of the Disciples (15:18–16:4)

If the world hates you (15:18). Jesus' disciples are to be known by their love; the world is characterized by hatred. The Qumran community stressed love within the brotherhood but hatred toward outsiders, preaching "everlasting hatred for the men of the pit" (1QS 9:21–22). Hatred in the world was experienced by Christians long before John wrote. The Roman historians Tacitus and Suetonius both called Christianity "a mischievous superstition" (*Annals* 15.44; *Nero* 16).

The following charges were regularly leveled against the early Christians: (1) insurrectionism (claiming Jesus is Lord); (2) cannibalism (eating Christ's body at the Lord's Supper); (3) immorality ("love feasts" [Jude 12], the kiss of love); (4) incendiaries (teaching that the elements will be dissolved and consuming fire will destroy the world [2 Peter 3:10]; thus Nero fastened the blame for the fire of Rome on the Christians); (5) disintegrating family relationships (divided families if the wife became a Christian but the husband did not).[494]

If they obeyed my teaching, they will obey yours also (15:20). As God assured Samuel, "It is not you they have rejected, but they have rejected me" (1 Sam. 8:7). Or as he told the prophet Ezekiel, "The house of Israel is not willing to listen to you because they are not willing to listen to me" (Ezek. 3:7).

Because of my name (15:21). The expression "because of my name" reflects Old Testament terminology pertaining to God and his great name.[495] The claim of Christians that Jesus—and he alone—is Lord (*kyrios*) pitted them against Roman imperial religion, which attributed this title to the Roman emperor. Domitian in particular, who probably reigned when John's Gospel was being written (A.D. 81–96), insisted on the designation *dominus et deus*, that is, Lord and God (cf. 20:28). However, John's Gospel is unequivocal that only those who know Jesus also know the Father.

They hated me without reason (15:25). The citation is from Psalm 35:19 or 69:4, the latter being more likely because Psalm 69 was widely regarded as messianic and frequently quoted elsewhere in the New Testament (see also 119:161, where the psalmist laments, "Rulers persecute me without cause"). In *b. Yoma* 9b, one of the causes for the destruction of the temple is given as "because therein prevailed hatred without cause," and "groundless hatred is considered as of even gravity with the three sins of idolatry, immorality, and bloodshed."

The Spirit of truth (15:26). In the present context, truth is required for the Spirit's role as a witness. At Qumran, the title "spirit of truth" was given to the leader of the forces of good against the forces of evil (e.g., 1QS 3:18). In 1QS 4:21, the expressions "spirit of holiness" (i.e., holy spirit) and "spirit of truth" occur in parallelism (see also the comments on 14:17).

You also must testify (15:27). In Old Testament prophetic literature (esp. Isaiah), God's end-time people are called God's "witnesses" to the nations (e.g., Isa. 43:10–12; 44:8). In the New Testament, believers are frequently promised the Spirit's help in times of persecution (Matt. 10:20; Mark 13:11; Luke 12:12). Particularly in Luke's writings, the Spirit is presented as vitally engaged in missionary outreach (Acts 1:8; cf. Luke 24:48; Acts 5:32; 6:10).

So that you will not go astray (16:1). Literally, "lest you be caused to stumble" (*skandalizō*). Encouraging words from a departing figure to stay true to the Lord God are a regular feature of Jewish farewell discourses. Note how decades after the composition of John's Gospel, Pliny the Younger, governor of Bithynia, wrote to the Roman emperor Trajan (A.D. 98–117):

> The method I have observed toward those who have been denounced to me as Christians is this: I interrogated them whether they were Christians; if they confessed it I repeated the question twice again, adding the threat of capital punishment; if they still persevered, I ordered them to be executed.... Others ... at first confessed themselves Christians,

and then denied it; true, they had been of that persuasion but they had quit it ... many years ... ago. They all worshipped your statue and the images of the gods, and cursed Christ (*Ep.* 10.96).[496]

Put ... out of the synagogue (16:2). See comments on 9:22.

A time is coming (16:2). The expression is reminiscent of prophetic or apocalyptic expressions such as "the days are coming."[497]

Anyone who kills you will think he is offering a service to God (16:2). This probably refers to Jewish rather than Roman persecution.[498] In his pre-Christian days, Paul certainly reflected such misguided zeal for his ancestral traditions.[499] Some rabbinic authorities held that slaying heretics was an act of divine worship: "If a man sheds the blood of the wicked it is as though he had offered an offering" (*Num. Rab.* 21:3 with reference to Num. 25:13). However, such kinds of judgments rarely became public policy. For the most part, Jewish persecution of Christians was spontaneous, with seasoned voices counseling moderation.[500] According to Josephus, the Jewish authorities (i.e., the high priest Ananus II) were responsible for the stoning death of James the brother of Jesus in A.D. 62 (*Ant.* 20.9.1 §200). Regarding the preparations for the martyrdom of John's own disciple, the church father Polycarp, we read that "these things happened with so great speed, quicker than it takes to tell, and the crowd came together immediately, ... and the Jews were extremely zealous, as is their custom, in assisting at this" (*Mart. Pol.* 13.1).

They will do such things because they have not known the Father or me (16:3). On the matter of passing judgment in want of all the facts, Epictetus writes, "When someone treats you ill or speaks ill of you, remember that he acts or speaks thus because he thinks that it is incumbent upon him. . . . If, therefore, you start from this point of view, you will be gentle with the man who reviles you. For you should say on each occasion, 'He thought that way about it'" (*Enchir.* 42).

The Work of the Holy Spirit (16:5–16)

The Counselor (16:7). See comments on 14:16.

I will send him (16:7). Old Testament prophetic literature is full of anticipation regarding the inauguration of the age of the kingdom of God by the pouring out of the Spirit.[501]

When he comes, he will convict (16:8). There are interesting parallels to this statement in Jewish documents. One first-century document says, "And the spirit of truth testifies to all things and brings all accusations. He who has sinned is consumed in his heart and cannot raise his head to face the judge [*kategoreō*]" (*T. Jud.* 20:5). *First Enoch* 1:9 (cited in Jude 15) deals with God's final judgment of the godless, where God will prove them guilty of all their godless works. Elsewhere Enoch functions as accuser of all the godless (cf. *Jub.* 4:23; 10:3–4, 17; *1 En.* 14:1). Another scribe (Michael?) has the task of writing down the transgressions of the seventy shepherds of the people and of reading aloud from this book at God's judgment (*1 En.* 89:62–63, 70; 90:17). The same terminology occurs in the Qumran scrolls where the term "rebuke" is used in a somewhat similar sense (e.g., 1 QS 9:16–17). Greek moralists (such as Philo) use the expression "to convict" (*elencheō*) primarily of the conscience. Occasionally, Philo speaks of the Word as an *elenchos* (e.g., *Worse* 146).

In regard to righteousness (16:10). Isaiah had confessed that all the "righteous acts" of people in his day were "like filthy rags" (Isa. 64:6). The world's (and Jewish) "righteousness" must thus be put in quotation marks; it is in fact the very opposite, *un*righteousness (cf., e.g., Rom. 2:12–24). This is what is here said to be prosecuted by the Spirit of truth in his legal function of *paraklētos*.

Prince of this world (16:11). See comments on 12:31.

Spirit of truth (16:13). See comments on 14:17; 15:26.

Guide . . . into all truth (16:13). Such divine guidance was already the psalmist's longing: "Show me your ways, O LORD, teach me your paths; guide me in your truth" (Ps. 25:4–5; cf. 43:3; 86:11); "may your good Spirit lead me" (143:10). Isaiah recounts how God led his people Israel in the desert by his Holy Spirit (Isa. 63:14) and predicts God's renewed guidance in the future (43:19). Wisdom literature applies guidance terminology to the figure of divine wisdom (Wisd. Sol. 9:11; 10:10, 17). The illuminating function of God's Spirit (or Wisdom) is also prominent in Philo, who writes, "For the mind could not have made so straight an aim if there was not also the divine spirit guiding it to the truth itself" (*Moses* 2.265). For Philo, Moses was the "teacher of divine things," who "has ever the divine spirit at his side, taking the lead in every journey of righteousness" (*Giants* 54–55). According to 1QS 4:2, "These are their [the spirits of light and darkness] paths in the world: to enlighten the heart of man, straighten out in front of him all the paths of justice and truth, establish in his heart respect for the precepts of God."

He will tell you what is yet to come (16:13). This same verb (*anangellō*, "declare, announce") occurs almost sixty times in Isaiah.[502] According to Isaiah, declaring things to come is the exclusive domain of Yahweh (Isa. 48:14). A close parallel to the present passage is Isaiah 44:7, where Yahweh challenges anyone to declare the things to come (cf. 42:9; 46:10). Another striking parallel is found in 41:21–29, where the idols of the nations are exhorted to interpret the meaning of past events and to "declare to us the things to come, tell us what the future holds, so we may know that you are gods" (41:22–23). In 45:19, Yahweh is said to declare truth—an expression combining two of the attributes of the Paraclete predicated on him in the present passage.

You will see me (16:16). The vision of God, denied as a possibility by John (apart from mediation through Jesus; 1:18; 5:37; 6:46) in keeping with Old Testament teaching (Ex. 33:20), is the aspiration of Hellenistic piety, and indeed most of the world's religions.

The Disciples' Grief Will Turn to Joy (16:17–33)

Weep and mourn (16:20). Both terms jointly refer to the loud wailing customary for mourning in the Near East. Similar terminology is already found in the Old Testament: "Do not weep for the dead king or mourn his loss" (Jer. 22:10).

Your grief will turn to joy (16:20). The Jewish feast of Purim celebrates "the time when the Jews got relief from their enemies, and . . . when their sorrow was turned into joy and their mourning into a day of celebration" (Est. 9:22). Old Testament Israel knew that it is God who is able to "turn their mourning into gladness" and to give them "comfort and joy instead of sorrow" (Jer. 31:13; cf. Isa. 61:2–3; 2 Esd. 2:27).

A woman giving birth to a child has pain because her time has come; but when her baby is born she forgets the anguish because of her joy that a child is born into the world (16:21). Everyone who has ever experienced or witnessed the birth of a child can relate to this illustration. In the prophetic portions of the Old Testament, the image of a woman in labor is common[503] and frequently applies to the coming of end-time salvation through the Messiah. The Day of the Lord is regularly portrayed as "a time of distress" (Dan. 12:1; Zeph. 1:14–15).

Intertestamental Judaism coined the phrase "the birth pains of the Messiah" to refer to the period of tribulation that precedes the final consummation.[504] This terminology is also used in Jesus' teaching on the end times, in which he speaks of "the beginning of birth pains" and times of "great distress" (Matt. 24:8, 21, 29 par.; cf. Rom. 2:9). The early church likewise saw present challenges in this larger perspective (Acts 14:22; 1 Cor. 7:26; 2 Cor. 4:17; Rev. 7:14).

You will rejoice (16:22). More literally, "your heart will rejoice." The same phrase occurs in Isaiah 66:14 in the context of the Lord's speaking words of comfort regarding Jerusalem (cf. 60:5). A general parallel is Psalm 33:21: "In him our hearts rejoice, for we trust in his holy name."

Figuratively . . . plainly (16:25). The term *paroimia* (translating Heb. *mašal* in the LXX) covers a wide range of parabolic and allegorical speech (e.g., Sir. 39:3; 47:17; see comments on John 10:6). However, the phrase *en paroimiais* does not necessarily mean "metaphorically" or "in a parable" but connotes the obscurity of Jesus' way of expression.

I came from the Father . . . going back to the Father (16:28). The present passage constitutes a Christological parallel to Isaiah's portrayal of the word of God in 55:11–12 (see comments on John 1:1).

You do not even need to have anyone ask you questions. This makes us believe that you came from God (16:30). Apparently, the disciples think that the promise of 16:23a has been fulfilled. In Jewish thought, the ability to anticipate questions and not needing to be asked is a mark of divinity. Thus Jonathan is said to swear to David by the God "who, before I have expressed my thought in words, already knows what it is" (Josephus, *Ant.* 6.11.8 §230). Elsewhere Jesus himself affirms, "Your Father knows what you need before you ask him" (Matt. 6:8).

You will be scattered (16:32). The present phrase alludes to Zechariah 13:7, a passage quoted in Matthew 26:31 par. Other Old Testament passages likewise refer to the scattering of God's flock.[505]

To his own home (16:32). The phrase also occurs in the LXX (Est. 5:10; 6:12), intertestamental literature (3 *Macc.*

6:27), and later in this Gospel (John 19:27). This probably refers to the disciples' temporary dwellings in Jerusalem rather than to their homes in Galilee.

You may have peace (16:33). See comments on 14:27.

I have overcome (16:33). The verb occurs only once in the LXX with God as the Conqueror (Ps. 51:4; cited in Rom. 3:4). It is also found in apocryphal and pseudepigraphical literature.[506]

Jesus Prays for Himself (17:1–5)

It was not uncommen for farewell discourses to conclude with a prayer (*Jub.* 22:28–30; Sir. 51:1–13; cf. *Jub.* 1:19–21; *4 Ezra* 8:19b–36). John 17 displays several thematic links with the Targums to Exodus 19–20.[507] More important still, Jesus' final prayer culminates John's portrayal of

GARDEN OF GETHSEMANE

A very old olive tree in the traditional site of the garden on the Mount of Olives.

Jesus as the one sent from the Father who, after completing his mission, will soon return to the one who sent him (cf. Isa. 55:10–11).

He looked toward heaven and prayed (17:1). See comments on 11:41.

Father (17:1). See comments on 11:41.

Glorify your Son that your Son may glorify you (17:1). The Old Testament says that God will not give his glory to another (e.g., Isa. 42:8; 48:11). Jesus' sharing his Father's glory thus implies that he is God. In a religious papyrus, a miracle worker prays, "Isis . . . glorify me, as I have glorified the name of your son Horus" (P. Lond. 121.503–504).[508] However, while the terminology is strikingly similar, in the wonder-worker's case he prays to be glorified *because* he has glorified the name of Horus, while Jesus prays to be glorified *in order that* he many glorify the Father.[509]

You granted him authority (17:2). God's granting of authority to Jesus marks the inbreaking of a new era (cf. Isa. 9:6–7; Dan. 7:13–14).[510]

All people (17:2). Literally, "all flesh," a Semitism.

This is eternal life: that they may know you (17:3). The Old Testament relates life after death to the knowledge of God (e.g., Jer. 31:34). Hosea records the divine lament, "My people are destroyed from lack of knowledge" (Hos. 4:6), while both Isaiah and Habakkuk envision a future day when "the earth will be full of the knowledge of the LORD as the waters cover the sea" (Isa. 11:9; Hab. 2:14). God's people are to acknowledge him in all their ways (Prov. 3:6) and to live lives

of wisdom (3:18; 11:9). The principle of wise living is also affirmed in later rabbinic teaching.[511]

"Knowing God" does not merely refer to head knowledge (the Greek conception). Rather, it means living in fellowship with God. Of course, God can also be known to a limited extent through creation (e.g., Wisd. Sol. 13:1–9; Rom. 1:18–25). But ultimately, knowledge of God is contingent on religious salvation, as was acknowledged even in Hellenistic Jewish literature: "For to know you is complete righteousness, and to know your power is the root of immortality" (Wisd. Sol. 15:3).

In the Qumran scrolls, "life" and "eternal knowledge" are set in close parallelism: "May he illuminate your heart with the discernment of life and grace you with eternal knowledge" (1QS 2:3; cf. 4:22; 11:3–4). The phrase "eternal life" is found in these writings as well (CD 3:20). In Hellenistic and oriental cults, it was the vision of God received by the initiate that was considered to be the source of life and salvation. Philo wrote, "holding that the knowledge of him is the consummation of happiness. It is also agelong life" (*Spec. Laws* 1.345; cf. *God* 143).

The only true God (17:3). This entire verse conforms closely to the pattern underlying 1 Corinthians 8:6: "there is but one God, the Father . . . and there is but one Lord, Jesus Christ." Similar expressions are also found in New Testament confessions of faith and liturgical formulas (e.g., 1 Thess. 1:9: "the living and true God"; 1 Tim. 1:17: "the only God"; 6:15–16: "God, the blessed and only Ruler . . . who alone is immortal"; 1 John 5:20: "the true God and eternal life"; Rev. 6:10: "Sovereign Lord, holy and true") as well as in Philo (*Alleg. Interp.* 2.68: "the only true God"; *Spec. Laws*

1.332: "the one true God . . . the Being who truly exists, even God"; *Embassy* 366: "the true God") and in other Jewish writings (*3 Macc.* 6:18: "most glorious, almighty, and true God"). See comments on John 5:44 ("the only God").

Jesus Christ (17:3). This phrase occurs elsewhere in this gospel only in 1:17; see also 1 John 4:2. It may strike the modern reader as curious that Jesus should call himself "Jesus Christ," but self-reference in the third person was common in antiquity (cf. John 21:24 and note).[512]

Before the world began (17:5). Preexistence is also ascribed to wisdom in intertestamental wisdom literature (e.g., Wisd. Sol. 7:25; 9:10–11) on the basis of its portrayal in the Old Testament book of Proverbs (esp. Prov. 8:23, 30); but see comments on John 1:1.

Jesus Prays for His Disciples (17:6–19)

You (17:6). Literally, "your name" (also in 17:26). God's "name" enshrines who God is (cf. Ex. 3:13–15). Because his name is glorious, God wants it to be made known.[513] In the Old Testament, knowledge of God's name implies a commitment of life (Ps. 9:10), and God's name is put on the central sanctuary (Deut. 12:5, 21). John takes over both aspects: Jesus' revelation of God's name to his followers must be met with obedience; and Jesus is shown to replace both tabernacle and temple, so that he has become the "place" where God has put his name (see also Isa. 55:13; 62:2; 65:15–16).

Speculation about the divine name was common in the Judaism of Jesus' day. In particular, people wondered about the angel of the Lord referred to in Exodus 23:20–21: "See, I am sending an angel ahead of you to guard you along the way and to bring you to the place I have prepared. . . . *My Name is upon him.*" In later Jewish literature, the name of God became enshrined in the sacred tetragrammaton (Yahweh), so that "the Name" served as a substitute for pronouncing this divine name.

The *Odes of Solomon* states that "the Messiah . . . was known before the foundations of the world, that he might give life to persons forever by the truth of his name" (41:15); moreover, God placed his name on the head of his people because they are free and they are his (42:20). In gnostic literature, "name" refers to the knowledge (*gnōsis*) mediated by the redeemer. This name is revealed only to certain individuals who thereby acquire a share in God's life, light, and joy.

I gave them the words you gave me (17:8). The portrayal of Jesus in the present passage is reminiscent of the description of the prophet like Moses in Deuteronomy 18:18.

Holy Father (17:11). The same phrase is found in *Odes of Solomon* 31:5. The concept goes back to Leviticus 11:44 (cf. Ps. 71:22; 111:9; Isa. 6:3). Similar addresses are found in Jewish literature: "O holy Lord of all holiness" (2 Macc. 14:36); "O Holy One among the holy" (*3 Macc.* 2:2); "You are holy and your Name is awesome" (*Shemoneh ʿEsreh* 3). Holiness is also ascribed to God in the book of Revelation (e.g., Rev. 4:8; 6:10). However, unlike in other Jewish contexts, Jesus' address of God as holy does not create a distance between him and God; for Jesus, God is his holy *Father*.

Protect them by the power of your name (17:11). The phrase "by the power of your name" is probably a Semitic expansion on "by [the instrumentality of] your name." Yet because God's name is powerful, it can be viewed as synonymous with power (see, e.g., Ps. 54:1, where "your name" and "your might" occur in parallelism). The psalmist knows that deliverance from his enemies and help in times of trouble are from the Lord: "Through your name we trample our foes" (44:5); "save me, O God, by your name, vindicate me by your might" (54:1); "our help is in the name of the LORD" (124:8).

The name you gave me (17:11). Exodus 23:21 says of the guardian angel of the people, "my Name is in him"; in Numbers 6:27, the "name" of Yahweh is "put on the Israelites" by the priestly blessing; according to Jeremiah 23:6, the "name" of the messianic King will be "The LORD Our Righteousness." As Paul sums it up, to Jesus God gave "the name that is above every name, that at the name of Jesus every knee should bow . . . and every tongue confess that Jesus Christ is Lord" (Phil. 2:9–10; cf. Rev. 19:12).

I protected them and kept them safe. . . . None has been lost (17:12). Jesus protected his disciples and kept them safe, just as Wisdom did Abraham: "Wisdom . . . preserved him blameless before God and kept him strong" (Wisd. Sol. 10:5). The juxtaposition of the verbs "protect" and "keep safe" reflects Semitic parallelism (see also Prov. 18:10)

The one doomed to destruction (17:12). Lit., "son of destruction." The expression can refer either to Judas's character[514] or his destiny.[515] The NIV rendering "doomed to destruction" suggests the latter, though of course both are true. The

noun "destruction" (*apōleia*) commonly refers in the New Testament to final condemnation. The expression "son of perdition" also occurs in 2 Thessalonians 2:3, there with reference to "the man of lawlessness," that is, the antichrist. This suggests that "son of destruction" labels Judas Iscariot as part of a typology of evil personages across the sweep of salvation history seeking to thwart God's sovereign purposes. The phrase "son of" is a Semitism,[516] though it is also attested in classical Greek.[517] Similar expressions (in the plural) are also found in the Qumran writings.[518]

So that Scripture would be fulfilled (17:12). The antecedent passage is probably Psalm 41:10 (applied to Judas in John 13:18). Other Old Testament passages fulfilled through Judas are Psalm 69:25 and 109:8 (cited in Acts 1:20).

Not that you take them out of this world but that you protect them from the evil one (17:15). Parallel wording is attested in rabbinic literature both for "take out of this world"[519] and for "protect from the evil one."[520] Moses (Num. 11:15), Elijah (1 Kings 19:4), and Jonah (Jonah 4:3, 8) all asked to be taken out of this world, but none of their prayers was answered (though Elijah was taken up to heaven at a later time).

Sanctify (17:17). The address "Holy Father" in 17:11 would suggest to the Jewish mind that holiness was also expected of Jesus' followers, according to the principle enunciated in the book of Leviticus (11:44; 19:2; 20:26).

Your word is truth (17:17). The present phrase is similar to Psalm 119:142: "Your law is true" (cf. 119:151, 160). David likewise acknowledged, "Your words are trustworthy" (2 Sam. 7:28; cf. Ps. 19:7). In common Jewish prayer, it was acknowledged that God sanctifies people through his commandments.

As you sent me into the world, I have sent them into the world (17:18). A partial Old Testament parallel is the instruction to Moses, who had himself been consecrated by God (Sir. 45:4) in order to consecrate others so that they too may serve God as priests (Ex. 28:41).

For them I sanctify myself, that they too may be truly sanctified (17:19). Jesus' sanctification "for" (*hyper*) others is similar to atonement passages elsewhere in the New Testament (e.g., Mark 14:24; John 6:51; 1 Cor. 11:24). It is also reminiscent of the Old Testament notion of "setting apart" sacrificial animals (e.g., Deut. 15:19).

Jesus Prays for All Believers (17:20–26)

My prayer is not for them alone (17:20). See the parallel in Deuteronomy 29:14–15: "I am making this covenant . . . not only with you . . . but also with those who are not here today."

So that the world may believe that you have sent me (17:21). The coordination between unity and love is paralleled by exhortations to brotherly love and harmony in Jewish testamentary literature, which attributes this parting concern to Noah (*Jub.* 7:26), Rebecca (*Jub.* 35:20), Isaac (*Jub.* 36:4), Zebulon (*T. Zeb.* 8:5–9:4), Joseph (*T. Jos.* 17:2–3), and Daniel (*T. Dan.* 5:3).

Brought to complete unity (17:23). The Qumran covenanters also saw themselves as a *yaḥad* ("union") and displayed a keen consciousness of their election.[521]

To let the world know that you sent me (17:23). This phrase is reminiscent of Old Testament passages such as Zechariah 2:9: "Then you will know that the LORD Almighty has sent me."

Before the creation of the world (17:24). Literally, "before the foundation of the world." The phrase "from the beginning of the world" was frequently used in Judaism.[522] A suggestive parallel is found in *Odes of Solomon* 41:15, where the Messiah is said to have been "known before the foundations of the world, that he might give life to persons forever by the truth of his name."

Righteous Father (17:25). The Old Testament commonly teaches that God is righteous and just.[523] With Jesus' betrayal and innocent suffering imminent, he affirms the righteousness of God his Father.

REFLECTIONS

JESUS' PARTING PRAYER IS FOR believers' love and unity, so that unbelievers may come to know him through them. The church has miserably failed to live up to this longing of Jesus' heart. It has constantly been plagued by painful divisions, competitiveness, and an unforgiving spirit. How can we expect unbelievers to be attracted to Jesus if this is the state of the company of his followers? We must repent and make it our ambition to promote love and unity with other Christians so that those outside the faith will see Christ in us.

I myself may be in them (17:26). Subsequent to the giving of the law at Sinai, the glory of God displayed on the mountain (Ex. 24:16) came to dwell in the midst of Israel in the tabernacle (40:34). As the Israelites moved toward the Promised Land, God frequently assured them that he was in their midst (29:45–46; Deut. 7:21; 23:14). In John's prologue, Jesus is said to have come to dwell (lit., "tabernacle") among his people (John 1:14; see comments), and now Jesus' earthly presence is about to be transmuted into his spiritual presence in his followers in keeping with Old Testament notions of a new covenant.

Jesus' Arrest (18:1–11)

The Gospels narrate two trials of Jesus, one Jewish and one Roman.[524] The former started with an informal hearing before Annas (18:12–14, 19–24), while Sanhedrin members were probably summoned in order to stage a more formal trial. A meeting of the highest Jewish body (Matt. 26:57–68; Mark 14:53–65) then led to formal charges and the sending of a delegation to Pilate (Matt. 27:1–2; Luke 22:66–71). The Roman trial consisted of an initial interrogation by Pilate (Matt. 27:11–14; John 18:28–38a), followed by an appearance before Herod (Luke 23:6–12) and a final summons before Pilate (Matt. 27:15–31; John 18:38b–19:16).

Though Jewish law contained numerous stipulations regarding legal proceedings against those charged with serious offenses, many such stipulations could be breached if the matter was judged to be urgent (including the possibility of mob violence). Another factor in Jesus' case was that executions could proceed on feast days but not on a Sabbath. Thus if Jesus' arrest took place on Thursday evening, little time remained if he was to be tried and put to death before the onset of the Sabbath at sundown of the following day. Moreover, Roman officials such as Pilate worked only from dawn until late morning, so that the Jews' case against Jesus had to be prepared overnight.[525]

The Kidron Valley (18:1). The Kidron Valley is frequently mentioned in the LXX and Jewish intertestamental literature.[526] Literally, the expression is "the brook [*cheimarros*] of Kidron," where "brook" refers to an intermittent stream that is dry most of the year but swells up during rainfalls, particularly in the winter (Josephus, *Ant.* 8.1.5 §17). The Kidron Valley, called "Wadi en-Nar," continues variously south or southeast until it reaches the Dead Sea (cf. Ezek. 47:1–12; Zech. 14:8).

An olive grove (18:1). To the east of the Kidron rises the Mount of Olives. The olive grove (*kēpos*, lit. "garden") on its slopes is called "Gethsemane" (meaning "oil press") in the Synoptics.[527] This garden may have been made available to Jesus and his followers by a wealthy person who supported Jesus' ministry. The phrase "there was" rather than "there is" may indicate that the garden had been destroyed by the time of the writing of John's Gospel.

Went into it (18:1). John's terminology ("went into it," later "went out") suggests a walled garden. According to Jewish custom (with reference to Deut. 16:7), Passover night was to be spent in Jerusalem, but in light of the large number of pilgrims, city limits were extended as far as Bethphage on the Mount of Olives (though Bethany lay beyond the legal boundary).[528]

A detachment of soldiers (18:3). A *speira* was a detachment consisting of a cohort of Roman soldiers.[529] A full cohort was led by a *chiliarchos* (lit., "leader of a thousand," rendered "tribune" or "commander") and consisted of one thousand men, though in practice it often numbered only six hundred.[530] The Romans could use surprisingly large numbers of soldiers even for a single person (like the 470 men protecting Paul in Acts 23:23), especially if they feared a riot. Roman troops were stationed in Caesarea, but during feast days gathered northwest of the temple by the fortress of Antonia. This enabled the Romans to keep a close eye on the large crowds during Jewish festivals and to quell any mob violence at the very outset.

Some officials from the chief priests and Pharisees (18:3). These "officials" (*hypēretai*) represented the temple police, the primary arresting officers. This unit was commanded by the captain of the temple guard (cf. Acts 4:1), who was charged with watching the temple at night (*m. Mid.* 1:1–2). Their arms and methods are recalled in a "street ballad":

Woe is me, for the house of Boethus:
  woe is me, for their clubs!
Woe is me, for the house of Annas:
  woe is me, for their whisperings!
Woe is me, for the house of Kdathros:
  woe is me, for their pen!
Woe is me, for the house of Ishmael
  (ben Phabi): woe is me, for their
  fist!
For they are the High Priests, and
  their sons the treasurers: their
  sons-in-law are Temple-officers,
  and their servants beat the people
  with their staves.[531]

The chief priests (made up predominantly of Sadducees) and the Pharisees are regularly linked in this Gospel (cf. Josephus, *Life* 5 §21).

Chief priests (18:3). The rubric of "chief [or high] priests" included the incumbent high priest, former high priests still living (such as Annas), and members of aristocratic families from whom high priests were chosen.[532]

They were carrying torches, lanterns and weapons (18:3). Torches (*lampas*) consisted of resinous strips of wood fastened together.[533] Lanterns (*phanoi*) were "roughly cylindrical terracotta vessels with an opening on one side large enough for a household lamp to be inserted, its wick facing outward; a ceramic ring—or strap—handle on the top permitted easy carrying. Occasionally lanterns may have had built-in lamps."[534] Roman soldiers carried both kinds of lighting devices,[535] and the temple guard went on their rounds with "lighted torches" (*m. Mid.* 1:2). While this was the time close to the full paschal moon, lanterns might still be needed to track down a suspect who (it probably was suspected) was hiding from the authorities in the dark corners of this olive grove. "*They* were carrying" does not mean that all are carrying torches; it would have been sufficient for only some to do so. Regarding the carrying of weapons, it may be noted that sometimes the temple guards were unarmed,[536] but in the present instance both they and the Roman soldiers take no chances.

I am he (18:5). Literally, "I am." In light of people's response, the phrase probably has connotations of deity.

And fell to the ground (18:6). Falling to the ground is regularly a reaction to divine revelation.[537] Legend has it that Pharaoh fell to the ground speechless when Moses uttered the secret name of God.[538] Falling to the ground also speaks of the powerlessness of the enemies when confronted with the power of God. The phrase is reminiscent of certain passages in the Psalms.[539] Jewish literature recounts the story of the attempted arrest of Simeon: "On hearing his voice they fell on their faces and their teeth were broken" (*Gen. Rab.* 91:6). The reaction also highlights Jesus' messianic authority in keeping with passages such as Isaiah 11:4: "He will strike the earth with the rod of his mouth; with the breath of his lips he will slay the wicked" (cf. 2 Esd. 13:3–4).

Malchus (18:10). The name Malchus is not uncommon in the first century A.D. It occurs several times in Josephus, almost entirely of Natabean Arabs[540] as well as in the Palmyrene and Nabatean inscriptions.[541] The name probably derives from the common Semitic root *mlk* (*melek* means "king").

Sword (18:10). According to Luke 22:38, Jesus' disciples possessed a total of two swords. The term "sword" (*machaira*)

may refer to a long knife or a short sword, with *rhomphaia* being the large sword. The fact that Peter's action is unforeseen suggests the short sword, which could be concealed under one's garments. It may have been illegal to carry such a weapon at Passover: "A man may not go out with a sword" (*m. Šabb.* 6:4; so the Sages with reference to Isa. 2:4, but not R. Eliezer [A.D. 90–130]: "They are his adornments").

right ▶

MODEL OF A ROMAN ERA SWORD

Right ear (18:10). Both Mark (14:47) and John use the term *ōtarion*, a double diminutive, equivalent to our "earlobe." It is possible that Peter deliberately chooses the right ear (which was considered to be the more valuable)[542] as a mark of defiance. While generally an injury to a slave would not have aroused much interest, Jesus shows concern even for this (by human standards) insignificant (Arab?) slave.

The cup (18:11). "Cup" serves here as a metaphor for death. In the Old Testament, the expression refers primarily to God's "cup of wrath," which evildoers will have to drink.[543] Similar terminology is found in later Jewish writings and the New Testament.[544] This imagery may have been transferred to the righteous, guiltless one taking on himself God's judgment by way of substitutionary suffering.[545]

this designation as well (see comments on 18:13). Presumably, he lived in the Hasmonean palace on the west hill of the city, which overlooked the Tyropoeon Valley and faced the temple. It is possible that Caiaphas and Annas lived in the same palace, occupying different wings bound together by a common courtyard.

The high priest (18:15–16). The sequence of references to "the high priest" in this chapter (esp. 18:13–14, 19, 24) shows that Annas is in view and that the courtyard (*aulē*) is the atrium connected with his house. The mention of a "girl on duty" confirms that the scene takes place outside the temple area, for there only men held such assignments (see also comments on 18:18). Caiaphas's quarters may have shared the same courtyard, so that even the second stage of the investigation would have been relatively private (though with at least some Sanhedrin members present). The formal action taken by the Sanhedrin (at about dawn) is not recorded in John's Gospel (cf. Matt. 27:1–2 par.).

The girl on duty . . . the girl at the door (18:16–17). On women gatekeepers, see 2 Samuel 4:6 (LXX) and Acts 12:13 ("servant girl named Rhoda").[550] The same word (*paidiskē*) is rendered "bondwoman" (in distinction from "free woman") in Galatians 4:22–31. Apparently, the female doorkeeper was a domestic female slave, probably of mature age, since her responsibility required judgment and life experience.[551]

It was cold (18:18). Nights in Jerusalem, which is only half a mile above sea level, can be cold in the spring.

The servants and officials (18:18). The soldiers have returned to their barracks, entrusting the role of guarding Jesus to the temple guards.

A fire (18:18). The presence of a fire confirms that these preliminary proceedings against Jesus take place at night, when the cold would incite people to make a fire to stay warm. Even at night, fires were not normally lit,[552] and night proceedings were generally regarded as illegal. Moreover, the fact that a fire was kept burning in the Chamber of Immersion so that the priests on night duty could warm themselves there and that lamps were burning even along the passage that led below the temple building (*m. Tamid* 1:1) suggest that the courtyard referred to in the present passage is private.

Jesus Before the High Priest (18:19–24)

The high priest (18:19). Again, Annas is referred to as "the high priest." The appropriateness of such a designation even after he was removed from office is confirmed both by the Mishnah (where the high priest is said to retain his obligations even when no longer in office; *m. Hor.* 3:1–2, 4) and Josephus (where Jonathan is called high priest fifteen years after his deposition; *J.W.* 2.12.6 §243; cf. 4.3.7–9 §§151–60). There may even be an element of defiance in the Jewish practice of continuing to call previous high priests by that name, challenging the Roman right to depose officials whose tenure was to be for life according to Mosaic legislation (Num. 35:25). Apparently, the seasoned, aged Annas still wielded considerable high priestly power while his relatives held the title.

Questioned Jesus (18:19). The fact that Jesus is questioned—a procedure considered improper in formal Jewish trials where a case had to rest on the weight of witness testimony (e.g. *m. Sanh.* 6:2)—suggests that the present hearing is informal (see comments on 18:21). On the Sadducees' reputation for judging in general, Josephus writes that "the school of the Sadducees . . . are indeed more heartless than any of the other Jews . . . when they sit in judgment" (*Ant.* 20.9.1 §199).

His disciples and his teaching (18:19). The question here addressed to Jesus indicates that the authorities' primary concern is theological, though a political rationale is later given to Pilate (cf. 19:7, 12). The Jewish leadership seems to view Jesus as a false prophet (see later *b. Sanh.* 43a), who secretly entices people to fall away from the God of Israel, an offense punishable by death (Deut. 13:1–11).[553] Apparently, Annas hopes Jesus might incriminate himself on those counts.

I have spoken openly to the world. . . . I always taught in synagogues or at the temple, where all the Jews come together. I said nothing in secret (18:20). Some see in the present statement an echo of the motif of Wisdom speaking to the people in public (Prov. 8:2–3; 9:3; Wisd. Sol. 6:14, 16; Bar. 3:37). More likely, Jesus is simply pointing to the public nature of his instruction, which has made it possible for the Jewish authorities to gather ample eyewitness testimony from those who have heard him teach. See further comment on "I said nothing in secret" below.

At the temple (18:20). This refers to the temple precincts, variously translated "temple courts" or "temple area" in the NIV.

I said nothing in secret (18:20). Note the earlier acknowledgment by the people of

Jerusalem that Jesus was "speaking publicly" (7:26). Jesus' words here echo Yahweh's in Isaiah 45:19; 48:16: "I have not spoken in secret." Socrates answered his judges similarly: "But if anyone says that he ever learned or heard anything privately from me, which all the others did not, be assured that he is not telling the truth" (Plato, *Apol.* 33B). The Qumran community, by contrast, preferred secret teaching, as did the mystery religions.

Why question me? Ask those who heard me. Surely they know what I said (18:21). Jesus' challenge is understandable especially if the questioning of prisoners was considered improper in his day (see comments on 18:19). This is further confirmed by the recognized legal principle that a person's own testimony regarding himself was deemed invalid (see 5:31). While an accused could raise an objection (which had to be heard: see 7:50–51; see also the apocryphal story of Susanna), a case was to be established by way of testimony, whereby witnesses *for* the defendant were to be questioned first (*m. Sanh.* 4:1; cf. Matt. 26:59–63 par.). If the testimony of witnesses agreed on essential points, the fate of the accused was sealed. This violation of formal procedure strongly suggests that Jesus' hearing before Annas is unofficial.

Ask those who heard me (18:21). Jesus is asking for a proper trial where evidence is established by interrogation of witnesses; the present informal hearing does not meet such qualifications. Such display of self-confidence before authority is in all likelihood startling. As Josephus tells us, those charged normally maintained an attitude of humility before their judges, assuming "the manner of one who is fearful and seeks mercy" (*Ant.* 14.9.4 §172).

One of the officials (18:22). The official (*hypēretēs*) in question is one of the temple guard who took part in Jesus' arrest (cf. 18:3, 12).

Struck him in the face (18:22). This is not the only ill-treatment Jesus has to endure during his Jewish trial before the Sanhedrin. According to Matthew, "they spit in his face and struck him with their fists. Others slapped him" (26:67). The word used here (*rhapisma*) denotes a sharp blow with the flat of one's hand (cf. Isa. 50:6 LXX). Striking a prisoner was against Jewish law.[554] Compare the similar incident involving Paul in Acts 23:1–5, where the high priest Ananias ordered those standing near Paul to strike him on the mouth.

Is this the way you answer the high priest? (18:22). A proper attitude toward authority was legislated by Exodus 22:28: "Do not blaspheme God or curse the ruler of your people" (quoted by Paul in Acts 23:5). See also Josephus, *Ag. Ap.* 2.24 §§194–95: "Anyone who disobeys him [the high priest] will pay the penalty as for impiety towards God himself."

If I said something wrong (18:23). Literally, "spoke in an evil manner," that is, "if I said something that dishonored the high priest." Jesus implicitly refers to the law of Exodus 22:28 (see previous comment) and denies having violated it. The LXX uses the expression "speak evil" for cursing the deaf and blind (Lev. 19:14), one's parents (20:9), the king and God (Isa. 8:21), and the sanctuary (1 Macc. 7:42).

Then Annas sent him, still bound, to Caiaphas the high priest (18:24). Before Jesus can be brought to Pilate, charges must be confirmed by the *official* high priest, Caiaphas, in his function as chair-

man of the Sanhedrin.[555] Just where the Sanhedrin met at that time is subject to debate.[556] A mishnaic source specifies the Chamber of Hewn Stone on the south side of the temple court (*m. Mid.* 5:4), while the Babylonian Talmud indicates that the Sanhedrin ceased meeting in this location "forty years" (not necessarily a literal time marker; e.g., *b. Yoma* 39a) prior to the destruction of the temple, moving to the marketplace.[557] Then again, "sent" need not imply movement to another building at all but may merely refer to changing courtrooms in the temple.

Peter's Second and Third Denials (18:25–27)

A relative of the man whose ear Peter had cut off (18:26). Being one of Jesus' disciples was not a legal offence, though it could have been surmised that open confession might lead to trouble, especially if Jesus is found guilty and executed (cf. 20:19). Of more immediate concern for Peter may have been the earlier incident in which he drew a weapon (perhaps carried illegally) and assaulted one of the high priest's servants (Malchus). Peter's denial of association with Jesus may therefore stem from a basic instinct of self-preservation and a self-serving desire on his part not to incriminate himself.

A rooster began to crow (18:27). While mishnaic legislation forbids the raising of fowl in Jerusalem (*m. B. Qam.* 7:7: "They may not rear fowls in Jerusalem"), it is unlikely this prohibition is strictly obeyed in Jesus' day.[558] Exactly when cocks crowed in first-century Jerusalem is subject to debate; estimates range from between 12:30 to 2:30 A.M. to between 3:00 and 5:00 A.M. Some have argued that reference is made here not to the actual crowing of a rooster but to the trumpet signal given at the close of the third watch, named "cockcrow" (midnight to 3:00 A.M.).[559] If so, Jesus' interrogation by Annas and Peter's denials would have concluded at 3:00 A.M. See comments on 13:38.

Jesus Before Pilate (18:28–40)

The palace of the Roman governor (18:28). Jesus is led to the Praetorium, the headquarters of the Roman governor. While based in Caesarea in a palace built by Herod the Great (cf. Acts 23:33–35), Pilate, like his predecessors, made it a practice to go up to Jerusalem for high feast days in order to be at hand for any disturbance that might arise. It is unclear whether Pilate's Jerusalem headquarters is to be identified with the Herodian palace on the western wall (suggested by the NIV's "palace") or the Fortress of Antonia (named after Mark Antony; Josephus, *J.W.* 1.21.1 §401) northwest of the temple grounds.[560]

Herod the Great had both palaces built, the former in 35 B.C. (on the site of an older castle erected by John Hyrcanus, see Josephus, *Ant.* 18.4.3 §91) and the latter in 23 B.C., whereby especially Philo identifies the (former) Herodian palace as the usual Jerusalem headquarters of Roman governors.[561] Yet the discovery of massive stone slabs in the Fortress of Antonia in 1870 has convinced some that it is this building that is in view (see further comments on 19:13).[562] On balance, the Herodian palace is more likely, especially in light of the above cited evidence from Philo and Josephus.[563]

Early morning (18:28). The expression "early morning" (*prōi*) is ambiguous. The last two watches of the night (from midnight to 6:00 A.M.) were called "cock-crow" (*alektorophōnia*) and "early morning" (*prōi*) by the Romans. If this is how the term is used here, Jesus is brought to Pilate before 6:00 A.M. This coheres with the practice, followed by many Roman officials, of starting the day very early and finishing the workday by late morning: "The emperor Vespasian was at his official duties even before the hour of dawn, and the elder Pliny, most industrious of Roman officials, had completed his working day, when Prefect of the Fleet, by the end of the fourth or fifth hour [i.e., 10:00 or 11:00 A.M.]. In Martial's account of daily life at the capital, where two hours are assigned to the protracted duty of *salutatio*, the period of *labores* ends when the sixth hour begins [noon]. Even a country gentleman at leisure begins his day at the second hour [7:00 A.M.]."[564] In light of Jewish scruples to try capital cases at night (see comments on 18:18), it is more likely that "early morning" means shortly after sunrise, when the Sanhedrin meets in formal session and pronounces its verdict on Jesus (Matt. 27:1–2 par.).

To avoid ceremonial uncleanness the Jews did not enter the palace; they wanted to be able to eat the Passover (18:28). Jews who entered Gentile

FORTRESS OF ANTONIA

A model of the fortress, which stood in the northwest corner of the temple grounds.

homes were considered unclean,[565] which would prevent them from celebrating the Passover. The present reference may not merely be to the Passover itself but to the Feast of Unleavened Bread, which lasted for seven days,[566] in particular to the offering (*hagigah*) brought on the morning of the first day of the festival (cf. Num. 28:18–19). "Eat the Passover" probably simply means "celebrate the feast" (cf. 2 Chron. 30:21).[567]

Pilate (18:29). See "Pontius Pilate."

Take him yourselves and judge him by your own law (18:31). Like Gallio after him (Acts 18:14–15), Pilate is not interested in being a judge of internal Jewish disputes.

But we have no right to execute anyone (18:31). Despite instances where the Jewish authorities are involved in executions, such as the stonings of Stephen

(Acts 7) and of James the half-brother of Jesus in A.D. 62 (Josephus, *Ant.* 20.9.1 §200) and the burning of a priest's daughter accused of committing adultery (*m. Sanh.* 7:2)—all of which involved lynch law or breaches of authority—the Sanhedrin did not have the power of capital punishment.[568] As Josephus reports, "The territory of Archelaus was now [A.D. 6] reduced to a province, and Coponius, a Roman of the equestrian order, was sent out as procurator, entrusted by Augustus with full powers, including the infliction of capital punishment" (*J.W.* 2.3.4 §117).

The same writer tells of a case where the high priest had sentenced some people to death by stoning, a sentence that was protested by some apparently for the reason that the Sanhedrin did not have the authority to impose the death penalty during the period of Roman rule in Judea. Sure enough, the high priest was deposed for his presumption (*Ant.* 20.9.1 §§197–203). This comports with the acknowledgment in Talmudic literature that the Jews had lost this power "forty years" before the destruction of Jerusalem.[569] Not only was this consistent with general Roman practice in provincial administration, capital punishment was the most jealously guarded of all governmental powers.[570]

Moreover, an equestrian procurator such as Pilate in an insignificant province like Judea had no assistants of high rank who could help him carry out his administrative and judicial duties. Thus, he must rely on local officials in minor matters while retaining the right to intervene in major cases, including "crimes for which the penalty was hard labor in mines, exile, or death."[571] Also, in handling criminal trials, the prefect or procurator was not bound by Roman law,

▶

PASSOVER SCENE

A model of the court of priests in the Jerusalem temple showing the altar of sacrifice.

which applied only to Roman citizens and cities. For this reason it is difficult to determine with certainty Pilate's motives in offering to give the case back to the Jewish authorities.

Kind of death he was going to die (18:32). Crucifixion was looked upon by the Jews with horror, as when Alexander Jannaeus had eight hundred of his captives crucified in the center of Jerusalem.[572] Execution on a cross was considered to be the same as hanging (Acts 5:30; 10:39), for which Mosaic law enunciated the principle, "Anyone who is hung on a tree is under God's curse" (Deut. 21:23; cf. Gal. 3:13). If Jesus had been put to death by the Sanhedrin, stoning would have been the likely mode of execution, since that is the penalty specified in the Old Testament for blasphemy,[573] the most common charge against Jesus in John. Other forms of capital punishment sanctioned by mishnaic teaching are burning, beheading, and strangling (*m. Sanh.* 7:1).

Pilate . . . asked him (18:33). In contrast to Jewish practice (see comments on 18:9 and 21), Roman law made provisions for

◀
PONTIUS PILATE INSCRIPTION

▶ Pontius Pilate

Pontius Pilate, governor of Judea, was appointed to his post by the emperor Tiberius in A.D. 26 and held this position for about ten years until A.D. 36/37.[A-28] According to Philo, Pilate owed his appointment to Sejanus, the commander of the Praetorian Guard in Rome (*Embassy* 159). If the chronology I presented in John 1 is correct, Pilate would have been governor for about seven years (the year of Jesus' trial being A.D. 33). The Synoptists use the generic title "governor" (*hēgemōn*) with regard to Pilate (e.g., Matt. 27:2, 11; Luke 20:20). Tacitus, the Roman historian, calls him *procurator* (*Ann.* 15.44); Josephus uses the equivalent expression *epitropos* (*J.W.* 2.9.2 §169). The famous Latin "Pilate inscription," found in Caesarea in 1961, identifies him as "prefect" (*praefectus*) of Judea: [PON]TIUS PILATUS [PRAEF]ECTUS IUDA[EA]E.[A-29]

Apparently, Pilate could act from a position of strength until the death of his mentor Sejanus (Oct.

18, A.D. 31), after which he had to tread much more lightly.[A-30] Since the Gospels portray Pilate's conduct at Jesus' trial as accommodating the Jews and as vulnerable personally, it is likely that his trial took place after A.D. 31 (i.e., in A.D. 33). Pilate was of equestrian rank, of lower nobility than senator, since Judea was considered to be a lesser imperial province.

Jesus' trial and crucifixion under Pilate is also attested by non-Christian sources, such as the Roman historian Tacitus, who writes, "Christ had been executed in Tiberius' reign by the procurator of Judea, Pontius Pilate" (*Ann.* 15.44). Pilate's tenure came to an end in A.D. 36/37, when he was deposed and sent to Rome by Vitellius, legate of Syria, on account of his brutal action in a Samaritan uprising (Josephus, *Ant.* 18.4.2 §§88–89).[A-31] He arrived in Rome after Tiberius's death (March 16, A.D. 37).

detailed questioning of persons charged with crimes, whether they were Roman citizens (*accusatio*) or not (*cognitio*).[574] These hearings were public and awarded the accused person with sufficient opportunity to defend himself against the charges, as seems to be presupposed in Jesus' case by the Synoptics.

The palace (18:33). See comments on 18:28.

Are you the king of the Jews? (18:33). "King of the Jews" may have been used by the Hasmoneans who ruled Judea prior to the Roman subjugation of Palestine. Josephus recounts that a golden vine or garden with the inscription "From Alexander, the king of the Jews" was given to the Roman general Pompey by Alexander, son of Alexander Jannaeus, and later transported to Rome and put in the temple of Jupiter Capitolinus (*Ant.* 14.3.1 §36). The title "king of the Jews" is also applied to Herod the Great (*Ant.* 16.10.2 §311).

Thus the designation "king of the Jews" has clearly political overtones, and Pilate's question is designed to determine whether Jesus constitutes a political threat to Roman imperial power.[575] Pilate's gubernatorial tenure was punctuated by outbursts of ethnic nationalism, which rendered him ever more alert to potential sources of trouble, especially since Judea was "infested with brigands" (*Ant.* 20.10.5 §215) and "anyone might make himself king as the head of a band of rebels" (*Ant.* 17.10.8 §285).[576]

My kingdom is not of this world. . . . But now my kingdom is from another place (18:36). Earlier, Jesus refused people's efforts to make him king (6:15). The answer given by the grandchildren of Jude, Jesus' half-brother, at a trial before Domitian echoes Jesus' words: "And when they were asked concerning Christ and his kingdom, of what sort it was and where and when it was to appear, they answered that it was not a temporal nor an earthly kingdom, but a heavenly and angelic one, which would appear at the end of the world" (Eusebius, *Eccl. Hist.* 3.20.6). Jesus' description of the nature of his kingdom echoes similar passages in Daniel (e.g., Dan. 2:44; 7:14, 27).

My servants (18:36). The term rendered "servant" (*hypēretēs*) has previously been used for the temple police. In the LXX, the expression refers to the minister or officer of a king (Prov. 14:35; Isa. 32:5; Dan. 3:46) or even kings themselves (Wisd. Sol. 6:4: "servants of his kingdom").

What is truth? (18:38). With this flippant remark, Pilate dismisses Jesus' claim that he has come to testify to the truth and that everyone on the side of truth lis-

REFLECTIONS

THE JEWISH LEADERS OF JESUS' day may well have known that Pilate, in the wake of his mentor Sejanus's demise, was in danger of losing his "friend of Caesar" status with the emperor in Rome, and they took full advantage of it: "If you let this man go, you are no friend of Caesar." Jesus did not play politics this way. In the face of accusations, he remained silent. When asked about his kingdom, he claimed that it was not of this world. Wherever you and I are empire-building, let us make sure the empire we are building is the kingdom of God.

tens to him. Rather than being philo- sophical in nature, Pilate's comment may reflect disillusionment (if not bitterness) from a political, pragmatic point of view. In his seven years as governor of Judea, he frequently clashed with the Jewish population. More recently, his position with the Roman emperor has become increasingly tenuous (see comments on 18:29).

He went out again to the Jews (18:38). Pilate returns to the outer colonnade (cf. 18:28–29).

I find no basis for a charge against him (18:38). (Cf. Luke 23:4.) Pilate's thrice-repeated exoneration of Jesus (cf. 19:4, 6) stands in blatant contrast with the actual death sentence pronounced in def- erence to the Jewish authorities.

It is your custom for me to release to you one prisoner at the time of the Passover (18:39). Literally, "at Passover."[577] There is little extrabiblical evidence for the cus- tom of releasing one prisoner at Passover. The practice may go back to Hasmonean times and may have been continued by the Romans after taking over Palestine.[578] The release probably served as a gesture of goodwill designed to lessen political antagonism and to assure people that "no one coming to Jerusalem would be caught in the midst of political strife."[579] One mishnaic passage, which stipulates that the Passover lamb may be slaugh- tered for a variety of people whose actual condition is uncertain, including "one whom they have promised to bring out of prison" (*m. Pesaḥ.* 8:6), suggests that such releases were common enough to warrant legislation. Roman law provided for two kinds of amnesty: pardoning a condemned criminal (*indulgentia*) and

acquitting someone prior to the verdict (*abolitio*); in Jesus' case, the latter would have been in view.[580]

No, not him! Give us Barabbas! (18:40). Generally, Zealot-style political extrem- ism was condemned. Yet here the Jews, at the instigation of the high priests, ask for the release of Barabbas, a terrorist, while calling for the death of Jesus of Nazareth, who has renounced all politi- cal aspirations. Apart from the irony of making such a one out as a political threat, this demonstrates both the influ- ence the Sanhedrin had over the Jewish people at large as well as the Jewish authorities' determination to have Jesus executed in order to preserve their own privileged position (11:49–52).

Barabbas (18:40). Nothing is known of this man apart from the Gospel evidence. "Barabbas" is not a personal name but a patronymic (like Simon *Barjonah*, i.e., "son of Jonah") that occurs also in the Talmud.[581] Very possibly John saw in this designation a play on words: Bar-abbas literally means "son of the father," and John has presented Jesus as the Son of the Father throughout the Gospel.

Taken part in a rebellion (18:40). Barab- bas was a *lēstēs* (lit., "one who seizes plun- der"). This probably refers not merely to a robber but to an insurrectionist, one who destabilized the political system by terrorist activity (cf. Mark 15:7). Luke indicates that Barabbas "had been thrown into prison for an insurrection in the city, and or murder" (Luke 23:19). Josephus frequently uses the term for those engaged in revolutionary guerilla warfare, who, harboring mixed motives of plun- der and nationalism, roamed the Jewish countryside in those volatile days. The term applies particularly to the Zealots, who had made armed resistance against Rome the consuming passion of their lives and who were committed to attain to national liberty by all means, including risk of their own lives.[582] In Matthew 27:16, Barabbas is characterized as "notorious" (*episēmos*), a word used by Josephus to describe Zealot leadership (John, son of Levi; *J.W.* 2.21.1 §585).

Jesus Sentenced to Be Crucified (19:1–16a)

After the Jewish phase of the trial and Jesus' interrogation by Pilate, we now enter the sentencing stage. The day is April 3, A.D. 33,[583] and Jesus' execution is imminent. Despite the Roman governor's thrice-repeated "I find no basis for a charge against him," Pilate yields to Jewish demands for Jesus' crucifixion. The preferred Roman capital punishment for non-Roman citizens, crucifixion is one of the most cruel and tortuous form of death invented and inflicted in human history. The mob's raucous relentlessness in asking for Jesus' execution contrasts with Jesus' quiet dignity in submitting to his fate in keeping with the will of the Father. As John points out, the events surrounding Jesus' crucifixion both confirm Jesus' kingship and fulfill Scripture.

Pilate (19:1). See "Pontius Pilate" at 18:29.

Had him flogged (19:1). From least to most severe, there were three forms of flogging administered by the Romans: (1) the *fustigatio*, a beating given for smaller offences such as hooliganism, often accompanied by a severe warning; (2) the *flagellatio*, a more brutal flogging to which criminals were subjected whose offenses were more serious; and (3) the *verberatio*, the most terrible form of this kind of punishment, regularly associated with other reprisals such as crucifixion.[584]

In the present instance, the flogging probably in view is the least severe form, the *fustigatio*, which is intended in part to appease the Jews and in part to teach Jesus a lesson.[585] After the sentence of crucifixion, Jesus is scourged again, this time in the most severe form, the *verber-*

▶ **Illegalities in Jesus' Trial Surfacing in John**

1a. Jewish trial before Annas
1. Jesus is questioned about his disciples and his teaching (18:19); but first witnesses must be produced to establish an accused person's guilt.
2. Jesus is struck in the face (18:22); he challenges his accusers to furnish testimony of actual wrongdoing (18:23).

1b. Jewish trial before Caiaphas
1. No details are provided by John (cf. 18:24, 28), so no illegalities can be determined from his account alone.

2. Roman trial before Pilate
1. No charges are brought against Jesus (18:29); the Jews merely call him a criminal they want to have executed (18:30–31). Pilate reiterates three times that he finds no basis for a charge against Jesus (18:37; 19:4, 6; similarly, Luke 23:4, 14, 22).
2. No witnesses are ever produced.
3. Jesus never actually stands trial.
4. The verdict is clearly based on political expediency, not evidence.

atio. This explains why Jesus is too weak to carry his own cross very far (see comments on 19:17). Also, the nearness of the special Sabbath means that the agony of crucifixion must be kept short in order not to interfere with religious festivities (19:31–33).[586]

A crown of thorns (19:2). Apparently, some branches are twisted together from the long spikes of the date palm or from the common thornbush (Isa. 34:13; Nah. 1:10),[587] shaped into a mock "crown," the radiant *stephanos* (Lat. *corona*) that adorns rulers' heads on many coins of Jesus' time.[588] The crown is also reminiscent of depictions of oriental kings worshiped as gods.[589] These thorns, up to several inches long, would sink into the victim's skull, which caused blood to gush out and distort a person's face, resulting in considerable pain.

A purple robe (19:2). Probably a military cloak is used as a mock royal robe.[590] The Matthean parallel (27:28) refers to a "scarlet robe," a red chlamys or outer cloak worn by the emperor, minor officials, and soldiers alike. John uses the term *himation*, which denotes a person's "outer clothing" or "robe." As in Mark 15:17, John gives the robe's color as purple, the imperial color (1 Macc. 8:14); yet in the book of Revelation, "purple and scarlet" are mentioned side by side (Rev. 17:4; 18:16). Because purple dye (taken from shellfish) was expensive, a genuine purple cloak was not as easily obtained as a red one.

Hail (19:3). The soldiers' greeting mimics the "Ave Caesar" extended to the Roman emperor. Their mocking of Jesus as king seems to copy scenes frequently featured on stage and in Roman circuses.[591] The game of "mock king," scratchings of which are preserved on the stone pavement of the fortress of Antonia (see comments on 19:13), was played by soldiers during the Roman Saturnalia.

Philo tells of people's mocking a certain madman named Carabas in the gymnasium of Alexandria in A.D. 38, who, dressed in a rug for a royal robe with a sheet of byblus as a diadem on his head and a papyrus "scepter" in his hand, received "homage" and was saluted as king and hailed as "lord," apparently in imitation of familiar pantomimes (*Flaccus* 36–42; c. A.D. 50).

Dio Chrysostom (A.D. 40–120) refers to a Persian custom in which "they take one of their prisoners, who has been condemned to death, set him upon the king's throne, give him the royal apparel, and permit him to give orders. . . . But after that they strip and scourge him and then hang him," for the purpose of showing "that foolish and wicked men frequently acquire this royal power and title and then after a season of wanton insolence come to a most shameful and wretched end" (*Regn.* 4.67–68).

Here is the man (19:5). "Man" may hark back to Old Testament messianic passages such as Zechariah 6:12: "Here is the

◀ *left*

CROWN OF THORNS

The branches of this tree contains the kind of thorns that may have been used in the construction of the degrading crown.

man whose name is the Branch."[592] In classical literature, the expression occasionally means "the poor fellow," "the poor creature."[593] To be sure, in his mock regal garments, Jesus must have been a heart-rending sight. In John's context, Pilate's statement may also accentuate Jesus' humanity.

You take him and crucify him (19:6). Pilate here uses sarcasm; he knows full well that the Jews do not have the authority to impose the death penalty; if they did, they would stone rather than crucify Jesus (see comments on 18:31).

We have a law, and according to that law he must die, because he claimed to be the Son of God (19:7). A Roman prefect was responsible both for keeping peace and for maintaining local law. "We have a law" may refer to Leviticus 24:16: "Anyone who blasphemes the name of the LORD must be put to death." Jesus has frequently been accused of blasphemy (John 5:18; 8:59; 10:31, 33); yet in both the Old Testament and other Jewish literature the claim of being God's Son need not be blasphemous and may refer to the anointed king of Israel (2 Sam. 7:14; Ps. 2:7; 89:26–27) or to the Messiah (4QFlor; see comments on 1:49).[594] Even Israel could be called God's son (Ex. 4:22; Hos. 11:1). In Greco-Roman circles, "son of god" frequently occurs in inscriptions as a title for the emperor, especially Augustus.[595]

When Pilate heard this, he was even more afraid (19:8). Alternatively, "very afraid." While Roman officials may have been cynical, they were also often deeply superstitious. In pagan ears, the designation "son of god" conjured up notions of "divine men," persons believed to enjoy certain divine powers. Two instances of such fear by a judge of one accused whom he came to recognize as a higher being are relayed by Philostratus (b. A.D. 172).[596] Ancient pagans concluded commonly enough that "the gods have come down to us in human form" (Acts 14:11). If Jesus was a "son of a god," Pilate may have reasoned, he might incur the wrath of the gods for having Jesus flogged (cf. Matt. 27:19).

Alternatively, the root of Pilate's apprehension may have been political. He may have feared that the Jewish leaders would report to Rome that he failed to respect local religious customs, which was an accepted principle of provincial administration (see the later incident recounted in Philo, *Embassy* 299–305 and the parallel in Josephus, *J.W.* 2.9.2–3 §§169–74).[597] This depiction of Pilate hardly fits with Josephus's portrayal of the early years of the Roman governor's tenure, where he ruthlessly broke up riots and stubbornly resisted Jewish demands. Yet John's account fits perfectly with Pilate's tenuous position subsequent to the execution of his mentor Aelius Sejanus in A.D. 31.[598] Another pertinent issue is the designation "friend of Caesar" (see comments on 19:12).

ECCE HOMO ARCH

An arch built by the emperor Hadrian in A.D. 135. It is located on the Via Dolorosa and is identified by tradition as the site where Pilate presented Christ to the crowd saying, "Behold the man!"

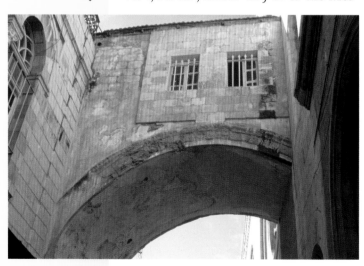

The palace (19:9). See comments on 18:28.

Where do you come from? (19:9). In a parallel recorded by Josephus, the Roman procurator Albinus summons the prophet Jesus, son of Ananias, who had proclaimed the destruction of Jerusalem and the temple, inquiring who he was and where he came from (*J.W.* 6.5.5 §305). During the course of his ministry, Jesus' origins have frequently been at issue in his dealings with his opponents (e.g., 7:27–28; 8:14; 9:29–30). On a literal level, Jesus' Galilean provenance places him under Herod Antipas's jurisdiction (cf. Luke 23:6–7). In the Johannine context, however, there are clearly spiritual overtones as well (18:36–37).

Jesus gave him no answer (19:9). Jesus' silence brings to mind the Suffering Servant of Isaiah: "As a sheep before her shearers is silent, so he did not open his mouth" (Isa. 53:7; cf. 1 Peter 2:22–23). If Nicodemus and the Jewish authorities could not understand where Jesus has come from, how can this Roman governor be expected to grasp Jesus' true origin? The Greco-Roman pantheon was replete with gods having sexual union with women resulting in human offspring; a mind saturated with such myths would have grave difficulty comprehending Jesus' relationship with his Father.

There was also a Greco-Roman tradition, harking back to Socrates, holding that silence constituted a virtue when faced by accusers. Thus Philostratus writes, "For my own part I am sure that silence constitutes a fourth excellence much required in a law-court" (*Life of Apollonius* 8.2; early third cent. A.D.). However, Philostratus also acknowledged that remaining silent did not prove advantageous to Socrates. In the same passage, Philostratus records one person's objection, "And what good did it do him, seeing that he died just because he would say nothing?" (see comments on John 18:38).

I have power (19:10). According to Josephus, Coponius, the first Roman governor of Judea (A.D. 6–9), "was sent out as

▶ Friend of Caesar

Pilate had reason to fear the threat of the Jewish leaders—who had conveyed their displeasure with Pilate to the emperor on earlier occasions—for Tiberius was known to act decisively when suspicions were cast on the conduct or loyalty of his subordinates.[A-32] By the time of Vespasian (A.D. 69–71), "friend of Caesar" had become virtually an official title; even in Jesus' day, the term may have had semi-technical force.[A-33]

It is possible that Pilate acquired "friend of Caesar" status through his mentor Sejanus,[A-34] especially in light of Tacitus's statement that "the closer a man's intimacy with Sejanus, the stronger his claim to the emperor's friendship" (*Ann.* 6.8). But since Sejanus has recently fallen from grace (executed October 18, A.D. 31), Pilate has ample reason to be concerned that his favored status with the emperor will likewise be removed.

In Hellenistic times, "friends of the king" was a special group honored by the ruler for their loyalty and entrusted by him with responsible tasks.[A-35] In the early empire, the "friends of Augustus" were a well-known group. Later, the inscription PHILOKAISAR, "friend of Caesar," frequently occurs on coins of Herod Agrippa I (A.D. 37–44; cf. Philo, *Flacc.* 40).

procurator, entrusted by Augustus with full powers, including the infliction of capital punishment" (*J.W.* 2.8.1 §117).

From above (19:11). In good Jewish manner, Jesus here uses "from above" as an expression for God.

From then on, Pilate tried to set Jesus free (19:12). Apparently Pilate remains unconvinced of Jesus' guilt. Perhaps also owing to his superstitious nature and because he is impressed by Jesus' courage in the face of death (considered virtuous in the Greco-Roman world), he is reluctant to have Jesus crucified. Yet, as in other instances, Pilate would eventually yield to Jewish demands (Philo, *Embassy*, 38.301–2).

Friend of Caesar (19:12). See "Friend of Caesar."

Caesar (19:12). Originally the cognomen of Gaius Julius Caesar, the name was taken over by Augustus, Caesar's great-nephew, and his successors. The shift from proper name to title (equivalent to "emperor") had certainly occurred

by the time of Vespasian and the Flavian rulers, who had no blood relations to the Julian dynasty. But an earlier date (supported also by the present reference) is likely. While Tiberius and Caligula could claim the name Caesar by virtue of adoption, Claudius could not. Moreover, already under Augustus, Judean coinage bore the name KAISAROS and a date, supporting the notion that "Caesar" functioned as an imperial title in Jesus' day.

The judge's seat (19:13). The Greek term *bēma* (originally "platform") denotes a judge's bench. This *bēma* or *sella curilis* normally stood in the forecourt of the governor's residence. It was elevated so that the judge could look over the spectators. Matthew depicts the entire trial with Pilate seated on the judge's seat and Jesus standing before him. Similar accounts are given of trials before the governors Festus (Acts 25:6, 17) and Florus (Josephus, *J.W.* 2.14.8 §301).

The Stone Pavement (19:13). The Greek term *lithostrōtos* may refer to different kinds of stone pavement, ranging from

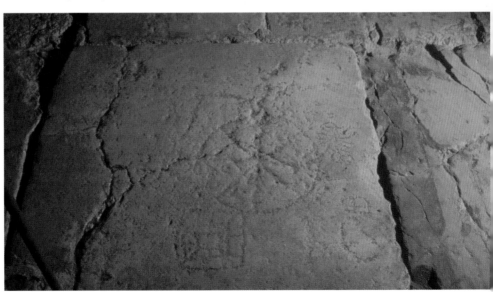

PAVEMENT FROM THE FORTRESS OF ANTONIA

The "Lithostratos"— a Roman era pavement stone found near the location of the fortress where Jesus carried his cross.

simple ones consisting of identical pieces to elaborate ones of fine mosaic. In light of the pavement's location in front of the governor's residence, where traffic would have been heavy, a simple pavement of large stones may be the most likely. A paved court measuring about 2,300 square yards has been excavated on the lower level of the fortress of Antonia, one of the two possible sites of the governor's residence (the other is Herod's Palace in the northwest part of the Upper City; see comments on 18:28).[599] The blocks making up this pavement are more than a yard square and a foot thick. This kind of structure may well have been famous as "the stone pavement." However, it is unclear whether the excavated pavement was part of the fortress of Antonia in Jesus' time.

Which in Aramaic is Gabbatha (19:13).
The meaning of "Gabath" (cf. Gibeah, birthplace of Saul; 1 Sam. 11:4) is given as "hill" by the Jewish historian Josephus (*J.W.* 5.2.1 §51).

Day of Preparation of Passover Week (19:14).
Some argue that "day of Preparation" refers to the day preceding *Passover*, that is, the day on which preparations for Passover are made (in the present case, Thursday morning). If so, John indicates that Jesus is sent to be executed at the time Passover lambs are slaughtered in the temple. The Synoptists, however, clearly portray Jesus and his disciples as celebrating the Passover the night prior to the crucifixion. Moreover, Matthew, Mark, Luke, and Josephus alike use "Preparation Day" to refer to the day preceding the Sabbath (Matt. 27:62; Mark 15:42; Luke 23:54; *Ant.* 16.6.2 §§163–64). The term used here should therefore be taken to refer to the day of

preparation *for the Sabbath* (i.e., Friday; cf. *Did.* 8:1; *Mart. Pol.* 7:1).[600]

If this is accurate, *tou pascha* means not "of the Passover" but "of Passover Week" (cf. NIV). Indeed, "Passover" may refer to the day of the actual Passover meal or, as in the present case, the entire Passover week (both Passover day and Feast of Unleavened Bread).[601] "Day of Preparation of Passover Week" is thus best taken to refer to the day of preparation for the Sabbath (i.e., Friday) of Passover week (see comments on 19:31). Thus all four Gospels concur that Jesus' Last Supper was a Passover meal eaten on Thursday evening (by Jewish reckoning, the onset of Friday).

About the sixth hour (19:14).
Reckoning time from dawn to dark, "sixth hour" is about noon. Mark 15:25 indicates that Jesus' crucifixion takes place at the "third hour," that is, about 9:00 A.M. But since people related the estimated time to the closest three-hour mark, any time between 9:00 A.M. and noon may have led one person to say an event occurred at the third (9:00 A.M.) or the sixth hour (noon).[602]

We have no king but Caesar (19:15).
The Old Testament frequently reiterates that Yahweh alone is the true king of Israel (e.g., Judg. 8:23; 1 Sam. 8:7). None of the foreign overlords qualified, be it Persian, Greek, or Roman. As Isaiah affirms, "O LORD, our God, other lords

CAESAR

A silver denarius with the image of the emperor Tiberius (A.D. 14–37).

besides you have ruled over us, but your name alone do we honor" (Isa. 26:13). The very feast of Passover, which the Jews are in the process of celebrating, is built on God's unique and supreme role in the life of the nation. The eleventh of the ancient Eighteen Benedictions prays, "Reign over us, you alone." Yet here, by professing to acknowledge Caesar alone as their king, the Jewish leaders betray their entire national heritage as well as deny their own messianic expectations based on the promises of Scripture. See also comments on John 19:12.

Handed him over to them to be crucified (19:16). The usual form of death sentence was *Ibis in crucem*, "On the cross you shall go" (Petronius, *Satyr.* 137). Latin literature usually uses the indirect expression *duci iussit*, "He ordered him to be led off" (e.g., Pliny, *Ep.* 10.96: "ordered . . . to be executed").[603] Upon pronouncement of the sentence, the criminal was first scourged, then executed (Josephus, *J.W.* 2.14.8 §308: "scourge before his tribunal [*bēma*] and nail to the cross"). The present statement is echoed by Tertullian, who says that the Jews extorted from Pilate a sentence giving Jesus up "*to them* to be crucified" (*Apol.* 21.18).

The Crucifixion (19:16b–27)

The soldiers took charge of Jesus (19:16). It was at this point that Jesus receives his second flogging, the brutal *verberatio*. In this form of punishment, the victim was stripped naked, tied to a post, and beaten by several soldiers with a whip "whose leather thongs were fitted with pieces of bone or lead or other metal." The scourgings were so severe that persons subjected to this torture sometimes died; others were left with

their bones and entrails exposed.[604] Josephus reports that a certain Jesus, son of Ananias, was brought before Albinus and "flayed to the bone with scourges" (*J.W.* 6.5.3 §304). Eusebius writes that certain martyrs at the time of Polycarp were "lacerated by scourges even to the innermost veins and arteries, so that the hidden inward parts of the body, both their bowels and their members, were exposed to view" (*Eccl. Hist.* 4.15.4).

Carrying his own cross (19:17). As Plutarch attests, "Each criminal who goes to execution must carry his own cross on his back" (*Sera Num. Vind.* 554 A/B). Artemidorus (2d cent. A.D.) likewise affirms that "the man who is to be nailed to it [the cross] carries it beforehand" (*Onir.* 2.56), as does Chariton (c. 25 B.C.– A.D. 50), who tells of the crucifixion of sixteen men, who "were duly brought out, chained together at foot and neck, each carrying his own cross. The executioners added this grim public spectacle to the requisite penalty as a deterrent to

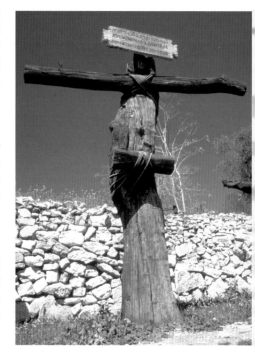

others so minded" (*Chaereas and Callirhoe* 4.2.7).

The person would carry his cross to the site of crucifixion, where the upright beam (*stipes*, which was about nine feet high) had already been staked into the ground. There the criminal would be made to lie with his back on the ground, his arms stretched out, and his hands, wrists, or forearms tied or nailed to the crossbar.[605] After this, the crossbar was stood up and affixed to the upright beam. To this beam, the person's feet were tied or nailed, often not very high off the ground, whereby the legs were bent and twisted so that a single nail was driven through both heels. An optional piece of wood (*sedecula*) served further to increase the victim's agony. Later Jewish literature draws parallels between the crucifixion and Isaac's carrying the wood "like one carries his stake [=cross] on his shoulder" (*Gen. Rab.* 56:3 on Gen. 22:6).

He went out (19:17). Jewish custom prescribed that stonings were to take place outside the camp or city.[606] By extension, the same principle applied to crucifixions (cf. Heb. 13:12).

The place of the Skull (which in Aramaic is called Golgotha) (19:17). Greek "Golgotha" transliterates the Aramaic expression for skull. The Latin equivalent (found in the Vulgate of all four Gospels) is "Calvary." The location may have derived its name from its skull-like appearance. A site just outside Gennath Gate, not far from the Church of the Holy Sepulchre, is the most likely option.[607] See comments on 19:13.

They crucified him (19:18). In ancient times, crucifixion was synonymous with horror and shame, a death inflicted on slaves (Cicero, *In Verrem* 2.5.65.168), bandits (Josephus, *J.W.* 2.13.2 §253), prisoners of war (*J.W.* 5.11.1 §451), and revolutionaries (*Ant.* 17.10.10 §295).[608] Josephus terms it "the most pitiable of deaths" (*J.W.* 7.6.4 §203; cf. 1.97), Cicero calls it "that cruel and disgusting penalty" (*In Verrem* 2.5.64.165). Those crucified were made a public spectacle, often being

GOLGOTHA

The center of this picture of a model of ancient Jerusalem focuses on Golgotha, where the Church of the Holy Sepulcher is today.

affixed to crosses in bizarre positions, and their bodies left to be devoured by vultures.[609] No Roman citizen could be subjected to this terrible punishment without sanction by the emperor.

For hours (if not days), the person would hang in the heat of the sun, stripped naked and struggling to breathe. In order to avoid asphyxiation, he must push himself up with his legs and pull with his arms, triggering muscle spasms causing unimaginable pain. The end would come through heart failure, brain damage caused by reduced oxygen supply, suffocation, or shock.[610] Atrocious physical agony, length of torment, and public shame combined to make crucifixion a most terrible form of death. The remains of a crucified man aged 24–28 years dating roughly to Jesus' day were found in north Jerusalem in 1968.[611] The crucifixion of Jesus is corroborated by extrabiblical writers. For example, according to the Roman historian Tacitus, Jesus was "executed in the reign of Tiberius by the procurator Pontius Pilate" (*Ann.* 44.3). The Jewish historian Josephus likewise reports that "Pilate . . . condemned [Jesus] to the cross" (*Ant.* 18.63–64).

With him two others—one on each side and Jesus in the middle (19:18). See Isaiah 53:12: "numbered with the transgressors." Matthew and Mark identify these two others as bandits (*lēstai*; Matt. 27:38 par.), possibly insurrectionists like Barabbas (Mark 15:7). While later Jewish legislation forbade condemning two persons on the same day (*m. Sanh.* 6:4: "two ought not to be judged in one day"), it is unlikely that this law was already in effect in Jesus' day, and if so, whether it would have been honored by the Romans. Earlier, the Jewish high priest

Alexander Jannaeus (88 B.C.) had crucified eight hundred persons at the same time (Josephus, *J.W.* 1.10.2 §97). The evangelists may find Jesus' crucifixion between two criminals reminiscent of Psalm 22:16: "a band of evil men has encircled me." According to Jewish convention, "when three persons were present, custom prescribed that the most honored take his place in the middle."[612]

Pilate had a notice prepared (19:19). Literally, "Pilate wrote a notice." The NIV rendering makes clear that Pilate probably did not write this notice himself but used the services of a literate slave.[613]

A notice prepared and fastened to the cross (19:19). This "notice" (the Latin word is *titulus*) was written on a board whitened with gypsum (*sanis, leukoma*). According to the Roman historian Suetonius, its purpose was the public exposition of the person's specific crime, presumably in order to deter others from committing similar acts. Thus the emperor Domitian had an unfortunate spectator dragged from his seat and thrown into the arena to dogs, with this placard (*titulus*): "A favorer of the Thracians who spoke impiously" (*Domitian* 10.1). However, while instances are known in which a person carried the notice around his neck or had it carried in front of him—such as "Attalus the Christian" during Marcus Aurelius's reign in the amphitheater in Lyons (Eusebius, *Eccl. Hist.* 6.44)—there is little or no evidence for the custom of affixing it to a cross.

Many of the Jews read this sign (19:20). The literacy level among first-century Palestinian Jews was high. "A pious Jew [in Jesus' day] . . . could read and write."[614]

The place where Jesus was crucified was near the city (19:20). See comments on 19:17.

The sign was written in Aramaic, Latin and Greek (19:20). If the order given reflects the order in which the inscriptions were written, Aramaic, the language most widely understood by the Jewish population of Palestine, would have taken pride of place. Of the three languages, Aramaic (see comments on 5:2) was the language commonly in use in Judea (cf. Acts 21:40); Latin was the official language of the Roman occupying force; and Greek was the "international language" of the empire, understood by most Diaspora Jews as well as by Gentiles.[615] By writing the sign in those three languages, the Romans ensured widest possible circulation of its contents, as a deterrent to every segment of the population.[616]

Aramaic: ישוע הנצרי מלך היהודים
Latin: IESUS NAZARENUS REX
    IUDAEORUM
Greek: ΙΗΣΟΥΣ Ο ΝΑΖΩΡΑΙΟΣ Ο
    ΒΑΣΙΛΕΥΣ ΤΩΝ ΙΟΥΔΑΙΩΝ

What I have written, I have written (19:22). "No longer faced with the possibility of mob unrest or a complaint to Tiberius, Pilate returns to his characteristic lack of cooperation."[617] Similar

words are recorded of the Seleucid ruler Demetrius: "And the things we have guaranteed to you have been guaranteed" (1 Macc. 13:38). This grammatical construction is also found in the Old Testament (Gen. 43:14: "if I am bereaved, I am bereaved"; Est. 4:16: "if I perish, I perish") and Jewish literature (*b. Menaḥ.* 3a: "what he has offered, he has offered"; *b. Ketub.* 96a: "what she seized, she seized"; *b. Yebam.* 106b: "what he did is done"). Similar phrases are also found in a Roman context.[618] The request of the Jewish authorities clashes with the Roman respect for written documents, a legal decision that could not be reversed. For John, Pilate's firmness may again relate to his speaking better than he knew, for Jesus is the King of kings and Lord of lords, and there is no other.

They took his clothes (19:23). In a collection of Roman law from the first century B.C. through the third century A.D. compiled in A.D. 530, we read that "on [a man's] condemnation to lose life . . . [his] property is confiscated." However, "neither may torturers claim these things of their own accord for themselves, nor their assistants ask for them, from those being stripped at the moment of execution; and governors . . . may . . . reward soldiers if they have performed bravely" (Justinian, *Digesta* 48.20).[619] Thus it appears that the soldiers were to take Jesus' clothes into custody but not necessarily arrogate them for themselves.

Romans normally stripped crucified persons naked. It is possible, however, that in deference to the Jewish dislike for public nudity Jesus was left with his underclothing (a dispute regarding whether a man about to be stoned should be completely stripped or not, involving R. Yehudah [c. A.D. 150], is recorded in

A BILINGUAL INSCRIPTION

This inscription is part of the mosaic floor of the fifth-century A.D. Jewish synagogue at Tiberias. The Greek (top) and Hebrew (bottom) text honor the major donor for the construction of the synagogue.

◀ *left*

m. Sanh. 6:3). This is suggested by the word *himatia*, which generally refers to the outer garment in distinction from the undergarment (called *chitōn*). People of that day wore a loin cloth, undergarments, the outer garment, a belt, a head covering, and sandals.[620]

Dividing them into four shares, one for each of them (19:23). It is unclear whether the soldiers overstepped legal bounds when dividing up Jesus' robe among themselves (see previous comment). "Four shares" indicates that the execution squad consisted of four soldiers, half the amount of the basic unit of the Roman army (i.e., eight soldiers sharing a tent [*contubernium*]), which was sometimes assigned to particular tasks (in Acts 12:4 Peter is "guarded by four squads of four soldiers each").[621] According to the Synoptics, a centurion was present as well. It is possible that additional soldiers were involved in preparing the other two men for crucifixion.

This garment was seamless, woven in one piece from top to bottom (19:23). Using a seamless piece of cloth precluded the possibility that two materials had been joined together, something forbidden in the Old Testament law. Such a garment could be woven without exceptional skill

and was not necessarily a luxury item. Josephus notes that the high priestly robe (*chitōn*) was "not composed of two pieces . . . [but] one long woven cloth" (*Ant.* 3.7.4 §161; cf. Ex. 28:31; Rev. 1:13), while Philo uses a robe as symbolic of the Logos, which binds all things together in unity (*Flight* 110–12). In the Old Testament, it was Joseph who was stripped of his robe (Gen. 37:3, 23), which in later Jewish thought was interpreted in salvific terms (*Gen. Rab.* 84:8).

That the scripture might be fulfilled (19:24). The passage referred to is Psalm 22:18.[622] On the "fulfillment quotations" in the latter half of John's Gospel, crescendoing in the passion narrative, see comments on John 12:38.

Near the cross of Jesus (19:25). Crucified persons may have been surrounded by family, friends, and relatives. According to one Talmudic passage, a rabbi stood under the gallows of a hanged disciple and wept (*b. B. Meṣiʿa* 83b).[623]

His mother, his mother's sister, Mary the wife of Clopas, and Mary Magdalene (19:25). The Greek wording allows for the reference to be taken to two, three, or four. The wording adopted by the NIV (which represents the most likely alternative) interprets there to be four women: (1) Mary, Jesus' mother (here, as elsewhere, not named in this Gospel; see comments on 2:1–5); (2) his mother's sister (perhaps Salome, the mother of the sons of Zebedee mentioned in Matthew and Mark); (3) Mary the wife of Clopas (cf. Luke 24:18?); and (4) Mary Magdalene (John 20:1–18; cf. Luke 8:2–3).

"Dear woman, here is your son." . . . "Here is your mother" (19:26–27). Jesus' mother, who is almost certainly

---

LOTS

Dice made of bone found in Jerusalem and dating to the early Roman period.

▼

widowed and probably in her early fifties with little or no personal income, was dependent on Jesus, her oldest son. In keeping with the biblical injunction to honor one's parents (Ex. 20:12; Deut. 5:16), Jesus makes provision for his mother subsequent to his death.

In the LXX, the adoption formula is generally "you are" rather than "here is," as in the present passage.[624] In antiquity, a dying person would ordinarily entrust his mother to another with a direct charge, such as the following: "I leave to you my mother to be taken care of."[625] Thus the second-century writer Lucian writes, "The bequest of Eudamidas was, 'I leave to Aretaeus my mother to support and cherish in her old age'" (*Toxaris* 22).

Dear woman (19:26). See comments on 2:4.

The Death of Jesus (19:28–37)

So that the Scripture would be fulfilled, Jesus said, "I am thirsty" (19:28). The allusion may be to Psalm 69:21: "They . . . gave me vinegar for my thirst." Another relevant psalm is 22:15: "My tongue sticks to the roof of my mouth." Psalm 69:21 is also cited in the Qumran hymn 1QH 12:11: "In their thirst they have given them vinegar to drink."

Wine vinegar (19:29). This cheap, sour wine was used by soldiers to quench their thirst (Mark 15:36; cf. Ps. 69:21). It differs from the "wine mixed with myrrh" Jesus was offered (and refused) on the way to the cross (Mark 15:23). While the latter was a sedative, "wine vinegar" prolonged life and therefore pain.

Put the sponge on a stalk of the hyssop plant (19:29). Hyssop is "a small bushy plant that can grow out of cracks in walls, a plant that 1 Kings 4:33 classifies as the humblest of shrubs."[626] It was used for the sprinkling of blood on the doorpost at the original Passover (Ex. 12:22). In the present instance, the branches at the end of the stalk would have formed a little "nest" into which the soggy sponge is placed. Since crucified people were not raised very high, the soldiers have to lift the stalk barely above their own heads.

Gave up (19:30). The same verb is used in Isaiah 53:12 to describe the death of the Suffering Servant: "His soul was *handed over* to death . . . and he was *handed over* because of their sins."

Day of Preparation (19:31). See comments on 19:14.

Special Sabbath (19:31). The Sabbath was special because it was the Sabbath of Passover week. An important sheaf offering was made on this day as well (Lev. 23:11).[627]

Because the Jews did not want the bodies left on the crosses during the Sabbath (19:31). The Romans left crucified persons on their crosses until death ensued (which could take days) and their bodies were devoured by vultures. Nevertheless, Roman law does seem to have allowed burial of crucified people, as a passage attributed to the first-century A.D. rhetorician Quintilian indicates: "But bodies are cut down from crosses, executioners do not prevent executed criminals from being buried" (*Decl.* 6.9; 2d cent. A.D.?). There is also evidence that at times, especially during feast days, bodies were taken down and given to relatives (Philo, *Flaccus* 83). The Jews' attitude was based on Deuteronomy 21:22–23 (cf. Josh. 8:29), according to which bodies of hanged criminals were not to defile the land by remaining on a tree overnight. According to Josephus, application of this passage was later extended to cover the crucified (*J.W.* 4.5.2 §317: "Even malefactors who have been sentenced to crucifixion are taken down and buried before sunset"; cf. Gal. 3:13).

They asked Pilate to have the legs broken and the bodies taken down (19:31). In order to hasten death, the crucifieds' legs (and sometimes other bones) would be smashed with an iron mallet, a practice called *crurifragium* ("breaking of bones"). This prevented the person from prolonging his life by pushing himself up with his legs to be able to breathe. Arm strength soon failed, and asphyxiation ensued. In the case of the body of a man crucified in the first century found north of Jerusalem (see comments on 19:18 above), one leg was fractured, the other broken to pieces.[628]

Pierced Jesus' side . . . bringing a sudden flow of blood and water (19:34).[629] The spear may have pierced Jesus' heart, resulting, either directly or via chest and lung, in the flow of blood and water.[630] The flow of blood and water underscores that Jesus died as a full human being.[631] The parallel 1 John 5:6–8 refers to "the Spirit, the water and the blood"; Jesus gave up his spirit when he died (John 19:30), leaving behind blood and water.

John also may be alluding to Exodus 17 and especially 19:6: "Strike the rock, and water will come out of it for the people to drink" (cf. Num. 20:11). Later Jewish thought held that Moses struck the rock twice, and that it yielded first blood, then water (*Ex. Rab.* 3:13 on Ex. 4:9). An allusion to the Passover may also be in view,[632] consisting of (1) the hyssop

(John 19:29); (2) the unbroken bones (19:33, 36); and (3) the mingled blood (19:34).[633] Moreover, Jewish sacrificial law required that the victim's blood not be congealed but flow freely at the moment of death so it could be sprinkled (*m. Pesaḥ.* 5:3, 5). Jewish law also insisted that the priest "slit the [lamb's] heart and let out its blood" (*m. Tamid* 4:2).

With a spear (19:34). Roman soldiers used primarily two kinds of weapons: a short sword for close combat, and a lance or javelin for attacks from a distance. The lance (*pilum*) was about three and a half feet long and was made up of an iron point or spearhead (*lonchē*) joined to a shaft of light wood.[634] Later the term *lonchē* (the word used in the present passage) came to be used for a spear or lance itself.

The scripture would be fulfilled: "Not one of his bones will be broken" (19:36). Remarkably, Jesus did not only escape the breaking of his legs (unlike those crucified with him), his body was also pierced by a spear, yet again without sustaining bone damage. Two sets of Scripture converge: (1) Psalm 34:20, depicting God's care for the righteous man: "He protects all his bones, not one of them will be broken"; and (2) Exodus 12:46 and Numbers 9:12, specifying that no bone of the Passover lamb may be broken (applied to Jesus in 1 Cor. 5:7; 1 Peter 1:19). Moreover, "in Jewish thought disfiguration was an obstacle to resurrection," which may further explain why John takes pains to stress that no bone was broken.[635]

As another scripture says, "They will look on the one they have pierced" (19:37). The passage in view is plainly Zechariah 12:10 (cf. Rev. 1:7). While the Hebrew of this passage appears to refer to the piercing of Yahweh himself (fig., with sorrow), later messianic interpretation developed this notion into the belief that the Messiah the son of Joseph would be pierced and people would look to Yahweh (*b. Sukkah* 52a). John, for his part, saw the fulfillment of Zechariah 12:10 at the crucifixion as confirmation that the Messiah was Jesus (cf. John 20:31). A related Old Testament figure that may have been in John's mind is that of the Suffering Servant of Isaiah 53:5, 10, who was "pierced for our transgressions" and "crushed" and "caused to suffer."

The Burial of Jesus (19:38–42)

Joseph of Arimathea (19:38). A member of the Sanhedrin (Mark 15:43; Luke 23:50), Joseph is wealthy (Matt. 27:57; cf. Isa. 53:9) yet "waiting for the kingdom of God" (Mark 15:43; Luke 23:51). Joseph's intervention fulfills another Scripture, "He was assigned a grave with the wicked, and with the rich in his death" (Isa. 53:9).[636] Of the several suggestions for the location of Arimathea,

none is in Galilee, which would make Joseph one of Jesus' Judean disciples.[637]

Asked Pilate for the body of Jesus (19:38). The Romans usually handed over executed criminals to the closest relative. In the case of crucifixion, however, the rotting bodies were left to the vultures, both as a stern public warning and as the epitome of shame. The Jews, by contrast, buried even such people; yet rather than allowing their corpses to desecrate previously buried ones (the result if placed in a family tomb), a separate burial site was provided just outside the city.[638] Doubtless the Jewish authorities' request that the bodies be taken down (19:31) presupposes this arrangement. Joseph of Arimathea, however, uses his position as member of the Sanhedrin to gain access to Pilate and to secure a more dignified burial for his master. Joseph's act takes some courage, since Jesus has been accused of subversive activities both against the Jews and the Romans.

Nicodemus (19:39). Like Joseph of Arimathea, Nicodemus is a member of the Sanhedrin, a "ruler" (see comments on 3:1; 7:50–52).

A mixture of myrrh and aloes, about seventy-five pounds (19:39). Literally, one hundred *litrai* (see comments on 12:3) or about sixty-five pounds (rather than seventy-five pounds as in the NIV). Myrrh, a fragrant resin used by Egyptians in embalming (Herodotus, *Hist.* 2.86; the Romans often cremated their dead), was turned by the Jews into a powder and mixed with aloes, itself a powder of aromatic sandalwood, with whom it is regularly associated in the Old Testament (cf. Ps. 45:8; Prov. 7:17; Song 4:14). In the Jewish context, the mixture was to overcome the smell of putrification. Judging from the narrative, Joseph takes care of legal matters while Nicodemus brings the spices. Very possibly, servants are used to carry the aromatic mixture, take Jesus' body down from the cross, transport it to the burial place, and prepare it for burial. During the times of Israel's monarchy, King Asa died and was laid on "a bier covered with spices and various blended perfumes" (2 Chron 16:14). Later, "five hundred servants carrying spices" participated in the funeral procession of Herod the Great (Josephus, *Ant.* 17.8.3 §199).

accordance with Jewish burial customs **(19:40).** "The two of them wrapped it" need not necessarily imply that Joseph and Nicodemus perform this task themselves. More likely, they use slaves in order not to contract ritual impurity (Num. 19:11: "unclean for seven days"), which would prevent them from celebrating the Passover (cf. John 18:28). Apparently, spices were spread along the linen wrappings (*othonia*; see comments on 11:44)[639] as well as underneath and perhaps around Jesus' body. Then the strips were wound around the corpse. Further spices may have been spread near the entrance of the tomb. In Jesus' day, burial clothes still tended to be luxurious; in around A.D. 90, R. Gamaliel II simplified procedures by having the dead buried in simple linen robes (*sadin*). Remarkably, the washing of Jesus' body, the most important service rendered to a dead person, is not mentioned by any of the evangelists.

The two of them wrapped it, with the spices, in strips of linen. This was in

At the place where Jesus was crucified (19:41). See comments on 19:17, 20.

▶

GARDEN TOMB

An alternative (although unlikely) site of Jesus' tomb. The tomb is associated with the site that General Charles Gordon suggested as the location of Golgotha in 1883.

There was a garden (19:41). The term for "garden" (*kēpos*) points to a more elaborate structure, such as an orchard or a plantation (cf. 18:1: "olive grove"; note the later mention of a gardener in 20:15). Later Jewish legislation discouraged the planting of fruit trees near burial sites. In Old Testament times, Manasseh king of Judah was buried in the family tomb in his "palace garden" (2 Kings 21:18), as was his son and successor Amon (2 Kings 21:26: "buried in his grave in the garden of Uzza [=Uzziah?]"). According to Nehemiah 3:16 (LXX; cf. Acts 2:29), the popular tomb of David was situated in a garden as well.

A new tomb, in which no one had ever been laid (19:41). Burying a crucified person in a fresh tomb was doubtless less offensive to the Jewish authorities than using a grave that had previously been used (cf. 19:38). The location of the tomb is probably on the site of the Church of the Holy Sepulchre (built by Constantine) rather than the popular "garden tomb."[640] The vestiges of a nearby garden were still visible in Cyril of Jerusalem's day (c. A.D. 350): "It was a garden where he was crucified. For though it has now been most highly adorned with royal gifts, yet formerly it was a garden, and the signs and the remnants of this remain" (*Catechesis* 14.5). The tomb's proximity to Golgotha and its location in a garden concur with speculation that the site of the crucifixion is just outside the second north wall of the city (comments on 19:17, "he went out"). In fact, one of the four openings in the north wall was the Garden Gate ("Gennath"; cf. Josephus, *J.W.* 5.4.2 §147). This (prestigious) area also housed the tombs of the Hasmonean high priests John Hyrcanus and Alexander Jannaeus (*J.W.* 5.6.2 §259; 5.7.3 §304). For information on tombs in first-century Palestine, see comments on 11:38.

Jewish day of Preparation (19:42). See comments on 19:14.

Since the tomb was nearby, they laid Jesus there (19:42). Sabbath was rapidly approaching, when all work must cease, including that of carrying spices or transporting a corpse.[641] While it was allowed for a dead body to remain without burial overnight if time was needed to obtain "a coffin and burial clothes" (*m. Sanh.* 6:5), the nearby tomb was a welcome instance of divine providence.

The Empty Tomb (20:1–9)

It is now Sunday morning, "the first day of the week." Mary Magdalene and several other women decide to attend to some unfinished business; carrying spices, they head for the tomb to anoint Jesus' body.

Mary Magdalene (20:1). Earlier, Mary was found near the cross as part of a group of women (19:25). Her surname suggests that she is from Magdala on the northwest shore of the Sea of Galilee, approximately seven miles southwest of Capernaum. Mary's witness was not used as significantly in the preaching of the early church as that of Peter, doubtless because evidence provided by a woman was held in lesser esteem (e.g., *m. Roš Haš.* 1:8).

Went to the tomb (20:1). Regarding mourning at a gravesite, see comments on 11:31. A seven-day mourning period was customary—though people would often visit tombs within three days after the burial—so that Mary may have remained at home had she not sought to complete

Gospel Accounts of the Resurrection

Four angelic announcement shown in one scale drawing

Matthew 28: 1–7   Mark 16:1–7   Luke 24:1–8   John 20:1–16

In the Gospel of Matthew account, Mary Magdalene and "the other Mary" set out for the tomb, but Mary Magdalene apparently entered the tomb later, by herself.

Verses 2, 3, and 4 refer to an earthquake, rolling back of the stone and the guards, even which took place before the women arrived,

possibly during the night. this gospel does not describe the actual entry of "the other Mary", but goes directly to the announcement of one angel, as in Mark and Luke, "He is not here; he has risen, just as he said. Come and see the place where he lay." **Matthew 28:1-7**

CARVED out of SOLID ROCK

CENTRAL CHAMBER

"As they entered the tomb, they saw a young man dressed in a white robe sitting on the right side ..." **Mark 16:5**

"The women ...entered ... suddenly two men in clothes that gleamed stood beside them." **Luke 24: 1-4**

KOKH

BENCH

FOLDED BURIAL CLOTH and LINEN

PIT

SLANTED TRACK for ROLLING STONE

Entrance dimensions average 36" high x 24" wide through the outer wall which was 18" thick. This creates a small tunnel, requiring a person to bend over upon entry, as describ in the Gospel accounts.

Reconstruction of the tomb of Joseph of
Arimathea based upon average measurements
of 62 Kokhim/Rolling-Stone tombs in Israel and
Jordan by E. L. Nitowski, Ph.D.

EAST →

OUTER COURT

HEIGHT OF
NATURAL ROCK/HILL
and STEP IS UNKNOWN

" Peter, ... <u>bending over</u> ...
saw the strips of linen ...
Luke 24:12

"the other disciple ...
<u>bent over</u> and looked ..."
John 20:5

"Mary (of Magdala) ... <u>bent over</u> to look
into the tomb and saw <u>two</u> angels in
white ... seated where Jesus' body
had been, one at the <u>head</u>
and the other at the <u>foot</u>."
John 20: 11,12

Two angelic beings are shown here seated on the
BENCH to illustrate the **John 20: 11, 12** account.
These same two angels are also drawn in a standing
position as they were seen by several women in
Luke 23:4. The **Mark 16:5** gospel noes only the angel
who spoke without specifically accounting for the other.

work left undone owing to the Sabbath (cf. 19:42). Rabbinic commentary, in the context of a dispute regarding whether intense mourning may be cut to two days in certain cases, cites the view of R. Bar Qappara (c. A.D. 200) that "on the third day ... mourning is ... at its height" (*Gen. Rab.* 100:7 on Gen. 50:10). According to a minor tractate in the Babylonian Talmud, one may "go out to the cemetery and examine the dead within three days and not fear [being suspected of] superstitious practices" (*b. Sem.* 8:1).

The stone had been removed from the entrance (20:1). One entered the cave tomb—which is probably horizontal rather than vertical (see comments on 11:38)—on ground level through a small doorway. This opening was usually no higher than a yard, so that people had to "bend down" to crawl in (20:5). Tombs could be sealed simply by a large stone rolled against the entrance, though more elaborate gravesites had a wheel-shaped "rolling slab" put in front, similar in effect to a sliding door (e.g., *b. Moʾed Qaṭ.* 27a).

The former is suggested in Jesus' case by the Synoptics (cf. Matt. 28:2). On the inside, larger tombs had a hallway leading to several burial chambers further back. Arrangements included (1) tunnels (*kōkīm*), into which the body was inserted head first; (2) semicircular niches (*arcosolia*), cut so as to leave a flat shelf or trough on or into which a body could be laid; (3) tombs where the body was placed on a bench that ran around three sides of the burial chamber. The second is most likely in Jesus' case (20:12).[642]

They have taken the Lord out of the tomb (20:2). Mary has no thought of resurrection. The charge of the Jewish leaders that Jesus' disciples stole his body (Matt. 27:62–66; 28:11–15) suggests that grave robbery was not uncommon. An inscription discovered in the neighborhood of Nazareth indicates that the emperor Claudius (A.D. 41–54) subsequently ordered capital punishment for those convicted of this crime.[643]

We don't know where they have put him (20:2). The plural "we" may indicate that Mary comes in the company of other women. This is further suggested by the fact that she goes to the tomb while it is still dark; for women would unlikely not venture outside the city by themselves at this time of day, especially during religious festivals when Jerusalem was crowded with visitors of uncertain character.[644]

He bent over and looked in at the strips of linen lying there (20:5). Apparently, by now there is enough daylight to see inside the burial chamber through the small, low opening in the cave tomb. The word "bend over" (*parakyptō*) is in the LXX regularly used for peering through a door or

◀

MAGDALA

Also known as
Migdal, this was
the site of the small
town on the west-
ern shore of the sea
of Galilee.

window.[645] For the "disciple Jesus loved," the linen strips (*ta othonia*; see comments on 19:40) are sufficient evidence that the body has not simply been moved. More-over, grave robbers certainly would not leave behind expensive linen wrappings or spices. "There" probably refers to the place where the body has been, on the *arcosolium* (see comments on 20:1).

The burial cloth that had been around Jesus' head (20:7). In contrast to Lazarus, who came out of the tomb still wearing his graveclothes (11:44), Jesus' resurrection body has apparently passed through the linen wrappings very much in the same way as he later is able to appear to his disciples in a locked room (20:19, 26). The grave clothes may have passed under the chin and been tied on top of the head to keep the corpse's mouth from falling open. According to talmudic tradition, "Formerly they were wont to uncover the face of the rich and cover the face of the poor . . . and the poor felt shamed; they therefore insti-tuted that everybody's face should be covered, out of deference for the poor" (*b. Mo'ed Qaṭ.* 27a).

The cloth was folded up by itself, sepa-rate from the linen (20:7). John draws attention to the care that has been taken in the way the tomb is left. The phrase "folded up" (NIV) may actually mean "rolled up" (*entylissō*), which either points to neatness or indicates that the cloth is still in the exact same position as when Jesus' body was wrapped in it. This rules out grave robbers, who would have acted in haste (and probably taken these items with them). Also, it renders the Jewish story of the disciples' stealing Jesus' body implausible, because they likewise would hardly have left the face cloth and linen wrappings behind.

Finally the other disciple . . . saw and believed (20:8). The fact that two men see the items mentioned in 20:5–7 renders the evidence admissible under the Jewish legal system (Deut. 17:6; 19:15).

(They still did not understand from Scripture that Jesus had to rise from the dead) (20:9). The singular "Scripture" (*graphē*) may indicate that a specific Old Testament text is in view—suggestions range from Psalm 16:10 to Isaiah 53:10–12 to Hosea 6:2—though it cannot be ruled out that the reference is to Scripture in its entirety (cf. Luke 24:25–27, 32, 44–47).

Jesus Appears to Mary Magdalene (20:10–18)

To their homes (20:10). Literally, "to them" (*pros autous*), that is, the things belonging to them, which means their homes (cf. Josephus, *Ant.* 8.4.6 §124). Elsewhere, John uses the equivalent expression *eis ta idia* (1:11; 16:32; 19:27; cf. Num. 24:25). In all probability, the "disciple Jesus loved" brought the good news of Jesus' resurrection to Jesus' mother whom he had taken "into his home" (19:27).

Crying (20:11). The term "to cry" (*klaiō*) denotes the loud wailing typical of people in the ancient Near East (see comments on 11:31). Mary weeps, not because Jesus has died, but because his body has vanished; abuse of the dead was considered an abhorrent offense. An Old Testament example is the Philistines' exposure of the bodies of Saul and his sons and the bodies' recovery and proper burial by the brave men of Jabesh-Gilead (1 Sam. 31:9–13).

Two angels in white (20:12–13). In that day and culture, angelic appearances were no less real than what in modern parlance is called "evidence." Angels or celestial visitors are often depicted as clad in white.[646] The appearance of angels in pairs is likewise not uncommon in descriptions of heavenly visitations.[647]

One at the head and the other at the foot (20:12). This probably refers to an angel sitting at either end of the burial shelf (see comments on 20:1).

The gardener (20:15). Apart from grave robbers or other mourners—neither of whom would have been likely visitors at this early morning hour—gardeners attending to the grounds where a tomb was located (cf. 19:41) would have been the only people around. Mary's guess indicates that at first blush the resurrected Jesus is indistinguishable from an ordinary person.

Carried him away (20:15). The expression "carry away" (*bastazō*) is found elsewhere in the context of disposing of a corpse (Josephus, *Ant.* 3.8.7 §210; 7.11.7 §287).

In Aramaic, "Rabboni!" (which means Teacher) (20:16). See comments on 1:38.

Go instead . . . and tell them (20:17). In light of the limitations placed on women's witness in first-century Judaism (*m. Roš Haš.* 1:8), Jesus' entrusting Mary with this important message is surely significant.[648]

Jesus Appears to His Disciples (20:19–23)

Were together (20:19). The location is probably a house in Jerusalem, presumably the same place where the disciples were when Mary Magdalene came to them with the news that she has seen the Lord (20:18; cf. Luke 24:33: "Jerusalem").

The disciples are probably still there to mourn. Also, the Feast of Unleavened Bread is still in progress.

With the doors locked for fear of the Jews (20:19). Concerning the plural "doors" (cf. 20:26), the reference may be to a door at the house entrance and one into the room. "Proper residences were equipped with bolts and locks. Bolted doors would prevent anyone from entering (a heavy bolt could be slid through rings attached to the door and its frame)."[649]

Peace be with you! (20:19). This common Jewish greeting (e.g., 1 Sam. 25:6), representing Hebrew *šālōm ʿalêkem* (repeated twice more in vv. 2, 26 below), is still used today. On "peace," see comments on 14:27. The expression "peace" may also function as a "formula of revelation." Thus when Gideon is gripped by fear at the sight of the angel of the Lord, the Lord says to him, "Peace! Do not be afraid. You are not going to die" (Judg. 6:23). Similarly, an angel reassures the frightened Daniel, "Peace! Be strong now; be strong" (Dan. 10:19). Jesus' greeting reassures any fears on the part of his followers related to their desertion of him prior to the crucifixion (John 16:32).

As the Father has sent me, I am sending you (20:21). This commissioning statement (cf. Matt. 28:18–20; Luke 24:46–49) climaxes the characterization of Jesus as the sent Son. Succession is important both in the Old Testament and in intertestamental literature. The most well-known Old Testament narratives involving succession are those featuring Joshua (following Moses) and Elisha (succeeding Elijah).

He breathed on them and said, "Receive the Holy Spirit" (20:22). The present reference represents a symbolic promise of the soon-to-be-given gift of the Spirit, not the actual giving of it (which happened fifty days later at Pentecost, see Acts 2). The Greek verb *emphysaō* means "breathe *on*" rather than "breathe *into*." The theological antecedent is Genesis 2:7, where the same verb and actual form is used.[650] There God breathes his Spirit into Adam at creation, which constitutes him as a "living being." Here, at the occasion of the commissioning of his disciples, Jesus constitutes them as the new messianic community, in anticipation of the outpouring of the Spirit subsequent to his ascension.

If you forgive anyone his sins, they are forgiven; if you do not forgive them, they are not forgiven (20:23). The second part of the present saying reads literally, "if you retain [anyone his sins], they are retained." In Matthew, this power is attributed to Peter in a universal, salvation-historical sense (Matt. 16:19; cf. Acts 1–12) and to the disciples in an inner-church context (Matt. 18:18).[651] Both evangelists may echo the reference to the one who is given "the key to the house of David" in Isaiah 22:22 (cf. Rev. 3:7).[652] If so, what is at stake is the authority to grant or deny access to God's kingdom.

In a Jewish context, the phrase "binding and loosing" originally described the activity of a judge who declared persons brought before him innocent or guilty, thus "binding" or "loosing" them from the charges made against them.[653] The rabbis used "binding" and "loosing" to declare what was forbidden or permitted by the law.[654] The same terminology was applied to the imposing or relieving of a ban or to a person's expulsion from or restitution to the synagogue.

If this meaning resonates in the present passage as well, Jesus would be declaring his new messianic community—not the Jewish leadership represented by the Sanhedrin and the Pharisees—as authorized to accept or deny acceptance into the believing (new) covenant community (cf. 9:22, 34, 35; 12:42; 16:2). On a secondary level, if Jewish nonmessianic synagogues in John's day have begun to expel Christians on a larger, more formal and organized scale, the present passage would serve as a reminder that Christians, not nonmessianic Jewish synagogues, now hold the key to membership in the messianic community.

Jesus Appears to Thomas (20:24–31)

Thomas (called Didymus) (20:24). See comments on 11:16.

The nail marks in his hands and put my finger where the nails were, and put my hand into his side (20:25). Apparently,

ROMAN NAILS

These iron nails were discovered in Judea and date to the Roman period.

Thomas thinks the disciples may have seen a ghost. Note that the Gnostics later taught Jesus only *appeared* to be human (the heresy of Docetism, from *dokeō*, "to seem"). Just as in the case of the incarnation (1:14), John takes pains to affirm that Jesus "came in the flesh" (a major concern in John's letters; cf. 1 John 4:2–3; 2 John 7), which entails also that his resurrection body is not merely that of a phantom or spirit apparition but a "fleshy" (albeit glorified) body.

A week later (20:26). Literally, "after eight days." This refers to Sunday, one week after Easter.

His disciples were in the house again (20:26). Now that the Feast of Unleavened Bread is over, the disciples would soon be returning home to Galilee (barring instructions to the contrary). See comments on 20:19.

My Lord and my God (20:28). "Lord" and "God" are frequently juxtaposed in the Old Testament with reference to Yahweh (e.g., Ps. 35:23–24). The expression seems to have made its way into Roman emperor worship via Mediterranean cults; an inscription dated 24 B.C. dedicates a building "to the god and lord Socnopaeus."[655] The most pertinent parallel is that of the Roman emperor Domitian (A.D. 81–96), who wished to be addressed as "dominus et deus noster" ("our lord and god"; Suetonius, *Domitian* 13.2). Only decades later, Pliny attests that Christians worshiped Christ as God (*Ep.* 10.96; before A.D. 115).

Because you have seen me, you have believed; blessed are those who have not seen and yet have believed (20:29). A saying attributed to R. Simeon b. Laqish

(c. A.D. 250) contrasts Israel (who saw) and the Gentile proselytes (who still had not fully believed) thus: "The proselyte is dearer to God than all the Israelites who stood by Mount Sinai. For if all the Israelites had not seen the thunder and the flames and the lightnings and the quaking mountain and the sound of the trumpet they would not have accepted the law and taken upon themselves the kingdom of God. Yet this man has seen none of all these things yet comes and gives himself to God and takes on himself the yoke of the kingdom of God. Is there any who is dearer than this man?" (*Tanḥ.* 6 [32a]).[656] However, this ethnic distinction is not found in John. Rather, the saying accentuates the different mode of existence between the followers of the earthly Jesus and those whose faith depends on their witness. See also 2 Esdras 1:37: "I call to witness the gratitude of the people that is to come, whose children rejoice with gladness; though they do not see me with bodily eyes, yet with the spirit they will believe the things I have said."

Jesus did many other miraculous signs in the presence of his disciples, which are not recorded in this book. But these are written that you may believe (20:30–31). On Jesus' signs in John's Gospel, see "Jesus' Signs in John's Gospel" at 2:1. Parallels to this type of concluding statement can be documented from both secular and intertestamental Jewish literature.[657] After describing God's creative work and the marvels of nature, one intertestamental book concludes a section with the words, "We could say more but could never say enough; let the final word be: 'He is the all'" (Sir. 43:27). Even closer in wording is 1 Maccabees 9:22: "Now the rest of the acts of Judas . . . and

the brave deeds that he did . . . have not been recorded, but they were very many."

Jesus is the Christ, the Son of God (20:31). See comments on 1:41, 49; 11:27.

By believing you may have life in his name (20:31). Regarding "life," see comments on 1:4. On "believing in his name," see comments on 1:12.

Jesus and the Miraculous Catch of Fish (21:1–14)

The present chapter, an epilogue mirroring in function the opening prologue, focuses primarily on two final issues: the special commissioning of Peter and the laying to rest of a rumor that the "disciple Jesus loved" would not die prior to Jesus' second coming.

Afterward (21:1). With the week-long Feast of Unleavened Bread now past, the disciples have left Jerusalem and returned to Galilee (cf. Luke 2:43).[658]

Sea of Tiberias (21:1). See comments on 6:1.

SEA OF GALILEE

▼

The sons of Zebedee (21:2). Their names are given in the Synoptics as James and John (e.g., Matt. 4:21 par.). Luke mentions that they were "Simon's partners" in fishing prior to being called by Jesus (5:10).

That night they caught nothing (21:3). Nighttime was the preferred time of day for fishing in ancient times, including first-century Galilee (e.g., Luke 5:5: "all night"). That way any fish caught before daybreak could be sold fresh in the morning.

Haven't you any fish? (21:5). The rare term translated "fish" (*prosphagion*) is not found elsewhere in biblical literature. The reference is most likely to a "bite to eat," which in first-century Galilee would often have been a piece of fish.

Throw your net (21:6). Three different kinds of net were used: one cast by hand; a trawlnet spread out from a boat and dragged through the water with cables on poles; and one stretched out in deep water. In the present instance, the trawlnet is most likely.[659]

Simon Peter . . . wrapped his outer garment around him (for he had taken it off) and jumped into the water (21:7–8). The "outer garment" in the present case is probably a fisherman's coat (*ependytēs*) that Peter wears in the morning chill. "For he had taken it off" is literally translated "for he was naked," but this may merely mean that Peter is wearing only his undergarment (so rightly the NIV), probably the short tunic of the Greek workman.[660] He tucks in his outer garment in order to be able to swim (rather than wade; the shoreline drops off rather rapidly at most parts of the lake) ashore more easily and to be properly dressed for greeting Jesus.[661]

Towing the net full of fish (21:8). The word for "towing" or "dragging" (*syrō*; used elsewhere in the New Testament only figuratively) occurs in connection with a trawlnet in Plutarch (*Soll. Anim.* 977.F).

About a hundred yards (21:8). Literally, "about two hundred cubits"; one cubit is about half a yard.

A fire of burning coals (21:9). See comments on 18:18.

With fish on it (21:9). The singular "fish" (*opsarion*) here may suggest there is just one large fish being cooked. But then Jesus encourages the disciples to bring some of the fish they just caught (21:10).

Full of large fish, 153 (21:11). Various attempts have been made to interpret the number 153 symbolically, but more likely it simply represents the number of fish counted. Large numbers elsewhere in John are meant literally as well (e.g., 2:6; 12:3). An abundant catch of fish was considered evidence of God's favor.[662]

Come and have breakfast (21:12). First-century Jews normally ate two meals a day (cf. Luke 14:12), with "breakfast" (*ariston*) being the first of these. It was generally eaten before starting a day's work (though it could be an early lunch as well; cf. Luke 11:37–38).

Jesus came, took the bread and gave it to them, and did the same with the fish (21:13). Jesus here performs the act of the Jewish host, pronouncing the blessing at a meal (cf. 6:11, 23).

Jesus Reinstates Peter (21:15–25)

Simon son of John (21:15). See comments on 1:42.

Feed my lambs. . . . Take care of my sheep. . . . Feed my sheep (21:15–17). Shepherd imagery abounds in the Old Testament, which is pervaded by a yearning for shepherds who are devoted to God, care for his sheep, and carry out his will (Isa. 44:28; Jer. 3:15; Ezek. 34; see comments on John 10). At Qumran, the metaphor is applied to the authoritative overseer (*mebaqqer*): "He . . . will heal all the strays like a shepherd his flock" (CD 13:9).

The term "feed" (*boskō*) regularly occurs in the LXX for feeding sheep (e.g., Gen. 29:7; 37:12); the metaphorical sense is found in Ezekiel 34:2. The two verbs "feed" and "take care of" are contrasted in Philo: "For those who feed (*boskō*) us supply nourishment . . . whereas those who tend (*poimainō*) have the power of rulers and governors" (*Worse* 8.25). Jointly, they span the fullness of the task given to Peter (cf. 1 Peter 5:1–3).

◀ *left*

FISH FROM THE SEA OF GALILEE

A SHEPHERD FEEDING HIS SHEEP NEAR JORDAN

▼

Jesus' Resurrection Appearances		
Location	Time	Reference
Empty tomb (Mary Magd. et al.)	Early Sunday morning	Matt. 28:1–10 par.; John 20:1–18
Road to Emmaus (two disciples)	Sunday noon	Luke 24:13–32
Jerusalem (Peter)	Sunday	Luke 24:34; 1 Cor. 15:5
Upper room (ten disciples)	Sunday evening	Luke 24:36–43; John 20:19–25
Upper room (eleven disciples)	Following Sunday	John 20:26–31; 1 Cor. 15:5
Sea of Galilee (seven disciples)	Later	John 21:1–23
Mountain in Galilee (eleven disciples)	Some time later	Matt. 28:16–20
Unknown (more than 500; James)	Some time later	1 Cor. 15:6–7
Mount of Olives (eleven disciples)	40 days after resurrection	Luke 24:44–49; Acts 1:3–8

Jesus' threefold repetition of his question may reflect the Near Eastern custom of reiterating a matter three times before witnesses in order to convey a solemn obligation, especially with regard to contracts conferring rights or legal dispositions. By analogy, Jesus' threefold question lends solemnity to the occasion of his commissioning Peter to his special shepherding task.

Stretch out your hands (21:18). In the ancient world, this expression (*ekteinō tas cheiras*) was widely taken to refer to crucifixion.[663] This is illustrated by the following passages: Epictetus, *Disc.* 3.26.22: "stretched yourself out like men who have been crucified"; Seneca, *Consol. ad Marciam* 20.3: "others stretch out their arms on a *patibulum*"; Dionysius of Halicarnassus, *Ant.* 7.69: "stretched out both his arms and fastened them to a piece of wood"; Tertullian, *De Pudic.* 22: "on the cross, with body already outstretched."

The "stretching" occurred when a condemned criminal was tied to the horizontal crossbar called *patibulum* (see comments on 19:17) and compelled to carry his cross to the place of execution. Patristic interpreters interpreted Isaiah 65:2 ("All day long I have held out my hands to an obstinate people") with reference to the crucifixion.[664]

To indicate the kind of death by which Peter would glorify God (21:19). By the time John wrote his Gospel, Jesus' prediction had been fulfilled. According to Clement of Rome (c. A.D. 96), Peter suffered martyrdom under Nero (A.D. 54–68; *1 Clem.* 5.4), probably during the final years of Nero's reign (c. A.D. 64–66).[665] Later, Tertullian (c. A.D. 212) asserts that Peter was crucified.[666]

"Lord, what about him?" . . . "If I want him to remain alive until I return, what is that to you?" . . . Because of this, the rumor

spread among the brothers that this disciple would not die. But Jesus did not say that he would not die (21:21–23). Interestingly, the final chapter of Matthew is likewise given to dispelling a rumor—in Matthew's case that the disciples stole Jesus' body (Matt. 28:11–15; cf. 27:62–66). It is not impossible that these final verses were penned by John's disciples subsequent to his death in order to counter the charge that Jesus' prediction had been proven erroneous by John's death. More likely is the suggestion that John himself, while still alive, seeks to lay to rest the rumor that Christ has promised to return during his lifetime.[667]

This is the disciple who testifies to these things and who wrote them down. We know that his testimony is true (21:24). This verse, in its formal, solemn posture, represents the signature and statement of autography also common in epistolary postscripts.[668] It comes on the heels of two retrospective references to "the disciple Jesus loved" in 21:7 and 20 and a third resumptive passage in 21:14. The function of the entire chapter is to confirm the Beloved Disciple as author of this Gospel and to substantiate the authority of his eyewitness account.

The present verse identifies the fourth evangelist, the author of John's Gospel, with the literary character of "the disciple Jesus loved." This figure, in turn, relates historically to John the apostle, the son of Zebedee. The present verse is cast in the third person in order to affirm the credibility of the author's own witness.[669] In the second part of the verse, the author shifts to the first person plural,[670] and in verse 25 to the first person singular (*oimai*, "I suppose"). Here the author strikes a more informal, familiar tone to underscore his personal involvement and not to appear unduly detached from the events recorded earlier (see also comments on 19:35; 1 John 1:1–4).

Jesus did many other things as well. If every one of them were written down, I suppose that even the whole world would not have room for the books that would be written (21:25). Hyperbolic statements such as these were well-established literary convention at the time in both Greco-Roman and Jewish literature. The Old Testament book of Ecclesiastes ends with the acknowledgment that the wise Teacher had searched out many proverbs but "of making many books there is no end" (12:9–12). The following saying is attributed to R. Yoḥanan ben Zakkai (c. A.D. 80): "If all the heavens were sheets, all the trees quills and all the seas ink, they would not suffice for recording my wisdom which I acquired from my masters" (*b. Sop.* 16:8).

Philo frequently resorts to the kind of hyperbole found in the present passage. In one of his works he writes, "Were he [God] to choose to display his own riches, even the entire earth with the sea turned into dry land would not contain (*chorēsai*) them" (*Posterity* 43.144). At another place he says, "their gifts are so boundless in number that no one, not even ... the world, can contain them" (*Drunkenness* 9.32). Once again, the Jewish philosopher comments, "He who should wish to describe ... the universe, would find life too short, even if his years were prolonged beyond those of all other men" (*Moses* 1.38.213).[671] Thus, John reinforces the selection principle already mentioned in 20:30–31 and further draws attention to the multitude of remarkable works performed by Jesus the Messiah (see comments on 20:30–31).

ANNOTATED BIBLIOGRAPHY

Commentaries

Barrett, C. K. *The Gospel According to St. John.* 2d ed. Philadelphia: Westminster, 1978.

Still one of the best commentaries on John, especially with regard to Greco-Roman backgrounds.

Brown, Raymond E. *The Gospel According to John.* 2 vols. AB 29A–B. New York: Doubleday, 1966, 1970.

Critical, yet extensive, including helpful excurses on major Johannine themes.

Carson, D. A. *The Gospel According to John.* Grand Rapids: Eerdmans, 1991.

One of the best evangelical commentaries on John now available, especially on difficult exegetical issues.

Moloney, Francis J. *The Gospel of John.* Sacra Pagina 4. Collegeville, Minn.: Liturgical, 1998.

The most recent thorough exegetical commentary, including helpful up-to-date bibliographies.

Morris, Leon. *The Gospel According to John.* NICNT. Rev. ed. Grand Rapids: Eerdmans, 1995.

The fruit of a lifetime of research on John's Gospel, this work is a model of judiciousness and even-handedness.

Ridderbos, Herman. *The Gospel of John: A Theological Commentary.* Trans. John Vriend. Grand Rapids: Eerdmans, 1997.

The new standard on theological synthesis. Less detailed than Carson, but more overtly theological in orientation.

Schnackenburg, Rudolf. *The Gospel According to St. John.* HTCNT. 3 vols. Trans. Kevin Smyth et al. New York: Crossroad, 1990 (1965, 1971, 1975).

Very thorough, moderately critical, always worth consulting. One caveat: Jewish background material is not always reliable and frequently seems to have been derived second-hand.

Special Studies

Bauckham, Richard. *The Gospels for All Christians: Rethinking the Gospel Audiences.* Grand Rapids: Eerdmans, 1997.

A seminal work on the universal orientation of the Gospels. Powerful refutation of the "Johannine community hypothesis."

Carson, D. A. "John and the Johannine Epistles." In *It Is Written: Scripture Citing Scripture,* eds. D. A. Carson and H. G. M. Williamson. Cambridge: Cambridge Univ. Press, 1988, 246–64.

A good starting point for the study of the Old Testament background to John's Gospel.

Charlesworth, James H., ed. *John and the Dead Sea Scrolls.* New York: Crossroad, 1991.

A helpful introduction to the relevance of Dead Sea Scrolls research for Johannine studies.

Culpepper, R. Alan, and C. Clifton Black, eds. *Exploring the Gospel of John. In Honor of D. Moody Smith.* Louisville, Ky.: Westminster John Knox, 1996.

A recent collection of essays that replaces more dated anthologies in relevance.

Köstenberger, Andreas. *The Missions of Jesus and the Disciples According to the Fourth Gospel.* Grand Rapids: Eerdmans, 1998.

An exegetical and theological study that endeavors to articulate a biblical theology of missions in the Fourth Gospel.

_____. *Encountering John. The Gospel in Historical, Literary, and Theological Perspective.* Grand Rapids: Baker, 1999.

A detailed introduction and survey of John's Gospel.

Pryor, John W. *John: Evangelist of the Covenant People: The Narrative and Themes of the Fourth Gospel.* Downers Grove, Ill.: InterVarsity, 1992.

Pryor shows convincingly that the substructure of John's narrative is salvation-historical, linking Jesus' new covenant community systematically with Old Testament antecedents.

Main Text Notes

1. For a general survey, see D. H. Johnson, "Logos," *DJG*, 481–84.

2. M. J. Harris, *Jesus As God* (Grand Rapids: Baker, 1992), 67.

3. For thorough discussion see Richard Bauckham, *God Crucified: Monotheism and Christology in the New Testament* (Grand Rapids: Eerdmans, 1998); Larry W. Hurtado, *One God, One Lord: Early Christian Devotion and Ancient Jewish Monotheism* (Philadelphia: Fortress, 1988).

4. Cf. E. C. Colwell, "A Definite Rule for the Use of the Article in the Greek New Testament," *JBL* 52 (1933): 12–21; Lane C. McGaughy, *Toward a Description Analysis of EINAI as Linking Verb in New Testament Greek* (SBLDS 6; Missoula, Mont.: Society of Biblical Literature, 1972).

5. See C. T. R. Wayward, "The Holy Name of the God of Moses and the Prologue of St. John's Gospel," *NTS* 25 (1978): 16–32.

6. See Thomas H. Tobin, "Logos," *ABD*, 4:348–56.

7. See D. H. Johnson, "Life," *DJG*, 469–71; G. F. Shirbroun, "Light," *DJG*, 472–73.

8. See also Isa. 42:6–7 and 49:6. Cf. John 12:46 with Matt. 4:16; Luke 2:32; 2 Cor. 4:6; Eph. 5:8; 1 John 1:5–7.

9. See Richard Bauckham, "Qumran and the Fourth Gospel: Is There a Connection?" in Stanley E. Porter and Craig A. Evans, eds., *The Scrolls and the Scriptures: Qumran Fifty Years After* (Sheffield: Sheffield Academic Press, 1997), 267–79.

10. Note that the Gk. word "understood" in v. 5 may actually mean "overcome" (see NIV footnote; cf. 12:35; 16:33).

11. See R. Kysar, "John, Gospel of," *ABD*, 3:886.

12. See Rom. 4:3, 20–24; Gal. 3:6; Heb. 11:8–12; James 2:23.

13. See esp. W. Horbury, *Jewish Messianism and the Cult of Christ* (London: SCM, 1998), 92–93, 99–100, who also discusses rabbinic interpretations.

14. See Charles H. Talbert, *Reading John* (New York: Crossroad, 1992), 74; cf. Elaine Pagels, "Exegesis of Genesis 1 in the Gospels of Thomas and John," *JBL* 118 (1999): 477–96.

15. For further discussion and relevant passages, see Köstenberger, "What Does It Mean to Be Filled with the Spirit?" *JETS* 40 (1997): 230.

16. See Ps. 5:7; 51:1; 69:16; 106:45; Lam. 3:22–23; see also 1QS 4:4.

17. See 3:16; Rom. 8:32; Gal. 4:4; see also Heb. 1:1–2; 2:2–3; 3:1–6.

18. See Hoehner, *Chronological Aspects*, 31–37; Finegan, *Handbook*, 340; B. Messner, "'In the Fifteenth Year' Reconsidered: A Study of Luke 3:1," *SCJ* 1 (1998): 201–11, with reference to the Roman historians Tacitus, *Ann.* 4.1, and Suetonius, *Tib.* 73, both of whom date the beginning of Tiberius's reign at A.D. 14 (the precise date is August 19, the day of Emperor Augustus's death); see comments on 2:20.

19. See R. A. Horsley, "Messianic Movements in Judaism," *ABD*, 4:791–97.

20. Matt. 16:14 par.; 17:3–4, 10 par.; 27:47, 49 par.; Sir. 48:10; *m. Šeqal.* 2:5; *m. Soṭah* 9:15; *m. B. Meṣiʿa* 1:8; *m. ʿEd.* 8:7; probably also 1QS 9:11. Quotations from the Mishnah are taken from H. Danby, *The Mishnah* (Oxford: Oxford Univ. Press, 1933).

21. See also Mark's conflation of Mal. 3:1 ("I will send my messenger") and Isa. 40:3 (also found in John 1:23 and Synoptic parallels) in Mark 1:2–3.

22. See Acts 3:22; 7:37; see also 1 Macc. 4:46; 14:41; *T. Benj.* 9:2.

23. Cf. J. Macdonald, *The Theology of the Samaritans* (Philadelphia: Westminster, 1964), 197–98, 362–71, 443.

24. C. S. Keener, *BBC* (IVPNTC; Downers Grove, Ill.: InterVarsity, 1993), 266.

25. E. W. Burrows, "Did John the Baptist Call Jesus 'The Lamb of God'?" *ExpTim* 85 (1974): 245–49.

26. Cf. D. Daube, *The New Testament and Rabbinic Judaism* (London: Athlone, 1956), 266–67.

27. This would seem to invalidate the recent claims, made by Mohammed Waheeb, an archaeologist heading the Jordanian excavations in the Jordan area, to have discovered the "Bethany beyond the Jordan" at a site about five miles north of the Dead Sea ("Site of Jesus' Baptism Found—Again," *BAR* 25/3 [1999]: 14–15). Cf. R. Riesner, "Bethany Beyond the Jordan (John 1:28): Topography, Theology and History in the Fourth Gospel," *TynBul* 38 (1987): 47; now succinctly presented in R. Riesner, "Archeology and Geography," *DJG*, 35–36; I am indebted to Riesner also for some of the following material.

28. For a general survey, see I. H. Marshall, "Lamb of God," *DJG*, 432–34.

29. Alternatively, the Baptist may have proclaimed Jesus as the apocalyptic warrior lamb who would bring judgment (cf. *1 En.* 90:9–12; *T. Jos.* 19:8; *T. Benj.* 3:8); cf. D. A.

Carson, *The Gospel According to John* (Grand Rapids: Eerdmans, 1991), 150. For the Baptist's message of judgment, see esp. Matt. 3:7–12; Luke 3:7–17.

30. See Num. 11:25; Judg. 3:10; 6:34; 11:29; 14:19; 1 Sam. 11:6; 16:13; 2 Chron. 15:1; 20:14.

31. Cf. Köstenberger, "What Does It Mean?" 229–30.

32. See Isa. 32:15; 44:3; Ezek. 36:25–27; Joel 2:28–32; cf. *Jub.* 1:23; 2 Esd. 6:26; *T. Jud.* 24:3; 1QS 4:20–21.

33. Cf. M. G. Abegg and C. A. Evans, "Messianic Passages in the Dead Sea Scrolls," in *Qumran Messianism*, ed. J. H. Charlesworth et al. (Tübingen: Mohr-Siebeck, 1998), 202.

34. Hoehner, *Chronological Aspects*, 37–38; idem., "Chronology," *DJG*, 119; C. J. Humphreys and W. G. Waddington, "The Jewish Calendar, a Lunar Eclipse and the Date of Christ's Crucifixion," *TynBul* 43 (1992): 351. For a dissenting voice, see Finegan, *Handbook*, 344–45, who places Jesus' birth in 3/2 B.C. (see pp. 278, 291), in which case Jesus would quite literally have been "about thirty years old." However, Finegan's date makes it hard to reckon with Herod's successors (according to a personal corespondence from H. Hoehner, dated Jan. 11, 2001).

35. For further rabbinic parallels, see Köstenberger, "Jesus As Rabbi in the Fourth Gospel," *BBR* 8 (1998): 119.

36. Cited in J. Lightfoot, *A Commentary on the New Testament from the Talmud and Hebraica* (Peabody, Mass.: Hendrickson, 1989 [1859]), 3:245.

37. J. Jeremias, *The Eucharistic Words of Jesus* (London: SCM, 1966), 45, n. 1.

38. For a general survey of this title, see L. W. Hurtado, "Christ," *DJG*, 106–17.

39. On messianism in the Old Testament, see Horbury, *Jewish Messianism and the Cult of Christ*, ch. 1.

40. See CD 2:12; 12:23–13:1; 14:19; 19:10–11; 20:1; 1QSa 2:14, 20; 4Q521 line 1; 11QMelch 2:18.

41. See *Pss. Sol.* 17:32; *1 En.* 48:10; 52:4; *4 Ezra* 7:28–29; 12:32; *2 Bar.* 29:3; 30:1; 40:1; 70:9; 72:2. Cf. J. C. O'Neill, *Who Did Jesus Think He Was?* (Leiden: Brill, 1995), 25–26; Abegg and Evans, "Messianic Passages," 191–94; Horbury, *Jewish Messianism*, ch. 2.

42. See O. Cullmann, "Πέτρος, Κηφᾶς," *TDNT*, 6:100–101.

43. For general (including archaeological) information on Bethsaida, see esp. F. Strickert, *Bethsaida: Home of the Apostles* (Collegeville, Minn.: Liturgical, 1998); H.-W. Kuhn and R.

Arav, "The Bethsaida Excavations: Historical and Archaeological Approaches," in *The Future of Early Christianity. Fs. H. Koester*, ed. B. A. Pearson (Minneapolis: Fortress, 1991), 77–106; "Searching for the New Testament Site of Bethsaida," *BAR* 48/4 (Dec. 1985): 207–16.

44. Cf. L. P. Trudinger, "An Israelite in Whom There Is No Guile: An Interpretive Note on John 1:45–51," *EvQ* 54 (1982): 117–20.

45. See 4Q246 2:1; cf. 1QSa 2:11–12; *4 Ezra* 7:28–29.

46. See G. F. Hawthorne, "Amen," *DJG*, 7–8.

47. See the discussion in Carson, *John*, 163.

48. Cf. M. Hengel, "The Dionysiac Messiah," in *Studies in Early Christology* (Edinburgh: T. & T. Clark, 1995), 293–331.

49. Cf. Riesner, "Bethany Beyond the Jordan," 46.

50. So R. H. Mounce, "Cana," *ISBE*, 1.585.

51. Cf. R. M. Mackowski, "'Scholar's Qanah.' A Re-examination of the Evidence in Favor of Khirbet-Qanah," *BZ* 23 (1979): 278–84; G. H. Dalman, *Sacred Sites and Ways* (London: SPCK, 1935), 101–6; R. Riesner, "Archeology and Geography," *DJG*, 36–37.

52. M. Avi-Yonah, *The World of the Bible: The New Testament* (Yonkers, N.Y.: Educational Heritage, 1964), 138.

53. See Riesner, "Bethany Beyond the Jordan," 47, referring to Mackowski, "Scholar's Qanah," 278–79. Cf. Dalman, *Sacred Sites and Ways*, 101.

54. See the helpful discussion of vv. 1–11 in Derrett, *Law in the New Testament*, 229–44.

55. See Jer. 31:12; Hos. 14:7; Amos 9:13–14; Matt. 22:1–14 par.; 25:1–13; *2 Bar.* 29:5; *1 En.* 10:19.

56. So Keener, *BBC*, 268.

57. Compare 19:26; the NIV softens Jesus' address by translating the phrase as "dear woman," but there is no equivalent for "dear" in the original.

58. See 4:21; 20:13, 15; cf. Matt. 15:28; Luke 13:12; 22:57.

59. Cf. R. E. Brown et al., eds., *Mary in the New Testament* (Philadelphia: Fortress, 1978), 188.

60. See Judg. 11:12; 2 Sam. 16:10; 1 Kings 17:18; 2 Kings 3:13; 2 Chron. 35:21.

61. Cf. Derrett, *Law in the New Testament*, 240–41.

62. Cf. 1 Esd. 8:20 and Bel 3 (Theod.); BAGD, 514 further lists several inscriptions and papyri.

63. L. Abbott, *Illustrated Commentary on the Gospel According to St. John* (New York/Chicago: A. S. Barnes & Co., 1879), 30.

64. See Roger Aus, *Water into Wine and the Beheading of John the Baptist* (Atlanta: Scholars, 1988), 15–17.

65. For general information, see J. C. H. Laughlin, "Capernaum: From Jesus' Time and After," *BAR* (Sept./Oct. 1993): 54–61, 90; A. Schlatter, *The History of the Christ* (Grand Rapids: Baker, 1997), 111–12.

66. On the relationship between this temple cleansing and that recorded by the Synoptics, see Köstenberger, *Encountering John* (Grand Rapids: Baker, 1999), ch. 5.

67. While this was not always possible for those living at a distance, Galileans were not so remote as to be prevented from attending regularly. See Ferguson, *Backgrounds*, 521.

68. Hoehner, *Chronological Aspects*, 60.

69. Cf. E. Stern et al., eds., *The New Encyclopedia of Archaeological Excavations in the Holy Land* (New York: Simon & Schuster, 1992), 2:744; A. Millard, *Discoveries from Bible Times* (Oxford: Lion, 1997), 243. See also *m. Kelim* 1:8 and Josephus, *Ant.* 15.11.5 §417; *J.W.* 5.5.2 §193; 6.2.4 §125.

70. On the temple tax, see Ex. 30:13–14; 2 Chron. 24:9; Neh. 10:32; Matt. 17:24–27 (cf. Josephus, *Ant.* 3.8.2 §§193–96).

71. Cf. *m. Šeqal.* 1:3: "On the 25th thereof [the month of Adar] they [the tables of the money-changers] were set up in the Temple." On Tyrian shekels, see P. Richardson, "Why Turn the Tables? Jesus' Protest in the Temple Precincts," in *SBL 1992 Seminar Papers*, ed. E. H. Loving Jr. (Atlanta: Scholars, 1992), 514–18. On the half-shekel offering, see J. Liver, "The Half-Shekel Offering in Biblical and Post-biblical Literature," *HTR* 56 (1963): 173–98.

72. Cf. C. K. Barrett, "The House of Prayer and the Den of Thieves," in *Jesus und Paulus*, ed. E. E. Ellis and E. Grässer (Göttingen: Vandenhoeck & Ruprecht, 1975), 13–20; C. A. Evans, "From 'House of Prayer' to 'Cave of Robbers': Jesus' Prophetic Criticism of the Temple Establishment," in *The Quest for Context and Meaning*, ed. C. A. Evans and S. Talmon (Leiden: Brill, 1997), 417–42. On Gentile worship at the Jerusalem temple, see "Appendix: Gentile Participation in Worship at Jerusalem," in E. Schürer, *The History of the Jewish People in the Age of Jesus Christ*, rev. and ed. G. Vermes et al. (Edinburgh: T. & T. Clark, 1979), 2:309–13 (henceforth Schürer, *HJP²*).

73. Moreover, the use of Tyrian shekels involved religious compromise, since these coins bore the image of the Tyrian god Melkart. P. M. Casey, "Culture and Historicity: The Cleansing of the Temple," *CBQ* 59 (1997): 306–32, esp. 313–15.

74. See W. J. Heard, "Revolutionary Movements," *DJG*, 688–98; M. Hengel, *The Zealots* (Edinburgh: T. & T. Clark, 1988).

75. See "Appendix B: The Fourth Philosophy: *Sicarii* and Zealots," in Schürer, *HJP²*, 2:598–606.

76. This reading of John 2:20 and a date of A.D. 30 for Jesus' first Passover and the temple cleansing are advocated by Hoehner, *Chronological Aspects*, 38–43; idem., "Chronology," *DJG*, 119; Humphreys and Waddington, "The Jewish Calendar, a Lunar Eclipse and the Date of Christ's Crucifixion," 351; Finegan, *Handbook*, 346–49.

77. Schürer, *HJP²*, 1:308–9.

78. See 1 Sam. 16:7; 1 Chron. 28:9; Ps. 139:1–18, 23–24; Jer. 17:10; Rom. 8:27; Heb. 4:12–13; Wisd. Sol. 1:6; *Pss. Sol.* 14:8; 17:25.

79. See also 1:48; 2:4, 19; 3:14; 4:17–18; 6:51, 70; 7:6; 8:28; 9:3; 10:15–18; 11:4, 14; 12:24, 32; 13:10–11, 38; 15:13; 21:18–19.

80. See Richard Bauckham, "Nicodemus and the Gurion Family, *JTS* 47 (1966): 1–37.

81. See A. J. Saldarini, "Sanhedrin," *ABD*, 5:975–80; G. H. Twelftree, "Sanhedrin," *DJG*, 728–32.

82. See Köstenberger, "Seventh Johannine Sign," 87–103.

83. For an extended discussion, see Carson, *John*, 191–96, esp. 194–95. See also W. L. Kynes, "New Birth," *DJG*, 574–76, esp. 575.

84. Cf. E. F. F. Bishop, "The Authorised Teacher of the Israel of God," *BT* 7 (1956): 81–83.

85. See e.g., Ps. 14:2; 33:14; 103:19. See C. R. Schoonhoven, "Heaven," *ISBE*, 2:654–65; J. D. Tabor, "Heaven, Ascent To," *ABD*, 3:90–91.

86. See Tabor, "Heaven, Ascent To," 3:91–94.

87. See R. A. Muller, "World," *ISBE*, 4:1115; J. Guhrt, "Earth, Land, World," *NIDNTT*, 1:525–26.

88. Ferguson, *Backgrounds*, 313–14.

89. The first is mentioned as early as Eusebius's *Onomasticon* (4th cent. A.D.). The second is defended by the eminent archaeologist W. F. Albright in *HTR* 17 (1924): 193–94, followed by B. W. Bacon, *JBL* 48 (1929): 50–55; see also J. Finegan, *The Archeology of the New Testament*, rev. ed. (Princeton, N.J.: Princeton Univ. Press, 1992), 70. R. Riesner ("Archeology and Geography," *DJG*, 35) suggests Ain Farah, eight miles northwest of Shechem.

90. For the role of the bridegroom's friend, see R. Gower, *The New Manners and Customs of Bible Times* (Chicago: Moody, 1987), 64–66.

91. R. Schippers, "Seal," *NIDNTT*, 3:497–501.

92. For Old Testament parallels, see Job 10:22 LXX; Isa. 26:14; Eccl. 9:9 LXX (cf. Ps. 33:13 cited in 1 Peter 3:10).

93. R. Riesner, "Archeology and Geography," *DJG*, 40.

94. Avi-Yonah, *World of the Bible*, 140.

95. "A city in Samaria" in Acts 8:5 may refer to Sychar as well; see Hengel, "Das Johannesevangelium als Quelle des antiken Judentums," in *Judaica, Hellenistica et Christiana* (WUNT 109; Tübingen: Mohr-Siebeck, 1999), 301.

96. Cf. J. Neyrey, "Jacob Traditions and the Interpretation of John 4:10–26," *CBQ* 41 (1979): 419–37; Dalman, *Sacred Sites and Ways*, 212–16.

97. Hengel, "Johannesevangelium als Quelle," 302, referring to Dalman.

98. Abbott, *Illustrated Commentary*, 52.

99. See *y. Šeb.* 9:9; *Lam. Rab.* 3:17; *y. Ber.* 8:5; *t. Ber.* 6:4–5. Cf. Köstenberger, "Jesus As Rabbi," 122.

100. See R. G. Maccini, *Her Testimony Is True* (JSNTSup 125; Sheffield: Academic Press, 1996), 131–44.

101. See D. Daube, "Jesus and the Samaritan Woman: The Meaning of *synchraomai* (Jn 4:7ff)," *JBL* 69 (1950): 137–47; idem, *NT and Rabbinic Judaism*, 373–82; J. D. M. Derrett, "The Samaritan Woman's Purity (John 4.4–52)," *EvQ* 60 (1988): 291–98.

102. See 4:15, 19, 49; 5:7; 6:34; 9:36; 12:21.

103. This is suggested by R. D. Potter, "Topography and Archaeology in the Fourth Gospel," in *Studia Evangelica I*, ed. K. Aland et al. (Berlin: Akademie, 1959), 331.

104. See esp. Neyrey, "Jacob Traditions," 421–22.

105. Cf. also Isa. 44:3; 49:10; 55:1; see also John 6:63; 7:38; Sir. 24:21; *1 En.* 48:1.

106. Cf. J. R. Díaz, "Palestinian Targum and the New Testament," *NovT* 6 (1963): 76–77.

107. Cited in Carson, *John*, 220.

108. Keener, *BBC*, 273.

109. Cf. C. H. Giblin, "What Was Everything He Told Her She Did?" *NTS* 45 (1999): 148–52.

110. So Hengel, "Johannesevangelium als Quelle," 307, 315.

111. For Samaritan views about Mount Gerizim, see J. Macdonald, *The Theology of the Samaritans* (London: SCM, 1964), 327–33.

112. See *Ant.* 11.8.4 §§321–24; cf. 13.9.1 §256. Josephus further attests to the temple's existence in 323 B.C., the year of Alexander the Great's death (*Ant.* 11.8.7 §346; cf. 11.8.3 §310). See Jeremias, *Jerusalem*, 352, n. 2. On archaeological excavations related to Mount Gerizim, see esp. Crown, *Samaritans*, 165–74.

113. R. Schnackenburg, *The Gospel According to St. John* (New York: Crossroad, 1990), 1:434, n. 44.

114. Avi-Yonah, *World of the Bible*, 141.

115. Bond, *Pontius Pilate*, 90.

116. Contra Keener, *BBC*, 273, who reads the present passage in terms of "racial reconciliation." But this does not square with the emphasis of the present passage on the Jews being *the source of salvation*.

117. For a helpful discussion contrasting biblical with Hellenistic concepts of God see Schnackenburg, *John*, 1:440.

118. Cf. Kippenberg, *Garizim und Synagoge*, 303, n. 216.

119. M. E. Boring, ed., *Hellenistic Commentary to the New Testament* (Nashville: Abingdon, 1995), 264–65.

120. Cf. J. Bowman, "Samaritan Studies," 298–308; repr. in *Samaritan Studies* (Manchester: Manchester Univ. Press, 1958).

121. See L. Morris, *The Gospel According to John*, rev. ed. (Grand Rapids: Eerdmans, 1995), 242–43, n. 67, for other primary quotes.

122. The spirit of open interchange between Jesus and his disciples—or even those of John the Baptist—is illustrated by passages such as 9:2; 11:8, 12, 16; 13:6–10, 36–38; 14:5, 8, 22; 21:21; also Matt. 9:14; 11:3; 13:10, 36; 15:12, 15; 17:10, 19; 18:21; 24:3 and the parallels in Mark and Luke.

123. See the discussion and references in Köstenberger, "Jesus As Rabbi," 120–22. Contra Keener, *BBC*, 274, who refers to "the general principle that one ought not to challenge one's teacher."

124. Gower, *New Manners and Customs*, 44.

125. See Köstenberger, "Jesus As Rabbi," 122–23.

126. H. Ridderbos, *The Gospel of John* (Grand Rapids: Eerdmans, 1997), 168, n. 194.

127. G. R. Beasley-Murray, *John* (WBC 36; Waco, Tex.: Word, 1987), 63.

128. Morris, *John*, 247.

129. Note Old Testament allusions in Josh. 24:13; Eccl. 2:18–21; Mic. 6:15 (cf. Matt. 25:24).

130. A. Deissmann, *Light from the Ancient East*, rev. ed. (London: Hodder & Stoughton, 1927), 364–65. Cf. Boring, *Hellenistic Commentary*, 268; Craig R. Koester "'The Savior of the World' (John 4:41)," *JBL* 109 (1990): 665–80, esp. 666–67.

131. Alternatively, "own country" may here refer to both Jewish Galilee *and* Judea in contrast to Samaria (see discussion in Carson, *John*, 234–38). See also W. D. Davies, *The Gospel and the Land* (Berkeley: Univ. of California, 1974), 321–31.

132. In the present instance, the "king" was probably Herod Antipas (cf. Mark 6:14), though Antipas did not technically hold that title but was tetrarch of Galilee (4 B.C.–A.D. 39). See H. W. Hoehner, *Herod Antipas* (SNTSMS 17; Cambridge: Cambridge Univ. Press, 1972).

133. See A. H. Mead, "The βασιλικός in John 4.46–53," *JSNT* (1985): 69–72.

134. Keener, *BBC*, 275. It has been speculated that the royal official is to be identified with Cuza, the manager of Herod's household mentioned in Luke 8:3.

135. See Dalman, *Sacred Sites and Ways*, 105.

136. See Köstenberger, *Missions of Jesus and the Disciples* (Grand Rapids: Eerdmans, 1998), 58–59, esp. n. 43.

137. On Ḥanina ben Dosa, see B. M. Bokser, "Wonder-Working and the Rabbinic Tradition: The Case of Ḥanina ben Dosa," *JSJ* 16 (1985): 42–92; G. Vermes, "Ḥanina ben Dosa: A Controversial Galilean Saint from the First Century of the Christian Era," *JJS* 23 (1972): 28–50; 24 (1973): 51–64.

138. R. M. Mackowski, *Jerusalem, City of Jesus* (Grand Rapids: Eerdmans, 1980), 81–83, even believes that behind the account of John 5:2–9 is the story of a pagan sanctuary that he argues was an Asclepieion; but this is categorically ruled out by Hengel, "Johannesevangelium als Quelle," 313. Nevertheless, Hengel does point to the significance of the Asclepios cult for John's Asia Minor audience (315). See also the ancient and bibliographic references cited in Boring, *Hellenistic Commentary*, 266–67.

139. So, e.g., Hengel, "Johannesevangelium als Quelle," 308, 321.

140. See 1 Kings 8:2, 65; 12:32; 2 Chron. 5:3; 7:8; Neh. 8:14, 18; Ps. 81:3; Ezek. 45:25; see also John 7:2, 10, 14, 37.

141. Helpful treatments include Avi-Yonah, *World of the Bible*, 142; J. Jeremias, *The Rediscovery of Bethesda* (Louisville, Ky.: Southern Baptist Seminary, 1966); Mackowski, *Jerusalem, City of Jesus*, 79–83; E. J. Vardaman, "The Pool of Bethesda," *BT* 14 (1963): 27–29; D. J. Wieand, "John V.2 and the Pool of Bethesda," *NTS* 12 (1966): 392–404. R. Riesner, "Archeology and Geography," *DJG*, 41, prefers the translation "There is in Jerusalem by the Sheep Pool the [site] with five porticoes called in Hebrew [i.e., Aramaic] Bethesda."

142. See Hengel, "Johannesevangelium als Quelle," 310–12.

143. The existence of these pools, if not the name "Bethesda," may be attested by the copper scroll from Qumran (3Q15), which dates from between A.D. 35 and 65. See Hengel, "Johannesevangelium als Quelle," 309–10.

144. The northern, smaller pool may go back to monarchial times; the southern pool may be that established in the second century B.C. by Simon the high priest (Sir. 50:3). For ancient sources, see Hengel, "Johannesevangelium als Quelle," 310. The site favored by most scholars is located under the Monastery of St. Anne in the northeast quarter of the Old City. Cf. Jeremias, *Rediscovery of Bethesda*; Vardaman, "Pool of Bethesda," 28. Regarding the archaeological identification of Bethesda, see esp. Wieand, "John V.2 and the Pool of Bethesda," 396–400.

145. See Hengel, "Johannesevangelium als Quelle," 315.

146. Some manuscripts read "Bethzatha" (preferred by Nestle/Aland) or "Bethsaida" (cf. 1:44; 12:21), but "Bethesda" is attested much more widely and is clearly the superior reading. Cf. Hengel, "Johannesevangelium als Quelle," 309: "One should by all means read 'Bethesda.'"

147. Barrett, *John*, 252–53; Hengel, "Johannesevangelium als Quelle," 313 (with further references in n. 74).

148. Hengel, "Johannesevangelium als Quelle," 316, with references to Jewish commentaries and targumim.

149. Abbott, *Illustrated Commentary*, 65–66.

150. See L. Morris, *The Lord from Heaven* (Downers Grove, Ill.: InterVarsity, 1974), 31–35; J. Jeremias, *New Testament Theology* (London: SCM, 1971), 61–67.

151. Cited in Boring, *Hellenistic Commentary*, 267.

152. See Num. 15:37–41; Deut. 6:4; 11:13–21. On the Jewish confession of God as "one God," called the *Shema* (from Heb. "to hear"), see Schürer, *HJP²*, 2:454–55. See also L. W. Hurtado, "First-Century Jewish Monotheism," *JSNT* 71 (1998): 3–26.

153. Cf. S. S. Cohon, "The Unity of God: A Study in Hellenistic and Rabbinic Theology," *HUCA* 26 (1955): 425–79, who also cites affirmations of God's uniqueness in *Sib. Or.* 3:11–12, 545–61; *Let. Aris.* 132–38; *Wis.* 13–15; Philo (*Moses* 1.75; *Decalogue* 52–81; *QG* 4.8); and Josephus (*Ant.* 2.5.4 §§75–76).

154. See Deut. 32:39; 1 Sam. 2:6; 2 Kings 5:7; Tobit 13:2; Wis. 16:13.

155. Schürer, *HJP²*, 2:455–63.

156. *1 En.* 37–71; esp. 49:4; 61:9; 62:2–6; 63:11.

157. See K. Rengstorf, "ἀπόστολος," *TDNT*, 1:414–20.

158. See Köstenberger, *Missions of Jesus and the Disciples*, 115–21.

159. See Gen. 2:7; Job 10:12; 33:4; Ps. 36:9.

160. See Carson, *John*, 259.

161. See *1 En.* 22:13; 51; *4 Ezra* 7:32; *2 Bar.* 30:1–2; 42:7–8; 50:2.

162. On the trial motif in John's Gospel, see Andrew T. Lincoln, *Truth on Trial: the Lawsuit Motif in the Fourth Gospel* (Peabody, Mass.: Hendrickson, 2000).

163. See John 5:45–47; also Luke 24:27, 44; Acts 13:27; 1 John 5:9.

164. The passage is attributed to R. Eliezer ha-Qappar (after A.D. 160). See also *Ex. Rab.* 1:20 (where God is said to bear witness to Moses) and Wisd. Sol. 1:6.

165. F. Kenyon, *Our Bible and the Ancient Manuscripts* (London: Eyre & Spottiswoode, 1939), 38, cited in Morris, *John*, 292.

166. The saying is attributed to Rabbah b. Bar Ḥanah in the name of R. Yoḥanan (c. A.D. 70).

167. See 12:38; 13:18; 15:25; 17:12; 19:24, 36–37.

168. See 1:45; 2:22; 3:10; 5:45–47; 12:41; 20:9; cf. Luke 24:27, 44–45 and Matthew's "fulfillment quotations." Cf. F. F. Bruce, *The Time Is Fulfilled* (Exeter: Paternoster, 1978), 35–53.

169. Jer. 29:25, 31; cf. Deut. 18:20; Jer. 14:14–15; 23:25; 29:9.

170. *Ant.* 20.5.1 §§97–99; 20.9.6 §§171–72; *J.W.* 2.13.4–6 §§258–65. Cf. P. W. Barnett, "The Jewish Signs Prophets—A.D. 40–70: Their Intentions and Origin," *NTS* 27 (1980–81): 679–97; O. A. Piper, "Messiah," *ISBE*, 3:332–33; A. S. van der Woude and M. de Jonge, "χρίω, Χριστός," *TDNT*, 9:509–27.

171. Morris, *John*, 294, n. 125, citing R. H. Strachan, *The Fourth Gospel* (London: SCM, 1955).

172. See Ex. 32:11–14, 30–32; Num. 12:13; 14:19–20; 21:7; Deut. 9:18–20, 25–29.

173. See *Ex. Rab.* 18:3 on 12:29, where Moses is called "a good intercessor."

174. Schnackenburg, *John*, 1:470, n. 139.

175. Another explanation for the name is the proximity of the nearby town Tell el-'Oreimeth, which was lyre-like in shape. See W. S. Lasor, "Galilee, Sea of," *ISBE*, 2:391–92. For general information, see also R. Riesner, "Archaeology and Geography," *DJG*, 37.

176. Avi-Yonah, *World of the Bible*, 143.

177. B. Malina and R. L. Rohrbaugh, *Social-Science Commentary on the Gospel of John* (Minneapolis: Fortress, 1998), 127.

178. Carson, *John*, 270.

179. Cf. D. Daube, *The New Testament and Rabbinic Judaism*, 46–51.

180. This reflects the view of both Hillel and R. Yoḥanan (cf. *b. Ḥul.* 105b, attributed to Abaye, c. A.D. 280–339).

181. R. E. Brown, *The Gospel According to John* (AB 29; Garden City, N.Y.: Doubleday, 1966), 1:234–35.

182. Beasley-Murray, *John*, 88; R. A. Horsley, "Popular Messianic Movements Around the Time of Jesus," *CBQ* 46 (1984): 471–95.

183. Carson, *John*, 275.

184. R. Bultmann, *The Gospel of John* (Oxford: Blackwell, 1971), 223–24.

185. See Matt. 26:10 par.; John 9:4; Acts 13:41 (quoting Hab. 1:5); 1 Cor. 16:10.

186. Cf. 1QS 4:4; 1QH 13:36; CD 1:1–2; 13:7–8.

187. Cf. Rom. 3:20, 27–28; Gal. 2:16; 3:2, 5, 10; cf. Phil. 3:6, 9.

188. See Ps. 78:24; 105:40; Neh. 9:15; Wisd. Sol. 16:20. Cf. Maarten J. J. Menken, "The Provenance and Meaning of the Old Testament Quotations in John 6:31," *NovT* 30 (1988): 39–56.

189. Logos: *Alleg. Interp.* 3.169–76; *Worse* 118; *Heir* 79; wisdom: *Names* 259–60; *Heir* 191.

190. NIV: "food of God"; see Lev. 21:6, 8, 17, 21, 22; 22:25.

191. Cf. H. Odeberg, *The Fourth Gospel* (Amsterdam: B. R. Grüner, 1968), 264–65, n. 3.

192. See Gen. 9:4; Lev. 17:10–14; Deut. 12:16. Cf. C. Koester, *Symbolism in the Fourth Gospel* (Minneapolis: Fortress, 1995), 98–100.

193. Talbert, *Reading John*, 138.

194. I. Abrahams, *Studies in Pharisaism and the Gospels* (Cambridge: Cambridge Univ. Press, 1917), 1:1–17, esp. 4.

195. Note the absence of the article before synagogue: Jesus taught "in synagogue" (similar to our "in church").

196. See Raymond E. Brown, *The Gospel According to John* (AB; Garden City, N.Y.: Doubleday, 1966, 1970), 1:297.

197. But cf. Ps. 16:10, applied to Jesus in Acts 2:27 and 13:35.

198. E.g., Ex. 15:11; Lev. 11:44–45; 19:2; 20:7; 1 Sam. 2:2; 6:20; Isa. 6:3; 8:13; 10:17; frequently in the Psalms.

199. D. A. Carson, *Matthew* (EBC 8; Grand Rapids: Zondervan, 1984), 239–40.

200. For helpful information on the particulars of the Feast, see Avi-Yonah, *World of the Bible*, 144. Old Testament references include Lev. 23:33–43; Num. 29:12–39; Neh. 8:13–18; Hos. 12:9; Zech. 14:16–19.

201. Odeberg, *The Fourth Gospel*, 279, cited in Morris, *John*, 353.

202. E.g., 1QS 8:4; 9:12–21; 10:1–5; 1QM 1:5, 11–12; 14:13: "the times indicated by your eternal edicts"; 15:5; 1QH 5:19–20; 9:16–20; 20:4–9.

203. For a general survey, see W. J. Heard, "Revolutionary Movements," 688–98.

204. Cf. esp. R. Riesner, *Jesus als Lehrer* (WUNT 2/7; Tübingen: Mohr-Siebeck, 1981), 97–245.

205. M. McNamara, *Targum and Testament* (Shannon: Irish Univ. Press, 1972), 142.

206. See also Rom. 2:13; Gal. 2:14; 3:10 (quoting Deut. 27:26), 12 (citing Lev. 18:5).

207. Cf. *m. Šabb.* 18:3; 19:1–3; *Tanḥ.* 19b.

208. E.g., Deut. 16:18–19; Isa. 11:3–4; Zech. 7:9.

209. Cf. W. A. Meeks, *The Prophet-King* (NovTSup 14; Leiden: Brill, 1967), 162–64.

210. Schürer, *HJP²*, 2:275–308; Jeremias, *Jerusalem*, 160–81.

211. See Deut. 28:25; 30:4; Neh. 1:9; Ps. 146 [147]:2; Isa. 49:6; Jer. 15:7; 41 [34]:17; Dan. 12:2; Judith 5:19; 2 Macc. 1:27; cf. *Pss. Sol.* 8:28; 9:2.

212. See Acts 14:1; 16:1; 18:4; 19:10, 17; 20:21; Rom. 1:16; 2:9, 10; 3:9; 10:12; 1 Cor. 1:22, 24; 10:32; 12:13; Gal. 3:28; Col. 3:11.

213. Note that there is a separate term for "Greek-speaking (or Grecian) Jews," the word *Hellē-nistēs*, which occurs in Acts 6:1 and 9:29.

214. Some rabbinic sources which may or may not reach back to the first century are *Pesiq. Rab.* 52:3–6; *t. Sukkah* 3:3–12. Cf. B. H. Grigsby, "'If Any Man Thirsts . . .': Observations on the Rabbinic Background of John 7, 37–39," *Bib* 67 (1986): 101–8.

215. See Lev. 23:36; Num. 29:35; Neh. 8:18.

216. See Josephus, *Ant.* 13.8.3 §245; *b. Sukkah* 48b; *m. Sukkah* 5:6; 2 Macc. 10:6.

217. Isa. 58:11; cf. Prov. 4:23; 5:15; Zech. 14:8.

218. Isa. 12:3; 44:3; 49:10; Ezek. 36:25–27; 47:1; Joel 3:18; Amos 9:11–15; Zech. 13:1.

219. See Neh. 9:15, 19–20; other relevant passages include Ex. 17:6; Ps. 105:41; Prov. 18:4; Isa. 43:19–20; 55:1; Jer. 2:13; 17:13; see also 1QH 16:4–40. Cf. M. J. J. Menken, "The Origin of the Old Testament Quotation in John 7:38," *NovT* 38 (1996): 160–75.

220. See *b. Sanh.* 37a; Ezek. 5:5; 38:12; *Jub.* 8:19.

221. Cf. I. Abrahams, *Studies in Pharisaism and the Gospels* (Cambridge: Cambridge Univ. Press, 1917), 1:11, referring also to Zech. 14:8.

222. Cf. J. Marcus, "Rivers of Living Water from Jesus' Belly (John 7:38)," *JBL* 117 (1998): 328–30.

223. See 2 Sam. 7:12–16; Ps. 89:3–4; Isa. 9:7; 11:1; 55:3; esp. Mic. 5:2.

224. Targumic parallels (probably of a later date) confirm that there were at least some rabbinic connections between Mic. 5:2 and Messiah's origin (see Beasley-Murray, *John*, 118, who also refers to *Pirqe R. El.* 3[2b]; *y. Ber.* 5a; and *Midr. Rab.* 51 on Lam. 1:16); see also R. E. Brown, *The Birth of the Messiah*, updated ed. (New York: Doubleday, 1993), 513, n. 2.

225. See Appendix E by G. F. Moore in F. Jackson and K. Lake, *The Beginnings of Christianity*, 5 vols. (1920–1933, repr. Grand Rapids: Baker, 1979), 1:439–45.

226. Cf. Josephus, *Ant.* 14.9.3 §167; *J.W.* 1.10.6 §209. Cf. S. Pancaro, "The Metamorphosis of a Legal Principle in the Fourth Gospel: A Closer Look at Jn 7, 51," *Bib* 23 (1972): 340–51.

227. *Ex. Rab.* 21:3, a rabbinic commentary on Ex. 14:15 attributed to R. Eleazar b. Pedat (d. A.D. 279).

228. For helpful discussions of the evidence, see B. M. Metzger, *A Textual Commentary on the Greek New Testament*, 2d ed. (New York: UBS, 1994), 187–89; D. B. Wallace, "Reconsidering 'The Story of Jesus and the Adulteress Reconsidered,'" *NTS* 39 (1993): 290–96.

229. See Isa. 60:19–22; Zech. 14:5b–8; cf. Rev. 21:23–24.

230. Keener, *BBC*, 285.

231. See Barrett, *John*, 335–37.

232. I owe this comment to Craig Blomberg's forthcoming book on the historicity of John's Gospel, to be published by InterVarsity Press, ad. loc.

233. See 1QS 3:7, 20–21; cf. 1QS 4:11; 1QM 13:12.

234. Jörg Augenstein, "'Euer Gesetz'—Ein Pronomen und die johanneische Haltung zum Gesetz," *ZNW* 88 (1997): 311–13.

235. See Dodd, *Interpretation of the Fourth Gospel* (Cambridge: Cambridge Univ. Press, 1953), 82.

236. Morris, *John*, 393, n. 24, citing Str-B 1:790.

237. Cf. S. Pancaro, *Law in the Fourth Gospel* (NovTSup 42; Leiden: Brill, 1975), 275–78; J. H. Neyrey, "Jesus the Judge: Forensic Process in John 8, 21–59," *Bib* 68 (1987): 512–15; C. Cory, "Wisdom's Rescue: A New Reading of the Tabernacles Discourse (John 7:1–8:59)," *JBL* 116 (1997): 104–5.

238. Morris, *John*, 393, n. 28, quoting Tenney.

239. Cf. A. J. Droge and J. D. Tabor, *A Noble Death: Suicide and Martyrdom among Christians and Jews in Antiquity* (San Francisco: Harper, 1991).

240. Cf. Odeberg, *Fourth Gospel*, 293–94.

241. See esp. 41:4; 43:10, 13, 25; 46:4; 48:12; cf. Deut. 32:39.

242. See Acts 13:22; 1 Sam. 13:14; 16:7; 1 Kings 11:4; cf. Jer. 3:15.

243. E.g. Plato, *Phaedo* 115.A.1; Dio Chrysostom, *Or.* 50.4.9.

244. See *Disc.* 4.1.114; cf. 1.19.9; 4.7.16–17. See Boring, *Hellenistic Commentary*, 282.

245. Cf. Jer. 4:4; 9:25–26; Ezek. 36:26–27.

246. See Gen. 21:9–10; 25:21–34; Rom. 9:6–13; Gal. 4:21–23.

247. On the importance assigned to ancestry in Judaism, see Jeremias, *Jerusalem*, 271–302.

248. See Philo's portrayal of Abraham in *Abr.* 70; *Migr.* 43; 132–33; *Heir* 24–27.

249. See H. Ridderbos, *Paul: An Outline of His Theology* (Grand Rapids: Eerdmans, 1975), 130–35, esp. 131, n. 98.

250. *Gen. Rab.* 22:6, citing Ps. 32:1; attributed to R. Berekiah in R. Simeon's name (c. A.D. 140–165).

251. See also 1QH 12:29–30: "He is in sin from his maternal womb, and in guilty iniquity right to old age."

252. See also Rom. 6:11–18; 7:7–25; see comments on John 13:27.

253. The saying is attributed to R. Nathan b. Abba in the name of Rab (d. A.D. 47).

254. See, e.g., Ezek. 16:15, 32–34; Hos. 1:2; 4:15; for the phrase "children of *porneia*," see Hos. 1:2; 2:6 [4] LXX.

255. Schnackenburg, *John*, 2:212, refers to Origen, *Contra Celsum* I.28; *Acts Pil.* 2.3–4; and later the *Toledoth Jeschu* (the legend of Pandera). Cf. J. P. Meier, *A Marginal Jew* (Garden City, N.Y.: Doubleday, 1991), 222–29, 245–52.

256. R. Joshua b. Ḥananyah (c. A.D. 90–130). The saying is attributed to R. Simeon b. Azzai (c. A.D. 120–140).

257. See J. Schneider, "ἥκω," *TDNT*, 2:926–28.

258. See Köstenberger, *Missions of Jesus and the Disciples*, 121–30.

259. Cf. J. R. Díaz, "Palestinian Targum and New Testament," *NovT* 6 (1963): 75–80; N. A. Dahl, "The Murderer and His Father (8:44)," *NorTT* 64 (1963): 129–62.

260. See Dan. 9:27; 11:31; 12:11; cf. Matt. 24:15 par.

261. See 2 Cor. 5:21; Heb. 4:15; 1 Peter 2:22 (citing Isa. 53:9); 1 John 3:5.

262. See Acts 8:9–11; Justin, *Apol.* 26:1–5; *b. Sanh.* 43a.

263. *b. Soṭah* 22a; the rabbis are R. Eleazar (A.D. 80–120), R. Jannai (c. A.D. 240), and R. Aḥa b. Jacob (c. A.D. 300).

264. B. J. Malina, *The New Testament World* (Atlanta: John Knox, 1981), 25–50.

265. See Ps. 88:48 LXX; Luke 2:26; Heb. 11:5; the close equivalent "will not taste death" is found in John 8:52.

266. See J. Behm, "γεύομαι," *TDNT*, 1:677; B. Chilton, "'Not to Taste Death': A Jewish, Christian, and Gnostic Usage," in *Studia Biblica* 1978, ed. E. A. Livingstone (JSNTSup 3; Sheffield: JSOT, 1980), 2:29–36.

267. Beasley-Murray, *John*, 138, paraphrasing Schlatter.

268. Beasley-Murray, *John*, 139.

269. Cf. M. J. Edwards, "'Not Yet Fifty Years Old': John 8:57," *NTS* 40 (1994): 449–54.

270. Cf. Daube, *The New Testament and Rabbinic Judaism*, 306.

271. See Matt. 9:27–31; 12:22–23; 20:29–34 par.; Mark 8:22–26.

272. Jeremias, *Jerusalem*, 118.

273. See Gen. 25:22; cf. *Gen. Rab.* 63:6, attributed to R. Yoḥanan (d. A.D. 279) and several colleagues.

274. See 6:28; Ps. 64:9; 66:5; 78:7; Jer. 51:10; Tobit 12:6, 7, 11; 2 Macc. 3:36; 1QS 4:4.

275. See Rom. 9:17; cf. Ex. 9:16; 14:4; Ps. 76:10.

276. *Sent. cod. Byz.* 532 = *Sent. Mono.* 1.385.

277. *b. B. Bat.* 126b; dated during the time of R. Ḥanina, who was a student of R. Yehudah ha-Nasi (d. A.D. 217).

278. See Deissmann, *Light from the Ancient East*, 135; K. Rengstorf, "πηλός," *TDNT*, 6:119. According to Boring, *Hellenistic Commentary*, 284, the inscription comes probably from the Asclepius temple on the island in the Tiber in Rome and dates to A.D. 138.

279. E.g., R. Aqiba (c. A.D. 130) in *t. Sanh.* 12:10.

280. Cf. D. Smith, "Jesus and the Pharisees in Socio-Anthropological Perspective," *TrinJ* 6 (1985): 151–56, building on the work of M. Douglas, *Purity and Danger* (London: Ark, 1984).

281. See *J.W.* 2.16.2 §340; 5.4.1 §140; 5.6.1 §252; 5.9.4 §410; 5.12.2 §505; 6.7.2 §363; 6.85 §401.

282. J. Ramsey Michaels, *John: A Good News Commentary* (San Francisco: Harper & Row, 1983), 150.

283. Cf. R. M. Mackowski, *Jerusalem, City of Jesus*, 56–58, 72, 74.

284. See *Gen. Rab.* 98:8; 99:8; *Tg. Onq.*: "till the time that the King, the Meshiha, shall come."

285. See Jeremias, *Jerusalem*, 116–19.

286. P. H. Davids, "Rich and Poor," *DJG*, 704.

287. A. Schlatter, *Der Evangelist Johannes*, 4th ed. (Stuttgart: Calwer, 1975), 227. Incidentally, the second group apparently disregards the fact that Pharaoh's magicians were able to perform miracles as well (Ex. 7:11, 22; 8:7; but cf. 8:18–19).

288. E.g., Acts 9:22; 18:28; Phil. 2:11. Cf. L. W. Hurtado, *One God, One Lord* (London: SCM, 1988), 112–13.

289. Schürer, *HJP*², 2:459–63.

290. See the analysis of the *birkath-ha-minim* in S. C. Mimouni, *Le judéo-christianisme ancien* (Paris: Cerf, 1998), 161–88, who argues that a form of the *birkath* was in use prior to the addition of *noṣrim* to the Palestinian recension (which he dates to around A.D. 90) in order to exclude Jewish Christians.

291. For a survey of the issues and further bibliographic references, see Boring, *Hellenistic Commentary*, 301–2.

292. See Josh. 7:19: "Give glory to the LORD. . . . Tell me what you have done" (see also 2 Chron. 30:8; Jer. 13:16; 1 Esd. 9:8; *m. Sanh.* 6:2).

293. Schnackenburg, *John*, 2:251, and Ridderbos, *John*, 345, n. 287 (referring to K. Rengstorf, "μαθητής," *TDNT*, 4:443), consider this to be a characteristic rabbinic self-designation, while Carson, *John*, 373–74, apparently following Barrett, *John*, 362–63, says this self-designation was not common.

294. See Rengstorf, "μαθητής," 4:443

295. Note also the close parallel to this verse in P. Eg. 2 (c. A.D. 150).

296. See Job 27:9; Ps. 34:15; 66:18; 109:7; Prov. 15:8, 29; 21:27; 28:9; Isa. 1:15; John 14:13–14; 16:23–27; 1 Peter 3:7; 1 John 3:21–22.

297. See similar analysis in Barrett, *John*, 365. For a Hellenistic parallel, see Philostratus, *Life of*

Apollonius 1.12 (after A.D. 217): "If you too really care for uprightness, go boldly up to the god and tender what prayer you will."

298. Plutarch, *Rom.* 22.1; Dionysius of Halicarnassus, *Ant. Rom.* 2.60.4; *Pomp.* 4.2.

299. For Greek parallels, see *aiōn*, MM, 16.

300. See Ps. 146:8; Isa. 29:18; 35:5; 42:7, 18.

301. See Isa. 6:10; 42:19; Jer. 5:21 (cf. Matt. 13:13–15 par.; esp. John 12:40). Cf. J. M. Lieu, "Blindness in the Johannine Tradition," *NTS* 34 (1988): 90.

302. W. Schrage, "τυφλός," *TDNT*, 8:281, 284–86.

303. For a general survey, see D. H. Johnson, "Shepherd, Sheep," *DJG*, 751–54.

304. Francis J. Maloney, *The Gospel of John* (Collegeville, Minn.: Liturgical, 1998), 307; cited by Blomberg in his forthcoming book on the historicity of John's Gospel, ad. loc.

305. G. Dalman, *Arbeit und Sitte in Palästina* VI (Gütersloh: Bertelsmann, 1939), 284–85.

306. Cf. C. T. Wilson, *Peasant Life in the Holy Land* (London: John Murray, 1906), 165; Dalman, *Arbeit und Sitte* VI, 250–51.

307. Cf. Dalman, *Arbeit und Sitte* VI, 249.

308. God by the hand of Moses and Aaron, Ps. 77:20; Isa. 63:11, 14; cf. Ps. 78:52.

309. Kim E. Dewey, "*Paroimiai* in the Gospel of John," *Semeia* 17 (1980): 81–99.

310. W. Barclay, *The Gospel of John*, rev. ed. (Philadelphia: Westminster, 1975), 2:58. Cf. E. F. Bishop, "The Door of the Sheep—John x.7–9," *ExpTim* 71 (1959–1960): 307–9.

311. See Gen. 28:17; Ps. 78:23; *1 En.* 72–75 (e.g., 72:2); *3 Bar.* 6:13.

312. See Matt. 7:7, 13–14; 18:8–9; 25:10 and par.; Acts 14:22.

313. E.g., Gen. 48:15; 49:24; Ps. 23:1; 28:9; 77:20; 78:52; 80:1; Isa. 40:11; Jer. 31:9; Ezek. 34:11–31. See J. G. S. S. Thomson, "The Shepherd-Ruler Concept in the Old Testament and its Application in the New Testament," *SJT* 8 (1955): 406–18.

314. E.g., Ps. 74:1; 78:52; 79:13; 95:7; 100:3.

315. Jer. 23:1–4; cf. 3:15; Ezek. 34; Zech. 11:4–17.

316. 2 Sam. 5:2; Ps. 78:70–72; Ezek. 37:24; Mic. 5:4; cf. *Pss. Sol.* 17:40–41; *Midr. Rab.* 2:2 on Ex. 3:1.

317. Isa. 63:11; cf. Ps. 77:20; *Midr. Rab.* 2:2 on Ex. 3:1.

318. See references in Barrett, *John*, 374.

319. E.g., Jer. 10:21; 12:10; 23:1–4; Ezek. 34; Zeph. 3:3; Zech. 10:2–3; 11:4–17; *1 En.* 89:12–76; 90:22–31; *T. Gad* 1:2–4.

320. Cf. Dalman, *Arbeit und Sitte* VI, 233–35.

321. See Ex. 3:7; 33:12, 17; Jer. 31:34; Hos. 6:6; 13:5; Nah. 1:7.

322. Boring, *Hellenistic Commentary*, 288, identifying the above quotation as a proverb in the

Corpus Paroemiographorum Graecorum; no date is provided.

323. Jer. 3:15; 23:4–6; Ezek. 34:23–24; 37:15–28; Mic. 2:12; 5:3–5; For a detailed discussion of the Old Testament background to 10:16, cf. Köstenberger, "Jesus the Good Shepherd Who Will Also Bring Other Sheep (John 10:16)," *Faith and Mission* 19/1 (Fall 2001), forthcoming.

324. See *Pss. Sol.* 17:40; *2 Bar.* 77:13–17; CD 13:7–9.

325. Cited in Boring, *Hellenistic Commentary*, 288.

326. See Köstenberger, *Missions of Jesus and the Disciples*, 162, n. 83, with reference to J. W. Pryor, *John: Evangelist of the Covenant People* (Downers Grove, Ill.: InterVarsity, 1992).

327. For a comparison of Luke's travel narrative (Luke 9:51–18:14) with John 10:22–11:57, see Blomberg in his forthcoming book on the historicity of John's Gospel, at 10:22.

328. Cf. Hengel, "Johannesevangelium als Quelle," 317.

329. 1 Macc. 1:59; cf. Dan. 11:31; Josephus, *Ant.* 12.7.7 §§320–21.

330. 1 Macc. 4:52–60; cf. 2 Macc. 10:5–8.

331. See further C. K. Barrett, *The New Testament Background: Selected Documents*, rev. ed. (London: SPCK, 1987), 139–41.

332. Cf. Hengel, "Johannesevangelium als Quelle," 318.

333. So ibid., 318.

334. See esp. D. L. Bock, *Blasphemy and Exaltation in Judaism and the Final Examination of Jesus* (WUNT 2/106; Tübingen: Mohr-Siebeck, 1998), esp. the six conclusions on 234–37.

335. The expression "Law" also covered the Psalter (for a broader conception of the term "the Law," see 12:34; 15:25; Rom. 3:10–19; 1 Cor. 14:21), just as "Torah" in rabbinic literature sometimes covers the Hebrew Scriptures in their entirety. Regarding this "generic sense" of Law, see S. Pancaro, *Law in the Fourth Gospel*, esp. 175–92.

336. See *b. ʿAbod. Zar.* 5a; sayings to this effect are attributed to R. Yose (c. A.D. 150) and Resh Laqish (third century A.D.). For a variation of the first view, see R. Jungkuntz, "Approach to the Exegesis of John 10:34–36," *CTM* 35 (1964): 556–65. The second position is held by J. A. Emerton, "Interpretation of Psalm 82 in John 10," *JTS* 11 (1960): 329–32, and idem, "Melchizedek and the Gods: Fresh Evidence for the Jewish Background of John 10:34–36," *JTS* 17 (1966): 399–401. For a variation of the third view, see A. T. Hanson, "John's Interpretation of Psalm 82," *NTS* 11 (1964–65): 158–62, and idem, "John's Interpretation of Psalm 82 Reconsidered," *NTS* 13 (1967): 363–67. See

further W. Gutbrod, "νόμος," *TDNT*, 4:1022–32, 1054–55.

337. For the charge of blasphemy against Jesus, see now the recent article by L. W. Hurtado, "Pre–70 C.E. Jewish Opposition to Christ-Devotion," *JTS* 50 (1999): 35–58, esp. 36–37.

338. See Ex. 28:41; 40:13; Lev. 8:30; 2 Chron. 5:11; 26:18.

339. The saying is attributed to R. Aḥa (d. A.D. 510) in the name of R. Jonathan (c. A.D. 200).

340. Cf. J. C. VanderKam, "John 10 and the Feast of the Dedication," in *Of Scribes and Scrolls*, ed. J. J. Collins and T. H. Tobin (Lanham, Md.: Univ. Press of America, 1990), 211–14.

341. Cf. E. Bammel, "John Did No Miracles: John 10:41," in *Miracles*, ed. C. F. D. Moule (London: Mowbrays, 1965), 197–202.

342. On the relationship between the two Bethanys referred to in John's Gospel, see W. H. Brownlee, "Whence the Gospel According to John?" in *John and Qumran*, ed. J. H. Charlesworth (London: G. Chapman, 1972), 167–74.

343. The name "Bethany" arose from a combination of the Hebrew word for "house," *beth*, and *ananyah*, whereby one of the two "an's" dropped out, a phenomenon known among linguists as syllabic haplology. Cf. W. F. Albright, "New Identifications of Ancient Towns: Bethany in the Old Testament," *BASOR* 9 (1923): 8–10.

344. Cf. C. S. Clermont-Ganneau, "Sarcophagi," *PEQ* 6 (1874): 7–10; C. H. Kraeling, "Christian Burial Urns," *BA* 9 (1946): 18, cited in F. F. Bruce, *The Gospel of John* (Grand Rapids: Eerdmans, 1983), 253; and Avi-Yonah, *World of the Bible*, 146.

345. Cf. Riesner, "Bethany Beyond the Jordan (John 1:28)," 44–45.

346. See H. Balz, "ὕπνος," *TDNT*, 8:552. Further references are provided by Gerald L. Borchert, *John*, vol. 1 (Nashville: Broadman & Holman, 1996), 352, and Barnabas Lindars, *The Gospel of John* (Grand Rapids: Eerdmans, 1972), 394.

347. Cf. J. A. Fitzmyer, *Essays on the Semitic Background of the New Testament* (London: G. Chapman, 1971), 369–70.

348. The original collection was compiled in Palestine by R. Eliezer b. Zadok (1st cent. A.D.). Later it was embellished and amplified by R. Ḥiyya (2d cent. A.D.). See also A. T. Hanson, "The Old Testament Background to the Raising of Lazarus," in *SE VI*, ed. E. A. Livingstone (Berlin: Akademie, 1973), 252–55.

349. But see Wisd. Sol. 19:3; *m. Ketub.* 4:4.

350. Brown, *John*, 1:424.

351. Cf. T. E. Pollard, "The Raising of Lazarus (John xi)," in *SE VI*, 434–43.

352. See Richard Bauckham, "Life, Death, and the Afterlife in Second Temple Judaism," in *Life in the Face of Death: The Resurrection Message of the New Testament* (Richard N. Longnecker, ed., Grand Rapids: Eerdmans, 1998), 80–95.

353. See Matt. 22:23–33 par.; Acts 23:8; Josephus, *J.W.* 2.8.14 §165; *Ant.* 18.1.4 §16. See A. Oepke, "ἀνίστημι, ἀνάστασις," *TDNT*, 1:370; F. Lang, "Σαδδουκαῖος," *TDNT*, 7:46–47.

354. See Schürer, *HJP²*, 2:456.

355. For a discussion of the Jewish doctrine of corporate personality see H. W. Robinson, *Corporate Personality in Ancient Israel* (Philadelphia: Fortress, 1964).

356. See Gen. 50:10; 2 Sam. 3:32; Jer. 38:15 LXX.

357. See G. Stählin, "θρηνέω," *TDNT*, 3:151–52.

358. See Ps. 6:2–3, 7; 18:5; 31:9–13; 38:10; 55:2, 4; 109:22; 143:4.

359. See Job 3:24; Ezek. 27:35; Mic. 2:6; 2 Macc. 4:37; Sir. 12:16; 31:13.

360. See Diodorus Siculus, *B. H.* 17.66.4; 27.6.1; Plutarch, *Cam.* 5.5; *Pyrrh.* 34.4; *Pomp.* 80.5; Josephus, *Ant.* 11.5.6 §162; *J.W.* 5.10.5 §445; 6.5.3 §304.

361. Avi-Yonah, *World of the Bible*, 147. For more information and examples of tombs from this period, see R. M. Mackowski, *Jerusalem: City of Jesus*, 20–21, 157–59.

362. Regarding the stone being laid across the entrance, see *m. ʾOhal.* 2:4.

363. For the use of spices in the burial process, see further J. N. Sanders, *A Commentary on the Gospel According to St John*, ed. and compl. by B. A. Mastin (London: Black, 1968), 274.

364. See W. Bingham Hunter, "Contextual and Genre Implications for the Historicity of John 11:41b–42," *JETS* 28 (1985): 53–70, who argues for a similarity in form with Jewish prayers of thanksgiving (*hodayot*).

365. Cf. H. van der Loos, *The Miracles of Jesus* (NovTSup 9; Leiden: Brill, 1965), 133–38; on the raising of Lazarus, ibid., 576–89.

366. See 12:27–28; 17:1, 5, 21, 24; Luke 11:2; 22:42; 23:34, 46.

367. Morris, *John*, 498.

368. Carson, *John*, 418–19; see also Beasley-Murray, *John*, 195.

369. About A.D. 90; cf. *b. Ketub.* 8b; *b. Moʾed Qaṭ.* 27b.

370. See Prov. 7:16; 31:22; Isa. 19:9; Ezek. 27:7.

371. See E. Lohse, "συνέδριον," *TDNT*, 7:861–62.

372. For further information on the Sanhedrin, see Schürer, *HJP²*, 2:199–226; Lohse, "συνέδριον," 7:861–71. Hengel, "Johannesevan-

gelium als Quelle," 330, questions whether the Sanhedrin had seventy members in Jesus' day as is frequently alleged; he rather favors the view that the composition of the Council depended on the respective ruling high priest, esp. in the period between A.D. 6 and 41.

373. Note also the absence of the definite article before *synedrion* in the Greek (which may imply "a gathering" rather than "the Sanhedrin"), though not too much should be made of this.

374. See Tobias Nicklas, "Die Prophetie des Kaiaphas: Im Netz johanneischer Ironie," *NTS* 46 (2000): 589–94.

375. See Hengel, "Johannesevangelium als Quelle," 332.

376. Cf. D. Daube, *Collaboration with Tyranny in Rabbinic Law* (London: Oxford Univ. Press, 1966), 18–47. M. Barker, "John 11.50," in *The Trial of Jesus. Fs. C. F. D. Moule*, ed. E. Bammel (SBT 2/13; London: SCM, 1970), 41–46, links Caiaphas's words with current messianic expectations.

377. See further C. H. Dodd, "The Prophecy of Caiaphas: John 11:47–53," in *More New Testament Studies* (Manchester: Manchester Univ. Press, 1968): 58–68.

378. See *J.W.* 1.2.8 §68; idem, *Ant.* 13.10.2 §§282–83; 13.10.7 §299; cf. *t. Soṭah* 13:5, with 13:6 referring to Simeon the Righteous (after 200 B.C.).

379. See Ps. 106:47; 107:3; Isa. 11:12; 43:5–7; 49:5; Jer. 23:3; 31:8–14; Ezek. 34:11–16; 36:24–38; 37:21–28; Mic. 2:12; cf. James 1:1.

380. Cf. J. Beutler, "Two Ways of Gathering: The Plot to Kill Jesus in John 11:47–53," *NTS* 40 (1994): 399–404.

381. R. Riesner, "Archeology and Geography," *DJG*, 49. But see W. F. Albright, AASOR 4 (1922–23): 124–33, who argues that the Ephraim mentioned in John is not Et-Taiyibeh but Ain Samieh, slightly to the northeast and lower in a valley.

382. Hoehner, *Chronological Aspects*, esp. 44, 63, 143.

383. W. Reinhardt, "The Population Size of Jerusalem and the Numerical Growth of the City," in *Palestinian Setting* (BAFCS 4; Grand Rapids: Eerdmans, 1995), 262–63. Josephus (*J.W.* 6.9.3 §422–25) provides the unlikely figure of over 2,500,000, on the basis of a census taken by Cestius in the 60s.

384. See Num. 9:6; 2 Chron. 30:17–18; John 18:28; cf. *m. Pesaḥ.* 9:1.

385. Keener, *BBC*, 294.

386. Keener (ibid.) mentions that a flask would normally contain no more than an ounce.

387. Cf. R. H. Harrison, *Healing Herbs of the Bible* (Leiden: Brill, 1966), 48–49.

388. W. Walker, *All the Plants of the Bible* (London: Lutterworth, 1958), 196.

389. See the illustration in A. Millard, *Discoveries from Bible Times*, 179.

390. Cf. J. Lightfoot, *A Commentary on the New Testament from the Talmud and Hebraica*, 3:376.

391. See the survey in L. A. Losie, "Triumphal Entry," *DJG*, 854–59.

392. Avi-Yonah, *World of the Bible*, 148.

393. W. R. Farmer, "The Palm Branches in John 12:13," *JTS* 3 (1952): 62–66.

394. Lit., "give salvation now," "O save!" (cf. 2 Sam. 14:4: "Help me, O king!"; 2 Kings 6:26).

395. See O. Michel, "ὄνος," *TDNT*, 5:284, n. 7; Ferguson, *Background*, 560–61.

396. This kind of conflation of quotations from the Old Testament is not uncommon in the New Testament (e.g., Matt. 27:9–10; Mark 1:2–3).

397. The saying is attributed to R. Meir (c. A.D. 150). Similarly, *Pirqe R. El.* 33, attributed to R. Eliezer (c. A.D. 90). See also 1 Cor. 15:37.

398. See Gen. 29:31, 33; Deut. 21:15; Matt. 6:24 par.; compare Luke 14:26 with Matt. 10:37.

399. See Köstenberger, "Jesus As Rabbi," 119, esp. n. 90.

400. E.g., Ps. 79:9; Isa. 63:14; 66:5; Ezek. 38:23.

401. Old Testament references to the "voice from heaven" include 1 Sam. 3:4, 6, 8; 1 Kings 19:13; and Dan. 4:31–32. For other examples of a "heavenly voice" in Jewish literature, see *1 En.* 65:4; *2 Esd.* 6:13, 17; *2 Bar.* 13:1; 22:1; *T. Levi* 18:6. See also Acts 9:4–6; 11:7, 9–10; Rev. 10:4, 8; 11:12; 14:2, 13; 18:4; 19:5; 21:3.

402. Cf. C. K. Barrett, *The Holy Spirit and the Gospel Tradition*, rev. ed. (London: SPCK, 1970), 39–40; G. H. Dalman, *The Words of Jesus* (Edinburgh: T. & T. Clark, 1902), 204–5.

403. Str-B 1:125, cited in Barrett, *Holy Spirit and the Gospel Tradition*, 39, n. 4. The *Tosafot* date to the twelfth or thirteenth century A.D.

404. Cited in Boring, *Hellenistic Commentary*, 292.

405. Cf. A. F. Segal, "Ruler of This World: Attitudes About Mediator Figures and the Importance of Sociology for Self-Definition," in *Jewish and Christian Self-Definition*, ed. E. P. Sanders (Philadelphia: Fortress, 1981), 2:245–68, 403–13.

406. See 1QS 1:18; 2:5, 19; 1QM 1:5; 4:2; 13:2, 4, 11–12; 14:9; 15:3; CD 12:2.

407. See A. S. van der Woude and M. de Jonge, "χρίω, Χριστός," *TDNT*, 9:509–17.

408. See 8:12; 11:9–10; cf. 1 John 1:6–7; 2:11; see also John 1:4–5, 7–9; 3:19–21; 9:4.

409. E.g., 1QS 1:9; 2:16; 3:13, 24; 1QM 1:1, 3, 9, 11, 13.

410. See 13:18; 15:25; 17:12; 19:24, 36. See C. A. Evans, "On the Quotation Formulas in the Fourth Gospel," *BZ* 26 (1982): 79–83; idem, "Obduracy and the Lord's Servant: Some Observations on the Use of the Old Testament in the Fourth Gospel," in *Early Jewish and Christian Exegesis*, ed. C. A. Evans and W. F. Stinespring (Atlanta: Scholars, 1987), esp. 225–26.

411. See Deut. 5:15; Isa. 40:10; 51:9; 52:10; 63:5; cf. Luke 1:51.

412. For a detailed account of the Jewish legal theory of envoys, see K. Rengstorf, "ἀπόστολος," *TDNT,* 1:414–20.

413. Cf. M. J. O'Connell, "The Concept of Commandment in the Old Testament," *TS* 21 (1960): 352.

414. See Finegan, *Handbook,* 357–58, who sees the Synoptics and John in conflict here and prefers the latter as "historically the more likely."

415. See further commentary on 18:28 and 19:14 below. For a thorough defense of the position taken here, see Carson, *Matthew,* 530–32; C. L. Blomberg, *The Historical Reliability of the Gospels* (Downers Grove, Ill.: InterVarsity, 1987), 175–80.

416. Cited in Keener, *BBC,* 297.

417. First-century B.C. and A.D. references include Plautus, *Most.* 267; Catullus, *Carm.* 12.3; Petronius, *Sat.* 28.4; Martial, *Epigr.* 12.70.1; and Juvenal, *Sat.* 14.22. The word originally referred to a piece of linen cloth and was applied to various specific things made of linen, such as handkerchiefs, towels, or curtains.

418. See Gen. 18:4; 19:2; 24:32; 43:24; Judg. 19:21; 1 Sam. 25:41.

419. See *T. Ab.* 3:7–9; *Jos. Asen.* 7:1. Cf. J. C. Thomas, *Footwashing in John 13 and the Johannine Community* (JSNTSup 61: Sheffield: JSOT, 1991), 35–40, who also cites instances of footwashing as part of hospitality in the Greco-Roman world (46–50).

420. Avi-Yonah, *World of the Bible,* 149, including a picture of fifth-century B.C. Attic pottery depicting this scene.

421. The term *niptēr* (only here in the New Testament) occurs elsewhere only in a Cyprian inscription from Roman times (cf. BAGD, 540). The longer expression *podaniptēr* ("footbath") is found in Herodotus 2.172 (5th cent. B.C.; cf. P66).

422. For further references and discussion, see Köstenberger, "Jesus As Rabbi," 122–23.

423. R. Yoḥanan (d. A.D. 279) in the name of R. Simeon b. Yoḥai (c. A.D. 140–165), with reference to Elisha's service of Elijah in 2 Kings 3:11.

424. *b. Ketub.* 96a; attributed to R. Joshua b. Levi (third century A.D.).

425. *Mek. Ex.* 21:2. This work may have been originally compiled on the basis of discussions between A.D. 135–150, with the final redaction taking place in the second half of the third century (G. Stemberger, *Introduction to the Talmud and Midrash,* 2d ed. [Edinburgh: T. & T. Clark, 1996], 255).

426. E.g., 1 Sam. 25:41; *Jos. Asen.* 20:1–5. See also the anecdote involving the mother of R. Ishmael (d. c. A.D. 135) recounted in Str-B 1:707.

427. Cf. Köstenberger, "Jesus As Rabbi," 117.

428. In Lev. 15:11, both terms are found side by side. On the distinctiveness in meaning between *louō* and *niptō,* see Thomas, *Footwashing,* 51, n. 25; A. Oepke, "λούω," *TDNT,* 4:305; F. Hauck, "νίπτω," *TDNT,* 4:947.

429. Barrett, *John,* 441.

430. Cf. *Cat. Min.* 67.1; *Pomp.* 55.6; see also Lucian, *Gallo* 7, 9; *Timon* 54; *Mort. Peregr.* 6.

431. E.g., a prophet's patience: James 5:10; cf. Philo, *Her.* 256.

432. E.g., the disobedience of Israel (Heb. 4:11); godless Sodom and Gomorrah (2 Peter 2:6; cf. Philo, *Conf.* 64).

433. 2 Macc. 6:28, 31; 4 Macc. 17:22–23: "atoning sacrifice"; Sir. 44:16; cf. Josephus, *J.W.* 6.2.1 §§103, 106.

434. Carson, *John,* 470.

435. See 2 Sam. 15:12. Cf. *b. Sanh.* 106b; attributed to R. Yoḥanan (d. A.D. 279).

436. J. H. Bernard, *A Critical and Exegetical Commentary on the Gospel of John* (Edinburgh: T. & T. Clark, 1928), 2:467.

437. Carson, *John,* 471; Morris, *John,* 553; Brown, *John,* 2:554; Barrett, *John,* 445.

438. Ferguson, *Backgrounds,* 338–39.

439. On the "disciple whom Jesus loved," see Köstenberger, *Missions of Jesus and the Disciples,* 154–61 (including further bibliographic references). For the identification of this disciple with John the son of Zebedee, see ch. 1 in Köstenberger, *Encountering John*; for the identification of this disciple with the Fourth Evangelist, see H. M. Jackson, "Ancient Self-Referential Conventions and Their Implications for the Authorship and Integrity of the Gospel of John," *JTS* 50 (1999): 1–34.

440. Cf. Jackson, "Ancient Self-Referential Conventions," 31.

441. Cf. G. H. R. Horsley, *New Documents Illustrating Early Christianity,* vol. 1 (North Sidney: Macquarie Univ. Press, 1981), 9 (= §1); vol. 2 (1982), 75 (= §2).

442. See *b. Pesaḥ.* 108a: "Even the poorest man in Israel must not eat until he reclines."

443. "The senior takes his place first, the second next above him, and then the third one below him" (b. Ber. 46b).

444. Morris, *John*, 555–56. See also Jeremias, *Eucharistic Words*, 48–49.

445. See *m. Pesaḥ.* 10:3.

446. Cf. Jeremias, *Eucharistic Words*, 54.

447. On acts of charity, see Jeremias, *Jerusalem*, 126–34. On begging, see ibid., 116–19.

448. The saying is attributed to Mar Zuṭra (d. A.D. 417); cf. Luke 21:2–4 par.

449. E.g., Matt. 8:20 par.; 17:24–27; Luke 8:3.

450. Ex. 12:8; cf. *m. Zebaḥ.* 5:8. Cf. Jeremias, *Eucharistic Words*, 44–46, who also cites *Jub.* 49:1, 12; *t. Pesaḥ.* 1:34 and other references.

451. Brown, *John*, 2:611. See also *T. Reub.* 1:3: "My children, I am dying and I go the way of my fathers."

452. Lev. 19:18; cf. Matt. 5:43. For a general survey, see L. Morris, "Love," *DJG*, 492–95.

453. *T. Gad* 6:1; cf. *T. Zeb.* 5:1, 8:5; *T. Jos.* 17:1–2; *T. Iss.* 7:6–7; *T. Sim.* 4:7; *T. Reu.* 4:5.

454. The rendering "mansions" (rather than "rooms"), which crept into English translations through Tyndale (1526) via the Vulgate, mistakenly suggests luxurious accommodations in modern parlance (Lat. *mansio* referred to a halting place, which was still the meaning of "mansion" in Tyndale's day). See Brown, *John*, 2:619.

455. On "father's house" as designating a (patriarchal) family in the LXX and extrabiblical literature, see J. McCaffrey, *The House with Many Rooms: The Temple Theme of Jn. 14, 2–3* (AnBib 114; Rome: Pontifical Biblical Institute, 1988), 50–51.

456. E.g., *1 En.* 39:4–5; 41:2; 71:16; *2 En.* 61:2. Cf. Luke 16:9, where Jesus speaks of his disciples' being "welcomed into eternal dwellings."

457. *Dreams* 1.256; cf. *Confusion* 78; *Heir* 274; *Moses* 2.288.

458. G. Schrenk, "πατήρ," *TDNT*, 5:997.

459. Walker, *Jesus and the Holy City* (Grand Rapids: Eerdmans, 1996), 186–90, esp. 188.

460. Similar language is used in Mark 10:40; 1 Cor. 2:9; Heb. 11:16; 1 Peter 1:4.

461. For specific rabbinic references and discussion, see Köstenberger, "Jesus As Rabbi," 120–22.

462. 1QS 4:2–17; cf. 2 Peter 2:2, 15, where "the way of truth" or "the straight way" is contrasted with "shameful ways" and "the way of Balaam."

463. Perhaps on the basis of Isa. 40:3; cf. 1QS 8:12–16; 9:19–20.

464. Acts 9:2; 19:9, 23; 22:4; 24:14, 22.

465. See Jer. 24:7; 31:34; Hos. 13:4. Cf. H. B. Huffmon, "The Treaty Background of Hebrew YĀDAʿ," *BASOR* 181 (1966): 31–37.

466. But see Ps. 9:10; 36:10; Dan. 11:32.

467. See 20:21. In another sense, it is the Spirit who is Jesus' "successor" (cf. v. 16). In 15:26–27, it is both the disciples and the Spirit.

468. See Deut. 5:10; 6:5–6; 7:9; 10:12–13; 11:13, 22.

469. See *New Docs* 4 §71.

470. Plato, *Phaed.* 65. A similar phrase is also found in Lucian, *Mort. Peregr.* 6.

471. Bammel, "Farewell Discourse," 108.

472. Cf. esp. Ps.-Plat. *Def.* 413a, cited in W. Foerster, "εἰρήνη," *TDNT*, 2:401.

473. Cf. L. Morris, *The Apostolic Preaching of the Cross*, 3d ed. (London: Tyndale, 1965), 237–44.

474. Beasley-Murray, *John*, 262.

475. On peace, see further W. Foerster, "εἰρήνη," *TDNT*, 2:400–17.

476. See BAGD, 592.

477. Cf. Josephus, *J.W.* 5.5.4 §210; *Ant.* 15.11.3 §395; *m. Mid.* 3:8; Tacitus, *Hist.* 5.5.

478. See 5:1–7; 27:2–6; cf. Ps. 80:8–16; Jer. 2:21; 6:9; 12:10–13; Ezek. 15:1–8; 17:5–10; 19:10–14; Hos. 10:1–2; 14:7; see also Sir. 24:17–23; 2 Esd. 5:23. An extensive allegorical depiction of Israel as a vine is also found in *Lev. Rab.* 36:2 (with reference to Ps. 80:9).

479. Since the Old Testament develops the vine metaphor in predominantly negative terms, the notion of the vine as the source of life for the branches is largely absent (but see Sir. 24:17–21).

480. E. M. Sidebottom, "The Son of Man As Man in the Fourth Gospel," *ExpTim* 68 (1956–57): 234, points to similarities in vocabulary between John 15 and the *mamšal* of the vine in Ezek. 17. Other parallels are adduced by B. Vawter, "Ezekiel and John," *CBQ* 26 (1964): 450–58. A general survey is found in R. A. Whitacre, "Vine, Fruit of the Vine," *DJG*, 867–68.

481. For Palestinian horticultural practice, see G. Dalman, *Arbeit und Sitte in Palästina* IV (Hildesheim: G. Olms, 1964), 312–13.

482. See Horace, *Epod.* 2.13: "cutting off useless branches with the pruning knife."

483. Cf. J. C. Laney, "Abiding Is Believing: The Analogy of the Vine in John 15:1–6," *BibSac* 146 (1989): 55–66, esp. 58–60.

484. See Ex. 25:8; 29:45; Lev. 26:11–12; Ezek. 37:27–28; 43:9. E. Malatesta, *Interiority and Covenant* (Anal. Bib. 69; Rome: Biblical Institute Press, 1978), esp. ch. 8; J. W. Pryor, "Covenant and Community in John's Gospel," *RTR* 47 (1988): 49–50.

485. F. Lang, "πῦρ," *TDNT*, 6:934–47, esp. 936–37 and 942.

486. E.g., Isa. 25:9; 35:10; 51:3; 61:10; 66:10; Zeph. 3:14–17; Zech. 9:9. See H. Conzelmann, "χαίρω, χαρά," *TDNT*, 9:362–63.

487. See G. Delling, "πληρόω," *TDNT*, 6:297–98; Conzelmann, "χαίρω, χαρά," 9:365.

488. For further references, see G. Stählin, "φίλος," *TDNT*, 9:151–54. See also Malina and Rohrbaugh, *Social Science Commentary*, 236.

489. For a study of the concept of friendship in Greco-Roman, Jewish, and early Christian literature with special focus on John's Gospel, see J. M. Ford, *Redeemer-Friend and Mother* (Minneapolis: Fortress, 1997).

490. *Jub.* 19:9; CD 3:2; *Apoc. Ab.* 9:6; 10:5; cf. James 2:23.

491. Philo, *Heir* 21; *Sacrifices* 130; *Cherubim* 49; *Moses* 1.156.

492. A similar contrast (between servants and sons) is found in Gal. 4:1–7 and Heb. 3:5–6.

493. See G. Quell and G. Schrenk, "ἐκλέγομαι," *TDNT*, 4:155–68.

494. See Matt. 10:34–38 par.; 1 Cor. 7:12–16. Cf. W. Barclay, *The Gospel of John*, rev. ed. (Philadelphia: Westminster, 1975), 2:183–85.

495. See 1 Sam. 12:22; 2 Chron. 6:32; Jer. 14:21; cf. Acts 5:41; 1 Peter 4:14; 1 John 2:12; Rev. 2:3.

496. See G. Stählin, "σκάνδαλον," *TDNT*, 7:339–58.

497. E.g., Isa. 39:6; Jer. 7:32; 9:25; 16:14; 31:31, 38; Zech. 14:1; 2 Esd. 5:1; 13:29; cf. Mark 2:20; Luke 19:43; 23:29.

498. See the use of "service to God" (*latreia*) with reference to Jewish worship in Rom. 9:4 and Heb. 9:1, 6. On Roman persecution, see comments on 16:1; see further M. Sordi, *The Christians and the Roman Empire* (London/New York: Routledge, 1994).

499. See Acts 8:1–3; 26:9–12; Gal. 1:13–14.

500. E.g., Acts 5:33–40; cf. *m. Sanh.* 9:6: "But the Sages say: [He shall suffer death] at the hands of Heaven."

501. E.g., Isa. 11:1–10; 32:14–18; 42:1–4; 44:1–5; Jer. 31:31–34; Ezek. 11:17–20; 36:24–27; 37:1–14; Joel 2:28–32; cf. John 3:5; 7:37–39.

502. Cf. F. W. Young, "A Study of the Relation of Isaiah to the Fourth Gospel," *ZNW* 46 (1955): 224–26.

503. See Isa. 13:8; 21:3; 26:17–18; 42:14; 66:7–13; Jer. 4:31; 6:24; 13:21; 22:23; 30:6; 49:22–24; 50:43; Mic. 4:9–10; cf. 2 Esd. 16:38.

504. E.g., *b. Sanh.* 98b; *b. Ketub.* 111a; 1QH 11:8–12; cf. Rev. 12:2–5. Cf. W. H. Brownlee, "Messianic Motifs of Qumran and the New Testament," *NTS* 3 (1956/57): 12–30, esp. 29.

505. E.g., Isa. 53:6; Jer. 23:1; 50:17; Ezek. 34:6, 12, 21.

506. See Wisd. Sol. 10:2; *Odes Sol.* 9:11; 10:4; 1 Esd. 3:12. J. E. Bruns, "A Note on John 16 33 and 1 John 2 13–14," *JBL* 86 (1967): 453, contends that John's portrayal of Jesus as victor echoes the pagan myth of Herakles, the conqueror of death and evil.

507. See Damiano Marzotto, "Giovanni 17 e il Targum di Esodo 19–20," *RivB* 25 (1977): 375–88.

508. Cited in Barrett, *John*, 390; cited also in Boring, *Hellenistic Commentary*, 303, where the source is identified as magical papyrus *PGM*, 7.500–504 (3d cent. A.D.).

509. Other relevant passages include Isa. 49:3; *Odes Sol.* 10:4; Phil. 2:9.

510. See also Matt. 11:27; 28:18; Wisd. Sol. 10:2.

511. See *b. Ber.* 63a, citing Prov. 3:6; *Song Rab.* I.4 §1, citing Hos. 4:6; *b. Makk.* 24a, citing Hab. 2:4.

512. Cf. H. M. Jackson, "Ancient Self-Referential Conventions," 24–31.

513. E.g., Ps. 22:22; Isa. 52:6; Ezek. 39:7.

514. E.g., Heb. "children of unrighteousness" becomes "children of perdition" in Isa. 57:4 LXX; the same phrase is found in *Jub.* 10:3.

515. Heb. "the people I have totally destroyed" becomes "the people of perdition" in Isa. 34:5 LXX.

516. See Matt. 23:15: "son of hell"; Eph. 5:6 = Col. 3:6 (textual variant): "those who are disobedient" = "sons of disobedience."

517. Cf. F. W. Danker, "The *huios* Phrases in the New Testament," *NTS* 7 (1960–61): 94, who cites a passage in Menander's *Dyscolos* (published as part of Papyrus Bodmer IV) that contains the word "madman" (lit., "son of madness," *odynēs huios*).

518. 1QS 9:16 and 10:19: "men of the pit"; CD 6:15 and 13:14: "sons of the pit."

519. *y. Ber.* 2:7: "God knows when it is the right time to take the righteous from the world."

520. *y. Peʾah* 1:1: "If a person guards himself from transgression once, twice, three times, thereafter, the Holy One, blessed be he, will guard him"; *Deut. Rab.* 4:4: "If you will keep the words of the law, I will guard you from the demons" (cf. Ps. 140:1; Matt. 6:13).

521. For a further discussion of Qumran parallels to the notion of unity in John 17, see Brown, *John*, 2:777.

522. *Gen. Rab.* 1:10; 2:5; *Lev. Rab.* 25:3; *Num. Rab.* 12:6; *Deut. Rab.* 10:2; *As. Mos.* 1:13–14. For further Jewish references, see F. Hauck, "καταβολή," *TDNT*, 3:620–21.

523. E.g., Ps. 116:5; 119:137; Jer. 12:1; cf. Rom. 3:26; 1 John 1:9; Rev. 16:5.

524. See the studies in *The Trial of Jesus*, ed. E. Bammel (SBT 2/13; London: SCM, 1970); B. Corley, "Trial of Jesus," *DJG*, 841–54.

525. On Roman and Jewish administrative policies in first-century A.D. Palestine, see now esp. P. Egger, *"Crucifixus sub Pontio Pilato"* (NTAbh NF 32; Münster: Aschendorff, 1997).

526. See 2 Sam. 15:23; 1 Kings 2:37; 15:13; 2 Kings 23:4, 6, 12; 2 Chron. 29:16; 30:14; Jer. 31:40; 1 Macc. 15:39, 41; cf. Neh. 2:15.

527. See Matt. 26:36; Mark 14:32. See J. B. Green, "Gethsemane," *DJG*, 265–68, esp. 267–68.

528. See Jeremias, *Eucharistic Words*, 55.

529. See Blomberg in his forthcoming book on the historicity of John's Gospel, ad. loc.

530. *Chiliarchos* was used to translate Latin *tribunus militum*, a commander of a cohort of 600 or even as few as 200 men (e.g., Polybius, *Hist.* 11.23; the LXX features twenty-nine instances of *chiliarchos* for civil or military officials).

531. Various versions circulated, depending on the high priests targeted: cf. *b. Pesaḥ.* 57a; *t. Menaḥ.* 13:21. The version cited is found in J. Klausner, *Jesus of Nazareth* (London: G. Allen & Unwin, 1925), 337. Ishmael b. Phabi was Annas's successor.

532. See Schürer, *HJP*², 2:203–6.

533. See the discussions in R. H. Smith, "The Household Lamps of Palestine in New Testament Times," *BA* 29 (Feb. 1966): 2–27; J. Jeremias, "*Lampades* in Matthew 25:1–13," in *Soli Deo Gloria*, ed. J. M. Richards (Richmond: John Knox, 1968), 83–87.

534. Cf. Smith, "Household Lamps," 7.

535. Cf. Dion. Hal., *Ant. Rom.* 11.40.2: "carrying torches [*phanous*] and lamps [*lampadas*]."

536. Cf. Josephus, *J.W.* 4.4.6 §293: "the majority were unarmed."

537. See Ezek. 1:28; 44:4; Dan. 2:46; 8:18; 10:9; Acts 9:4; 22:7; 26:14; Rev. 1:17; 19:10; 22:8.

538. Eusebius, *Praep. ev.* 9.27: "the king . . . bade Moses tell him the name of the God who sent him, scoffing at him: but Moses bent down and whispered in his ear, and when the king heard it he fell speechless." The legend is attributed to Artapanus, *Concerning the Jews* (prior to first century B.C.?). Cf. R. G. Bury, "Two Notes on the Fourth Gospel," *ExpTim* 24 (1912–13): 233.

539. See Ps. 27:2; 35:4; cf. 56:9; see also Elijah's experience, 2 Kings 1:9–14.

540. See *Ant.* 1.15 §240; 13.5.1 §131; 14.14.6 §390; 15.6.2–3 §§167–175; *J.W.* 1.14.1 §276; 1.15.1 §287; 1.18.4 §360.

541. Hence the suggestion that Malchus was an Arab; cf. 1 Macc. 11:39: "Imalkue the Arab"; Josephus, *Ant.* 13.5.1 §131: "Malchus the Arab," referring to an earlier namesake. See Brown, *John*, 2:812; BAGD, 489–90.

542. Cf. BAGD, 174.

543. E.g., Ps. 75:8; Isa. 51:17, 22; Jer. 25:15–17; Ezek. 23:31–34; Hab. 2:16.

544. See 1QpHab 11:10–15: "cup of YHWH's right hand," "cup of God's anger"; Rev. 14:10; 16:19; 18:6.

545. Cf. G. Delling, "*Baptisma Baptisthēnai*," *NovT* 2 (1957): 92–115, esp. 110–15; L. Goppelt, "πίνω, ποτήριον," *TDNT*, 6:149–53.

546. Cf. E. M. Smallwood, "High Priests and Politics in Roman Palestine," *JTS* 13 (1962): 14–34.

547. See note on 13:23 and Köstenberger, *Encountering John*, ch. 1.

548. See Morris, *John*, 666, n. 37.

549. E.g., 2 Kings 10:11; Ps. 55:13; cf. Luke 2:44: "relatives and *friends*"; see also *New Docs* 4.44; Homer, *Iliad* 15.350: "kinsmen."

550. MM 295 cite inscriptions dating from 14 B.C. and A.D. 34.

551. Cf. Lady W. M. Ramsay, "Her That Kept the Door," *ExpTim* 27 (1915–16): 217–18, 314–16 and the supplement by J. Mann, pp. 424–25, pertaining to Talmudic literature.

552. Cf. A. N. Sherwin-White, *Roman Society and Roman Law in the New Testament* (Oxford: Oxford Univ. Press, 1963), 45.

553. The charge that Jesus leads the people astray surfaces earlier in John's Gospel: e.g., 7:12, 47.

554. Morris, *John*, 670; Keener, *BBC*, 307.

555. See P. S. Alexander, "Jewish Law in the Time of Jesus: Towards a Clarification of the Problem," in *Law and Religion*, ed. B. Lindars (Cambridge: J. Clarke, 1988), 44–58, esp. 46–49; Schürer, *HJP*², 2:199–226.

556. See the discussion in J. Blinzler, *The Trial of Jesus* (Cork: Mercier, 1959), 112–14.

557. *b. Šabb.* 15a; *b. Sanh.* 41b; *b. ʿAbod. Zar.* 8b.

558. Jeremias, *Jerusalem*, 47–48.

559. Cf. J. H. Bernard, *A Critical and Exegetical Commentary on the Gospel According to St. John* (Edinburgh: T. & T. Clark, 1928), 2:604.

560. Acts 21:35, 40; see the extensive description in Josephus, *J.W.* 5.5.8 §§238–46; both locations are mentioned in *Ant.* 15.8.5 §292. Cf. the discussion in Brown, *John*, 2:845.

561. *Embassy* 306: "the house of the governors"; see also the incident involving Pilate taking place in that location recounted in *Embassy* 299–305.

562. Cf. L. H. Vincent, "L'Antonia, palais primitif d'Hérode," *RB* 61 (1954): 87–107.

563. Cf. C. Kopp, *The Holy Places of the Gospels* (Edinburgh/London: Nelson, n.d. [1963]), 368–39. Brown, *John*, 2:845, also notes that the term *aulem*, used in Mark 15:16 to describe the Praetorium, occurs frequently in Josephus with reference to the Herodian

Palace but never with regard to the Fortress of Antonia.

564. See also Seneca, *De ira* 2.7.3: "All these thousands hurrying to the forum at break of day." Cf. Sherwin-White, *Roman Society*, 45, with primary references.

565. *m. ᵓOhal.* 18:7: "The dwelling-places of Gentiles are unclean"; cf. Num. 9:7–14; 31:19.

566. See Luke 22:1: "the Feast of Unleavened Bread, called the Passover"; see further notes on 19:14, 31.

567. Cf. C. C. Torrey, "The Date of the Crucifixion According to the Fourth Gospel," *JBL* 50 (1931): 239–40. Contra Keener, *BBC*, 307–8, who says different calendars or John's "making a symbolic point" account for the apparent discrepancy between John and the Synoptics.

568. See the discussion in Barrett, *John*, 533–35; Hengel, "Johannesevangelium als Quelle," 330; and Paul Winter, *On the Trial of Jesus* (Berlin: de Gruyter, 1974).

569. *y. Sanh.* 1:1; 7:2; on "forty years," see note on v. 24 above; this probably refers to A.D. 6. See also Simon Legasse, *The Trial of Jesus* (London: SCM, 1997), 54–56.

570. Cf. Sherwin-White, *Roman Society*, 24–47, esp. 36.

571. A. N. Sherwin-White, "The Trial of Christ," in *Historicity and Chronology in the New Testament* (London: SPCK, 1965), 99, summarized by Brown, *John*, 2:848.

572. Josephus, *J.W.* 1.4.6 §97; 4QpNahum 1:6–8: "the Angry Lion [who filled his den with a mass of corpses, carrying out rev]enge . . . , who hanged living men [from the tree, committing an atrocity which had not been committed] in Israel since ancient times, for it is horrible for the one hanged alive from the tree."

573. Lev. 24:16; cf. John 10:33; Acts 7:57–58; *m. Sanh.* 7:4; 9:3.

574. Cf. Sherwin-White, *Roman Society*, 13–23.

575. Cf. E. Bammel, "The Trial before Pilate," in *Jesus and the Politics of His Day*, ed. E. Bammel and C. F. D. Moule (Cambridge: CUP, 1984), 417–19.

576. Cf. E. E. Jensen, "The First Century Controversy Over Jesus as a Revolutionary Figure," *JBL* 60 (1941): 261–72, esp. 261–62.

577. The expression refers to the entire festival in Deut. 16:1–2; Ezek. 45:21; Luke 2:41; 22:1; John 2:13, 23; 6:4; 11:55; Acts 12:4; Josephus, *Ant.* 17.9.3 §213; cf. *y. Pesaḥ.* 9:5: "and [the first Passover in Egypt was observed for] one night [only], whereas the Passover of [successive] generations is observed for the entire seven [days]."

578. Cf. Josephus, *Ant.* 20.209; Livy, *History* 5.13; *b. Pesaḥ* 91a. See Josef Blinzler, *The Trial of Jesus* (Westminster: Newman, 1959), 218–21.

579. C. B. Chavel, "The Releasing of a Prisoner of the Eve of Passover in Ancient Jerusalem," *JBL* 60 (1941): 273–78 (the quotation is from p. 277).

580. Keener, *BBC*, 309.

581. Cf. J. J. Twomey, "'Barabbas Was a Robber,'" *Scr.* 8 (1956): 115–19.

582. G. Bornkamm, "λῃστής," *TDNT*, 4:257–62.

583. Humphreys and Waddington, "The Jewish Calendar, a Lunar Eclipse and the Date of Christ's Crucifixion," 331–51, with particular reference to the lunar eclipse occurring on that day (cf. Mark 15:33).

584. For ancient references on flogging and torture, see Malina and Rohrbaugh, *Social-Science Commentary*, 263.

585. Sherwin-White, *Roman Society*, 27–28.

586. Similar floggings are recorded in Acts 22:24 (cf. 16:22) and in Josephus, *J.W.* 2.306.

587. The former is favored by E. Ha-Reubéni, "Recherches sur les plantes de l'évangile," *RB* 42 (1933): 230–34; the latter by H. J. Hart, "Crown of Thorns in John 19:2–5," *JTS* 3 (1952): 66–75; E. R. Goodenough and C. B. Welles, "The Crown of Acanthus?" *HTR* 46 (1953): 241–42; and Avi-Yonah, *World of the Bible*, 151, suggest acanthus.

588. C. Bonner, "The Crown of Thorns," *HTR* 46 (1953): 47–48.

589. Hart, "Crown of Thorns," 66–75, esp. 71–74.

590. Carson, *Matthew*, 573.

591. Cf. P. Winter, *On the Trial of Jesus*, 2d ed. (Berlin/New York: de Gruyter, 1974), 148–49.

592. Cf. W. A. Meeks, *The Prophet-King* (NovTSup 14; Leiden: Brill, 1967), 70–71.

593. Demosthenes, *Mid.* 91; *De Falsa Leg.* 198; 4th cent. B.C.

594. O. Michel, "Son," *NIDNTT*, 3:637.

595. A. Deissmann, *Bible Studies* (Edinburgh: T. & T. Clark, 1901), 167.

596. *Life Apollonii* 1.21: "'By the gods,' he asked, 'who are you?' this time altering his tone to a whine of entreaty"; 4.44: "careful not to fight with a god."

597. Yet see P. L. Maier, "Episode of the Golden Roman Shields at Jerusalem," *HTR* 62 (1969): 109–21.

598. See H. W. Hoehner, "Chronology," *DJG*, 121. Contra Keener, *BBC*, 311; Brown, *John*, 2:891, who conjectures that "perhaps the tremors that presaged the fall of Sejanus were already felt by sensitive political observers, and Pilate feared that soon he would have no protector at court," thus placing Jesus' trial and crucifixion prior to Sejanus's demise in October, A.D. 31.

599. See Avi-Yonah, *World of the Bible*, 152.

600. C. C. Torrey, "The Date of the Crucifixion According to the Fourth Gospel," *JBL* 50 (1931): 227–41 (including his critique of Str-B 2:834–85 on 235–36); A. J. B. Higgins, "Origins of the Eucharist," *NTS* 1 (1954–55): 206–9; Cullen I. K. Storey, "The Mental Attitude of Jesus at Bethany: John 11.33,38," *NTS* 37 (1989): 51–66; Blomberg, *The Historical Reliability of the Gospels*, 177–78; Morris, *John*, 708; Ridderbos, *John*, 606.

601. Cf. Josephus, *Ant.* 14.2.1 §21; 17.9.3 §213; *J.W.* 2.1.3 §10; Luke 22:1; see comments on 18:28.

602. See Craig Blomberg, *The Historical Reliability of the Gospels*, 180; Morris, *John*, 708; see also comments on John 1:39.

603. Cf. Sherwin-White, *Roman Society*, 27.

604. Carson, *John*, 597.

605. The upper palm of the hand is considered most likely by F. T. Zugibe, "Two Questions About Crucifixion," *BRev* 5/2 (1989): 41–43.

606. See Lev. 24:14, 23; Num. 15:35–36; Deut. 17:5; 21:19–21; 22:24; Acts 7:58; cf. Luke 4:29.

607. See R. Riesner, "Archeology and Geography," *DJG*, 43; J. E. Taylor, "Golgotha: A Reconsideration of the Evidence for the Sites of Jesus' Crucifixion and Burial," *NTS* 44 (1998): 180–203. Gordon's Calvary is ruled out by A. Parrot, *Golgotha and the Church of the Holy Sepulchre* (London: SCM, 1957), 59–65.

608. Cf. M. Hengel, *Crucifixion* (Philadelphia: Fortress, 1977); J. B. Green, "Death of Jesus," *DJG*, 147–48; Malina and Rohrbaugh, *Social-Science Commentary*, 263–64; David W. Chapman, "Perceptions of Crucifixion among Jews and Christians in the Ancient World" (Ph.D. diss., University of Cambridge, 2000).

609. Seneca, *Consol. ad Marciam* 20.3 (A.D. 37–41); Pliny, *Hist. Nat.* 36.107–18; Josephus, *J.W.* 5.11.1 §451; Philo, *Dreams* 2.213.

610. The latter (shock) is strongly argued by Zugibe, "Two Questions," 41: "Shock is unquestionably the cause of Jesus' death on the cross," referring also to a surgeon's opinion, who contends, "there is overwhelming evidence that Christ died from heart failure due to extreme shock caused by exhaustion, pain and loss of blood."

611. The man's name is incribed on his bone ossuary as Yehoḥanan ben Hagkol. See J. H. Charlesworth, "Jesus and Jehoḥanan: An Archaeological Note on Crucifixion," *ExpTim* 84 (1972–73): 147–50.

612. Cf. Str-B 1:835, with primary references.

613. For a reconstruction of the sign, see Avi-Yonah, *World of the Bible*, 153.

614. Cf. Riesner, *Jesus als Lehrer*, 199.

615. Inscriptions warning Gentiles against entering the inner temple were written mainly in Greek (see comments on 2:14).

616. Polyglot notices were common in the Hellenistic era. Examples include those cited by Josephus (*Ant.* 14.10.2 §191: "both Greek and Latin" [47 B.C.]; *J.W.* 6.2.4 §125: "in Greek characters and in your own" [Hebrew]), and the *Res Gestae Divi Augusti* (prior to A.D. 13), which existed not only in Latin but also in Greek. See also Est. 8:9. Blinzler, *Trial of Jesus*, 254–55, also refers to Roman tombstones still extant today.

617. Keener, *BBC*, 313.

618. Cicero, *Epist. Quint. Fratr.* 1.2.2; 1.2.13: *scripsi, scripsi* (59 B.C.).

619. The ruling is attributed to the "deified Hadrian" (A.D. 117–38).

620. Cf. H. Daniel-Rops, *Daily Life in Palestine at the Time of Christ* (London: Weidenfeld & Nicolson, 1962), 211–18.

621. Cf. Keener, *BBC*, 313.

622. For the use of Ps. 22 in ancient Jewish writings, see Str-B 2:574–80.

623. Cf. E. Stauffer, *Jesus and His Story* (London: SCM, 1960), 111–12 and 179, n. 1.

624. See Ps. 2:7: "You are my Son; today I have become your Father"; Tobit 7:12: "you are her brother, and she is your sister." On the Code of Hammurabi, see R. de Vaux, *Ancient Israel* (New York: McGraw-Hill, 1961), 112–13.

625. M.-J. Lagrange, *Évangile selon Saint Jean*, 2d ed. (Paris: J. Gabalda, 1925), 494, cited in Brown, *John*, 2:907.

626. Brown, *John*, 2:909. There is some uncertainty as to the exact species of hyssop referred to here: see the discussion in J. Wilkinson, "Seven Words from the Cross," *SJT* 17 (1964): 77; W. E. Shewell-Cooper, *Plants and Fruits of the Bible* (London: Darton, Longman & Todd, 1962), 75–76; and F. G. and P. A. Beetham, "A Note on John 19:29," *JTS* 44 (1993): 163–69.

627. Cf. Str-B 2:582.

628. Cf. N. Haas, "Anthropological Observations on the Skeletal Remains from Giv'at ha-Mivtar," *IEJ* 20 (1970): 38–59; J. Zias and E. Sekeles, "The Crucified Man from Giv'at ha-Mivtar," *IEJ* 35 (1985): 22–27; H. Shanks, "New Analysis of the Crucified Man," *BAR* 11 (Nov./Dec. 1985): 20–21.

629. Cf. J. Wilkinson, "The Incident of the Blood and Water in John 19.34," *SJT* 28 (1975): 149–72.

630. See the summary in Carson, *John*, 623–24, and the fuller treatment in Beasley-Murray, *John*, 355–58. For further discussion, see P. Barbet, *A Doctor at Calvary* (New York: P. J.

Kennedy, 1953); W. D. Edwards et al., *Journal of the American Medical Assocation* 255 (1986): 1455–63; A. F. Sava, "Wound in the Side of Christ," *CBQ* 19 (1960): 343–46.

631. See *Lev. Rab.* 15:2 on Lev. 13:2: "Man is evenly balanced, half of him is water, and the other half is blood."
632. *m. Pesaḥ.* 5:5–8; cf. *m. ʾOhal.* 3:5.
633. Cf. J. M. Ford, "Mingled Blood from the Side of Christ, John 19:34," *NTS* 15 (1969): 337–38.
634. Avi-Yonah, *World of the Bible*, 154.
635. Cf. D. Daube, *The New Testament and Rabbinic Judaism*, 325–29.
636. For a survey of funerary customs in antiquity and a discussion of the likely location of Jesus' burial site, see J. B. Green, "Burial of Jesus," *DJG*, 88–92.
637. One possibility is the Judean village Ramath-aim-Zephim (cf. 1 Sam. 1:1).
638. See Josephus, *Ant.* 5.1.14 §44: Achan "given the ignominious burial proper to the condemned." Cf. *m. Sanh.* 6:5.
639. See further F. N. Hepper, "Flax and Linen in Biblical Times," *Buried History* 25 (December 1989): 105–16.
640. Cf. Taylor, "Golgotha," 180, referring also to G. Barkay, "The Garden Tomb—Was Jesus Buried Here?" *BAR* 12/2 (March/April 1986): 40–53, 56–57.
641. In emergency situations it was probably permissible to wash and anoint a dead person's body even after sundown; cf. the cases adjudicated in *m. Šabb.* 23:4–5.
642. See Brown, *John*, 2:982–83.
643. Text in Barrett, *New Testament Background*, 15.
644. Morris, *John*, 734.
645. Judg. 5:28; Prov. 7:6; Song 2:9; Sir. 14:23; 21:23.
646. Dan. 10:5–6; Ezek. 9:2; Rev. 15:6; cf. *1 En.* 87:2.
647. E.g., in 2 Macc. 3:26, where two "splendidly dressed" young men appear to Heliodorus; cf. Acts 1:10: "two men (i.e., angels) dressed in white."
648. Cf. R. G. Maccini, *Her Testimony Is True* (JSNTSup 125; Sheffield: Sheffield Academic Press, 1996), 207–33.
649. C. S. Keener, *BBC*, 317.
650. See also 1 Kings 17:21; Ezek. 37:9; Wisd. Sol. 15:11; cf. Philo, *Opif.* 135.
651. The Greek words used for "binding and loosing" in Matthew are *deō* and *lyō*; John has *aphiēmi* for "forgive" and *krateō* for "retain."
652. J. A. Emerton, "Binding and Loosing—Forgiving and Retaining," *JTS* 13 (1962): 325–31.
653. A. Schlatter, *Der Evangelist Matthäus*, 5th ed. (Stuttgart: Calwer, 1959), 511.
654. Cf. Str-B 1:738–41; H. Büchsel, "δέω," *TDNT*, 2:60–61; Lightfoot, *A Commentary on the New Testament from the Talmud and Hebraica*, 2:237–41; G. Dalman, *The Words of Jesus*, 213–17.
655. Cf. Deissmann, *Light from the Ancient Near East*, 361–62.
656. Cited in Barrett, *John*, 574.
657. See Bultmann, *John*, 697–98, n. 2.
658. Cf. C. F. D. Moule, "The Post-Resurrection Appearances in the Light of Festival Pilgrimages," *NTS* 4 (1957–58): 58–61.
659. G. Dalman, *Arbeit und Sitte in Palästina VI* (Hildesheim: G. Olms, 1964 [1939]), 346–51, esp. 349. See also Keener, *BBC*, 318.
660. Avi-Yonah, *World of the Bible*, 155.
661. See *t. Ber.* 2:20: "where people stand naked, he may not greet [his fellows] there."
662. *T. Zeb.* 6:6: "Therefore the Lord made my catch to be an abundance of fish; for whoever shares with his neighbor receives multifold from the Lord."
663. See Beasley-Murray, *John*, 408–409; Hengel, *Crucifixion*, esp. ch. 4.
664. *Barn.* 12; Justin, *Apol.* 1.35; Irenaeus, *Dem.* 79.
665. 1 Peter 5:13 places Peter in Rome not much earlier.
666. *Scorpiace* 15: "Peter is struck [i.e., his legs are broken to hasten the crucified's death]. . . . At Rome Nero was the first who stained with blood the rising faith. Then is Peter girt by another, when he is made fast to the cross." Blomberg in his forthcoming book on the historicity of John's Gospel also cites *Acts Pet.* 37–39 and Eusebius, *Eccl. Hist.* 3.1.
667. Cf. Jackson, "Ancient Self-Referential Conventions," to whom I am indebted also in my note on 21:24. On the present verse, Jackson writes, "Verse 23 . . . makes perfectly good sense as a corrective from a living Beloved Disciple anxious to dispel what he feels are overly enthusiastic eschatological inferences being drawn by some from Jesus' words" (21–22).
668. See Gal. 6:11; Col. 4:18; 2 Thess. 3:17; Philem. 19.
669. "This is the disciple," "his testimony." Compare the high-priestly prayer, where Jesus refers to himself as "Jesus Christ" (17:3) and Thucydides's practice of introducing himself in the third person (1.1.1 and 5.26.1) and of referring to himself as "Thucydides" (4.104–7: "Thucydides, the son of Oloros, who composed this history"). Cf. Jackson, "Ancient Self-Referential Conventions," 27; see also 28–30 on Josephus.
670. An "associative collective," where the "you" subsumed under the "we" are the book's

Christian readers but where the "I" included in the "we" is the author (ibid., 23–24).

671. Other later examples are cited in Boring, *Hellenistic Commentary*, 308.

Sidebar and Chart Notes

A-1. See esp. Henry Mowvley, "John 1$^{14-18}$ in the Light of Exodus 33^7–34^{35}," *ExpTim* 95 (1984): 135–37.

A-2. There are two major possibilities for the dating of Jesus' ministry, A.D. 26–30 or 29–33, with the latter set of dates to be preferred. See H. W. Hoehner, *Chronological Aspects of the Life of Christ* (Grand Rapids: Zondervan, 1977); idem., "Chronology," *DJG*, 118–22. A less detailed but congruent chronology is found in J. Finegan, *Handbook of Biblical Chronology* (rev. ed.; Peabody, Mass.: Hendrickson, 1998), 352.

A-3. For the dating of the four Passovers between A.D. 29 and 33 mentioned above, see Humphreys and Waddington, "Jewish Calendar," 368, likewise settles on Friday, April 3, A.D. 33, as the most likely date of Jesus' crucifixion, with reference to Hoener, *Chronological Aspects*, 44, 114, and P. Maier, "The Dates of the Nativity and the Chronology of Jesus' Life," in J. Vardaman and E. M. Yamauchi, eds., *Chronos, Kairos, Christos; FS Finegan* (Winona Lake, Ind.: Eisenbrauns, 1989), 125 and Table 1.

A-4. For a defense of the temple cleansing as a sign in John's Gospel, see Köstenberger, "The Seventh Johannine Sign: A Study in John's Christology," *BBR* 5 (1995): 87–103.

A-5. Cf. S. Safrai, "Home and Family," in *The Jewish People in the First Century*, vol. 2, eds. S. Safrai and M. Stern (Philadelphia: Fortress, 1987), 728–92; J. D. M. Derrett, *Law in the New Testament* (London: Darton, Longman & Todd, 1970), 227–38; E. Ferguson, *Backgrounds of Early Christianity*, 2d ed. (Grand Rapids: Eerdmans, 1993), 68–69; D. J. Williams, "Bride, Bridegroom," *DJG*, 86–88.

A-6. On Jesus' "natural family," see esp. R. Bauckham, *Jude and the Relatives of Jesus in the Early Church* (Edinburgh: T. & T. Clark, 1990), 5–44.

A-7. Epiphanius suggests Jesus' brothers were sons of Joseph by a previous marriage; Jerome conjectures they were cousins; but the most likely explanation (already suggested by Helvidius) is that they were the sons of Joseph and Mary, younger half-brothers of Jesus.

A-8. See D. F. Watson, "Wine," *DJG*, 870–73.

A-9. See Gen. 27:28, 37; Deut. 7:13; Judg. 9:13; Ps. 104:15; Prov. 3:10; Song 7:9; Isa. 55:1; 65:8; Joel 3:18; Zech. 9:17; cf. Matt. 26:27–29 par.

A-10. See Deut. 32:32–33; Ps. 60:3; 75:8; Prov. 4:17; 23:29–35; Isa. 5:22; 51:17; Jer. 25:15; Hos. 7:5; Rev. 14:10.

A-11. For a general survey, see M. O. Wise, "Feasts," *DJG*, 234–41.

A-12. On the New Testament characterization of the Jerusalem temple, see esp. P. W. L. Walker, *Jesus and the Holy City* (Grand Rapids: Eerdmans, 1996). A general survey is found in M. O. Wise, "Temple," *DJG*, 811–17.

A-13. Cf. M. Goodman, "A Note on Josephus, the Pharisees and Ancestral Tradition," *JJS* 50 (1999): 17–20.

A-14. See S. Westerholm, "Pharisees," *DJG*, 609–14.

A-15. The considerable literature on Samaritans includes: A. D. Crown, ed., *The Samaritans* (Tübingen: Mohr-Siebeck, 1989); J. Jeremias, "The Samaritans," in *Jerusalem in the Time of Jesus* (London: SCM, 1969), 352–58; J. A. Montgomery, *The Samaritans* (New York: Ktav, 1907; repr. 1968); H. G. M. Williamson, "Samaritans," *DJG*, 724–28. See also H. K. Bond, *Pontius Pilate in History and Interpretation* (SNTSMS 100; Cambridge: Cambridge Univ. Press, 1998), 71–73, 89–93 (esp. 71, n. 69).

A-16. The saying is attributed to the later R. Yannai (c. A.D. 240); the insult "Samaritan" is listed together with "people of the land" (Jews ignorant of the law), "a boor," and "a magician."

A-17. This listing does not imply endorsement as the likely site of Jesus' tomb. The Garden tomb rather provides a setting not dissimilar to the kind of tomb Jesus would have been laid in.

A-18. See, e.g., 5:16, 18; 7:1; 8:48; 10:31, 33; 11:8; 19:12.

A-19. Cf. E. Stern, ed., *The New Encyclopedia of Archaeological Excavations in the Holy Land*, 1:291–96, esp. 292–95, with extensive bibliography; J. C. H. Laughlin, "Capernaum: From Jesus' Time and After," *BAR* 19 (September/October 1993): 55–61, 90, with other helpful bibliographical references.

A-20. For a complete list of high priests from 200 B.C. to A.D. 70, see Jeremias, *Jerusalem*, 377–78. For a list of high priests from 37 B.C. to A.D. 68, see E. M. Smallwood, "High Priests and Politics in Roman Palestine," *JTS* 13 (1962): 31–32.

A-21. Cf. Hengel, "Johannesevangelium als Quelle," 327.

A-22. On these excavations, see esp. W. Horbury, "The 'Caiaphas' Ossuaries and Joseph Caiaphas," *PEQ* 126 (1994): 33–48; E. Stern, ed., *The New Encyclopedia of Archaeological Excavations in the Holy Land*, 2:756. On John's portrayal of Caiaphas and Annas his father-in-law, see now esp. Hengel, "Johannesevangelium als Quelle," 322–34.

A-23. The following is adapted from F. J. Moloney, *The Gospel of John* (Collegeville, Minn.: Liturgical, 1998), 377–78 (for further bibliography, see 389–91). See also E. Bammel, "The Farewell Discourse of the Evangelist John and Its Jewish Heritage," *TynBul* 44 (1993): 103–16; W. S. Kurz, "Luke 22:14–38 and Greco-Roman and Biblical Farewell Addresses," *JBL* 104 (1985): 251–68; idem, *Farewell Addresses in the New Testament* (Collegeville, Minn.: Liturgical, 1990); A. Lacomara, "Deuteronomy and the Farewell Discourse (Jn 13:31–16:33)," *CBQ* 36 (1974): 65–84; R. W. Paschal Jr., "Farewell Discourse," *DJG*, 229–33, esp. 232.

A-24. E.g., Gen. 49; Josh. 23–24; 1 Sam. 12; 1 Kings 2:1–12; 1 Chron. 28–29.

A-25. E.g., *T. 12 Patr.*; *As. Mos.*; cf. *Jub.* 22:10–30; 1 Macc. 2:49–70; Josephus, *Ant.* 12.6.3

§§279–84. For Greco-Roman farewell passages, see Malina and Rohrbaugh, *Social Science Commentary*, 221–22.

A-26. *m. Hor.* 3:4; cf. *m. Meg.* 1:9; *m. Mak.* 2:6; *t. Yoma* 1:4.

A-27. *b. Pesah.* 57a; *t. Menah.* 13:18 "the powerful men of the priesthood."

A-28. See H. W. Hoehner, "Pontius Pilate," *DJG*, 615–17.

A-29. Cf. J. Vardaman, "A New Inscription which Mentions Pilate as 'Prefect,'" *JBL* 81 (1962): 70–71.

A-30. E.g. Josephus, *J.W.* 2.9.2 §§169–74; *Ant.* 18.3.1 §§55–62; Luke 13:1 (?).

A-31. Cf. E. M. Smallwood, "The Date of the Dismissal of Pontius Pilate from Judaea," *JJS* 5 (1954): 12–21.

A-32. Cf. Suetonius, *Tiberius* 58; Tacitus, *Ann.* 3.38.

A-33. Cf. E. Bammel, "*Philos tou Kaisaros*," *TLZ* 77 (1952): 205–10, who consequently insists on a post-A.D. 31 crucifixion date for Jesus.

A-34. See comments on 19:8 above; on Sejanus's anti-Semitism, see Philo, *Embassy* 159–61.

A-35. 1 Macc. 2:18; 3:38; 10:65; 11:27; 3 Macc. 6:23; Josephus, *Ant.* 12.7.3 §298.

ACTS

by Clinton E. Arnold

Acts as a Second Volume

"Acts" is the second installment of Luke's two-volume account of the ministry, death, and resurrection of Jesus (volume 1) and the story of the beginning of the early church (volume 2). It is an account of God's plan of salvation consummated in Jesus Christ and going out to all peoples—both geographically (from Jerusalem to Samaria, Syria, Asia Minor, Greece, and Italy) and ethnically (not only to Jews, but now embracing Gentiles of every nationality). The book of Acts reflects the continuation of Jesus' ministry after his death and exaltation (Acts 1:1).

COASTLINE OF
MYRA IN LYCIA
(ASIA MINOR)

> ▶ **Acts**
> # IMPORTANT FACTS:
>
> - **AUTHOR:** Luke. He was a coworker of the apostle Paul, who ministered with him in Troas and Philippi, accompanied him with the collection to Jerusalem, and was with him during his Caesarean and Roman imprisonments. He was a physician who may have come from Syria.
> - **PART TWO OF A TWO-VOLUME WORK:** Luke's Gospel is the first half of a single two-volume work ("Luke-Acts"), sharing purpose, themes, and theology with the book of Acts.
> - **CENTRAL THEME OF LUKE-ACTS:** Luke seeks to show that *God's great plan of salvation has come to fulfillment in the life, death, resurrection, and ascension of Jesus the Messiah, and continues to unfold as the Spirit-filled church takes the message of salvation from Jerusalem to the ends of the earth.*
> - **OTHER KEY THEMES:**
>   1. Promise-Fulfillment: The age of salvation has arrived in Jesus the Messiah.
>   2. The Age of the Spirit: The sign of the new age is the coming of the Spirit in the ministry of Jesus and the early church.
>   3. The gospel is "good news" for all people, regardless of race, gender, or social status.
> - **PURPOSE IN WRITING:** To defend and legitimize the claims of the church as the authentic people of God in the present age. To help believers grow in their faith and to inspire their evangelistic zeal.
> - **RECIPIENT:** Theophilus, but intended for a larger Christian audience.

Acts is not a comprehensive history of the church, but rather a focused history centering on the beginnings and early development of the church in Jerusalem, the ministry of the apostle Peter (and to some degree, John), and a rather extensive account of the way God used the apostle Paul to take the gospel to Asia Minor, Greece, and Rome. A complete history of the church would have told us about the ministries of the other apostles, the development of the church in Galilee, the story of the spread of Christianity to Egypt, the origins of the church in Rome, and a variety of other topics.

Luke's primary burden is to give testimony to the fact that God's salvation has arrived in and through the Lord Jesus Christ. This salvation is the fulfillment of Israel's hope and is now being sent to Gentiles and to people throughout the entire world.

Luke

Although Luke never names himself as the author of Acts, ancient historians are unanimous in their assertion that Luke was the author of Acts and the third

Gospel. The earliest evidence comes from a late second-century papyrus (P^{75}) that has the phrase "the gospel according to Luke" at the end of the scroll. The church father Irenaeus gives fairly extensive testimony about Luke:

> Luke also, the companion of Paul, recorded in a book the Gospel preached by him . . . . But that this Luke was inseparable from Paul, and his fellow-labourer in the Gospel, he himself clearly evinces, not as a matter of boasting, but as bound to do so by the truth itself.[1]

After summarizing the passages in Acts where Luke includes himself in the story (the so-called "we" sections), Irenaeus adds these remarks: "As Luke was present at all these occurrences, he carefully noted them down in writing, so that he cannot be convicted of falsehood or boastfulness."[2]

Another important ancient source, a second-century prologue to the Gospel of Luke, gives additional historical information: "Luke was a Syrian of Antioch, by profession a physician, the disciple of the apostles, and later a follower of Paul until his martyrdom. He served the Lord without distraction, without a wife, and without children. He died at the age of eighty-four in Boeotia [a region in central Greece], full of the Holy Spirit."[3] Eusebius and Jerome contain similar historical traditions about Luke.[4]

Paul refers to Luke three times in his letters.[5] The references in Philemon and Colossians place Luke with Paul in Rome during his imprisonment, which represents historical data that line up with the text of Acts. It was probably during this time that Luke engaged in writing his two-volume work while he served with the apostle Paul as his "fellow worker." In the Colossians passage, Paul speaks of Luke as the "doctor," but we know nothing else about Luke's background, training, or practice as a physician. The apostle extols Luke's faithfulness in 2 Timothy 4:1 when he says, "Only Luke is with me." Paul wrote this comment during his second imprisonment in Rome when he faced his impending martyrdom for the cause of Christ.

In summary, Luke was probably a Gentile Christian, possibly of Syrian (and thus Semitic) origin. He may have been a Jewish sympathizer ("God-fearer") prior to his conversion as his familiarity with Judaism and the Greek Old Testament might suggest. The story of when and how he was converted is unknown.

Theophilus—Luke's Literary Patron

In his introductions both to the Gospel and to the book of Acts, Luke addresses himself to a man named Theophilus. This individual is already a follower of Christ and Luke writes to him so that he may "know the certainty" of the things he has been taught (Luke 1:4). Acts is thus not an evangelistic tract, a defense brief for Paul's trial, or a piece of literature for its own sake. Acts is written by a believer to help another believer and probably a great many more.

In describing Theophilus as "most excellent," Luke uses the term *kratistos*, an expression typically used as a title of respect for a person of high social status and wealth, often a person of equestrian rank in Roman society. Paul uses this title, for instance, to respectfully address the Roman procurators of Judea (Acts 24:3; 26:25). The equestrian order ranked only below the senatorial order in status and had a minimum wealth qualification of four hundred thousand sesterces.[6] It may well be that as a zealous new believer with a significant amount of wealth, Theophilus desires to use his resources for the sake of the cause of Christ. He finds opportunity for doing so by functioning as a literary patron for Luke.[7]

A possible reconstruction might look something like this: Theophilus is a new believer from the equestrian order in Rome—excited about his new faith, anxious to spread the word, and eager to learn more and grow. He meets Luke shortly after his arrival in Rome with Paul. Luke has already planned to write both the Gospel and Acts, but is unable both to support himself and devote his time to the arduous and time-consuming task of writing. As Theophilus gets to know Luke and hears of his plans, he becomes convinced (not least by the leading of the Holy Spirit) that he should use his resources to subsidize Luke for the period it would take to write the two volumes and then to support the publication of the work. Theophilus personally wants to benefit from Luke's account as a means of facilitating his own knowledge and growth as a Christian, but he also realizes that there are numerous others who could benefit similarly from such a production. Theophilus thus gives generously to support Luke in this endeavor and then funds scribes to make copies of the manuscript for distribution to churches.

Luke's Opportunity For Writing

Luke was uniquely positioned to write this two-volume work. He was a Gentile who had excellent training in Greek, knew the art of rhetoric, had superb research and compositional skills, and was familiar with the conventions of historical writing in the Hellenistic tradition (along the lines of Polybius and Thucydides). Yet Luke also had a strong familiarity with Judaism and the Greek Old Testament, which may have come as a result of involvement in a synagogue prior to becoming a Christian.

Since Luke was not one of the Twelve, he was not an eyewitness to the life and ministry of Jesus or the earliest days of the church. But Luke was a gifted researcher and had the time and opportunity to gather written sources and interview eyewitnesses. When Luke accompanied Paul to Jerusalem in A.D. 57 with the Gentile-Christian delegation, he probably had no idea that he would be spending the next two years in Palestine while Paul was in custody in Caesarea. Yet this time provided him with ample opportunity to collect the information he needed to write his planned acount.[8] From Caesarea, Luke probably made repeated visits to Jerusalem to interview the leaders of the church (including a number of the apostles) and likely also had the opportunity to speak with believers who came to Caesarea to visit Paul in his chains.

The time in Caesarea would also have afforded him with many occasions to dialogue with the apostle Paul, who was in a light form of custody and was permitted visitors. After Paul's release, Luke accompanied him on the voyage to Rome, which Luke writes about in great detail as a participant in the events.

Why Did Luke Write Acts?

Luke's intention in writing Acts may best be summed up as "an account of Christian beginnings in order to strengthen faith and give assurance that its foundation is firm."[9] He does this on two levels: (1) by helping his readers understand the story of God's work in and through Jesus of Nazareth and the beginnings of the early church as a means of informing and establishing their beliefs, and (2) by providing them with instruction and inspiration—through moving examples—that will inform their lifestyles, affections, and priorities in life. More specifically, here are a few of the principal ways that Luke hopes to encourage and build up believers:

- He wants to give his readers further confidence in the truthfulness and reliability of their faith (Luke 1:4).
- He wants his readers to recognize that the advent of Christianity is according to God's plan. God himself providentially guided all of the events surrounding the development and growth of the church.[10]
- He wants to assure his readers that God's salvation has come both to Jews and to Gentiles of every social class and background. It represents the fulfillment of divine promises recorded throughout the Hebrew Scriptures. A new era of human history has begun.[11]
- He wants to inspire ongoing evangelistic outreach, prepare his readers with a better understanding of the heart of the gospel (the *kerygma*), and provide them with instructive models on how to proclaim it in a variety of circumstances—whether in a synagogue or in a room full of Greek philosophers.[12]
- He wants to encourage a greater dependence on the Spirit.
- He wants his readers to know that in spite of intense opposition and suffering, their faith is secure and the word of God will prevail.[13]

◄

When Did Luke Write This Book?

Luke probably wrote the Gospel and Acts during the two-year period of Paul's imprisonment in Rome: A.D. 60–62 (shortly after the last recorded events in Acts).[14]

Introduction (1:1–5)

Luke begins the second volume of his account of the person of Jesus Christ by recalling a series of incredible events immediately following the resurrection. Jesus appeared to his followers over a period of forty days. These appearances served to guarantee the reality of his coming to life again after his painful and torturous death. The Lord also used this time to instruct his disciples about the plan of God and their crucial role in it. He instructs them to wait for a short period of time until they would receive the abiding manifestation of God's empowering presence—the Holy Spirit.

My former book (1:1). The book of Acts complements the Gospel of Luke as the second part of his two-volume work. It was common in Greek, Latin, and even Jewish literature for an author to divide his work into volumes and begin the first with a preface for the whole. The succeeding volumes would each begin with a shorter preface summarizing with a few words the contents of the previous volume.[15] The Jewish historian Josephus, for instance, begins the second volume of his polemic against Apion with a comment similar to Luke's: "In the former book, most honored Epaphroditus, I have demonstrated."[16]

Theophilus (1:1). Luke wrote for the benefit of a person named Theophilus (see "Introduction" and comments on Luke 1:1).

All that Jesus began to do and to teach (1:1). The word "began" conspicuously implies that what Jesus did in his public ministry on earth until the time he was crucified was only a start. Jesus would now continue his proclamation of the kingdom of God and his redemptive ministry by working through his people. This continuation of Jesus' work is the story of Acts.

Gave many convincing proofs that he was alive (1:3). In the final chapter of his Gospel (Luke 24), Luke records some of these appearances (see comments on Luke 24:1–53). The apostle Paul records that Jesus appeared not only to the twelve apostles and to James, but even to five hundred brothers at the same time (1 Cor. 15:5–7). Paul adds that among these five hundred, many were still alive, meaning that anyone who needed eyewitness verification of this incredible claim of bodily resurrection from the dead could easily obtain it.

Spoke about the kingdom of God (1:3). The kingdom of God was the central message of Jesus' teaching during his three-year ministry. It continues to be the central theme of his teaching after his resurrection. The kingdom, however, took a substantially different form than what his Jewish followers were expecting.

The gift my Father promised, which you have heard me speak about (1:4). The Old Testament prophets announced the pouring out of the Holy Spirit in connection with the new covenant. Isaiah 32:15 looks forward to a time when "the Spirit is poured upon us from on high." God says through Ezekiel that, "I will put my Spirit in you" (Ezek. 37:14; cf. 36:27). On the day of Pentecost, Peter specifically connected the outpouring of the Spirit with the prophecy of Joel 2:28–32. Jesus gave his most extensive teaching about the coming Holy Spirit to his disciples in the night before he was crucified (John 14–16).

▶

MODERN JERUSALEM

The Muslim Dome of the Rock is prominent on the temple mount.

The Ascension (1:6–11)

Responding to a question that reveals the disciples' ongoing confusion about the nature of the kingdom of God, Jesus declares what is truly central to God's plan for the immediate future. First, this is not the time that God is coming in judgment on the nations and establishing a political earthly reign. Jesus warns his followers even to avoid speculating about the timing of this event; only the Father knows when this will happen. Second, they will soon receive the fulfillment of the new covenant promise of the Holy Spirit. Third, the Spirit will empower them to serve as witnesses of Christ throughout the world. As witnesses, they will testify to Jesus as the Messiah and to his sacrificial death on the cross, his resurrection, and his offer of salvation to all who believe. This task will not be limited to the borders of Israel. Rather, Christ calls them to take their testimony to the entire world.

Forty days after his resurrection, Jesus ascends to the Father. Two angels appear and assure the disciples that Jesus will return.

Are you at this time going to restore the kingdom to Israel? (1:6). Israel at this time was under the political domination of Rome. Most Jews were unhappy with this situation and longed for the time that God would sovereignly intervene in fulfillment of the prophetic texts and remove these impure and arrogant Gentiles from power. The nation took matters into their own hands in A.D. 66 and inaugurated a war with the Roman forces that eventually led to the destruction of Jerusalem and the temple. It appears that the disciples still did not completely understand the nature of this phase of the kingdom plan that Jesus was inaugurating. In fairness to them, however, we need to realize that they had not yet received the indwelling presence of the Holy Spirit. After Pentecost, there was no more misunderstanding about this issue.

In Jerusalem, and in all Judea and Samaria, and to the ends of the earth (1:8). The itinerary Jesus establishes becomes the outline for the book of Acts: "in Jerusalem" (Acts 1–7), "in all Judea and Samaria" (8:1–11:18), and the rest of the book tracks the spread of the gospel through Asia Minor, Greece, and on to Rome.

The ends of the earth (1:8). In a first-century Jewish manner of speaking, this could be a reference to Rome.[17] It is significant in this regard that Luke draws the book of Acts to a conclusion with Paul reaching Rome. Yet it is likely that Luke intends for his readers to see this commission from the Lord as extending far beyond the city of Rome or even the boundaries of the Roman empire. From the perspective of a Roman, the capital city was not on the extremities of the earth, but was rather the center. The empire itself extended far to the north

REFLECTIONS

THE TASK OF TAKING THE GOSPEL to the ends of the earth remains unfinished. As many as 12,000 distinct cultural groups around the world remain unreached, having no church in their language and culture. What is your church doing to support this ongoing mission given to us by the risen Lord? What role will you play?

▶

glory of God (the *shekinah*). It was like the cloud that covered the tent of meeting when the glory of the Lord filled the tabernacle (Ex. 40:34) and the cloud that enveloped Jesus and the other two figures with him when he was transfigured in the presence of three of his disciples (Luke 9:34–36).

Two men dressed in white (1:10). These two men are actually angels. These messengers could manifest their appearance in dazzling white as the two did at the tomb: "Suddenly two men in clothes that gleamed like lightning stood beside them" (Luke 24:4). The fact that there are two is significant for establishing their credibility as witnesses in a Jewish context. The Jewish law stipulates that "a matter must be established by the testimony of two or three witnesses" (Deut. 19:15).

Will come back in the same way (1:11). The angels assure the amazed disciples not only that Jesus will return, but that it will be in a similar fashion. This accords with what Jesus himself taught: "At that time men will see the Son of Man coming in clouds with great power and glory" (Mark 13:26).

(as far as the province of Britannia, modern Great Britain) and a great distance to the west (Spain and Gaul). We know that the apostle Paul planned to preach the gospel as far as Spain (see Rom. 15:24). Jesus here echoes the language of Isaiah 49:6, which anticipates the light of the gospel extending throughout the inhabited earth: "I will also make you a light for the Gentiles, that you may bring my salvation to the ends of the earth."

A cloud hid him from their sight (1:9). This is not a normal cloud. Rather, it is a special cloud that shrouds the divine

The Disciples Wait and Pray (1:12–14)

In roughly the ten days between Jesus' ascension and the coming of the Spirit, the disciples devote themselves to prayer. They meet together in a private room where they spend long hours together calling on the Lord. Their sense of anticipation must have been high in light of Jesus' promise of an outpouring of the Spirit.

The Mount of Olives (1:12). Luke indicates that Jesus ascended not from within

▶

the city walls of Jerusalem, but from the Mount of Olives (see "Mount of Olives" at Luke 19:29). Following Jesus' ascension, the disciples return to the city.

A Sabbath day's walk (1:12). This Jewish expression referred to a distance between a half and three-quarters of a mile. The Rabbinic sources stipulate that a Sabbath day's journey was not to exceed two thousand cubits. Given that a cubit was about twenty-two inches, this would be a limit of 3,666 feet (a mile is 5,280 feet). The distance between the temple and the Mount of Olives was within this range.

They went upstairs to the room (1:13). The group met together in an upstairs room of a private home in Jerusalem. Most likely this was a home owned by someone sympathetic with the movement. To accommodate a crowd of this size (later 120 people meet in the room), the home was probably owned by a fairly wealthy person. Archaeologists have recovered the remains of a few homes in the Herodian quarter from this period owned by wealthy citizens.[18] One of these homes, the so-called "Palatial Mansion," had a room that measured thirty-six by twenty-one feet (nearly seven hundred square feet). Early Christian tradition, however, identifies this home with the "Cenacle" (see "The 'Cenacle'").

The women (1:14). This refers to the same women who visited the tomb of

---

CENACLE

An historical tradition locates the "upper room" in the Cenacle on Mount Zion.

▶ The "Cenacle"

Christian tradition identifies a place called the "Cenacle" as the "upper room" where the 120 disciples met. The site of the *cenaculum,* a Latin expression meaning "dining room," is today located within the church of the Dormition (built in 1900) on Mount Zion in the southwest corner of the city near the Zion Gate. Although there is nothing visible on this site today that constitutes the upper room at the time of the apostles, there is historical evidence that demonstrates Christian veneration of this site as the location of the home with the upper room since the first century.[A-1] The church father Epiphanius notes that there was "a little church of God" on this site since the time of the emperor Hadrian.[A-2]

Beginning in 1971, excavations were undertaken in this area under the direction of M. Broshi.[A-3] The team found remains of a number of Herodian-era homes that would have been two- and three-story structures. The excavators also discovered a variety of water installations (rock-hewn and barrel-vaulted cisterns, pools, and baths), pottery, a sword, and a few fresco fragments. The finds are consistent with the historical evidence that this was a densely populated portion of the city with wealthy inhabitants living in splendid private homes.

One of these homes—and possibly the site identified as the "Cenacle"—may well have been the location of the upper room. It suggests that a wealthy follower of Jesus opened up his home as a meeting place for this group. Who owned this home is uncertain, but someone such as Mary, the mother of John Mark, is a distinct possibility.[A-4]

Jesus and discovered it was empty: Mary Magdalene, Joanna, and Mary (the mother of James) (see Luke 24:10).

Mary the mother of Jesus (1:14). This is the final time that Mary is mentioned in the New Testament. It is meaningful that the last image we have of her is in prayer.

His brothers (1:14). These brothers are named in only one place in the New Testament (Mark 6:4). They were James, Joseph (or Joses), Judas, and Simon. Before the cross, they were skeptical of his claims (see John 7:5), but now they are devoted to him. James will become the leader of the Jerusalem church and Judas (or Jude) will become the author of a New Testament letter.

Peter Addresses a Group of 120 (1:15–26)

In the ten days between Jesus' ascension and the coming of the Spirit, many of Jesus' followers meet in the upper room of a Jerusalem home and wait on God in prayer. During this time, Peter addresses the group regarding Judas Iscariot and announces the necessity of choosing a man to replace Judas in the special min-

istry that the Lord had entrusted to the Twelve. After calling on the Lord in prayer, the group is sovereignly guided to select a man named Matthias to serve as one of the twelve apostles. These twelve men would serve an important role as witnesses of the resurrection of Jesus, vindicating his claim of being the Messiah of Israel, who died on the cross for the sins of the world.

A hundred and twenty (1:15). It may be significant that according to Jewish tradition, it was necessary to have a hundred and twenty men in a city to have a legitimate Jewish community. The Mishnah says, "And how many should there be in a city that it may be fit to have a Sanhedrin? A hundred and twenty men."[19]

Judas (1:18). On the surface it appears that Luke's account of Judas's death differs from Matthew's in a few places. Matthew says that Judas is remorseful after his betrayal of Jesus, returns the thirty silver coins to the chief priests, and then hangs himself. The chief priests then use the money to buy a potter's field for the burial of foreigners (Matt. 27:1–10). Luke simply states that Judas buys a field with the money and there suffers a terrible fall. Rather than seeing two contradictory stories here, it is better to consider how the various elements combine to give us a more complete picture of what actually happened, especially regarding who buys the field (the priests or Judas?) and how Judas dies (by hanging himself or by taking a nasty fall?). Many interpreters throughout church history as early as Augustine have suggested that the Jewish leaders themselves buy the field in Judas's name (thus explaining Luke's, "Judas bought a field"). It is possible that the leaders pur-

MODEL OF A FIRST-CENTURY JERUSALEM HOME
▼

chase the land before Judas's death, since no clear relative time coordinates are given for the purchase of the property and Judas's death. At some point after the priests take possession of the property, Judas decides to commit suicide on this piece of land. It is not surprising that he chooses to take his life there, given his frustration with the priests, initially expressed by his throwing the money into the temple (Matt. 27:5). He manages to devise a way to hang himself, but the rope (or tree branch) breaks under his weight, which results in his body tumbling to the ground (presumably on a rocky surface) and suffering fatal trauma.[20]

They called that field in their language Akeldama, that is, Field of Blood (1:19). *Akeldama* is a compound Aramaic expression. Over the centuries, many have identified Akeldama with a Jewish cemetery located about a half mile south of the Old City of Jerusalem, where the Hinnom Valley joins the Kidron Valley.

In this area, archaeologists have uncovered roughly eighty burial caves, most of which date to the Herodian period (37 B.C.–A.D. 70). Most archaeologists today would discount the identification of this area with the potter's field. The principal reason is that this was not a likely site for a potter's field or as a cemetery for strangers; rather, this was a burial place for the wealthy and priestly families of Jerusalem. One of the tombs probably belonged to the high priest Annas, who held office from A.D. 6–15.[21]

It is written in the book of Psalms (1:20). Peter quotes from two Psalms that he regards as predicting Judas's demise (Ps. 69:25) and the need to find someone to replace him (Ps. 109:8). Because these Psalms were authored by David, Peter understands them messianically and sees in them information that speaks directly to their situation.

It is necessary to choose this apostolic ministry (1:21, 25). Because Jesus had

AKELDAMA, THE FIELD OF BLOOD

The traditional site of Akeldama, the "field of blood," in the Hinnom Valley near the monastery of St. Onuphrius.

chosen *twelve* men to function as his witnesses, Peter and the others consider it essential that an additional witness be chosen by Jesus himself. The term "apostle" comes directly from the Greek word *apostolos* ("one who is sent; a messenger") and is used throughout the New Testament to designate someone sent by Christ to convey a message. The replacement for Judas needs to be one who had a close association with Jesus and the eleven from the beginning of Jesus' public ministry. Above all, this person would function as a witness to the fact of the bodily resurrection of Jesus and the saving significance of this event. These Twelve would pass on as well as safeguard the true tradition about Jesus. This "apostolic ministry" would be significant in laying the foundations for the church.

Joseph called Barsabbas (also known as Justus) (1:23). The name "Bar-Sabbas" is Aramaic for "Son of the Sabbath." We do not know if this was a nickname expressing his former zeal for Sabbath observance or a given name. His proper name was Joseph, but he also took a Roman (Latin) name, Justus.

Matthias (1:23). The lot fell to a man named Matthias. His name is an abbreviated form of "Mattathias," meaning, "the gift of God." The church historian Eusebius reports a tradition that Matthias had been one of the Seventy sent out by the Lord.[22] We know nothing else about either of these men.

They cast lots (1:26). By the casting of lots, Jesus himself would supernaturally make the choice, just as he had chosen the Twelve in his earthly ministry. When they prayed, they specifically asked the Lord Jesus to choose: "Show us which of these two you have chosen" (1:24). The typical method for casting lots involved writing the two names on stones, placing them into a jar, and shaking it until one fell out.[23] This decision-making procedure was not unusual in a Jewish context. The book of Proverbs says, "The lot is cast into the lap, but its every decision is from the LORD" (Prov. 16:33). Examples of this practice can be found in the Old Testament, for instance, in the distribution of responsibilities for working in the temple of the Lord (1 Chron. 26:14–16). After the coming of the Spirit on the day of Pentecost, we do not find this method used again elsewhere in the New Testament.

The Day of Pentecost (2:1–13)

The time finally came when the Lord poured out his Spirit on all the believers. It happened during the Feast of Weeks (which the Greeks called "Pentecost")—a time when many were once again gathered in Jerusalem. The Spirit did not come in a quiet and imperceptible way, but manifested his presence like a surging wind and like tongues of fire. The recipients of the Spirit were then empowered for witness and began immediately by magnifying the greatness of God. Leaving the upper room and moving into the streets, the disciples continued to speak and attracted a large crowd. The Jews who listened could not believe what they heard—Galileans speaking in languages and dialects they could not possibly have known.

▶

LOTS

Dice made of bone found in Jerusalem and dating to the early Roman period.

The coming of the Spirit marked the beginning of the church. The presence of the Spirit is what makes a person a Christian. The event fulfilled prophecies that spoke of the last days and that the Spirit would be imparted (see Isa. 32:15 and Joel 2:28–32). The last days had now arrived.

The day of Pentecost (2:1). The term "Pentecost" is a transliteration of the Greek word *pentēkostē*, which means "fiftieth." It referred to the fiftieth day after the Passover festival when the Jews celebrated the Feast of Weeks—the annual harvest festival (see Lev. 23:15–21 and Deut. 16:9–12). This was the second of three festivals (the others being Passover and Tabernacles) that all Jewish males were required to attend in Jerusalem (Deut. 16:16). It occurred in early summer after the conclusion of the grain harvest. This was a joyous occasion when the Israelites expressed their thanks to God for his provisions through the year and renewed their commitment to him. Later Jewish tradition associated this festival with the giving of the law at Sinai. If this tradition dated as early as the first century, the coming of the Spirit at Pentecost would underscore the Spirit's role in fulfilling and superseding the Mosaic law. This was also an opportune time since Pentecost was the next occasion after Passover that a large crowd would be assembled in Jerusalem.

The blowing of a violent wind ... tongues of fire (2:2–3). The Spirit is associated here with two symbols that often symbolized the manifestation of the presence of God. In Ezekiel's vision of the valley filled with dry bones, the life-giving breath of God comes as a wind and makes these dead bodies live again (Ezek. 37:1–14). This prophecy is linked to the new

covenant promise of the indwelling Spirit (Ezek. 37:14). Alluding to Ezekiel's vision, Jesus himself described the coming Holy Spirit as a wind (John 3:8).

During the period of the Exodus, God appeared to Moses as fire. When the Lord revealed himself to Moses the first time, it was in a burning bush (Ex. 3:2–5). God called Moses to be his agent for rescuing the people of Israel from their bondage in Egypt and assured Moses of his enabling presence. After the Exodus, God appeared to Moses again on Mount Sinai. The Lord "descended on it in fire" and gave the law to Moses (Ex. 19:18).

With both the wind and the fire, Luke is careful to point out that the coming of the Spirit was *like* these two common natural phenomena. There was no actual wind or fire. Violent wind and fire represent powerful forces; a divine wind bringing life and fire from above suggests the empowering presence of God.

The image of tongues is probably meant to convey both the miraculous speaking in other languages that the disciples were about to accomplish as well as the ability the Spirit would provide to proclaim the gospel with power.

Staying in Jerusalem (2:5). Numerous Jews from all over the Mediterranean world came to this important festival. The population of Jerusalem swelled from about one hundred thousand inhabitants to around a million during each of the three festivals.[24] Many would stay in private homes and inns, but the majority would have camped in tents both within the city walls and in the vicinity of the city.[25]

In his own language (2:6). Since the time of Alexander the Great, who spread Greek culture all the way to Mesopotamia and beyond, Greek was the official language.

Official documents and letters were written in Greek from countries as far apart as Persia to Spain and North Africa to Gaul. Nevertheless, most people were multilingual and could also speak a local language. It was these local languages and dialects that the Holy Spirit enabled these believers to speak fluently, uttering praises to God.

Galileans (2:7). The majority of Jesus' followers at this point were from Galilee, where he had spent most of his time in his public ministry. The Galileans often bore the brunt of disparaging comments and stereotyping. Most Jewish Galileans were bilingual, speaking both Aramaic and Greek (with some also speaking Hebrew). They would not be capable of speaking the languages and dialects of the various countries represented in Jerusalem on this day.

Parthians . . . Arabs (2:9–11). Luke only gives us a representative list of the countries from which many Jewish pilgrims came. He does not mention many other countries from which a contingent of Jews would have arrived, such as Syria, many of the other Asia Minor territories (Galatia, Caria, Lydia, Cilicia), any territories in Greece (Macedonia, Achaia), other parts of North Africa, or the island of Cyprus.

Converts to Judaism (2:11). This is a translation of the Greek word *prosēlytoi*, from which we get "proselyte." For a male Gentile to become a proselyte, he was required to (1) be circumcised, (2) perform a baptismal rite of purification, and (3) offer a sacrifice at the Jerusalem temple. Only the latter two requirements were mandated for women. Most Gentiles attracted to the one true God preferred the looser requirements in obtaining the status of "God-fearer," especially the men, who could then avoid the rite of circumcision.

Our own tongues (2:11). Each person heard God exalted in his or her own native language or dialect.

THE ROMAN WORLD

The map shows the fifteen locations mentioned in Acts 2:9–11.
▼

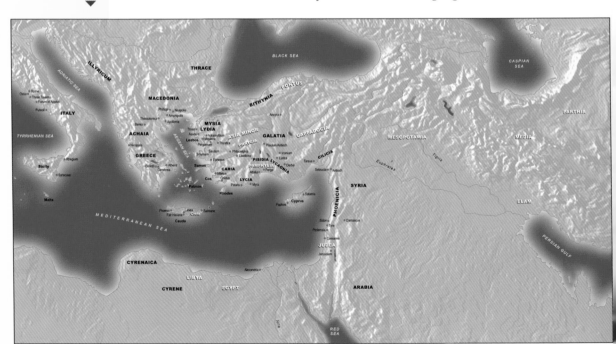

The Countries and Languages Refleccted in Acts 2:9–11		
Country	**Local Dialects**[A-5]	**What Is Known About Judaism There**[A-6]
1. Parthia 2. Media 3. Elam 4. Mesopotamia	Aramaic, *Parthian, Iranian*	It was to these countries in the East—in the area of modern-day Iran and Iraq—that the tribes of Israel were exiled over seven hundred years earlier under the Assyrians (722 B.C.) and later under the Babylonians (586 B.C.). Although they were given permission to return to Israel during the Persian empire (5th cent. B.C.), many chose to stay. By the time of the first century, the number of Jews in this region may have numbered in the hundreds of thousands.
5. Judea	Aramaic, Hebrew	This was the Roman province to which Jerusalem belonged. Jews from all of the surrounding villages streamed to Jerusalem for the festivals.
6. Cappadocia 7. Pontus 8. Asia 9. Phrygia 10. Pamphylia	*numerous local dialects include Phrygian, Pisidian, Lydian, Carian, Lycian, Celtic, Lycaonian, and others.*[A-7]	These five countries were all ethnic territories within the Roman province of Asia Minor (modern-day Turkey). There are numerous literary texts and archaeological evidences illustrating the extensive Jewish presence in Asia Minor from the second century B.C. The earliest Jewish presence can be traced to the late sixth or fifth century B.C.
11. Egypt	Coptic	This was the largest Jewish community in the world at that time. The largest community was in the city of Alexandria, where there may have been as many as a hundred thousand Jews.
12. Libya (Cyrene)	Latin, *Numidian*	There is considerable evidence for Jewish presence in North Africa, especially in the city of Cyrene.
13. Rome	Latin	Jews established a colony in Rome during the second century B.C. The Roman general Pompey brought a great number of Jews to the city from Palestine in 62 B.C. The Jewish population in Rome swelled to as high as twenty thousand by the first century A.D. Those who became Christians at Pentecost returned to Rome and planted the church there—the same church that Paul wrote to in his letter to the Romans.
14. Crete	Greek	This large Greek island had a sizeable Jewish population dwelling primarily in the area of Gorytna. In the second century B.C., they faced persecution from the Cretans, but later secured Roman support. The first-century Jewish writer Philo said that the islands of Euboea, Cyprus, and Crete were "full of Jewish colonies."[A-8]
15. Arabia	Nabatean (a branch of Aramaic), Aramaic, Arabic[A-9]	This would refer to the Nabatean Arabs who lived to the east of the Jordan River and to the south of Palestine. Their capital was Petra, about fifty miles south of the Dead Sea. There is ample evidence of Jewish presence in the key cities (Petra, Hegra) and in the territory.[A-10]

They have had too much wine (2:13). The literal translation of this phrase from the Greek is, "they are filled with sweet wine."

Peter Stands Up and Preaches the Gospel (2:14–36)

Reversing his previous public denial of Jesus, Peter now stands up in front of this large crowd and boldly declares that Jesus is in fact the awaited Messiah of Israel and the sovereign Lord. He cites three passages from the Old Testament demonstrating that the Messiah would be a descendent of David, that he would rise from the dead, and that he would be exalted to the right hand of God. He proclaims that these have all been fulfilled in Jesus of Nazareth.

The actual message Peter gave was probably much longer than what was recorded here. Luke provides us with an accurate abbreviation of this important address.

Peter ... addressed the crowd (2:14). Peter takes the opportunity to address the gathered crowd by responding to their accusation that the followers of Jesus are drunk. Flanked by the eleven other apostles and inspired by the Holy Spirit, Peter embarks on a long address that elicits an incredible response with many people putting their faith in Jesus. Peter begins by pointing out the absurdity of thinking that over a hundred people would be drunk at nine o'clock in the morning.

In the last days, God says, I will pour out my Spirit (2:17). He immediately explains that what they are witnessing is nothing less than the outpouring of the Spirit predicted in Joel 2:28–32. This coming of the Spirit marks the beginning of the last days. The "age to come" has

arrived and the new covenant blessing of the Holy Spirit is now visibly manifest among those who have put their faith in Jesus.

Your sons and daughters will prophesy (2:17). According to the prophecy, one of the key features of the Spirit's coming would be men and women prophesying. What the crowd was hearing on the day of Pentecost was one form of prophetic utterance.

I will show wonders in the heaven above (2:19). The text of Joel also predicts the occurrence of miraculous signs in space involving the sun and the moon. These astral phenomena, however, will occur in connection with the coming future Day of the Lord. While the coming of the Spirit marks the beginning of the age to come and the commencement of the last days, the signs in heaven will point to the conclusion of the present evil age and the return of the Lord in judgment.

Everyone who calls on the name of the Lord will be saved (2:21). Joel's prophecy is not one of utter gloom and despair. It holds out the bright hope that anyone who calls on the name of the Lord will be saved.

Jesus of Nazareth (2:22). Peter now moves from his explanation about the outpouring of the Spirit to a proclamation of the person of Jesus Christ. He speaks specifically about Jesus' miraculous deeds (which point to the fact that God was active in him) and his violent death. Peter assumes that the crowd was familiar with Jesus' works of power—whether they would publicly admit it or not. He explains, however, that the death of Jesus was not something unexpected. It was an integral part of the plan of God.

God raised him from the dead (2:24). Peter then affirms the reality of Jesus' resurrection from the dead. He does not present an apologetic for an empty tomb at this point, but rather focuses on the Jewish issue of the resurrection as fulfillment of prophecy. To accomplish this, he cites Psalm 16:8–11, a psalm ascribed to David.

You will not abandon me to the grave, nor will you let your Holy One see decay (2:27). Peter's argument hinges on Psalm 16:10, where David declares that he would not be left in the grave nor would his body experience decay. Under the inspiration of the Spirit, Peter argues that this could not refer to David himself because he did in fact die and his tomb is present in Jerusalem for all to see. Rather, this psalm is a prophecy about the greater descendent of David who would sit on David's throne—Jesus the Messiah—whose body did not remain in a tomb nor did it experience decomposition because God raised him from the grave. Peter declares that he and all those with him are eyewitnesses to the fact that Jesus was resurrected.

His tomb is here to this day (2:29). The Jewish historian Josephus confirms that David's tomb was still present in Jerusalem in the first century. He tells the story about a Jewish priest named John Hyrcanus entering the tomb and taking out three thousand talents of silver to give to the invading Syrian king in 134 B.C. with the hope that the invasion could be forestalled.[26] Hearing of this, Herod the Great made a secretive entry into the tomb at night to retrieve more of this treasure. He did not find any money, but he found many gold furnishings. When he tried to penetrate further into the tomb, two of his guards were killed by what he considered to be an act of divine judgment. He fled the tomb and built a white marble monument hoping that this would help to make amends for his indiscretion.[27]

In 1913, the French archaeologist, Raymond Weill, discovered nine burial tombs in the southern portion of the City of David. He identified the largest and most magnificent of these as the tomb of David. This tomb was hewn out of rock and measured over fifty-two feet long, eight feet wide, thirteen feet high at the front and lowering to six feet at the deepest portion. Many archaeologists today dismiss Weill's identification because no corroborating evidence dating the tomb to the time of David has been discovered.[28] Nevertheless, other scholars believe that a reasonable case can be made that this is, in fact, David's tomb.[29]

The Lord said to my Lord: "Sit at my right hand" (2:34). Peter goes on to further establish that Jesus had ascended to heaven and once again argues that this was in fulfillment of prophecy, citing Psalm 110:1, the most frequently cited Old Testament passage in the entire New Testament. The Psalm speaks of the exaltation of Jesus to the right hand of God where he wields kingly authority over his enemies. Peter implicitly understands the address of the Psalm, the Lord said to my Lord, as God speaking to David's Lord, that is, to Jesus.

Both Lord and Christ (2:36). For Peter, the bottom line of his entire message is that Jesus is both Messiah (Christ) and Lord. As Messiah, he is the fulfillment of Israel's expectations for a descendent of David to come and sit on the throne. As Lord, Jesus is at the right hand of God and is *the* sovereign.

A Great Response to the Message (2:37–41)

The crowd had listened intently to everything Peter declared. Rather than rejecting what Peter said about who Jesus was and what he had accomplished on the cross, they became profoundly aware of their own sinfulness. Many in this crowd, no doubt, were among those in the Passover mob who yelled "Crucify! Crucify!" when Pilate mockingly presented Jesus to them as their king (John 19:14–15). They now plead with Peter and the other apostles to tell them how they should respond to his words.

Peter directly tells them to repent and to express their commitment to Christ through baptism. He assures them that Christ would forgive their sins and endow them with the promised Holy Spirit.

The response to this Spirit-inspired message is astonishing. Three thousand Jews from all over the Mediterranean world receive Christ. They are immediately baptized and become the first converts in the beginnings of a movement that would spread rapidly throughout the extent of the Roman empire and ultimately all over the world.

They were cut to the heart (2:37). Luke uses a term that literally means, "to be stabbed (with a knife)." It came to be used to express deep anxiety or profound regret. This is the only time the word is used in the New Testament.

Repent (2:38). This became the central call of early Christian preaching. Repentance (*metanoia*) involves primarily a radical change in a person's central affections, convictions, and life direction. It signifies a recognition that one's life has been oriented around self and sinful pursuits and an embracing of God's will and priorities.

The call to repent is a continuation of Jesus' own ministry introduced by John the Baptist with his call to repentance (Luke 3:3) and repeatedly urged by Jesus himself in his earthly ministry (Luke 13:3, 5; 24:47).

Be baptized. . . . Those who accepted his message were baptized (2:38, 41). From the beginning, baptism has been the central rite performed for incorporating new believers into the church. The word itself is a Greek term, a transliteration of *baptizō*, meaning "to dip (in water)," "immerse," "sink," or "drench."[30]

What Peter calls for here in conjunction with their repentance is an entirely new rite for the people of God. This is appropriate since baptism is associated with the new covenant and the gift of the Holy Spirit. There was some similarity in form, however, to contemporary practices in Judaism. Gentile converts to Judaism were required to be purified in a ritual bath. There is also evidence that many Jews throughout the land performed daily washings in special pools as a way of maintaining ritual purity. This was particularly true at Qumran, where numerous ritual baths (*miqva'ot*) have been discovered.

There were many places in Jerusalem where these new believers could have been baptized. A number of ritual baths were located within the walls of the temple as well as a number of installations west of the temple mount. There were also six large pools in Jerusalem (mentioned by Josephus): the pool of the Towers, the Strouthion Pool, the Sheep's Pool (Bethesda), the Serpents' Pool, Solomon's Pool (the Pool of Siloam), and the Pool of Israel.[31]

In the name of Jesus Christ for the forgiveness of your sins (2:38). This baptism is a one-time rite. It is also specifically a baptism in the name of Jesus Christ. The apostle Paul later characterizes it as vividly symbolizing a participation in Christ's burial and resurrection (Rom. 6:3–4). Identification with Christ—and not the water itself—is the basis for the forgiveness of sins (Acts 2:38).

For all who are far off (2:39). This phrase is an allusion to Isaiah 57:19 where the Prophet points to a day when it will be said, "Peace, peace, to those far and near." Peter applies this promise to all of the Jews who have come from faraway lands and are now recipients of the Spirit of peace. At this point he may not realize it, but the intent of the application of this promise is for Gentiles as well. God will show him this by a vision and by involving him in the conversion of the Gentile household of Cornelius (Acts 10). Paul will apply this prophecy to the inclusion of Gentiles into the one body of Christ (Eph. 2:13).

The Early Christian Experience and Practice (2:42–47)

Luke gives us the first of a series of summary statements about the life and Spirit-directed vitality of these early Christians (see also in 4:32–35; 5:12–16; 9:31; 12:24). So much was happening so fast, but these new believers were committing themselves to learning more about Jesus, praying, worshiping, and

---

▶ Foundational Elements of Early Christian Life

In a summary statement, Luke lists four key features that characterize the lives of the first Christians. These believers made as a matter of the highest priority "devoting themselves" to these practices:

1. Instruction: The Apostles' Teaching: The twelve apostles had a significant role in the beginnings of the church. They passed on to these new Jewish believers a full account of Jesus' life and teaching. This would have included much of what came to be recorded in the four Gospels. In addition to this, they would have helped provide a new perspective on the Old Testament, explaining how Jesus was the fulfillment of many prophecies. Throughout the early history of the church, grounding new believers in the apostles' teaching was a major priority.

2. Fellowship: It was important to these early believers to spend much time together. These hours would have been passed in discussing the apostles' teaching, encouraging and challenging each other, and enjoying one another in the family bond that the Spirit created. This "fellowship" also extended to a tangible manifestation of love for one another that found expression in sharing with the poorer members of this new community.

3. Worship: The Breaking of Bread: This expression refers both to sharing ordinary meals together (furthering their fellowship) and to remembering the significance of the death of the Messiah by celebrating what came to be known as "the Lord's Supper." At this stage, the Lord's Supper was held in conjunction with a common meal in homes throughout the city. This remembrance would have been a time of quiet reflection, as well as an occasion for expressing thanks to the risen Jesus and praising him for what he had accomplished.

4. Prayer: The first Christians spent much time before the Lord in prayer. They prayed privately, but they often prayed together as a group. It appears that many maintained the Jewish pattern of setting aside three times a day for focusing on prayer. Some continued to go to the temple and pray at the customary Jewish hours of prayer. Their prayers probably centered on blessing and praising God as well as asking him for guidance and for boldness in proclaiming the Gospel.

enjoying a vibrant community life. They were also committed to proclaiming Jesus as the Messiah to others and God was powerfully at work through their testimony. Every day more people were confessing Jesus and joining their community.

Wonders and miraculous signs (2:43). The Spirit of God works through the twelve apostles to perform many healings and to cast demons out of people. These miracles contribute to the development of a climate of receptivity to the gospel message.

All the believers were together (2:44). They did not all move into a communal living arrangement together, but rather they develop a strong sense of community. They confess a common Lord, spend much time together, share with one another, and participate in a common vision and purpose.

REFLECTIONS

"FELLOWSHIP" AND SPENDING
time together regularly to deepen relationships and serve one another is a significant challenge facing the church—especially in the larger churches of heavily populated areas. Work schedules, the pull of entertainment, and the proliferation of various activities undermine community. The result is that believers sometimes feel disconnected, uncared for, and unloved. Many Christians even see church as something that you do only once a week. What steps can be taken to develop more true fellowship among believers?

Had everything in common (2:44). Sometimes a false impression is gained that these early Christians sold everything they owned when they joined the church. This was, in fact, the practice of the Qumran community on the Dead Sea. When someone joined that group, his property and earnings were all handed over to a trustee in the community and it became part of a common fund.[32] This is not the case, however, for these first believers. Their commitment to Jesus and the work of the Spirit in their lives produce in them a completely new attitude to their property. No longer are they motivated to amass wealth for themselves, but they now view what they have as resources for the cause of Christ and for the care of his people. The verb tense for "selling" (the imperfect) implies that there was not one big sale of goods upon a person's conversion, but that individuals sold portions of their personal and real property as needs in the community surfaced. This was entirely voluntary and not mandated by the apostles.

The temple courts (2:46). The Greek text reads simply, "in the temple." Luke does not specify here exactly which part of the temple precincts these three to four thousand believers met each day, but later he tells us that they met "in Solomon's Colonnade" (see comments on 5:12).

In their homes (2:46). Some of the wealthier members of the church owned private residences in the city of Jerusalem. Rather than sell their homes, they opened them up for the Christians to meet. Private homes were the principal meeting places of early Christians for the first three centuries of the church's existence.

◄

A WEALTHY HOME

A model of a typical affluent family house in Herodian upper Jerusalem.

Recent excavations in Jerusalem on the Western Hill (part of the Upper City) have resulted in the discovery of a residential district in the ancient city. There were many houses in this area that would have belonged to the wealthier inhabitants of the city.[33] It is not known whether any of these homes were the places where one or more of the groups of early Christians gathered, but they do help us to see the kind of setting for some of the home groups (see "The 'Cenacle'").

◄

ENTRANCE TO A MIQVEH

The entrance to a ritual bath in the remains of a Herodian-era home on the western hill in upper Jerusalem.

Peter and John Heal a Lame Beggar (3:1–10)

Some time after the day of Pentecost—perhaps as much as a couple of years later (Luke does not tell us)—an amazing incident happens near a gate in the temple courts. Two of the apostles, Peter and John, are confronted by a lame beggar who asks them for money. They, in turn, manifest the healing power of Jesus to restore the paralyzed limbs of this destitute man. Cured of his paralysis, the man promptly makes a spectacle in the temple courts by demonstratively praising God for his healing. Such an incident of healing is not out of ordinary in these early days and months of the church. Luke has previously said that they are commonplace in the ministry of the apostles (see 2:43). Luke chooses to tell us about this episode because it attracts a large crowd and gives Peter

HEROD'S TEMPLE
20 B.C. – A.D. 70

Living quarters for priests were within this colonnaded enclosure

Rooms within walls

F. Sanctuary

CUBITS

FEET

4 cubits = 6 feet.

1 cubit = 18 inches

D. Israel Court
(for Jewish men) *under colonnades*

E. Priests' Court

Chamber of hewn stone (possible Sanhedrin council room)

Laver

Altar

Chamber of the Hearth

Nicanor Gate

Lepers' Court

Colonnades went all around Women's Court with upstairs balcony

(cutaway view)

Levite choirs performed on steps

Oil Storage

C. Women's Court

Pharisee and Tax Collector
Lk 18:10-14

Wood Storage

Nazirites Court

Widow's Offering
Mk 12:42

Beautiful Gate

Lame man healed
Acts 3:6-8

Chel (Rampart)

Chel

"No entry" laws were posted in 3 languages

Soreg—
a low wall surrounding temple (location uncertain) with 13 places of entry

Triumphal Entry
Mt 21:15

Soreg

No Gentiles permitted inside of Soreg boundary

B. Sacred Enclosure

A. Gentiles' Court

Dimensions are stated in history (Josephus and the Mishnah) but are subject to interpretation, and all drawings vary.

another unique opportunity to proclaim the gospel.

The time of prayer—at three in the afternoon (3:1). According to Josephus, the priests at the temple "twice each day, in the morning and about the ninth hour [= 3 P.M.]" offer the daily animal sacrifice prescribed by the law of Moses (see Num. 28:1–8) and referred to in Judaism as the *tamid*.[34] Following an offering of incense, a sacrificial lamb is slaughtered on the altar. This is accompanied by the priest presenting a cereal offering (an unleavened loaf of wheat flour and oil) and a drink offering (a libation of wine). The priests then lead those in attendance in a time of singing and prayer. The Mishnah describes this time of prayer following the sacrifice:

> When he stooped to pour out the drink offering the Prefect waved the towel and Ben Arza [a priest] clashed the cymbal and the levites broke forth into singing. When they reached a break in the singing they blew upon the trumpets and the people prostrated themselves [in prayer]; at every break there was a blowing of the trumpet and at every blowing of the trumpet a prostration [in prayer]. This was the rite of the daily whole-offering in the service of the House of our God.[35]

In these early stages of the church, the apostles and the other believers (who were all Jewish) continue to observe the set times of worship in the Jerusalem temple.

A man crippled from birth (3:2). It was not at all surprising to find poor and handicapped people begging for a handout in Jerusalem and particularly near the temple. Charitable giving was viewed as particularly meritorious when it was done here.[36]

The temple gate called Beautiful (3:2). This is most likely one of the gates in the Court of Women, either on the west side leading to the Court of the Israelites (also called the Corinthian gate or the gate of the Sanctuary) or on the east side leading to the Court of the Gentiles. Both of these gates were exceptionally grand and ornate in appearance, appropriately fitting the description "beautiful." Josephus describes their size and splendor well:

> Of the gates nine were completely covered with gold and silver, as were the posts and lintels, but the one outside the Sanctuary was of Corinthian bronze, and far more valuable than those overlaid with silver or even with gold. Every gateway had double doors, each half being 45 feet high and 22-1/2 wide. On the inner side

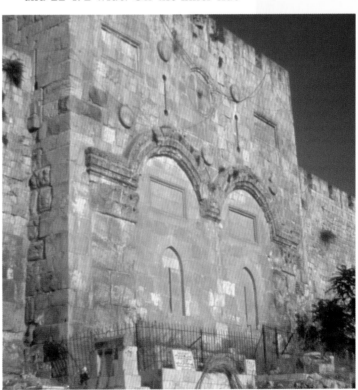

▶

**THE GOLDEN GATE
(THE BEAUTIFUL
GATE)**

A reconstruction
of the gate as seen
in the Jerusalem
temple model.

Asclepius) or helper spirits to attempt their healings. Peter calls on the power of the exalted Lord. This healing marks yet another instance of the ongoing work of Christ through the church as Luke has announced at the beginning of his work when he says that his Gospel is an account of "all that Jesus *began* to do and to teach" (1:1).

The man's feet and ankles are miraculously strengthened—in fact so much so that he is able to run and jump. Staying close to the apostles' side, the man accompanies them into the temple courts unable to contain his exuberance over what God has done for him. Because all of the onlookers know well the pitiable state of the man before, they are astonished and wonder what has happened.

Peter Speaks at the Temple (3:11–25)

Taking advantage of this singular opportunity, Peter addresses the crowd. They give their full attention to Peter because there is incontrovertible evidence standing right before them that Peter and John could exercise some kind of supernatural power. What is this power that healed the crippled man so dramatically? Is this a sign to them from God?

In his message, Peter strongly emphasizes that the healing is performed in the power of the risen Jesus. He testifies to the crowd that Jesus is indeed the anticipated Messiah and offers his point on the basis of many Old Testament prophetic texts that find their precise fulfillment in the ministry of Jesus. This is not strictly an informational speech. Peter stresses to the crowd their guilt before God in rejecting the Messiah and, in fact, joining the rest of the mob in demanding his death. Peter then tells

however the gateways widened out, and on either hand there was a gate-room 45 feet square, shaped like a tower and over 60 feet high. Each room was supported by two pillars 18 feet round. The other gates were all of the same size, but the one beyond the Corinthian gate, opening out from the court of the Women on the east and facing the gate of the Sanctuary, was much bigger; for its height was 75 feet, that of the doors 50, and the decoration was more magnificent, the gold and silver plates being extremely thick.[37]

In the name of Jesus Christ of Nazareth, walk (3:6). Hoping to get a charitable handout from Peter and John as they pass through the gate, the lame man receives far beyond what he could have imagined. Staring at him, Peter says, "In the name of Jesus Christ of Nazareth, walk." By this statement, Peter acts not on his own authority, but he is appealing to the risen Jesus to manifest his healing power. Jesus himself, by contrast, heals on the basis of his own authority during his earthly ministry. Other itinerant healers of the time call on various kinds of deities (such as them that it is not too late for them to be reconciled to God if they repent of their sin and turn to God by embracing the risen Jesus as the Messiah who will forgive their sin and come again to fulfill God's kingdom program on earth.

Solomon's Colonnade (3:11). The entire temple platform was surrounded by beautiful colonnades on the perimeter of the outer court. The colonnade on the east side is referred to as "Solomon's Colonnade" (or "portico," "stoa," or "porch"). On the other side of the eastern temple wall would have been a steep hillside descending to the Kidron Valley. Josephus provides us with a detailed description of the colonnade:

> The colonnades were all double, the supporting pillars were 37 -1/2 feet high, cut from single blocks of the whitest marble, and the ceiling was panelled with cedar. The natural magnificence of it all, the perfect pol-

ish and the accurate jointing afforded a remarkable spectacle, without any superficial ornament either painted or carved. The colonnades were 45 feet wide and the complete circuit of them measures three quarters of a mile, Antonia being enclosed within them.[38]

This eastern colonnade would then have extended for over three hundred yards. One part of this large area apparently became a popular meeting spot for the first Christians in Jerusalem (see also Acts 5:12). The entire colonnade was destroyed during the Jewish war (A.D. 66–70); only the temple platform remains.

The God of Abraham, Isaac and Jacob (3:13). Peter seizes this unique opportunity to address the crowd and begins by immediately clarifying that the man is not healed by any inherent powers that he or John possesses. He points them to

SOLOMON'S COLONNADE

A model of the Royal Stoa as it would have appeared from the northeast.

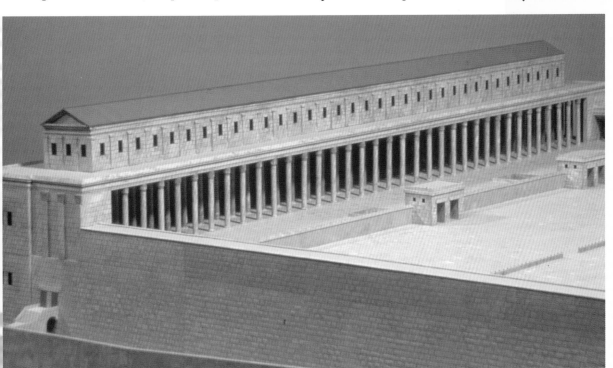

the one God that they all worship—the God who reveals himself to Moses at the burning bush as "I Am" (Yahweh), the God of Abraham, Isaac, and Jacob" (see Ex. 3:4–6).

Servant Jesus (3:13). Yet Peter attributes the healing to God's glorified servant, Jesus. For the Jew, "Servant" is a significant expression. It is an allusion to the Servant Songs of the prophet Isaiah. Isaiah 52:13 says that the servant "will be raised and lifted up and highly exalted." Yet this will only follow a period of suffering.

The author of life (3:15). Peter immediately moves on to speak of the suffering the Servant of God experienced. Peter directly accuses the assembled crowd of handing Jesus over to be killed. Presumably many of those present in this crowd are among those who join with the throng in demanding before the Roman proconsul that Jesus be crucified. Their assent makes them guilty of the most heinous crime imaginable. Peter accuses them of the amazing paradox of killing the author of life. This title points to Christ as the source of life, a function normally ascribed to the Father in the Old Testament. Using the same words, the writer of Hebrews later refers to Jesus as "the author of salvation" (Heb. 2:10). Jesus does not remain in the grave, however, for God raises him. Peter and John are now eyewitnesses of this important fact.

Peter once again makes it clear that it is the power of the risen Christ, represented by his name, that has healed the man. Belief in the person and the power of Jesus, not any kind of magic or personal power, has made the man well.

Foretold through all the prophets (3:18). Peter tells them that they acted in ignorance, although this is no excuse before

God. It was in the predetermined plan of God that Jesus would die. For most Jews this would have been difficult to see. Where does it explicitly state in the Old Testament that the Messiah would suffer? Part of the difficulty for many Jews is that they do not understand some of the prophecies in the Old Testament as pointing to the Messiah and therefore do not expect a *suffering* Messiah. For instance, most Jews interpret the Suffering Servant in Isaiah 52–53 as referring to themselves (in a corporate sense): They are the ones who have suffered and there is atoning significance to their suffering. Jesus, however, has used the language and imagery of the Suffering Servant to characterize his own mission (see, for example, Mark 10:45). He would be the representative of the people who would die an atoning death. This prophecy of Isaiah then becomes a central part of early Christian preaching to demonstrate that the Messiah would suffer and die. Yet there are other Old Testament texts that speak in a typological or prophetic way of the suffering of the Messiah.[39] The whole sacrificial system, in fact, points to a final and effective sacrifice.

REFLECTIONS

"I KNOW DEEP DOWN THAT I WILL still pay for some of the terrible things I have done." This is the sentiment that some Christians cling to in their hearts (often secretly) because of sinful choices and behaviors prior to coming to know Christ or even after becoming a Christian. Yet this notion is patently false. God wipes away the *entire* record of our sinful misdeeds.

So that your sins may be wiped out (3:19). As in his preaching at Pentecost, Peter now calls on the people to repent and turn to God so that their sins could be wiped out. This is a rare and colorful word that only appears in the Gospels and here in Acts. The term (*exaleiphō*) is used in the contemporary literature for the erasure or blotting out of a written record. The point is that there would no longer be any record of their complicity in the death of Jesus or any of their transgressions before God. Paul uses the same word in Colossians 2:14 to describe the forgiveness of sins.

Times of refreshing (3:19). By repenting and turning to God's plan in Jesus as the Messiah, Peter announces that there will be a future blessing. They will be able to participate fully in the future times of refreshing when Jesus returns and the kingdom of God is fully realized. This will be the time when God restores everything, establishing his order on earth.

He must remain in heaven until the time comes (3:21). Peter's comment indicates that a certain amount of time must elapse until the Messiah returns. As Jesus said, "No one knows about that day or hour, not even the angels in heaven, nor the Son, but only the Father" (Matt. 24:36).

All the prophets . . . have foretold these days (3:24). In this latter part of Peter's message, he appeals to further prophetic texts that point to the Messiah. He begins with a prophecy of Moses who pointed to a coming "prophet like me" that would arise and lead God's people (see Deut. 18:15–19). He also points to the covenant promise that God made with Abraham indicating that God would bless the nations through Abraham's offspring (Gen. 12:3; 22:18; 26:4). For Peter, Jesus the Messiah is the means by which this promise will be realized. At this point, it is doubtful that Peter appreciates the full scope of this promise and that he will soon be proclaiming the gospel to Gentiles (see Acts 10). The first opportunity for responding to these blessings will be extended to Abraham's physical descendants, the Jews.

Peter and John Are Arrested (4:1–22)

The apostles' continued proclamation of Jesus in the temple courts and the incredible number of his followers cause great concern among the Jewish leaders. The crucifixion of the leader of the movement has by no means put a stop to it. After arresting Peter and John, the high court of Israel interrogates the two witnesses. The rulers are overwhelmed by their boldness and persuasive appeal and so order them never to speak about Jesus again.

The captain of the temple guard (4:1). The wording of the NIV text can give the impression that there is an armed temple security force distinct from the priesthood. There is, however, no professional police force; security is handled by the priests. This official (*stratēgos*) is a priest who is second in authority to the chief priest. He stands at the high priest's right hand during the Day of Atonement ritual and whenever the high priest offers the daily sacrifice.[40] He supervises the day-to-day activities of the temple and is in charge of keeping order. He possesses the legal right to make an arrest. The potential military skill of this official is well illustrated by the example of Eleazar (captain of the temple guard in A.D. 66), who was made a general in the Jewish war of independence.[41]

The Sadducees (4:1). Well known through their repeated appearances in the Gospels (see "Sadducees" at Luke 5:24), the Sadducees were a wealthy group of politically influential Jews, many of whom were priests. They held a more moderate attitude toward the Torah than the Pharisees or the Essenes and tended to be more open to Greek cultural influences (Hellenism). The name of this group most likely derives from Zadok, the high priest under David (the first Old Testament reference is 2 Samuel 8:17, where he was co-priest with Abiathar; his descendants held the priestly office in Jerusalem since Solomon's time).

Later in Acts 23:8, Luke tells us that the Sadducees refuse to accept the belief in a future resurrection of the dead, a view espoused by the Pharisees. This is confirmed by Josephus.[42] The Sadducees may have considered the idea of a resurrection as a liberal innovation since it is not perfectly clear in the Torah. Josephus says that "according to their teaching, souls perish together with bodies."[43]

The number of men grew to about five thousand (4:4). A short time earlier following Peter's sermon on the day of Pentecost, the community of believers in Jerusalem has increased by three thousand (2:41). To this number are added two thousand more. The fact that Luke uses the term *anēr* for men (versus the more generic *anthrōpos*), indicates that he has not included all of the women and young people in his figure.

The rulers, elders and teachers of the law (4:5). These three groups composed the Jewish ruling council, the Sanhedrin (see "The Sanhedrin" at 4:15). "Rulers"

(*archontes*) refers specifically to the high priest and the chief priests, the most prominent of whom are specifically named in verse 6. "Elders" (*presbyteroi*) is a special term used to designate the lay members of the council. These were probably representatives of the aristocratic families in Jerusalem and tended to ally themselves with the Sadducees.[44]

The final expression (*grammateus*) is translated by most other versions as "scribes." They were a professional class of scholars invested with the responsibility of interpreting, teaching, and preserving the Jewish law. They were esteemed as the spiritual leaders of the people and, for the most part, were allied with the Pharisees (although there were undoubtedly some scribes associated with the Sadducees).

Annas the high priest (4:6). Annas retired from his high priesthood some twenty years earlier. He bore the title "high priest" only in an emeritus sense. Nevertheless, his age, experience, and family associations gave him significant personal authority. Annas became high priest in A.D. 6 and served in that capacity for nine years (until A.D. 15). He played a significant part in the trial of Jesus (see John 18:13–14).

Caiaphas (4:6). Joseph Caiaphas became high priest in A.D. 18 and was able to retain his position for nineteen years (until A.D. 37). He was the son-in-law of Annas (John 18:13). As high priest, he not only officiated at the temple, but served as president of the Sanhedrin and as the political head of the Jewish nation.

John, Alexander and the other men of the high priest's family (4:6). All of these men were "rulers" in Jerusalem as members of the Sanhedrin. It is likely that

John (or Jonathan) was one of the five sons of Annas who later succeeded his brother-in-law as high priest in A.D. 37.[45] A recently discovered ossuary inscription found in the vicinity of Jerusalem mentions John. It reads: "Yehoḥanah, daughter of Yehoḥanah [John], son of Theophilus the high priest."[46] The Theophilus of this inscription, who began his service as high priest in A.D. 37, is the father of John.

By what power or what name did you do this? (4:7). These leaders of the Sanhedrin do not question the reality of the healing; the evidence is apparently beyond dispute. They assume, however, that the miracle is not done on the basis of power from the one true God. It was common in the Greco-Roman world to call on various deities, helper spirits, and magical names and symbols to effect healing. In response, Peter makes it clear that the healing has nothing to do with magic, but only with the Lord Jesus Christ.

He is "the stone you builders rejected, which has become the capstone" (4:11). Peter not only responds to their question, but offers an incisive rebuke. He claims that their rejection of Jesus and Jesus' current place of honor in God's plan fulfills Psalm 118:22, which he cites. By appealing to this passage, Peter follows the lead of Jesus himself (see Matt. 21:42). The force of this quotation and rebuke may be underlined by the fact that the scribes are described as "builders" in rabbinic literature.[47]

"Capstone" is an interpretation of the expression "head of the corner." As one author describes, "It expresses rather the

◄

CORNERSTONE

Herodian-era masonry in Jerusalem.

▸ The Appointments of Annas and Caiaphas (According to Josephus)

The Jewish historian Josephus gives a succinct account of the deposition of Annas from the high priesthood and the appointment of Caiaphas in the context of the Roman governorship of Judea:

Tiberius Nero, [Caesar Augustus's] wife Julia's son, succeeded. He was now the third emperor; and he sent Valerius Gratus to be procurator of Judea, and to succeed Annius Rufus. (34) This man deprived Ananus of the high priesthood, and appointed Ismael, the son of Phabi, to be high priest. He also deprived him in a little time, and ordained Eleazar, the son of Ananus, who had been high priest before, to be high priest: which office, when he had held for a year, Gratus deprived him of it, and gave the high priesthood to Simon, the son of Camithus; (35) and when he had possessed that dignity no longer than a year, Joseph Caiaphas was made his successor. When Gratus had done those things, he went back to Rome, after he had tarried in Judea eleven years, when Pontius Pilate came as his successor.[A-11] function of a main, often oversized, stone used at an important spot in the joining of two walls of a building, to bear their weight and stress."[48] This usage is well-illustrated by the *Testament of Solomon:* "So Jerusalem was being built and the temple was moving toward completion. Now there was a gigantic cornerstone which I [Solomon] wished to place at *the head of the corner* to complete the Temple of God."[49]

Unschooled, ordinary men (4:13). The point of their criticism is that Peter and John both lack formal scribal training in the law. This is seen clearly in the Greek where the contrast is between *grammateis* and *agrammatoi,* that is, between scribes and those without scribal training.

Judge for yourselves whether it is right in God's sight to obey you rather than God (4:19). Peter and John let it be known that they will defy the injunctions of the Sanhedrin if the council rules to

prohibit them from proclaiming the gospel of Jesus Christ. They portray their decision as choosing to obey God rather than men thereby implying that the Sanhedrin's ruling on this matter is not from God. This is an extraordinarily bold and audacious statement. All Jews were accustomed to viewing the Sanhedrin as the final and binding interpreter of the Hebrew Scriptures. These two men, without any scribal training, now challenge the validity of the Sanhedrin's ruling and undermine the integrity of the supreme ruling body of all Israel.

A similar statement was uttered by Socrates when he stood trial in Athens and was ordered to stop teaching his philosophy or "if you are caught doing so again you shall die." Socrates declared, "Men of Athens, I respect and love you, but I shall obey the god rather than you, and while I live and am able to continue, I shall never give up philosophy or stop exhorting you and pointing out the truth to any one of you whom I may meet."[50]

▶ The Sanhedrin

The Sanhedrin was the ruling body of the Jewish people. It was composed of seventy people plus the high priest, who presided over the council. Although Palestine was ultimately under the control of the Romans through the appointed procurator, the emperor had granted the Jews a great deal of self-governing powers. The Sanhedrin was essentially a senate that directly governed the eleven districts (*toparchies*) of Judea. The group made judicial rulings and conducted the administrative affairs of Judea. But the decisions of the Sanhedrin carried substantial weight for Jews scattered throughout the Mediterranean world. It was the final board for deciding on matters connected with the Jewish law.

In the New Testament era, the Sanhedrin was controlled by the chief priests (most of whom were

Sadducees) and the wealthy nobility of Jerusalem. The Pharisees had increasing representation on the council through some of their scribes who retained seats. The Pharisaic popularity with the masses, however, gave their voice significant power on the council.

The Sanhedrin met in a building to the west of the southern end of the temple precincts near the so-called Xystus/*Lishkath ha-Gazith* (an open square close to the palace).[A-12] The Talmud describes the council chamber as "like a great basilica."[A-13] A bridge led directly from the Sanhedrin's council building across the Tyropoeon valley directly to the temple mount. This bridge has been identified by archaeologists as "Wilson's Arch."[A-14] The council building and the bridge were completely destroyed by the Romans in A.D. 70.

It is not certain whether Peter would have been familiar with this statement (although Luke would probably have known it). The principle of obedience to God's commands as a matter of paramount importance, however, is deeply rooted in the Old Testament. After Saul's failure to obey God by completely routing the Amalekites, for instance, the prophet Samuel told Saul, "Does the LORD delight in burnt offerings and sacrifices as much as in obeying the voice of the LORD? To obey is better than sacrifice . . . . For rebellion is like the sin of divination, and arrogance like the evil of idolatry" (1 Sam. 15:22–23). The repeated mistake of many of the leaders of Israel in generations past was in following "the stubborn inclinations of their evil hearts" rather than obeying God (Jer. 7:23–26). This is how Peter and John interpret the stubbornness and intransigence of Israel's present leadership in not only refusing to recognize Jesus as Messiah, but also by ardently opposing the proclamation of this good news.

The Believers Gather and Pray for Confidence to Proclaim the Gospel (4:23–31)

Peter and John immediately return to their fellow believers and report all that has transpired in the hearing before the Sanhedrin. Undoubtedly feeling dismayed at the intransigence of the Jewish leaders and rather intimidated by the threats, they lift their voices as a group before God in prayer. Surprisingly, they don't ask for protection, but for boldness to continue sharing Christ. They also ask God to continue to manifest his healing power, as he has just done with the crippled man, to demonstrate the authenticity and source of the message they are proclaiming.

Sovereign Lord (4:24). The group addresses God as *despota*, from which is derived the English word "despot." But there are no overtones of tyranny in the Greek expression, only the idea of one who wields absolute and sovereign power. This same way of addressing God is found elsewhere in the New Testament (e.g. Luke 2:29; Rev. 6:10) and in the Greek Old Testament (Gen. 15:2, 8; Josh. 5:14). When Jeremiah was called by God as a prophet, he addressed God: "'Ah, Sovereign LORD (*despota*),' I said, 'I do not know how to speak; I am only a child.' But the LORD said to me, 'Do not say, "I am only a child." You must go to everyone I send you to and say whatever I command you. Do not be afraid of them, for I am with you and will rescue you,' declares the LORD" (Jer. 1:6–8).

Why do the nations rage? (4:25). These believers remind God of what he said through David in Psalm 2, a psalm that early Christians applied to Christ because of its reference to the "anointed one" and the similarities to their own situation. The raging of the "nations" (lit., the "Gentiles") is seen to correspond to the Romans who sentenced Jesus to death by crucifixion. The "peoples" of Israel conspired with the Romans to execute this sentence. The actions of the "kings" and "rulers" find their fulfillment in Herod and Pontius Pilate. This Herod is not Herod the Great, but his son, Herod Antipas.

Against his Anointed One (4:26). Their rage is directed at God's *christos*, his Messiah. In its original context, Psalm 2 refers to David as God's "anointed" king. Here it is interpreted as fulfilled in the descendent of David "whom you [God himself] anointed" (4:27). This becomes an explicit identification of Jesus of Nazareth as the Messiah and, of course, is what the Sanhedrin adamantly rejects.

They did what your power and will had decided beforehand should happen .... Stretch out your hand (4:28, 30). "Your power" is the NIV interpretation of "your hand." The hand of God is a common image in the Old Testament to represent the power and strength of God. It is by God's "mighty hand" that Pharaoh was forced to free the Israelite captives (see Ex. 3:19–29; 6:1; 7:4–5). When Moses stretched out his hand over Egypt, God performed many miraculous signs and wonders through him (see Ex. 8:5; 9:22; 10:12). The psalmist writes reassuringly, "Though I walk in the midst of trouble, you preserve my life; you stretch out your hand against the anger of my foes, with your right hand you save me" (Ps. 138:7).

The place where they were meeting was shaken (4:31). After these believers pray, God gives them this unmistakable sign that he has heard them and that he is present with them. The psalmist observes, "Nations are in an uproar, kingdoms fall; he lifts his voice, the earth melts [lit., *is shaken*]. The LORD Almighty is with us" (Ps. 46:6–7). The earth shakes when the Lord is present: "Tremble [lit., *shake*], O earth, at the presence of the Lord, at the presence of the God of Jacob" (Ps. 114:7).

The Community Experience of the Early Believers (4:32–37)

The Holy Spirit is powerfully at work in transforming the lives of these new believers and shaping this new community. Unity, generosity, and powerful witness are some of the key characteristics of this group.

They shared everything they had (4:32). See comments on 2:44.

There were no needy persons among them (4:34). At this early stage in the life of the church, the basic needs for day-to-day life of each person are met by the generosity of members of the community. About fifteen years later (A.D. 47–49) during the reign of Claudius, however, the Jerusalem church as well as the entire city and the whole surrounding area of Judea faced a terrible famine. This same principle of generosity was then exhibited by other churches. The believers at Antioch put together a relief fund for the sake of the churches in Judea (see 11:28–30; 12:25). Similarly, at the beginning of his second missionary journey, Paul began raising funds for the impoverished Christians in Judea to which the churches of the provinces of Galatia, Asia, Macedonia, and Greece gladly contributed. Detailed reference to this collection can be seen 1 Corinthians (16:1–4), 2 Corinthians (8–9), and Romans (15:25–27).

Put it at the apostles' feet (4:35). By placing the money at the feet of the apostles, these believers are recognizing and submitting to their authority. In the Old Testament and Judaism, feet are sometimes referred to in contexts where someone's authority is stressed.[51] This image is also used to stress the authority of Christ over all things.[52] Falling at someone's feet is a sign of respect and compliance (Est. 8:3; 1 Sam. 25:24). By laying their money at the feet of the apostles, these believers are recognizing the authority of the apostles to administer the funds however they see fit.

CYPRUS

REFLECTIONS

EXTRAORDINARY GENEROSITY AND a caring sensitivity to the poor characterized the life of the early church. These virtues are quite contrary to our natural tendency to focus on ourselves. It is the presence of the Holy Spirit that prompts a desire to give. Are you allowing the Spirit to warm the coldness of your heart? Do you periodically contribute to your church's common fund for the poor? Are you responsive when you hear of someone in need?

Joseph, a Levite from Cyprus, whom the apostles called Barnabas (which means Son of Encouragement) (4:36). Luke gives both a positive and negative example of contributions to the community life—Joseph and Ananias. Joseph is a Levite originally from the island of Cyprus (see comments on 13:4) but now apparently resides in Jerusalem. Clement of Alexandria reports that Barnabas was one of the seventy disciples sent out by Jesus (Luke 10:1).[53] The nickname "Barnabas" is most likely derived from the Aramaic expression *bar* (son of) *nabi* (prophet).[54] As such, "Son of Exhorta-

tion" is a better translation of the following expression than the NIV, "Son of Encouragement." The nickname thus expresses the apostles' recognition of Joseph's giftedness and ability as a preacher or missionary. This is precisely the role that Joseph/Barnabas assumes later in Acts when he becomes a prophet/teacher in the church at Antioch (Acts 13:1) and a missionary to his homeland (Cyprus) and to the province of Galatia with the apostle Paul (Acts 13–14).

Ananias and Sapphira (5:1–11)

The earliest church in Jerusalem gets off to a grand and exciting start. Incredible opposition comes from outside the church, but God works miracles, the proclamation of the gospel prevails, and the church continues to grow. Now there is a sudden change. There is a significant disruption from within when two members of the community sin and face sudden and direct divine retribution. But the opposition is not strictly from within. Satan is back on the scene attempting to derail what God is doing by exerting his powerful evil influence on these followers of Jesus.

Ananias (5:1). With a twist of irony, the name Ananias is derived from a Hebrew name meaning, "God is merciful." Apart from his appearance here, we know nothing else about Ananias or his wife.

Sapphira (5:1). Her name is a common Hebrew name meaning "beautiful." Her name is attested on a number of first-century Jewish ossuaries (containers for the bones of the dead).

He kept back part of the money for himself (5:2). Ananias and his wife own a valuable piece of property, sell it, and give a portion of the money to the apostles while retaining some of the money for themselves. So far, there is nothing at all wrong with their actions. In fact, they are another exemplary illustration of the wealthier members of the community contributing to the well being of the whole. The relatively uncommon word that Luke uses for "kept back" (*nosphizō*) highlights a similarity between this episode and the sin of Achan in Joshua 7. Joshua gave the people of Israel firm instructions not to take as personal plunder any of the articles of the city of Jericho that had been dedicated to the Lord (Josh. 6:18–19). Achan sinned by taking some of the devoted materials and hid them in his tent. He lied and deceived the community, suffering his own death as a consequence. In a similar way, Ananias keeps back what he represents to the apostles as devoted to the Lord and lies to the leaders of the community.

Satan has so filled your heart (5:3). Although Ananias devises the plan and suffers the consequence for acting it out, Satan plays a role in this drama as well. This is his first recorded appearance after the death and resurrection of Christ when he suffered a massive defeat. He is portrayed here as actively opposed to God by attempting to destroy the wellbeing of this new community. He does so by his classic activity of enticing an individual to sin and defy God. He tried to derail Jesus at the outset of his ministry by tempting him in the desert (Luke 4:1–13), by influencing Judas to betray Jesus (Luke 22:3), and by enticing Peter to deny Jesus (Luke 22:31–32). He will continue his efforts unabated against the

church and its mission. For Luke, the contrast here is in being filled with the Holy Spirit (see 4:31 as well as 2:4; 4:8; 13:52).

You have lied to the Holy Spirit (5:3). The sin of Ananias does not have to do with what percentage of the sale price of his property he gives to the apostles. His transgression is in lying to Peter and the apostles by misrepresenting the gift as the entire sale price. His lie is interpreted as a lie to the Holy Spirit because of the Spirit's dynamic presence in the body of believers and its leaders.

After it was sold, wasn't the money at your disposal? (5:4). This statement makes it clear that Ananias is under no obligation to give all or part of the money to the apostles. The practice of selling property to meet the needs of the community is strictly a Spirit-led voluntary expression of love for one another. It is not an experiment in communism or socialism. Neither is it an attempt to model the Christian community after the pattern of the Dead Sea community of Essenes as represented in the Dead Sea Scrolls.

When Ananias heard this, he fell down and died (5:5). The language of this passage points to divine judgment (not simply a sudden heart attack caused by the stress of the situation[55]). The same unique verb used here for dying is also used to refer to the death of Herod Agrippa I (in 12:23) when the Lord strikes him down through an infestation of worms.

The young men came forward, wrapped up his body, and carried him out and buried him (5:6). These young men (neōteroi) do not hold any kind of special office. They are merely young believers who are willing to help serve the church in any way they can. It is customary for the deceased to be buried on the same day as the day of death. It is unusual for Ananias' wife to know nothing of it. This can be explained, in part, by the supposition that Ananias is given a rapid and unceremonious burial without the traditional mourning as a result of the community's recognition that he has been struck down by the hand of God (see Lev. 10:1–5), as happened also in Israel's history with Achan (Josh. 7:25).[56]

How could you agree to test the Spirit of the Lord? (5:9) This deception goes beyond lying. They are "testing" (peirazō) the Spirit of God. The people of Israel have done the same through their rebellion in the desert after God redeems them from their bondage in Egypt (Ex. 17:2; Deut. 33:8).

The whole church (5:11). This is the first time that the word "church" (ekklēsia) is used to designate the Christian community in Luke's writings. As tempting as it might be to base the meaning on the etymology of the word and arrive at "called out ones" (from ek, "out of," and kaleō,

"call"), this is clearly not the background of the word. The word has a long history of usage in the Greek language for simply designating an "assembly" of people (as it is used in Acts 7:38) or, specifically, the assembly of citizens of a Greek city-state (and thus parallel in meaning to the Greek dēmos, from which is derived the English term "democracy").[57] This Greek term was used by the Greek translators of the Hebrew Scriptures to render the Hebrew term qāhāl, referring to the "assembly" of Israel, the people of God. This can be illustrated by a passage such as Deuteronomy 31:30: "And Moses recited the words of this song from beginning to end in the hearing of the whole assembly (ekklēsia) of Israel."[58] Luke reflects the early Christian application of this term to the Christian community.

Signs, Wonders, and the Growth of the Church (5:12–16)

God works powerfully through the apostles to bring healing and deliverance to many unbelieving Jews. This makes the crowds more receptive to the message they are proclaiming and many turn their hearts to Christ. Nevertheless, great awe fills the hearts of the local Jews and causes them to be apprehensive about joining the Christian meetings in the temple courts.

Solomon's Colonnade (5:12). See comments on 3:11.

No one else dared join them (5:13). Because people in Jerusalem hear about the Ananias and Sapphira episode, they have great respect for the Christians (especially the apostles), but they are also somewhat fearful. Whenever the believers meet in the colonnaded area of the temple courts to worship and hear the teaching of the apostles, unbelieving Jews are afraid to join their meetings. They are probably concerned that a half-hearted allegiance may cause them to experience the same kind of demise as the couple who are struck dead.[59] Nevertheless, many people continue to hear the gospel through the outreach and preaching of the apostles and the believing community and respond in faith to Christ.

So that at least Peter's shadow might fall on some of them as he passed by (5:15). In Jewish and Hellenistic folk belief, a shadow was believed to carry spiritual

power. This could be harmful as well as beneficial depending on who or what cast the shadow. Cicero relates a belief that by touching the shadow of a criminal, harm would come to a person.[60] Another ancient writer wrote that a person or an animal could be injured if something violent was done to their shadow.[61] The Mishnah warns Jews of the danger of passing under the shadow of an Asherah[62] or the shadow of a corpse[63]; to do so rendered one unclean. In the present case, some of the people believe that Peter's shadow will convey a miraculous and beneficial power of healing. This does not mean that Peter believes this or condones it. The apostles, as well as Luke, tend to oppose a magical way of viewing spiritual power. Nevertheless, God in his mercy allows these people to be healed—a sign that ultimately attracts them to the message of the gospel.

Those tormented by evil spirits (5:16). The word translated "tormented" (*ochleō*) was used in Judaism to refer to any kind of trouble or affliction an evil spirit might cause. The book of Tobit says: "If a demon or evil spirit gives trouble to any one, you make a smoke from these [a fish liver and heart] before the man or woman, and that person will never be troubled again."[64] The crucial difference here is that the apostles never burned fish entrails or used any other magical means of deliverance. They relied strictly on the power and authority of the resurrected Christ.

"Evil spirits" is literally "unclean spirits." Jews commonly made a distinction between "clean" (*katharos*) and "unclean" (*koinon* or *akathartos*). Numerous laws determined what made a person ritually or morally impure. These included such things as the consumption of certain

---

SOLOMON'S COLONNADE

A portion of the Royal Stoa as it is reconstructed in the Jerusalem Temple model.

▼

kinds of foods, contact with a corpse, idolatry, and sexual promiscuity. Jews also regarded evil spirits as unclean, presumably because they promoted idolatry and enticed the people of God to defile themselves through a variety of impure actions. One Jewish document notes, "If you continue to do good, even the unclean spirits will flee from you."[65] Zechariah looked forward to the day when God would remove the "unclean spirit" from the land (Zech. 13:7). Jesus commonly referred to demons with this phrase.[66]

The Apostles Are Arrested and Then Set Free By an Angel (5:17–26)

Continuing to disobey the orders of the Jewish leaders to quit talking about Jesus, Peter and John are arrested again, but this time with the rest of the apostles. God dramatically intervenes by sending an angel to free them from their custody.

The party of the Sadducees (5:17). See comments on 4:1.

Filled with jealousy (5:17). The Jewish leaders are certainly jealous, but the word *zēlos* implies more than this. Behind it stands an Old Testament and Jewish tradition of zeal for the law, the temple, and the honor of God. Phineas the priest, grandson of Aaron, became legendary in Israel because of the way he burned with zeal for the law. When the men of Israel were indulging in sexual immorality with Moabite women and began worshiping their idols, Phineas drove a spear through an Israelite man and his Moabite companion. God commended Phineas because "he was zealous for the honor of his God" (Num. 25:13). Phineas was extolled to the people of

Israel during the time of the Maccabean revolt (1 Macc. 2:54). Here the high priest and the Sadducees are ready to resort to violence to squash this new movement that they perceive to be a threat to the honor of God.

They arrested the apostles (5:18). This time the Jewish officials arrest not only Peter and John, but all the apostles.

The public jail (5:18). In addition to Herod's prison on the west side of the city and a prison in the fortress of Antonia, the Sanhedrin had a place of incarceration either in the temple or below the building where it met (i.e., the Xystus or "the Gazith").[67]

An angel of the Lord (5:19). The entire group of apostles is able to escape from confinement in the prison through the direct intervention of an angel sent by God. In the Old Testament, "the angel of the Lord" appears at key times in Israel's history to guide, guard, and to reveal. For example, the angel of the Lord appeared to Moses in the burning bush (Ex. 3:1–6). The angel of the Lord also stopped Abraham from slaughtering Isaac, encouraged and strengthened Gideon and Elijah, and fought the Assyrian forces of Sennacherib.[68] Many have thought that some of the angel of the Lord passages in the Old Testament refer to the work of the preincarnate Jesus as the Logos.[69] Here it is clearly not a reference to the risen Christ, who mediates his presence directly or through the Holy Spirit, but to a special unnamed angel dispatched directly from the Father.

Stand in the temple courts (5:20). The angel tells the apostles to proclaim the gospel not throughout the cities and villages of Judea, but specifically "in the temple." The temple had been the center of spiritual life for the Jewish people, but that has now come to an end for God's people. No longer is it necessary for the daily animal sacrifices to be performed: One final sacrifice has been offered. No longer will the people of God need to stream to Jerusalem annually for the Passover celebration: Jesus has offered himself as the ultimate Passover sacrifice. No longer will there be a need for the Day of Atonement ritual: Jesus has provided atonement through his blood shed on the cross. All that had been represented by the temple has now reached its final purpose and fulfillment in Christ.

The full message of this new life (5:20). The temple was sometimes described by Jews as "the house of our life."[70] God has now intervened to bring *new* life to his people but apart from the temple.

The officers (5:22). These are the "attendants" or "servants" of the *stratēgos*, the captain of the temple guard (see comments on 4:1). They were not a specially trained Roman police force, but a group of Jewish Levites and priests responsible for security in the temple precincts.

The Apostles Appear Before the Sanhedrin (5:27–42)

Confronted with yet another miraculous event, it seems that the leaders finally recognize the hand of God on this movement, yet they remain staunchly opposed. Some members of the council want the apostles put to death not only because of their opposition to the Messianic sect, but also due to their own vindictiveness at the apostles' accusation of their complicity in the death of Jesus. One moderating voice among the Jewish rulers, however, advises proceeding with caution and discernment. Gamaliel's counsel prevails and the Apostles are flogged and released.

Determined to make us guilty of this man's blood (5:28). This is indeed the same council who a short time earlier sentenced Jesus of Nazareth to death. The chief priest and members of the Sanhedrin regarded Jesus' death as just punishment due to him for blaspheming God (Mark 14:63–64). They vehemently object to the apostles' accusation that there were other motives for inflicting the death penalty on Jesus.

The God of our fathers (5:30). This way of addressing God demonstrates that Peter does not now dissociate himself from his Judaism, but still embraces it as his heritage. "The Christian faith is the fulfilment, not the contradiction, of Judaism, if Judaism is rightly understood."[71] This was a common way of referring to God in the Old Testament and Judaism.[72] The title distinguished the one true God from the gods of the nations and highlighted the personal nature of God, who directly revealed himself to the patriarchs.

By hanging him on a tree (5:30). The "tree" does not indicate a live tree, but the wood used to construct a stake or a pole. Peter's remarks echo Deuteronomy 21:22–23: "If a man guilty of a capital offense is put to death and his body is hung on a tree, you must not leave his body on the tree overnight. Be sure to bury him that same day, because anyone who is hung on a tree is under God's curse." Of course, Jesus was accursed, but thereby freed us from the curse that the law brought on us (see Gal. 3:13–14).

Prince (5:31). As used here, this title is similar to "Lord" (*kyrios*). In the Greek Old Testament, "prince" (*archēgos*) was also used to refer to the head of a tribe (Num. 10:4), a commander in an army (1 Chron. 26:26), or a leader among the people (Isa. 3:6–7) (see comments on 3:15).

Savior (5:31). The prophet Isaiah declares, "The LORD has made proclamation to the ends of the earth, 'Say to the Daughter of Zion, See, your Savior comes'" (Isa. 62:11). Peter now announces to the chief priest and all the members of the Sanhedrin that the Savior has arrived. The Old Testament often speaks of God as Savior for his mighty deliverance of the people of Israel from their slavery in Egypt (see Ps. 95:1). Now the title is applied to Jesus, the Son of God, who has delivered people from a different type of bondage.

A Pharisee (5:34). One of the three major sects of Judaism, the Pharisees constituted the single most important party and come closest to representing "normative Judaism." In essence, Pharisaism was not a political party or a party of the "clergy." It was a lay society that emphasized a rigorous commitment to obeying the Torah. Not only was every word of the written Torah binding, but also the interpretation and explanation of Torah provided by the Scribes. Josephus notes, "the Pharisees have imposed on the people many laws from the tradition of the fathers not written in the Law of Moses."[73] A strong rivalry existed between

TORAH SCROLL

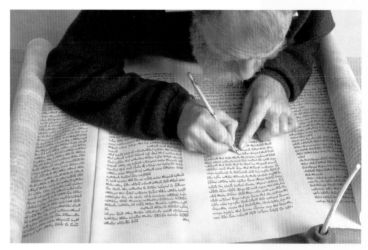

▶ Rabban Gamaliel, the Elder

Gamaliel was famous in Judaism, recognized as the greatest teacher of his day (roughly A.D. 25–50). He was the grandson of Hillel, for whom an entire school of thought was named within Pharisaism. Among Christians, he is best known for his role as the spiritual father and teacher to the young Saul of Tarsus (Acts 22:3).

Although some scholars have erroneously regarded him as the president of the Sanhedrin at this time (an office that properly belonged to the high priest), he was nevertheless the most respected man of the Sanhedrin and the leader of the Pharisaic party.[A-15] It is said in the Mishnah that, "when Rabban Gamaliel the Elder died, the glory of the Law ceased and purity and abstinence died."[A-16]

The Mishnah refers to him repeatedly appealing to his authority for many of the laws regulating the Sabbath, certificates of divorce, the recitation of blessing at a meal, harvesting, tithing, dough offerings, among many others.

Gamaliel also left a significant legacy through his descendants. His son Yeshua served as high priest in A.D. 63–65. Another son, Simeon, became a famous rabbi who is cited repeatedly throughout the Mishnah. His grandson, Gamaliel II, also became a famous rabbi allegedly training over a thousand disciples.

the Pharisees and the Sadducees because the latter saw only the Torah as binding, not the many oral traditions of the Pharisees. Although the Sadducees had significant influence because of their wealth and control of the priesthood, the great majority of the people sided with the Pharisees, seeing them as the upholders of the law (see "Pharisees" at Luke 5:24).

Theudas (5:36). There is no information about this Theudas outside of the New Testament. There were many insurgents after the death of Herod the Great (4 B.C.) and, presumably, he was one of them. This Theudas has sometimes been confused with another revolutionary leader of the same name who led an uprising during the procuratorship of Cuspius Fadus (A.D. 44–46), but this does not take place for another ten years (if Josephus' dating of this Theudas can be trusted[74]). Nevertheless, the story of this later Theudas is instructive as an example of the insurgent activity.

Judas the Galilean (5:37). Gamaliel refers to the seditious activities of a man who came on the scene shortly after Herod the Great's son Archelaus was deposed from his rulership of Judea and a Roman procuratorship was established (A.D. 6). Josephus explains what happened: "The territory of Archelaus was brought under direct Roman rule, and a man of equestrian rank at Rome, Coponius, was sent as procurator with authority from Caesar to inflict the death penalty. In his time a Galilean named Judas tried to stir the natives to revolt, saying that they would be cowards if they submitted to paying taxes to the Romans, and after serving God alone accepted human masters. This man was a rabbi with a sect of his own, and was unlike the others."[75] Josephus credits Judas the Galilean and his companion, Sadduk the Pharisee, with the rise of the entire Zealot movement—the fourth Jewish "philosophy" that ultimately led to the revolt against Rome.

In the days of the census (5:37). Josephus informs us that this census took place under the direction of P. Sulpicius Quirinius, the governor of the Roman province of Syria. This is the same Quirinius who earlier directed a census on behalf of Caesar Augustus at the time of Jesus' birth (see comments on Luke 2:1). Quirinius came into Judea, now part of the Roman province of Syria, to take account of its wealth and to assess it for the purposes of taxation. The Jewish people were upset with this action, but the high priest Joazar intervened and

▶ A Later Theudas (according to Josephus)

Now it came to pass, while Fadus was procurator of Judea, that a certain magician, whose name was Theudas, persuaded a great part of the people to take their effects with them, and follow him to the river Jordan; for he told them he was a prophet, and that he would, by his own command, divide the river, and afford them an easy passage over it; and many were deluded by his words. However, Fadus did not permit them to make any advantage of his wild attempt, but sent a troop of horsemen out against them; who, falling upon them unexpectedly, slew many of them and took many of them alive. They also took Theudas alive, and cut off his head, and carried it to Jerusalem. This was what befell the Jews in the time of Cuspius Fadus's government.[A-17]

▶ Instructions on Flogging

An entire tractate of the Mishnah—*Makkoth* (stripes)—is devoted to delineating the infractions that warrant flogging as well as the methods and procedures for carrying it out. The following excerpt explains how it is to be done:

> How do they scourge him? They bind his two hands to a pillar on either side, and the minister of the synagogue lays hold on his garments . . . so that he bares his chest. A stone is set down behind him on which the minister of the synagogue stands with a strap of calf-hide in his hand, doubled and re-doubled, and two other straps that rise and fall are fastened thereto. . . . He must give him one-third of the stripes in front and two-thirds behind; and he may not strike him when he is standing or when he is sitting, but only when he is bending low, for it is written, "the judge shall cause him to lie down" [Deut. 25:2]. And he that smites, smites with his one hand with all his might. . . . If he dies under his hand, the scourger is not culpable.[A-18]

As the accused suffers his beating, another person stands by and reads from Deuteronomy 28:58–63 ("If you do not carefully follow all the words of this law. . .") repeatedly throughout the beating.

---

quelled their fears somewhat with a stirring appeal. It was this census that prompted Judas to revolt and excited the Jews about fighting for liberty from foreign rule and oppression. He admonished the people to take action by insisting that "taxation was no better than an introduction to slavery."[76]

But if it is from God, you will not be able to stop these men (5:39). Gamaliel gives sound and temporizing advice to the council—something that did not happen when Jesus stood before the same group. His comments echo the instructions given in the Torah about discerning a prophet that was sent from God: "You may say to yourselves, 'How can we know when a message has not been spoken by the LORD?' If what a prophet proclaims in the name of the LORD does not take place or come true, that is a message the LORD has not spoken. That prophet has spoken presumptuously. Do not be afraid of him" (Deut. 18:21–22). A later rabbi reflects a similar principle: "R. Johanan the Sandal-maker said: Any assembling together that is for the sake of Heaven shall in the end be established, but any that is not for the sake of Heaven shall not in the end be established."[77]

Had them flogged (5:40). Rather than let the apostles go again with a stern warning, the council orders a severe beating. The word used here, *derō*, literally means to "flay, skin," but it has come to be used in a figurative sense for a flogging. The law governing flogging is given in Deuteronomy 25:1–4, which limited the number of lashes to forty. This was later reduced by the synagogue to thirty-nine, as Josephus attests: "But for him that acts contrary to this law, let him be beaten with forty stripes, save one, by the public executioner; let him undergo this punishment, which is a most ignominious one for a free man."[78]

From house to house (5:42). Apart from the large gatherings in the temple courts, the thousands of believers in Jerusalem regularly meet in smaller groups in private homes throughout the city. For those who have become Christians, there is a lot to learn—all that Jesus has said and done as well as a fresh perspective on the Hebrew Scriptures in light of their fulfillment in Christ. Apparently the apostles divide up the task of teaching by each going to a set group of homes where believers gathered. The teaching responsibilities for the apostles is enormous (see comments on 2:46).

The good news that Jesus is the Christ (5:42). The heart of the apostles' evangelistic message is that Jesus of Nazareth is indeed the longed-for Messiah of Jewish expectation.

The Neglect of the Greek-Speaking Widows (6:1–7)

A serious problem arises that threatens to undo the unity of the church during a time of great growth. A sharp schism has developed between two social groups within the church. The early characterization of the Christian community as "one in heart and mind" (4:32) has given way to partiality and strife.

This passage describes how the apostles handle this problem and resolve the conflict. They do so by appointing additional leaders for the church. These new leaders possess a strong blend of practical savvy and Spirit-inspired living. By handling this problem effectively, the church continues to grow even more.

Disciples (6:1). The term "disciple" (*mathētēs*) is used regularly in the Gospels to refer to a follower of Jesus of Nazareth. Even though Jesus is now exalted to the right hand of the Father, his followers are still referred to as "disciples." The word itself is surprisingly rare in the Old Testament (only one time; 1 Chron. 25:18), but master-disciple relationships were common in the Old Testament and Judaism, as we see in the relationship between prophets and their students (e.g. 1 Sam. 19:20–24; 2 Kings 4:1, 38) and the rabbis and their students. The common Old Testament way of referring to the relationship is by the term "follow" (*akoloutheō*). In the Greek world, however, the term "disciple" was commonly used. At the time of the New Testament era, it was frequently used in

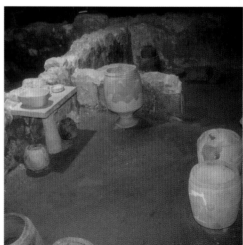

the sense of an "adherent," such as we might find in the relationships between the philosopher Socrates and his students (or after his death, those who commit their lives to his teaching).[79]

Complained (6:1). The word for complaint (*gongysmos*) is colorful and strong. Luke probably chooses it to recall the griping of the Hebrews when they were in the desert shortly after God provided them a miraculous deliverance through Moses (see Ex. 16:7–9; Num. 11:1).

The Grecian Jews . . . Hebraic Jews (6:1). "Grecian Jews" is a rather imprecise translation of an expression that means "Greek-speaking Jews." The term *hellenistēs* frequently means "Greek-speaking" in a variety of ancient literature.[80] The church father Chrysostom reports that Luke uses the term "Hellenists" for "those speaking Greek."[81] The contrast here is with those who did not speak Greek fluently: "the Hebraic Jews"(*hebraioi*). This latter group is designated as "Hebrews" because they were much more comfortable with Hebrew or Aramaic.

Jews who were raised in Palestine spoke Aramaic as their native tongue. This was a Semitic language that had many similarities to Hebrew. Aramaic was the dominant language of the Near East for centuries before the time of Christ. Many Jews in Palestine, especially in Jerusalem and Judea, continued to use Hebrew (as evidenced for instance in the Dead Sea Scrolls). Most would also probably have learned some measure of Greek—this is now the language of the Roman empire—but certainly would not have felt as comfortable in this language as their native tongue.[82]

Many Jews raised outside of Palestine, such as in North Africa, Egypt, and Asia Minor, would never have learned Hebrew.

Their principal language would have been Greek. When they settled in Jerusalem, these "Hellenists" would have enjoyed meeting together in a synagogue where the Scriptures were read in Greek, prayer was in Greek, and conversation was in Greek.

It is doubtful that there were any serious doctrinal differences between the "Hellenists" and the "Hebrews" at this stage. These "Hellenists" tended to be just as zealous about the temple, the law, and the festivals as any Jew raised in Jerusalem (Saul/Paul is a good case in point).[83] There may have been some cultural differences, however, that further distinguished them from the "Hebrews," such as taste in foods, musical styles, and literature. The "Hebrews," on the other hand, in their efforts not to be tainted by Hellenistic culture, may have been more isolationist and ethnocentric, perhaps going to great lengths to avoid contact with other Jews who did not accept their own outlook and interpretation of purity regulations.[84]

The daily distribution of food (6:1). Many Jews immigrated to Jerusalem to spend their final years in the Holy City and die there. Often the men preceded their wives in death, and the widows were then left with no immediate family to support them and care for their daily needs. There is some evidence that widows even traveled from Diaspora locations to Jerusalem. There is a higher proportion of women's names in Greek ossuary (a burial box for bones) inscriptions.[85]

Jerusalem leaders had put together an organized system of relief for the destitute. Rabbinic literature testifies to the existence of both a daily and a weekly distribution of relief. The daily distribution (*tamḥûy*) typically consisted of bread, beans, and fruit. The weekly distribution (*quppāh*) consisted of food and clothing.[86] Although the rabbinic evidence is later than the New Testament, there is little doubt that some sort of organized relief was in place in Jerusalem at this time. The widows in Acts, however, are Christian Jews and are deriving aid from their new Christian community. Presumably the apostles have instituted a similar kind of system of relief to that offered by the temple officials.

Luke does not tell us who is to blame for this discriminatory treatment faced by the Greek-speaking Jewish widows. The apostles, however, do not undertake a blame-finding investigation. They immediately seek a solution to the problem through finding men of integrity to serve as leaders to provide leadership to the relief effort in the church.

To wait on tables (6:2). The verb translated "to wait" is *diakonein* from which is derived *diakonoi* ("deacons"). Consequently, some have assumed that this passage provides the background to the office of "deacon" in the early church.[87]

This is not the case. First of all, the word *diakoneō* was widely used with the simple and non-technical sense of "to serve." Such is the case in Mark 10:45, when Jesus said of himself: "The Son of Man did not come to be served, but to serve, and give his life as a ransom for many." Second, it is unlikely that Luke would tell the story about the origin of the office and never use the term "deacons" (*diakonoi*) for the first office holders.[88] In this situation, an *ad hoc* group of leaders is formed to take care of a pressing matter in the church.

Choose seven men (6:3). There is some precedent in Judaism for choosing seven men to lead. When Josephus took command of Galilee, he appointed seven magistrates in every town of the region.[89] This reflects an implementation of his understanding of Deuteronomy 16:18 ("Appoint judges and officials for each of your tribes in every town"): "Let there be seven men to judge in every city, and these such as have been before most zealous in the exercise of virtue and righteousness."[90] There is also some later rabbinic evidence for the appointment of seven men to carry out various kinds of tasks.[91]

Known to be full of the Spirit and wisdom (6:3). These men need to excel not only in natural abilities to administrate and lead, but they need to demonstrate the presence of the Holy Spirit in their lives. This experience of the life in the Spirit is the mark of the new age and the fulfillment of Old Testament prophecy.

To prayer and the ministry of the word (6:4). The Twelve want to devote more time to prayer. Their time in prayer probably includes but greatly exceeds the typical Jewish practice of praying three times a day. Their "ministry of the word"

THE APOSTLES HAD AN ENORMOUS
work load in these early days of the church. They were responsible for teaching and ministering to thousands of people. On top of this, problems often surfaced that required their attention, time, and wisdom. With such a busy schedule, it would have been easy to let their times of prayer slip away. Yet the apostles realize that because of the size and significance of their responsibilities, they needed to spend more time in prayer. They leave a wonderful example to us as we face busy schedules and extensive responsibilities.

would have included both evangelistic proclamation (which, in a Jewish context, would have involved demonstrating that Jesus was the Messiah based on the Old Testament) and teaching the many thousands who recently embraced Jesus as Messiah and joined the Christian community. Integral to this ministry would be passing on the tradition of Jesus—giving accounts of his ministry and faithfully reciting his teaching.

Stephen (6:5). See comments on 6:8.

Philip, Procorus, Nicanor, Timon, Parmenas, and Nicolas (6:5). The surprising twist to this story is that it appears that the people choose seven men who are "Hellenists." That is, they all come from the offended group within the church. Each of the seven men has a Greek name (amply attested by occurrences in Greek inscriptions and literature). The fact that Nicolas is a convert to Judaism and is thus a Gentile indicates that the others are Greek-speaking Jews.

Beyond this passage, nothing further is known about Procorus, Nicanor, Timon, and Parmenas. Some of the church fathers believed that Nicolas is the founder of the heretical sect of the Nicolaitans referred to in Revelation 2:6, 15.[92] There is no evidence to support this assertion. It is more likely that some make an unwarranted connection because of the similarity of names. Philip, as we will see in Acts 8, becomes a zealous ambassador of the gospel in Samaria and later in Caesarea (21:8).

A convert to Judaism (6:5). See comments on 2:11.

Laid their hands on them (6:6). The practice of the laying on of hands in the Old Testament often occurred in the context of sacrifice and symbolized the transfer of sins from the offender to the sacrificial being.[93] The clearest example of this is when Aaron placed his two hands on the head of the scapegoat (Lev. 16:21). But the laying on of hands also took place for the conferral of blessing, as when Jacob blessed each of his sons (Gen. 48:18), and for the conferral of authority on a successor, as when Moses commissioned Joshua (Num. 27:18–23; Deut. 34:9). The latter example became important in rabbinic Judaism as a model for its ordination practice.[94] The laying on of hands in this passage, however, is not a rite of ordination. It represents a conferral of authority and blessing on these seven leaders. They are already full of the Spirit, but now they are commissioned to fulfill a special responsibility in the community.

A large number of priests became obedient to the faith (6:7). It must have been encouraging to the Christian community in Jerusalem to see many priests becoming followers of Jesus. Luke does not specify if some of these individuals are from the high priestly families or whether all come from the order of ordinary priests (like John the Baptist's father Zechariah). The ordinary priests, living throughout Palestine, were organized into twenty-four different rotations, with each group coming and serving a two-week stint (in addition to serving at the three pilgrim festivals). There are many ordinary priests—J. Jeremias estimates eighteen thousand, a number that might even be low[95]—who serve the Jerusalem temple.

It is also possible that among these new converts were Essene priests, with perhaps some from the Qumran community. The original core of this community was of priestly descent. Some Essenes were residents in Jerusalem and may have occupied an area of the city known as the "Essene Quarter."[96]

The Story of Stephen (6:8–15)

Luke now tells the remarkable story of one of these seven men. Although we never see Stephen waiting on tables, we find him doing many of the things the apostles themselves are doing. His bold proclamation of the Word and his success make him a threat to the Jerusalem leaders. He is arrested and interrogated. Like Jesus, he faces false witnesses whose testimony leads to his conviction and death. Whereas earlier, the apostles face imprisonment and flogging for their proclamation of Jesus as Messiah, now the persecution reaches a much higher level.

Stephen (6:8). Luke devotes a significant amount of space to telling the story of this exemplary, Spirit-filled man (6:8–8:2). He has a rather common Greek name that means, "crown" or "wreath." The victor in an athletic contest is crowned with a *stephanos* (see 1 Cor. 9:25). We know nothing of his life prior to his appearance here in Acts. As the others, he is likely a Greek-speaking Jewish settler in Jerusalem originally from somewhere in the empire.

Great wonders and miraculous signs among the people (6:8). Because of his faith and his receptivity to the Spirit's work, God is able to do powerful works through Stephen. These probably include miraculous healings and the casting out of unclean spirits among the unbelieving Jews. Because of these remarkable signs, he is likely gaining a strong and receptive hearing for his proclamation of the gospel.

The Synagogue of the Freedmen (6:9). The term "freedmen" is a translation of the Greek word *Libertinoi*, itself a transliteration of the Latin *Libertini*. This is an expression used to designate emancipated slaves. This particular synagogue thus probably consisted of Jews from Rome who were freed from slavery and migrated back to Jerusalem. They banded together and formed their own synagogue where they could worship and praise God in Greek.

During the many battles that took place in Palestine leading up to the conquering of Palestine by the Romans (63 B.C.), many Jews were captured, taken to Rome, and sold as slaves. Philo refers to a Jewish sector of the city of Rome populated mainly by emancipated Jewish slaves who had gained Roman citizenship.[97] The Roman historian Tacitus refers to four thousand Gentile "freedmen" (*libertini*) in Rome who became tainted with the superstitions of the Jewish rites.[98] Many of these assuredly became proselytes.

Jews of Cyrene and Alexandria as well as the provinces of Cilicia and Asia (6:9). The language of the passage in Greek is somewhat ambiguous. There are three possibilities for understanding what Luke is referring to: (1) there is one syna-

gogue—the *Libertinoi*—comprised of Jews from four regions; (2) there are two synagogues—one called the *Libertinoi* consisting of members from Cyrene and Alexandria and another synagogue with members from Cilicia and Asia; or (3) there are five synagogues—the one called *Libertinoi* consisting of emancipated Jews from Rome as well as four other synagogues associated with Jews from each of the other four geographical areas. The evidence slightly favors the third view, in part because the *Libertinoi* most likely refers to emancipated Jews from Rome.[99] We know from Acts 24:12 that there is more than one synagogue in the city. We also know based on other sources that Jews often formed synagogue congregations based on their places of origin.[100]

The synagogue of the Alexandrians is mentioned a number of times in rabbinic literature. A passage in a Jewish Tosephta speaks of a rabbi purchasing the "synagogue of the Alexandrians."[101] Interest-

▶ Archaeological Evidence of a First-Century Jewish Synagogue in Jerusalem

In December 1913, French archaeologist R. Weill discovered a well-preserved Greek dedicatory inscription of a synagogue. The discovery was made on the southeast hill of Old Jerusalem, the hill of Ophel. The inscription has been dated to the first century A.D., sometime in the period prior to the destruction of Jerusalem in A.D. 70. This valuable stone is now housed in the Rockefeller Museum.[A-19] The text of the inscription reads as follows:

> Theodotus, son of Vettenus, priest and archisynagogos [ruler of the synagogue], son of an archisynagogos, grandson of an archisynagogos, constructed the synagogue for the reading of the law and the teaching of the commandments and the guest-room and the (upper?) chambers and the installations of water for a hostelry for

those needing (them) from abroad, which was founded by his fathers and the elders and Simonides.[A-20]

In the location where the inscription was discovered, some sparse remains of the synagogue can still be seen. Portions of walls, pavement, stones decorated with rosettes, and the remains of three ritual baths (*miqva'ot*) are all part of the ancient synagogue.[A-21]

The name "Vettenus" is Roman and may suggest that the father of Theodotus had lived in Rome and received Roman citizenship from the *Vettena* family. This and other factors have led many scholars to think that the synagogue of this inscription is, in fact, the "Synagogue of the Freedmen" in Acts 6:9.[A-22] ingly, the parallel passage in the Babylonian Talmud refers to it as the synagogue of the Tarsians (i.e., Cilicians).[102] There is no direct evidence of a Cyrenian synagogue, but archaeologists have discovered the burial place of a Jewish family from Cyrene in Jerusalem.[103]

Words of blasphemy against Moses (6:11). The first accusation that the witnesses bring is that Stephen is speaking against the Jewish law. There is nothing in Stephen's address to indicate that he attacks the law. The fact that Luke refers to the witnesses as *false*, indicates that he disagrees with their charge.

Sanhedrin (6:12). See "The Sanhedrin" at 4:11.

Speaking against this holy place (6:13). The false witnesses also accuse Stephen of speaking against the temple. The evidence for this charge is the claim that Stephen says that "Jesus of Nazareth will destroy this place." This echoes the false charge brought against Jesus in his trial (Mark 14:57–59). While it is true that Jesus said that the temple would be destroyed and "not one stone will be left on another" (Luke 21:6), this is a long way from saying that Jesus himself would destroy it. Interestingly, the community behind the gnostic *Gospel of Thomas* attributes the destruction of the temple to Jesus.[104]

Stephen Speaks to the Sanhedrin (7:1–53)

In reading through this lengthy address, one may wonder what it has to do with the charges brought against Stephen and why Luke takes the space to record it in all of its details. At first glance it seems merely to be a tedious recounting of the history of Israel.

A closer examination of the speech in light of ancient rhetoric, however, demonstrates that this is a powerful address aimed at refuting the charges leveled against Stephen, namely, that he is blaspheming God, speaking against the law/Moses, and denouncing the temple. Rather than responding to the charges directly and enumerating the reasons why they are false, Stephen responds subtly, yet forcefully, through the indirect route of *insinuation*.[105] He selectively recounts Israelite history in such a way that the audience must infer a correlation between calloused Israel's rejection of Joseph and Moses and their own rejection of Jesus. Stephen begins, however, by establishing common ground with his hearers by reciting their common ancestry in the celebrated patriarch Abraham.

A second crucial theme Stephen develops is that God has not limited the manifestation of his presence and glory to one location, by inference, the temple. God appears to Abraham in Mesopotamia, to Joseph in Egypt, and to Moses in the Sinai Desert. It is therefore inappropriate to claim that the presence of God is isolated to one man-made building. The implication is not that Solomon was wrong in building the temple or that there was something inherently remiss in the whole temple cult, but the attitudes of the Jewish people were wrong if they could not see the glory of God in the person of Jesus, the Messiah. Thus, at the end of his address, Stephen directly and incisively accuses them of obstinately rejecting and opposing God's work in and through Jesus who has fulfilled the law.

Although the speech is long in comparison to others in Acts, it is not a transcript of what Stephen says. It is more aptly described as a summary, or précis of the address. It represents a valuable

**THE SITE OF
HARAN**

piece of direct evidence of how the "Hellenists" (the Greek-speaking Jewish Christians) now understood the Old Testament in light of Jesus's coming, his death, and resurrection. In substance, it probably differs little or not at all from what the "Hebraists" or one of the Twelve would have said.

If one wonders how Luke would have known the content of this message, at the end of the chapter Luke points us to someone who was there and witnessed the entire set of proceedings—Saul of Tarsus, his future coworker and traveling companion.

The high priest (7:1). This is Caiaphas, the same high priest who presided over the trial of Jesus. He remained in office until A.D. 36—four or five years after this episode.

The God of glory (7:2). For the people of Israel, the "glory" of God was the visible manifestation of his presence among them. This is exhibited by the cloud that

settled on Mount Sinai (Ex. 24:15–18). After the Israelites constructed the tabernacle, the cloud covered it and "the glory of the LORD filled the tabernacle" (Ex. 24:34–35). A special manifestation of the presence of God appeared on the ark of the covenant. When the ark was captured, it was exclaimed, "the glory has

**THE ANCIENT
NEAR EAST**

Haran was located near the northern Euphrates river.

departed from Israel" (1 Sam. 4:21–22). Ultimately, God mediated his presence and glory through the temple in Jerusalem: "When the priests withdrew from the Holy Place, the cloud filled the temple of the LORD. And the priests could not perform their service because of the cloud, for the glory of the LORD filled his temple" (1 Kings 8:10–11). The later Rabbis refer to this manifestation of glory as the *Shekinah*, a word that never appears in the Bible.[106]

For many first-century Jews, the Jerusalem temple was the singular place on earth where God was present in his glory.[107] Throughout his appeal to the Jews, Stephen will demonstrate that both historically and especially now, God regularly manifested his presence outside of the temple. He concludes his address by reporting his own vision of the glory in association with Jesus the Messiah at the right hand of the Father in heaven (Acts 7:56).[108]

The covenant of circumcision (7:8). Circumcision is the removal of the male foreskin. Jews performed this operation as a religious ritual on their children out of obedience to the command of God as it was delivered to Abraham (Gen. 17:2, 10–14). God instituted circumcision as a symbol of his agreement with Israel. Cir-

cumcision came to be understood in Israel as representing their salvation and their ethnic identity as Jews, the chosen people of God. Stephen has nothing disparaging to say about circumcision in his comments. On the basis of his speech, it is impossible to accuse him of speaking against the law (and thus Moses).

Joseph (7:9). Stephen delivers a concise rehearsal of the story of Joseph in verses 9–16. The principal idea that he communicates here is how the patriarchs rejected Joseph, but God was with Joseph and worked through him to save all the descendants of Jacob from the horrible famine afflicting the land.

Their bodies were brought back to Shechem and placed in the tomb that

▸ Stephen and the Old Testament

In his recounting of Israel's history, Stephen makes ample use of the Old Testament, quoting portions of at least twenty-two verses from Genesis, Exodus, Deuteronomy, Isaiah, and Amos. A comparison of these citations with the forms of the Old Testament text demonstrate that he is using the Greek version of the Bible, known as the Septuagint (LXX). This is consistent with the fact that Stephen was one of the "Hellenists" (a Greek speaker).

F. F. Bruce aptly comments about Stephen's knowledge and use of the Old Testament: "The speech is no mere catena of quotations, studiously put together; the Old Testament wording is reproduced with a spontaneity which suggest that the author has the narrative at his fingertips and is able to use it with a striking freshness and freedom."[A-23]

Abraham had bought from the sons of Hamor (7:16). Technically, Jacob was buried near Hebron (south of Jerusalem) "in the field of Machpelah near Mamre" (Gen. 23:19), as were the other patriarchs, according to Josephus.[109] Joseph, however, was buried in Shechem (in Samaria) "in the tract of land that Jacob bought for a hundred pieces of silver from the sons of Hamor" (Josh. 24:32).

Moses (7:20). Stephen devotes the greatest portion of his address—twenty-six verses—to telling the story of Moses (7:17–42). This revered deliverer of Israel and the situation he faced are similar to the story of Jesus and the situation he faced with Israel. Both were God's anointed deliverers, but both face rejection by the people of God.

Moses was educated in all the wisdom of the Egyptians (7:22). The Old Testament says nothing about the education of Moses in Egypt. In Exodus 2:1, Pharaoh's daughter took young Moses as her son; in the next verse he is "already grown." There are some statements and traditions in Judaism about Moses' education. Josephus simply says that Moses "was educated with great care."[110] Philo has a lengthy description of the kind of education that Moses received. It is difficult to assess the historical accuracy of Philo's account, although one scholar suggests that he portrays Moses as the "genius, idealised man."[111]

Powerful in speech (7:22). Moses himself claims, "O Lord, I have never been eloquent, neither in the past nor since you have spoken to your servant. I am slow of speech and tongue" (Ex. 4:10). Moses' protest to God should not be taken too seriously. The remainder of the biblical account of his life shows him to be confident and forceful in his addresses to Pharaoh and the Israelites. One Jewish tradition states that "by his words he performed swift miracles" (Sir. 45:3).

Moses thought that his own people would realize that God was using him to rescue them, but they did not (7:25). Stephen explains the response of the Jewish people to Moses in a way that his own hearers' refusal would recognize Jesus of Nazareth as their God-appointed rescuer. Their furious response to his

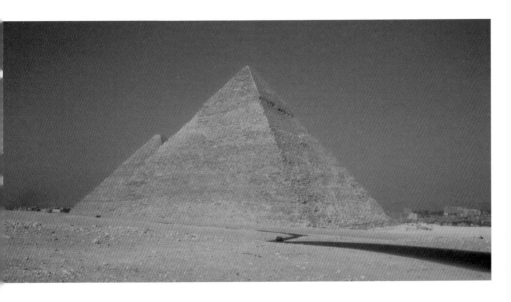

EGYPT

The pyramids at Giza.

▶ **The Education of Moses in Egypt (According to Philo)**

Therefore the child being now thought worthy of a royal education and a royal attendance.... And immediately he had all kinds of masters, one after another, some coming of their own accord from the neighbouring countries and the different districts of Egypt, and some being even procured from Greece by the temptation of large presents. But in a short time he surpassed all their knowledge, anticipating all their lessons by the excellent natural endowments of his own genius....

Accordingly he speedily learnt arithmetic, and geometry, and the whole science of rhythm and harmony and metre, and the whole of music, by means of the use of musical instruments, and by lectures on the different arts, and by explanations of each topic; and lessons on these subjects were given him by Egyptian philosophers, who also taught him the philosophy which is contained in symbols, which they exhibit in those sacred characters of hieroglyphics, as they are called, and also that philosophy which is conversant about that respect which they pay to animals which they invest with the honours due to God....

And all the other branches of the encyclical education he learnt from Greeks; and the philosophers from the adjacent countries taught him Assyrian literature and the knowledge of the heavenly bodies so much studied by the Chaldeans. And this knowledge he derived also from the Egyptians, who study mathematics above all things, and he learnt with great accuracy the state of that art among both the Chaldaeans and Egyptians.[A-24]

▶
ROSETTA STONE

An Egyptian monument inscription dating to 196 B.C. written in hieroglyphic Egyptian, demotic Egyptian, and Greek.

message indicates that they completely understand his insinuation.

Holy ground (7:33). The remembrance of Moses approaching God on "holy ground" in the Sinai may serve as yet another reminder that the Jerusalem temple is not the only place where God mediates his glory and presence.[112]

He received living words (7:38). Stephen makes no critical remarks about the law, contrary to the false charge leveled against him. In fact here he describes the Torah as "living words (*logia*)" (see Rom. 3:2). A similar thought appears in Psalm 119:50 using the same term: "Your promise (*logia*) gives me life (NRSV)." When Moses gave the law to the people of Israel, he declared: "Take to heart all the words I have solemnly declared to you this day, so that you may command your children to obey carefully all the words of this law. They are not just idle words for you—they are your life" (Deut. 32:46–47). The rabbis declared regarding the law: "The more study of the Law the more life."[113]

Gave them over (7:42). God was personally involved with Israel throughout their history. They were able to enter the promised land and conquer the enemy tribes because God handed them over (*paradidōmi*) to Israel (Ex. 23:31; Num. 21:2). On the other hand, when his people went their own way and defied him, God gave them over to the sword (Ps. 78:61) or to their enemies (Ps. 106:41). This is in fact what happened when Israel was exiled under Nebuchadnezzar (Jer. 22:25). As judgment and as discipline, God allowed his people to follow the dictates of the power of sin and its consequences excluding them from receiving his enabling grace (see also Rom. 1:24–32; Eph. 4:19).

To the worship of the heavenly bodies (7:42). Stephen's specific accusation is that God handed them over to the "forces of heaven." This refers to evil spirits and wicked angels who tempted Israel to worship the planets, stars, and idols as gods (see Jer. 7:18, 19:13 in the LXX). In the various religions of the neighboring peoples, the planets and stars were thought to be gods.

You have lifted up the shrine of Molech and the star of your god Rephan (7:43). Stephen quotes Amos 5:25–27 in support of his contention that Israel succumbed to idolatry. The Septuagint form of the text that Stephen uses differs somewhat in this passage from the Hebrew Masoretic text. Instead of "Molech" and "Rephan"(the LXX reading), the Hebrew refers to "Sakkuth your king, and Kaiwan your star-god." Both Sakkuth and Kaiwan were Assyrian deities, the latter associated with the planet Saturn (a planet the Romans also worshiped as a god).[114] The variant names may imply an association of the deities. It was common in antiquity for one national group to identify their gods with the similar gods of another nation.

Molech was a prominent Canaanite deity revered as a god of the underworld. Devotees offered children as burnt offerings to the god, probably for some divinatory purpose.[115] In disobedience to the explicit prohibitions in the Torah (Lev. 20:2–5), some of the Israelites worshiped Molech. The Israelite kings Ahaz and Manasseh sacrificed their children by fire to this god.[116] Child sacrifice associated with the worship of Molech was a persistent problem in Israel.[117] Rephan is never mentioned elsewhere in the Old Testament, but the name is an Egyptian form of "Saturn."

Joshua (7:45). The name "Joshua" may here be significant because his namesake is the "Righteous One" of verse 52 whom the Jewish leaders are rejecting. The Hebrew term *Yēšûăʿ* (the name of Joshua) is translated into Greek in the Septuagint as *Iēsous*.[118] In other words, it is the same Greek term that lies behind the translation of both "Joshua" and "Jesus." Now, a second "Joshua" offers to redeem them and lead them into the kingdom, conquering their (spiritual) enemies. Unfortunately, they have rejected him.

The Most High does not live in houses made by men (7:48). Some scholars have interpreted this sentence to mean that David's desire to build a temple and, consequently, Solomon's work in constructing it were seriously misguided and contrary to God's plan. One commentator goes so far as to say that "Israel's decision was a misguided act in that it made Yahweh like a heathen idol."[119]

This is not the point, however, that Stephen is trying to make. His essential idea, rather, is that God is transcendent and cannot be thought of as limited to a building. The tabernacle, as Stephen asserts, was built according to a divine plan—God sanctioned it. Stephen gives

▶

THE TABERNACLE

A model of the tabernacle and its precincts.

no indication that the construction of the Jerusalem temple was outside the will of God.

When Solomon offered his prayer of dedication for the temple, he recognized that God cannot be confined to it: "But will God really dwell on earth? The heavens, even the highest heaven, cannot contain you. How much less this temple I have built!" (1 Kings 8:27). This point is similarly made in Stephen's quotation of Isaiah 66:1–2. Ben Witherington sums it up well when he concludes: "The point of all three of these verses is not that God's presence can't be found in the temple (clearly Acts 2–4 shows it can), but that God's presence can't be confined there, nor can God be controlled or manipulated by the building of a temple and by the rituals of the temple cultus or the power moves of the temple heirarchy. What is being opposed is a God-in-the-box theology that has magical overtones."[120]

You stiff-necked people (7:51). Stephen uses the language of the Old Testament to describe the intransigence of the Jewish leaders he is addressing. He implicitly compares the leaders of the Sanhedrin to the Israelites in the desert who demanded that Aaron make them a golden calf to worship as their god (Ex. 32). The Lord repeatedly spoke of them to Moses as a "stiff-necked" people worthy of death (Ex. 33:3, 5; 34:9; Deut. 9:6, 13). They refused to recognize their awesome deliverance and God's continued presence with them as well as his leading them to a far better place.

Uncircumcised hearts and ears (7:51). Although these Jewish leaders are physically circumcised in obedience to the law, Stephen accuses them of disobedience to the weightier part of the law that demands a responsive heart to God's revelation. An "uncircumcised heart" is the description in the Torah for those who were disobedient to God and inflated with stubborn pride (Lev. 26:41). The prophet Jeremiah blamed the unresponsiveness of God's people to the call to repent on their "uncircumcised ears" (Jer. 6:10) and spoke repeatedly of the circumcised Israelites as having "uncircumcised hearts" (Jer. 4:4, 9:26).

Was there ever a prophet your fathers did not persecute? (7:52). The Old Testament speaks of numerous prophets that were persecuted and killed by wayward Israelite leaders. Jezebel was accused of "killing off the LORD's prophets" while the prophet Obadiah took a hundred prophets and hid them in caves (1 Kings 18:4). The prophet Elijah told the Lord that he fled to the desert to hide because "the Israelites have rejected your covenant, broken down your altars, and put your prophets to death with the sword. I am the only one left, and now they are trying to kill me too" (1 Kings 19:10). There are other similar complaints in the Old Testament.[121] Jesus himself carried on this protest (Matt. 23:31; Luke 13:34), as did Paul (1 Thess. 2:15) and the author of Hebrews (Heb. 11:32, 36–37).

Jewish tradition contains many stories about the persecution of the prophets. An entire book, *Martyrdom of Isaiah*, purportedly describes the events leading up to and including Isaiah's martyrdom. It portrays Isaiah's martyrdom as follows: "Because of these visions, therefore, Beliar was angry with Isaiah, and he dwelt in the heart of Manasseh, and he sawed Isaiah in half with a wood saw" (*Mart. Isa.* 5:1). The church fathers Justin Martyr and Tertullian also speak of Isaiah being sawed in half.[122]

The Righteous One (7:52). For Luke, this is an important messianic title of Jesus. The most relevant background is Isaiah 53:11: "By his knowledge my righteous servant will justify many, and he will bear their iniquities." Although this title does not figure prominently in the Jewish messianic expectation of the era, Jesus continually referred to himself using the language and imagery of Isaiah 53. This passage also became a key text for the early Christians in understanding the nature of Jesus' messianic mission. For Stephen to assert Jesus' righteousness is a further insult to the leaders of the Sanhedrin since they have aggressively sought Jesus' death.

The law that was put into effect through angels (7:53). Stephen turns the tables on his accusers by charging them with disobeying the law. By rejecting the Messiah, they have rejected the heart and essence of the law itself. This passage refers to angelic involvement in the giv-ing of the law to Moses. The idea first appears in Deuteronomy 33:2, where God is portrayed as accompanied by angels in his appearance on Sinai.[123] The angelic involvement in the giving of the law apparently was a widespread conviction among the rabbis.[124] Paul and the author of Hebrews also refer to the participation of angels in the bestowal of the law (Gal. 3:19; Heb. 2:2). Once again, how can Stephen's opponents accuse him of speaking against the law when he clearly understands it to be an angel-attended revelation of God in accord with Jewish tradition and when he embraces the core of it?

Stephen Is Martyred (7:54–8:1a)

The reaction to Stephen's address is severe. Far from being persuaded and joining the Christian movement, the crowd responds violently. They rush Stephen, drag him out of the city, and stone him to death. This is no official

▶

A PLACE OF STONING

The so-called "Tomb of Absalom" built during the Herodian era in the Kidron Valley near Jerusalem. It may have been a traditional place of stoning.

trial. It has all the marks of a lynching. The scene most likely takes place within two years after the death of Jesus and thus occurs in A.D. 31 or 32.[125]

Stephen becomes the first Christian martyr. He dies as a result of his faith that Jesus of Nazareth is the long-awaited Messiah, that he is risen from the dead and stands at the right hand of the Father. He dies for his bold testimony on behalf of his exalted Lord.

Stephen's speech and the violent response by the Jewish leaders initiates a significant break between the new messianic movement (later to be known as Christianity) and official Judaism. Whereas the early Christians often met in the temple (see 2:46; 3:1), this now will no longer be possible.

Gnashed their teeth (7:54). The grinding of the teeth as an expression of anger and rage was common in Judaism. David says that "the wicked plot against the righteous and gnash their teeth at them."[126] This was his own experience as well: "Like the ungodly they maliciously mocked; they gnashed their teeth at me. O Lord, how long will you look on? Rescue my life from their ravages" (Ps. 35:16–17).

Jesus standing at the right hand of God (7:55). Jesus' present position at the right hand of the Father is strongly attested in early Christianity (see comments on 2:33–34).[127] His exalted place of prominence is seen as the fulfillment of Psalm 110:1: "The LORD says to my Lord: 'Sit at my right hand until I make your enemies a footstool for your feet.'" What is unusual here is that Jesus is portrayed as standing, not sitting. There have been a variety of explanations offered: Jesus stands to welcome Stephen; Jesus rises to make intercession for Stephen; Jesus gets up to come

to Stephen's aid; Jesus stands as a witness in the judgment against Stephen's murderers and as an advocate in Stephen's defense; Jesus is standing to perform his duties as priest in the heavenly temple. We can only speculate as to the precise reason that Jesus is standing, but common to all these is the fact that Jesus is actively watching, involved, and responding to the needs of his people from his exalted position at the Father's side.

It is also significant to recognize how the Jewish leaders respond to his vision. If Stephen is right and Jesus is now standing at the right hand of God, then they must be horribly in error and the Sanhedrin has become God's enemy. In their eyes, this explanation is not only wrong, but must be stopped at all costs.

I see heaven open (7:56). This is the language of visionary experience as well illustrated by the beginning of Ezekiel: "In the thirtieth year, in the fourth month on the fifth day, while I was among the exiles by the Kebar River, the heavens were opened and I saw visions of God" (Ezek. 1:1). In John's Gospel, Jesus saw heaven open "and the angels of God ascending and descending on the Son of Man" (John 1:51). Behind Jesus' vision at the outset of his ministry is the imagery of Jacob's ladder (Gen. 28:12). There is divine commerce between heaven and earth with God revealing himself in a new way through the Son. Now that Jesus has completed his earthly ministry, heaven is open again, but now the Son of Man is in the presence of God watching and involved with his people.

The Son of Man (7:56). This is one of the few times outside of the Gospels that the expression "Son of Man" is used of Jesus (see also Rev. 1:13; 14:14). Within the Gospels, Jesus commonly used the phrase as a Semitic way of referring to himself ("a man such as I") as well as a title associating him with the coming "one like a son of man" (see Dan. 7:13; *1 En.* 46–53; see "Son of Man" at Mark 2:12).[128] In the former usage, Jesus frequently spoke of the suffering he would experience as, for instance, in Mark 8:31: "He then began to teach them that the Son of Man must suffer many things." Here Stephen may have used the expression to emphasize that his vision is of the suffering Son of Man (whom these Jewish leaders conspired to kill), who now stands vindicated at the right hand of God and yet will come as their final judge.

Began to stone him (7:58). The group can tolerate Stephen no longer. Convicted by what he said, but not to repentance, they respond in rash violence. Violating a Roman provincial law requiring the authorization of the Roman governor to prosecute a capital offense (see

John 18:31), they seize Stephen and drag him out of the city to stone him. Not even bothering to take a vote on his guilt or innocence, they join in anger to respond to what they perceive to be outrageously blasphemous statements. According to the Old Testament, blasphemy was a capital offense punishable by stoning (Lev. 24:14–16).

The witnesses laid their clothes (7:58). According to rabbinic law, the witnesses were required to take the lead in stoning the condemned person. Here they take off their cloaks to enable them to better carry out the sentence.

A young man named Saul (7:58). With a dramatic twist, Luke here introduces the principal character of the second half of his book. "Saul" is his Hebrew name, a name he shares with one of Israel's illustrious kings, with whom he also shared a common lineage from the tribe of Ben-

▶ Rabbinic Regulations For Stoning

Although Stephen's stoning was not the result of a carefully prosecuted trial, some aspects of the rabbinic regulations governing a sentence of stoning are insightful for understanding the scene in Acts 7. The instructions are given in Mishnah, *Sanhedrin* 6:1–4:

When sentence [of stoning] has been passed they take him forth to stone him. The place of stoning was outside [far away from] the court, as it is written, 'Bring forth him that hath cursed without the camp' (Lev. 24:14)....

When he was about ten cubits from the place of stoning they used to say to him, "Make thy confession," for such is the way of them that have been condemned to death to make confession, for every one that makes his confession has a share in the world to come....

When a man was four cubits from the place of stoning they stripped off his clothes. A man is kept covered in front and a woman both in front and behind....

The place of stoning was twice the height of a man. One of the witnesses knocked him down on his loins; if he turned over on his heart the witness turned him over again on his loins. If he straightway died that sufficed; but if not, the second [witness] took the stone and dropped it on his heart. If he straightway died, that sufficed; but if not, he was stoned by all Israel, for it is written, "The hand of the witnesses shall be first upon him to put him to death and afterward the hand of all the people" (Deut. 17:7).

jamin.[129] The name "Paul" (first mentioned in 13:9) is his Roman name (see comments on 13:9).

As a "young man" (*neanias*), Saul is anywhere from twenty-four to forty years of age.[130] This is consistent with the fact that he refers to himself as an "old man" in Philemon 9 (written in the early 60s), a designation that commonly meant over fifty years of age. The most likely inference, then, is that Saul is born sometime in the first decade—A.D. 1–10.[131]

Having been born in Tarsus (in the province of Cilicia), Saul came to Jerusalem for his schooling. He studied with the famous rabbi Gamaliel (see comments on 22:3) and may well have been a part of the Cilician synagogue (see comments on 6:9). It is unlikely that he is an actual member of the Sanhedrin yet—he is too young—but he is certainly associated with its members and on a fast track for becoming a member.

Lord Jesus, receive my spirit (7:59). Echoing the words of Psalm 31:5—"Into your hands I commit my spirit"— Stephen breathes his last breath. He apparently has confidence that he will be ushered immediately into the presence of Jesus. His words also echo those of Jesus on the cross, who utters, "Father, into your hands I commit my spirit" (Luke 23:46). Stephen, however, commits his spirit directly to Jesus, whom he refers to as "Lord"—a title Jesus shares with the Father. This demonstrates his exalted view of Jesus as God.

Lord, do not hold this sin against them (7:60). Stephen follows the example of his Lord who, as he was hanging on the Roman cross, uttered, "Father, forgive them, for they do not know what they are doing" (Luke 23:34).

The Church Faces Persecution (8:1b–3)

Stephen's address to the Jewish leaders serves as a catalyst for a more intense campaign of public persecution against Christians in Jerusalem. Christians are drug from their homes, imprisoned, and possibly even killed. Fearing for their lives, the Christians leave the city and move to towns and villages throughout Judea and Samaria. Ironically, one of the principal antagonists in this persecution is Saul of Tarsus. On the surface, this may appear to be a huge setback for the Jesus movement. But God is using this great evil as a means of spreading the gospel to "all Judea and Samaria" (1:8).

A great persecution (8:1). The body of Jewish leaders who try and kill Stephen—the members of the Sanhedrin as well as leaders from the Hellenistic synagogues—now unleash their hostilities against the entire church, both Hellenists and Hebrews.

All except the apostles were scattered (8:1). The vast majority of Christians flee the city of Jersusalem. Luke informs us earlier that over five thousand men have become believers, not including all of the women and children (4:4). There is thus a sudden departure of five to ten thousand people leaving the city. For the wealthier Christians who are hosting the meetings of the church in their homes, this no doubt meant abandoning their houses and property.

The twelve apostles choose to stay, not because they are any less the objects of attack, but probably because of their commitment to remain as witnesses in the city. Knowing that their lives are in grave danger, the Twelve are nevertheless unconcerned about the possibility of suffering and death for the sake of Christ.

Godly men buried Stephen and mourned deeply for him (8:2). The men probably bury Stephen shortly before the outbreak of persecution and their own flight from the city. Their mourning actually goes against Jewish custom, which disallows open lamentation and only permits silent mourning for a person who is stoned.[132]

Saul began to destroy the church (8:3). One of the principal leaders in this flare-up of persecution is Saul of Tarsus. Later on this man admits in his letters "how intensely I persecuted the church of God and tried to destroy it" (Gal. 1:13; see also Phil. 3:6). Luke uses a rather colorful word that is here translated "destroy" (*lymainomai*). In the literature where it appears, it is often used to describe a person torn up by wild animals, such as lions, wild pigs, leopards, and wolves.[133]

Philip's Ministry in Samaria (8:4–8)

In a few brief verses, Luke tells the story of how the good news of Christ spreads from Jerusalem to Samaria (see 1:8). This happens through the proclamation of another one of the seven leaders chosen to wait tables—Philip.

The Samaritans stood on the fringes of Judaism. They were not Gentiles, but neither were they properly Jews (either in terms of religious convictions or in terms of ethnicity). Incredible tension and downright hatred typically characterized the attitudes of Jews toward Samaritans and vice-versa (see "Samaritains" at 8:5).

For the Samaritans to respond to the gospel and receive the Spirit at the hands of the Jewish-Christian leaders of the church marks a radical step for the church, a step toward fulfilling the vision Jesus had for the church of a people who are not excluded on the basis of race and other human-constructed barriers. On the other hand, it would fan the flames of anger even more on the part of the Jewish leaders in Jerusalem.

Those who had been scattered (8:4). The thousands of Christian Jews who leave Jerusalem travel to cities and villages throughout Judea and Samaria. They simply do not go looking for a safe haven until the persecution subsides; they go with a strong sense of mission proclaiming Jesus as Messiah.

Philip (8:5). Philip is the second of the seven "Hellenists" whose story Luke now tells (see comments on 6:5).[134] How fascinating it would be to hear how God used the other five. We know nothing of Philip's life prior to his choice as one of the seven leaders in Acts 6. God uses him

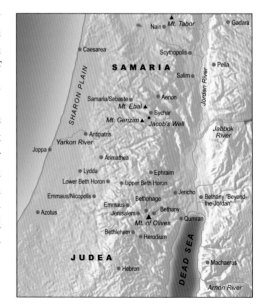

in amazing ways to reach Samaritans with the gospel as well as a Gentile God-fearer from Africa. Luke reports that Philip eventually settled in Caesarea, where he married and had four daughters, each of whom exercised a prophetic gift (8:40; 21:8–9). According to church tradition, he moved to Hierapolis, which is near Colosse, about a hundred miles due east of Ephesus.[135] The situation for him and his family in Caesarea may have become too dangerous for them as the conflict between Jews and Gentiles grew as a prelude to the Jewish war that began in A.D. 66.[136]

A city in Samaria (8:5). Samaria was a region that contained a number of cities. Luke does not specify which of these cities Philip visits, whether it is Sebaste (the ancient city of Samaria), Gitta, Shechem, Sychar, Neapolis, or even another Samarian city. Least likely is the city of Sebaste, which essentially became a Greek city when it was resettled with Greek (Macedonian) soldiers after Alexander the Great. After the ancient city of Samaria was destroyed by the

Jewish freedom fighter John Hyrcanus and his sons (107 B.C.),[137] it was later rebuilt in the style of a Greek city, and Herod dedicated it to the Roman emperor by renaming it *Sebastos* (a Greek title of respect bestowed on the emperor meaning "venerable" or "august" (cf. the Latin *augustus*).[138]

Proclaimed the Christ there (8:5). Philip goes to a Samaritan city and begins proclaiming that Jesus is the Messiah. Some of the Samaritans may have already heard of Jesus through the woman he had spoken to at the well in a town called Sychar (John 4:1–26). On that occasion, the Samaritan woman confessed to a belief in a coming Messiah that she shared with other Samaritans (John 14:25). Jesus directly told her his identity: "I who speak to you am he."

Not accepting any of the prophetic books, Samaritans based their messianic expectation on one passage—Deuteronomy 18:15—where Moses said, "The LORD your God will raise up for you a prophet like me from among your own brothers." They described him as the

REMAINS AT SAMARIA

(left) The Roman theater in Sebaste.

(right) The Roman forum.

▶ **Samaritans**

The Samaritans[A-25] viewed themselves as Israelites, true remnants of the tribes of Ephraim and Manasseh, who maintained a monotheistic faith and upheld the Torah as holy scripture. They kept the rite of circumcision, regularly observed the Sabbath and the Jewish festivals, and honored Moses as the greatest of the prophets.

The Jews, however, viewed the Samaritans as "half breeds"—descendants of Mesopotamian (Gentile) colonists who settled in the area and intermarried with the Jews remaining there after the Jewish exile by Assyria (2 Kings 17:24–31).[A-26]

At the heart of the schism between Jews and Samaritans in the first century was the fact that Samaritans rejected the Jewish temple worship. Three centuries earlier, they had constructed their own temple on Mount Gerizim. They also rejected all of the Hebrew Bible except the first five books of Moses.

The hostility intensified in the century before Christ when John Hyrcanus destroyed their temple (107 B.C.) and devastated many of their cities. Under the Syrian ruler Antiochus Epiphanes (167 B.C.), they had requested that their temple be dedicated to Zeus Hellenios, thus identifying Zeus with Yahweh.[A-27]

The Jewish rabbi Ben Sira refers to the Samaritans as "the foolish people that live in Shechem."[A-28] Jews regarded Samaritans on the same level as Gentiles in ritual and purity matters. Not only did Jews prohibit intermarriage with Samaritans, but they did not even allow a Samaritan to convert to Judaism.[A-29] The apostle John summarizes the situation well when he says, "Jews do not associate with Samaritans" (John 4:9).

Taheb (an Aramaic term meaning "Returning One"), who would come and restore the true worship on Mount Gerizim.

Evil spirits came out of many (8:7). Just as the twelve apostles cast out evil spirits and healed the sick (see comments on 5:16), Philip continues the same ministry. Luke makes a distinction between the casting out of spirits and physical healing here (see comments on 8:9).

Simon, the Magician (8:9–25)

One episode that stands out in Philip's ministry in Samaria is his encounter with a wonder-working man named Simon. Capable of exhibiting tremendous spiritual power, Simon has garnered a significant following in Samaria. Yet Luke portrays the power of God working through a disciple of Jesus as vastly superior. In fact, Simon recognizes the greater power at work in and through Philip and wants it for himself, but for the wrong reasons. In this story, Luke demonstrates that the desire to obtain spiritual power—fundamental to magic—is a profoundly inadequate motive for joining the Christian movement. Magic is a poison and imprisons the soul.

A man named Simon (8:9). In terms of extrabiblical evidence, we have little accurate information about Simon. This is due in large measure to a legend that developed in the early church attributing the rise of the Gnostic heresy to Simon.

Luke, however, says absolutely nothing about Simon being a gnostic or as holding any of the worldview assumptions that are typical of Gnosticism. Most scholars today, therefore, regard it as highly unlikely that Simon is the first gnostic. They characterize Simon in terms that do not go beyond Luke's: Simon is a Samaritan who practices magic and has significant influence on people.

Justin, Irenaeus, Origen, Tertullian, and Eusebius are among those church fathers who attribute the beginning of Gnosticism to Simon.[139] It is doubtful, however, that Gnosticism as a religious system of redemption actually came into existence until late into the first century or even into the second century.[140]

Practiced sorcery (8:9). Literally, Luke says Simon practices "magic" (*mageia;* 8:11). In the ancient world, magic was not the art of illusion. Magic was predicated on the reality of spiritual forces (both personal and impersonal) and the belief that they could be coerced and manipulated. A magician was someone who had a deep knowledge of the spirit world and could prescribe the right incantation, formula, or ritual to obtain the desired results. Although no hard examples of first-century Samaritan practices of magic survive today, over 230 papyrus documents have been discovered illustrating the practice of magic generally for the Greco-Roman period.[141]

The divine power known as the Great Power (8:10). Justin Martyr attests to this description of Simon (see "Simon, the Magician" at 8:9). It is not likely that Simon is setting himself up as a rival of

---

▶ **The Rise of the Legend of Simon as the Founder of Gnosticism (Justin Martyr)**

In his volume defending the Christian faith, Justin Martyr (A.D. 110–165) wrote briefly about Simon. Although aspects of his account may be true, Justin is the first to portray Simon as a gnostic. Justin's account is believed and uncritically passed on by many of the other church fathers. Justin provides the following description of Simon:

> There was a Samaritan, Simon, a native of the village called Gitto, who in the reign of Claudius Caesar, and in our royal city of Rome, did mighty acts of magic, by virtue of the art of the devils operating in him. He was considered a god, and as a god was honoured by you with a statue, which statue was erected on the river Tiber, between the two bridges, and bore this inscription, in the language of Rome: "To Simon the holy God" (*Simoni Deo Sancto*).
>
> And almost all the Samaritans, and a few even of other nations, worship him, and

acknowledge him as the first god; and a woman, Helena, who went about with him at that time, and had formerly been a prostitute, they say is the first idea (*ennoia*) generated by him.[A-30]

The portions of Justin's portrayal of Simon that are often regarded as historically plausible are: (1) Simon came from the Samaritan town of Gitta; (2) he was a magician; (3) he attracted a significant following in Samaria; (4) he was worshiped as a god.

The statue that Justin saw has been discovered, but it was not dedicated to Simon, but rather a Roman deity called Semo (*Semoni Sancto Deo*). This false identification may not have originated with Justin.[A-31]

Subsequent writers expand on his consort Helena, whom they identify with the second god of Gnosticism, i.e. *ennoia, sophia,* the "demiurge" or creator god.

Yahweh in the Samaritan cities and thereby attempting to supplant the worship at Mount Gerizim. Simon is simply a magician who is presenting himself as a "Great Power," which in Jewish and Samaritan culture is equal to saying that he is a "Great Angel." In Asia Minor, an inscription set up in honor of the moon-god Men extols him as "the Great Power" of the invisible God.[142]

They were baptized (8:12). Given the great hostility between Jews and Samaritans, it is surprising to see Philip go so far as to baptize them. Baptism is the ritual of incorporation into this new community. The people that Judaism did not allow into their community, the newly constituted people of God, are now embraced on an equal footing.

Simon himself believed and was baptized (8:13). On the surface, it appears that Simon also responds to Philip's preaching, but Luke gives us reason to doubt the sincerity of his convictions in the following verses. Jesus warns about basing one's faith only on signs and wonders: "Now while he was in Jerusalem at the Passover Feast, many people saw the miraculous signs he was doing and believed in his name. But Jesus would not entrust himself to them, for he knew all men" (John 2:23–24).

They sent Peter and John to them (8:14). Peter and John remain in Jerusalem with the other ten apostles in spite of the terrible threat to their lives. It must come as a shock to them to hear that Samaritans are embracing Jesus as Messiah and entering the community of believers. John, after all, was one of the two disciples who asked Jesus if he should call down fire from heaven on the inhospitable Samaritans who refused to provide lodging for them (Luke 9:52–56). How much more the Sanhedrin and leaders from the Hellenistic synagogues would be upset with Christians when they found that they were now receiving Samaritans into their fellowship!

Peter and John placed their hands on them, and they received the Holy Spirit (8:17). Peter and John journey to Samaria to find out for themselves. Satisfied with the genuineness of their commitment, they lay their hands on these new Samaritan believers and the Holy Spirit comes on them. The intermediate agency of the apostles in this instance raises many ques-

▶ A Magical Spell

The following text is a portion from a Greek magical papyrus discovered in Egypt and now housed in the British Museum in London. The passage from the papyrus gives some indication of the worldview and technique that stood behind the practice of magic in the time of Jesus and the apostles.

Come to me, spirit that flies in the air, called with secret codes and unutterable names, at this lamp divination which I perform, and enter into the boy's soul, that he may receive the immortal form in mighty and incorruptible light, because while chanting, I call, "IAŌ ELŌAI MARMACHADA MENEPHŌ MERMAI IĒŌR AIEŌ ĒREPHIE PHEREPHIŌ CHANDOUCH AMŌN EREPNEU ZŌNŌR AKLEUA MENĒTHŌNI KADALAPEU IŌ PLAITINE RE [an additional seventeen magical names are called upon]."[A-32]

If this is similar to the kind of magic that was being practiced by Simon and others in Samaria, it is not surprising that Philip was casting spirits out of many people.

tions since the Spirit is normally presented as coming at the moment of belief. It is doubtful that this means that the Spirit only comes when the apostles bestow it on new believers (and thus now through ordained clergy who are under the authority of the church in apostolic succession). Nor does this appear to be a special filling of the Spirit for empowerment for witness. The uniqueness of this event can only be appreciated in light of the historical and cultural setting. Because of the longstanding antipathy between the Samaritans and Jews, apostolic participation and confirmation is needed.[143] Peter and John can leave Samaria having no doubts whatsoever about God's inclusion of the Samaritans in this new community of believers joined to Jesus, the Messiah. The conversion of the Samaritans represents the first giant step toward fulfilling Jesus' instructions about witness in Acts 1:8.

He offered them money (8:18). Consistent with his function as a magician (or shaman), Simon wants to purchase the ability to bestow the Spirit on people, presumably so he can charge people for the gift.[144] It is from this situation that the English term "simony" was coined to refer to the buying or selling of a church office.

You are full of bitterness (8:23). The translation of the NIV—"you are full of bitterness"—appears inconsistent with the context. Peter does not see anger and bitterness in Simon: The man is giddy with excitement over the prospect of obtaining this new-found spiritual

power. The literal wording of the phrase, however, is "you are in a gall (poison) of bitterness" (*cholē pikrias*). Peter's language echoes Moses' warnings to the people of Israel when they renewed the covenant with God: "Make sure there is no man or woman, clan or tribe among you today whose heart turns away from the LORD our God to go and worship the gods of those nations; make sure there is no root among you that produces such bitter poison (*cholē kai pikria*)" (Deut. 29:18 LXX). Simon is not bitter; rather, he is full of a bitter poison.[145] This is consistent with the next line that describes him as a "captive to sin." Both expressions suggest that Simon himself has not experienced the redeeming and transforming work of the Spirit.

Peter and John returned to Jerusalem, preaching the gospel in many Samaritan villages (8:25). Peter and John are so utterly convinced of the genuineness of God's work among the Samaritans that they begin proclaiming the gospel of

◄ *center*

SAMARITAN MONEY

Samaritan silver coin dating from the fourth century B.C.

SHECHEM AND MOUNT GERIZIM

▼

Christ to them. We cannot underestimate what a radical shift of thinking this is for them. If word of this reaches the Sanhedrin, the Jewish leaders will be incensed. This is the last mention of the apostle John's activity in Luke's account.

Philip and the Ethiopian Eunuch (8:26–40)

Before his ascension, Jesus said that the disciples would be witnesses to "the ends of the earth" (1:8). The conversion of the Ethiopian marks an enormous stride forward toward the fulfillment of this goal. To Greeks and Romans, Ethiopia was at the ends of the earth. In describing Poseidon's trip to the Ethiopians, Homer said that they lived "at the world's end."[146] Herodotus claimed that Ethiopia "stretches farthest of the inhabited lands in the direction of the sun's decline."[147]

The conversion of the Ethiopian also represents the inaugural step of the gospel going out to the Gentiles. In many ways, this is a more radical step forward than the conversion of Cornelius and his household. Not only is the Ethiopian a Gentile, but he is from a distant land and in some ways an outcast with respect to Judaism since, as a eunuch, he is regarded as in a constant state of ritual impurity.

For Luke, the mission of the church is out of control—that is, out of the control of the human agents. From beginning to end, this passage shows the work of God in directing every aspect of the outreach.

The desert road—that goes down from Jerusalem to Gaza (8:26). Whether Philip remains and ministers in Samaria or returns with the apostles to Jerusalem, Luke does not tell us. What is important, however, is that Philip is divinely directed to the road leading to southwest Palestine—the area well-known in the Old Testament as the territory of the Philistines. Gaza itself is one of the five cities of the Philistines. Although it had been destroyed by the Jewish ruler Alexander Jannaeus, it had recently been rebuilt by the Roman governor Gabinius.[148]

In 1838, the famous archaeologist E. Robinson suggested that the site of the Ethiopian's baptism is near Tell el-Hesi (about forty miles southwest of Jerusalem and twenty miles northeast of Gaza), and his guess has recently received additional support.[149] Tell el-Hesi is located on a Roman road that led from Jerusalem to Gaza. There is also a

▶

ETHIOPIA, GAZA, AND JERUSALEM

◄

spring at the site that is an important source of water for the area. This proposal can be nothing more than an educated guess, but it does fit the details of the text.

An Ethiopian (8:27). In the Greco-Roman period, "Ethiopia" referred to the land south of Egypt—what is today the Sudan and modern Ethiopia.[150] In Old Testament times, this was the land of Cush (see Est. 1:1; 8:9; Isa. 11:11). The term "Ethiopia" has come to mean the land of the "Burnt-Faced People," indicating their black skin.

The man whom Philip encounters is most likely from the kingdom of Nubia located on the Nile River between Aswan and the Fourth Cataract (a waterfall-like area of rapids). The capital of this region is Meroe.

An important official in charge of all the treasury (8:27). Regardless of his status as a eunuch (which may have been a pre-

requisite for his position), this man is a finance minister in a government. As such, he is a man of high social standing, which is consistent with the fact that he travels in style.

Candace, queen of the Ethiopians (8:27). Although "Candace" is a female name in English-speaking circles, it was a title then. *Kandakē* is the transliteration of a Nubian word for "queen."[151]

This man had gone to Jerusalem to worship (8:27). This is an incredible journey for this man and his retinue to undertake. If he covered an average of twenty-five miles per day, the trip to Jerusalem would have taken anywhere from 48–60 days and round trip, 96–120 days. The journey would have taken considerably longer if he stopped for any length of time in the cities along the way. This man is earnestly seeking the God of Israel and spends a great deal of time to go and worship him.

It is unlikely that this man is a prose-lyte (impossible if he is not only castrated but dismembered, because of the requirement for circumcision) since Luke typically points out those who are full proselytes (see 6:5). He may more accurately be described as a "God-fearer" or a "sympathizer."

But how has he become acquainted with Judaism? There is ample evidence of a Jewish presence in Upper (southern) Egypt beginning in the second century B.C. and extending through the second century A.D.[152] One papyrus letter even attests to a synagogue in the city of Thebes.[153] It is unknown if the Jewish Diaspora extended as far south as Nubia and the city of Meroe. If a synagogue was present in Meroe, there is a simple explanation as to how this Ethiopian became a God-fearer. If this man traveled extensively (as it seems he was accustomed to), he may have come into contact with Jews anywhere in Egypt.

As a Gentile God-fearer, he could not have taken part in the temple services in Jerusalem. At the most, he could be admitted into the Court of the Gentiles.

▶ The Social Status of a Eunuch

This Ethiopian is described by Luke as a "eunuch," which most likely means that he had been castrated and possibly even dismembered.[A-33] This is not surprising for a male who holds a high position in the government of a queen or for an official over a king's harem. In the book of Esther, for example, a eunuch named Hegai was in charge of Xerxes's harem (Est. 2:3, 14, 15).

Nevertheless, there was a stigma attached to being a eunuch in ancient societies. Ancient writers speak of the regret that eunuchs felt over their condition as well as occasions of social ostracization.[A-34]

In Judaism, the law excluded eunuchs from public worship: "If a man's testicles are crushed or his penis is cut off, he may not be included in the assembly of the Lord" (Deut. 23:1). Such a man was judged to be physically blemished and in a permanent state of ritual impurity (Lev. 21:20; 22:24).

Josephus reflects the attitudes of some (probably Pharisaic) Jews toward eunuchs:

Let those that have made themselves eunuchs be had in detestation; and do you avoid any conversation with them who have deprived themselves of their manhood, and of that fruit of generation which God has given to men for the increase of their kind; let such be driven away, as if they had killed their children, since they beforehand have lost what should procure them; for evident it is, that while their soul is become effeminate, they have withal transfused that effeminacy to their body also. In like manner to you treat all that is of a monstrous nature when it is looked on; nor is it lawful to geld man or any other animals.[A-35]

By contrast, the prophecy of Isaiah held out hope for eunuchs: "To the eunuchs who keep my Sabbaths, who choose what pleases me and hold fast to my covenant—to them I will give within my temple and its walls a memorial and a name better than sons and daughters; I will give them an everlasting name that will not be cut off. And foreigners who bind themselves to the LORD to serve him, to love the name of the LORD, and to worship him, all who keep the Sabbath without desecrating it and who hold fast to my covenant—these I will bring to my holy mountain and give them joy in my house of prayer. Their burnt offerings and sacrifices will be accepted on my altar; for my house will be called a house of prayer for all nations" (Isa. 56:3–8).

Perhaps the fact that this eunuch was reading this scroll indicated that he was familiar with this passage and found hope in it. Philip can now proclaim its fulfillment.

Perhaps the Ethiopian came for one or more of the three great pilgrim festivals (Passover, Pentecost, or Tabernacles).

Sitting in his chariot (8:28). If the Ethiopian is able to sit and read on his journey, he does not come alone. Whether he comes with one other person or a retinue, Luke is silent. The Greek word translated "chariot" (*harma*) was frequently used for chariots of war, but could also be used of some type of carriage for a long journey (as Joseph used on his trip from Egypt to Hebron to bury his father; Gen. 46:29). We really have no way of knowing what this vehicle really looked like.

Reading the book of Isaiah the prophet (8:28). The fact that the Ethiopian possesses a scroll of Isaiah demonstrates that he is a person of means. Such documents were expensive since they had to be produced by hand. The man is probably reading a Greek version of the text of

◀

CHARIOT

An ancient depiction of a horse-drawn chariot on a coin.

Isaiah since it is doubtful that he knows Hebrew. It was common for people to read aloud in antiquity both because of the way the text was written (there were no word divisions or punctuation) and to aid the memory.

The Spirit told Philip (8:29). From beginning to end of this episode, Luke stresses God's guidance—first by an angel and then by the Holy Spirit. God used a similar pattern in leading Peter to Cornelius (10:3, 19). Philip does exactly what the Spirit led him to do by running to the carriage, initiating a conversation with the man, and then joining him in the carriage.

He was led like a sheep to the slaughter (8:32). Of all the passages in the Old Testament that the Ethiopian could have been reading, there is no single chapter more appropriate for explaining the work of Christ than Isaiah 53. Although many Jews thought of their own experience as fulfilling much of the suffering and martyrdom themes of the passage, Philip declares that the passage finds its decisive fulfillment in one person—Jesus. First-century Jews did not interpret the suffering servant of Isaiah 53 as a prophecy about the coming Messiah.[154]

Luke cites only verses 7–8 from the chapter, but assuredly, Philip explains to

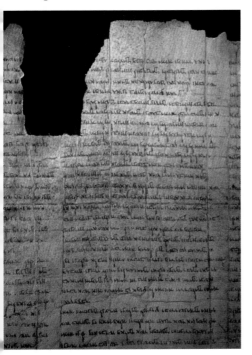

◀ *left*

ISAIAH SCROLL FROM QUMRAN

the Ethiopian how Jesus has fulfilled every aspect of the entire fourth servant song (Isa. 52:13–53:12). This passage enables Philip to describe Jesus' coming as a humble servant, the fact of his suffering and death, the meaning of his suffering and death ("he was pierced for our transgressions" [v. 5]; the Lord has laid on him the iniquity of us all" [v. 6]), and his resurrection ("after the suffering of his soul, he will see the light of life and be satisfied" [v. 11]).

Who can speak of his descendants? For his life was taken from the earth (8:33). Much of the Isaiah 53:7–8 passage that Luke cites would properly be interpreted as references to the suffering of the Messiah. Philip probably explained the last line ("for his life was taken up from the earth") as a reference to Jesus' resurrection and exaltation (see also Isa. 53:10). The rhetorical question, "Who can speak of his descendants?" thus is not a lament over the fact that the Messiah never marries and has children, but rather that he now has a host of spiritual offspring.[155] This eunuch, who was once deprived of full membership in Judaism, is now to be

TEL EL-HESI

The area Edward Robinson identified as the place where the Ethiopian was baptized.

▼

REFLECTIONS

THIS PASSAGE PROVIDES SOME helpful guidelines for all believers who seek to share their faith:[A-36]

1. Be sensitive to the prompting of the Spirit.
2. Be prepared to share your faith across cultures.
3. Witnessing is most effective to people whose hearts have already been prepared by God.
4. Start with their questions.
5. The basis for witnessing should be the words of Scripture.
6. The focus of witnessing needs to be the person of Christ.
7. Invite a response.

fully incorporated into the family of the Messiah.

Told him the good news about Jesus (8:35). Philip does not limit himself to the Isaiah passage, which merely serves as the starting point to explain how Jesus of Nazareth has come in fulfillment of Old Testament promises. This constitutes the "good news" or "gospel" (*euangelion*) of the Christian message.

Why shouldn't I be baptized? (8:36). It was the normal practice of the earliest church for baptism to follow immediately after conversion (2:38, 41; 8:12, 13). The fact that the Ethiopian asks for baptism reveals how much Philip has taught this man in a short amount of time. Surely Philip has taught him that baptism is now understood as the rite that represents his identification with the death of Jesus (and, consequently, its atoning significance) and incorporates him into the community of believers. Because the Ethiopian introduces his question with "what hinders me?" he may be alluding to the fact that he has indeed been hindered from becoming a proselyte in Judaism because of his physical blemish.

The Spirit of the Lord suddenly took Philip away (8:39). The word that Luke uses here (*harpazō*) is the same word used by Paul to refer to the Lord Jesus "snatching up" (or rapturing) people to meet him in the air at his second coming (1 Thess. 1:17). Although it is hard for us to imagine the Holy Spirit physically moving Philip from one location to another, this indeed appears to be what happened.[156] This is not without precedent in the Bible. The Spirit of the Lord transported Elijah from one place to another (1 Kings 18:12; 2 Kings 2:16).

Went on his way rejoicing (8:39). Joy is one of the hallmarks and signs of new life in the messianic era (see Luke 2:10; 8:13; Acts 2:46). Rejoicing is anticipated by the prophets (see Isa. 51:11; 55:12). This observation also serves as evidence that the Ethiopian receives the Holy Spirit (see Rom. 14:17). We know nothing more about the Ethiopian but can presume that he returns to his homeland and proclaims Jesus as Messiah to all of the Jews and God-fearers he knows. This may have been the decisive introduction of the gospel into Nubia. Irenaeus (A.D. 120–202) says this much: "This man was also sent into the regions of Ethiopia, to preach what he had himself believed."[157]

Philip, however, appeared at Azotus (8:40). Azotus (Ashdod in the Old Testament) was about twenty miles north of Gaza, twenty miles south of Joppa, and two and a half miles inland from the

Mediterranean. It was on the "Via Maris," the main coastal road leading from Gaza to Joppa. In the early first century, the city became part of an imperial estate belonging to the empress Livia (the wife of Caesar Augustus).[158] Philip continues to proclaim the gospel in this city as well as in the various coastal towns between Azotus and Caesarea. This includes Jamnia, Antipatris, and possibly the more inland cities of Lydda and Joppa (where Peter later ministered (9:23–43; 10:5–23). This is not the last that we hear of Philip. Luke records a visit that both he (assuming the "we" includes Luke) and Paul had with him twenty years later in Caesarea (21:8).

The Lord Appears to Saul on the Road to Damascus (9:1–9)

After introducing Saul in connection with the death of Stephen and the outbreak of persecution against Christians, Luke now returns to him and describes his dramatic conversion and call to serve. Saul becomes the most important figure in the spread of the gospel to the ends of the earth (1:8).

He went to the high priest and asked him for letters (9:1–2). The high priest in Jerusalem at this time was Caiaphas, the son-in-law of Annas (see John 18:13), who officiated between A.D. 18–37. He is the same high priest who took a leading role in the trial of Jesus, insisting that he was guilty of blasphemy and worthy of death (Matt. 26:57–68). This is also the same high priest who tried Peter and John and

sternly warned them about spreading the gospel (Acts 4:1–21, esp. v. 6). Given the history of his antipathy to Jesus and his followers, Caiaphas is more than glad to grant the request of the zealous young persecutor of Christians.

Saul asks the high priest for extradition documents that will authorize him to apprehend Jews who confess Jesus as the Messiah and have fled Jerusalem. This is an extreme measure, but extreme actions have already been taken by the Jerusalem leaders to crush the movement. Rome granted this level of authority to the high priest for dealing with internal matters. The precedent was set by a letter that the Roman proconsul wrote much earlier to the ruler of Egypt: "Therefore if any pestilent men have fled to you from their country, hand them over to Simon the high priest, that he may punish them according to their law" (1 Macc. 15:21). This right was upheld by Julius Caesar and is now applied by the high priest to stop the new pestilence

▶ Damascus

Damascus was located about 135 miles northeast of Jerusalem on the verge of the Syrian Desert.[A-37] It was about sixty miles northeast of the Sea of Galilee and fifty-five miles inland (due east of the coastal town of Sidon). Today the ancient city lies buried beneath the modern city of Damascus, the capital of Syria.

Situated along the banks of the Barada river with fertile soil, the area around the ancient city was a rich agricultural region. The city gained its importance, however, by its function as the major station along the busy trade route connecting Jerusalem to Mesopotamia and the east. All Jews traveling from Babylon to Jerusalem would have passed through this city.

By New Testament times, the city was under Roman control (belonging to the Roman province of Syria) and thoroughly influenced by Greek culture—the streets of the city were laid out in typical Hellenistic fashion (a Hippodamian layout). There was a gymnasium and a theater, and the principal language of the city was Greek. Damascus was, in fact, a principal city of the Decapolis ("ten cities"), a loose federation of Greek cities east of the Jordan river and the Sea of Galilee. Coins from the city demonstrate that the people worshiped Artemis, Athena, Nike, Tyche, Helios, and Dionysus.[A-38]

There was a sizeable Jewish population in the city attested to by Josephus's report that ten to eighteen thousand Jews were killed there at the outbreak of the Jewish revolt (A.D. 66).[A-39]

that has spread all the way to the frontierland of Damascus.

Synagogues in Damascus (9:2). There were many synagogues in the city of Damascus. This was necessary because there was a large Jewish population. We understand the size of this population by a report from the Jewish historian Josephus. He informs us that during the Jewish war of A.D. 66–70 (roughly thirty years later), over eighteen thousand Jews were killed in the city of Damascus.

These synagogues had a strong power of attraction to many in the Gentile populace (especially many women). They were drawn in by the strong ethical standards of the Jews and their claim to be in a covenant relationship with the one true God. Many Gentiles attached themselves to the synagogues by turning their backs to polytheism and embracing the god of Israel. These Gentile God-fearers and proselytes were often among the first to become Christians, accepting the Christian proclamation that Jesus is the awaited Messiah.

Evidently the persecution of Christians in Judea resulted in some of the Greek-speaking Jewish-Christians fleeing to Damascus. Filled with the Holy Spirit and passionate about their conviction that Jesus is the Messiah, they began proclaiming this good news among the synagogues of Damascus. A good number of Jews and probably many Gentile God-fearers were giving their hearts to Christ and committing themselves to this new movement.

The persecution of Christians thus backfired in the face of the chief priest and the Jewish ruling council. It served to spread the messianic movement as far as Damascus. Incensed at what was happening, the Jewish leaders commission Saul to journey to Damascus and extradite the Judean Jews to Jerusalem, where they will stand trial.

DAMASCUS

▼

The Way (9:2). The early Christians often referred to themselves as "the Way." This is derived from the notion that Jesus the Messiah is the way of life or the way of salvation. Jesus, in fact, spoke of himself in these terms: "I am the way and the truth and the life. No one comes to the Father except through me" (John 14:6).

There are no written records of the beginnings of the church in Damascus. It undoubtedly started in the Jewish community. Some speculate that Galileans who heard Jesus and subsequently became Christians traveled to Damascus as the first to proclaim Christ. Jews from Damascus itself may have heard Jesus during his earthly ministry or have been present at the day of Pentecost. The Jews who fled Jerusalem, however, are clearly impacting the city for the cause of Christ.

Take them as prisoners to Jerusalem (9:2). In light of Saul's "murderous threats" (9:1) and the death of Stephen, the lives of these Jewish Christians are in definite danger.

A light from heaven flashed around him (9:3). The light is a special manifestation of the divine presence and glory. No doubt Saul sees himself as a beneficiary of the messianic promise of Isaiah 9:2: "The people walking in darkness have seen a great light; on those living in the land of the shadow of death a light has dawned." For Saul, the more important light is the recognition of Jesus as the Messiah. The fact that the light appears "from heaven" points to Jesus as exalted to the right hand of God.

Saul, Saul, why do you persecute me? (9:4) Jesus directly addresses Saul in Aramaic (*Saoul* is the Aramaic form of his name; *Saulos*, as in 9:1, is the Greek form). Jesus asks Saul a question that he will never forget and that will have a revolutionary impact on every aspect of his life. The question presupposes that Jesus is resurrected and alive (he is not in the grave), that he is in a close relationship with the people who embrace him as Messiah and Lord (he is not a messianic pretender), and that by persecuting Christians, Saul is actually persecuting the Lord and standing in the way of what God is accomplishing in fulfillment of Old Testament promises. What a shattering realization!

The men traveling with Saul (9:7). Although the identity of these men is not explicitly stated, they may have been fellow official representatives of the Sanhedrin. They hear something, but do not know or understand what the Lord says to Saul.

For three days he was blind (9:9). Unable to see after this dramatic encounter, the traveling companions lead Saul by the hand to the city of Damascus. Overwhelmed by what has happened and full of grief at actually opposing the God he is so zealously trying to serve, Saul refuses to eat or drink for three days.

He spends much of this time in prayerful, repentant reflection on the course of his life, the claims of the followers of Jesus, and the messianic texts of Scripture. At some point during these three days, the Lord appears to him again in a vision (cf. 9:12).

Ananias Meets With Saul (9:10–19a)

Following his direct appearance to Saul, the Lord uses one Jewish believer from Damascus to minister to Saul.

Ananias (9:10). He is a Jew living in Damascus who has put his faith in Jesus as the Messiah based on the preaching of Jewish Christians who come to the city prior to Saul. Today in the city of Damascus, there is a chapel bearing the name of Ananias. The tradition that this chapel marks the site of Ananias' home dates back to Byzantine times. Based on the location, the actual house of Ananias may have been situated directly on the wall.[159]

A vision (9:10, 12). In the days that followed Jesus' appearance to Saul in a brilliant light on the road to Damascus, the Lord gives further guidance through two visions. First, he appears to this Damascene believer, Ananias, and gives him specific directions to meet Saul and how to minister to him. Then the Lord again appears to Saul, but this time in a vision, and informs him that someone is coming to meet him and restore his sight. The word that is used for vision (*horama*) indicates something that is actually seen as opposed to something that is purely imaginary. The Lord will once again use a double vision as a means of reaching the Gentile household of Cornelius through the apostle Peter (Acts 10:1–

REFLECTIONS

ALTHOUGH FEW CHRISTIANS HAVE experienced a blinding flash of light and a vision of the ascended Christ reaching out to them as a catalyst prompting their conversions, most of us can reflect on people, events, and circumstances that show God's initiative in reaching us with his love in the gospel. Salvation is truly the result of God's initiative. We have done nothing to earn it.

23). It is significant to observe that Saul receives the vision during a period when he has spent considerable time in prayer.

The house of Judas on Straight Street (9:11). Judas is presumably not a Christian, but Paul's Jewish host with whom he has made arrangements prior to leaving Jerusalem. "Straight Street" is actually one of the main roads going through Damascus (the *cardo maximus*), the main east-west route through the city. Part of this street has been discovered by archaeologists. It was colonnaded and was about fifty feet wide. Today it is known as the *Darb el-Moskatim*.[160]

STRAIGHT STREET

The eastern end of the street looking west at the east gate of Damascus. ▼

Tarsus (9:11). Saul was not originally from Jerusalem or even from Palestine. He came from an Asia Minor city in the province of Cilicia called Tarsus (see 22:3). From a grammar school age, however, Saul lived in Jerusalem and there received his education.

Place his hands on him (9:12). In the Old Testament, the laying on of hands is done in connection with a special commission (as Moses did when he conferred the leadership of the nation on Joshua; Num. 27:23) or with the imparting of a blessing (as Jacob did on his sons just before he died; Gen. 48:14). Jesus often laid his hands on people as he healed them: "When the sun was setting, the people brought to Jesus all who had various kinds of sickness, and laying his hands on each one, he healed them" (Luke 4:40). Here the Lord instructs Ananias to confer the divine blessing of healing on Saul by laying his hands on him.

"Lord," Ananias answered, "I have heard many reports" (9:13). Well-informed of Saul's violent persecuting activity against the Jewish Christians, Ananias understandably objects to the instructions. He has not heard that the Lord appeared to Saul on the Damascus road.

Your saints (9:13). This is the first time that this expression is used to refer to Christians. It is here found on the lips of a believer in Damascus. The term reflects the proper understanding that the new covenant people of God have been made holy and pure before God by the forgiveness achieved in Jesus' death on the cross. It also conveys the idea that believers are especially devoted to God.

This man is my chosen instrument (9:15). The Lord overrules all of Ananias's objections and tells him that Saul has been specially chosen as an ambassador of the gospel. God will use Saul to take the gospel particularly to the Gentiles, but also to Jews and even to kings.

How much he must suffer for my name (9:16). The Lord also informs Ananias that this one who has inflicted much suffering on Christians now will experience much suffering himself as he carries out his divinely ordained mission. Saul/Paul himself later enumerates the variety of ways he eventually suffered for the cause of Christ (2 Cor. 11:23–33).

He could see again (9:18). Obeying the Lord Jesus, Ananias locates the house and does exactly as the Lord has told him. Ananias greets Saul and lays hands on him, and Saul regains his sight. Saul's physical blindness has similarities to the spiritual blindness he experienced before his conversion. Saul later reflects, "The god of this age has blinded the minds of unbelievers, so that they cannot see the light of the gospel of the glory of Christ, who is the image of God" (2 Cor. 4:4). The illumination of Christ, however, frees Saul of his spiritual blindness and he wholeheartedly embraces Jesus as the Messiah and Son of God.

Filled with the Holy Spirit . . . and was baptized (9:17–18). At this time, Saul is filled with the Holy Spirit, who will empower this newly commissioned apostle to proclaim the gospel and endure the suffering. Saul is then immediately baptized, presumably by Ananias. In later church tradition, there is a one- to three-year delay for baptism, which follows a long period of instruction. The New Testament pattern appears to be that the rite is performed in a short time after a person professes faith in Christ. It is also important here to observe that Paul experiences the work of the Spirit in his life prior to his baptism.

Saul Immediately Proclaims Jesus in Damascus (9:19b–25)

In one of the greatest reversals in history, the man who once persecutes followers of Jesus now begins proclaiming him as the Son of God and as the long-awaited Messiah among the Jews in the synagogues of Damascus.

At once he began to preach in the synagogues (9:20). Because the first letter of Saul/Paul was written nearly seventeen years later, some have assumed that he spent these years in prayer, study, and reflection before engaging in ministry. But this is not true. Saul begins his preaching almost immediately, only after spending some time with his new brothers and sisters in the Lord.

Oddly enough, some of the Jews in these Damascus synagogues have probably been in contact with members of the Jerusalem Sanhedrin and are anxious for the help Saul will bring in, putting a stop to the encroaching influence of this new movement. Yet now here Saul is passionately advocating the very thing he has come to crush.

Filled with the Spirit and gaining a deeper appreciation day-by-day of the marvelous fulfillment of the Old Testament expectation in Jesus, Saul's presentation of Jesus as the Messiah becomes more and more powerful. Many of the Jews resistant to his preaching have great difficulty providing a credible response to Saul's message. It is possible that it is at this time that he receives the first of his five synagogue beatings mentioned in 2 Corinthians 11:24.

Son of God (9:20). A central part of Saul's teaching is declaring Jesus as the Son of God. This does not mean that Jesus is God's Son in any sort of physical sense. The background of this phrase needs to be understood in its Old Testament context of God's special relationship with the anointed king of Israel. The Lord had a unique relationship with David and promised him that one of his descendants would be king of Israel in the future, that he would have a glorious and eternal reign, and that he would enjoy a relationship of sonship to the Father: "I will establish the throne of his kingdom for ever. I will be his father, and he shall be my son."[161] To announce that Jesus is *the* Son of God is to proclaim the arrival of the anointed king (the "Messiah") who will reign on the throne of David.

[Mission to Arabia (Gal. 1:17)]. If we compare this account to Paul's later own words in Galatians 1, we find that he leaves Damascus shortly after his conversion to journey to "Arabia." This is not to be identified with the Arabian peninsula occupied today by Saudi Arabia, but refers to the vast kingdom of Nabatea (see comments on Gal. 1:17). The Nabateans lived in the land south of Damascus and southeast of Palestine. Today their land is located within parts of southern Syria, Jordan, the Negev of Israel, the Sinai, and the northwestern region of Saudi Arabia. The capital of this vast empire was the city of Petra, about fifty miles south of the Dead Sea.

Because of his commission to reach Gentiles with the gospel, Paul probably spends time in the major cities of Nabatea, such as Petra and Hegra, where there were Jewish synagogues and where he could present the gospel to the Gentile

God-fearers and proselytes. His method for reaching Gentiles throughout his ministry is by first preaching the Messiah in the Jewish synagogues. Here he finds many Gentiles who have already come to believe in the one God of Israel and have gained some familiarity with the Old Testament. He probably spends as much as one and a half to two years in this region.[162]

▶

ARABIA (NABATEA)

PETRA

▼

Why does he go to this region? This appears to have been an area where Jewish Christians had not yet taken the gospel after they were scattered from Jerusalem by persecution. In fulfilling the principle of not "building on someone else's foundation" (Rom. 15:20), Saul goes to this neighboring area where Christ has not yet been preached.

After many days had gone by (9:23). Luke chooses not to relate the account of Saul's trip to Arabia, but this is the time it likely occurs. After his one or two years in Nabatea, Saul returns to Damascus for the second phase of his ministry there, where he faces the conspiracy for his death and has to flee.

The Jews conspired to kill him . . . . But his followers took him by night and lowered him in a basket through an opening in the wall (9:23–25). Astonished that their ally from Jerusalem joins this dangerous Messianic sect, the Jewish leaders from the synagogues are so incensed that they begin to make plans to kill Saul. This is not a surprising move on their part since precedent has already been set for killing vocal leaders of this movement (e.g. Stephen; 7:54–8:1). Now they see for themselves Saul's persuasive appeal on behalf of Jesus. Something needs to be done as soon as possible to stop the spread of his influence in their city. He himself describes this incident in 2 Corinthians 11:32:

> In Damascus the governor under King Aretas had the city of the Damscenes guarded in order to arrest me. But I was lowered in a basket from a window in the wall and slipped through his hands.

It is no contradiction that Saul says that the governor under King Aretas is after him and Luke says that the Jews are conspiring against him. The most likely explanation is that both groups are out to get him.[163] Aretas IV was the king of the Nabateans, ruling over them from 9 B.C. to A.D. 40. The "governor" under him was properly an *ethnarch*, that is, a ruler over the Nabateans living in the city of Damascus. Saul's preaching throughout Nabatea evidently stirred up a significant amount of antipathy against him from the Jews living in the area. As happened in other cities during Saul's missionary journeys, they probably complained bitterly to the local officials and represented Saul as a threat. The two groups then—the Jewish leaders and the local Nabatean leaders—collude against Saul in the city of Damascus. His life is in danger and he has to leave the city.

Becoming aware of their plan, Saul's fellow believers hatch a plan to usher him out of the city. They stealthily lower him in a basket through a window under the cover of darkness so he can escape on foot.

Saul Goes to Jerusalem (9:26–31)

To Jerusalem (9:26). Saul immediately departs for Jerusalem. He tells us why in his letter to the Galatians. He wants to become acquainted with Peter (Gal. 1:18)—the most significant leader in the Jerusalem church. Presumably he stays in Peter's home there. These two weeks give them much time to become more personally acquainted.

Saul hears about Peter's three years of accompanying the Lord Jesus in his earthly ministry and many of the details of Jesus' teaching and deeds. Peter, in turn, hears the details of Saul's miraculous conversion and his proclamation of Jesus as Messiah in Damascus and throughout Nabatea (Arabia).

He tried to join the disciples (9:26). Saul soon finds out that there is still much suspicion about the authenticity of his conversion. Knowing all too well the violence Saul has exhibited toward the believers in Jesus, the Christians in Jerusalem are understandably fearful of him. Many consider Saul's conversion a clever ruse to trap them and persecute them. Presumably, he stays with relatives after his arrival into the city before he becomes acquainted with Peter.

More disciples than the twelve apostles are apparently in Jerusalem at this time. Roughly three years has passed since the outbreak of persecution against the church (see Gal. 1:18–20). Apparently the intensity of the persecution has subsided to a sufficient degree that a number have returned to the city.

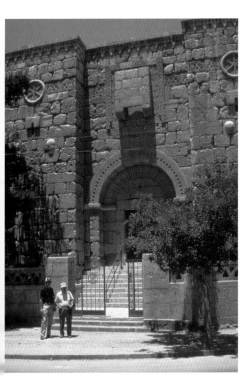

◀ *left*

A WALL AT THE MODERN CITY OF DAMASCUS

Barnabas took him and brought him to the apostles (9:27). Barnabas, a Jew from Cyprus who became a follower of Christ (see comments on 4:36), intervenes. Believing Saul's story, he takes him to the apostles and explains the details of his conversion. This reduces the cloud of suspicion surrounding Saul. He is then able to meet with groups of Christians and even begins proclaiming Christ in Jerusalem. According to Galatians 1:18, Peter and James (the Lord's brother, not one of the Twelve) are the only apostles Saul meets at this time.

right ▶

JERUSALEM TO TARSUS

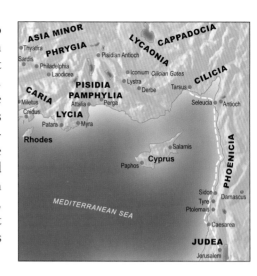

Debated with the Grecian Jews (9:29). Saul proclaims Christ particularly among the Jews who are not from Jerusalem but who come from various parts of the Greek-speaking world (see comments on 6:1, 9). For the most part, these zealous Jews outrightly reject Saul's message and are prepared to put him to death—the very thing Saul himself did to such blasphemous people a few years earlier.

Sent him off to Tarsus (9:30). Knowing the reality of the threats from the non-Christian Jews, believers in Jerusalem usher Saul to the coastal city of Caesarea.

This is only a stop-off point for Saul's ultimate destination—Tarsus of Cilicia. To go to Tarsus is to go home for Saul.[164] He may have had family and friends living there since he spent his earliest years there before being sent to Jerusalem for his education. The extensive Jewish population of the area along with the many Gentile sympathizers to Judaism provide an ideal mission field for him to continue fulfilling his divinely given commission. He probably spends between three and four years in Tarsus and the neighboring cities of Cilicia before going to Antioch in 39 or 40 A.D.[165]

TARSUS

(left) A view of the Taurus mountains from the city of Tarsus (looking in the direction of the Cilician gates).

(right) The gate of Cleopatra at Tarsus.

▼

Peter Heals Aeneas and Dorcas (9:32–43)

Luke now shifts his focus away from Saul and back to Peter, partly in preparation to narrate the conversion of the Gentile household of Cornelius. Peter does not remain resident in Jerusalem, but becomes a missionary. After ministering to the new believers in Samaria (8:14–25), he apparently returns to Jerusalem for a period of time (8:25) and then begins traveling to villages in Judea and Samaria. He presumably evangelizes and provides these new converts with apostolic teaching.

Lydda (9:32). Lydda, known as Lod in the Old Testament, was located eleven miles southeast of Joppa (Tel Aviv).[166] The main road from Jerusalem to Joppa passed through this city. Lydda was the chief city over one of the eleven districts (or toparchies) into which Judea was divided.[167] The population was almost exclusively Jewish.[168] Luke does not tell us how this city was evangelized. It may have been reached by the Christians dispersed from Jerusalem following the persecution (8:1, 4) or even by Philip (8:40). Today the ancient city is covered by modern buildings, which have prevented any extensive archaeological work.[169] After the Jewish war, Lydda became an important center for rabbinical learning.

Aeneas (9:33). Luke does not explicitly state whether Aeneas is a believer. His ethnic background is most likely Jewish. Although the name "Aeneas" appears in Palestinian inscriptions, it was also a well-known Greek name.

▶ Tarsus

Tarsus was the principal city of the province of Cilicia located in the southeastern portion of Asia Minor (in modern-day Turkey).[A-40] Ideally situated about ten miles north of the coast of the Mediterranean Sea on the Cydnus River, Tarsus was an important center for commerce. The city served as the nexus point between the interior of Asia Minor and Syria as well as for trade from the Mediterranean. To the north of Tarsus lay the rugged Taurus mountain range with peaks averaging a height of seven thousand feet. There was only one viable pass over the mountains from Tarsus—a narrow gorge called the Cilician Gates.

Stoic philosophy and rhetoric flourished in Tarsus. It was home to four famous Stoic philosophers: Antipater, Archedemus, Athenodorus Cordylion, and Athenodorus of Tarsus. The latter, a friend of Cicero, had even served as the court philosopher for the emperor Caesar Augustus. Strabo said that the Tarsians' zeal for learning surpassed that of Athens or Alexandria.[A-41] In spite of Tarsus' fame for Stoic philosophy, it remains doubtful that Saul had received any formal Stoic education there.

As with any other city of the time, there were an abundance of cults in Tarsus. Most important to the city was the god Sandas, an old Cilician god of war and the weather. He was frequently identified with the Greek hero/god Heracles (in Greek mythology he was born of a human mother and Zeus). There was also a large Jewish population in the province of Cilicia and in the city of Tarsus.

The modern city of Tarsus occupies the ancient site thereby preventing little archaeological work from being undertaken. Excavations conducted a generation ago on the southeastern extremity of the modern city turned up nothing from the Roman period, but archaeologists have recently discovered 250 coins dating as early as the second century B.C.,[A-42] although most date between the third and fifth centuries A.D.[A-43]

Jesus Christ heals you (9:34). Not using any healing formulas, incantations, or rituals, Peter declares that Aeneas will be healed by the power of Jesus Christ. Peter is not a shaman or a magician (like Simon), but is an earthly representative of the living and powerful Christ.

Sharon (9:35). Sharon is a large coastal plain in northern Palestine. Joppa lay at the southern end of this plain that extends north about thirty miles to Caesarea Maritima and inland nearly ten. After the building of Caesarea by Herod and a new network of roads, the population of this area grew considerably.

Joppa (9:36). The seaport where Jonah once boarded a boat to flee from the mission God had called him to (Jonah 1:3), this city became a site for the spread of Christianity and the location where Peter is used by God to raise a woman from the dead.[170] Located about thirty-five miles northwest of Jerusalem and eleven miles northwest of Lydda, Joppa served as the main port for Jerusalem and all of Judea. Ancient Joppa (or Jaffa) was located within the modern city of Tel Aviv. When Herod the Great built his new port at Caesarea Maritima, Joppa became far less significant (although it later regained its

significance when the port at Caesarea deteriorated and fell into disuse in the late Byzantine period). Although many modern buildings cover the ancient site, the modern visitor's center covers the remains of some Roman-era structures.

Joppa was a rather dangerous port because of the rocky breakwater about a hundred yards offshore. Sudden high winds from the north resulted in many ships being dashed against the rocks.[171] The population of Joppa was predominately Jewish. Consequently, it later became a revolutionary center in the Jewish war against the Romans in A.D. 66.[172]

Tabitha (which, when translated, is Dorcas) (9:36). "Tabitha" is an Aramaic name that means "gazelle." "Dorcas" is a Greek translation of the name. The fact that she has a Greek name illustrates the level of Greek influence in Palestine.

Her body was washed (9:37). It was common in the cultures of antiquity to wash and anoint a body in preparation for burial. This was also true in Judaism: "They may make ready on the Sabbath all that is needful for the dead, and anoint it and wash it."[173]

He got down on his knees and prayed (9:40). Peter does not have some inherent power and ability to heal. He calls on God to give him direction on how to respond to this situation and for the ability to do what God wants him to do.

A tanner named Simon (9:43). It is significant that Peter stays with a tanner, since this was viewed as a despised trade in Judaism. One rabbi even exclaimed, "Woe to him who is a tanner."[174] Tanners were suspected of immorality because

LYDDA, SHARON, AND JOPPA
▼

◀

JOPPA

Looking at the modern city of Tel Aviv from the site of Joppa.

women worked in the trade. Many were repulsed by the trade simply because of the stench of working with animal carcases. Jews also had concerns about the ritual purity of tanners because of their contact with dead bodies.[175] At this point, not yet having his vision of unclean animals let down from heaven in a sheet, Peter is still concerned about maintaining Jewish ritual purity.

The Conversion of Cornelius (10:1–48)

The conversion of Cornelius and his household represents the decisive step forward in the spread of Christianity to the Gentiles. Cornelius was not the first Gentile to receive Christ, however. Already a Gentile proselyte (6:5), an Ethiopian Gentile (8:26–39), and some converts of Philip (8:40) have become followers of Christ. But this situation is unique because of the involvement of the apostle Peter (the recognized leader of this new movement) and God's miracu-

lous superintending of the events (including God's revelation to Peter that he had declared all foods pure).

This significant event probably occurs sometime between A.D. 39–40. This means it happens roughly ten years after the death and resurrection of Jesus and about seven years after Paul's conversion.

Caesarea (10:1). Caesarea Maritima was a major seaport city about sixty miles northwest of Jerusalem. Politically it functioned as the provincial capital of Judea and was home to the Roman governors.[176] The city had only recently been built by Herod the Great over the former site of a coastal town called Strato's Tower and occupied 235 acres within the perimeter wall.

Herod commissioned an army of workers to begin work on the city and the harbor in 23 B.C. and actually completed the immense undertaking in a decade. He spared no expense in fulfilling his vision of creating a major international port that rivaled Alexandria and

Piraeus (the port of Athens). In creating the first artificial harbor in the ancient world, Herod's engineers made use of a new sophisticated technology. Creating immense wooden forms, the engineers made much of the harbor and breakwater with a type of concrete that hardened underwater.

He patterned the city itself on the style of a Roman provincial capital with

▶ **CAESAREA MARITIMA AND ITS ENVIRONS**

▶ ## The City of Caesarea
IMPORTANT FACTS:

■ Population: over 50,000

■ Prominent Religions: Tyche (Fortuna); Ephesian Artemis (Diana); Apollo; Dionysus; Isis; Serapis; Demeter; Mithras; Ruler cult (Augustus and Roma); Judaism

■ The major port city for Palestine

■ A city recently constructed by Herod the Great (begun in 23 B.C.)

■ Seat of the Roman Government for the Province of Judea

all of the amenities (including temples, theater, market, hippodrome, and an amphitheater). The beautiful four thousand-seat theater was located at the south end of the city with the seats facing the Mediterranean. Archaeologists estimate that the seating capacity around the oval track of the hippodrome was thirty thousand. The city was laid out on the Hellenistic grid model with streets that ran north-south and east-west. The infrastructure of the city included an intricate sewer system and an abundant water supply. Herod's engineers designed an immense aqueduct that brought water from mountain springs (at Shuni) some six miles to the north. Most of the aqueduct was carried on high arches, but part of it is through a quarter of a mile long tunnel, which was bored through a sandstone ridge.

Herod named the city after Caesar Augustus, the reigning emperor. Josephus tells us of the great honor he bestowed on Caesar: "On rising ground opposite the harbour-mouth stood Caesar's temple, of exceptional size and beauty; in it was a colossal statue of Caesar, no whit inferior to the Olympian Zeus which it was intended to resemble, and one of Rome comparable with the Hera of Argos. Herod dedicated the city to the province, the harbour to those who sailed these seas, and the honour of his new creation to Caesar: Caesarea was the name he gave it."[177]

The city had great significance for Christianity not only because of Luke's portrayal of the conversion of the Gentile family of Cornelius, but also as the place where Origen (A.D. 185–254) and Eusebius (A.D. 260–340) lived and taught. For Jews, painful memories were associated with Caesarea. At the outset of the Jewish war in A.D. 66, the Gentile citizens of the city massacred nearly the entire population of Caesarea's Jews.[178]

A man named Cornelius (10:1). Cornelius may have been a descendant of one of the ten thousand slaves freed by the Roman general L. Cornelius Sulla Felix in 82 B.C.[179] It is not uncommon for freedmen to take on the family name (*gens*) of their emancipator. On the other hand, "Cornelius" was a rather common Latin name.

He was a fairly wealthy man of status living in a beautiful city. Evidently he has been stationed in Caesarea for a long period of time because he possesses a home, his family is with him, and he has been there long enough to perform many generous deeds for the Jewish community. It is also possible that he has retired from the military and has chosen to settle in Caesarea. Nothing is known of this man outside of the biblical account.

A centurion (10:1). "The centurions are the principal professional officers in the Roman army."[180] They served as the commanding officers over troops of eighty to a hundred men and are paid well. "The financial attraction of the centurionate,

▶ Archaeology in Caesarea

Caesarea Maritima has been a major focus of archaeological excavation since 1950 by groups from Israel, Italy, and the United States.[A-44] Since 1971 a consortium of nearly two dozen colleges and universities known as the Joint Expedition to Caesarea Maritima (JECM) has been excavating the land site. In 1980, an international consortium was formed to carry out underwater excavations of the ancient harbor. Known as CAHEP—"the Caesarea Ancient Harbour Excavation Project"—and headed by A. Raban (University of Haifa) and R. L. Hohlfelder (University of Colorado)—this group made significant discoveries relating to the ancient harbor. *National Geographic* magazine featured Caesarea Maritima as the cover story of a 1987 issue and produced a video-documentary of the work there.[A-45] Work at Caesarea is now done under the auspices of the Combined Caesarea Expeditions (CCE), a joint initiative of the University of Maryland and the University of Haifa.[A-46]

Among some of the sigificant discoveries on the site of the ancient city were the remains of a synagogue, an underground Mithraeum, and many statues, inscriptions, and coins. The synagogue building dates to the fourth century A.D., but it incorporates walls from a much earlier synagogue structure that dates to the Herodian era. Excavators found the

capital of a column engraved with a Jewish menorah. The Mithraeum, an underground structure for performing rituals in honor of the Persian god Mithras, was built in the late first century from a converted subterranean warehouse vault.

In addition to discovering well-preserved statues of Tyche and Artemis, archaeologists found a horde of thirty-seven hundred bronze Roman coins (dating to the mid-fourth century). Of the inscriptions found at the site, three are particularly significant: (1) a Latin stone inscription from the theater that mentions "Pontius Pilate," (2) a Latin inscription on the aqueduct that commemorates the presence of the tenth Roman legion at Caesarea, and (3) fragments of a Hebrew inscription on the mosaic floor of the synagogue that listed the twenty-four priestly courses.

◀ **CAPITAL WITH MENORAH FROM CAESAREAN SYNAGOGUE**

however, was that the pay was probably some sixteen times that of the basic legionary salary. In short, a centurion had both considerable military and social status and wealth."[181] As a centurion, Cornelius was also a Roman citizen. The historian Polybius (1st cent. B.C.) says of centurions: "They wish centurions not so much to be venturesome and daredevil as natural leaders, of a steady and sedate spirit. They do not desire them so much to be men who will initiate attacks and open the battle, but men who will hold their ground when worsted and hard pressed and be ready to die at their posts."[182]

The Italian Regiment (10:1). This is the earliest reference (c. A.D. 40) to the *Cohors II Italica voluntariorum civium Romanorum* (the "Second Italian Cohort of Roman Citizens"), known from Latin

CAESAREA MARITIMA

(top) Remains of the ancient harbor.

(bottom left) Ruins near the harbor.

(bottom right) The theater. The aqueduct is visible in the top right of the photo.

▶ Josephus's Description of Caesarea

Herod Rebuilds "Strato's Tower": "Herod noticed on the coast a town called Strato's Tower, in a state of decay, but thanks to its admirable situation capable of benefiting by his generosity. He rebuilt it entirely with limestone and adorned it with a most splendid palace. Nowhere did he show more clearly the liveliness of his imagination."

The Creation of the Immense Harbor: "The city lies midway between Dora and Joppa, and hitherto the whole of that shore had been harbourless, so that anyone sailing along the Phoenician coast towards Egypt had to ride the open sea when threatened by the southwest wind; even when this is far from strong, such huge waves are dashed against the rocks that the back-wash makes the sea boil up a long way out. But the king by lavish expenditure and unshakable determination won the battle against nature and constructed a harbour bigger than the Piraeus [the harbor of Athens], with further deep roadsteads in its recesses. The site was as awkward as could be, but he wrestled with the difficulties so triumphantly that on his solid fabric the sea could make no impression, while its beauty gave no hint of the obstacles encountered. He first marked out the area for a harbour of the size mentioned, and then lowered into 20 fathoms of water blocks of stone mostly 50 feet long, 9 deep, and 10 broad, but sometimes even bigger."

The Breakwater: "When the foundations had risen to water-level he built above the surface a mole 200 feet wide; half this width was built out to break the force of the waves and so was called the Breakwater; the rest supported the encircling stone wall. Along this were spaced massive towers, of which the most con-spicuous and most beautiful was called Drusium after Caesar's step-son."

The Situation of the Port; The Colossal Statues and the Towers: "There was a row of arched recesses where newly-arrived crews could land, and in front of these was a circular terrace forming a broad walk for those disembarking. The harbour-mouth faced north, as in that locality the north wind is the gentlest, and on either side rose three colossal statues standing on pillars; those on the left of ships entering were supported by a solid tower, those on the right by two upright stones clamped together, even higher than the tower of the other side."

Houses and Streets: "Adjoining the harbour were houses, also of limestone, and to the harbour led the streets of the town, laid out the same distance apart."

Caesar's Temple and Statue: "On rising ground opposite the harbour-mouth stood Caesar's temple, of exceptional size and beauty; in it was a colossal statue of Caesar, no whit inferior to the Olympian Zeus which it was intended to resemble, and one of Rome comparable with the Hera of Argos. Herod dedicated the city to the province, the harbour to those who sailed these seas, and the honour of his new creation to Caesar: Caesarea was the name he gave it."

Other Public Works and the Games: "The rest of the buildings—theatre, amphitheatre, and market-place—were on a scale worthy of that name. The king also instituted four-yearly games and called them too after Caesar, gracing the first contest—held in the 192d Olympiad—with the personal gift of very valuable prizes, the royal bounty extending not only to the winners but to those who came second and third."[A-47]

Roman Military Command Structure	
Roman Military Title	Amount of Men
1. Century	100
2. Maniple	200 (two Centuries)
3. Cohort	600 (three Maniples)
4. Legion	6000 (ten Cohorts)

inscriptions.[183] This cohort was present in Syria during the Jewish revolt (A.D. 66–70) and remained there for an extended period of time following the war. It was likely made up of Roman citizens who were in some sense "Italian." Some of the soldiers were possibly local Syrian recruits or freedmen.[184]

Devout and God-fearing (10:2). Cornelius turns his back to the gods of the military (such as Mithras) and the household gods of Rome and embraces the one true God of Israel as the object of his devotion. He attaches himself to the synagogue (without becoming a full proselyte), sharing his wealth with those in need (in the Jewish community) and praying regularly.

At about three in the afternoon (10:3). This was a set Jewish time of prayer. We can assume that Cornelius is praying at this time and receives the vision in the context of prayer. The time is also further evidence that Cornelius is not simply dreaming.

He had a vision (10:3). Cornelius distinctly sees an angel appear and speak to him by name. Throughout this early period in the spread of Christianity, God frequently uses angels to give direction to his servants.[185]

As a memorial offering before God (10:4). Just as the Old Testament describes the smoke of a burnt offering ascending to the presence of the Lord (see Lev. 2:2), Cornelius's generous giving and his regular and sincere prayers are pleasing to the Lord. This is consistent with the way prayer is described elsewhere in the Old Testament: "May my prayer be set before you like incense; may the lifting up of my hands be like the evening sacrifice" (Ps. 141:2). God receives Cornelius's prayer and giving as acceptable offerings from this Gentile man who responds according to the light of revelation he has received through the synagogue. Now God will give him the full revelation of Jesus Christ.

Send men to Joppa (10:5). Joppa is about thirty miles south of Caesarea.

About noon (10:9). Noon, or "the sixth hour," is not one of the normal Jewish times of prayer (although Daniel sets aside three times a day to pray; see Dan. 6:10). Peter here illustrates the practice of the apostles and the early Christians to pray frequently.

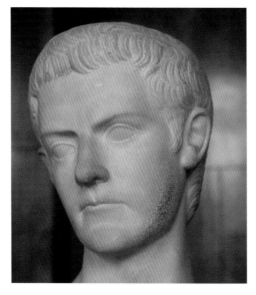

▶

CALIGULA

A marble bust of the renown emperor who reigned A.D. 37–41.

Peter went up on the roof to pray (10:9). Palestinian homes typically had flat roofs with access from an outdoors stairway. It was common for the occupants to climb the stairs to the roof and sit on the top of the house, especially in the summertime, to benefit from a cool breeze. Peter goes to the roof at noon time probably to find a place where he can pray undisturbed.

He fell into a trance (10:10). Whereas Cornelius has a vision (*horama*) in which an angel of the Lord appears to him, Peter falls into a trance (*ekstasis*) and has a vision of heaven opening. The term literally means "to stand outside of yourself" and refers to a state of being brought about by God "in which consciousness is wholly or partially suspended."[186] The same word is used to describe the vision Daniel sees on the banks of the Tigris River after fasting for three weeks and interceding for the people of Israel (Dan. 10:7).

He saw heaven opened (10:11). Stephen experiences the same phenomenon (see comments on 7:56).

Something like a large sheet (10:11). The term *othonē*, translated here as "sheet," refers to a linen cloth. Linen had a variety of applications with a sheet (such as a bed sheet) being just one. The term is used often in ancient literature for the sails of a ship, as in *Martyrdom of Polycarp* 15:2: "like the sail (*othonē*) of a ship filled by the wind." The sheet Peter sees is suspended by its four corners and filled with a large number of animals.

All kinds of four-footed animals, as well as reptiles of the earth and birds of the air (10:12). In this vision, Peter sees all kinds of animals. This description is reminiscent of the summary of animal life at

bottom left

ROOFS

These are homes in the village of Der Samet in the area of Hebron. Inhabitants sleep on the roofs during the hot summer nights.

JOPPA

The modern site of Joppa (or, Jaffa).

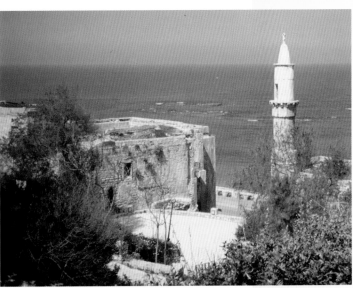

the beginning of creation (Gen. 1:24). The Torah, however, prohibited the Israelites from eating certain animals. A detailed set of criteria for determining which animals were clean and which were to be regarded as unclean is given in Leviticus 11. There are four basic criteria:

- Land animals had to both chew the cud and have a split hoof.
- Sea creatures had to have fins and scales.
- Winged insects had to have jointed legs to hop.
- Birds of prey, reptiles, and other crawlers were off limits.

Among those animals the Israelites could not eat were camels, rabbits, pigs, eagles, vultures, owls, weasels, rats, and lizards. Peter sees many of these prohibited (and "unclean") animals in the sheet, presumably mingled together with animals that are ritually pure.

I have never eaten anything impure or unclean (10:14). It is to Peter's credit that he has never eaten any of the pro-

hibited animals. As an observant Jew of his time, Peter exercises great sensitivity not to defile himself with any food that will render him ceremonially impure. God has clearly revealed in the law that he should not eat any of them: "Do not defile yourselves by any of these creatures. Do not make yourselves unclean by means of them or be made unclean by them. I am the LORD your God; consecrate yourselves and be holy, because I am holy" (Lev. 11:43–44). Peter's reaction to the vision and his perplexity are entirely understandable.

"Unclean" (*akathartos*) is the typical description in the law for the prohibited animals; "impure" (*koinos*) never appears. *Koinos* is more often translated as "common." It comes to be used in later Judaism for the foods that Gentiles would eat. "The opposite is that which is sanctified or dedicated *[hagios]* and hence withdrawn from ordinary use."[187]

Jewish literature is filled with examples of people who refused to defile themselves by consuming "common" or unkosher food. Note a few examples from the period around the Maccabean revolt that show the intensity of commitment to avoid unclean foods:

- Antiochus Epiphanes ordered everyone in his kingdom (which included Israel) to give up their ancestral customs "that all should be one people" (1 Macc. 1:41). This included a specific command to "sacrifice swine and unclean (*koina*) animals." The commitment not to defile themselves with impure food was so strong in Israel that many gave their lives to obey it: "But many in Israel stood firm and were resolved in their hearts not to eat unclean food. They chose to die rather than to be defiled by food or to profane the holy covenant; and they did die" (1 Macc. 1:62–63).

- Eleazar, priest during the Maccabean period, was praised for not defiling himself, although he was martyred: "O priest, worthy of the priesthood, you neither defiled your sacred teeth nor profaned your stomach, which had room only for reverence and purity, by eating defiled foods" (4 Macc. 7:6).

The question of *why* God originally designated certain animals as ceremonially unclean is difficult to answer. The Old Testament never explicitly or implicitly tells us. It is inadequate to speculate that God selected a kosher menu as a means of protection for his people from food-borne diseases in an age before refrigeration. It is possible that God originally willed to keep Jews and Gentiles apart in order to unite them in a special way in the messianic age. There was, in fact, a strain of messianic expectation in Judaism that anticipated the declaration of all animals as clean: "All the animals which in this world are declared unclean, God will in the future [that is, in the days of the Messiah] declare clean."[188]

Do not call anything impure that God has made clean (10:15). The full implication of the coming of Christ and the inauguration of the new covenant has not yet dawned on Peter. God is lifting the distinction between clean and unclean foods—a boundary that separates Jews from Gentiles.

The prophets anticipated a time when God would cleanse anyone who worshiped him. The new covenant promise of Ezekiel anticipated a time when God would cleanse his people from impurity and place his Spirit in them: "I will sprinkle clean water on you, and *you will be clean; I will cleanse you from all your impurities* and from all your idols. I will give you a new heart and put a new spirit in you; I will remove from you your heart of stone and give you a heart of flesh. And I will put my Spirit in you and move you to follow my decrees and be careful to keep my laws. You will live in the land I gave your forefathers; you will be my people, and I will be your God" (Ezek. 36:25–28). Zechariah envisioned a day when there would be an abundant source of cleansing in Israel: "On that day a fountain will be opened to the house of David and the inhabitants of Jerusalem, *to cleanse them from sin and impurity*" (Zech. 13:1).

This time has now arrived in the person of Jesus. In fact, Jesus declared all foods to be clean during his ministry: "Don't you see that nothing that enters a man from the outside can make him 'unclean'? For it doesn't go into his heart but into his stomach, and then out of his body. (In saying this, Jesus declared all foods 'clean.')" (Mark 7:15–16). Jesus emphasized that it is actually sinful thoughts and tendencies that defile people rather than what they eat: "He went on: 'What comes out of a man is what makes him "unclean." For from within, out of men's hearts, come evil

TEMPLE TO CAESAR AUGUSTUS

The remains of a temple at Caesarea built by Herod in honor of the namesake of the city.

thoughts, sexual immorality, theft, murder, adultery, greed, malice, deceit, lewdness, envy, slander, arrogance and folly. All these evils come from inside and make a man "unclean"'" (Mark 7:20–25).

God now impresses the reality of this teaching of Jesus on Peter by means of this vision. Of course, this is a critical time. The Gentiles are now to be incorporated into the new people of God.

The Spirit said to him (10:19). From beginning to end, God has been directly involved in orchestrating this entire set of events. The direct guidance of the Spirit is characteristic of ministry in this new covenant era (Joel 2:28; Acts 2:17) and especially of the early Christian mission (see, e.g., Acts 13:2; 16:6).

He is a righteous . . . man (10:22). Cornelius is not "righteous" in the Pauline sense of justified before God. The expression here (*dikaios*) means that he is living as an observant Jew would live at that time by giving heed to and obeying the Mosaic law.[189]

Peter invited the men into the house to be his guests (10:23). Although it was not unlawful for Peter to host Gentile guests in the home, he certainly risks ritual defilement according to Jewish tradition. In general, Jews tried to minimize their contact with Gentiles. This is well illustrated by an exhortation given in the book of *Jubilees:*

> Separate yourself from the gentiles, and do not eat with them, and do not perform deeds like theirs. And do not become associates of theirs. Because their deeds are defiled, and all of their ways are contaminated, and despicable, and abominable (*Jub.* 22:16).

Peter's warm invitation to these men may indicate that he is beginning to understand what the Lord is teaching him about ritual impurity. The much greater test for him, however, will be to enter the home of a Gentile (see 10:25).

Brothers from Joppa went along (10:23). Six fellow Jewish believers from Joppa accompany Peter (see 11:12). This is significant because they will witness the Gentiles receiving the Holy Spirit and will be able to corroborate Peter's story to Jewish believers in Jerusalem.

CAESAREA

(left) Site of the ancient harbor.

(right) The Roman aqueduct.

▼

As Peter entered the house (10:25). In Jewish tradition, entering the home of a Gentile would render one ritually unclean. The Mishnah makes this clear: "The dwelling-places of Gentiles are unclean."[190] The fact that Peter enters the home of this Roman soldier is a big step for Peter and normally would have been an unusual surprise for these Gentiles. Yet God has prepared both Peter and Cornelius for this encounter.

Cornelius met him and fell at his feet in reverence (10:25). In Near Eastern cultures, prostrating oneself before a king or superior is a sign of great respect. The word *proskyneō* is often used "to designate the custom of prostrating oneself before a person and kissing his feet, the hem of his garment, the ground, etc."[191] But because Peter responds by saying, "Stand up, I am only a man," Cornelius probably looks on Peter as a divine messenger, an angel. The apostle John also responds to an angel in this fashion (Rev. 19:10; 22:8–9).

It is against our law for a Jew to associate with a Gentile or visit him (10:28). After being careful all of their lives not to associate with Gentiles in a way that would render them ritually impure, Peter and his six Jewish companions must face a deep inner turmoil. On the one hand, their consciences are sorely troubled by entering into this house and possibly defiling themselves, yet on the other hand, they have a strong awareness that God himself is directing them to do so.

Jews typically did not enter a Gentile home (even that of a God-fearer) because they did not practice the same level of caution as observant Jews did to ensure that only kosher foods were eaten and that they were prepared in the proper way. There was also always the risk that the home may have had a household idol or other trappings of pagan idolatry. The best way for a Jew to be protected was never to enter a Gentile home.[192]

God has shown me that I should not call any man impure or unclean (10:28). The vision demonstrates to Peter that the Torah distinction between clean and unclean animals no longer applies. He can now kill and eat an animal that has previously been regarded as ritually impure. As he has reflected on his vision over the past four days, he has recognized that one of the implications of this new divine decree is that *people* who are previously thought of as ritually defiled because they do not observe Jewish food laws are no longer to be regarded as impure. There is an entirely new situation for Gentiles (and for Jewish attitudes toward Gentiles) made possible by the coming of the Messiah.

Then Peter began to speak (10:34). Verses 34–43 consist of a summary of the message that Peter gives to Cornelius and all those who gathered at his home. In a real sense, the message is the summary of the heart of the preaching of the apostles (what has often been referred to as the *kerygma* ["the proclamation" of the apostles]). It also serves as a general outline to the contents of the four Gospels.

God does not show favoritism (10:34). According to Peter, God has never shown partiality toward one group of people over another. This is not a new idea in Judaism; it has always been in the Torah: "For the LORD your God is God of gods and Lord of lords, the great God, mighty and awesome, who shows no partiality and accepts no bribes" (Deut. 10:17; see also 2 Chron. 19:7). This was a truth that many Jews had lost sight of, including Peter. "Exclusivism as practiced by many first-century Judean Jews was a development of the intertestamental period that had gone beyond the intent of God."[193]

Accepts men from every nation who fear him and do what is right (10:35). The term "accepts" (*dekton*, more properly translated "acceptable") is used frequently in the context of the presentation of sacrifices in the worship of Israel. It was incumbent on worshipers to bring sacrifices that were "acceptable" to the Lord (see Lev. 1:3–4; 19:5). Practicing righteousness in a Jewish context was understood as observing the law, not simply in the sense of being a good person. This passage is clearly not teaching that fearing God and observing the law merits salvation, otherwise Peter's following sermon about the the work of Jesus and receiving forgiveness of sins through his name would be unnecessary. What Peter is expressing is that fearing God and seeking to follow his ways puts a person in an "acceptable state (of repentance) to hear and receive the message of salvation and release from sins."[194] Cornelius still needs salvation.[195]

You know the message God sent (10:36). Cornelius and his guests certainly have heard about Jesus and know something about what he has taught. How fascinating it would be to know what level of contact they may have had with Jesus and what kinds of reports they heard about him.

The good news of peace through Jesus Christ (10:36). The gospel is a message of peace with God, made possible not by achieving ritual purity through observing the law, but by the work of Jesus, the Messiah. This is a fulfillment of Isaiah 57:19, where a day is envisioned when it is declared, "Peace, peace, to those far and near." Peter alluded to this passage in his preaching on the day of Pentecost (see comments on Acts 2:39).

The Old Testament prophets envisioned "peace" (*šālôm*) in the messianic age. Peter's preaching here makes an allusion to the promise of Isaiah 52:7: "How beautiful on the mountains are the feet of those who bring good news, who proclaim peace, who bring good tidings, who proclaim salvation, who say to Zion, 'Your God reigns.'"

The Old Testament notion of peace goes well beyond a cessation of strife and war. It refers to a holistic sense of well-being and fulfillment. This depends on being in a close relationship with God, experiencing his gracious presence, finding strength and encouragement in him, and being free from his judgment and condemnation.[196]

You know what has happened throughout Judea (10:37). A more literal translation would be, "You know the word (or saying) about what has happened throughout Judea." The term *rhēma* ("word") is used here in a similar way to *logos* (which appears in 10:36) to refer to the account of the ministry, death, burial, and resurrection of Jesus. This is a common usage for *rhēma*, which cannot always be pressed to mean a spoken word.

God anointed Jesus of Nazareth (10:38). Peter's words here echo and fulfill Isaiah 61:1–2: "The Spirit of the Sovereign LORD is on me, because the LORD has anointed me to preach good news to the poor. He has sent me to bind up the brokenhearted, to proclaim freedom for the captives and release from darkness for the prisoners." Jesus read these words at the outset of his ministry when he spoke in the synagogue at Nazareth (Luke 4:17–21). The "anointing" occurred when the Spirit came on Jesus at his baptism by John and empowered him to carry out his work as God's deliverer.

Healing all who were under the power of the devil (10:38). The "freedom for the captives" and "release from darkness for the prisoners" referred to in the prophecy of Isaiah 61:1 finds its fulfillment in the exorcisms of Jesus and in his death and resurrection. Both Jews and Gentiles alike have fallen under the sway of the evil one. Not all are demonized and in need of exorcism, but many have been blinded to the revelation of God through the deceiving work of the devil.

Because God was with him (10:38). The source of Jesus' power is not the devil or Beelzebub (as the Pharisees accuse him), nor is he claiming to be a shaman endowed with magical powers. The one true God is at work in and through Jesus of Nazareth.

We are witnesses of everything he did (10:39). This is the unique testimony that Peter (and the other eleven apostles) can provide. For three years they had watched Jesus, heard him speak on repeated occasions, received personal training and instruction from him, and saw him after he rose from the dead. This is why the teaching of the twelve apostles (see 2:42) is so important to the early church.

The country of the Jews (10:39). This refers to the areas of Galilee and Judea.

By hanging him on a tree (10:39). See comments on 5:30.

By us who ate and drank with him after he rose from the dead (10:41). The fact that Jesus took food "proves the physical reality of the body of the risen Jesus."[197] Luke describes this in much more detail at the end of his Gospel (see Luke 24:36–43). Jesus did not appear to the disciples as a bodiless spirit-being (as later Docetism and Gnosticism would teach).

God appointed as judge of the living and the dead (10:42). Jesus is not only the redeemer, but he is also the end-time judge (see also 17:31). Such is the right accorded to the "son of man" figure in

313

Acts

CAESAREA

(left) The south end of the hippodrome.

(right) The theater.

Daniel's prophecy: "He was given authority, glory and sovereign power; all peoples, nations and men of every language worshiped him" (Dan. 7:14).

The Holy Spirit came on all who heard the message (10:44). The Spirit comes on all of these Gentiles with visible and unmistakable signs (the speaking in tongues). In this instance, Peter does not lay his hands on them and ask God to impart the Spirit (as he and John had done for the Samaritans; see comments on 8:15). The Spirit comes spontaneously on them, presumably in response to their faith in the message about Jesus that Peter has just explained to them. Many scholars aptly refer to this event as "the Pentecost of the Gentiles."

The circumcised believers who had come with Peter were astonished (10:45). The Torah-observant Jews recognize the remarkable significance of this event. God is now accepting Gentiles on the same basis that he did the Jews—on the sole basis of believing in Jesus Christ for the forgiveness of sins. These Gentile believers will not be required to be circumcised, offer sacrifices, observe the Jewish festivals, or keep Jewish dietary laws as a means of entering or maintaining their position in the new people of God.

REFLECTIONS

SINCE GOD MAKES NO ETHNIC, CULTURAL, OR SOCIAL distinctions in his new community, we do not have the right to make them either. Unfortunately, the church has had a very difficult time learning this lesson. The church often returns to the boundary-making discrimination that characterized much of Judaism in Jesus' time. Since God shows no favoritism, work hard at breaking down the walls that may exist in your own heart toward others who are different.

Peter Reports to Jerusalem (11:1–18)

When Peter returns to Jerusalem, he is confronted by law-observant Jewish Christians concerned about his involvement with the Gentiles. Peter recounts to them and the Jerusalem church leaders all that happened, emphasizing God's clear direction.

The apostles and the brothers throughout Judea (11:1). Apparently the intensity of the persecution has subsided and some of the Jewish Christians have returned to live and minister in Jerusalem.

The circumcised believers (11:2). On the surface, it seems that this expression refers to all Jewish Christians living in Jerusalem since all male Jews are circumcised on the eighth day after their birth (this is the sense in 10:45). Yet here it appears to imply more. It refers to those Jewish believers in the Jerusalem church who are zealous for the law and want to uphold its requirements for all who believe. This includes the laws regulating purity and uncleanness as well as an insistence on circumcision. The apostle Paul later comes into conflict with this group during his ministry in Antioch of Syria. He describes how Peter succumbs to the influence of "the circumcision group" after some of their members arrive in that city. Paul becomes incensed when Peter begins refusing to eat with the Gentile believers (see Gal. 2:12). At this earlier stage, Peter is less conflicted about eating with Cornelius and his household and never hints that any of them should be circumcised. This may be due in part to Cornelius's sensitivity to have kosher meals prepared for his guests (since he is a God-fearer), but more importantly, it is probably due to the freshness of the vision God gives to Peter, which he now relates to the Jerusalem believers.

Ate with them (11:3). The complaint of these law-conscientious Jews focuses on Peter's entry into a Gentile house and eating with them, something not explicitly said in 10:48 but certainly implied. They cannot understand how Peter, a prominent leader of the church, could so flagrantly violate the law. Of course, they have not been given the vision Peter received nor have they been in Caesarea to witness the Gentiles' experience of the Spirit coming on them after they put their faith in Christ.

Peter began and explained everything to them (11:4). In verses 4–17, Luke summarizes the entire Cornelius episode that he has narrated in Acts 10. Repetition is a technique used by ancient writers to emphasize the importance of key events (see comments on Acts 10).

All your household will be saved (11:14). The Roman *familia* often consist of three generations living together. Cornelius may have had his parents and possibly even grandparents living with him in addition to his own children. The slaves are also considered an integral part of the household.[198]

You will be baptized with the Holy Spirit (11:16). John the Baptist proclaimed that Jesus would baptize his followers with the Holy Spirit (Luke 3:16), and Jesus himself reiterated this shortly before he ascended to heaven (Acts 1:5). This was fulfilled on the day of Pentecost for the Jewish believers. The episode of the Spirit's coming on the household of Cornelius—"as he had come on us at the

beginning" (11:15)—stresses that Jews and Gentiles now have equal access to the new covenant blessing of the Spirit solely on the basis of faith in Jesus Christ.

They had no further objections (11:18). After Peter carefully explains to them all that has happened and how God himself superintended these events, the rest of the apostles and possibly many from the circumcision group are satisfied. This only lasts for a time. A few years later, the circumcision group asserts the indispensibility of circumcision for salvation (see 15:1).

God has granted even the Gentiles repentance unto life (11:18). The Jerusalem leaders recognize that the events surrounding Cornelius are not an isolated exception. This event has wide-ranging implications that extend to the Gentiles as a class of people.

The Establishment of the Church in Antioch (11:19–30)

Luke now tells the story of the first major turning of Gentiles to the Christian faith. This takes place in Antioch, the capital city of the Roman province of Syria.

NIGHT IN MODERN JERUSALEM

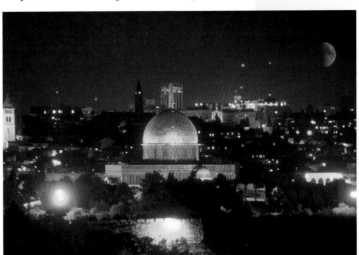

Those who had been scattered by the persecution (11:19). Luke told us earlier about this persecution (8:1, 4), which apparently led to thousands of Christians leaving Jerusalem. Some apparently traveled much further than Judea and Samaria.

Traveled as far as Phoenicia (11:19). Phoenicia was a stretch of land along the Mediterranean coast west of Damascus and belonging to the Roman province of Syria. Much of ancient Phoenicia today lies within the borders of Lebanon. The principal cities of Phoenicia were Acco, Aradus, Berytus, Byblos, Dora, Heliopolis, Ptolemais, Tyre, and Sidon. There is inscriptional evidence of Jewish settlements in a number of the Phoenician cities.[199] In a letter King Agrippa I wrote to the emperor Claudius, he referred to the presence of Jewish colonies in the land of Phoenicia and on the island of Crete.[200] The

southern portion of Phoenica lay seventy-five miles northwest of Jerusalem. The northern region of Phoenicia was about a hundred miles south of Antioch, Syria.

Cyprus (11:19). See comments on 13:4.

Men from Cyprus and Cyrene (11:20). Among the Jewish Christians in Jerusalem who were scattered by the persecution are some who originally came from the island of Cyprus and northern Africa. Roman Cyrenaica was due south of Greece across the Mediterranean Sea on the African continent. Luke is probably referring here to the Roman province of Cyrenaica rather than the city of Cyrene.

Began to speak to Greeks (11:20). These Greek-speaking Jewish Christians from the Diaspora make their way to the city of Antioch and take a bold step. Based on the

PHOENICIA

▼

▶ Antioch on the Orontes

Nearly three hundred miles north of Jerusalem in the province of Syria was a city—Antioch on the Orontes—that became a major center for Christianity as it spread to the Gentile world.[A-48] Antioch was the third largest city in the Roman empire with a population between a quarter and a half-million people.[A-49] The city also had a sizeable Jewish population, estimated between thirty and fifty thousand.[A-50]

The city lay in a fertile plain near the foot of Mount Silpius with the Orontes river flowing through it and continuing on a distance of fifteen miles to the sea. Antioch was a major junction for roads coming from the east (Aleppo), the south (the Lebanon, Damascus, and Palestine), and the north (Tarsus and the whole of Anatolia). At the mouth of the river, it was served by its port city, Seleucia Pieria.

About five miles south of the city at the natural springs supplying water to the city was a famous

park called Daphne where there was a sanctuary dedicated to the god Apollo. A variety of ecstatic rites were held there in the name of this deity.

There was a period of significant hostility against the Jews in the summer of A.D. 38. Many Jews were killed and their synagogues were burned. In response, the Jewish high priest in Jerusalem (Phineas) retaliated by sending thirty thousand men to Antioch attacking and killing many Gentiles in the city. The trouble only ended once the emperor intervened.[A-51]

Antioch had a bad reputation for its morality. A passage in Juvenal bemoans the influence Antioch had on Rome: "The waters of Syrian Orontes flowed into the Tiber." Yet it was through this city that God worked to spread the good news of salvation throughout the empire.

precedent set by Peter, which they have undoubtedly heard about, they begin to proclaim the gospel directly to the non-Jewish Greek-speakers of Antioch.

Luke does not tell us if these Gentiles are predominantly God-fearers linked to the synagogues of the sizeable Jewish population in Antioch or if they are Gentiles with virtually no exposure to Judaism and still adherents of the local religions. If they preach primarily to Gentile God-fearers, it is only a matter of time until more Gentiles—friends, family members, and neighbors of the initial wave—respond to the gospel. Most of these people turn to Christ from adherence to Apollo, Artemis, Zeus, Tyche, or the Syrian cults of Baal and the mother goddess—some of the popular deities of the city. We can safely assume that a good number of the Jews in the city also turn to Christ during this period.

The Lord's hand was with them (11:21). "The hand of the Lord" is a common Old Testament metaphor for the manifestation of God's presence and power. The "hand of the LORD" was on Elijah (1 Kings 18:46) and Elisha (2 Kings 3:15), enabling them to do amazing feats. Ezra experienced the power and blessing of "the hand of the LORD" on his life. Luke says that "the hand of the Lord" was with John the Baptist (Luke 1:66). Clearly to Luke the outreach efforts of these Hellenistic Jewish Christians cannot be explained in any way other than God's being with them and blessing their efforts.

They sent Barnabas to Antioch (11:22). When news of the conversion of these Gentiles reaches Jerusalem, they send Barnabas both to investigate what they are hearing and to facilitate the work there. Luke does not tell us why Peter does not travel to Antioch. The apostles

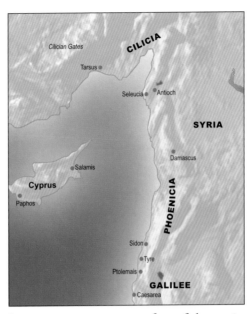

have a great amount of confidence in Barnabas. Like some of the Jewish-Christian evangelists that go to Antioch, Barnabas is also originally from Cyprus (see comments on 4:36). The fact that the apostles send Barnabas indicates that, at least to some degree, they feel a responsibility to exercise a level of leadership for the movement, especially to ensure the ongoing unity of the church. Upon arriving, Barnabas finds ample evidence that God has been powerfully at work

REFLECTIONS

CHURCH LEADERS OFTEN SPEND a great deal of time and effort searching for new strategies for doing effective outreach in their communities. Books, conferences, and seminars present a variety of models for reaching a neighborhood with the gospel. Luke reminds us here that it is not so much the strategy that is most important, but the work of God. In doing outreach, our greatest concern should be, "Is the hand of the Lord with us?"

bringing these Gentiles to himself. There is no hint that Barnabas criticizes any facet of the work there. Rather, he rejoices and joins with the brothers in proclaiming the gospel and teaching the new Gentile believers.

Barnabas went to Tarsus to look for Saul (11:25). As numerous people begin turning to Christ and as Barnabas sees the potential for continued effective outreach, his thoughts turn to Saul. Here is a man who was trained as a rabbi and extremely competent in the Scripture, who was able to argue effectively and proclaim the gospel in Greek, and most importantly, who had received a commission from the Lord to reach the Gentiles. Barnabas was one of the first Jerusalem disciples to believe in the authenticity of Saul's conversion and confidently introduced him to the apostles (9:27). Because of the danger to his life in Jerusalem, Saul's fellow believers helped him leave the city safely so he could go to Tarsus in Cilicia. There he remained proclaiming Christ in his home region.

With Tarsus being over a hundred miles away, Barnabas's trip takes many days. The difficulty is compounded by the fact that he does not know precisely where Saul is. The word translated "to look for" (*anazēteō*) implies the search entails some difficulty. It is often used in the context of hunting for criminals or fugitive slaves.[201] But Barnabas successfully locates Saul and is able to convince him to join him in the work at Antioch.

For a whole year Barnabas and Saul met with the church (11:26). This may mean that Barnabas and Saul work together for a year in the church before they travel to Jerusalem on their famine relief visit (c. A.D. 44–45). It is more likely, however, that Barnabas had Saul come to Antioch much earlier (c. A.D. 39). In this case, they spend a year working intensively with believers in Antioch and then Paul or both of them journey to other cities in Syria where they proclaim the gospel and plant churches,

Circus

Palace

Orontes River

Eastern Gate

Tetrapylon

Nympheum

Theatre of Caesar

Street of Herod and Tiberius

Mt. Silpius

Amphitheatre

Jewish Community

Road to Seleucia

To Daphne

while maintaining their involvement with Antioch. They most likely reach the principal Syrian cities of Seleucia Pieria, Apameia, and Laodicea as well as other towns and villages in the province.[202]

The disciples were called Christians first at Antioch (11:26). Disciples, believers, servants of Christ, those who are "in Christ," saints, and followers of "the Way" are some of the ways Christians refer to themselves in this early period. It appears that the term "Christians" (*christianoi*) was created by non-Christians in Antioch as a way of distinguishing them from Jews (and possibly other religious groups). In the only other places in the New Testament where the term is used, it is used by non-Christians referring to the followers of Jesus (26:28; 1 Peter 4:16). The name itself is formed on the analogy of "Herodians" (*herodiani*—the adherents and clients of the house of Herod; see Matt. 22:16) and *caesariani* (the servants of Caesar). For these new believers in Antioch, however, the new designation reveals their allegiance to the Messiah (*christos*), Jesus of Nazareth. The very fact that the local population coins a name for this new movement attests to its growth in the city. The new name for believers apparently becomes a popular self-designation only in the period after the New Testament attests, interestingly, by Ignatius, a famous church leader from Antioch.

Prophets came down from Jerusalem to Antioch (11:27). The gift of prophecy was commonly practiced in the early church. Luke specifically names Agabus (11:28; 21:10), Judas and Silas (15:32), the four daughters of Philip (21:8–9),

> ## ▸ The City of Antioch
> ## IMPORTANT FACTS:
>
> - Population: about 300,000 (the third largest city in the Roman empire)
> - Religions: Apollo, Artemis, Isis, Zeus, Tyche, the Syrian cults of Baal, the mother goddess, Judaism, the emperor cult (in addition to many other gods and goddesses)
> - Commercial Importance: agriculture (esp. grain, olives, and grapes), trade between East and West
> - Political Importance: a free city, but under Roman rule, capital of the Roman province of Syria
> - Cultural Importance: became the center for the spread of Christianity to non-Jews

▸ How Long Was Saul in Tarsus and Then in Antioch?

An accurate chronology of Saul's first seventeen years as a believer (c. A.D. 33–49) is difficult to construct. He does not write any letters during this period and only makes a handful of references to this time in his later letters (especially in Gal. 1–2). Luke gives only a few details that can help. Fortunately, we are on much firmer ground for putting together an accurate chronology for the period following the Jerusalem council until his imprisonment in Rome (A.D. 49–62).

Estimates for how long Saul was in Tarsus range from three years (A.D. 36–39) to ten years (A.D. 37–47). Similarly, estimates for how long he ministered in Antioch and in Syria range from ten years (A.D. 39–49) to one to two years (A.D. 47–49).[A-52]

If the mission of the Hellenistic Jewish Christians to Antioch began early (c. A.D. 36 or 37) and Barnabas went there a short time later, it is more convincing to think of Barnabas looking for Paul's help within a year after his arrival.

▶**The Anti-Jewish Upheaval in** A.D. **38–41**

During the infant years of the church at Antioch (which began in A.D. 36 or 37), a horrible tempest of hostility toward Jews raged in Alexandria and spilled over into Palestine and Syria. In the autumn of A.D. 38, mobs of citizens in Alexandria, Egypt, took part in a bloody rampage against the Jewish inhabitants of that city. Many Jews were tortured and killed, synagogues, homes, and businesses were destroyed, and numerous other atrocities were perpetrated against the Jews. Much of the crisis was sparked by the emperor Gaius Caligula's insistence that he be worshiped as a god.[A-53]

The conflict spread to Judea in late A.D. 39 when Caligula arrogantly ordered the Syrian governor P. Petronius to set up his image in the Jerusalem temple. The Jews were horrified and threatened all-out war against the Roman forces if the abominable act was carried out. Fortunately, Petronius defied Caligula's orders and, before the emperor could respond, the emperor was assassinated.[A-54]

In Antioch at roughly the same time (A.D. 39–40), Gentile hostility toward Jews boiled over into violence. Many Jews were killed and their synagogues burned down. According to the *Chronicle* of Malalas, when news of this reached Jerusalem, the high priest Phineas dispatched an army of thirty thousand Jews who traveled to Antioch and attacked and killed many Gentiles in the city. The emperor then intervened and had Phineas beheaded.[A-55]

Nevertheless, in spite of this uproar, the church at Antioch—consisting of Jews and Gentiles in one unified community—continued to grow significantly. It was during this period that the apostle Paul came and began to serve the church with Barnabas.

and leaders of the church at Antioch (13:1). Paul speaks extensively about prophecy in 1 Corinthians 14 and teaches that prophets, together with the apostles, have laid the foundation of the early church (Eph. 2:20). Two early Christian writings have much to say about how to discern a false prophet.[203] Among the criteria mentioned are: Does he exibit the Lord's ways? Does he ask for money? Is his life inconsistent with his prophecies? Is he gentle, quiet, and humble? Does he refrain from evil? Hermas warns that the false prophet is actually inspired by a spirit from the devil.[204]

Agabus (11:28). Luke singles out one of the prophets and mentions him by name, possibly because of his accurate predictions. He not only prophesies the impending famine, but thirteen years later in Caesarea prophesies Paul's arrest in Jerusalem (21:10–11). Because he appears in one of the "we" sections of Acts, Luke meets him personally. We know nothing else about this important figure in the early church.

Through the Spirit predicted (11:28). Luke clearly sees that one important aspect of prophecy is prediction. Receiving inspiration from the Holy Spirit of God, the prophet simply declares what he hears. The New Testament prophet did not need to descend into an oracle chamber, invoke the deity with any kind of formula or incantation, go into an ecstatic

◄

TARSUS

The Cleopatra gate.

trance, observe a period of taboos, or go through any preparatory ritual.

A severe famine would spread over the entire Roman world (11:28). There is abundant ancient evidence attesting food shortages and greatly inflated food prices during the reign of Claudius (see below).[205] The word translated "famine" in this verse (*limos*) can also mean "death" or "severe shortage."[206] Obviously Antioch is not affected as badly as Jerusalem and Judea, otherwise they would not have been able to provide substantial help.

Rome began to experience a scarcity of food in the winter of A.D. 40–41, the beginning of Claudius's reign. This general disruption in the food supply is attributed to declines in the production of grain in Egypt, the principal grain supplier for Rome and much of the Mediterranean region. Crop failures in Egypt grew particularly severe in the period of A.D. 45–47.[207] One writer indicates that the crisis was felt in all of Syria in A.D. 44.[208]

But Jerusalem and Judea were the hardest hit of all during this time. This was exacerbated by still other factors. When the emperor Gaius Caligula ordered

◄

ROMAN STREET IN TARSUS

A recently excavated cardo in the city.

his statue to be erected in the Jerusalem temple in late A.D. 39, the Jews refused to plant their crops.[209] Indeed, they were ready to die rather than allow their temple to be profaned. The next year was a sabbatical year, which kept their ground out of production and intensified the food shortage. Just three years later, in A.D. 44–45, Judea strongly felt the adverse effects of the more general food shortage and the resultant exorbitant prices for grain that was in short supply and in high demand.

Of course the Jewish Christians in Jerusalem, ostracized from the temple and any official relief efforts tied to the temple, were especially vulnerable. Now more than ever they needed to depend on the generosity and true fellowship of the larger Christian community.

This happened during the reign of Claudius (11:28). Claudius reigned from January 15, A.D. 41 to October 13, A.D. 54, assuming power at the age of fifty immediately after the assassination of Caligula. His full name is Tiberius Claudius Nero Germanicus. Suetonius says of Claudius that, "nearly the whole of his childhood and youth was so troubled by various diseases that he grew dull-witted and had little physical strength; and on reaching the age at which he should have won a magistracy or chosen a private career, was considered by his family incapable of doing either."[210] He was made emperor by the Roman army against his will in a comical series of events. He ruled

BUST OF THE
EMPEROR
CLAUDIUS

Roman Emperors	
Emperor	**Date of Reign**
Octavian "Augustus"	31 B.C.–A.D. 14
Tiberius	14–37
Gaius "Caligula"	37–41
Claudius	41–54
Nero	54–68

▶ Ancient Testimony About the Great Famine

Among the ancient accounts of food shortages during the reign of Claudius, two are rather striking. The first, by the Roman historian Suetonius, illustrates the severity of the food shortage in Rome: "Once, after a series of droughts had caused a scarcity of grain, a mob stopped Claudius in the Forum and pelted him so hard with curses and stale crusts that he had difficulty in regaining the Palace by a side-door; as a result he took all possible steps to import grain, even during the winter months— insuring merchants against the loss of their ships in stormy weather."[A-56]

In the second account, the Jewish historian Josephus tells of how Queen Helena of Adiabene (a small kingdom in north Mesopotamia) came to the aid of Jews in Jerusalem in A.D. 44. Helena and her son, King Izates, had just converted to Judaism. This passage shows that some food was available for those who had the money to purchase it: "Now her coming was of very great advantage to the people of Jerusalem; for whereas a famine did oppress them at that time, and many people died for want of what was necessary to procure food withal, Queen Helena sent some of her servants to Alexandria with money to buy a great quantity of corn, and others of them to Cyprus, to bring a cargo of dried figs; and as soon as they were come back, and brought those provisions, which was done very quickly, she distributed food to those that were in want of it, and left a most excellent memorial behind her of this benefaction, which she bestowed on our whole nation; and when her son Izates was informed of this famine, he sent great sums of money to the principal men in Jerusalem."[A-57] for many years, however, and was the emperor responsible for the expulsion of Jews from Rome in A.D. 49.

Each according to his ability, decided to provide help (11:29). The way the community responded to the need is similar to the way Paul encouraged the church in Corinth to give for a subsequent collection.[211]

To the elders (11:30). One might expect the funds from Antioch to be taken to Jerusalem and laid at the feet of the apostles (4:35, 37; 5:2). In the decade that has elapsed since the beginning of the Jerusalem church, a leadership structure emerges that worked in conjunction with the unique authority of the twelve apostles. Following the pattern of the local synagogues, the early Christians identified leaders for their household groups and retained the name "elders" (*presbyteroi*). They probably retained many facets of the role and function of elders in the synagogue structure. Luke does not tell us how the elders related to the apostles or the seven, nor does he indicate whether there was a higher group of elders serving as leaders of the entire collection of churches in Jerusalem and Judea. This latter idea could follow from the fact that there were elders over the Jewish people in the Holy Land (see 4:5, 8, 23). By this time, many of the apostles may have already left Jerusalem to proclaim Jesus as the Messiah in distant cities.

Chronology of the Early Years of Saul of Tarsus		
Year	Event	Location of Saul
33	• conversion of Saul	
34	• Saul in Damascus and Arabia (36–39?)	Saul in Damascus and Arabia
35	• conversion of Cornelius (?)	
36	• Saul visits Peter in Jerusalem • Jewish-Christian mission to Antioch	Saul in Tarsus and Cilicia
37		
38	• Barnabas goes to Antioch	
39	• Barnabas gets Saul	Saul in Antioch and Syria
40		
41		
42		
43	• Death of James, the apostle	
44	• Death of Agrippa I	
45		
46	• Jerusalem collection visit	
47	• 1st Missionary Journey	1st Missionary Journey
48		
49	• Council at Jerusalem	

Sending their gift . . . by Barnabas and Saul (11:30). This is the second time Saul travels to Jerusalem after his conversion. The previous time was three years after his conversion for the purpose of becoming acquainted with Peter (see comments on Acts 9:26 and Gal. 1:18). Now, between eight and ten years later, he goes again as an emissary of the church at Antioch to bring relief.

There is much discussion among Bible scholars as to whether this is the visit that Saul/Paul refers to in Galatians 2:1–10 or whether the Galatian passage describes his next visit for the Jerusalem council. The weightier arguments are in favor of identifying this famine-relief visit with the details Paul describes in Galatians 2:1–10,

not least because the results of the council decision are not communicated in Galatians. This reconstruction also fits better with the overall sequence of events Paul describes in Galatians 1–2.[212]

If this is the case, Paul uses this same time to "set before [the authorities in Jerusalem] the gospel that I preach among the Gentiles" (Gal. 2:2). Apparently some dissension has already surfaced with a handful of law-observant Jewish Christians who have gone to Antioch to investigate how faithful Paul and the Antioch believers are to the law, presumably circumcision, purity regulations, and observance of Jewish festivals and rites (Gal. 2:4). Paul raises this issue with the leadership of the Jerusalem church in an informal way, and they reaffirm Paul and Barnabas in their work among the Gentiles (Gal. 2:9).

Herod Agrippa I Persecutes the Church (12:1–25)

This chapter dramatically portrays the power of God working to ensure the success of the church and its mission despite violent opposition. God directly intervenes by sending an angel to free the apostle Peter from his imprisonment and stems the persecution by striking down the king of the land. Herod the Great murdered the innocent children of Bethlehem to oppose God's work; now his descendant embarks on a murderous tirade against the leaders of the church.

King Herod (12:1). This is not Herod the Great who ruled Israel at the time of the birth of Jesus. This is his grandson, Herod Agrippa I.[213] Agrippa's father is Aristobulus, son of Mariamne, the favorite of Herod the Great's many wives. Born in 10 B.C., Agrippa's father was killed when Agrippa was three years

The House of Herod	
Herod the Great	• ruled Palestine from 37 B.C.–4 B.C.
Herod Archelaus	• son of Herod the Great and Malthace • ruled Judea from 4 B.C.–A.D. 6; following his oppressive reign, Roman governors ruled Judea
Herod Antipas	• son of Herod the Great and Malthace • ruled Galilee and Perea as a "tetrarch" from 4 B.C.–A.D. 39
Herod Philip	• son of Herod the Great and Cleopatra of Jerusalem; half-brother of Antipas • ruled the northern portion of Herod the Great's domain (Gaulanitis, Auranitis, Batanea, Trachonitis, Paneas, and Iturea) from 4 B.C.–A.D. 34
Herod Agrippa I	• grandson of Herod the Great • grew up in Rome with future emperor Claudius • ruled Palestine from A.D. 41–44
Agrippa II	• son of Agrippa I and Cypros • ruled Palestine from A.D. 50 through the Jewish War (A.D. 66–70) • because he sided with the Romans during the war, the emperor Vespasian bestowed on him rulership over all his previous realm (A.D. 75–100) • his death ended the Herodian family

◀ *left*

violent action against the church is not clear. Verse 3 may indicate that he is sensitive to the denunciation of the messianic sect by his fellow Jews and seeks to please them by his actions. The most effective way of dealing with this new group is through robbing it of its leaders.

He had James, the brother of John, put to death with the sword (12:2). This is James, the son of Zebedee, one of the twelve apostles. He is the first of the Twelve to die for the cause of Christ. This is the last time John is mentioned in the book of Acts. According to church tradition, the apostle John at some point moved to the capital city of Asia Minor, Ephesus, where he served the church for many years and from where he wrote his three letters and his Gospel.[215] "With the sword" probably indicates that James is beheaded. This was the tradition in church history.[216] It was a common Roman form of execution.[217] It also illustrates the extent of authority Agrippa had been granted by Rome, that is, to use "the law of the sword" (*ius gladii*).[218] It is important to recall that Jesus told James and John that they would share his "cup" and share his "baptism" (referring to his martyr's death) when they quarreled over

old because of the irrational suspicions of Herod the Great. Agrippa was raised in Rome where he grew up with Claudius, the future emperor, and Drusus, son of the emperor Tiberius. His imperial connections served him well later in life. Because of lavish spending, he returned to Palestine as a poor man and held no significant position of power until Gaius Caligula became emperor in A.D. 37. Because Agrippa earlier endeared himself to Caligula, the new emperor gave him the title "king" and put him in charge of territory in northern Palestine. After the death of Herod Antipas in A.D. 39, Caligula added Galilee and Perea to his domain. When his childhood friend Claudius became emperor in A.D. 41, Agrippa's kingdom was extended to include Judea and Samaria. He ruled as a client king over Israel for a little over three years (A.D. 41–44).

The Pharisees appreciated Agrippa both because he was a descendant of the Hasmoneans (through his mother) and because he scrupulously kept Jewish customs. Josephus says, "He loved to live continually at Jerusalem, and was exactly careful in the observance of the laws of his country. He therefore kept himself entirely pure: nor did any day pass over his head without its appointed sacrifice."[214]

Arrested some who belonged to the church, intending to persecute them (12:1). What motivates Agrippa to take

Four "James" in the Early Church	
James, the father of Judas	• his son, Judas, was one of the twelve apostles (Luke 6:16; Acts 1:13)
James, the son of Alphaeus	• one of the twelve apostles (Luke 6:15; Acts 1:13)
James, the brother of John	• the son of Zebedee (Luke 5:10; 9:28, 54) • one of the twelve apostles (Acts 1:13) • killed by Herod Agrippa (Acts 12:2)
James, the brother of the Lord	• half-brother of the Lord Jesus; son of Mary and Joseph (Acts 12:17; 15:13; 21:18; 1 Cor. 15:7; Gal. 1:19; 2:9, 12; James 1:1; Jude 1)

who would sit at Jesus' right hand and his left (Mark 10:39). Jesus' words are now fulfilled for James.

This pleased the Jews (12:3). The Sanhedrin, the elders of the people, and many Jews living in Jerusalem and Judea continue in their hostile attitudes toward the followers of Jesus. This encourages Agrippa to follow through with his violent intentions toward the church.

The Feast of Unleavened Bread (12:3). This is one of the great pilgrim festivals of Judaism that swelled the population of Jerusalem from a hundred thousand upward to a million people.[219] The Feast of Unleavened Bread occurred in conjunction with the celebration of Passover. Commemorating the Exodus from Egypt and the miraculous deliverance of the first-born Israelite children, Passover was celebrated every spring beginning on the thirteenth day of Nisan with the slaughter of the lamb and the taking of the Passover meal (on the evening of the fourteenth day). The Feast of Unleavened Bread began on the next day and was celebrated for seven consecutive days (see Ex. 12–13). During this period, leaven (or yeast) was avoided altogether as a reminder of the haste with which God's people fled Egypt.

Four squads of four soldiers each (12:4). Luke relates the high level of security placed on Peter. This is not suprising since stories of the arrest and previous escape of the apostles are probably known to Agrippa (see comments on 5:17–42). These are most likely Roman soldiers and not the temple guard. It was common Roman procedure to have four squads of soldiers keep watch in succession throughout the night. One Roman writer explains, "And because it used to seem impossible for sentries to maintain successful watches, the watches therefore were divided into four parts by the waterclock, so that it not be necessary to stand watch for more than three night-time hours."[220]

Herod intended to bring him out for public trial after the Passover (12:4). The text literally says, "To bring him up to the people after the Passover." There has been some debate as to whether this implies a trial or simply a public execution. Regardless of whether Agrippa plans some half-hearted attempt at a public hearing or not, the intent is clear based on how he handles James: Peter's life will end immediately after Passover. Significantly, it is Passover some ten years previously that Jesus faced a farce of a trial and his death (see Luke 22:1–2).

Peter was kept in prison (12:5). Although Luke does not explicitly state what prison, most scholars think it was probably in the Fortress of Antonia.

The church was earnestly praying to God for him (12:5). News of the imprisonment of Christians, the death of James, and now the impending execution of Peter grips believers throughout Jerusalem and Judea. They respond by meeting in homes and praying fervently and passionately for one of their beloved leaders.

Between two soldiers, bound with two chains (12:6). There is variation in the manner of chaining prisoners, but at night, as Lucian reports, the prisoner "had to be fully secured by his bonds."[221] On the last night prior to his execution, God intervenes in a dramatic and unmistakable way: An angel enters the prison and releases Peter.

He struck Peter on the side (12:7). Deep in sleep, Peter is not roused by the illu-mination of the cell caused by the presence of the angel of the Lord. The angel does more than nudge Peter to wake him; the word for "struck" (*patassō*) suggests a strong blow. The word is often used in contexts where one is struck in a fight, such as when Moses struck down the Egyptian (Ex. 2:12).

The iron gate leading to the city (12:10). One exit of the Antonia Fortress led to the temple; the other led into the city. An addition in the manuscript tradition inserts, "They went down seven steps" (Codex D). Most scholars agree that this likely reflects an authentic historical reminiscence, but since the Antonia Fortress was totally destroyed in the Jewish war, it is difficult to verify this information.

From everything the Jewish people were anticipating (12:11). Shortly after Pentecost, the Christians in Jerusalem are "enjoying the favor of all the people"

R E F L E C T I O N S

IT IS DIFFICULT TO UNDERSTAND WHY GOD MIR-aculously intervened to save Peter, but did not do so to rescue James from the murderous hands of Agrippa. Luke makes no direct attempt to address this question here, yet it is a question that we ask from time to time when a loved one is taken from this world. Part of the answer lies in perspective. This life is only a temporary and partial experience of what God has in store. There is another place, far better, where Jesus himself has gone after he suffered an excruciatingly painful death (Acts 1:11). Stephen received a glimpse of this new existence when "heaven was opened," and he saw Jesus just prior to his own unjust murder (Acts 7:55–56). Peter was given an additional thirty years to live. For him, these years were dedicated to serving his Lord in flareups of suffering, but with the anticipation of "an inheritance that can never perish, spoil or fade—kept in heaven for you" (1 Peter 1:4).

(2:47). Over the last decade, the tide of opinion has changed dramatically.

He went to the house of Mary (12:12). This is the first and only reference in the New Testament to this Mary, the mother of John Mark. It is noteworthy that no mention is made of her husband. Perhaps he has died or possibly has not become a Christian.[222] Mary must be one of the wealthier members of the church. The passage suggests that she owns a sizeable home—it was large enough to host a considerable gathering of people to pray and it had an outer courtyard with a gate (see "The 'Cenacle'" at 1:13).[223] The forecourt is reminiscent of the high priest's house (Matt. 26:71).

This is further evidence that the Jerusalem church met in a network of homes throughout the city. The entire church of Jerusalem was clearly not present since Peter later instructs those present to tell James and the brothers about his miraculous release (12:17). How

many believers are still in Jerusalem at this time is difficult to know. At one point there are thousands (see Acts 2:41; 4:4), but then the violent persecution hits that forced virtually all but the apostles to leave the city (Acts 8:2–3). Apparently many have returned.

John, also called Mark (12:12). Luke here introduces a young man who will become a significant figure in the book of Acts and early Christianity. Like Saul/Paul, he has both a Jewish name (John) and a Roman name (Mark). Paul identifies him as the cousin of Barnabas (Col. 4:10). After returning from Jerusalem to Antioch with Paul and Barnabas, he became one of their missionary traveling companions (Acts 12:25; 13:5). For some unstated reason, he left them in the middle of their journey and returned to Jerusalem (13:13). This led to a sharp disagreement between Paul and Barnabas over Mark's suitability for ongoing missionary service—an irresolvable dis-

---

▶ John Mark in Later Church History

Among other achievements, Mark is credited with writing the second Gospel and preaching the gospel in Egypt.

Regarding the Gospel, Eusebius says: "When, at Rome, Peter had openly preached the word and by the spirit had proclaimed the gospel, the large audience urged Mark, who had followed him for a long time and remembered what had been said, to write it all down. This he did, making his Gospel available to all who wanted it."[A-58] Papias, a church leader in Hierapolis (Asia Minor), reaffirms this tradition and describes Mark as "Peter's interpreter" who "wrote down accurately everything he remembered,

though not in order, of the things either said or done by Christ."[A-59]

According to Eusebius, after Mark writes his Gospel, he travels to Rome where he proclaims the gospel and is "the first to establish churches in Alexandria."[A-60] It is highly unlikely that Mark is the first to establish churches there. As with Rome, Christianity probably gains its initial foothold in Egypt shortly after the outpouring of the Spirit in Jerusalem on the day of Pentecost. The widespread character of the tradition that Mark ministers in Egypt, however, lends to its credibility.[A-61] agreement that led to each of these leaders going separate ways (15:37–41). Whatever misgivings Paul has about Mark later evaporated, for Paul instructed Timothy to "get Mark and bring him with you, because he is helpful to me in my ministry" (2 Tim. 4:11).

A servant girl named Rhoda (12:13). Her name means "rose." It is a name that is well-attested in Greek, found in inscriptions naming women from Athens, Miletus, Mysia (Asia Minor), and Antioch.[224] It is doubtful that she is a literal slave. The term *paidiskē*, here translated "servant," can mean a "young woman."[225]

It must be his angel (12:15). When those in the prayer meeting hear Rhoda's exclamation of who is at the door, they do not believe her and some think it is Peter's angel. Many Jews believed in the notion of an angel who was closely associated with a person and could even take on that person's appearance. Note the book of Tobit, where the angel Raphael took on the disguise of Azarias (a relative of Tobit's) and became a guide for Tobit's son, Tobias (Tobit 5:4–16). Jesus himself spoke of angels associated with children: "See that you do not look down on one of these little ones. For I tell you that their angels in heaven always see the face of my Father in heaven" (Matt. 18:10). This led to a belief in the church about angels assigned to people for their lifetimes and who from time to time intervene on their behalf.[226]

Tell James (12:17). James, the son of Zebedee, has been executed by Agrippa. This refers to James, the brother of the Lord. The Gospels say little about this James. In fact, together with the rest of his siblings, he exhibits concern about

Jesus' activities and teaching at the outset of his ministry—"he is out of his mind" (Mark 3:21). Apparently after Jesus' death and resurrection, James has a massive change of heart, perhaps triggered by Jesus' personal appearance to him (1 Cor. 15:7). At the beginning of Acts, he and his brothers are portrayed as joining together with the apostles in prayer as they await the promised outpouring of the Holy Spirit (Acts 1:14). Throughout the early years of the church, James stayed in Jerusalem and became a significant leader in the church. He helped the church navigate its way through the difficult issues handled in the Jerusalem council.[227] The Jewish historian Josephus refers to James in one passage: "James, the brother of Jesus, who was called the Christ."[228]

Then he left for another place (12:17). Luke is deliberately vague about where Peter goes. This is a signal in the narrative that Peter's story, though unfinished, will no longer occupy Luke's attention in the development of his account of the spread of the gospel.[229] The most pressing concern for Peter (and for the church) is for Peter to escape to a place where Herod cannot harm him.

Ordered that they be executed (12:19). According to the Code of Justinian, guards faced the same punishment that the escaped prisoner was sentenced to receive.[230]

To Caesarea (12:19). On Caesarea, see comments on 10:1.

He had been quarreling with the people of Tyre and Sidon (12:20). This is the only ancient account of this conflict. Josephus is silent about it. Presumably it had something to do with the food supply to the cities.

Tyre and Sidon were the principal cities in the territory of Phoenicia and, in the Roman era, were under the jurisdiction of the Roman governor of Syria. Both were coastal cities. Tyre was a little over fifty miles north of Caesarea, whereas Sidon was about twenty miles north of Tyre.

Blastus, a trusted personal servant of the king (12:20). Blastus is otherwise unknown in any accounts of Herod Agrippa.

They depended on the king's country for their food supply (12:20). Phoenicia relied heavily on Galilee for its supply of food. This was true a thousand years earlier when Solomon supplied Hiram, king of Tyre, with wheat and olive oil year after year (2 Kings 5:9–12; see also Ezek. 27:17). Because of the famine afflicting Judea, the need in Tyre and Sidon was particularly acute.

Herod, wearing his royal robes (12:21). Josephus provides a much fuller and par-

---

▶The Missionary Travels of Peter

Based on other passages in the New Testament letters, it appears that Peter began a period of widespread missionary activity. Where he went immediately, we do not know, but he was back in Jerusalem for a brief period in A.D. 46, where he met with Saul during the famine relief visit (Gal. 2:9). He was in Antioch of Syria not much later where he ran into conflict with Paul (Gal. 2:11–15) and was back in Jerusalem in A.D. 49 for the Jerusalem council. Some have suggested that he may have even visited Corinth sometime between A.D. 52–55 on the basis of a faction in Corinth that claimed they were "of Cephas" (1 Cor. 1:12). The origin of this group, however, could be explained on other grounds.

According to 1 Corinthians 9:5 (written in A.D. 54/55), Peter had a wife who accompanied him in his missionary travels. He must have spent considerable time in northern and central Asia Minor (the provinces of Pontus, Galatia, Cappadocia, Asia, and Bithynia) since he addressed two letters to believers in these regions (1 and 2 Peter). It is doubtful that Peter ministered in Rome for any extended period of time in the 40s or 50s (although we cannot completely rule out a brief visit). When Paul wrote to the Roman church he never mentions Peter or alludes to any foundation-laying work that he had done there (see Rom. 15:20).[A-62] In A.D. 60–61, when Paul wrote his so-called captivity letters, there is no mention of Peter or inclusion of any greetings from Peter.

At some point, probably in the early 60s, Peter did journey to Rome and it was from there that he wrote his two letters. He cryptically refers to Rome in the first letter as "Babylon" (1 Peter 5:13). Eusebius reports that Peter and Paul were in Rome at the same time during this period and eventually lost their lives as martyrs under the Neronian persecution.[A-63]

allel account of the death of Agrippa I (see "Josephus's Account of the Death of Agrippa I"). According to Josephus, Herod appeared in front of the people early on a sunny morning wearing an unusual robe made entirely of silver. As the bright morning sun shone on the robe and reflected brightly off of it, Herod gleamed in dazzling splendor. The effect on the people was precisely as Herod intended. They acclaimed him as a god. This is certainly not unusual for the time. Emperors were often honored as gods after their deaths. Gaius Caligula, however, was at this time insisting that people worship him as a god during his reign. Herod sought no less an honor.

This is the voice of a god, not of a man (12:22). The gathered crowd (the *dē-mos*)—the citizens of Caesarea and possibly also including the delegations from Tyre and Sidon—begins to acclaim Agrippa as a divine being. Ironically, hun-

dreds of years earlier, the ruler of Tyre dared to consider himself a god. God warned him through the prophet Ezekiel that his insolence would lead to his sudden demise and death: "This is what the Sovereign LORD says: 'In the pride of your heart you say, "I am a god; I sit on the throne of a god in the heart of the seas." But you are a man and not a god, though you think you are as wise as a god. . . . Because you think you are wise, as wise as a god I am going to bring foreigners against you, the most ruthless of nations; they will draw their swords against your beauty and wisdom and pierce your shining splendor. They will bring you down to the pit, and you will die a violent death'" (Ezek. 28:2, 6–8). Many Jewish and Christian interpreters see in this prophetic oracle a deeper reference to the fall of Satan himself.

He was eaten by worms and died (12:23). Herod dies a gruesome and painful death. Josephus claims that he suffered five days before he died. The one and only true God utterly humiliates this arrogant earthly ruler, who has not only opposed the work of God on earth, but also dared to put himself in the place of God. There has been a variety of suggestions based on known afflictions involving worms to explain the nature of Herod's death. Luke's point, however, is that an angel strikes him down.

According to Josephus, Herod Agrippa dies three full years after the accession of Claudius.[231] This puts his death in A.D. 44.

But the word of God continued to increase and spread (12:24). The early church is facing incredible opposition. There is a severe famine in Judea, the Sanhedrin and Jewish leaders persecute believers and

◀ *left*

A KING'S THRONE

King Tut's throne in the Cairo Museum.

chase them out of Jerusalem, and now, the king of Palestine himself executes a principal leader of the movement and threatens more. Nevertheless, nothing will stop the spread of the Word of God. God himself intervenes in history to guide and protect his people as they carry out their divinely appointed task.

When Barnabas and Saul had finished their mission, they returned (12:25). This verse draws to conclusion Luke's brief account of the famine relief visit of Saul and Barnabas to Jerusalem (11:27–30). They return to Antioch taking John Mark with them.

Saul and Barnabas Are Commissioned (13:1–3)

As the church at Antioch is worshiping and seeking the Lord, the Holy Spirit clearly directs them to send two of their gifted leaders on an evangelistic mission.

▶ Josephus's Account of the Death of Agrippa I

Now, when Agrippa had reigned three years over all Judea, he came to the city Caesarea, which was formerly called Strato's Tower; and there he exhibited shows in honor of Caesar, upon his being informed that there was a certain festival celebrated to make vows for his safety. At which festival, a great multitude was gotten together of the principal persons, and such as were of dignity through his province.

On the second day of which shows he put on a garment made wholly of silver, and of a contexture truly wonderful, and came into the theatre early in the morning; at which time the silver of his garment being illuminated by the fresh reflection of the sun's rays upon it, shone out after a surprising manner, and was so resplendent as to spread a horror over those that looked intently upon him; and presently his flatterers cried out, one from one place, and another from another (though not for his good), that he was a god; and they added, "Be thou merciful to us; for although we have hitherto reverenced thee only as a man, yet shall we henceforth own thee as superior to mortal nature."

Upon this the king did neither rebuke them, nor reject their impious flattery. But, as he presently afterwards looked up, he saw an owl sitting on a certain rope over his head, and immediately understood that this bird was the messenger of ill tidings, as it had once been the messenger of good tidings to him; and fell into the deepest sorrow. A severe pain also arose in his belly, and began in a most violent manner.

He therefore looked upon his friends, and said, "I whom you call a god, am commanded presently to depart this life; while Providence thus reproves the lying words you just now said to me; and I, who was by you called immortal, am immediately to be hurried away by death. But I am bound to accept of what Providence allots as it pleases God; for we have by no means lived ill, but in a splendid and happy manner."

When he said this, his pain was become violent. Accordingly he was carried into the palace; and the rumor went abroad everywhere, that he would certainly die in a little time.

But the multitude presently sat in sackcloth, with their wives and children, after the law of their country, and besought God for the king's recovery. All places were also full of mourning and lamentation. Now the king rested in a high chamber, and as he saw them below lying prostrate on the ground, he could not himself forbear weeping. And when he had been quite worn out by the pain in his belly for five days, he departed this life, being in the fifty-fourth year of his age, and in the seventh year of his reign.[A-64]

This excursion takes about two years—A.D. 47–48.

There were prophets and teachers (13:1). This group of five apparently are the leaders of the church at Antioch. Luke describes them here in terms of their ministry function rather than simply "elders" (*presbyteroi;* see 11:30) or "overseers" (*episkopoi;* see 20:28). As teachers, they pass on the teachings of Jesus, tell the stories of his deeds and explain them, and teach and interpret the Old Testament in light of what has taken place in the ministry and work of Christ on the cross.

What is most notable about these five is their racial, cultural, and social diversity. Two are from northern Africa, one is from Cyprus, and the other is from Cilicia (Tarsus). Only one is from the Holy Land and not one is from Antioch or Syria. One is clearly from the upper class society of Palestine, while the others are from the Hellenistic Diaspora.

Barnabas (13:1). See comments on 4:6 and 11:22.

Simeon called Niger (13:1). *Niger* is the Latin term for "black" (the Greek term, not used here, is *melas*). This clearly implies that Simeon's complexion is darker than most Syrians. He probably comes from somewhere in northern Africa.

Lucius of Cyrene (13:1). The team of leaders in the church at Antioch includes another individual from northern Africa. Lucius is most likely one of the Hellenistic Jews, originally from Cyrene, who fled Jerusalem at the outbreak of the persecution and went to Antioch to proclaim the gospel to Gentiles (see 11:20). Although some think he may be the same Lucius that Paul refers to as his relative in Romans 16:21, there is no evidence to support this identification.

Manaen (who had been brought up with Herod the tetrarch) (13:1). Although Luke does not tell us where Manaen is from, he refers to his high social status. Manaen was raised as a foster-brother (*syntrophos*) of Herod Antipas, son of Herod the Great and Malthace, who ruled Galilee from 4 B.C. to A.D. 34. Luke is the only source for this information; Josephus never mentions Manaen. Did Manaen ever hear Jesus when he taught in Galilee? When did he become a follower of Christ? Did Manaen ever try to reach his childhood friend with the gospel of Christ? These are intriguing questions for which we have no answers. Manaen is undoubtedly an important source of information for Luke.

While they were worshiping the Lord and fasting (13:2). What is significant to notice here is that the choosing of Saul and Barnabas is not due to the church's careful planning and strategizing. The Holy Spirit directly leads the church to send these two men out on an important mission. The context for receiving this special guidance of the Spirit is the community's gathering for worship. The fact

> ## REFLECTIONS
>
> **IN MANY WAYS, THE CHURCH AT ANTIOCH IS A "MODEL** church"—the kind of example our churches should strive to emulate. It is a church with a plurality of gifted leaders who zealously and selflessly serve the Lord. It is a multi-ethnic church reflecting the fact that the gospel is not for just one particular group. And it is a church of people who worship the Lord with sincere hearts, sensitive to the leading of the Spirit, and obedient to the Lord's directives.

that they are also fasting may imply that they are earnestly seeking the Lord's guidance. In Judaism, fasting sometimes accompanied a period of deep and sincere waiting on the Lord (see Neh. 1:4; Luke 2:37). The specific words from the Spirit probably come to them in the form of a prophecy.[232]

They placed their hands on them (13:3). See comments on 6:6.

The Mission to the Island of Cyprus (13:4–12)

CYPRUS

▼

The men decide to go to the island of Cyprus for their first outreach into Gentile territories. This is a logical place to start since Barnabas originally came from this island.

Seleucia (13:4). Seleucia Pieria, near the mouth of the Orontes river, was the port city for Antioch. The Syrian capital was located fifteen miles upriver from Seleucia. The city was also the home port for a fleet of Roman imperial naval vessels. The city was founded and named after Seleucus I Nicator in 300 B.C., one of Alexander the Great's generals.[233] The upper city was built on the slope of Mount Pierius and was a well fortified acropolis.

Sailed from there to Cyprus (13:4). It is about a seventy-five mile boat trip from Seleucia to Salamis, Cyprus.

Salamis (13:5). Salamis is the largest city on the island. It is located on the east coast and is the natural entry point for anyone traveling from Syria. Among the Roman-era archaeological discoveries on the ancient site are a gymnasium, a theater, an aqueduct, and a large temple complex of Zeus.[234]

In the Jewish synagogues (13:5). Apparently the Jewish population in the city is large enough to support more than one synagogue. It is here that the missionary team begins in their efforts to reach the island with the good news of Jesus Christ.

The apostle to the Gentiles inaugurates his missionary work by proclaiming the gospel in Jewish synagogues. There are two reasons Paul has for this practice. First, he maintains the conviction that

▶ The Island of Cyprus

Cyprus is the third largest island in the Mediterranean following Sicily and Sardinia.[A-65] At its widest and longest points, it measures 138 miles long and sixty miles wide.

The island has a long and rich history that can be traced back as far as 6000 B.C. to neolithic era settlements. It features prominently in Greek and Roman era literature. In 22 B.C. it came into the possession of the Roman empire and was governed by Roman proconsuls who lived in the city of Paphos.

Jewish settlers migrated to Cyprus from the time of Alexander the Great onward. There is ample evidence of substantial Jewish presence on the island throughout the period leading up to the New Testament era.[A-66] In the early part of the second century in the reign of Trajan (A.D. 98–117), Jews on the island took up arms against the rest of the population and massacred thousands of Gentiles.[A-67]

Cyprus was home to Barnabas (see Acts 4:36). He would therefore have known the territory, the synagogues, and many of the people there.

CYPRUS

Remains of the temple of Apollo at Curium, Cyprus.

the gospel should first be presented to the Jews and then to the Gentiles (Rom. 1:16). The second reason is more pragmatic. The easiest way of reaching the Gentile community is by presenting the gospel to the Gentile proselytes and God-fearers who gathered regularly in the synagogues. These Gentiles have already turned from their idols and are seeking the one true God. All that they need to hear is that the promises for them have now been fulfilled in Jesus, the Messiah. The conversion of these Gentiles, in turn, provides a natural segue for reaching the larger Gentile community. This is a principle that had been effective in Antioch.

John was with them as their helper (13:5). As the cousin of the Cypriot Barnabas, John Mark also has some knowledge of the island and its population. The term "helper" (*hypēretēs*) is used of any kind of subordinate assistant. His help includes assisting Barnabas and Paul with the daily needs, but also probably

extending to involvement in preaching and teaching (see the use of the word in Luke 1:2 and Acts 26:16).[235]

They came to Paphos (13:6). After proclaiming the word in Salamis (for which Luke provides no report as to their success), they journey roughly 106 miles (115 Roman miles) westward to the other side of the island to the city of Paphos.[236] It is entirely possible that they stop in cities and villages along the way—

SALAMIS

The breakwater of the ancient harbor at Salamis, Cyprus.

such as Tremithus, Citium, Amathus, Curium, and Palaipaphos—and proclaim the gospel in these places. Luke's account is abbreviated at this point; his intent is to set the stage for telling the story about Elymas and Sergius Paulus.

Paphos was the capital city of Cyprus and seat of the Roman provincial procurator. This *Nea Paphos* ("New Paphos") is to be distinguished from the *Palaipaphos* ("Old Paphos"), which was located about ten miles southeast. The old city was a famous sanctuary of the goddess Aphrodite. *Nea Paphos* was the principal port city for the western side of the island and the seat of the provincial administration. Archaeologists have discovered the remains of three enormous Roman villas, two temples, a theater, and an amphitheater in the city.[237]

A Jewish sorcerer and false prophet (13:6). This man is not a member of the Persian priestly caste (a common usage of *magos*). He is a popular magician, or shaman, who in many respects is similar to the Samaritan Simon (see 8:9–25; also Sceva in 19:14) in his beliefs and techniques. The fact that he is known as a magician indicates that he has been reputed as having extensive esoteric knowledge about spirit forces and how to manipulate them through incantations, rituals, and formulas. Luke's reference to him as a "false prophet" may indicate that he practices revelatory magic or divination as a means of fortune telling. Luke here draws on the Old Testament traditions about lying prophets (see Jer. 23:9–32) as a means of characterizing this man.[238] The fact that he is Jewish is not a surprise. Many Jews engaged in various forms of magical practices in the Greco-Roman era. In fact, Jewish magic was famous in antiquity.[239] Josephus gives an account of the Roman procurator Felix securing the services of a Jewish magician from Cyprus to use spells in his quest to secure the attraction of Drusilla, with whom he fell madly in love.[240]

Bar-Jesus (13:6). The name of this person is "the son of Jesus (or Joshua)." *Bar* is an Aramaic expression meaning "son of." It is unlikely that this magician has taken the same name as Jesus of Nazareth. "Jesus/Joshua" was a common Hebrew name (see Col. 4:11) and is the name of the father of Elymas.

An attendant of the proconsul (13:7). It was not unusual for Roman leaders to

PAPHOS

(left) Remains of a fourth-century A.D. church commemorating the apostle Paul's visit.

(right) Ruins of the ancient city.

▼

▶ A Spell For Divining the Future

Among the many Greek magical papyri that have been discovered, some contain examples of revelatory magic, or divination. This particular text illustrates how this was done and connects it with prophecy:

> Whenever you seek divinations, be dressed in the garb of a prophet, shod with fibers of the doum palm and your head crowned with a spray from an olive tree—but the spray should have a single-shooted garlic tied around the middle. Clasp a pebble numbered 3663 to your breasts, and in this way make your invocation ... [an invocation follows] ... "Stay allied, lord, and listen to me through the charm that produces direct vision which I do today, and reveal to me concerning those things I ask you through the lamp divination for direct vision which I do today, I, [name of the conjurer], IY EYĒ OŌ AEĒ IAEĒ AIAĒ E AI EY ĒIE ŌŌŌŌŌ EY ĒO IAŌAI."[A-68]

have "spiritual advisors" who were astrologers and magicians. Caesar Augustus frequently consulted soothsayers and magicians.[241] The emperor Tiberius retained the services of an astrologer from Alexandria named Claudius Thrasyllus, whom he made a member of his household and whose many predictions he trusted.[242] Emperor Nero also employed the services of astrologers, including Balbillus (the son of Thrasyllus), who predicted the future for him.[243] Nero also followed the advice of a magician named Tiridates, who led him to perform a ritual of initiation.[244]

Sergius Paulus (13:7). A Latin inscription discovered in Rome makes explicit mention of this man. His full name is given as "Lucius Sergius Paullus." He is listed along with four other men as a director of water management for the Tiber river in Rome.[245] The men were responsible for managing the flow of the river to prevent the disastrous flooding that sometimes occurred in the city. The inscription explicitly mentions that he served in this capacity during the reign of Claudius. Since the title "censor" is not used in the inscription of Claudius (a title he gained in A.D. 47), the inscription can be dated to the early period of Claudius's reign, A.D. 41–47. The dating suggests that Sergius Paulus served as proconsul of Cyprus either just before his position in Rome or just after.[246]

He and his son, who bare the same name, are mentioned on yet another inscription. In the 1912 excavation of the city of Pisidian Antioch, Sir William Ramsay discovered an inscription (dated in the

JEWISH MAGICAL AMULETS

These medieval amulets were intended to protect people from evil spirits.

▼

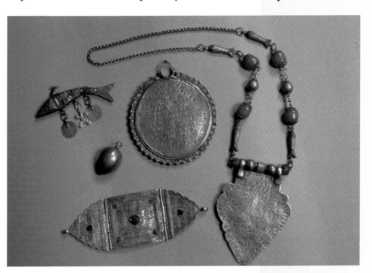

▶

This first-century A.D. inscription, found in Pisidian Antioch, honors the son of the proconsul of the island of Cyprus.

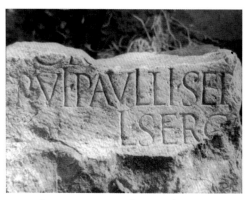

period A.D. 60–100) that read: "To Lucius Sergius Paullus the younger, son of Lucius, one of the four commissioners in charge of the Roman streets, tribune of the soldiers of the sixth legion styled Ferrata, quaestor." Apparently the son of the proconsul of Cyprus became an important Roman official in Pisidian Antioch, the very place the apostle Paul and his companions travel to next.[247] It is possible that the Sergii Paulli family, although ultimately of Italian origin, were native to Pisidian Antioch.[248] The fact that the mis-

sionary team goes directly from Cyprus to Pisidian Antioch may have something to do with the proconsul's family connections in that city.[249]

Elymas the sorcerer (for that is what his name means) (13:8). There are two possibilities for understanding the origin of the name "Elymas." It may be derived from the Aramaic word *haloma*, meaning "one who dreams" (in the sense of receiving visions). Or it may come from a Semitic word related to the Arabic *'alim*, which means "wise man." In this sense it would have much in common with our translation of *magoi* from the East as "wise men" in the birth narrative of Jesus (Matt. 2:1).[250]

Saul, who was also called Paul (13:9). Up to this point, Luke only refers to the apostle by his Hebrew name, "Saul." Now, as the apostle begins his mission to the Gentiles, Luke will refer to him as

Roman Names				
PRAENOMEN	**NOMEN GENTILE**	**COGNOMEN**	**SUPERNOMEN**	
(an individual's name identifying the person within the family—similar to our first name)[A-69]	(family name—similar to our surname)	(additional family name designating a branch of the family—used as the ordinary personal name)	Signa (Nickname)	Hebrew Name
Lucius	Annaeus	**Seneca**		
Marcus	Tullius	**Cicero**		
Gaius	**Julius**	**Caesar Germanicus**	Caligula ("little boots")	
Gaius	Octavius	**Caesar** ("**Augustus**" a title)		
Tiberius	Julius	Caesar Augustus		
Tiberius	**Claudius**	Nero Germanicus		
Nero	Claudius	Caesar		
(Lucius)	Sergius	Paullus		
?	?	**Paullus**		**Saul**

"Paul." The change probably reflects the historical reality that Paul himself begins using his Roman name as he ventures into Gentile territory with the gospel. In addition, it may be that Paul wants to avoid using his Hebrew name since, in Greek, *Saulos* is an adjective that refers to "the loose, wanton gait of courtesans or Bacchantes."[251]

It was common for Roman citizens to have three names: the praenomen, nomen, and cognomen (see the chart below). "Paul" is the apostle's Roman cognomen. Since Paul gained his citizenship at birth (see 22:26–29), it is a matter of speculation to determine how his parents or grandparents received their citizenship. Scholars suggest two different ways that Paul's ancestors may have gained their prized Roman citizenship. (1) F. F. Bruce suggests that it may have been bestowed on Paul's father or grandfather by one of the Roman generals (Pompey or Antony) known to have been in control of the province of Cilicia in the first century B.C. and for whom his relative rendered some outstanding service to the Roman cause. Bruce suggests that if the citizenship was bestowed by Mark Antony, Paul's full name would have been: Marcus Antonius Paullus.[252] (2) Alternatively, Paul's ancestors may have gained their citizenship after being freed as enslaved prisoners of war (perhaps enslaved during the Roman general Varus's campaign against Jews in Galilee in 4 B.C. or even in earlier Roman excursions into Palestine).[253]

You are a child of the devil (13:10). By trying to turn the proconsul away from the faith and opposing the missionary group, Elymas shows his true colors. Far from being a "son of Jesus" (the savior) he is a "son of the devil" (the enemy). The language here is reminiscent of what

Jesus told the Jewish leaders who opposed him and sought to kill him: "You belong to your father, the devil, and you want to carry out your father's desire" (John 8:44). Paul also recognizes that the devil is source of the spiritual power behind the magic and divination that Elymas practices.

The hand of the Lord (13:11). It is not by counter-magic or personal vindictiveness that Elymas is struck blind. God himself intervenes in this situation to thwart this opponent of the gospel (see comments on 4:28).

For a time you will be unable to see (13:11). A temporary blindness came on Saul when he was confronted by the Lord (9:9). "For a time" may imply that the blindness will be removed if and when Elymas turns to the Lord in repentance.

He believed (13:12). The mission to Cyprus is a success. The Roman proconsul of the entire island puts his faith in Jesus. We know nothing more about the subsequent history of Sergius Paulus, Elymas, or the others who become believers on Cyprus at that time. This would certainly be an exciting series of stories.

The Mission to Antioch of Pisidia (13:13–52)

Paul and Barnabas continue the mission to the Gentiles in south-central Asia Minor. This is a natural westward extension of Paul's previous work in the nearby province of Cilicia (where his home city of Tarsus was located). In this section, Luke records a lengthy summary of one of Paul's messages that he delivers in a local synagogue.

PERGA IN PAMPHYLIA

(left) Remains of the Hellenistic-era towers marking the beginning of the colonnaded street.

(right) The remains of the main street through this port city.

▼

Perga (13:13). Leaving Cyprus, Paul and his two companions journey over 150 miles by boat to the south coast of Asia Minor. Coming to the Cestrus river, they travel five miles up the river to the port of Perga.[254] Luke does not tell us how long they stay in the city or whether they proclaim the gospel there at this time. On the return trip, they share the gospel in the city.

Perga was one of the leading cities of Asia Minor. It had a sizeable population evidenced in part by its fourteen thousand-seat theater. It also boasted a large stadium, many Roman baths, a large gymnasium, and three aqueducts sup-

plying water to the city. The principal deity of the city was Artemis (associated with the Ephesian Artemis), also known as the Queen of Perga. The remains of her famous temple in Perga have not yet been discovered. There were presumably many Jews in the city and a synagogue. Philo speaks of a colony of Jews in the province (*Embassy* 281) and Jews from Pamphylia were present in Jerusalem on the day of Pentecost (Acts 2:10).

In Pamphylia (13:13). Pamphylia is a small Roman senatorial province located west of the province of Cilicia (where Paul was from). In A.D. 43, Pamphylia combined with Lycia (a province to the west) to form a joint Roman province. It was enclosed by the Mediterranean Sea to the south and the territory of Pisidia to the north.

John left them to return to Jerusalem (13:13). Luke gives no indication as to why John Mark leaves, but Paul regards it as desertion and it becomes an issue that divides Paul and Barnabas later (see 15:37–39). There are numerous suggestions as to why John Mark leaves, many relating to his youthful inexperience: He is homesick; he is having difficulty living and ministering in a strange culture; or, he is unwilling to take the rugged hundred-mile journey northward to Antioch. Some assume there are other reasons for the departure: He resents the fact that Paul is assuming more of the leadership over his cousin Barnabas; he thinks the plan is to stay in Pamphylia and resents the sudden decision to go to Antioch; or, he feels increasingly uncomfortable with the nature of this mission to Gentiles. We will never know for sure.

Pisidian Antioch (13:14). Pisidian Antioch technically lay in the territory of Phrygia but was called "Antioch towards Pisidia" to distinguish it from another Antioch in Phrygia that was on the bank of the Maeander river. Today the site lies just north of the modern city of Yalvaç. Pisidia was a mountainous region in southern Asia Minor stretching some 120 miles east to west and fifty miles north to south. The mountains would have made it a difficult journey for Paul and Barnabas and may be one of the reasons why he was ill

---

▶ Antioch (Near Pisidia)

Antioch was a prosperous city in central Asia Minor in the ancient territory of Phrygia, but now the Roman province of Galatia.[A-70] It was regarded as the most important Roman colony in Asia Minor. The city lay just west of the rugged Taurus mountain range. This colony was a miniature Rome in the midst of Asia Minor and was even organized into seven districts.[A-71] Antioch was second in importance in Galatia only to Ancyra, the capital city of the Roman province.

In addition to a large population of local indigenous Anatolian peoples, Antioch also had many Roman citizens. It was home to many Roman senators and equestrians. Sometime after Paul's visit, Sergius Paulus, the proconsul of Cyprus, took up residence there. The city had a large imperial sanctuary constructed to serve the emperor cult. Other surviving Roman structures from the New Testament period include a large bathhouse, an aqueduct, the remains of a street system and a decorated city gate. Paul's visit would have occurred at the climax of an era of building and development in the city. One expert on the city notes, "Antioch would have appeared to Paul as a model of the capital itself."[A-72]

The principal deity of the city was the moon-god Mên, called Mên Askaênos. Remains of the second-century B.C. sanctuary can still be seen on the hill called Karakuyu, about an hour's climb above the city (2.5 miles southeast). Inscriptions also attest to the worship of Jupiter (*Iuppiter Optimus Maximus*), Dionysus, and Asklepios in the city. There was also a strong Jewish presence in the city most of whom came c. 200 B.C. when two thousand Jewish families (perhaps more than ten thousand people) were forcibly resettled in Phrygia and Lydia from Babylon.[A-73]

The ruler cult was of paramount importance in the city. Construction of the imperial temple in honor of the city's founder, Caesar Augustus, began during the reign of Tiberius. A triumphal arch celebrating Augustus's Pisidian victories was completed in A.D. 50, just after Paul's initial visit. An expert on the Roman site notes: "There is no doubt that the imperial temple and the associated buildings provided the main focus for the public and religious life of the colony." [A-74]

Since 1991, the site has been excavated by teams led by Turkish archaeologist Mehmet Taschalan. Excavations have focused on a bathhouse, the imperial sanctuary, the theater, and the east section of the main road (the *decumanus maximus*). Taschalan's team has also discovered a stadium (measuring 208 yds. by 33 yds.) in a valley west of the city.[A-75] when he first preached the gospel to them (see Gal. 4:12). The territory of Pisidia was now included in the large Roman province of Galatia.[255] In fact, "the region around Derbe, Lystra, Iconium, and Antioch was all part of the province of Galatia in the mid-first century A.D."[256]

They entered the synagogue and sat down (13:14). There would have been significant variety in synagogue architecture in the first century throughout the Mediterranean world. In general, however, most would have had stone benches built along two or three of the walls and rows of wooden benches in the middle of the structure.[257] The seating was segregated according to men and women. There is also evidence of a hierarchical seating order with more distinguished members sitting in the front and younger and less distinguished members seated in rows behind them.[258] Archaeologists have not yet discovered the synagogue remains in the city.

After the reading from the Law and the Prophets (13:15). According to the

Mishnah, the synagogue service includes a recitation of the *Shema* and the *Shemoneh ʿEsreh* (the Eighteen Benedictions), a reading from the Torah and the Prophets, and the "lifting up of the hands" (the blessing of the priests).[259] Philo stresses the importance of the message that follows the reading of the Scriptures: "Accordingly, on the seventh day there are spread before the people in every city innumerable lessons of prudence, and temperance, and courage, and justice, and all other virtues; during the giving of which the common people sit down, keeping silence and pricking up their ears, with all possible attention, from their thirst for wholesome instruction; but some of those who are very learned explain to them what is of great importance and use, lessons by which the whole of their lives may be improved."[260]

A message of encouragement (13:15). This is a technical expression for a synagogue sermon following the reading of the Scriptures.[261]

Please speak (13:15). It is not surprising that the synagogue officials would invite Paul to speak. Here in their midst is a rabbi who was trained under Gamaliel in Jerusalem.

Standing up, Paul motioned with his hand and said (13:16). Standing and motioning is what one expected of a good orator delivering a synagogue sermon.

You Gentiles who worship God (13:16). The synagogue in Antioch already has attracted many Gentiles sympathetic to the worship of the one God of Israel (see comments on 2:11).

PISIDIAN ANTIOCH

The Roman road through the middle of the city.

▼

The God of the people of Israel chose our fathers (13:17). Paul begins his message with a historical retrospect touching on the exodus, the conquest, the period of the judges, and the monarchy of David. Luke probably gives us merely an outline of what Paul says in his address. This sketch of the history of Israel establishes common ground with his synagogue audience and lays the foundation for what he will soon say about Jesus as the messianic descendant of David.

He overthrew seven nations in Canaan (13:19). These seven nations are "the Hittites, Girgashites, Amorites, Canaanites, Perizzites, Hivites and Jebusites, seven nations larger and stronger than you" (Deut. 7:1).

All this took about 450 years (13:20). This 450 years would represent four hundred years in Egypt (Gen. 15:13), forty years in the desert (Num. 14:33–34), and ten years conquering the land (Josh. 14:1–5).

I have found David son of Jesse a man after my own heart (13:22). This verse represents a combination of portions

◀

PISIDIAN ANTIOCH

Overview of the excavation of the Byzantine church recently identified as the previous site of the Roman-era Jewish synagogue.

▶ The Organization of a Synagogue

There was no "pastor" of a synagogue as we would have in a contemporary church. The reading of the scriptures, the preaching, and public prayers were given by members of the assembly. Most synagogues would have had the following leadership structure:[A-76]

- *Archontes* ("leaders") or *Presbyteroi* ("elders")— These were the chief leaders of the synagogue in charge of its direction and oversight. It appears that this position was held for a year at a time. Although both titles are attested in the inscriptions, *archontes* was used far more often to denote these leaders.

- *Archisynagōgos* ("ruler of the synagogue")— This officer had the special responsibility of organizing the public worship for each Sabbath and for all of the additional meetings of the synagogue. This leader was selected from among the *archontes*. Usually there was one person who held this office, but on occasion, as here, there were two.

from two Old Testament passages about David: Psalm 89:20 ("I have found David") and 1 Samuel 13:14 ("a man after his own heart").

From this man's descendants (13:23). The Old Testament is clear that the coming Messiah would be a descendant of David (2 Sam. 7:12–16; Ps. 89). The prophet Jeremiah revealed: "'The days are coming,' declares the LORD, 'when I will raise up to David a righteous Branch, a King who will reign wisely and do what is just and right in the land. In his days Judah will be saved and Israel will live in safety. This is the name by which he will be called: The LORD Our Righteousness'" (Jer. 23:5–6; see comments on 2:14–36).

The Savior Jesus (13:23). See comments on 5:31.

Whose sandals I am not worthy to untie (13:25). Rabbi Joshua ben Levi teaches that "all manner of service that a slave must render to his master, the pupil must render to his teacher—except that of taking off his shoe."[262] By contrast, because of Jesus' infinite superiority, John did not feel he was even worthy to perform a task that was considered too menial for most disciples to perform for their masters.

The people of Jerusalem and their rulers did not recognize Jesus (13:27). Both the crowds and the leaders of the Jewish people in Jerusalem—the members of the Sanhedrin, the chief priests, the elders, and the scribes—bore guilt for inciting the death of Jesus at the hands of the Romans. They refused to believe the claims of Jesus and did not recognize that he was the anticipated Messiah of Israel. Paul's hope is that his audience in Antioch does not make the same mistake as their compatriots in Jerusalem.

Executed . . . laid him in a tomb . . . raised him from the dead . . . was seen (13:28–31). Paul presents the heart of the gospel message in these four verses. This is the essence of the *kerygma*, the early Christian preaching (see 1 Cor. 15:3–4).

The tree (13:29). The cross is often referred to as "the tree" by the early Christians. This reflects a connection with Deuteronomy 21:22–23: "If a man guilty of a capital offense is put to death and his body is hung on a tree, you must not leave his body on the tree overnight. Be sure to bury him that same day, because anyone who is hung on a tree is under God's curse." In his letter to these people (and probably also in his preaching), Paul clarifies that Christ redeems us from the curse pronounced by the law on our human sinfulness by himself becoming a curse for us by dying on a tree (Gal. 3:14).

For many days he was seen (13:31). Paul stresses the role of Jesus' many post-resurrection witnesses. They can vouch for the authenticity and reliability of the message Paul is proclaiming.

PISIDIAN ANTIOCH

The Roman aqueduct bringing water to the city. ▼

What God promised our fathers he has fulfilled for us (13:32–33). Paul insists that Jesus of Nazareth fulfills the promises of the Old Testament recorded in Psalm 2:7; 16:10; and Isaiah 55:3 (see comments on Acts 2:27–31).

Everyone who believes is justified (13:39). In his first sermon recorded in Acts, Paul proclaims his well-known doctrine of justification (*dikaioō*) by faith (see Rom. 3:28; 5:1; Gal. 2:16). There is a judicial (or forensic) background to this important theological concept that is well-illustrated in Deuteronomy 25:1: "When men have a dispute, they are to take it to court and the judges will decide the case, acquitting (*dikaioō*) the innocent and condemning the guilty." Applied to people who put their faith in Christ, "justification" means that they have been acquitted of all their guilt before God. This acquittal is tantamount to having all of one's sins forgiven.

From everything you could not be justified from by the law of Moses (13:39). On the surface it appears that Paul implies that the Mosaic law is capable of justifying people in spite of certain sins, but not others. This is not at all what Paul is saying. Paul makes it clear in his letters that the Mosaic law is unable to bring ultimate acquittal for any of the sins they have committed.

Take care that what the prophets have said does not happen to you (13:40). Concerned that the members of the synagogue in Antioch may scoff at his message and reject it, Paul uses the words of Habakkuk 1:5 to warn them about the dire consequences of dismissing what he has to say. In that context, the prophet derided the people of Israel for not recognizing that the impending invasion of Babylon was God's own doing—it was an act of judgment against his people. Paul echoes the words of this passage to warn these people that it is once again a dangerous proposition to ignore what God is doing, but in this instance through Jesus of Nazareth, who has come as Messiah and Savior. The common thread between the two situations is that God acts in surprising ways.

PISIDIAN ANTIOCH

The ruins of the temple of Augustus.

On the next Sabbath almost the whole city gathered (13:44). The initial response to Paul's message is excellent. Many Jews and Gentile proselytes show keen enthusiasm. Invited to speak again on the following Sabbath, Paul and Barnabas are astounded that the synagogue is overflowing with Gentiles who want to hear the gospel. This event illustrates the effectiveness of Paul's strategy of reaching Gentiles through the synagogue. These believing Gentiles can immediately go and reach family, friends, neighbors, and coworkers.

They were filled with jealousy (13:45). The leading members of the synagogue who disagree with Paul's message are provoked by his success in attracting Gentiles to their synagogue. This may stem from their own inability to attract as many or possibly from a concern about their synagogue being defiled by impure Gentile sinners. The latter concern may also be connected to their perception of Paul's relaxed attitude about the Jewish law in his explanation of the Scriptures, especially as it relates to the Gentiles.

Light for the Gentiles (13:47). Paul declares his focus on the Gentiles as fulfilling the divine directive as related in Isaiah 49:6 that God calls his servant to be a light to the Gentiles. Jesus himself alluded to the wording of this passage in Acts 1:8 by stating that the gospel goes to the far reaches of the inhabited world.

All who were appointed for eternal life believed (13:48). This is one of the clearest statements affirming absolute predestination found anywhere in the New Testament.[263] Jews commonly believed that God enrolled his people in a book of life. This is attested in the Torah itself: "The LORD replied to Moses, 'Whoever has sinned against me I will blot out of my book'" (Ex. 32:33). The prophet Daniel spoke of a future deliverance for "everyone whose name is found written in the book" (Dan. 12:1).[264] The expression "eternal life" can literally be rendered "life in the age (to come)." This new age has dawned in the life and work of Jesus.

The word of the Lord spread . . . they stirred up persecution (13:49–50). The Jews and Gentiles who believe do not keep the good news to themselves, but begin telling others throughout the south Galatian region. By contrast, the unbelieving Jewish leaders harden in their opposition and do all they can to get Paul and Barnabas out of the area.

The God-fearing women of high standing (13:50). These are probably Roman (Italian) women from the colonial families settled there by Augustus—aristocratic provincial elite who become Jewish sympathizers.[265] Similarly, the leading men are most likely Roman officials.

They shook the dust from their feet in protest (13:51). Jesus commended this action to the Twelve and the seventy when he sent them out on their respective missions as a symbolic protest against those who rejected their message (Luke 9:5; 10:11). The symbol was expressed in first-century Judaism as a means of ridding oneself of the impurities of walking through Gentile lands.[266] For Jesus and the apostles, the Gentiles were not intrinsically impure—only those who refused to receive the gospel of the Messiah's saving work (see comments on Acts 18:6).

The Evangelization of Iconium (14:1–7)

After their mixed reception at Antioch, the missionary partners travel nearly a hundred miles to Iconium where they receive a similar response to their preaching.

Went as usual into the Jewish synagogue (14:1). Paul begins his outreach in Iconium at the Jewish synagogue in spite of the fact that he angrily turns to the Jewish leaders in Antioch of Pisidia and

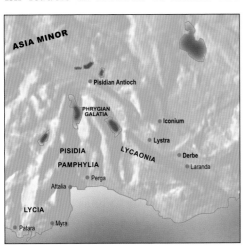

exclaims, "We turn now to the Gentiles" (13:46). Because of the presence of Gentile God-fearers, the synagogue is the best place to begin his witness to the Gentiles.

The Jews who refused to believe stirred up the Gentiles (14:2). This is precisely the response he encounters in Antioch (14:46, 50) and will later experience in Thessalonica (17:5) and elsewhere. Many Jews as well as Gentiles respond to the gospel.

Miraculous signs and wonders (14:3). The people of the city see miraculous things happen as Paul and Barnabas minister here. These signs and wonders no doubt include healings and exorcisms. As at other times in the outreach of the early church, God intervenes in these dramatic ways to demonstrate the authenticity of the message about his grace that these two missionaries are proclaiming. These miracles serve as background to a comment Paul later makes to the Galatian believers in his letter: "Does God give you his Spirit and work miracles among

◀ *left*

SOUTH GALATIA

▶ Iconium

The city of Iconium lay about ninety miles east southeast of Antioch and roughly 150 miles due south of Ancyra (modern Ankara, the capital city of Turkey).[A-77] It was part of the Roman province of Galatia, but for many years was regarded as the easternmost city of the ethnic territory of Phrygia. The Phrygian dialect was still spoken there as inscriptions dating as late as the second century A.D. attest.[A-78]

The city was friendly to Rome and was honored by the emperor Claudius sometime shortly before Paul's visit. Iconium was situated on a major trade route (the *Via Sebaste*),[A-79] which linked the Syrian east to Ephesus and served as an important com-

mercial city for the area. Numismatic evidence attests to the establishment of a Roman colony (*Colonia Iulia Augusta Iconiensum*) in the city during the reign of Vespasian (A.D. 69–79).[A-80] Agriculture flourished in the fertile plateau area encompassing Iconium and water was plentiful. The city was, therefore, prosperous and growing.

There is evidence that the population worshiped the Asia Minor mother goddess Cybele, Herakles (Hercules), Zeus Megistos (Jupiter Optimus Maximus), as well as Apollo.[A-81] From Luke, we know that there was a Jewish community and a synagogue in the city. Numerous inscriptions attest to the fact that Christianity became deeply rooted in this city.

you because you observe the law, or because you believe what you heard?" (Gal. 3:5).

With the apostles (14:4). Luke here explicitly labels Paul and Barnabas "apostles," as he does again in verse 14. Apparently, Luke uses the title in two different ways: someone who travels with Jesus in his earthly ministry, has seen him risen from the dead, and constitutes one of "the Twelve"; and someone set apart by the Holy Spirit for an evangelistic mission and then commissioned and "sent out" by the local church.[267]

The Lycaonian cities (14:6). In A.D. 25, the "Lycaonian cities" of Lystra and Derbe were incorporated into the Roman province of Galatia. Luke, how-

ever, demonstrates his knowledge of the former territorial divisions, to which the local populace was still sensitive. The territory of Lycaonia reached northeast nearly as far as Iconium and bordered Cilicia on the south, Cappadocia to the east, Phrygia and the former ethnic territory of Galatia to the north, and Pisidia and Isauria to the west.[268] Another of the principal cities of Lycaonia was Laranda, located about twenty miles east southeast of Derbe in the direction of Tarsus.

The Evangelization of Lystra (14:8–21a)

Undaunted by the threats of stoning and persecution, Paul and Barnabas travel on to the cities of Lystra and Derbe. An unusual situation surfaces at Lystra where the two are mistaken to be gods.

Lame from birth and had never walked (14:8). Luke's statement about the severity of the handicap highlights the "wonder" (see 14:3) of this healing. For the man to walk and jump, God has to restore bone mass and a significant amount of muscle.

In the Lycaonian language (14:11). While these people know Latin and Greek, they still retain facility in their

LYSTRA

The tel of the ancient city (center right).

▼

▶ Lystra

The city of Lystra had a fairly recent history, having been established by Augustus in 26 B.C. and made a Roman colony (*Colonia Iulia Felix Gemina Lustra*) in A.D. 6, the southernmost colony in this portion of Asia Minor.[A-82] It was located roughly twenty miles south of Iconium, but a day's journey off the main road, the *via Sebaste*. It was never an important city in this portion of Asia Minor.

The Roman influence in this city is seen by the predominance of Latin inscriptions. The raising of livestock (especially sheep) and agriculture were the principal occupations in this region. This is consistent with the discovery of a coin in Lystra from the time of Augustus depicting the Ceres, the goddess of vegetation.[A-83] native Anatolian dialect, which Luke refers to as *Lykaonisti*. Usage of this dialect in the area around Lystra persisted until as late as the fifth century A.D. and beyond.[269] There is evidence that two Christian monasteries in Constantinople (Byzantium) founded in the sixth century used the Lycaonian language in their liturgy.[270] Inscriptions in the dialects of other nearby Anatolian languages also survive (namely, Carian, Sidetic, and Pisidian).

The gods have come down to us in human form (14:11). The famous first-century Roman poet Ovid tells a story about Zeus and Hermes taking mortal form and visiting an elderly couple in their humble Phrygian countryside home. Leading up to this, Zeus and Hermes visited a thousand homes seeking shelter and rest but were repeatedly spurned, their true identities being concealed. It was not until they came to the home of Philemon and Baucis that they found hospitality. The old couple welcomed the two visitors, fed them well, and prepared for them a place to rest. Not knowing that they were entertaining gods "in the guise of human beings," the old couple finally learned the identity of their heavenly visitors. The gods then led Philemon and Baucis to the top of a hill and mercifully spared them from a devastating flood sent in judgment on the inhospitable inhabitants of the region. Their humble home was miraculously transformed into a marble temple.[271] If this local legend was known to the inhabitants of Lystra, it may help to explain their identification of the missionaries as Zeus and Hermes and their eagerness to honor them.

There is also inscriptional evidence from Lystra attesting the local worship of Zeus and Hermes. A stone relief found at Kavak (in the territory of Lystra) depicts Hermes accompanied by the eagle of Zeus. In the city of Lystra, a stone was discovered that portrays Hermes and a second god (possibly the earth-god *Gē* or Zeus *Epēkoos*).[272]

Barnabas they called Zeus, and Paul they called Hermes (14:12). Although Zeus (Jupiter) is the head of the pantheon of gods, it is not surprising that Paul is associated with Hermes (Mercury) instead of

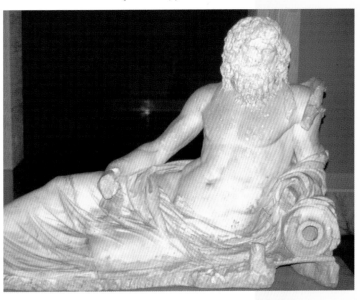

Zeus. Hermes was widely regarded as the messenger of Zeus. One ancient writer describes Hermes as the god "who is the leader in speaking."[273]

The priest of Zeus (14:13). Another group of manuscripts uses the plural, "the priests of Zeus," which more accurately reflects the historical situation. It was common for such temples to have a college of priests.[274]

Whose temple was just outside the city (14:13). The temple has not yet been discovered. Archaeologists, however, have found many statues and inscriptions attesting the worship of Zeus and Hermes in this region. None of these, however, dates any earlier than the third century A.D.[275]

Brought bulls and wreaths to the city gates (14:13). The bulls are brought to be sacrificed. Such animals were typically adorned with garlands on their way to be slaughtered.[276]

They tore their clothes (14:14). In Jewish culture, extreme grief is often expressed by tearing one's clothes. It was an outward expression of what the person was feeling inwardly. "The destructive action reveals the sudden and sharp emotion that overshadows all ordinary concerns, such as care for appearance and possessions."[277] Reuben and Jacob both tore their clothes when they thought Joseph had been killed (Gen. 37:29, 34). Many of Israel's leaders tore their clothes when God's honor was impugned.[278] When the Sanhedrin heard an account of blasphemy against God, the judges "stand up on their feet and rend their garments, and they may not mend them again."[279] This is what the high priest did at the trial of Jesus (see Matt. 26:65; Mark 14:63).

Men, why are you doing this? (14:15). This question marks the beginning of a short address that Paul gives to the crowd, wherein he appeals to them to desist in their acclaiming of him and Barnabas as gods, and points them to the one true God. What Luke records in the span of these three verses is a brief summary of what is likely a longer address. This is not exactly an evangelistic message, at least from what we know of it, because it makes no mention of Jesus or the elements of the *kerygma*—the message of the death, resurrection, and exaltation of Christ, drawing the implications of this event for the forgiveness of sins and a relationship with God.

There are similarities between this address and his message to the Greeks on the Areopagus in Athens (see 17:22–30). These are the only two occasions where Luke records Paul's preaching to non-Jews. In both instances Paul contextualizes his message to people who do not know the Scriptures. The apostle stresses natural revelation (focusing on God as Creator and the providential sustainer of the world) and the emptiness of idolatry while avoiding a recounting of Israel's history or how Jesus fulfills Jewish prophecies about a coming Messiah.

From these worthless things (14:15). Jews typically regarded idolatry as "empty" (*mataios*). One Jewish writer writes, "For just as one's dish is useless when it is broken, so are the gods of the heathen, when they have been set up in the temples."[280] Another Jewish writer asserts that "men themselves are much more powerful than the gods whom they vainly worship."[281]

The living God (14:15). Frequently throughout the Old Testament, the one God of Israel is described as "the living God." Joshua tells the people of Israel as they enter the promised land that "the living God is among you."[282] A popular story is told in Palestinian Judaism shortly before the birth of Christ about Daniel challenging the Persian king about his worship of the statue of Bel, the patron deity of Babylon: "The king revered it and went every day to worship it. But Daniel worshiped his own God. So the king said to him, 'Why do you not worship Bel?' He answered, 'Because I do not revere idols made with hands, but the living God, who created heaven and earth and has dominion over all living creatures.'"[283] This story well depicts the Jewish attitude toward idols.

Paul's comments are offensive to these Gentile worshipers of Zeus. The implication of what Paul says is that other gods, including Zeus and Hermes, are not alive.

Who made heaven and earth and sea and everything in them (14:15). This line repeats the same words we find used in support of the fourth commandment enjoining Israel to keep the Sabbath holy: "For in six days the LORD made the heavens and the earth, the sea, and all that is in them, but he rested on the seventh day" (Ex. 20:11). But God is also extolled as Creator in these words in other Old Testament and Jewish contexts.[284]

In the past, he let all nations go their own way (14:16). Throughout the history of Israel, God directly and repeatedly intervened by revealing himself to them, making them his own people, redeeming them from slavery, guiding and leading them, bestowing on them his law, speaking to them through the prophets, and giving them promises of a bright future. God did not respond to the Gentile nations in the same way, but he did not leave them without a witness. Paul's comments here echo what he says elsewhere to the Greeks on the Areopagus (17:30) and to the Romans in his letter (Rom. 1:28).

He has shown kindness by giving you rain from heaven (14:17). God's witness to the Gentile nations is not through

REFLECTIONS

PAUL'S COMMENTS ABOUT OTHER RELIGIONS WOULD solicit a hostile reaction today in the contemporary climate of pluralism. To infer that worshipers of other gods are devoted to "empty" things and neglect the living and true God would be viewed today as intolerant and inflammatory. It is important to realize that Paul was no angry man who said these things out of an unstable or uncharitable personality. He came to these people in love earnestly desiring for them to recognize and acknowledge the one true God. In Paul's understanding, there were not many paths that led to the same ultimate reality. There was one path and many deceptive counterfeits.

their religions, which Paul has characterized as "worthless." The living God's providential care for the nations by providing them with land, rain, crops, and the enjoyment of life is a sufficient testimony to point these people to a greater reality. A Jewish rabbi said that if a person sees "mountains, hills, seas, rivers and deserts he should say, 'Blessed is the author of creation,'" and "for rain and good tidings he should say, 'Blessed is he, the good and the doer of good.'"[285]

Paul's remarks here may have functioned as a direct polemic against the local cult religions. Zeus was popularly worshiped as the god of weather and the one who provided vegetation.[286]

Some Jews came from Antioch and Iconium (14:19). It is surprising that Paul's Jewish opponents from Antioch (near Pisidia) travel a hundred miles to oppose him in Lystra. Do they receive word from Jews living in Lystra about what is transpiring there? Contact between the cities of Antioch and Lystra, in spite of the distance, is evidenced in part by a statue of Concordia that the people of Lystra erected in the city of Antioch.[287]

They stoned Paul and dragged him outside the city (14:19). There is great irony in the fact that the apostle goes from being venerated as a god to an object of derision whom the people try to kill. Luke does not say why they do not attempt to stone Barnabas as well. It may point to the role Paul is playing in the events—especially in the speaking. Since stoning was a distinctively Jewish form of punishment, we can assume that these Jewish opponents from Antioch and Iconium threw the rocks while the Gentile crowd from Lystra looked on.

But after the disciples had gathered around him, he got up and went back into the city (14:20). Since the crowd supposes that Paul is dead, the apostle probably is seriously injured—at least stoned in the head and knocked unconscious. Some interpreters have thought that God works a miracle in raising Paul up in response to the prayers of these who "had gathered around him." This may be the case.

They preached the good news in that city (14:21). Luke says nothing about any of

▶ Derbe

Very little is known about the ancient city of Derbe either from literary evidence or from archaeology. The site was only positively identified in the late 1950s when two inscriptions were discovered on the site that mentioned the city (although Sir William Ramsay had erroneously identified a different site as Derbe in the late 1800s). One of the inscriptions, the shaft of a large statue base and weighing nearly a ton, reads: "The Council and the People of Claudio-Derbe...." The other inscription, dating to the fourth or fifth century, also gives evidence of Christianity in the city: "The most God-loving Michael, bishop of Derbe."

The site of Derbe is located about sixty-five miles southeast of Iconium (thirty miles east of the area originally suggested by Ramsay) at modern Devri Scehri. The mound where the city is situated, Kerti Hüyük, still has not been excavated.[A-84]

the events surrounding the ministry of Paul and Barnabas in Derbe. Yet he does say that many people there become followers of Christ.

Revisiting and Strengthening the New Galatian Churches (14:21b–23)

Then they returned to Lystra, Iconium and Antioch (14:21). After being expelled from Antioch, plotted against in Iconium, and nearly stoned to death in Lystra, it is a tribute to God's power in their lives that Paul and Barnabas even consider stepping foot in those cities again. They are willing to risk their lives for the sake of the gospel, however, and their love and concern for the well-being of these new converts drive them to take incredible risks.

Appointed elders for them in each church (14:23). Knowing that these fledgling communities need leadership to facilitate their continuing growth in the Lord, Paul and Barnabas appoint *presbyteroi*. The plural suggests that a group of gifted men is selected for each church and share equally in the task of leading the respective congregations.[288] Paul's model for this form of leadership comes from the synagogue pattern and from how he sees the network of house churches structured in Jerusalem (see comments on 11:30).

Returning to Antioch, Syria (14:24–28)

Rather than continuing to other cities in Asia Minor to proclaim the gospel, the two decide to return to their sending church in Antioch of Syria. Luke does not state why they decide to return at this juncture, but it may have had to do

with a sense of accomplishment of their work in south Galatia and a desire to solicit further support for a more extensive future trip.

They went down to Attalia (14:25). Attalia served as the harbor for Perga, the capital of the Roman province of Pamphylia. Although Luke does not explicitly tell us that Paul's boat came into Attalia when they first arrived in this region (see 13:13), this was probably his point of entry. This time, however, Paul and Barnabas spend some time preaching the gospel in Perga (five miles upriver from Attalia), although we have no report of the response.

They sailed back to Antioch (14:26). The journey has now come full-circle, and these two emissaries return to the church in Syria that sent them out.

The door of faith to the Gentiles (14:27). The missionary report alludes to the language of Jesus, who described himself as "the door" to salvation (John 10:9). At the heart of Paul's preaching is the presentation of faith as the means by which one enters the door and receives justification and forgiveness of sins (see Acts 13:39).

They stayed there a long time (14:28). It is impossible to know exactly how long the two stay in Antioch and resume their ministry to the many believers there. It is certainly less than a year and may have been just a few months. It is during this time and prior to the Jerusalem Council that Paul receives word that a group of Jewish believers zealous for the law visits the new believers in south Galatia and begin to subvert his teaching. In response, Paul writes his first letter—Galatians.

The Jerusalem Council (15:1–29)

For many years, the Jewish people welcomed Gentiles into their covenant community provided that they turned from their idols to the one true God and adhered to the Jewish law—most notably by being circumcised. Now that the Messiah of Israel has come and an ingathering of Gentiles into the newly con-

stituted people of God is happening, a number of law-observant Jews are wondering why Paul and the church at Antioch are not insisting that the Gentile converts keep the law. This issue becomes divisive and threatens to split the movement. The wisest course of action is to convene a meeting with the leaders of the Jerusalem church and reach a mutual understanding that will govern the movement as more and more Gentiles put their faith in Jesus Christ.

Some men came down from Judea to Antioch (15:1). A faction within the Jerusalem church consisting of believers who have been Pharisees (see 15:5) are disturbed about the way Gentiles are being admitted into the church. They are upset that Gentile believers are not being circumcised as commanded by the law. To make sure that the Antioch church is not lax in its fidelity to God's law, a group of them make the three hundred-mile journey to Syria to press this issue. Verse 24 makes it clear that they are not authorized by the leaders of the Jerusalem church.

Unless you are circumcised, according to the custom taught by Moses, you cannot be saved (15:1). These Jewish believers, committed to the law of God, make it clear to the leaders of the church at Antioch that circumcision is essential to salvation. They are not excluding Gentiles from becoming authentic members of the people of God; they are simply insisting that they be circumcised.

Sharp dispute (15:2). The apostle Paul is equally convinced that circumcision is *not* necessary as a sign of the covenant for the newly constituted people of God. For Paul, this is not an issue on which the two

▶ The Perspective of a Pharisaic Jewish Believer on Circumcision

Circumcision was a sign and seal of the covenant relationship between God and his people. It began with God's covenant to Abraham and was thought to continue forever: "You are to undergo circumcision, and it will be the sign of the covenant between me and you . . . my covenant in your flesh is to be an everlasting covenant. . . . Any uncircumcised male, who has not been circumcised in the flesh, will be cut off from his people; he has broken my covenant" (Gen. 17:10, 13–14).

In the two centuries leading up to the time of Christ, circumcision became a hallmark of Israel's distinctiveness in relationship to the Gentile nations. The Syrian rulers had tried to forbid circumcision to the men of Israel. The Maccabean freedom fighters, in turn, reasserted the indispensability of circumcision and fought to retain this rite. Circumcision became the principal symbol of being a Jew. This attitude is well illustrated in the book of *Jubilees* (c. 180–170 B.C.): "Anyone who is born whose own flesh is not circumcised on the eighth day is not from the sons of the covenant which the Lord made for Abraham since he is from the children of destruction. And there is therefore no sign upon him so that he might belong to the Lord because he is destined to be destroyed and annihilated from the earth and to be uprooted from the earth because he has broken the covenant of the Lord our God."[A-85]

When the Maccabees successfully revolted against the Syrians, they would not permit any Gentiles to remain in the country unless they were circumcised: "Hyrcanus . . . permitted them to stay in that country, if they would circumcise their genitals, and make use of the laws of the Jews; and they . . . submitted to the use of circumcision, and the rest of the Jewish ways of living; at which time therefore this befell them, that they were hereafter no other than Jews."[A-86]

Circumcision thus became the principal rite for Gentile proselytes to perform. The book of Judith (2d cent. B.C.) tells of a Gentile (an Ammonite) who joined the covenant people of God: "And when Achior saw all that the God of Israel had done, he believed firmly in God, and was circumcised, and joined the house of Israel, remaining so to this day."[A-87]

For these Pharisaic Jewish Christians, there was no clear indication that Jesus had abolished circumcision. Gentiles should enter the family of God not only by putting their faith in Jesus of Nazareth as the Messiah, but also by accepting the law, just as Gentiles had done historically. How, then, could the most important sign of the covenant be neglected?

▶ Gentile Attitudes About Circumcision

Gentiles were culturally predisposed to avoid circumcision. Although public nudity was acceptable in the context of the baths, gymnasia, and athletic events, circumcision was viewed as repugnant. "Circumcision became the target of horror, contempt, scorn, and ridicule."[A-88] Antiochus IV Epiphanes (c. 160 B.C.) outlawed circumcision with a penalty of death: Mothers with their circumcised babies were killed.[A-89] Philo writes that Jews were often ridiculed because of circumcision.[A-90]

One scholar observes: "Cultural pressure against circumcision manifested itself in several ways. Since Jews were widely known to be circumcised, they were frequently ridiculed and ostracized. The Greek gymnasium or the Roman bath, both favorite institutions of those who could afford them, presupposed public nudity. The severe social stigma against circumcision discouraged Jews from participating."[A-91] parties should amiably "agree to differ." This is central to the gospel and needs to be settled by the principal leaders of the church—the apostles and elders in Jerusalem.

They traveled through Phoenicia and Samaria (15:3). This three hundred-mile journey is not an overnight ride. It takes a minimum of twenty days and probably takes them a month, given their stops along the way. The fruit of the evangelism of those Jerusalem believers scattered by the persecution is now seen (see 11:19). Communities of believers have been established not only in the territory of Phoenicia, but also in Samaria (see 8:5–25). Paul and Barnabas stop and fellowship with a number of these groups of believers. They encourage them by telling them the story of numerous Gentile conversions in Antioch, on the island of Cyprus, and in the regions of Cilicia and southern Galatia.

Believers who belonged to the party of the Pharisees (15:5). Not surprisingly, those who are the most vocal opponents of Paul's position were Pharisees prior to their conversion. In accepting Jesus as the Messiah of Israel, they have not changed their distinctive views about the law.

And required to obey the law of Moses (15:5). Here we find that the issue actually involves more than circumcision. The Pharisaic believers want the Gentiles to observe the entire law of Moses as a condition of membership in the people of God. This includes especially the laws regulating ritual purity, Sabbath observance, and the celebration of the key Jewish festivals. In the letter he writes to the Galatians just prior to the council, Paul explains the implications of the Pharisaic believers' view: "Again I declare to every man who lets himself be circumcised that he is obligated to obey the whole law" (Gal. 5:3).

The apostles and elders met to consider this question (15:6). Of the Twelve, Luke only explicitly mentions Peter, but presumably at least some of the others are present (see comments on 11:30). The fact that leaders from the church at Antioch travel to Jerusalem and meet with the leaders there shows the ongoing oversight for the entire movement exerted by the Jerusalem church and the commitment of both churches to be unified in the essential aspects of the gospel.

SAMARIA

The place of sacrifice on Mount Gerizim.

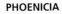

PHOENICIA

The modern city of Sidon.

Some time ago God made a choice (15:7). Peter, the principal leader among the Twelve, stands up and addresses the entire group. He begins by calling them to reflect back on the beginning of the Christian movement when God sovereignly chooses him to explain the gospel to Cornelius and his household some ten years ago.

He accepted them by giving the Holy Spirit to them (15:8). Peter does not take a "middle of the road" position on the issue. He presents a case firmly on the side of Paul and opposed to the Pharisaic believers. His argument is that God poured out his Spirit on Cornelius and his household before they received circumcision (and actually even before they received water baptism). For Peter, this signified God's sovereign decision to incorporate Gentiles into the one people of God solely on the basis of faith apart from a requirement of circumcision or law obedience.

He purified their hearts by faith (15:9). "Purification" and cleansing (*katharisas*) from sin no longer comes from the blood of the sacrifices, but by putting one's trust in the Messiah, who has poured out his blood to make purification for sin.[289]

You try to test God (15:10). Whether they do so wittingly or unwittingly, Peter accuses his Pharisaic brothers of putting God to the test by requiring circumcision and law-obedience of Gentile believers. Testing God is tantamount to unbelief. The Israelites repeatedly tested God in the desert by distrusting him and grumbling against what he was doing among them.[290] God himself has decided to free Christians (Jewish and Gentile) from the former obligations of circumcision and law-observance. To insist on these rites and practices now, in light of the significance of the cross and resurrection of Christ, is to ignore the significance of what God has done and to blatantly provoke him.

Putting on the necks of the disciples a yoke (15:10). A yoke is a harness put around the neck and front quarters of a large animal enabling it to pull a farm implement or a wagon. It comes to represent any kind of burden someone endures and, in some instances, an image of bondage. Sin, for instance, is a yoke around a person's neck (Lam. 1:14). Jews referred to the law of Moses as a yoke, but one that protected them from the dangers of this world. The Mishnah says, "He that takes upon himself the yoke of the Law, from him shall be taken away the yoke of the kingdom [that is, the troubles that come from the earthly rulers] and the yoke of worldly care; but he that throws off the yoke of the Law, upon him shall be laid the yoke of the kingdom and the yoke of worldly care."[291] Peter, however, takes a much more negative view of the law—especially in terms of the numerous rituals, purity regulations, and various observances—viewing it as an inappropriate

YOKE

The man is plowing his field in the Nile Valley with a pair of bulls harnessed to a wooden yoke.

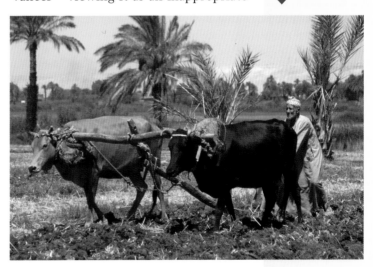

burden to place on Gentiles as a condition for their salvation.

Neither we nor our fathers have been able to bear (15:10). The law, taken together with the protective "fence" of traditions and regulations the Pharisees have built around it, is beyond human ability to keep. In this, Peter reflects the teaching of his master, who said to the Pharisees, "You load people down with burdens they can hardly carry, and you yourselves will not lift one finger to help them" (Luke 11:46).

We believe it is through the grace of our Lord Jesus that we are saved (15:11). The main point of Peter's argument is not how difficult the law is to keep, but rather its irrelevance now for salvation. Peter states unequivocally that salvation—for Jews as well as for Gentiles—is through grace and not by successfully completing the various requirements of the law. In this he is perfectly in line with Paul, who also stresses that salvation was a gift of God's grace (Eph. 2:8–9; Gal. 2:15–16). For Peter, the case of Cornelius and his household is paradigmatic. Their reception of the Spirit upon exercising faith in the Lord Jesus is sufficient evidence to convince him that God now receives Gentiles as his new covenant people solely on the basis of faith.

The whole assembly became silent (15:12). The silence of the crowd of believers may imply that the majority are

---

▶ **The Jerusalem Council and Galatians**

There has long been a debate in biblical scholarship over the relationship between Acts 15 and Galatians 2:1–10. On the surface, the correspondence between the two chapters suggests that Galatians 2 represents Paul's report about the conference to the Galatian Christians: It speaks of Paul and Barnabas going up to Jerusalem; a meeting with James, Peter, and John; a discussion about the Gentile mission and the role of circumcision; and an agreement reached by all the parties involved. This means that Galatians is written well after the Jerusalem council. Many who take this view see the letter written to Christians in the northern ethnic territory of Galatia, especially in the cities of Ankyra, Tavium, and Pessinus (places not mentioned by Luke in Acts).

A closer examination of the two texts, however, leads to the conclusion that the two passages are not referring to the same events. First, Acts 15 speaks of a meeting with the apostles, elders, and the entire church; the meeting in Galatians 2 is held privately with the "pillars" of the church. Second, Galatians says nothing about the so-called "Apostolic Decree." Third, Paul's dispute with Peter (Gal. 2:11–21) is less likely to occur after the Jerusalem Council than before. Fourth, Luke speaks of three visits that Paul makes to Jerusalem: first (Acts 9:26–29), second (Acts 11:27–30; 12:25), and third (Acts 15). Paul refers to the events of Gal 2:1–10 as occurring on his second visit (Gal 2:1), i.e. the famine relief visit, not the Jerusalem Council visit.

In light of this evidence, it is best to see the events spoken of in Galatians 2 as having taken place on Paul's previous trip to Jerusalem recorded in Acts 11:30 and 12:25. This is the time when Paul and Barnabas take a relief gift to Christians in Jerusalem on behalf of the church at Antioch. It is a time conducive to a private meeting with James, Peter, and John to discuss the outreach to the Gentiles. This view is then understood as Paul writing Galatians just after his mission to Antioch, Iconium, Lystra, and Derbe (the southern part of the Roman province of Galatia) just prior to the Jerusalem Council.[A-92] convinced by Peter and agree with him.[292] It must be remembered, however, that Luke does not give us a full account of the proceedings in Jerusalem, an account that would have taken many pages. Now the group listens to Paul and Barnabas describe the ways God has been at work through them in reaching Gentiles. The "signs and wonders" give further evidence of God's own sovereign inclusion of Gentiles on the basis of faith and not through fulfilling the requirements of the law.

James spoke up (15:13). On James, see comments on 12:17. He appears to have become one of the most significant leaders in the Jerusalem church. Like Peter, he does not lend his support to the position of the Pharisaic believers. He agrees with Paul and Barnabas in affirming that circumcision and law-obedience are not essential for obtaining salvation.

Simon (15:14). James refers to Peter by his Hebrew name (see 2 Peter 1:1).

Taking from the Gentiles a people for himself (15:14). God originally chose Israel, not the Gentiles (*ethnē*), to be his special people: "For you are a people holy to the LORD your God. Out of all the peoples (*ethnē*) on the face of the earth, the LORD has chosen you to be his treasured possession" (Deut. 14:2). James recognizes that there has been a fundamental change in the way God constitutes his people. Yet this change is not unanticipated, since Zechariah 2:11 predicted a future period when "many nations [*ethnē*] will be joined with the LORD in that day and will become my people." Once again, the conversion of Cornelius and his household is seen to mark this development in the plan of God.

I will return and rebuild David's fallen tent (15:16). James appeals to Amos 9:11–12 to provide further support for what Peter has said and what actually happened in the case of Cornelius and the many other Gentiles who believed the gospel and received the Spirit. This prophecy anticipates Gentiles becoming a part of God's people when the house of David is restored. The royal line of David reigning over Israel came to an end when Jehoiachin and Zedekiah were exiled to Babylon (2 Kings 24:15–25:7). This prophecy anticipates a reestablishment of David's kingdom. The Qumran community also understood this passage in a messianic sense.[293]

The coming of Jesus marks the restoration of "David's fallen tent." The conviction that Jesus of Nazareth is David's descendant who assumes the throne is at the heart of the gospel message (see Acts 2:29–36; 13:22–23).

That the remnant of men may seek the Lord, and all the Gentiles who bear my name (15:17). With the coming of Jesus as the Davidic Messiah, the extension of his reign over the Gentiles has now taken place. They enter the covenant people of God not by "becoming Jews," however, but as Gentiles by putting their faith in Jesus. The "remnant" is more properly translated "all other peoples"— that is, all the various ethnic groups comprising the Gentiles. There are many Old Testament prophecies that speak of the conversion of the nations in the messianic age.[294]

We should not make it difficult for the Gentiles (15:19). James comes down squarely on the side of Peter, Paul, and Barnabas. Because of his relationship with Peter as one of the "pillars" of the Jerusalem church (Gal. 2:7), it is doubtful that this decision reflects a change in his thinking from a position similar to the Pharisaic brothers. This meeting in Jerusalem appears to be the catalyst for formalizing a conviction that the Jerusalem leadership already holds, but that significantly challenges the Jewish believers who belong to the Pharisaic party.

The term translated "make it difficult" (*parenochleō*) is a strong, colorful, and somewhat pejorative term only appearing here in the New Testament. It is used in the Old Testament to describe what the lions could have done to Daniel (Dan. 6:19, 24 LXX) and to portray Delilah's nagging of Sampson (Judg. 16:16).

Telling them to abstain from (15:20). The focus of the debate now shifts away from the question of what is essential for salvation to one of how to help Gentile believers break away from their idolatrous pre-Christian practices. Each of these four instructions relates to dangers associated with involvement in idolatry. James wants to make sure that these Gentiles make a clean break with their past when they embrace the living and true God. The instructions are, therefore, guidelines to assist their growth as believers, knowing full well that the Gentiles will continue to face significant cultural and spiritual pressures stemming from their past immersion in idolatry and ongoing association with family, friends, and coworkers still involved with it. These guidelines are a practical help in the spiritual and moral battle these Gentiles will face.

Later, in a similar vein, Peter wrote a letter to Gentiles in the northern portion of Asia Minor, encouraging them to abstain from certain practices: "Dear friends, I urge you, as aliens and strangers in the world, to abstain from sinful desires, which war against your soul" (1 Peter 2:11). The apostle John abruptly ended his first letter with the warning, "Dear children, keep yourselves from idols" (1 John 5:21).

It is important that we do not view the so-called "Apostolic Decree" as a compromising effort of the Jewish leaders to get the Gentiles to obey at least some of the Jewish law. The decree is not at all a matter of law-obedience for the sake of obtaining salvation. Nor is the decree a concession to the law-oriented consciences of Jews who want the Gentiles to meet them halfway as a means of expressing cultural sensitivity and thereby promoting unified table fellowship. The latter view cannot explain why these four specific prohibitions are selected as opposed to others. In other words, why didn't the council restrict Gentiles from eating pork in the presence of Jewish believers?

Food polluted by idols (15:20). The Greek word *alisgēma* should not be limited to food, but should be understood as referring to any kind of contact with idolatrous practices. The church father Gregory of Nyssa describes well what James is referring to: "The pollution around the idols, the disgusting smell and smoke of sacrifices, the defiling gore about the altars, and the taint of blood from the offerings."[295] In his revelation on Sinai, the Lord explicitly prohibited the worship of other gods in the first two of the Ten Commandments (Ex. 20:2–6) and forbade offering sacrifices to idols (Lev. 17:7). This is one aspect of the law that is never repealed.

From sexual immorality (15:20). The term *porneia* is used in Judaism to refer to any kind of sexual activity outside the bond of marriage.[296] *Porneia* is roundly condemned throughout the New Testament.[297] The sexual mores of the Greek and Roman world were much more lax than what was expected and practiced in Judaism and early Christianity. This was certainly one area where new Gentile believers needed admonishment. But illicit sexual activity also occurred in connection with the worship of other gods.[298] Growing as a disciple of Christ meant leaving the sensual delights associated with idolatry.

From the meat of strangled animals and from blood (15:20). These prohibitions are often interpreted in light of Leviticus 17:10–16. In this context, both Israelites and resident Gentile aliens were commanded not to eat blood or any animal from which the blood had not been drained. But this view does not do justice to the precise wording of this text.

"The meat of strangled animals" is an interpretive translation of the Greek word *pnikton*, which simply means "choked" or "strangled." The term neither appears in Leviticus 17 nor anywhere else in the Old Testament, but is known and used in connection with pagan idolatry.[299] Both Jews and the early Christians are convinced that demonic spirits were involved in idolatry. When writing to the Corinthians, the apostle Paul wrote, "The sacrifices of pagans are offered to demons, not to God, and I do not want you to be participants with demons" (1 Cor. 10:20). In commenting on this passage, the church father Origen observes that demons especially like blood and sacrificial animals that have been strangled:

> As to things strangled, we are forbidden by Scripture to partake of them, because the blood is still in them; and blood, especially the odour arising from blood, is said to be the food of demons. Perhaps, then, if we were to eat of strangled animals, we might have such spirits feeding along with us.[300]

Similarly, Basil the Great, explains how demons savor the smell of burning blood from the burnt offering of a strangled animal:

> The demon sits in the idol, to which sacrifices are brought, and partakes of a part of the blood that has evaporated into the air as well as of the steam rising from the fat and from the rest of the burnt-offering.[301]

The so-called decree from the Jerusalem church may, therefore, best be understood as a set of guidelines to protect new Gentile believers from the many dangers of idolatry.[302] The intent of

◀ *left*

AN IDOL

Statue of the goddess Aphrodite.

these latter two prohibitions may help these Gentile believers avoid demonic influence that could arise after consuming sacrificial food.

For Moses has been preached in every city from the earliest times (15:21). James concludes his address by pointing out that the law of Moses is read in the synagogues on a regular basis in all the cities of the Mediterranean world where there are Jewish communities, which is certainly all major cities. Philo observes that "each seventh day there stand wide open in every city thousands of schools [viz., synagogues]" where anyone can come and hear the law of Moses being taught.[303]

The literal translation of this clause is, "Moses has those who are preaching him." Perhaps James concludes in this way to provide a contrast: There will continue to be those who proclaim Moses in the synagogues throughout the empire, burdening the Gentiles with the requirements of the law for salvation (Acts 15:19), but we will preach a message of grace based on faith in the work of Christ (15:11). James is not trying to reassure the Pharisaic Christians that the Gentile converts will learn the law of Moses in all of their respective cities. This wrongly assumes that these Gentiles will be attending the synagogue services every Sabbath.

They chose Judas (called Barsabbas) (15:22). What Peter and James say appears to gain the consensus of the Jerusalem church. They then choose two representatives from the church to travel to Antioch with Paul and Barnabas to communicate to the Gentile believers what has happened in the proceedings and to pass on the letter. Of Judas, also called Barsabbas (as was Joseph in 1:23), nothing else is known in the New Testament or later church history.

Silas (15:22). Silas is the shortened form of the name "Silvanus." He is here identified as a leader (*hēgoumenos*) in the Jerusalem church, which probably implies that he was an "elder" (*presbyteros*). It is not known whether he was from a Pharisaic background. Paul gains a great deal of confidence in this leader as they spend time together in Jerusalem and Antioch. Silas becomes a fellow missionary with Paul and helps to plant the churches in Philippi, Thessalonica, and Corinth (see the references to him in 16:19–18:5). He is mentioned by Paul in three of the letters.[304] He is not mentioned again after Paul leaves Corinth for Ephesus and then Jerusalem (unless the "Silas" Peter refers to in 1 Peter 5:12 is the same person). Luke comes into contact with Silas at Troas and journeys with the team to Philippi (see Acts 16:10–12). Silas may have been an important source of information for Luke about the early years of the Jerusalem church and the Jerusalem Council.

Some went out from us without our authorization and disturbed you (15:24). Luke now reveals that "the men who came down from Judea to Antioch" did so without the blessing and approval of the apostles and elders of the Jerusalem church. Some interpreters suggest that the Jerusalem church sent them on a "fact-finding" mission, but that they drastically overstepped their authority by insisting on circumcision and law observance.[305] The arrival of this law-oriented delegation in Antioch corresponds with the arrival of a similar delegation in the churches of Galatia (Gal. 1:7). Both had the same disruptive impact.

It seemed good to the Holy Spirit (15:28). There was a widespread conviction among the leaders of the Jerusalem church that the Holy Spirit led them in making these decisions. Given the gravity of this decision and its implications for the future direction of the church, it is especially significant to have this unanimity on discerning how the Spirit is directing them.

The Church at Antioch Receives the News (15:30–33)

They gathered the church together and delivered the letter (15:30). Letters are typically read aloud to groups in antiquity. They are not duplicated and distributed.

Glad for its encouraging message (15:31). Their worst fears—that the Pharisaic Christian delegation represent the convictions of the Jerusalem congregation—are alleviated. The Gentile Christians in Antioch now rejoice in a reaffirmation of the genuine unity with the Jerusalem church. They are probably also encouraged by the letter giving wise

guidance to stimulate their growth in the faith.

Who themselves were prophets, said much to encourage and strengthen the brothers (15:32). Luke now informs us that Judas and Silas are prophets. Although Christians often think of prophecy primarily in terms of revelatory insight into future events, there is a strong edificatory function in prophecy, as exhibited here (see 1 Cor. 14:3).

Paul Returns to South Galatia (15:36–40)

Let us go back and visit the brothers in all the towns (15:36). Paul's proposal to Barnabas is to return and visit all of the new believers from their recent trip across the island of Cyprus as well as Antioch, Iconium, Lystra, and Derbe in the southern part of the Roman province of Galatia.

They had such a sharp disagreement that they parted company (15:39). Apparently Paul is still upset about John Mark's sudden departure during their initial journey to Asia Minor (see 13:13). He does not see John Mark as a suitable coworker for the kind of rigorous mission work they will be engaging in. The word translated "sharp disagreement" (*paroxysmos*) is a rare and colorful word. It is used only twice in the Greek Old Testament—in both instances to express "the furious anger" of God.[306] Whatever it is that so exasperated Paul about John Mark was overcome in the next few years and the two are completely reconciled. He was with Paul ten years later during his Roman imprisonment (Col. 4:10; Philem. 24), and Paul asked for him during his subsequent imprisonment in terms expressing his high esteem: "Get Mark and bring him with you, because he is helpful to me in my ministry" (2 Tim. 4:11).

Barnabas took Mark and sailed for Cyprus (15:39). Accompanied by Mark, Barnabas returns to his native island to continue the evangelization of the cities and villages that he began with Paul. This is the last that we hear of Barnabas in the biblical record.

Paul chose Silas and left (15:40). Not wanting to travel alone and aware of the significant giftedness of Silas, Paul contacts him (he is presumably still in Jerusalem) and asks him to be his coworker in the mission. Because of Silas's prominent role as a leader in the Jerusalem church, he is an important voice for the churches in Galatia disturbed by the Pharisaic Christians insisting on circumcision and law observance.

He went through Syria and Cilicia (15:40). Rather than taking a boat from Seleucia to Attalia, Paul decides to take an overland route. This enables him to visit and encourage churches that he and others had previously established in these

regions, including his hometown of Tarsus (see 9:30; 11:25). This rugged route takes him through a narrow mountainous pass called the "Cilician Gates."

Revisiting the Galatian Churches (Acts 16:1–5)

A disciple named Timothy (16:1). During Paul's initial visit to Lystra, members of three generations of one family come to faith in Jesus Christ—a grandmother (Lois), a mother (Eunice), and a son (Timothy) (see 2 Tim. 1:5). This young man, Timothy, has taken root and grown so much in his faith and the knowledge of the Lord that Paul now wants him to accompany him and Silas in their missionary efforts.

Timothy becomes Paul's most valuable coworker over the span of the next fifteen years. He works alongside Paul in the evangelization of Philippi, Thessalonica, Berea (Acts 17:14–15), Corinth (18:5; 2 Cor. 1:19), and Ephesus (Acts 19:22). During Paul's Ephesian ministry, Timothy serves as Paul's emissary to the Corinthian church for handling some of the problems that surface there (1 Cor. 4:17; 16:10). In a similar way, he serves the Philippian church (Phil. 2:19) and

right ▶

ANTIOCH OF SYRIA TO SOUTH GALATIA

the Thessalonian church (1 Thess. 3:2, 6). He is also named as a cowriter of Paul's second letter to the Corinthians (2 Cor. 1:1; Phil. 1:1) as well as his letters to the Thessalonians (1 Thess. 1:1; 2 Thess. 1:1), the Colossians (Col. 1:1), and to Philemon (Philem. 1). Shortly before the end of his life, Paul writes Timothy two personal letters: One gives a variety of instructions for exercising leadership in the church at Ephesus (1 Tim.) and the other offers significant advice and encouragement to the young coworker as Paul awaits death in a Roman prison (2 Tim.). Paul's affection for him is summed up well in a remark he makes to the Philippian church: "As a son with his father he has served with me in the work of the gospel" (Phil. 2:22).

It appears that Timothy is known to the writer of Hebrews. The reference to him in that book refers to his recent release from prison (Heb. 13:23).

Whose mother was a Jewess and a believer, but whose father was a Greek (16:1). The fact that Timothy has a Greek father and has not been circumcised suggests that he was not brought up in a strictly observant Jewish household. Such a mixed marriage between a Jew and a Greek was illegal in Jewish law.[307] According to rabbinic texts, descent is reckoned from the mother's line in the event of an illegal marriage, which means that Timothy is regarded as a Jew by the Jewish community.[308] It was not uncommon to find mixed marriages in the Diaspora. The tense of the verb in the passage suggests that Timothy's father has died.

He circumcised him because of the Jews who lived in that area (16:3). Some think Paul is grossly inconsistent in this action. After all, he comes from the Jerusalem Council, where circumcision and law

obedience are deemed unnecessary. But it must be recognized that Paul's purpose in circumcising Timothy is not to ensure him or others of the fact that he is now saved; Timothy is already a vibrant believer. His purpose is strategic. The Jews who live in the area know that Timothy is a Jew, but they would regard him

◀

DERBE

The countryside south of Derbe from on top of the ancient site.

LYSTRA INSCRIPTION

The name "Lystra" appears in this inscription at the Konya museum.

▼

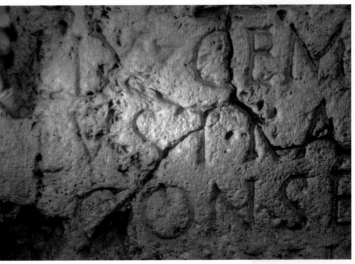

as an apostate since he is not circumcised. If Paul wants to continue to have access to the synagogues, here and elsewhere, as a part of his evangelistic strategy, he needs to make Timothy acceptable to Jews. This action accords well with what Paul says elsewhere about the overriding concerns of the gospel: "Though I am free and belong to no man, I make myself a slave to everyone, to win as many as possible. To the Jews I became like a Jew, to win the Jews. To those under the law I became like one under the law (though I myself am not under the law), so as to win those under the law" (1 Cor. 9:19–20). There was nothing inherently evil now in circumcision. It is a matter of indifference as long as it is not mistakenly taken as essential to salvation (1 Cor. 7:19).

They delivered the decisions (16:4). Paul by no means ignores the outcome of the Council's decisions. He faithfully passes these on to the churches in every city. In this regard, Silas fills a vital role in confirming and explaining the Jerusalem church's decisions to Jewish Christians. As a leader of the Jerusalem church, he commands a great deal of respect. Four cities were evangelized in Paul's first visit to this area. It is possible that these new believers shared their faith in other

towns and villages in south Galatia since then, resulting in communities of believers in other places.

Paul's Vision of a Man in Macedonia (Acts 16:6–10)

The region of Phrygia and Galatia (16:6). This expression is better translated "the region of Phrygian Galatia" (also known as Phrygia Paroreius). Phrygia here serves as an adjective modifying Galatia.[309] When the Romans created the political province of Galatia in 25 B.C., they incorporated a portion of the ethnic territory of Phrygia. The rest of Phrygia was included in the Roman province of Asia.[310] In 16:1, Luke tells us that Paul came to Lystra and Derbe (not in Phrygian Galatia). Now Paul continues his journey through Phrygian Galatia (this includes the cities of Iconium and Antioch). This interpretation of the phrase stands in contrast to the view of some other interpreters who do not take Phrygia as an adjective here and interpret Galatia as a reference to the northern ethnic territory of Galatia. They would then see this as a highly abbreviated reference to Paul evangelizing the cities of Ancyra, Tavium, and Pessinus.[311] But this is unlikely since this region of north Galatia lies over 125 miles northeast of any route between Lystra and the region of Mysia.[312]

Kept by the Holy Spirit from preaching the word in the province of Asia (16:6). Paul apparently follows the principal Roman road called the *Via Sebaste* from Lystra to Antioch. From there, he probably intends to take the road that runs due west through Apamea, Colossae, and Laodicea to the Asia Minor capital of Ephesus.

They came to the border of Mysia (16:7). Paul now journeys northwest from Antioch along the major road to either Cotiaeum or further north to Dorylaeum. Both of these cities are close to the ancient territories of Mysia and Bithynia. Mysia is part of the Roman province of Asia Minor and is bordered by Lydia to the south, Phrygia to the east, and Bithynia to the north. Two of the principal cities of Mysia are Adramytium and Pergamum.

They tried to enter Bithynia (16:7). Bithynia is a territory in northern Asia Minor that forms a dual Roman province with Pontus.[313] Because Ephesus is closed to him, it is not surprising that Paul wants to enter this region since the city of Byzantium (later to become Constantinople) is located here as well as other important cities such as Nicomedia (the seat of the Roman government), Nicaea, and Prusa. Although Paul never has the

opportunity to preach the gospel in this region, the apostle Peter later spends time evangelizing in Bithynia and Pontus (see 1 Peter 1:1).

Paul had a vision of a man of Macedonia (16:9). When Paul reaches Troas, he cannot go any farther west by land and the Lord has directed him not to go north or south. Is he to stay in Troas? Where is he to go? In the midst of this quandary, the Lord gives him a night vision that

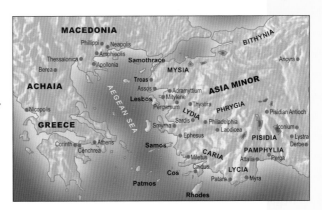

▶ Alexandria Troas

Paul and his companions come to Troas after the Holy Spirit prevents them from going north to Bithynia or south to Mysia or Ephesus. Paul also spends some time there after his Ephesian ministry (Acts 20:5–6).

Troas was properly called "Alexandria Troas" or "Alexandria" of the Troad.[A-93] It was believed that the Troad was the area originally under Trojan rule during the time of Homer. The city was originally called Antigoneia, but was renamed in honor of Alexander the Great. The city was located on the west coast of Asia Minor about ten miles south of the ancient city of Troy (Ilium) and was the major seaport for northwest

Asia Minor because of its artificial harbor.

Augustus made the city a Roman colony, the only one he established in western Asia Minor. By Paul's time Strabo spoke of Troas as "one of the famous cities of the world."[A-94] The city had a temple dedicated to the god Smintheus, a god of healing and associated with Asclepios.

The ruins are located on a site called Eski Stamboul and remain unexcavated. Recently, however, E. Schwertheim and C. Özgünel have jointly inaugurated an expedition to conduct a thorough site survey.[A-95]

provides him with clear direction. There have been some creative guesses as to the identity of this man of Macedonia, ranging from Luke to Alexander the Great. It is unlikely that the Lord gives him a vision of any particular person other than the fact that the man is clearly identifiable as a Macedonian.

We got ready (16:10). Luke's narrative now abruptly changes from the third person ("he" and "they") to the first person ("we"). The best explanation for this is that Luke, the author of Acts, now joins the team of Paul, Silas, and Timothy. It is possible that Troas was Luke's home although there is a strong historical tradition that Luke is from Antioch of Syria.[314] Some speculate that Luke lives in Philippi and that, as an itinerant doctor, he travels between Philippi and Troas.[315] Wherever he is from, Luke is already a believer and an ardent supporter of this missionary outreach to the Gentiles. He travels with the team to Philippi and apparently remains there after the other three leave (this is where the "we" passages end for a time).

The Evangelization of Philippi (Acts 16:11–40)

Luke tells the exciting and dramatic story of the creation of the church in Philippi by giving three vignettes involving people who come in contact with the gospel. One is a prominent, wealthy, Gentile businesswoman who is already a Jewish sympathizer and attached to the local synagogue. The second is a low-status slave girl who is being exploited for spirit-inspired divination abilities. Luke never says that she puts her faith in Christ, but the account of Paul's encounter with her demonstrates the power of Christ over the realm of the demonic. The final episode involves a Roman official charged with keeping Paul and Silas in custody. He is ready to commit suicide until the missionaries intervene and give him hope rooted in Jesus Christ.

▶ Macedonia

The region of Macedonia had an illustrious history as the homeland of Philip II of Macedon and his son, Alexander the Great. From Philip's time on, Macedonia was a leading center and purveyor of Greek culture. The territory lay between the Balkans and the Greek peninsula.[A-96] In spite of its distinctiveness, Macedonia was often considered to have been a part of Greece.

Caesar Augustus (Octavian) made Macedonia a Roman senatorial province in 27 B.C., but this was later combined into one large province with Achaia by Tiberius. In A.D. 44, six years before Paul's visit, the emperor Claudius once again separated Macedonia into a distinct senatorial province. Macedonia was divided into four separate districts with the cities Amphipolis, Thessalonica, Pella, and Pelagonia as the administrative centers of each. Augustus established four cities in the province as Roman colonies: Philippi, Kassandreia, Dion, and Pella.

Numerous gods and goddesses were worshiped throughout this province, including Zeus, Apollo, Artemis, Bendis (goddess of the forests and fertility), the Cabiri, *Theos Hypsistos* ("God most high"), Herakles, Dionysus, the Egyptian deities Serapis and Isis, and *Dea Syria* (Atargatis).[A-97] The emperor cult and the cult of *Roma* (the deified personification of Rome) were also well established. The New Testament is the most important witness for a Jewish presence in Macedonia.

◄

SAMOTHRACE

Ruins of the ancient city on the island.

Sailed straight for Samothrace (16:11). Samothrace is a small island (sixty-nine square miles) in the northern Aegean sea lying twenty-five miles south of the Thracian coast. The name reveals the island's historical connection with Thrace—it is the "Samos" ("height" or "mountain") of Thrace. This reflects the fact that a mountainous peak rises to a height of 5250 feet on the island. The mountain makes the island visible for boats passing through the Hellespont and provides a safe anchorage on the north side of the island. On the way to Macedonia, Paul's boat apparently spends the night at this port. The island is best known as the center of worship for the cult of the Cabiri.

The next day on to Neapolis (16:11). Neapolis (modern Kavála) is the principal port city for this district of Macedonia and serves its main city, Philippi, which is located nine miles inland. After landing here, Paul most likely takes the famous Roman highway called the *Egnatian Way* to Philippi. The road continues west from Philippi through Amphipolis and Thessalonica and on to the Adriatic sea. One scholar rightly notes, "The mention of the seaport and the island of Samothrace are unnecessary detail in the account of the trip to the main destination of Philippi . . . but it is detail that is understandable in an alleged eyewitness account."[316]

NEAPOLIS

The modern harbor at Kavala, the site of ancient Neapolis.

▼

A Roman colony (16:12). Augustus created the Roman colony of Philippi expressly for the purpose of making homes for his military veterans. He was also motivated by a desire to establish a military presence in this strategic area and to further the cultural and political Romanization of Macedonia. Philippi had a sizeable population of Latin-speak-

▶ Philippi

Properly known as *Colonia Julia Augusta Philippensis,* Philippi was famous in antiquity as the place commemorating the victory of Octavian (later called Caesar Augustus) over the murderers of Julius Caesar, Brutus, and Cassius in 42 B.C.[A-98] Following the battle, Augustus made Philippi a Roman colony and renamed it after his daughter.

The city was founded nearly four hundred years earlier and called *Krenides* because of the springs in the area. It was located not far from the base of Mt. Pangaion, where there were a number of productive gold mines. Shortly after it was established, the town was taken over by the rising Greek leader, Philip of Macedon (father of Alexander the Great), who renamed it after himself.

The Roman colony occupied a vast portion of the plain of Datos. It was a wealthy city because of the mines, its relationship to Rome, and its commer-

cial importance on the *Via Egnatia.* The population would have consisted of a mixture of Greeks, Romans, native Thracians, and foreigners.

Emperor worship thrived in the city, but so did the worship of Greek, Roman, Thracian, Egyptian, and Asia Minor deities. Among the most prominent were Dionysus, Bendis (a local Thracian deity), Artemis, Apollo Comaeus, Isis, Liber Pater, Hercules, the Thracian Horseman, and the cult of the emperors (Augustus, Livia, and Claudius).

Among the remains of Philippi visible today is a theater (built in the 4th cent. B.C. and altered by the Romans in the third cent. A.D.), two Byzantine era churches (Basilica A = c. A.D. 500; Basilica B = c. A.D. 560), some scant remains of the ancient forum, and the foundations of the sanctuary dedicated to the Egyptian deities.

ing Roman citizens. Colonies were often initially established with between two and five thousand men.[317] The citizens were probably extended the privilege of the *ius Italicum*, giving them the same rights as colonies in Italy and *immunitas* (exemption from direct taxation).

The leading city of that district of Macedonia (16:12). Politically, Philippi was not the leading city. Thessalonica was the seat of the Roman procounsul for the entirety of Macedonia and Amphipolis the center of Roman administration for this one of the four districts of Macedonia. By this expression "first city" (*prōtē polis*), Luke accurately conveys the local sense of pride in Philippi as the "leading city"—even over the regional capital.

We went outside the city gate to the river (16:13). The "river" (*potamos*) refers either to the River Gangites or to a stream that flows a short distance away from the city's west gate.[318]

A place of prayer (16:13). Many commentators assume that there was no synagogue in Philippi and that there was simply an area by the river Gangites that the Jews had agreed to meet each Sabbath. But there may have been a synagogue building there. The Greek term *proseuchē* can mean "prayer," but in Jewish circles it was also a common term for "a house of prayer," that is, a synagogue. By referring to the Philippian synagogue as a *proseuchē*, Luke simply reflects what they likely called it, similar to the usage of Jews in Palestine and Egypt.[319] Jews commonly built syn-

agogues outside of cities near the sea or by rivers to facilitate their ritual washings. A recently discovered grave stele from the western cemetery of Philippi mentions the presence of a synagogue in the city: "Nikostratos Aurelios Oxycholios himself furnished this flat tomb and if someone lays down on it a dead body of others, he will give a fine to the synagogue."[320] The inscription, however, dates to a time later than Paul's ministry in the city—probably to the early third century.

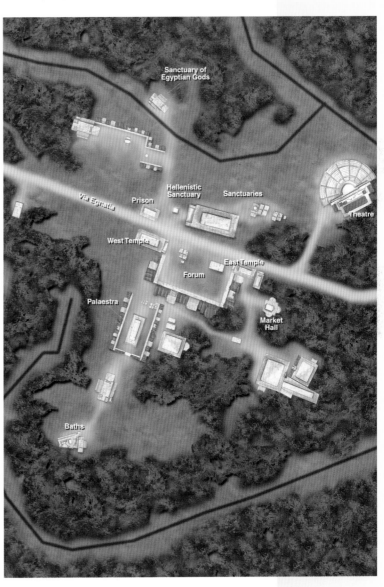

Began to speak to the women who had gathered there (16:13). Although Luke does not deny that men are present (according to Jewish law, ten men were required to form a synagogue[321]), he focuses on the women who are in attendance at the synagogue on that day. This remark provides a bridge to speak about one prominent woman who places her faith in Christ.

A woman named Lydia (16:14). The name "Lydia" could be an ethnic nickname for this woman—Lydia was the ethnic territory in western Asia Minor where the city of Thyatira was located. There are inscriptions, however, that attest to Lydia as a proper name in Asia Minor, such as one referring to Julia Lydia Laterane of Ephesus, "high priestess and daughter of Asia."[322]

A dealer in purple cloth from the city of Thyatira (16:14). The dyeing of fabrics in the city of Thyatira was well known in the ancient world, which included a long history. Homer speaks of purple-dyeing taking place in the regions of Lydia and Caria as early as his time.[323] Pliny notes that the practice was invented by the Lydians in the city of Sardis.[324] Seven

right ▶

PURPLE DYE

Shellfish from which a purple fluid was extracted and used in the production of dye.

RIVER NEAR PHIIPPI

▼

inscriptions have now been discovered that attest to a guild of dyers in Thyatira.[325] One inscription even speaks of the guild of purple dyers in Thessalonica honoring one of their members who was Thyatiran.[326] Two inscriptions discovered in Philippi mention "sellers of purple."[327] Purple dye was commonly made from a marine shellfish called a *Murex*, but there is also evidence that dyers from this area used the root from a madder plant.

It is not surprising to find a woman undertaking such business in Macedonia or in Asia Minor. Women had begun taking on significant business and civic roles in these areas. Evidently, Lydia had moved to Philippi and set up a business of selling dyed fabrics to Romans in the colony. Her business was apparently doing well if she owned a house large enough to accommodate Paul and his team in addition to the members of her household.

A worshiper of God (16:14). Lydia is not a Jew, but she becomes exposed to the God of Israel through the local synagogue and places her faith in him. Many more women were God-fearers in the ancient world than men. Of all the Jewish inscriptions discovered thus far that mention God-fearers, about 80 percent are women.[328]

She and the members of her household were baptized (16:15). After listening to Paul's teaching about Jesus as the Messiah, Lydia and her entire household believe the gospel and are immediately baptized. Her household includes any of her children still living at home and her domestic servants. It is most likely that she has been widowed, although we cannot rule out the possibility that she is divorced (keeping in mind that divorce was less common than it is now).

Come and stay at my house (16:15). Just as Peter stayed at the house of the Gentile Cornelius, Paul, Silas, Timothy, and Luke now stay at the home of a single Gentile businesswoman. For Silas, as an elder from the Jerusalem church, this is undoubtedly a difficult step to take in light of his former Jewish scruples about Gentile impurity.

A slave girl who had a spirit by which she predicted the future (16:16). This young girl receives her inspiration from what Luke literally calls a "python spirit" (*pneuma pythōn*). The Python dragon or serpent was associated with the oracle sanctuary at Delphi, about eighty miles northwest of Athens. In the story of the origin of the cult, Apollo killed this large snake that was guarding the entrance to the oracle cave. Apollo then became the guardian and patron of this sanctuary, which was an entrance to the underworld. During the Greco-Roman era, people came from all over the Mediterranean world to consult the priestesses of Apollo (called *pythia*) for advice. The Pythia descended into the oracle grotto to seek inspiration from the god by allowing herself to be possessed by a spirit. She then arose and uttered the god's instructions to the inquirer—first in an ecstatic, gibberish speech and then typically in the form of Greek verse.[329] The first-century writer Plutarch, himself a priest of the Delphic god, refers to the priestesses as *engastrimythoi* ("belly talkers") because of the sound of their voices as the god or spirit spoke through them.[330]

These men are servants of the Most High God (16:17). "Most High" is a title given to God in the Old Testament emphasizing his sovereignty. The LXX often translates ʾelyôn with *hypsistos,* as in Deuteronomy 32:8, "when the Most High (ʾelyôn/hypsistos) gave the nations their inheritance. . . ."[331] Some scholars suggest that the young girl is referring not to the God of Israel, but to a deity known in the Greco-Roman world as *Theos Hypsistos.* This is, at least, how Philippian Gentiles who hear the girl's screams might understand her.[332] The worship of such a deity, sometimes associated with Zeus, is well attested in inscriptions. It is more likely, however, that the indwelling python spirit rightly recognizes the connection of Paul and his companions to the one true God. This explains, in part, the reason why the slave girl harasses the missionaries. This is also consistent with the way one of the spirits manifesting in the Gerasene demoniac responds to Jesus with the exclamation: "What do you want with me, Jesus, Son of the Most High (*theos hypsistos*) God" (Luke 8:28; Mark 5:7).

In the name of Jesus Christ I command you to come out of her! (16:18). Paul discerns in this slave girl an evil spirit, or demon, that enables her to practice divination. Following the example of Jesus and based on the authority of his name, Paul firmly commands the demon to leave, and it promptly obeys.

PHILIPPI

(left) Small temples cut into the rock hillside near the theater in honor of Artemis and Silvanus.

(right) Temple ruins.

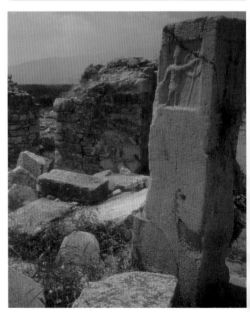

Paul's method leaves an impression of awe and curiosity on many who witness the event. His method differs sharply from other exorcists, who performed rituals (often involving animal viscera and blood), used various substances, uttered strings of unintelligible sounds, and invoked a number of deities and helper spirits (they frequently included Hekate, the goddess of the underworld). It also was unusual for any other pagan shaman/exorcist to seek to remove a "python spirit," which was thought to be a good and helpful spirit, not a malevolent one. Of course for Paul, this is part of the deception of idolatry. This attitude toward a Python spirit is consistent with his Jewish background, which taught that a person who has a Python and "speaks from his armpits" has "a familiar spirit."[333]

In the subsequent history of the church, "python spirits" are seen as evil and are subject to exorcism. Origen speaks of some who "have been under the influence of the demon called Python, i.e. the ventriloquial spirit, from the commencement of their existence."[334] Another early church leader observes, "For pythons prophesy, yet they are cast out by us as demons and put to flight."[335]

Realized that their hope of making money was gone (16:19). The passage literally reads, "their hope of making money had gone out of her," which highlights the fact that her fortune telling was not a gimmick, but was dependent on the python spirit that lived within her. This poor girl was doubly exploited—by the spirit and by those who owned her.

Dragged them into the marketplace to face the authorities (16:19). The missionaries are taken to the *agora*, or, as the Romans called it, the *forum*. There they are accused before the *stratēgoi*, the equivalent of the Latin *duoviri* (lit., "the two men")—the two principal city officials in any Roman colony. They are responsible for judging cases and wielding the power to inflict punishment. Helmut Koester comments that the use of this term here "reveals Luke's good knowledge of the local situation."[336]

These men are Jews . . . advocating customs unlawful for us Romans to accept or practice (16:20). Luke previously explained the real motive of the accusers was that they were furious about their loss of potential income. When they now bring their case to the judges, however, they begin their case with racial comments. This is not surprising since anti-Jewish feelings were common among the Romans.[337] Tacitus goes so far as to denounce the Jews by saying that "they have a hostile hatred of all men."[338]

▶An Example of a Roman Beating

Cicero gives an account of a man named Gaius Servilius who suffered an official beating from Roman *rhabdychoi* (Latin = *lictors*): He was beaten "till finally the senior lictor Sextius . . . took the butt end of his stick, and began to strike the poor man violently across the eyes, so that he fell helpless to the ground, his face and eyes streaming with blood. Even then his assailants continued to rain blows on his prostrate body. . . . Such was the treatment he then received; and having been carried off for dead at the time, very soon afterwards he died."[A-99]

The principal charge, however, is not exactly a fabrication. Roman law prohibited the adoption of foreign cults: "No one shall have gods for himself, either new or foreign gods, unless they are officially recognized."[339] In practice, this law was typically overlooked, but it was a convenient and effective charge for the owners of the slave girl.

Stripped and beaten . . . thrown into prison (16:22–23). Paul and Silas receive a severe punishment. They are handed over to the *rhabdychoi* ("rod bearers") and shackled in the city prison. It appears that Timothy and Luke somehow escape this punishment, possibly because they are not as actively engaged in the preaching and in the exorcism as their companions, or possibly because they are not Jews. It is curious why Paul and Silas do not invoke their Roman citizenship at this point to avoid this painful and degrading punishment. It is worth remembering, however, that Paul's principal allegiance is to Christ, not to Rome. Paul knows that if a church is successfully established in Philippi, these new believers will assuredly face hostile opposition from the local populace (as indeed was the case not only here, but in Thessalonica and elsewhere). Not all of these people would be protected from punishment by Roman citizenship. His suffering demonstrates that the gospel is for all people, not just Roman citizens, and that it is worth suffering for (see Phil. 3:20). This is only one of three occasions in which Paul faced this kind of beating (2 Cor. 11:25).

He put them in the inner cell and fastened their feet in the stocks (16:24). The inner cell was typically reserved for those who committed serious crimes and for those of low social status. The magistrates intended to demoralize and humiliate the two men.[340]

A set of Roman leg stocks was found in the Gladiators Barracks at Pompeii, Italy, and illustrate the kind of mechanism securing Paul and Silas. It was a long metal comb with spaces between each of the teeth for the legs of a number of prisoners to be placed. A metal rod was inserted into the holes in the top of each tooth and anchored to the floor. The bar pressed tightly on the legs and made it impossible for the prisoners to shift positions to avoid discomfort. Sleep was only possible

PHILIPPIAN JAIL

(left) Ruins of the structure that is traditionally identified as the prison where Paul stayed.

(right) An inner cell.
▼

through laying or sitting on the floor. The stocks were not only a security measure, but were also a form of torture.[341]

Singing hymns to God (16:25). In spite of the indignity, shame, and physical pain they suffer, both from the severe beating as well as from the leg stocks and the repulsive conditions of the inner cell, Paul and Silas find joy in their Lord. This is as much a demonstration of the power of the Spirit as the exorcism they have just performed. Among the hymns they sing are probably not only some of the Old Testament Psalms, but also new compositions in honor and praise of Christ (Col. 3:16).

A violent earthquake (16:26). There is nothing surprising about an earthquake rocking this region. It was prone to more severe earthquakes than it is today. What is surprising, though, is the timing of the quake and its impact on the prison; that is, it loosens the leg stocks from the floor of the prison.

Sirs, what must I do to be saved? (16:30). The potential escape of all of the prisoners causes the jailer to fear for his own life as a penalty for the escape of any of his wards while he is on duty. Faced with the ultimate question of life—"What happens when I die?"—the jailer asks Paul and Silas. Most likely the jailer has heard some of the hymns Paul and Silas sang and possibly overheard them sharing the gospel with other prisoners. So, at his moment of crisis, he has heard enough to know that these two men have the answers.

He was filled with joy (16:34). Rejoicing is a common response for those who believe the gospel (e.g., the new believers in Jerusalem, 2:46; the Ethiopian, 8:39;

the Gentiles at Pisidian Antioch, 13:48, 52) and a sign of the presence of the Holy Spirit.[342]

When it was daylight (16:35). The hours between midnight and 7:00 A.M. are eventful for Paul and Silas: a major earthquake (and presumably a number of aftershocks), preventing a suicide, leading the jailer to Christ, having their wounds treated, sharing the gospel with the jailer's family, baptizing them, and enjoying a meal with this family of new believers. The weary and wounded missionaries now have another big day in front of them.

Release those men (16:35). Perhaps the magistrates originally only desired to hold the men overnight as a deterrent to their activities. But they may also have now connected the earthquake with the two men and want them out of town as soon as possible.[343] Greeks and Romans often saw natural phenomena, such as earthquakes, as omens and signs from the gods.

Even though we are Roman citizens (16:37). Roman law prohibited Roman citizens from receiving the kind of treatment Paul and Silas suffered. The Roman historian Livy writes, "The Porcian law alone seems to have been passed to protect

ROMAN SWORDS

Models of ancient Roman swords.

the persons of the citizens, imposing, as it did, a heavy penalty if anyone should scourge or put to death a Roman citizen."[344] The later Julian laws upheld the Porcian laws: "Also liable under the *Lex Julia* on public violence is anyone who, while holding *imperium* or office, puts to death or flogs a Roman citizen contrary to his [right of] appeal."[345] It is not surprising, then, that the magistrates are greatly alarmed.

Then they left (16:40). Luke apparently remains in Philippi since he does not here say, "then *we* left." Because he is not Jewish and not at the center of the controversy, Luke is not likely under the same pressure to leave. It is also possible that he is already known in the city as a medical doctor. The circumstances provide him with the opportunity to stay and help these new believers grow in the faith. Luke reappears in the narrative in 20:5–6 some six or seven years later. He is still in Philippi, but joins Paul for his trip to Jerusalem at the conclusion of the so-called third missionary journey.

Reaching Thessalonica (Acts 17:1–9)

Taking the famous Egnatian Way—the road leading west from Byzantium to the Adriatic sea—Paul, Silas, and Timothy travel a hundred miles from Philippi to Thessalonica. The party decides to spend no time in the cities of Amphipolis and Apollonia (except for a possible stayover of a night in each city). Amphipolis is situated on a hill surrounded on three sides by the river Strymon. As beautiful and significant as these cities are, Paul desires to go to the strategic center for the province—Thessalonica. From there, the entire province can hear the gospel message, as in fact happened (see 1 Thess. 1:8).

Thessalonica (17:1). The city was named after the half-sister of Alexander the Great when it was founded in 315 B.C. by her husband Cassander. It became the seat for the Roman governor and the capital for the entire province of Macedonia. Possessing a fine harbor, Thessalonica

▶ The Gods and Goddesses Worshiped at Thessalonica

Just like any other city in the Mediterranean world, Thessalonica had an array of cults.[A-100] The Greek deities Zeus, Asclepius, Aphrodite, and Demeter were popular among the people. Archaeologists have discovered the remains of a sanctuary in the sacred cult area of the city devoted to the Egyptian god Sarapis. This deity was worshiped as one who healed the sick, worked miracles, broke the powers of astral fate, and could speak to his followers in dreams. Many of the inscriptions found at this site also point to the worship of the Egyptian goddess Isis.

By far the most popular cult of the city was the cult of the Cabirus. Not well known, this cult had a wild, bloody, and sexually perverse set of features. The central myth of this cult involved two brothers killing a third, decapitating the body, and burying the head at Mount Olympus. One of the key symbols of the cult was the male genitals. In a similar way, the cult of Dionysus gave prominence to phallic symbolism in addition to the drunken revelry that went along with the celebrations of the god. These two cults certainly had a powerfully negative impact on the social ethics of the city. Converts from these cults had a long way to go in appropriating a distinctively Christian lifestyle.

In addition to these traditional deities, the Thessalonians also revered the Roman rulers as divine. During the reign of Caesar Augustus, a temple was built for the ruler cult to honor Augustus and his successors.

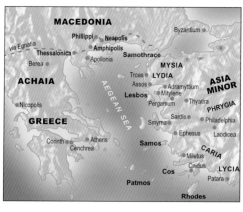

Jewish synagogue (17:1). Archaeologists still have not discovered the remains of the synagogue. A few Jewish inscriptions, however, have been discovered in the city. An inscription published in 1994 that dates to the third century A.D. actually points to the existence of a number of synagogues in the city. The inscription on a sarcophagus (a stone coffin) warns intruders that if anyone places another body in it, they will be liable for a fine of seventy-five thousand denarii "to the synagogues."³⁴⁸

became the chief seaport of Macedonia. Although we do not have precise figures about the population of the city, Strabo notes that it was the most populous city in Macedonia.³⁴⁶ The modern city of Salonica (or Thessaloniki) occupies the site of the ancient city and thereby hinders the undertaking of any extensive archaeological work. With a population of over a half-million, the modern city is the second largest city of Greece.³⁴⁷

Three Sabbath days (17:2). The total length of Paul's stay in Thessalonica may actually have been longer than three weeks; this is merely how long his welcome lasts in the synagogue. We know that he stays long enough to receive a monetary gift from the Philippians (Phil. 4:16) and that he spends time working in the city to earn his support (1 Thess. 2:9).

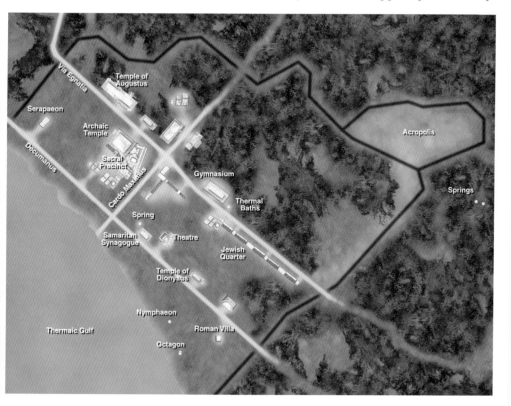

His stay in the city, however, lasts no more than a couple of months.

This Jesus I am proclaiming to you is the Christ (17:3). Over the course of three Sabbaths, Paul attempts to persuade the Thessalonian Jews that Jesus of Nazareth, who was put to death under Pontius Pilate, is indeed the Messiah that they were anticipating. This is particularly difficult since most Jews expected a Messiah that came with power and broke the chains of Roman rule. It is thus necessary for Paul to explain to them where the Old Testament teaches that the Messiah must suffer and die. The key text is the fourth servant song, Isaiah 52:13–53:12.

God-fearing Greeks (17:4). These are Gentiles who have already turned from their gods and goddesses and embraced the one true God. Now, together with some of the Jews, they respond to the gospel.

Prominent women (17:4). These women are probably both Jew and Gentile. Inscriptional evidence points to women participating in all levels of society (although not to the same degree as men) and conducting business in the province.

Jason (17:6). Paul's host may have been a Jew converted during Paul's preaching in the synagogue. His name is a Greek equiv-

REFLECTIONS

PAUL'S CHURCH PLANTING EXPErience in Thessalonica was not ideal from our perspective. What would we think of a church planter who stayed for only a few weeks and provoked the wrath of the city officials and numerous people? Although the persecution forced Paul to leave (in large measure out of concern for the safety of the small nucleus of Thessalonian Christians), God remained powerfully at work. A few months later Paul writes a letter to them rejoicing because of their faith, hope, love, and active proclamation of the gospel—and that in a context of ongoing persecution. We are not alone in the work of the ministry.

THE HARBOR AT MODERN THESSALONICA

alent to the Hebrew names Joshua or Jeshua.[349] Jason's home probably becomes a meeting place for a house church.

Caesar's decrees (17:7). The Roman Caesars issued decrees (*dogma*) warning anyone about predicting a change of ruler over the empire. Caesar Augustus issued an edict in A.D. 11 explicitly forbidding the use of astrology to predict his or anyone else's day of death.[350] The emperor Tiberius reaffirmed this decree (*dogma*) by putting to death foreigners who ignored it.[351]

In response to these decrees, some cities pledged their commitment to the Caesar by offering oaths of loyalty. A good example of such an oath comes from the city of Paphlagonia in Asia Minor (dated to 3 B.C.):

> I swear . . . that I will support Caesar Augustus, his children and descendants, throughout my life, in word, deed and thought . . . that in whatsoever concerns them I will spare neither body nor soul nor life nor children . . . that whenever I see or hear of anything being said, planned or done against them I will report it . . . and whomsoever they regard as enemies I will attack and pursue with arms and the sword by land and by sea. . . .[352]

These oaths help us see how violence toward Paul and his companions could easily be formed.

Another king, one called Jesus (17:7). Because Paul's preaching about Jesus includes references to him as "Lord," the fact that he has a "kingdom," and that he is coming again in judgment, it is easy to

POLITARCHAI
INSCRIPTION

▶ The City Officials

Luke uses a rather uncommon word to refer to the civic officials—the term *politarchai*. Earlier generations of critical scholars argued that the choice of this term by the author of Acts demonstrates his unreliability as a historian. They observed that *politarchai* does not appear in the Greek inscriptions of the first century (or before), whereas it does appear in second century and later literary documents. This is taken as evidence that "Luke" is writing well into the second century and using terminology familiar to him from his own setting.

Archaeology has dramatically vindicated Luke's reliability on this issue. A total of seventy inscriptions have now been discovered that make use of this term. Over three quarters of these are from Macedonia and over half of those are from the city of Thessalonica. Some of these inscriptions date to the first century and a few date as early as the third century B.C.[A-101]

The term appears to have been used primarily in Macedonia as the title for the chief magistrates in the cities. Thus, Luke not only chooses an appropriate term to refer to the local officials at Thessalonica, but appears to have carefully selected the precise title that the Thessalonians are using.

see how Paul's words can be turned against him as a threat to the Roman Caesar. Furthermore, Paul's proclamation about the Day of the Lord and the impending return of Christ (the *parousia*) easily signals to those who hear that he is predicting a change of ruler in direct defiance of the decrees of Caesar.

Thrown into turmoil (17:8). The mob creates an uproar in the city that has big implications for the ongoing life of this infant church. First, Jason and others from his household come under legal trouble and presumably ongoing scrutiny. Second, Paul's life is now in danger and his presence possibly places the lives of the other Christians in jeopardy as long as he remains in the city. This makes it impossible for him to return. Third, the evidence of Paul's letter to the Thessalonians suggests that some of these new believers do, in fact, lose their lives as a result of this local persecution (see 1 Thess. 4:13).

In Berea (17:10–15)

Leaving the Via Egnatia, which goes west to the Adriatic, Paul's friends take him to

Berea, about forty-seven miles southwest of Thessalonica on the road to Athens. Some scholars think that Paul may have originally intended to take the Egnatian Way to the west coast and from there to take a boat to Italy and on to Rome. The fact that Emperor Claudius has recently expelled the Jews from Rome (in A.D. 49) may also contribute to the decision to go south.

Berea (17:10). Lying twenty-five miles inland from the Aegean coast, Berea is situated at the foot of Mount Bemius (Mount Vermion; 6614 feet) and on a tributary of the Haliacmon River at an elevation of 591 feet. The site is occupied by the modern city of Veria. Nevertheless, there have been many archaeological discoveries, including the remains of houses, public buildings, roads, graves, statuary, and inscriptions.[353] Archaeological evidence points to the worship of Zeus Hypsistos, Hermes, Asclepius, and Herakles in this city.[354]

They went to the Jewish synagogue (17:10). As with Thessalonica, no synagogue remains have yet been discovered. A couple of Jewish inscriptions have been found, but these date much later than the time of Paul.

More noble character (17:11). Luke contrasts the response of the Bereans to that of the Thessalonians. He commends the fact that they check Paul's preaching against the testimony of Scripture and are eager to learn. The term he chooses only appears here in the New Testament and is the comparative form of *eugenos*, which can mean "one of noble birth" or simply "noble" or "excellent." An eagerness to learn about God, to discern how he is working, and to evaluate it in light of written revelation is a more excellent path than an emotive response based on faulty knowledge and cultural bias.

Many of the Jews believed (17:12). Paul's preaching once again generates a good response, but this time especially with the Jews. Word quickly reaches the Thessalonian Jews who oppose Paul, and they travel to Berea to try their same methods of stopping him that worked in their own city. Unfortunately, they find success, and Paul is forced to leave the city. He is escorted to the coast by some concerned Christian brothers and from there departs to Athens. There are many possible ports along the coast that Paul may use to catch a boat—Dion, Methone, Makragialos (Pydna), or Aliki.

Luke gives no indication of the amount of time Paul spends in Berea. The circumstances of his stay and the overall chronology of this time suggests no more than a month or two. Although we have no record of Pauline correspondence to this city, we do know that he gains a valuable companion from one of his converts, a man named Sopater (see 20:4).

In Athens (17:16–21)

Athens (17:16). After disembarking at the harbor of Piraeus, Paul walks to

◀

ATHENS

The modern harbor of Piraeus.

Athens and enters the famous city through one of the northwest gates. The size of Athens can be appreciated by the fact that the wall that surrounded the city had a circumference of five to six miles.

As Paul journeys into the heart of the city, he feels a sense of awe at the impressive architecture and grandeur of the immense buildings from this center of Hellenistic culture. What he only heard about previously, he now sees firsthand. Entering the city, the Hephaesteum first comes into view. This is a beautiful Doric style temple dedicated to the god Hephaestus and the goddess Athena built between 449–444 B.C. Just across from this is the Stoa of Attalus, a two-storied colonnaded building gifted to the city c. 150 A.D. by Attalus, King of Pergamum.

Towering above all, however, is the magnificent Parthenon, a Doric temple dedicated to Athena Polias (447–438 B.C.) and sitting atop the Acropolis as a crown. The rectangular temple measures 228 feet by 101 feet (23,000 square feet) and includes Doric columns that stand thirty-four feet high with a diameter at the base of six feet. The columns support a roof made of richly ornamented slabs of

ATHENS

(top left) The temple of Athena Nike.

(top right) Tower of the Winds.

(bottom left) The Parthenon.

(bottom right) A column capital of the Temple of Hephaestus with the agora in the background.
▼ ▶

marble depicting a variety of scenes. Inside the temple stands a thirty-nine-foot high statue of Athena.

The Acropolis itself, a large limestone plateau measuring 1050 feet by 512 feet and rising 512 feet high, stands impressively at the center of the city. The sides of this rocky crag are steep on every side but the west. Also on the Acropolis is the Erechtheum (built 421–405 B.C.) for the worship of Athena and Poseidon, the temple of Athena Nike ("Athena who brings victory") built 427–424 B.C., and the Propylaea (built 437–432 B.C.)—a monumental roofed gateway on the west side of the Acropolis.

As Paul takes in all of these grand sights, he first passes through the Greek Agora ("market place") and then the Roman Agora. Standing prominently in the Roman market is a forty-foot octagonal structure housing a waterclock and sundials known as the Horologion. It is also called "The Tower of the Winds" because it contains carved representations of the eight wind gods below the cornice.

The city was full of idols (17:16). Every building in the city and, indeed, every-where Paul turns have a representation of some god or goddess. The fact of idolatry is nothing new to Paul. He saw it on the streets of Tarsus as a young child; it was present in Damascus, Antioch, and all the cities where he planted churches. There is something about the pervasiveness of it in Athens that causes him to grieve deeply. The spiritual darkness of this city is a tremendous obstacle to the gospel.

The synagogue (17:17). In the midst of such an idolatrous city is a Jewish community that met to worship the one true God. Many Jewish burial inscriptions have been discovered in Athens that

▶ **The City of Athens**
IMPORTANT FACTS:

- Religion: pluralistic, with many gods and goddesses
- Political Importance: free city, but under Roman rule
- Cultural Importance: the historic cradle of Greek civilization and culture, the premier "university town" of the empire

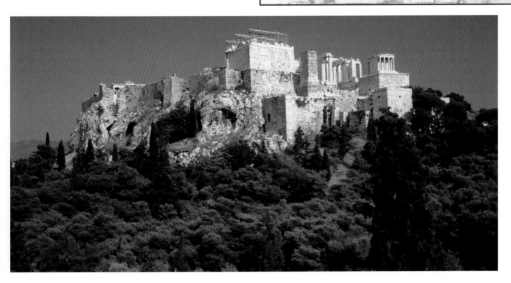

◀

THE ACROPOLIS

attest to the Jewish presence. They range in date from the second century B.C. to the third century A.D., but a high proportion of them date to the first century A.D.[355]

God-fearing Greeks (17:17). Even in Athens, there are Gentiles who have forsaken their deities and turned to God. These Gentiles now hear Paul contend that Jesus is the fulfillment of Israel's messianic hope. In contrast to his accounts of Thessalonica and Berea, Luke

does not tell us the response Paul receives about his preaching in the synagogue at Athens.

The marketplace (17:17). The Greek agora had once served Athens as the center for democratic assemblies. Now as a city under Roman imperial rule, democratic rule is a relic of the classic past. The Greek agora is now filled with altars, statues, and temples. Paul probably spends time presenting the gospel in the Roman agora, the area used for buying and selling and other commercial purposes.[356] There is no shortage of people to talk to in this busy place.

Epicurean and Stoic philosophers (17:18). At some point during Paul's brief stay in Athens, he encounters adherents of two of the most popular philosophical schools.[357] Intrigued by what Paul is saying, these philosophers invite him to address a larger gathering of people.

The Stoics derived their name from the *stoa poikilē* (the "painted colonnade") in the Greek agora. Their founder Zeno

▶ The "Idols" of Athens

There were numerous gods and goddesses worshiped at Athens—more than will be named here. Listed are a few that can be attested by archaeological evidence or because they are mentioned in ancient literature describing Athens.[A-102]

Greek: Athena, the patron goddess of Athens, was probably the most popular with temples and edifices dedicated to her. Certainly every deity of the Greek pantheon was worshiped here. These included Zeus, Hera, Apollo, Ares, Artemis, Aphrodite, Asclepius, Athena Nike, Athena Polias, Castor and Pollux, Demeter, Dionysus, the Erinyes, Eros, Ge, the Graces, Hades (Pluto), Hephaestus (Vulcan), Hekate, Heracles, Hermes, Hestia, Pan,

Persephone, and Poseidon. A vast number of images of Hermes could be found all over the city and particularly in the agora. Numerous images of lesser deities and heroes are also found throughout the city.

Asia Minor: Cybele.

Roman: The Romans identified the gods and goddesses in their pantheon with similar deities in the Greek pantheon. Thus, Jupiter is identified with Zeus, Mars with Ares, etc. Thus, the counterparts of the Roman deities were worshiped in Athens.

Ruler Cult: In 27 B.C., the cult of "Roma" (the divinization of Rome) and the cult of Caesar were established in Athens.

(340–265 B.C.) is from the island of Cyprus. Stoicism is an influential school of thought that was prevalent in the first century and focused on a moral earnestness.

The Epicureans, named after their founder Epicurus (340–270 B.C.), are an often misunderstood group today. While it is true that they say, "Pleasure is the beginning and end of living happily," their understanding of pleasure was not that of unrestrained lust and a party mentality. Their understanding of pleasure chiefly involved "living in accord with nature"; for them, this involved a fairly disciplined and ordered lifestyle. Diogenes Laertius clarifies the Epicurean understanding of "pleasure":

> When, therefore, we maintain that pleasure is the end, we do not mean the pleasures of profligates and those that consist in sensuality, as is supposed by some who are either ignorant or disagree with us or who do not understand, but freedom from pain in the body and from trouble in the mind. For it is not continuous drinkings and revellings, nor the satisfaction of lusts, nor the enjoyment of fish and other luxuries of the wealthy table, which produce a pleasant life, but sober reasoning, searching out the motives for all choice and avoidance, and banishing mere opinions.[358]

The Epicurean philosophy did not attract many adherents among the common people. Most Epicureans were wealthy and educated, that is, from the upper classes of life.

This babbler (17:18). The philosophers use a colorful word to describe Paul from typical Athenian slang, the term *spermologos*.[359] This word was commonly used to describe a person who went around the market picking up scraps. Some philosophers used it when referring to a person who picked up scraps of learning here and there.

To Agora
House of Arrhephori
Areopagos
Erechtheum
Belvedere
Porch of Caryatids
Altar of Rome and Augustus
Propylaia
Sacred Way
Monument of Agrippa
Temple of Athena Nike
Parthenon
Temple of Themis
Stoa
Sacred Spring
Odeon of Herodes Atticus
Stoa of Eumenes
Theatre of Dionysus
Odeon of Perikles
Orchestra
Stoa
Altar
Roman Baths

Foreign gods . . . Jesus and the resurrection (17:18). Although they view Paul demeaningly, these philosophers are curious about the non-Greek Eastern deities he is proclaiming. This interest is nothing new for Greeks and Romans. They embraced many of the gods and goddesses coming from the Orient, including Persian, Anatolian, Egyptian, and Syrian deities.

The philosophers misunderstand Paul to be proclaiming two gods. The wording of Luke's text can be interpreted to mean that they think Paul is teaching about a god named "Jesus" and a goddess named "Anastasis" (the Greek word meaning "resurrection"). The idea of a bodily resurrection from the dead is a strange idea to a Greek during this time.

The term that is used here for foreign gods is the Greek word *daimonia*, elsewhere translated "demons," with the meaning "evil spirits." The Greeks, however, used the word in a neutral sense to refer to the gods.

The Areopagus (17:19). The name means "hill of Ares" (the Greek god of war). The Romans identified Ares with their god of war, Mars, which resulted in the alternative translation, "Mars Hill." The hill was adjacent to the Acropolis with only a ravine separating the two. Standing 378 feet high, this rocky hill

---

▶ Stoic Beliefs

Creation: The world has been created out of fire, the foundational element. From fire came air, from air water, and from water earth. The balance achieved by these elements is attributed to *logos,* the impersonal forces that create and hold together.

God: The Stoics are pantheistic materialists (god is in everything). They may refer to the supreme god as Zeus, but they can also equate him with fate, nature, *logos,* and the "world soul" (with the universe understood as a living organism). The gods of the popular religions exist, but their mythologies are only a crude expression of the truth.

ΖΗΝΩΝ Ο ΚΙΤΙΕΥΣ

ZENO

The founder of Stoicism.

Soul: The soul is corporeal, similar to the human body. The closest comparison to the soul is warm breath of a human.

◀

Sin: There is no concept of sin. Error is nothing more than the failure of attaining the ideal, or acting contrary to the laws of nature. There is no concept of offending the will of an all-holy, righteous being.

Fate: We all live in the grip of the relentless pull of fate. Although we have no control over destiny, we do have the power to control our selves and our wills.

Ethics: The pursuit of virtue is the primary good. To be virtuous is to live in harmony with reason (logos) and to be at one with nature.

Afterlife: The Stoics believe in a limited survival after death, but not in the sense of a personal, individual existence. Individual human souls will ultimately be absorbed into the basic elements in periodic cosmic conflagrations. Seneca says, "We whose souls are blessed and who have shared in eternity . . . will be changed into our former elements."[A-103]

Hell: There is no underworld or place of torture for those who die.

was once the foundation for the supreme court of ancient Athens, but now no buildings remain on the site.[360]

Originally, the Areopagus was the ruling council for the city of Athens. As a democratic form of government progressively came into prominence, the powers of the council began to wane (around the 6th cent. B.C.). When Roman power became dominant in Greece, the Areopagus was reinstated as the governing body of the city. There is some question as to whether this council met on the hill or at a different location in the city (such as the Royal Stoa, the *Stoa Basileios*).[361] It is not likely, however, that Paul is standing before this governing body in an official trial. Paul appears informally before a group of people—including Stoics, Epicureans, and other philosophers—who evidently meet on the hill to dialogue and debate on various issues.

Talking about and listening to the latest ideas (17:21). Luke's comment about the Athenians passing their days away discussing the latest ideas is culturally appropriate; this is what some Greek writers said about them. The Greek historian Thucydides records an observer reproaching the Athenians by saying: "You are the best people at being deceived by something new that is said."[362]

Paul Addresses the Areopagus (17:22–34)

Taking advantage of a unique opportunity to proclaim the gospel, Paul

---

▶ Epicurean Beliefs

Creation: The world developed out of a collection of atoms in space that operate according to natural laws. There is not a divine creation. Epicureanism is an essentially materialist worldview.

God: Gods exist, but they live outside the world in interstellar spaces. They do not intervene in the affairs of humanity, so there is no place for providence or prayer. Nor is there any reason to fear them. Because they are superior beings, they are worthy of worship and honor. Because so little attention is paid to the gods, the Epicureans are called "atheists" by their contemporaries.

Soul: The soul is like the body in that it is composed of atoms. It is thus corporeal. According to Lucretius, once it separates from the body, it has no existence.[A-104]

EPICURUS

Sin: There is no concept of sin. The avoidance of actions that produce pain is a major objective of the Epicurean.

Ethics: The chief goal of human existence is to live in accord with nature. This involves understanding the physical laws of the universe and living in a consistent manner with these. Pleasure is in accord with nature and instructs us how to live in harmony with her. Pleasure represents the absence of pain.

Community: Friendship in community is a primary source of pleasure.

Afterlife: There is no life after death. When the body dies, the soul also disintegrates. According to Epicurus, "Death is nothing to us; for the body, when it has been resolved into its elements, has no feeling, and that which has no feeling is nothing to us."[A-105] Epicureans do not accept the idea of a bodily resurrection.

Hell: There is no underworld or place of torture for those who die.

addresses a large gathering of people at the Areopagus.[363] Luke provides us with an apt summary of what Paul says. This message is of great importance because it gives us insight into how the apostle communicates the gospel to non-Jews— in this instance, Greek philosophers and people who worship a variety of other gods.

The thrust of his address is in response to the observation of the Epi-

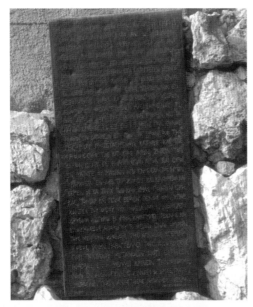

▶

AREOPAGUS (MARS HILL)

(right) A bronze plaque with the text of Paul's speech on the hillside.

(bottom) The location of the ancient Areopagus.

▼

cureans and Stoics that "he seems to be advocating foreign gods" (17:18). Paul tactfully yet firmly declares that he is proclaiming the one true God.

It is striking to see the ways that Paul tailors his message to communicate to these people. This message contrasts considerably with what Paul said when he spoke in the synagogue at Antioch of Pisidia (13:16–41). There he recounted Israel's history and peppered his sermon with quotations from the Old Testament.

Here he employs an entirely different strategy. Recalling the numerous statues, temples, and altars he has seen in his walks through the agora and around the city, he finds an entrée with the people by referring to the altar "TO AN UNKNOWN GOD." He thereby capitalizes on their concession of at least some ignorance of ultimate reality.

When Paul says, "Now what you worship as something unknown I am going to proclaim to you" (17:23), he does not imply by this statement that they are already unconsciously worshiping the one true God. This merely serves as a means to raise for them the most basic question of life: Who is God?[364]

In the first part of his message, he confidently states that the God he proclaims is indeed the supreme God who is Creator, Lord of all, and the source of life. Up to this point, many of his listeners are inclined to believe what he is saying (except, of course, the Epicureans). Paul then reveals that this God is not aloof from his creation, but has established it in a way that humanity seeks after him. To support his denial of the utter transcendence of God, Paul cites lines from two Greek poets, Epimenides and Aratus (see below).

Lest we think that Paul has watered down his gospel by adapting it so readily to his Greek audience, we need to take a deeper look at what he actually says. Apart from the lines he quotes from the two Greek poets, the language, imagery, and concepts in his sermon are derived from the Old Testament. His entire message is thoroughly rooted in a biblical worldview and not in a Greek polytheistic, pantheistic, or dualistic worldview. The following chart shows the Old Testament references to many of Paul's statements.

What Paul says about the one true God is, by implication, a biting critique of idol worship. On this, many of the Epicureans and some of the Stoics agreed. But the larger part of the people, who are immersed in the worship of the various gods and goddesses, find what Paul says hard to accept.

Very religious (17:22). The word that Paul uses here—the comparative form of *deisidaimonia*—can be translated "superstitious" in the sense that they revere many gods and fear the possibility of offending them. This may be the sense that Paul intends because he calls attention to the altar dedicated to an "unknown god." It is possible, however, that Paul means nothing more than that they are devoted to many gods. This comment shows that Paul's audience includes many people who are not Stoics or Epicureans since the remark is not

Paul's Dependence on the Old Testament in the Areopagus Address	
Statement	**Old Testament Reference**
God made the world and everything in it (v. 24)	Gen. 1–2; Isa. 42:5; Jer. 10:12, 16
Lord of heaven and earth (v. 24)	Ex. 20:11; Isa. 42:5 (see also Matt. 11:25)
God does not live in temples built by hands (v. 24)	1 Kings 8:27 (see also 2 Cor. 5:1)
God does not need anything from the people he has created (v. 25)	1 Chron. 29:14; Ps. 50:7–15
God as the source of "breath" (v. 25)	Gen. 2:7; Isa. 42:5
God appointed the eras for the successive nations (v. 26)	Deut. 32:8; Dan. 2:36–45 (see also Luke 21:24)
God established national boundaries (v. 26)	Deut. 32:8; Ps. 74:17
God desires that people would seek him (v. 27)	Ps. 14:2; Prov. 8:17; Isa. 55:6; 65:1; Jer. 29:13
God is not far away (v. 27)	Ps. 145:18; Jer. 23:23–24
God is not like an image made out of gold, silver, or stone (v. 29)	Deut. 5:8; Ps. 115:2–8; Isa. 37:19; 44:9–20
God has overlooked such ignorance (v. 30)	(see Rom. 3:25)
God calls men now to repent (v. 30)	Isa. 59:20; Jer. 15:19; Ezek. 14:6; 18:30, 32; (see also Matt. 3:2; 4:17; Acts 2:38; 3:19)
God will judge the world (v. 31)	Ps. 9:8; 96:13; 98:9; Isa. 66:16; Jer. 25:31 (see also Matt. 11:22, 24; 12:36)
God has appointed a man who will judge (v. 31)	(see John 5:22, 27, 30)

typical of either school of thought. In fact, the Epicureans speak demeaningly of people who are "superstitious."

An altar with this inscription: TO AN UNKNOWN GOD (17:23). Although archaeologists have still to discover an altar with this inscription, ancient writers clearly attest to the existence of such altars:

> *Pausanias* (2d cent. A.D.): "The Athenians have another harbor at Mounychia with a temple of Mounychian Artemis, and one at Phaleron, as I said, with Demeter's sanctuary beside it. The temple of Athena Skiras is also here, and one of Zeus further off, *and altars of the 'Unknown gods,'* and of heroes, and the children of Theseus and Phaleros."[365]

> *Philostratus* (late 2d cent. A.D.): Athens is a place "where altars are set up in honor even of unknown gods."[366]

> *Diogenes Laertius* (3d cent. A.D.): This Epicurean author reports that "nameless altars" (*anōnymous bōmous*) can be found in different parts of Athens. These were set up in honor of gods whose names had been forgotten or

local deities whose names were unknown. Epimenides had ostensibly appeased these unknown gods to avert a plague afflicting Athens.[367]

People living during this time were afraid of what might happen if they did not properly honor a local deity. They could bring sickness or misfortune on their household or city by not giving the god or goddess the proper veneration. On the other hand, by honoring the deity, one might experience benevolence and blessings from the deity. By setting up altars even to unknown gods, people could be sure that they were not unwittingly neglecting to honor one of the gods.

He determined the times (17:26). By establishing the providence of God over the course of history, Paul clearly distinguishes his view of a personal God from the fatalism of the Stoics and the impersonal view of the Epicureans. These comments also show God to be more concerned about his creation than what is popularly thought to be true about the Greek gods.

For in him we live and move and have our being (17:28). This appears to be a citation from a poem attributed to Epimenides (c. 600 B.C.):

> *They fashioned a tomb for thee,*
> *O holy and high one—*
> *The Cretans, always liars, evil beasts,*
> *idle bellies!—*
> *But thou art not dead; thou livest and*
> *abidest for ever,*
> For in thee we live and move and
> have our being.[368]

Epimenides was originally from the island of Crete, but came to Athens and taught about the gods and allegedly per-

ALTAR TO AN IDOL

The altar of Zeus Agoraios in the Athenian agora.

▼

formed many wonders. By quoting this line, Paul seems to give tacit approval to a pantheistic conception of God (such as held by the Stoics). This is not the case, however. This pagan concept of God is correct only up to a certain point. The God Paul proclaims is not so immanent in humanity (as salt infuses water) that individuals are in fact divine. Otherwise his comments about the impending judgment and the resurrection of the dead make no sense. The line also bolsters his argument against idolatry in that idols lack life, they cannot move, and they have no real existence.

We are his offspring (17:28). Paul's next quotation is from a Stoic philosopher who is originally from the city of Soli in Cilicia (not far from Tarsus). Aratus (315–240 B.C.) also traveled to Athens where he learned his Stoicism from Zeno, the founder of the philosophy. In an astronomical poem, entitled *Phaenomena*, Aratus speaks of Zeus:

> *Let us begin with Zeus. Never,*
>   *O men, let us leave him*
>   *unmentioned.*
> *All the ways are full of Zeus, and all*
>   *the market-places of human*
>   *beings.*
> *The sea is full of him; so are the*
>   *harbors.*
> *In every way we have all to do with*
>   *Zeus, for we are truly his*
>   *offspring.*[369]

Once again, Paul cites a pagan philosopher and agrees with his conception of divinity up to a point. Yet, as we already noted, Paul is not a pantheist. He conceives of men and women as created in the image of God, but not actually participating in the divine nature. If people bear this divine likeness, it is inconsistent to create inanimate objects as representations of the gods. Paul then uses these two quotations to bolster his criticism of the idolatry that vexes his soul.

He commands all people everywhere to repent ... he will judge the world (17:30–31). Paul does not soft-pedal the demands of the gospel. Repentance for these people involves above all turning from their gods to serve the living and true God (see the pattern of the Thessalonians that Paul commends; 1 Thess. 1:9). The God Paul proclaims will bring history to a conclusion and there will be a time of judgment by the resurrected Jesus.

A few men became followers of Paul and believed (17:34). Paul's overall response is discouraging. Only "a few" believe. Perhaps this is enough for the beginnings of one house church (although we have no other indications that a church is started at this time). Because of the increasing tendency in Greek thought toward a rigorously dualistic view of the person—a strong separation between the material and immaterial—the notion of a reanimation of the physical body is considered repugnant. Why be joined again with that which is inferior and base? Consequently, this idea is rejected.

Dionysius, a member of the Areopagus (17:34). Luke's comment about Dionysius makes it clear that at least some official members of the ruling council are present when Paul speaks. In his history of the church, Eusebius records a tradition stemming from another Dionysus from Corinth (c. 170 A.D.). He further informs us that Dionysius the Areopagite who, as related in the Acts, was converted to the faith by the Apostle Paul, was the first to be appointed Bishop of Athens.[370]

In Corinth (18:1–17)

Although not forced to leave Athens, Paul wants to get to Corinth—the strategic center of the province of Achaia. He stays in this city for eighteen months, longer than he has spent in any other place during his mission. Many people, both Jews and Gentiles, turn to Christ during this important ministry. Following a period of intense opposition to the gospel from certain Jews, the Roman ruler over the province of Achaia makes a critical decision imposing a bearing on the legal freedom of Christianity for the next decade.

Corinth (18:1). The city of Corinth had a rather tumultuous history leading up to the time of the apostle Paul.[371] The orig-

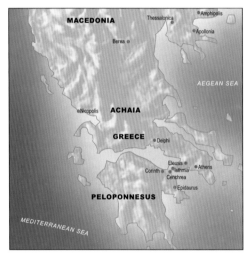

MACEDONIA
AND ACHAIA

inal (Greek) city of Corinth was wiped off the map by the Roman general L. Mummius and his troops in 146 B.C. because the city was part of a confederacy aligned against Rome. The city was not rebuilt immediately and the site lay largely unoccupied for a century. Due to its strategic location overlooking the isthmus connecting the Peloponnesus to central Greece, Julius Caesar city rebuilt the city and established it as a Roman colony in 44 B.C. The city rapidly grew and acquired a distinctively Roman character.

By the time of Paul's arrival, Corinth is serving as the capital of the Roman province of Achaia (which encompasses Athens). The province includes the whole of the Peloponnese as well as territories on the other side of the isthmus (such as Epirus, Aetolia, and Thessaly). The city is also a thriving commercial center because it controls the important trade route between east and west as well as the land route between northern Greece (and Macedonia) and the Peloponnese.

Corinth was served by two ports—five miles to the east was Cenchrea on the Saronic Gulf with access to the Aegean Sea and two miles to the north was Lechaeum on the Gulf of Corinth leading to the Adriatic Sea.

The immorality in the city was renowned in antiquity and often associated with the cult of Aphrodite. The first-century historian Strabo claims that the temple owned a thousand prostitutes:

> And the temple of Aphrodite was so rich that it owned more than a thousand temple-slaves, courtesans, whom both men and women had dedicated to the goddess. And therefore it was also on account of these women that the city was crowded with people and grew rich; for instance, the ship-captains freely

▶ The City of Corinth
IMPORTANT FACTS:

- Population: 80,000–100,000[A-106]
- Prominent Religions: Apollo, Athena, Isis, Serapis, Asclepius, Aphrodite, Demeter and Kore; Tyche (Fortuna); the Ruler Cult; Judaism
- Roman Colony
- Seat of the Roman Government for the Province of Achaia

CORINTH

An aerial view of the ancient city of Corinth from the top of the Acrocorinth.

▶ Archaeological Remains in Corinth

The site of ancient Corinth is unoccupied and there are extensive remains. Since 1896, the American School of Classical Studies has been the principal entity conducting excavations at Corinth.

The foundation and columns of a sixth century Doric temple (possibly for Apollo) is the most noticeable structure one sees today in arriving at the site. Just east of the temple is the well-preserved Lechaeum Road that leads from the forum to the harbor (about two miles away). On the east side of this road, just before reaching the forum, is the fountain of Peirene, the collection and distribution point of the city's water supply. The large rectangular forum had two stoas (colonnades)—one on the northwest and another on the south running the entire length of the forum. A large square stone platform stands on the south side of the forum that has been identified as the *rostra* (or *bēma*), the speaker's platform from where an official announcement might be made or a civic official might address an assembly.[A-107]

The remains of temples and shops line each of the sides of the forum. Some remains on the west side of the forum of the temple have been provisionally identified as belonging to Aphrodite (Venus), the Clarian Apollo, Tyche (Fortuna), and Hercules. Still further west are the scant remains of a large temple constructed during the reign of Claudius that was probably the site of the imperial cult temple.

Archaeologists have recently focused their efforts on the sanctuary of Demeter and Kore, which is located just south of the city on the slope leading to the ascent to the Acrocorinth. Some thirty-six dining halls have been identified at the sanctuary along with the discovery of much cookware. Recently, archaeologists discovered eighteen curse tablets in one of the rooms of the sanctuary that date to the first or second century A.D.

In the far north part of the city (a half mile north of the forum), archaeologists have found the remains of a sanctuary of the healing god Asclepius. This structure would have pre-dated the Roman colony, but was probably still in use as an Asclepion during Paul's time. Excavators have found many terra-cotta replicas of human body parts (such as arms, legs, eyes, ears, breasts, and genitals) apparently donated to the temple as expressions of gratitude for the god's healing. More recently, they have unearthed about four thousand oil lamps in the fountain adjacent to the Asclepion (the Fountain of Laerna). The lamps appear to date substantially later than the New Testament era. Some of the lamps are inscribed with the line: "Angels who dwell on these waters."[A-108] squandered their money, and hence the proverb, "Not for every man is the voyage to Corinth."[372]

Although the relevance of Strabo's claim for the New Testament period has sometimes been disputed by modern scholars, his testimony likely reflects accurately on the social situation of Corinth at the time of Paul.[373] The women of Aphrodite extended their lascivious trade not only in the temple on the Acrocorinth (the 1900-foot mountain just south of the city), but throughout the city as well. In the pre-Roman era of Corinth, there were a series of expressions people used in the Greek-speaking world built on the word

Corinth to refer to various kinds of sexual activities: "to act the Corinthian" (*korinthiazomai*) means practicing fornication; "Corinthian companions" (*korinthiai hetairai*) and "Corinthian girls" (*korinthiai korai*) were prostitutes.[374]

Aquila . . . with his wife Priscilla (18:2). Not long after arriving in the city, Paul develops a close friendship and ultimately a life-long partnership with a Christian couple who have recently arrived from Rome.[375] They work with Paul for the duration of his stay at Corinth, accompany him to Ephesus, and later return to Rome after the death of Emperor Claudius. Aquila is originally

CORINTH

(top) The Lechaeon Road leading into the Roman city with the Acrocorinth in the background.

(bottom left) Columns from the ancient temple of Apollo.

(bottom right) The Corinthian canal, which was dug across the isthmus in modern times.

from Pontus, a region of northern Asia Minor along the coast of the Black Sea. The name Priscilla is a diminutive and familiar form of Prisca.

Claudius had ordered all the Jews to leave Rome (18:2). Aquila and Priscilla had no choice about departing from Rome. The Roman emperor actually took the radical step of ordering every Jew to leave Rome immediately. This was nothing new for the Jews. A similar expulsion occurred twenty years earlier under the reign of Tiberius.[376] There were also significant ethnic tensions between the Jews and Gentiles in Alexandria and other cities in the empire.

From the first year of his reign (A.D. 41), Claudius looked with suspicion on the Jews. The Roman historian Dio Cassius notes this when he writes:

> When the Jews had again multiplied to a point where their numbers made it difficult to expel them from the city without a riot, he did not directly banish them, but forbade

them to gather together in accordance with their ancestral way of life.[377]

Eight years later (A.D. 49), Claudius was no longer tolerant and decided to rid the city of the Jews altogether. In his biography of Claudius, Suetonius corroborates Luke's account by verifying this expulsion: "Because the Jews at

REFLECTIONS

RACISM IS NOTHING NEW. THE Jews living in the Mediterranean world in the first century knew a lot about it. Priscilla and Aquila were the victims of racism. Although what they suffered was unjust and discouraging, God worked in a powerful way through these evil circumstances. Had they not left Rome, they would not have met Paul and had a vital partnership role in planting the churches in Corinth and Ephesus.

To Lechaeum Harbor

North Market

Theatre

Temple of Apollo

Odeum

Fountain of Peirene

Temple

Northwest Stoa

Agora

Temples

Central Shops

Berna

Temple

South Basilica

To Acrocorinth

Rome caused continuous disturbances at the instigation of Chrestus, he expelled them from the city."[378] The identity of "Chrestus" is most likely "(Jesus) Christ." This suggests that there were heated debates among the Jews in the synagogues in Rome with the Jewish Christians who contended that Jesus is the Messiah (*Christos*), which did not go unnoticed by the Roman authorities.

Tentmaker (18:3). Paul discovers that Aquila and Priscilla also work in the same trade, so they join forces. "Tentmaking" is the literal translation of the Greek word *skēnopoios* and involves working with leather as the primary material from which tents are made, [379] although there is some evidence that the word implies that Paul works with various kinds of fabrics.[380] The work also includes the making and repair of a large range of leather and woven goods. Tents were needed for the many travelers staying in the city and for the sailors who usually lived in tents while their boats were docked. People also needed skilled workers to repair their torn or broken tents. One scholar suggests that since the Isthmian Games were held in the spring of A.D. 51, the trio probably had plenty of demand for their products.[381]

Paul most likely learned his trade skills in his preparation to be a rabbi. These teachers were expected to support themselves by some form of labor. According to Rabbi Gamaliel III, "An excellent thing is the study of Torah combined with some secular occupation, for the labor by them both puts sin out of one's mind. All study of the Torah which is not combined with work will ultimately be futile and lead to sin."[382]

The synagogue (18:4). In the early part of this century, archaeologists discovered an inscription preserved on a block of white marble that probably served as the lintel over a doorway. The inscription simply read: "The Synagogue of the Hebrews." It is possible that the inscription dates to the time of Paul, but it could date as late as the second century. Archaeologists have also uncovered seven other inscriptions from Corinth confirming the Jewish presence in the city. Among these inscriptions, some being in Hebrew, one contains an engraving of the seven-branched menorah and one has the title, "ruler of the synagogue" (*archisynagōgos*).[383]

Silas and Timothy came from Macedonia (18:5). Silas and Timothy remained in Macedonia (with the churches of Philippi, Thessalonica, and Berea) while Paul continued on to Athens and then to Corinth. Now they return and bring Paul good news about how all the new believers in this area are doing in their walk with the Lord in spite of the most trying of cir-

SYMBOLS OF JEWISH PRESENCE IN CORINTH

(top) Three menorahs adorn a column from a fourth-century A.D. synagogue.

(bottom) "The Synagogue of the Hebrews" inscription.

▼ ▶

cumstances. Paul also receives at this time a substantial monetary gift from the new church at Philippi that enables him to leave his tentmaking and devote all of his energies to proclaiming the gospel (see 2 Cor. 11:9; Phil. 4:16).

He shook out his clothes in protest (18:6). As he experienced elsewhere, his regular proclamation of Jesus as Messiah in the synagogue met with a positive response from a few Jews and God-fearing Gentiles, but a hostile reaction on the part of other Jews within the synagogue. When some of the opposition become abusive and make blasphemous statements (presumably about the Lord Jesus Christ), Paul leaves the synagogue, departing with a dramatic gesture of shaking the dust off his garments. This symbolic act has precedent in the Old Testament (see Neh. 5:13) and in Judaism as a way of distancing oneself from the sinful and rebellious actions of a people. Jesus himself advised the Twelve on their mission to "shake the dust off your feet" when a home or a town did not receive them (see Matt. 10:14).

Your blood be on your own heads! I am clear of my responsibility (18:6). Paul's action here needs to be seen in close connection with his words of condemnation that echo the language of the prophet Ezekiel (see Ezek. 33:5).

Titius Justus, a worshiper of God (18:7). After Paul leaves the synagogue, the core of new believers begins meeting next door at the home of a Gentile God-fearer. These probably are times of considerable tension as members of the two groups pass each other on the street.

In Romans 16:23, Paul speaks of the church as meeting in the home of a man named Gaius. This may be the same per-son as Titius Justus and means that Luke only refers to him by his Roman *nomen* (Titius) and *cognomen* (Justus), not by his *praenomen* (Gaius). Paul says that Gaius is one of the Corinthian converts that he baptized himself.

Crispus (18:8). In spite of the initial resistance of many synagogue members, there is a dramatic reversal. The synagogue ruler himself embraces Jesus as Messiah along with his entire household. Apparently many other Corinthians also become believers at this time, which probably includes many of the Jews from the synagogue. This is certainly a major blow to the Jewish opposition and probably helps to precipitate even more hostility. In 1 Corinthians 1:14, Paul tells us that he personally baptized Crispus.

A vision (18:9). The Lord grants Paul an encouraging vision, directing him to stay in the city. The apostle remains in Corinth for a period of eighteen months.

While Gallio was proconsul of Achaia (18:12). Much is known about this man from literature outside the Bible including the writings of Tacitus, Pliny, Dio Cassius, and Seneca.[384] L. Iunius Gallio Annaeanus, his full Roman name, was actually the brother of the famous Stoic

◄

THE GALLIO INSCRIPTION

philosopher Seneca, who spoke of him with admiration and love. He was a well-known jurist and had important connections with the Roman emperor and others in power.

Gallio served as the Roman proconsul (*anthypatos*) of the province of Achaia. Consequently, any decision he made would have more widely ranging implications than a decision made by a local civic official (such as the *politarchēs* at Thessalonica).

In the early part of this century, an important inscription explicitly naming Gallio was discovered in the Greek city of Delphi.[385] This inscription has been the single most important piece of evidence enabling us to date Paul's stay in Corinth with accuracy. The inscription itself is dated, which thereby enables us to fix a precise date on Gallio's proconsulship in Corinth, and thereby also the time of Paul's eighteen-month ministry in the city. The inscription reads:

> Tiberius [Claudius] Caesar Augustus Germanicus, [Pontifex maximus, in his tribunician] power [year 12, acclaimed Emperor for] the 26th time, father of the country, [consul for the 5th time, censor, sends greeting to the city of Delphi.] I have for long been zealous for the city of Delphi [and favorable to it from the] beginning, and I have always observed the cult of the [Pythian] Apollo, [but with regard to] the present stories, and those quarrels of the citizens of which [a report has been made by *Lucius] Junius Gallio* my friend and [pro]consul [of Achaia].[386]

We know from other sources that the 26th acclamation of Claudius took place during the first half of his twelfth year as emperor. His accession occurred on January 25 in A.D. 41, which means that this inscription would be dated somewhere in the period of January 25 to July 31, A.D. 52. Thus, Gallio was serving in Corinth during this time. He probably became proconsul in the spring of A.D. 51 (the season when proconsuls typically took office) and served in this capacity for about a year. Because Paul stayed in Corinth "for some time" (18:18) after this incident, it probably occurred within the first few months of his ministry there.

The Jews made a united attack on Paul (18:12). Jewish opposition to Paul's preaching continues to grow in Corinth. At one point, a group from the synagogue forcefully apprehend Paul and take him before the Roman proconsul, where they charge him with violating their own law (the Torah). The real essence of their complaint before Gallio is the Jews' contention that the Jesus movement is not a legitimate form of Judaism and, therefore, should not come under the same legal protection under Roman law.

I will not be a judge of such things (18:15). Gallio, however, sees things differently and interprets their complaints against Paul as a matter of intramural debate. Annoyed that they bring this issue before him, Gallio summarily dismisses them and instructs them to settle the matter themselves. This decision constitutes an important precedent for the legal freedom of the early Christians, at least until midway into Nero's reign, when matters grew exceedingly worse for the church. At this point Christianity is judged to be a sect within Judaism and, therefore, a legal religion (*religio licita*) by a Roman governor with expertise as a jurist.[387]

They all turned on Sosthenes the synagogue ruler and beat him (18:17). Sosthenes, possibly the successor to Crispus as ruler of the synagogue, is among the Jews who seized Paul and brought him before Gallio. When matters did not go in their favor before Gallio and they are ordered to leave, Sosthenes becomes the brunt of a fierce attack by a group of Corinthian Gentiles. Such flare-ups of anti-Jewish sentiment were not uncommon in the cities of the empire. Furthermore, Gallio may have given tacit approval to this hostility toward the Jews as an action consistent with the emperor's anti-Semitism.[388] This is a tragic turn of events for the Jewish community.

Paul's Initial Ministry In Ephesus (18:18–23)

In the early spring of A.D. 52, Paul decides to leave Corinth and return to the Roman province of Syria. Here he visits his "home church," the church at Antioch, and journeys to Jerusalem, possibly for the festivals of Passover and Pentecost. Paul is also

THE END OF
THE SECOND
MISSIONARY
JOURNEY
▼

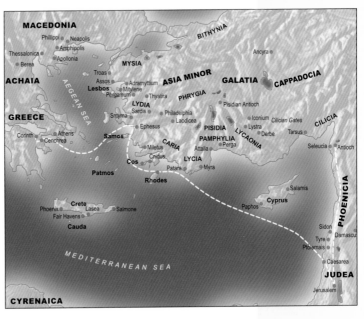

motivated to go to Jerusalem so that he can properly conclude a Nazirite vow he has taken. His shorn hair is an offering he takes to the temple.

Departing from Corinth's eastern port, he is accompanied by his coworkers Aquila and Priscilla. Evidently they make plans to begin working in Ephesus, the capital city of Asia Minor, which Paul had tried to reach previously (16:6). Silas and Timothy presumably remain in Corinth to continue giving leadership and help to the fledgling church.

He had his hair cut off . . . because of a vow (18:18). Paul has apparently initiated a Nazirite vow; the period of this special consecration has now come to a conclusion. The roots of the Jewish tradition of the Nazirite vow are explained in Numbers 6:1–21 and elaborated on in the rabbinic literature. [389] It was common in Judaism for a person to take a Nazirite vow for a fixed period of time, such as thirty days. This kind of vow involved abstaining from wine, avoiding impurity (such as contact with the dead), and leaving one's hair uncut. When the period of the vow was finished, the hair was shaved and brought to the Jerusalem temple as an offering, where the person would also make a sacrifice.

Luke does not explain why Paul has taken this vow. It may have been an expression of faith and commitment to the Lord for the challenge of the new circumstances of proclaiming the gospel in Corinth in the midst of heavy opposition. It may also have been a way for Paul to express his thanksgiving to God for his hand of blessing on the Corinthian ministry and for keeping him safe, just as God had promised to do in the vision. The passage clearly shows that Paul does not abandon Jewish traditions altogether. He finds this form helpful to express his devotion and commitment to the Lord.

Cenchrea (18:18). At some point during Paul's ministry a church was planted in this eastern port city of Corinth. Phoebe, a deaconness of the church, carried the letter Paul later wrote to the Roman Christians (Rom. 16:1). The site of Cenchrea has been found and excavated to a limited extent. The artificial breakwaters for the harbor are still visible in addition to many of the harbor buildings. These include a variety of warehouses and several temples. One has been identified as a sanctuary of the Egyptian goddess Isis.

They arrived at Ephesus, where Paul left Priscilla and Aquila (18:19). After arriving in Ephesus, Paul immediately begins preaching in the Jewish synagogue. He is met with a favorable reception, so much so that the people beg him to return to the city after his trip to Syria. This provides a good opening for Aquila and Priscilla, who settle in the city, secure a home, start a business, and begin ministering the gospel of Jesus Christ to the people in the synagogue. This couple has a solid and fruitful ministry in the city in

CENCHREA

Harbor remains at the ancient port city.

▼

Traveled from place to place throughout the region of Galatia and Phrygia (18:23). On his return trip to Ephesus, Paul opts to take an overland route rather than sail so he can visit the many churches he had a hand in starting throughout Asia Minor. At Galatia, he most likely revisits the churches at Antioch, Iconium, Lystra, and Derbe.

◀ *left*

THE REGION OF GALATIA AND PHRYGIA

the intervening months until Paul returns. It is likely that a number of people turn to Christ as a result of their ministry, and they begin hosting a church in their home.

When he landed at Caesarea, he went up and greeted the church and then went down to Antioch (18:22). Paul lands at the beautiful seaport of Caesarea Maritima (see comments on 10:1). Paul travels from there to Jerusalem (this is the meaning of "he went up and greeted the church") and then makes the long trek to the city of Antioch. In one concise statement, Luke condenses a lengthy and probably eventful journey. In fact, Paul's travels recorded in 18:22–23 (Corinth to Ephesus to Caesarea to Jerusalem to Antioch and then to Ephesus) span a distance of about fifteen hundred miles.

During his visit to Jerusalem, Paul hears about and sees the conditions resulting from a famine that ravages the country. When he returns to the churches he plants, it is with a sense of urgency for mounting a relief collection for helping the Jerusalem and Judean believers in their dire need. Luke himself gives us no details about Paul's visits to Jerusalem and Antioch. From the time he drops off Aquila and Priscilla until he rejoins them in Ephesus may have been as much as a year.

The Ministry of Apollos in Ephesus (18:24–28)

During Aquila and Priscilla's ministry in Ephesus while Paul is in Syria, a Jewish man from Egypt named Apollos[390] (short for Apollonius) comes and speaks in the synagogue. He is an incredibly capable speaker, but more importantly, he believes that Jesus is the Messiah. Oddly, however, he has not heard the full extent of Jesus' teaching, and probably has not heard about Jesus' resurrection, nor has he experienced the empowering of the Holy Spirit in his life.

Learned man (18:24). Apollos knows the Old Testament well, probably in the

ALEXANDRIA, EGYPT

▼

Greek version known as the Septuagint. The word *logios* can also mean "eloquent," and this is also a characteristic of his speaking. Apollos has been trained in the art of rhetoric and may have functioned as a Jewish sophist—an itinerant teacher. He most likely comes to Ephesus as a businessman, like many other Egyptians.

Explained to him the way of God more adequately (18:26). Seeing his openness to Jesus, Aquila and Priscilla invite Apollos into their home and give him a complete account of the cross, resurrection, and Pentecost events. This also includes a clear explanation of the nature of Jesus' atoning sacrifice. Evidently, Apollos responds with enthusiasm and delight and thus enters into a new understanding of the nature of God's salvation and the experience of the new covenant blessing of the promised Holy Spirit.

right ▶

EPHESUS AND WESTERN ASIA MINOR

Wanted to go to Achaia (18:27). As Apollos becomes more acquainted with Priscilla and Aquila, they presumably tell him of their ministry in Corinth and the struggles they have there with unbelieving Jews. Apollos most likely takes this as a challenge and makes plans to travel to Achaia to proclaim the gospel. Upon

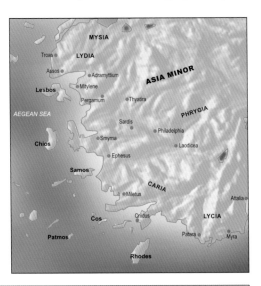

▶ Alexandria

Founded by Alexander the Great in 331 B.C., the city of Alexandria subsequently became the capital of Egypt and eventually eclipsed Athens as the cultural and educational center of the Hellenistic world.[A-109] Alexandria was the second largest city of the Roman empire with a population of over a half million people. Located in lower Egypt on the Mediterranean Sea, Alexandria's port was the connection point for shipping between India and Rome. The enormous lighthouse (328 feet high) on the small island of Pharos at the opening of Alexandria's two artificial harbors was acclaimed by early writers as one of the Seven Wonders of the ancient world.

There was a large Jewish community in Alexandria—possibly numbering in excess of a hundred thousand—and many synagogues. The Jews were accorded special privileges in the city, but there were occasional flare-ups of intense anti-Jewish sentiment. The most serious of these happened in A.D. 38, under the Roman prefect Flaccus, when there was severe rioting against the Jews that resulted in the destruction of synagogues and property as well as the loss of life.

It was at Alexandria where the Hebrew Scriptures were translated into Greek. [A-110] This was also home for the famous Jewish writer Philo, whose writings combined Old Testament ideas with Greek philosophy.

There is no written record recounting the story of how Christianity began in Egypt and in Alexandria. Undoubtedly it started early, perhaps shortly after Pentecost. The earliest papyrus fragments of our New Testament were discovered in Egypt. Unfortunately, Alexandria became a major center for Gnosticism in the second century.

arriving there, he uses his rhetorical skills and knowledge of the Scripture to persuade the Jews that Jesus is the promised Messiah. Apollos's ministry has a deep impact on the Corinthian church, as we can see from Paul's first letter to the Corinthians. After Paul returns to Ephesus, Apollos comes and ministers alongside the apostle (see 1 Cor. 16:12).

Paul and the Disciples of John the Baptist in Ephesus (19:1–7)

Because of the city's strategic importance to the spread of the gospel in Asia Minor, Paul earnestly desires to minister for an extended period of time in Ephesus. As it turns out, he stays in Ephesus for about three years, twice as long as he spent in any other place in his apostolic travel. The apostle comes to the city by traveling an overland route from Antioch. This takes him across Asia Minor to this beautiful coastal city.

Ephesus (19:1). Numerous inscriptions refer to Ephesus as "the first and greatest metropolis of Asia." This is not an empty boast. Ephesus was clearly the leading city of the most prosperous region of the Roman empire. With a population of a quarter million, Ephesus ranked only behind Rome, Alexandria (Egypt), and Antioch (Syria) in size.[391]

For about 150 years, Ephesus served as the seat of the Roman administration for Asia Minor. As the Romans built their famous network of roads throughout the province, they numbered their milestone markers from Ephesus. Economically, one ancient writer calls Ephesus "the greatest commercial center in Asia this side of the Taurus river."[392] Another speaks of Ephesus as the most prosperous commercial center of the time, con-

trolling the financial affairs of western Asia Minor.[393] The location of Ephesus on a natural port helped the city achieve its prominence in commerce and flourish during the days of the Roman empire.

There he found some disciples (19:1). Immediately upon his arrival in Ephesus, Paul faces a unique situation. He discovers a group of men who claim to be followers of Jesus, but they are familiar only with what John the Baptist announced and possibly a small amount of independent information about him. They have put their faith in Jesus, but apparently do

EPHESUS
▼

not know about his death, resurrection, and the outpouring of the Holy Spirit.

This is an incredible circumstance since over twenty years has passed since John the Baptist announced the coming of Jesus. If these men are Jews, it is unlikely they have traveled to Jerusalem for one of the pilgrimage feasts in the intervening years, where they could have

inquired further and received more information about Jesus Christ.

Nevertheless, these men have acted on the limited information they heard and believe in Jesus. Luke does not tell us whether they worship in the synagogue or if they have created their own group. They lack, however, the new covenant experience of the Holy Spirit in their lives. Without the Spirit's presence, one is not a true Christian.[394]

The Holy Spirit came on them (19:6). Paul teaches these men, and after their response, he baptizes them into the Lord Jesus Christ. They receive the Holy Spirit, which immediately manifests his presence by enabling them to speak in tongues and prophesy.

This is the only situation we find in the New Testament or early Christian literature of a group of people who are aware of Jesus only through John the Baptist's teaching (though see 18:25). It

---

▸ The City of Ephesus
IMPORTANT FACTS:

- Population: about 250,000
- Religion: official covenant with the Ephesian Artemis, up to fifty other gods and goddesses worshiped
- Port City
- Seat of the Roman Government for Asia Minor
- Location of the Temple of Artemis—one of the Seven Wonders of the Ancient World

---

▸ Archaeology In Ephesus

Archaeologists have been working at the site of ancient Ephesus for well over a hundred years. Excavation of the city first began in 1863 under the directorship of J. T. Wood, who had been commissioned by the British Museum to find the ancient temple of the Ephesian Artemis. Since 1895, the Austrian Archaeological Institute in Vienna has assumed primary responsibility for the systematic exploration of the site and has sent teams every year. They publish their discoveries annually in a journal sponsored by the Institute.[A-111]

In recent years, teams have been excavating and working to preserve a set of terraced dwellings near the city center. These were thought to be the homes of wealthy citizens. Most of these lavish houses had three floors, which surrounded a columned open area in the center. The rooms were decorated with

frescoed walls and mosaic floors depicting a variety of scenes from the Greek classics.

Over thirty-five hundred inscriptions have been discovered in the city. During the 1980s they were combined into a seven-volume anthology called *Die Inschriften von Ephesos* ("The Inscriptions of Ephesus").[A-112] Most of these inscriptions date from the Roman period and provide much helpful insight into the political, social, religious, and cultural life of the city.

The foundations and walls of numerous buildings have now been identified. These include temples of various gods and goddesses, two marketplaces, gymnasiums, bathhouses, a library, and fountains. Since Ephesus has been an uninhabited site for centuries, much has been preserved.

is important to see that their partial knowledge is not enough for a genuine Christian experience and the reception of the Spirit. In the gracious providence of God, however, they gain the opportunity to hear the complete story and enter into a relationship with the Spirit of God.

Preaching in the Synagogue and the Hall of Tyrannus (19:8–10)

As is his custom, Paul begins teaching in the Jewish synagogue. He uses it as a strategic starting point in fulfilling his commission from the Lord to take the gospel to the Gentiles in Ephesus. Every synagogue has a number of Gentiles already attracted to the one true God of Israel.

The synagogue (19:8). The synagogue at Ephesus has not yet been discovered by archaeologists. This is due in part to the fact that the section of the city where most Jews likely lived has not yet been excavated. Archaeologists, however, have discovered a few inscriptions that confirm the presence of a Jewish synagogue in the city:

- There is a fragment of a stone block (possibly from a synagogue at Ephesus) that is inscribed with a menorah and bears the inscription, "the altar."[395]
- Another inscription reads: "May the years of the rulers of the synagogue (*archisynagogoi*) and of the elders (*presbyteroi*) be many!"[396]

The Jewish historian Josephus confirms that there was a Jewish presence in the city. In fact, he claims that the Ephesian Jews were granted citizenship in the city.[397] Josephus also records many documents granting Jews in Ephesus certain privileges, such as exempting them from certain duties because of their Sabbath-keeping obligations.[398] Three tomb inscriptions have also been discovered that come from the Jewish community in Ephesus, one of them honoring a Jew who had been a "chief doctor" in the city.[399] All the available evidence suggests that the Jews in Ephesus were well integrated into the civic and social life of the city and did not experience the same level of hostility toward them that Jews faced in other cities (such as Alexandria).[400] Luke tells us that Paul spoke in the synagogue for three months, "arguing persuasively about the kingdom of God."

The lecture hall of Tyrannus (19:9). After opposition to his teaching grows too intense in the synagogue, Paul is able to secure the use of a lecture hall in the city for his teaching. Although a variety of buildings have been discovered by archaeologists, we have yet to find one with the name of "Tyrannus" attached to it. One ancient tradition (the Western text of Acts) explains that Paul teaches "from the fifth hour to the tenth," that is, from 11:00 A.M. until 4:00 P.M.

THE HARBOR OF EPHESUS

Only an outline of the harbor is visible today since the Cayster River has filled it with silt.

If this tradition is true, we can surmise that Paul spends the mornings plying his leatherworking trade in the workshops (see Acts 18:3). Then he engages in a daily period of intense teaching in this public hall at a time that is normally reserved for a meal and rest. During the evening he returns to work or spends time meeting with people house to house.

All the Jews and Greeks who lived in the province of Asia heard the word of the Lord (19:10). By teaching in this fashion in a public place, Paul is able to touch the lives of many people who are curious about his message. In fact, because so many people travel to Ephesus on business, the gospel message spreads all over the province. Presumably at this time, groups of people begin meeting in homes on the Lord's Day to worship Christ, learn about him, and fellowship together. Most likely Epaphras is one of those who hears, becomes a Christian, and proclaims the gospel in his hometown of Colosse. Similarly, others from such Asia Minor cities as Pergamum, Sardis, and Philadelphia hear Paul's preaching and return to their cities to plant churches. What an exciting time to see the spread of the gospel. Luke could have filled a whole volume with stories about Paul's ministry in Ephesus.

God Does Extraordinary Miracles Through Paul (19:11–12)

Luke continues to tell us what a remarkable time of ministry this was. Paul heals the sick and casts out demons—apparently on a regular basis (the imperfect tense of the verb "did" underlines this). The power does not come from Paul, however; it comes from God. Luke emphasizes that God is performing these extraordinary works of spiritual power "through Paul."

Handkerchiefs and aprons (19:12). Some of the sick people never come into direct contact with Paul. Their caregivers merely bring them handkerchiefs and aprons that Paul has touched, and the people are healed. The word for "handkerchief"(*soudarion*) probably refers to a face cloth for wiping perspiration, and the word translated "apron" (*simikinthion*) generally means a belt, but can refer to any article of clothing that has been in contact with the apostle's skin.[401] This practice looks "magical" in orientation, such that an object is charged with a power (like electricity) and released when it comes into contact with a sick person. Indeed, this view was prevalent in the common belief of the day and in the local occultism. Various kinds of objects were thought to be spiritually charged, and other objects could be empowered for use in a variety of purposes. What is important to see here is that (1) this method does not come from the initiative of Paul; it appears that the people assume things would work this way; and, (2) God chooses to manifest his healing power in spite of this deficient understanding of spiritual power. As we will see below, God dramatically teaches the Ephesian Christians about the futility of their magical practices and assumptions.

The evil spirits left them (19:12). As in the teaching of Jesus, we see here an assumption that the demonic realm is real and that there is a close association of demonic presence with certain illnesses. We do not know, however, whether Paul is here ministering to people who turn to Christ or to those who have yet to believe. Clearly the power of God is superior to the power of the enemy, who can be summoned to depart.

A Failed Exorcism and the Public Renunciation of Magic (19:13–20)

Ephesus was the hot place of ministry for a number of itinerant Jewish exorcists. This may correspond to the fact that this city had a reputation for being a center for magical and occult practices (see below). These men apparently developed special ability in effectively dealing with evil spirits. In this instance, however, their techniques are woefully inadequate.

Tried to invoke the name of the Lord Jesus (19:13). People who practiced magical incantations invoked any name thought to be laden with spiritual power. Because of the reputation surrounding Jesus as a mighty exorcist, it is of little surprise to find someone adding his name to their repertoire of names in the formula. We know of at least one magical incantation text that illustrates this tendency. This passage is from an Egyptian magical papyrus that dates to the late Roman period. Note the use of various kinds of rituals, the strings of magical names, and the way the name of Jesus is thrown into the mix:

> A tested charm of Pibechis [a legendary magician from Egypt] for those possessed by daimons: Take oil of unripe olives with the herb mastigia and the fruit pulp of the lotus, and boil them with colorless marjoram while saying, "IOEL OS SARTHIOMI EMORI THEOCHIPSOITH SITHEMEOCH SOTHE IOE MIMIPSOTHIOOPH PHERSOTHI AEEIOYO IOE EO

▶ Jewish Magic in Antiquity

Among many Gentiles, Jewish magic was famous in antiquity.[A-113] Certain Jews had a reputation for having power to manipulate evil spirits. Jewish magic is well illustrated in many different sources.

Jewish amulets. There are numerous magical amulets that are of a distinctively Jewish character. Many invoke Jewish angels and have various kinds of Jewish symbolism engraved on them. Most of these are made to protect people against the attacks of demonic powers.

Incantations and exorcism techniques associated with Solomon. There are many accounts of Jewish belief that Solomon's unsurpassed wisdom applied to dealing with evil spirits. Josephus notes of Solomon: "Now so great was the prudence and wisdom which God granted Solomon that he surpassed the ancients, and even the Egyptians.... And God granted him knowledge of the art used against demons for the benefit and healing of men. He also composed incantations by which illnesses are relieved, and left behind forms of exorcisms with which those possessed by demons drive them out, never to return."[A-114]

Many of these incantations and exorcism formulas are compiled into a document that becomes known as *The Testament of Solomon*.[A-115] The *Testament* purports to explain how Solomon manipulated evil spirits to force them to do the work of building the temple. Imbedded in this plot are many loosely related formulas, recipes, and incantations for dealing with evil spirits when they caused all kinds of physical infirmities and perpetrated other evils.

Jewish involvement in magical practices continued through the centuries and is well attested in the "Kabbalistic" and "Hekhaloth" texts.

CHARI PHTHA [Ptah is the Egyptian creator god], come out from (the name of the victim). The phylactery: On a time lamella write "IAEO ABRAOTH IOCH PHTHA MESENPSIN IAO PHEOCH IAEO CHARSOK," and hang it on the patient. It is terrifying to every daimon, a thing he fears. After placing the patient opposite to you, conjure. This is the conjuration: "I conjure you by the god of the Hebrews, Jesus, IABA IAE ABRAOTH AIA THOTH ELE ELO AEO EOY IIIBAECH ABARMAS IABARAOU ABEL-BEL LONA ABRA MAROIA BRAKION, who appears in fire, who is in the midst of land, snow, and fog, TAN-NETIS; let your angel, the implacable, descend and let him assign the daimon flying around this form, which god formed in his holy paradise, because I pray to the holy god, calling upon AMMON IPSENTANCHO."[402]

Sceva, a Jewish chief priest (19:14). We know of this person only from Luke. Whether he is recognized by leaders in the local synagogue is unknown.

He gave them such a beating (19:16). The itinerants working with the demonized man in Ephesus face unbelievably powerful resistance from the victim. The demon taunts them by saying through the man, "Jesus I know, and I know about Paul, but who are you?" He then physically assaults the exorcists and they flee. The account clearly shows that it is not adequate merely to rely on formulas and names thought to be full of supernatural power. These exorcists have no relationship to Jesus. As Paul reiterates in his letters on many occasions, it is not out of his own personal power that he ministers, but out of the empowering presence of the Lord Jesus Christ working through him. For Paul, spiritual power is found in solidarity or union with Christ.

This became known to the Jews and Greeks living in Ephesus (19:17). Word of this dramatic situation spreads rapidly to people living in the city. Folks regard the name of Jesus with great respect and even fear. Surely people feel a sense of vulnerability if these Jewish exorcists were injured by this demonized man. Yet, what a stark contrast Paul provides in his regular ministry of exorcism. Certainly many people realize that nothing like this ever happens to him.

Many of those who believed (19:18). Even the Christians of Ephesus are moved to fear by this episode involving Sceva. Many of these believers come forward and openly confess their wicked deeds. This statement demonstrates that there are many who did not make a clean break with the past. They continued to be involved in occult arts in spite of their belief in Christ.

Sorcery (19:19). Many Christians in Paul's day are still wearing amulets, reciting magical invocations, and possessing papyrus scrolls of magical formulas and recipes. In the ancient world, "magic" (*mageia*) or "sorcery" (*perierga*) was a way of controlling various sorts of spirits. By knowing the right names, performing the appropriate rituals, or saying the appropriate incantations, one could command spirits to manifest themselves, to provide protection from other malicious spirits, to provide success, to compel the attraction of the opposite sex, or to effect a curse.

Brought their scrolls together and burned them publicly (19:19). Having never renounced their involvement in the occult arts, God brings conviction on the hearts of many of these new Christians. They go to their homes and gather together all of their papyrus scrolls of magical formulas (and presumably all other paraphernalia associated with magical practices), and burn them in front of a large assembly of believers.

Fifty thousand drachmas (19:19). Some of the people apparently sit down and calculate the value of the scrolls accord-

ing to their current market rate. The amount comes to fifty thousand drachmas, roughly the equivalent of fifty thousand days' wages. Another way of looking at this is that it would require over 150 people working a full year to equal the financial value of these scrolls. This strongly suggests that *many* Christians bring *many* scrolls out to the burning. Certainly they could have sold these documents and provided ample funds for the fledgling Christian community; however, it is worth no amount of money to these Christians to allow these scrolls to continue in circulation.

In this way the word of the Lord spread widely and grew in power (19:20). Luke ends this account on a triumphal note. These events in Ephesus demonstrate that the power of God is mightier than any other power. Writing to Christians in this area five to eight years later, Paul says of Christ that God exalted him to a position "far above all rule and authority, power and dominion, and every title that can be given" (Eph. 1:21). No spirit,

◀ *left*

A LEAF FROM A MAGICAL PAPYRUS

This is identified as *PGM* LXX and is housed at the University of Michigan.

▶ Magic and the Occult In Ephesus

Ephesus was renown as being something of a center for magical practices in the Mediterranean world.[A-116] The practice of magic was everywhere—it was part of the fabric of common "folk belief"—but Ephesus acquired a significant reputation for it.

This reputation was perpetuated, in part, by the so-called "Ephesian Letters" (*Ephesia Grammata*). These were actually six names—*askion, kataskion, lix, tetrax, damnameneus,* and *aisia*—thought to be laden with protective power for warding off evil demons. One ancient writer says that the "magi" instructed people possessed by evil spirits to repeat to themselves the magic words in order to drive the demons out.[A-117] There was a story that circulated

about an Ephesian wrestler who traveled to Olympia to compete in the games. This wrestler wore the "Ephesian Letters" on an ankle bracelet while he competed and was winning every match. Finally an opponent from Miletus discovered the bracelet and protested, whereupon the item was removed by the officials. The Ephesian wrestler then fell to three successive defeats by his Milesian opponent.

No magical papyri have been discovered in Ephesus. But this has more to do with the fact that the climate of this area is not conducive to the preservation of papyri. Nevertheless, a variety of magical amulets, gems, and inscriptions have been discovered in the city.

demon, god, goddess, or any other supernatural agent that anyone cares to name can come close to rivaling the Lord Jesus Christ.

REFLECTIONS

OUR FAMILIES, FRIENDS, COMMUNITY, culture, and pre-Christian religious beliefs have an amazing staying power over our lives. An important part of the discipleship process is confronting and replacing the ungodly aspects of what we believe and how we live. Whether it is trafficking in magic or the idolatry of greed, it is essential that we repudiate the evil and replace it with a pure commitment to Christ and his ways.

Paul's Plans (19:21–22)

To Jerusalem (19:21). Paul now makes plans to return to Jerusalem. Luke does not tell us why he intends to go there, but based on Paul's letters we know that he initiates a collection from among the churches for the relief of impoverished Christians there.[403]

Through Macedonia and Achaia (19:21). These are the Roman provinces in Greece where Paul planted churches—in Philippi, Thessalonica, Berea, and Corinth. All of these churches are participating in the famine relief collection.

Rome (19:21). We know from the end of Acts that Paul finally arrives at Rome. Even at this early stage, Paul has a strong

▶ The Problem of Christian Magic and Syncretism

The Ephesian Christians provide us with a marvelous example of forsaking everything to gain Christ and hold firmly to him. We cannot underestimate, however, how difficult this sort of renunciation was for people who had grown up with household gods and magical formulas and spells. Surely the apostle Paul taught the importance of leaving behind these idolatrous objects and devoting oneself to Christ alone. Yet no amount of preaching appears to have convinced these Ephesians in the earliest stage of their walk with the Lord. God used a dramatic event to help them see the futility and danger of holding on to their occult practices.

Not all Christians in the early history of the church followed the example of the Ephesians. Many continued to worship their idols alongside Jesus and to call on other spiritual powers in magical

invocations. This is probably what was happening at Colosse when Paul denounced their practice of invoking angels (Col. 2:18).

In recent years, more papyrus documents have been discovered that may aptly be called "Christian magic." Most of these papyrus texts have been discovered in Egypt and are written either in Greek or Coptic (an Egyptian language). Many have now been translated into English in a volume titled, *Ancient Christian Magic*.[A-118] The texts are highly syncretistic—that is, they blend Christianity with occultism and various other religious practices and beliefs. What is striking in these texts is how the name of Jesus is invoked in a formula alongside angels and pagan deities. For example, one text calls upon: "Hor, Hor, Phor, Eloei, Adonai, Iao, Sabaoth, Michael, Jesus Christ. Help us and this household. Amen."

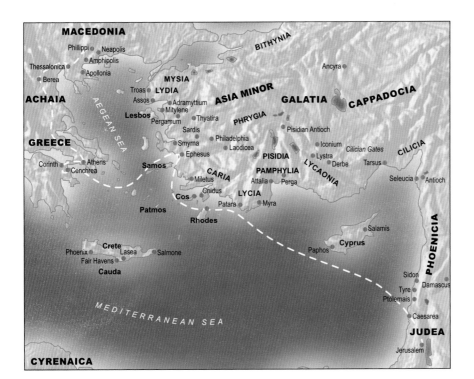

◄

PAUL'S INTENDED JOURNEYS

Macedonia to Achaia to Jerusalem.

desire to go to the capital city to minister the gospel. He has no idea what lies before him.

Timothy and Erastus (19:22). Anticipating an imminent departure, Paul sends two members of his ministry team ahead of him to the churches at Philippi and Thessalonica. Although it is easy to think of Paul as working alone, we must remember that he has a strong team concept of ministry. This is the only mention of Timothy in connection with Paul's ministry at Ephesus. From his correspondence to Corinth (he writes 1 Corinthians while he is in Ephesus), we learn that the apostle uses Timothy as an emissary in continuing ministry to the Corinthians while he is in Ephesus. Timothy travels there at least once to help the church deal with certain issues (see 1 Cor. 4:17; 16:10–11). Paul's other companion, Erastus, is probably a different person from the Erastus mentioned in Romans 16:23 as the city treasurer of Corinth.

Opposition From the Cult of the Ephesian Artemis (19:23–41)

Shortly after Paul decides to leave Ephesus, he faces the most heated opposition to his ministry in the city yet.[404] A huge mob forms at the instigation of some local businessmen and they begin shouting their adherence to the local patron goddess of the city, Artemis of Ephesus. The success of Paul's ministry and the growth of the church is now seen as a significant threat to this famous cult.

A silversmith named Demetrius (19:24). In the late 1800s an inscription found in Ephesus and dated to the mid-first century was published by a British scholar. The inscription honored a group of men who had served as "temple wardens" (*neopoios*). One of those honored was a man from Ephesus named "Demetrius, son of Menophilos, and grandson of Tryphon." While some scholars have argued for a positive identification

▶ The Cult of the Ephesian Artemis

Artemis of Ephesus, known to the Romans as Diana of Ephesus, was the principal deity of the huge metropolis of Ephesus and popular throughout the Mediterranean world. In fact, the Greek writer Pausanias notes that she was worshiped more widely than any other deity he knew.[A-119] She was worshiped as the great "mother goddess" and was thereby closely related to the main mother goddess of Asia Minor, Cybele (also called "the great mother" [*magna matēr* or *ma*]).

As a mother goddess Artemis possessed fertility and reproductive power that caused the earth to blossom with life of all kinds. She was the goddess of childbirth and a nourishing mother to all. Animals and wildlife were also a part of her domain and under her control.

Her grand temple in Ephesus was lauded by ancient writers as one of the Seven Wonders of the World. The structure of the cult was integrally interwoven into the fabric of daily life and culture. The temple actually functioned as the banking and financial center for the province. Large amounts of money were deposited and borrowed from the Artemision. The cult also owned substantial amounts of property in the area. One of the twelve calendar months was named after her—the month of Artemision—and during this month an annual festival was held in her honor.

The worshipers of Artemis regarded her as supreme among all the gods and goddesses. They honored her as "first among thrones," "savior," "Lord," "Queen of the World," and "the heavenly goddess."

Her cultic image is richly ornamented in the oriental style.[A-120] The first thing one notices is the rows of bulbous objects on her chest. Although some have interpreted these as numerous female breasts, the shape does not suggest this; others have suggested ostrich eggs, steer testicles, grapes, nuts, and acorns. Whatever they are supposed to be, they probably represent in some way her role as a goddess of fertility. The ferocious lions on her arms depict her mighty power.

The skirt of Artemis is adorned with a series of frightful-looking creatures that appear to be in a posture of surrender to the goddess. These probably represent more than her dominion over wildlife in nature. These animals may be understood as representing the harmful spirits of nature over which Artemis wielded authority.

Although the Ephesian Artemis was not widely known as a goddess of magic, she does appear to have a close association with the magical practices of the time. As a supremely powerful deity, she could exercise her power for the benefit of her adherents who faced attacks from opposing powers and spirits. In the magical papyri, she is virtually identified with Hekate (the goddess of witchcraft) and Selene (the moon goddess) and ascribed with power over the spirits of the underworld. Many magical amulets have been discovered bearing the image of the Ephesian Artemis.

Her power extended also to the stars, which were widely believed to be animated by spirit powers and tied to a person's fate. In fact, the symbols of the Zodiac were prominently depicted on the cultic image of Artemis as a necklace.

Those who worshiped Artemis believed they were devoted to an awesome, unrivaled deity, who could not only help them in the daily affairs of life but could also provide them with protection from evil powers and break the bonds of fate.

between this Demetrius and the one mentioned in Acts, it is impossible to be certain. The text here could be referring to another person of the same name, since Demetrius was a popular name. Nevertheless, the possibility remains that this is indeed the same person.

Silver shrines (19:24). These were not simply statuettes of the goddess, but depictions of her sitting on her throne in the center of the temple. Archaeologists have not yet discovered any of these sil-

ver shrines. Presumably, most of them were melted down and the silver reused as they were discovered over the centuries. These shrines were probably sold to people to use primarily as dedicatory offerings. They would have been brought to the temple and offered to the goddess.

Workmen in related trades (19:25). Inscriptions found at Ephesus have brought to light the existence of numerous trade guilds in the city. Presumably there are also craftsmen who make less

THE EPHESIAN ARTEMIS

(left) A beautiful marble statue of the goddess found under the town council building at Ephesus.

(right) The image depicts lions on her arms and the Zodiac on her chest.

(bottom) Ghoulish creatures are represented on her cultic vestment.

◀ ▼

▶ Archaeological Discovery: An Inscription Attesting the Guild of Silversmiths

A Greek inscription discovered at Ephesus dating to the time of the emperor Claudius in the mid-first century gives solid evidence for the existence of silver shrine makers and a whole guild of silversmiths (*argyrokopoi*).

> This tomb and the area around it and the subterranean vault belong to M. Antonius Hermeia, silversmith, shrine-maker (*neopoios*), and Claudia daughter of Erotion, his wife. No one is to be put in this tomb except the aforementioned. If anyone does dare to put in a corpse or excise this text, he shall pay to the silversmiths at Ephesus 1000 denarii. Responsibility for this tomb rests with the association of silversmiths, and Erotion dedicated 50,000 denarii. The legacy was provided in the 6th month, on the appointed day.[A-121]

In addition to this text, at least seven other inscriptions have now been discovered making some reference to silversmiths. One of these texts (inscribed on a column) suggests that the shops of the silversmiths were located on the Arcadiane Street—the street that ran from the theater to the harbor.[A-122] Another reads, "may the guild of the silversmiths flourish!"[A-123]

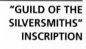

"GUILD OF THE SILVERSMITHS" INSCRIPTION

A reference to the guild is made on seventh and eighth lines.

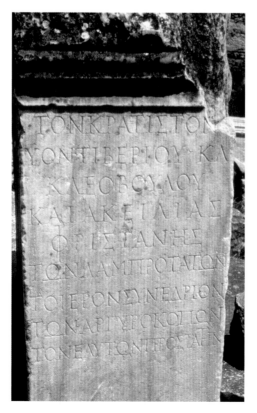

expensive shrines of Artemis out of terra cotta and marble.

A good income from this business (19:25). It is interesting to note that the catalyst for the great disturbance can be traced back to an economic incentive. These businessmen are losing money and feel they can turn things around by changing public opinion.

Paul has convinced and led astray large numbers of people (19:26). This is an insight into the tremendous success of the gospel in penetrating this strategic city. The loss of business to these shrine-makers is also an indication that many of the new Christians are people who turn to God directly from idols.

Worshiped throughout the province of Asia and the world (19:27). This is no exaggeration on the part of Demetrius. The Ephesian Artemis was worshiped throughout the Mediterranean world.

Great is Artemis of the Ephesians (19:28). Demetrius' speech to the trade workers of the city has its intended effect. The people are furious and begin chanting their support for the goddess. What starts as a meeting of trade workers quickly attracts numerous others from the city, who join in the chorus of protest.

The theater (19:29). The crowd assembles at the theater, though we do not know if this is where the meeting originates. The central location of the theater and the numerous people shouting in concert would certainly attract others. The theater, which overlooked the harbor, could hold up to twenty-four thousand people. There is no way of determining the approximate number of people who are involved in this uproar, but it is not inconceivable that it is numbered in the thousands. This is underlined by Luke's comment that, "soon the whole city was in an uproar."

The officials of the province (19:31). When Paul wants to speak to the assembled mob in the theater, some fellow believers and friends of his who are civic officials prevent him. The expression

▲
THEATER AT EPHESUS

◀
ARTEMISIUM

The scant ruins of the Artemis temple at Ephesus.

"officials of the province" (NIV) is an interpretive translation of the Greek word *Asiarchēs* (a combination of the Greek words for "Asia" and "ruler"). Over a hundred references to Asiarchs have now been counted in the many inscriptions found on the west coast of Asia Minor.[405] These people were wealthy, aristocratic Roman citizens who held this high provincial Roman office for an indeterminate period of time. Some of the Ephesian Asiarchs were important benefactors of the city, providing money for public works, setting up honorary statutes of civic and Roman officials, and subsidizing embassies to Rome on the city's behalf. Although we do not know the exact duties of their official service, they were people of great influence who had often served in a variety of important public offices. Because there was no separation of religion and state, they probably bore some responsibilities regarding the cult of the Ephesian Artemis.

The fact that some of the Asiarchs are friends of Paul suggest that they may be Christians. It is possible that the house churches of Ephesus met in the larger homes of these people. It is also possible that Paul becomes acquainted with some of them as his customers in his tent-making business.

The Jews pushed Alexander to the front (19:33). In the beginning, many Gentiles view Christianity as a form of Judaism. In fact, most Christians viewed themselves as a form of Judaism. But the non-Christian Jews of the city want to dissociate themselves from this Christian movement. The Jewish effort to have the assembly hear from one of their representatives is unsuccessful, however. This fiasco results in a furthered frenzied response by the crowd, who continue shouting "Great is Artemis of the Ephesians" for two hours.

The city clerk (19:35). The "city clerk" (*grammateus*) is the elected head of the city council. He functions much like a mayor to the city. Recognizing the danger the citizens are putting the city in with respect to the Roman authorities, the city clerk appeals to the noisy crowd for calm and advises a more cautious approach to the burgeoning Christian movement. By doing so, he exemplifies the duty of an excellent civic official. The Roman historian Dio Chrysostom, addressing leaders in Tarsus, describes the ideal ruler of a city:

> But I say that the counsellor who is a good counsellor and fit to be leader of a city should be prepared to withstand absolutely all those things which are considered difficult or vexatious, and especially the vilifications and anger of the mob. Like the promontories that form our harbours, which receive the full violence of the sea but keep the inner waters calm

ASIARCH INSCRIPTION

This inscription makes reference to an *Asiarch* and speaks of a man named Salutaris as a "lover of Artemis."

▼

and peaceful, so he too should stand out against the violence of the people, whether they are inclined to burst into a rage or abuse him or take any measure whatever, and he should be wholly unaffected by such outbursts.[406]

The people listen to him, and the tension of the volatile setting is defused. When he finishes speaking, he simply dismisses the assembly.

Paul Travels to Macedonia and Greece (20:1–6)

The next six verses are a highly abbreviated summary of nearly two years of activities by Paul. He pours his efforts into visiting many of the churches he has established to encourage them and help them in their growth and development.

After encouraging them, said good-by (20:1). After nearly three years of ministry in Ephesus, Paul decides to leave. This is not a sudden or forced departure. He tells the Corinthians that he has planned to stay in Ephesus through Pentecost (1 Cor. 16:8), which in the year 55

falls on May 25.[407] Now he wants to revisit his churches and begins gathering a collection for the impoverished Christians in Jerusalem.

After leaving Ephesus, he apparently travels first to Troas, a fact that we learn from 2 Corinthians, which he writes a short time later in Macedonia: "Now when I went to Troas to preach the gospel of Christ and found that the Lord had opened a door for me, I still had no peace of mind, because I did not find my brother Titus there. So I said good-by to them and went on to Macedonia" (2 Cor. 2:12–13). Before leaving Ephesus, Paul sends Titus to Corinth to deal with a difficult situation. Paul himself has just visited Corinth and faces a hostile response. He writes them what he terms a "sorrowful letter" (2 Cor. 2:3–9), which is now lost. At this point, Paul is anxious about the situation in Corinth and awaits news from Titus (2 Cor. 7:5–7).

Set out for Macedonia. He traveled through that area (20:1–2). During this time, he revisits the churches in Philippi, Thessalonica, Berea, and presumably others that were established on the basis of their witness in the region. It may have been during this period that Paul travels to the west coast and proclaims the gospel in Illyricum (Rom. 15:19), a Roman province on in the northwest portion of the Balkan peninsula along the Adriatic sea. Paul writes 2 Corinthians while he is in Macedonia.

Arrived in Greece, where he stayed three months (20:2–3). This probably refers to Corinth rather than Athens (or any other Greek city). While in Corinth, he is able to deal personally with the

MACEDONIA

Phillipi • • Neapolis
Thessalonica • • Amphipolis
• Apollonia
Berea •

ACHAIA

AEGEAN SEA

GREECE

Corinth • • Athens
Cenchrea

Troas •

Assos •
Lesbos • • Adramyttium
• Mitylene
Pergamum • • Thyatira

MYSIA

ASIA MINOR

LYDIA   PHRYGIA

Sardis •
Chios   • Smyrna   • Philadelphia
• Laodicea
• Ephesus

Samos

CARIA

• Miletus

Cos   • Cnidus   LYCIA

Patmos   Patara •   • Myra

Rhodes

◀ *left*

PAUL'S TRAVELS TO MACEDONIA, GREECE, AND ASIA MINOR

deep concerns that he writes about in 2 Corinthians and to gather the final portions of his collection for the Jerusalem church. It is also during this time that he writes his substantive letter to the church at Rome. In it, he expresses his plans to visit them shortly as he anticipates a journey to Spain.

The Jews made a plot against him (20:3). We know nothing about this plot. It may have involved not only plans to kill him, but also to take the large amount of money Paul is carrying with him. Apparently Paul wants to first visit the church in Antioch (Syria) before going on to Jerusalem. Now his plans take an abrupt change, and he returns overland to Philippi.

He was accompanied by (20:4). For his trip to Jerusalem with the collection, Paul takes with him seven delegates from churches in Macedonia, Asia, and south Galatia. Two of the companions he names here, Sopater and Secundus (we know nothing else about them, unless Sopater is the same person as Sosipater in Rom. 16:21). Luke later joins Paul in

Philippi and accompanies him to Rome. It is not known whether Silas is still in Corinth (Acts 18:5) or whether he has left and journeyed elsewhere. On Timothy, see comments on 16:1. These delegates go ahead of Paul to Troas and wait for him there.

Aristarchus (20:4). A convert from Paul's ministry at Thessalonica (or possibly as a product of the early Thessalonian Christians' evangelization), Aristarchus joins Paul in his Ephesian ministry, as also has Gaius from Derbe (19:29). He also later visited Paul during his Caesarean imprisonment and accompanied him on his eventful voyage to Rome (27:2). Evidently, he was imprisoned with Paul in Rome and was with him when he wrote to the Colossians (Col. 4:10) and to Philemon (Philem. 24).

Tychicus (20:4). Tychicus, an Ephesian believer, later ministers to Paul during his Roman imprisonment. He was with Paul when he wrote his letters to the Ephesians and to the Colossians and carried those letters to the churches (Eph. 6:21; Col. 4:7). He remained faithful to Paul and was an important emissary for him (2 Tim. 4:12; Tit. 3:12).

Trophimus (20:4). The only other time we hear about this Ephesian is when Paul was accused of taking him into the temple precincts (21:29).

We sailed from Philippi . . . joined the others at Troas (20:6). Paul now leaves Macedonia with Luke (note the "we") and joins the other delegates in the northern Asia Minor city of Troas. It is now early spring (April of A.D. 57),[408] which Luke dates by reference to the Feast of Unleavened Bread.

REFLECTIONS

THE APOSTLE PAUL DOES NOT work alone. He is a team player and team developer. He is constantly investing himself into the lives of other people who will share the work of the ministry with him and continue it in his absence. This same priority and method should characterize the work of Christian leaders today.

Eutychus Falls and Is Healed (20:7–16)

As a direct result of his preaching after Paul left Ephesus (2 Cor. 2:12–13), a community of believers had been established in Troas (on Troas, see Acts 16:7). Paul feels an obligation to visit them and encourage them before he travels on to Jerusalem. During his short stay, God works an amazing miracle through the hands of the apostle.

On the first day of the week we came together to break bread (20:7). This is a

clear reference to the fact that the early Christians began meeting on the first day of the week to worship (Sunday), rather than on the Sabbath day (Saturday). A similar reference occurs in 1 Corinthians 16:12, where Paul encourages the believers in Corinth to set aside some money when they gather on the first day of every week. "Breaking bread" refers to the early Christian practice of sharing a meal together followed by a time of worship when those gathered remember the significance of the death of Jesus by partaking of bread and wine (see comments on Acts 2:42).

Kept on talking until midnight (20:7). This does not imply that the believers have met throughout the day and into the night. Slaves and artisans may not have been free from their work-related responsibilities to meet until the evening, so they may not have gathered together until this time. This is a unique opportunity for Paul and for the Christians of this city, and they want to make the most of their brief time together.

The upstairs room ... the third story (20:8–9). Luke's description suggests that the meeting is held in the third floor room of a Roman *insula*. This was typically a three-story building that had apartments on the top two floors and shops at the street level. Most of the population of the major cities lived in these multi-storeyed tenement blocks.[409] This so-called "house church" is actually an "apartment church."

Eutychus (20:9). This young man, whose name means "fortunate," succumbs to his body's weariness after a day of work and the late hour of the night.

Was picked up dead (20:9). Luke clearly states that he is dead, not that he "appeared to be dead" (see 14:19).

Threw himself on the young man (20:10). Similar to Peter when he raised Tabitha (9:36–41), Paul brings this young man back to life. The essence of this story is also similar to Elijah's raising of the widow of Zarephath's son (1 Kings 17:17–24) and Elisha's restoring the life of the Shunammite woman's son (2 Kings 4:33–36). In both instances, the prophets lay on the young men they were attempting to bring back to life. We may assume that Paul calls out to God in a way similar to Elijah: "O LORD my God, let this boy's life return to him!" (1 Kings 17:21).

Sailed for Assos (20:13). The group of eight men (the seven mentioned in 20:4 plus Luke) board their ship at the port while Paul stays behind to squeeze as much time out of his visit as possible. He knows an overland shortcut that enables him to get to the next port of call before the ship leaves from there. The port city of Assos is twenty miles south of Troas. Aristotle once lived in this city and it is also the birthplace of the Stoic philosopher Cleanthes.

Mitylene . . . Kios . . . Samos (20:14–15). The ship leaves the port of Assos and sails to Mitylene, about thirty miles south of Assos and only ten miles off the Asia

Minor mainland. Mitylene is the capital and port city of the island of Lesbos, the third largest Aegean island (629 square miles) after Crete and Euboea. Leaving there, the boat sails south skirting the coastline and "right through" (*antikrys*) the passage separating the island of Kios from the mainland. Contrary to the NIV translation, the boat probably does not dock at Kios. At the narrowest point, Kios is only five miles from the mainland of Asia Minor. The boat passes by Ephesus and eventually comes to the island of Samos. The island is only a mile from the mainland. Leaving the port city of Samos, the boat then makes its way roughly twenty miles to the city of Miletus.

In a hurry to reach Jerusalem, if possible, by the day of Pentecost (20:16). Having spent nearly three years in Ephesus, it is extraordinarily difficult for Paul to visit without spending significant time meeting with people and dealing with problems and issues. In A.D. 57, Pentecost falls on May 29.[410] It has been nearly twenty-five years since the outpouring of the Holy Spirit on that important Pentecost after Jesus' resurrection. The offering Paul is carrying and the Gentile delegates that accompany him will be a significant symbol of God's work in reaching Gentiles.

Paul Speaks to the Ephesian Elders (20:17–38)

Paul takes advantage of his stay in Miletus to meet with the Ephesian elders to encourage them and advise them in their important ministry. As with the other addresses that Luke records in Acts, this is merely a précis of a much longer talk that Paul gives. Luke provides us with the highlights and central points of Paul's talk. This is the only occasion thus far in Acts where Luke himself is actually present at one of the messages that he records and can thereby now write as an eyewitness to the event and from memory (and possibly notes) on what Paul says.

This message is also unique in being the only speech given by Paul in Acts that

▶ Miletus

The city of Miletus was located just thirty miles due south of Ephesus.[A-124] Miletus was also a harbor city and, during the pre-Roman era, was a more significant city in Asia Minor than Ephesus. Situated on a small peninsula, Miletus actually had three harbors.

There is a well-preserved theater in the city that was capable of accomodating fifteen thousand people. Both Josephus and archaeology confirm a strong Jewish presence in the city.[A-125] On the fifth row of the theater, an inscription was discovered that reads, "the place of the Jews and the God-fearers (*theosebion*)." The inscription suggests that Jews and God-fearers were viewed as two distinct but related groups who were held in high esteem by the city. The theater management granted to them the privilege of a special section of seats.[A-126] is addressed explicitly to Christians. The Miletus address is thus much more comparable to Paul's letters, all of which are addressed to Christians. It is not surprising, then, that there are numerous themes in this speech that amply parallel similar statements and themes in the letters.[411]

Paul sent to Ephesus for the elders of the church (20:17). Paul does not neglect the Ephesian church in this fortuitous few days he would be in Miletus. He decides to gather the leadership of the church and meet solely with them. It would take one to two days to get the message to Ephesus and at least two days for them to get to Ephesus. On "elders" (*presbyteroi*), see 11:30.

I served the Lord with great humilty and with tears (20:19). It is sometimes easy to think of Paul as a thick-skinned, cognitively-oriented, driven personality. This statement gives a unique perspective on the tender side of Paul. In verse 31, he repeats the fact that he serves them with many tears. Paul has a huge capacity to love and embrace those who came into the body of Christ. Paul invariably develops a great deal of affection for these new believers and is deeply grieved when they lapse morally or are taken in by some kind of false teaching.

"Humility" was not a virtue that is emulated in the Greco-Roman world and was often thought of as a sign of weakness in an individual. Paul seeks to embody a servant model of leadership that he learns from the Lord Jesus.[412]

Severely tested by the plots of the Jews (20:19). Luke reveals nothing about any Jewish plots against Paul in Ephesus, although it would be surprising if he does not face opposition from the zealous members of the synagogue there. Fresh

on Paul's mind is the fact that he is not able to take a boat directly from the port of Corinth (Cenchrea) to Syria precisely because of a plot on his life (20:3). He has also faced many other violent outbursts against him in most of the cities where he has proclaimed the gospel.

Publicly and from house to house (20:20). The Ephesians have fond memories of the hours they spent learning from Paul in the Hall of Tyrannus. But this passage makes it clear that Paul exercises his teaching ministry also "from house to house." This also reveals something of the organization of the Ephesian church as a network of house churches.

Compelled by the Spirit, I am going to Jerusalem (20:22). Paul here uses the imagery of being chained or tied up like a prisoner, but in this instance by the Holy Spirit. This is the same word used to describe Paul's binding in chains when he is later taken into custody by the Romans in Jerusalem (22:29) or the chains with which people try to shackle the Gerasene demoniac (Mark 5:3). The metaphor underlines Paul's conviction that he is under a divine imperative to get to Jerusalem.

In every city the Holy Spirit warns me (20:23). The Judean prophet Agabus soon warns Paul that he will be bound and arrested if he goes to Jerusalem (21:10–11). Prophets in Tyre warn of the same fate awaiting Paul (21:4). Presumably, the Spirit speaks similarly through prophets in Corinth, Troas, Philippi, and elsewhere to the same effect.

I am innocent of the blood of all men (20:26). Paul's words here echo the image of the watchman in Ezekiel: "Son of man, speak to your countrymen and say to them: 'When I bring the sword against a land, and the people of the land choose one of their men and make him their watchman, and he sees the sword coming against the land and blows the trumpet to warn the people, then if anyone hears the trumpet but does not take warning and the sword comes and takes his life, his blood will be on his own head."[413] Like the faithful watchman in Ezekiel, in proclaiming the kingdom of God, Paul has warned the people in the cities where he ministers about the impending judgment.

The flock . . . be shepherds (20:28). The concept of a flock of sheep as an image of the community of God's people has deep Old Testament roots. Israel is God's special "flock" and the sheep of his pasture (Ezek. 34). God gave stern warnings to the shepherds who tended his flock through the prophets Jeremiah and Ezekiel (Jer. 23:1–4; Ezek. 34:1–31). The main concern in Ezekiel is that the shepherds have become so concerned about feeding themselves that their sheep have not been well fed, have roamed the hillsides unprotected, and have become prey for the wild animals. Because of this dreadful situation, God himself becomes the shepherd for his sheep. God's role as the shepherd of his people is beautifully expressed in Psalm 23. Jesus claims to have fulfilled this distinctive role as "the good shepherd" (John 10:1–18). Peter, as a representative of all Christian leaders, is three times enjoined by Jesus to "take care of my sheep" (John 21:15, 16, 17).

Of which the Holy Spirit has made you overseers (20:28). The apostle Paul may appoint leaders in the churches (14:23), but ultimately the decisions for leaders

are based on the prior appointment by the Holy Spirit. Luke does not tell us how Paul discerned this decision of the Spirit—whether through prophecy, a strong inner leading of the Spirit both in himself and in those who are to be appointed, or by a recognition of the Spirit's work in their lives granting giftedness and abilities that are clear leadership qualities.

Overseers (20:28). The leaders of the church at Ephesus are first called "elders" (20:17) and now referred to as "overseers." This verse demonstrates that "elders" (*presbyteroi*) and "overseers" (*episkopoi*) are not two distinguishable groups of leaders in the first-century church. The function and role of these leaders is intimately associated with the meaning attached to the image of "shepherd." The term *episkopos* was widely used in the ancient Greco-Roman world. There are instances of it used of people who managed buildings or cargo on a boat.[414] There were also market overseers who judged between fair and shady dealings.[415] Inscriptional evidence points to the use of *episkopoi* as a designation for community officials in Rhodes.[416] The

A SHEPHERD WITH HIS SHEEP

A SHEPHERD WITH HIS SHEEP
▼

term is also used in the Greek Old Testament and Judaism for various kinds of leaders of the people (e.g., Neh. 11:9, 14, 22). Philo even refers to Moses as an *episkopos* who keeps watch over the condition of the soul.[417]

Savage wolves will come (20:29). The prophet Ezekiel complains that the rulers of Jerusalem are "like wolves tearing their prey" (Ezek. 22:27). Similarly, Zephaniah pronounces woe over Jerusalem's rulers because they "are evening wolves, who leave nothing for the morning" (Zeph. 3:3). Jesus warns his disciples about the coming of false prophets who "come to you in sheep's clothing, but inwardly they are ferocious wolves" (Mark 7:15). Jesus also stresses the protection the shepherd provides since a "hired hand" runs away when he sees a wolf coming leaving the sheep vulnerable to the wolf's attack (John 10:12–13).

"SAVAGE WOLVES WILL COME"

Even from your own number men will arise and distort the truth (20:30). Paul may be speaking prophetically here—the Spirit has revealed to him that a struggle for the truth will ensue within the Ephesian church. If not, perhaps Paul sees some tendencies within members of the church that disturb him. His prediction indeed proves to be correct. Less than ten years later, an unhealthy teaching

emerged in the Ephesian church that he instructed Timothy to deal with.[418] Toward the end of the first century, the Ephesian church struggled with an outbreak of docetic teaching that the apostle John fought against in his letters (see esp. 1 John 2:19; 2 John 7).

So be on your guard! (20:31). A good shepherd will keep the flock secure from all dangers. This command reaffirms the need for the Ephesian *presbyteroi/episkopoi*/shepherds to be vigilant over the large community of believers in their care. The word used in this context literally means to "watch" (*grēgoreō*). After Nehemiah built the walls of Jerusalem, he stationed men on the walls and on the gates to "watch" (Neh. 7:3). During the Jewish revolt in the second century B.C., the Jewish commander Jonathan learned that the enemies from Syria were preparing to attack and so "commanded his men to be alert [*grēgoreō*] and to keep their arms at hand so as to be ready all night for battle" (1 Macc. 12:27). Jesus repeatedly instructed his disciples to "watchfulness" (Mark 13:34, 35, 37).

These hands of mine have supplied my own needs and the needs of my companions (20:34). Paul did not avail himself of his apostolic right to be financially supported in his ministry, although financial gifts were sent to him from time to time (2 Cor. 11:8; Phil. 4:14–18). He worked hard in a trade to support himself, not only during his Ephesian ministry, but also in other places that he ministered.[419] This is the one place we learn that his work helped support others on his team. Paul was sensitive to the potential danger of being compared with other kinds of itinerants (such as the Cynics) who exploited people financially.

We must help the weak (20:35). Generosity with money, food, and material possessions is a hallmark of the early church and a virtue that Paul enjoins his congregations to practice (see also Eph. 4:28). "The weak" probably refers to those in the church who are not able to entirely support themselves. Paul is elsewhere clear that able-bodied people must work so they have adequate resources to purchase food and shelter (2 Thess. 3:6–15). Nevertheless, there are some in the church who cannot survive without substantive help from their brothers and sisters in the community of believers.

Remembering the words the Lord Jesus himself said (20:35). Jesus' teaching, "It is more blessed to give than to receive," is not present in any of the four Gospels. Paul is apparently here quoting a saying of Jesus that is only known in oral tradition or in a written source that is not preserved. There are a variety of similar statements made by other people in Jewish, Greek, and early Christian literature.[420] A principle of reciprocity is deeply ingrained in Greco-Roman culture, that is, one must give in equal measure to what one has received. Paul's exhortation strikes out at this idea and encourages believers to give to those who cannot give in return.[421]

They would never see his face again (20:38). Paul intends to visit Jerusalem and travel from there to Rome and on to Spain in his efforts to reach Gentiles with the gospel of the Lord Jesus Christ (Rom. 15:24–29). At this point, Paul does not know that he will travel to Italy in Roman custody and face trial in the capital city of the empire. If the Pastoral Epistles are to be dated to shortly after this imprisonment, it appears that Paul does, in fact, have the opportunity to see the Ephesians again (1 Tim. 1:3).

The Journey From Asia Minor to Jerusalem (21:1–16)

After the tearful good-bye, Paul departs with his eight companions on a boat and travels to Jerusalem. Luke describes some of the stops along the way. Paul is able to meet with believers in a variety of locales, but he is also served twice with prophetic warnings that he will face suffering in Jerusalem.

We had torn ourselves away from them (21:1). The verb expresses the difficulty and anguish both groups experienced in having to be separated. It is comparable to the weaning of a child from his mother's breast (see Isa. 28:9 where the passive construction of the same verb is used).

Cos (21:1). The group boards a vessel that skirts the coastline and takes them as far as the southern Asia Minor coastal city of Patara, from where they board a larger boat that takes them to Palestine.

Cos is a small island in the Aegean (112 square miles: twenty-seven miles long and between one and seven miles wide) that is part of the Sporades group

COS

The shoreline of the island.

▼

MILETUS TO
JERUSALEM

MACEDONIA
Phillippi • • Neapolis
Thessalonica • Amphipolis
• Berea • Apollonia
ACHAIA
GREECE
Corinth • • Athens
• Cenchrea
BITHYNIA
Ancyra •
MYSIA
Troas • LYDIA
Assos • Adramyttium ASIA MINOR GALATIA CAPPADOCIA
Lesbos • Mitylene
Pergamum • Thyatira PHRYGIA
Sardis •
• Philadelphia • Pisidian Antioch
Smyrna • • Laodicea • Iconium Cilician Gates
• Ephesus PISIDIA • Lystra • Derbe Tarsus • CILICIA
Samos CARIA PAMPHYLIA LYCAONIA Seleucia • • Antioch
• Miletus • Cnidus Attalia • Perga
Cos • Cnidus LYCIA
Patmos • Patara • • Myra
Rhodes
• Salamis
Phoenix • Crete • Lasea Cyprus
Fair Havens • • Salmone Paphos •
Cauda
• Sidon
Tyre • • Damascu
Ptolemais •
PHOENICIA
• Caesarea
JUDEA
• Jerusalem
CYRENAICA
MEDITERRANEAN SEA
AEGEAN SEA

RHODES

"St. Paul's Bay" at
Lindos, Rhodes.

of islands. At the narrowest point, it is less than five miles from the Asia Minor mainland and the city of Halicarnassus. Cos may be best known for being the location of the school of medicine founded by Hippocrates in the fifth century B.C.[422]

Rhodes (21:1). After spending the night in Cos, they travel another sixty miles to the island of Rhodes. This is the largest island (540 square miles) of the Sporades and the fourth largest island currently belonging to Greece. Rhodes lies twenty miles off the coast of Asia Minor. The harbor of Rhodes was the site of the great "Colossus" (a hundred-foot statue of the sun god Helios), one of the Seven Wonders

of the ancient world. However, the Colossus was later destroyed by an earthquake in the third century B.C.

Patara (21:1). Patara is one of the principal cities of the Roman province of Lycia and the seat of the Roman proconsul. The port was an important shipping port for the Alexandrian grain vessels.[423] It was located on the mouth of the Xanthus River a few miles south of the city of Xanthus. At this port, Paul finds a cargo ship that is scheduled to make a non-stop ocean crossing to Phoenicia. The four hundred-mile voyage would have taken between three and five days depending on the wind.

We landed at Tyre (21:3). On Tyre, see comments on 12:20. On Phoenicia, see comments on 11:20.

Finding the disciples there (21:4). The verb Luke uses here suggests that Paul searches for the believers. These people most likely received the gospel from the Jerusalem Christians who traveled to Phoenicia after the outbreak of persecution (11:19).

Through the Spirit they urged Paul not to go on to Jerusalem (21:4). Paul has told the Ephesian elders that he is "compelled by the Spirit" to go to Jerusalem. There is probably no contradiction here. It appears that the Spirit is telling prophets in a variety of places that Paul will face suffering and imprisonment in Jerusalem. The prophets conclude, out of their natural human concern, that Paul should not go to Jerusalem in order to avoid the persecution.[424] Paul, however, is thoroughly convinced that the Spirit is leading him to go. He is willing to suffer anything for the sake of Christ.

And their wives and children accompanied us out of the city (21:5). This is a touching observation that demonstrates how Paul endears himself to entire families of believers.

Landed at Ptolemais (21:7). Paul and his companions reboard their ship and sail south down the coastline to Ptolemais, the southernmost Phoenician port.[425] This city, located about eight miles north of Haifa, was known as Acco in the Old Testament era (Judg. 1:31); Ptolemy II Philadelphus (282–246 B.C.) later renamed it after himself. During the Roman era, Acco-Ptolemais came under the direct control of the Roman proconsul of Syria. Emperor Claudius refounded the city, improved its port, and settled many veterans there. Josephus regarded the city as the western boundary of Galilee.[426] Under Nero, the city became a Roman colony. The Gentile population of the city was consistently hostile to the Jews. This reached a boiling point roughly nine years later at the outbreak of the Jewish war when the inhabitants of this city massacred two thousand Jews.[427] As at Tyre, Paul is able to locate a group of believers and spend time with them.

We reached Caesarea (21:8). Staying only one day at Ptolemais, the party then makes the thirty-mile trip (probably by boat) to the beautiful port city of Caesarea (see comments on 10:1).

Stayed at the house of Philip the evangelist (21:8). Luke refers to Philip here as an "evangelist," the only time he uses the word in the book of Acts (see comments on 8:5; see also Eph. 4:11; 2 Tim. 4:5). No doubt part of the reason for this designation is based on the astonishing ways God used him to reach many Samaritans (8:4–25) and the Ethiopian official (8:26–40). Following his ministry to the Ethiopian and evangelistic work in Azotus, Philip traveled to Caesarea (8:40). Apparently he settled in the city, married (if he was not married earlier), and raised a family. Perhaps many in the city of Caesarea have come to know Christ as a result of Philip's ministry. Whatever his means of generating income, it has been adequate for him to purchase a home that is large enough to host this group of nine men. In the spirit of Christian hospitality, Philip opens his home to this group. Philip probably proves to be an important source of information to Luke about the early days of the church in Jerusalem.

Four unmarried daughters who prophesied (21:9). The church historian Eusebius, quoting an Ephesian church leader from the second century, reports that Philip later moved with his daughters to Hierapolis in Asia Minor (near Colosse

PTOLEMAIS (ACCO)

Ancient ruins at this important port city.

▼

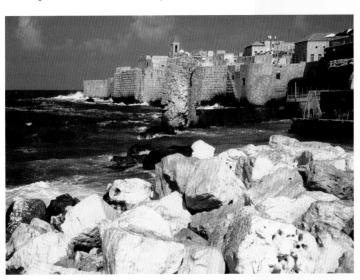

and Laodicea). Two of the daughters never married and remained in Hierapolis until their deaths; another daughter "lived in the Holy Spirit and rests in Ephesus."[428] The fact that Philip's daughters prophesy further demonstrates the fulfillment of Joel 2:28 ("your sons and your daughters will prophesy") that Peter quoted in his message on the day of Pentecost nearly twenty-five years earlier. Women continued to exercise prophetic gifts, as seen in the church at Corinth (1 Cor. 11:5).

A prophet named Agabus came down from Judea (21:10). The Jerusalem prophet, Agabus, now meets with Paul a second time. Whereas in the first instance, he predicted the coming of a severe famine (11:27–28), this time he predicts Paul's arrest in Jerusalem.

He took Paul's belt (21:11). Agabus acts out what he believes the Spirit to be telling him about Paul's impending arrest and custody. The way he does this is reminiscent of how Old Testament prophets sometimes delivered their messages, as, for example, Isaiah did when he went around stripped and barefoot for three years as a sign of what Assyria would do to the Egyptian and Cushite captives.[429]

And will hand him over to the Gentiles (21:11). The words were not fulfilled precisely as they are recorded here. When the Jews seized Paul, the Romans actually intervened and took him into their custody. Ultimately, however, the Jewish leaders were responsible for Paul's Roman custody, and in this way the prophecy was fulfilled.

Breaking my heart (21:13). The Caesarean Christians are deeply upset that Paul will shortly be facing persecution in Jerusalem and do their best to dissuade him from going to the capital city. Although compelled by the Spirit and determined to go, despite the threat of suffering, Paul is affected by their pleas. The word used here is found in the context of women pounding on clothes with stones as they wash them to get them clean.[430] Nevertheless, he remains obedient to the leading of the Spirit of God.

We got ready and went up to Jerusalem (21:15). The term used for getting ready (*episkeuazō*) is used by some ancient authors for saddling and packing horses for a trip.[431] It may imply that the group made the sixty-four-mile journey to Jerusalem on horseback.

ANCIENT BELT BUCKLES

These Roman-era buckles were discovered in the excavations at Masada.

The home of Mnason (21:16). The group travels to the home of an apparently wealthy Jerusalem believer named Mnason, who has a house sufficiently large to accommodate Paul's entourage of nine plus some from Caesarea.[432] Mnason came from the island of Cyprus (like Barnabas) and is most assuredly a Jew. He is strong enough in his faith not to worry about opening his home up to Gentiles from Macedonia and Asia Minor and face the dangers of ritual impurity (from a Jewish perspective). His commitment to Christ has given him a new perspective on Gentiles. It is possible that his name is a shortened and Grecized form of the Jewish name Menahem or Manasseh.[433]

One of the early disciples (21:16). This can be viewed one of three ways: (1) He is one of the disciples of Jesus during his earthly ministry and may have been one of the 120 in 1:15; (2) he is one of the early converts of the preaching of the apostles in Jerusalem; or (3) he is one of the converts of Paul and Barnabas in their missionary journey to Cyprus. One of the first two options is most likely. As one who has been a foundational member of the Jerusalem church, Mnason proves to be an important source of information to Luke for his writing during this visit. This value is all the greater for Luke's first volume if Mnason had been a disciple of Jesus.

Paul Meets With the Jerusalem Church (21:17–26)

Paul and the delegates presumably make it to Jerusalem in time for the Pentecost celebration of A.D. 57. But the celebration of this festival is far less significant to Luke than the warm and supportive reception Paul receives by the Jerusalem church and the deliberations about how to handle the problem of negative perceptions about Paul and his ministry by many Jewish believers in Jerusalem.

The brothers received us warmly (21:17). In light of the turmoil that will follow, Luke stresses the fact that Paul and his eight Gentile companions receive a warm reception by their fellow Christians in Jerusalem. Certainly not all Jerusalem Christians are opposed to Paul.

Went to see James, and all the elders were present (21:18). Absent is mention of any of the twelve apostles. Apparently Peter and John are away from Jerusalem in other places of service as are the other apostles. James has surfaced as the most prominent leader of the Jerusalem church (on James, see comments on 12:17; on elders, see comments on 11:30). Some have suggested that James is now functioning as a president over a kind of Christian "sanhedrin" with as many as seventy elders, but this is speculative.[434]

Paul and his group probably present to the leaders the collection of funds for the relief of the poor and suffering Jerusalem Christians.[435] What Paul hopes to be the high point of his visit to Jerusalem is quickly overshadowed by the controversy brewing about him and his attitude toward the Jewish law.

When they heard this, they praised God (21:20). The leadership of the Jerusalem church is solidly in support of Paul and the ministry he has among the Gentiles. This is not a begrudging support; they genuinely give thanks to God for the many Gentiles who have become Christians and for the numerous communities of believers that have been established throughout Asia Minor, Macedonia, and Achaia.

How many thousands of Jews have believed (21:20). God has not only been powerfully at work through Paul, but also through the Jerusalem believers. Evangelistic efforts have resulted in thousands of Jews embracing Jesus as the Messiah. This is certainly fantastic news for Paul, who a year or so earlier had told the Romans, "Brothers, my heart's desire and prayer to God for the Israelites is that they may be saved" (Rom. 10:1) and that he could wish himself cut off from Christ if it would lead to the people of Israel turning their hearts to Jesus (Rom. 9:3). Paul no doubt "praised God" for this encouraging result.

All of them are zealous for the law (21:20). These new believers have not yet matured in their faith to the point that they share the same outlook as their leaders on the law. The difficulty is compounded further by the ongoing presence of the Pharisaic Jewish believers who had already troubled the churches at Antioch and south Galatia some eight to ten years earlier. These "Judaizers," no doubt, had made efforts to orient the new believers toward their position in the "battle for

the law" being waged within Judean Christianity. The position of James and the elders was also increasingly difficult in light of the fervency about fidelity to the law in prevailing Jewish culture.

You teach all the Jews . . . to turn away from Moses (21:21). The principal charge is that Paul is literally teaching "apostasy from Moses." Of the specific charges that are levelled, there is no indication in Paul's letters that Jewish Christian parents should no longer circumcise their children nor is there any indication that Paul is actively teaching that Jewish Christians should altogether cease being Torah-observant. As long as circumcision is not performed as a rite that is essential for salvation, Paul has no difficulty with Jews continuing to practice this procedure. Paul, of course, has actually been the one responsible for Timothy's circumcision—and Timothy is present in the delegation (16:3).

These Jerusalem Jewish Christians apparently are living by the conviction that when people receive Jesus as the Messiah and are indwelt by the Spirit, they need to continue (if Jews) or take on (if Gentiles) the Jewish law with its rites and observances. Their position is not as extreme as the "Judaizers" who contend that obedience to the law, especially circumcision, is essential for salvation (15:1, 5).

These Jewish believers have heard that Paul is radically opposed to what they regard as a fundamental part of their Christian life. Their assumptions regarding Paul are only partly, not entirely, wrong. Paul probably does not *insist* on Torah observance for converted Jews in the Gentile cities and, no doubt, some begin to live on a principle of freedom from the law.

What shall we do? (21:22). James and the Jerusalem elders are in a difficult situation. On the one hand, they are in agreement with Paul theologically and want to affirm his work among the Gentiles. On the other, they want to continue to reach Jerusalem and Judean Jews with the gospel of Christ and not give a cause for deeper division within the Jerusalem church.

Four men with us who have made a vow .... pay their expenses (21:23–24). James and the elders come up with a plan that they think will demonstrate to the Jewish Christian believers in Jerusalem that Paul is at least to some degree law-observant and certainly not opposed to the law in ways that they assume. The plan involves supporting four Jewish-Christian men in the fulfillment of their Nazirite vows (see Num. 6:2–21; *m. Naz.*).

The purpose of the Nazirite vow was to dedicate oneself to the Lord for a set period of time. A Jewish man took a Nazirite vow typically for a thirty-day period, but sometimes longer (as in the case of Samson) or shorter periods (such as seven days) were also possible. During this time the Nazirite abstained from wine (or anything from the vine), scrupulously avoided any contact with a corpse, and left his hair uncut. At the end of the period of his special consecration to the Lord, he shaved off his dedicated hair and offered it at the temple. He was also required to present an offering of a year-old male lamb, a year-old ewe lamb, a ram, a basket of bread, and various grain and drink offerings (see Num. 6:14–17). These offerings resulted in a considerable expense to the Nazirite. Paul apparently helped subsidize the cost of these sacrifices. This kind of participation in the

▶ Jerusalem: Nine Years Before the War

Nine years after the events of Acts 21, a massive Jewish revolt against Rome broke out in Galilee and Judea (A.D. 66). It culminated with the legions of Titus laying seige to the holy city and killing thousands upon thousands of Jews, tearing down the walls of the city, and utterly destroying the massive temple complex.

Many Jews had grown weary of Roman rule in Palestine and despised their ongoing presence. The Roman procurator Felix (A.D. 52–59) had been a rather inept ruler and showed little sensitivity to Jewish concerns, especially in his massacre of many Jews when the Egyptian false prophet led thousands astray. There were many other less severe confrontations with the Romans that struck the flames of antipathy toward them. One such incident occurred when a Roman soldier found a copy of the Jewish law, tore it in two, and threw it on a fire during the procuratorship of Cumanus (A.D. 48–52).

Josephus's remarks about this incident reveal the fervor for the law that characterized this period: "The Jews, as if their whole country was in flames, assembled in frantic haste, religious fervour drawing them together irresistibly."[A-127]

Apocalyptic hopes were high that God would mightily intervene with his Messiah and crush these Gentile sinners who had little or no respect for the Jewish law. These hopes led to many false messiahs and assorted revolutionaries appearing on the scene. It is during this time that a group called the *Sicarii* (see "Terrorists" at Acts 21:37) surreptitiously plunged their knives into those who did not measure up to their zeal for the law.

Such was the atmosphere in Jerusalem during the time when many Jews were coming to faith in Jesus as Messiah. In spite of receiving Jesus, they would have felt tremendous pressure to maintain their fidelity to the law.

expenses was not without precedent. Herod Agrippa I at one time paid the expenses of a group of poor Nazirites.[436]

Join in their purification rites (21:24). In addition to paying the expenses of the four Nazirites, James urges Paul to join in their purification rites. This probably does not mean that Paul is also completing a Nazirite vow at this time, but that he is completing a special purification ritual (see, e.g., Num. 8:21; 19:12; 31:19). Paul's seven-day purification rite, with washings on the third and seventh days, is consistent with a Jewish understanding that a Jew who took a trip outside of the Holy Land and into Gentile territories would become ritually impure.[437] Such a cleansing was essential for Paul, according to Jewish tradition, since he would be entering the temple to assist with the Nazirite ceremony. He apparently times the final sprinkling on the seventh day of his purification so that it would coincide with the completion of the Nazirite vows of the four men. Paul's willingness to support the Nazirites and to undertake the purification rites himself illustrates his principle of becoming "all things to all men" for the sake of the gospel (1 Cor. 9:22–23).

R E F L E C T I O N S

FOR THE SAKE OF THE GOSPEL, IT MAY BE IMPORTANT for us (and our fellow believers) to engage in certain practices, wear special clothing, or wear our hair in a particular way—as long as it is not inconsistent with the gospel. Believers trying to reach the youth culture on Hollywood Boulevard, for instance, should dress differently than those trying to share Christ in a retirement community. The goal is for the progress of the gospel to be the driving passion of every believer.

As for the Gentile believers, we have written to them our decision (21:25). James once again reiterates that he and the elders of the Jerusalem church stand by their previous decision. What they have recommended to Paul is a practical maneuver, not a reassertion of the importance of the law for salvation. James reiterates the elements of the so-called decree, which the leadership of the Jerusalem church still affirm as essential for Gentile believers to facilitate their growth in the faith by ensuring that they have made a decisive break with idolatry and all that is associated with it.

Jews From Ephesus Provoke Hostility Against Paul (21:27–40)

The prophecy of Agabus is now to be fulfilled. Paul is bound and taken into Roman custody after he is nearly killed by a mob of Jews who wrongly think he has defiled the temple. Luke does not report on what happened to the delegates who accompany Paul. They do not appear to have been arrested; they probably return to their homes after they realize that Paul will be in custody for some time. Luke may have remained in Palestine for the next two years (A.D. 57–59), possibly gathering information for his two-volume work. He is with Paul in Caesarea (27:1) and will accompany him on his voyage to Rome.

Jews from the province of Asia (21:27). These are no doubt Jews from the city of Ephesus who have rejected Jesus as Messiah and are resentful of the influence Paul has exerted on the Jewish community of their city. It is ironic that they, not Jerusalem Jews, are the main instigators of the commotion that followed.

▶ The Boundary Warnings to Gentiles in the Temple

There was a stone wall that separated the court of the Gentiles from the inner courts of the temple (such as the holy area, the women's court, the court of the Israelites, and the court of the priests). Warning signs were posted along this wall prohibiting the Gentiles from entering. Josephus describes the stone wall and these notices:

> Anyone passing through this towards the second court found it enclosed within a stone balustrade 4 1/2 feet high, a perfect specimen of craftsmanship. In this at equal intervals stood slabs announcing the law of purification, some in Greek and some in Roman characters. No foreigner was to enter the holy area—this was the name given to the second court.[A-128]

Two of these stone warning tablets have been discovered by archaeologists. One complete tablet written in Greek is on display in the Archaeological Museum in Istanbul, Turkey. Half of another is housed in the Rockefeller Museum in Jerusalem. The inscription reads: "No foreigner is to enter within the forecourt and the balustrade around the sanctuary. Whoever is caught will have himself to blame for his subsequent death."[A-129]

Defiled this holy place (21:28). The Jews from Asia Minor stir up all the other Jews in the temple precincts. They claim that Paul has led Trophimus, a Gentile believer from Ephesus, from the court of the Gentiles into the inner courts of the temple, which was prohibited to Gentiles. Paul certainly has not done this, but the charge is believable to the masses.

They dragged him from the temple, and immediately the gates were shut (21:30). Paul is apparently seized by the temple police, dragged out of the Court of Women into the Court of the Gentiles, and has the doors shut behind him.[438] One cannot help but notice the irony of God's ordained messenger to bring light to the Gentiles now being shut out of the most holy place of Judaism—the place where God mediated his grace to his people for centuries. In Paul's view as well as Luke's, the temple is no longer the place to receive God's grace; God's grace is now supremely manifested and available in the Lord Jesus Christ.

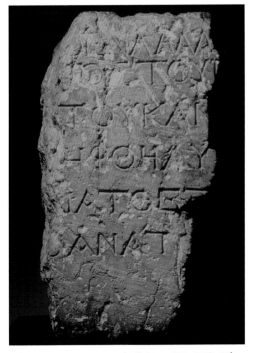

They were trying to kill him (21:31). The Jews are ostensibly within their legal rights to have Paul executed for the crime they are convinced he is guilty of, although there is no evidence in Josephus or elsewhere for anyone being killed for

▶

FORTRESS OF ANTONIA

A model of the fortress, which stood in the northwest corner of the temple grounds.

this offense. The Romans, however, do not look favorably on this frenzied mob justice.

The commander of the Roman troops (21:31). The commander, a *chiliarch* named Claudius Lysias (cf. 23:26), is in charge of a thousand Roman soldiers. Josephus informs us that a Roman cohort was always stationed at the fortress of Antonia "and at the festivals they extended along the colonnades fully armed and watched for any sign of popular discontent."[439] A

cohort typically consisted of 760 infantry troops and 240 cavalry.

He at once took some officers and soldiers and ran down to the crowd (21:32). The fortress of Antonia was located just outside the northwest corner of the temple precincts. The structure rose sixty feet high with three towers reaching seventy-five feet high and a fourth, just over a hundred feet. It gave the Romans a vantage point to watch over all that happened in the temple courts. Josephus notes: "Where

▶ Josephus's Account of the Egyptian Rebel

The exploits of the Egyptian revolutionary, whom the Roman *chiliarch* refers to, is described in detail by Josephus.

> A greater blow than this was inflicted on the Jews by the Egyptian false prophet. Arriving in the country this man, a fraud who posed as a seer, collected about 30,000 dupes, led them round from the desert to the Mount of Olives, and from there was ready to force an entry into Jerusalem, overwhelm the Roman garrison, and seize supreme power with his fellow-raiders as bodyguard. But Felix anticipated his attempt by

> meeting him with the Roman heavy infantry, the whole population rallying to the defence, so that when the clash occurred, the Egyptian fled with a handful of men and most of his followers were killed or captured; the rest of the mob scattered and stole away to their respective homes.[A-130]

There is a discrepancy in the two stories over the numbers involved. Most scholars think that Luke's figure of four thousand as more reliable given Josephus's tendency to exaggerate numbers.[A-131] This occurred when Felix was procurator of Judea (A.D. 52–59).

▶ "Terrorists"

The "terrorists" led by the Egyptian pseudo-Messiah (Acts 21:38) were a loosely organized political extremist group that surfaced in Palestine during the procuratorship of Felix. "Terrorist" is the NIV translation of the Greek word *sikarios,* which is a loanword from Latin (*sicarius*). In Latin, a *sica* is a dagger, and thus, the Sicarii were "dagger men."[A-132] Josephus provides us with an informative description of this violent group:

> Another type of bandit sprang up in Jerusalem, known as 'Sicarii.' These men committed numerous murders in broad daylight and in the middle of the City. Their favourite trick was to mingle with festival crowds, concealing under their garments small daggers with which they stabbed their opponents. When their victims fell, the assassins melted into the indignant crowd, and through their plausibity entirely defied detection. The first to have his throat cut by them was Jonathan the high priest, and after him many were murdered every day. More terrible than the crimes themselves was the fear they aroused, every man hourly expecting death, as in war.[A-133]

it joined the Temple colonnades stairs led down to both, and by these the guards descended."[440]

Bound with two chains (21:33). Paul's wrists are secured with manacles and he is bound to two soldiers.[441]

He ordered that Paul be taken into the barracks (21:34). Paul is taken up the stairs and into the fortress of Antonia.

Kept shouting, "Away with him!" (21:36). The crowd means more than merely "Get him out of here"; they desire him to be led away to his death. Paul is experiencing the same response from the crowd that Jesus faced (see Luke 23:18; John 19:15).

Do you speak Greek? (21:37). The Roman official appears surprised when Paul addresses him in Greek. It was not astonishing to him that a Jew from Palestine would know Greek. Most Jews have probably learned at least some Greek. In

listening to Paul, the tribune most likely discerns that Paul knows the language as well as any native Greek speaker. This may lead the tribune to conclude that Paul is not a local Judean revolutionary.

From Tarsus in Cilicia (21:39). On Tarsus, see comments on 9:30.

A citizen of no ordinary city (21:39). On the surface, it seems astonishing that Paul would reveal his Tarsian citizenship to the Roman official before disclosing his Roman citizenship. Yet in the ancient world, there was significant status attached to citizenship in an important city, such as Tarsus. Mention of his civic citizenship would have increased the esteem with which the tribune held him and perhaps incline the official to accede to Paul's request to address the people.

◀

ROMAN MILITARY DAGGER

A model of a dagger similar to what the Sicarii may have used.

Had Paul mentioned his Roman citizenship at this juncture and this were announced to the assembled crowd, it would only have inflamed their passions against him even more.[442] Yet there was a strong Jewish community in Tarsus which, at one point, even sent legates to help provoke the Jewish rebellion against Rome.[443]

He said to them in Aramaic (21:40). "Aramaic" is the NIV translation of the Greek expression *hebrais dialektos*. This can be interpreted to mean that Paul speaks to the crowd in (Mishnaic) Hebrew,[444] but it more likely means that he addresses them in the closely related Aramaic language. Aramaic is a Semitic language closely related to the Hebrew, which was widely spoken throughout ancient Palestine, Nabatea, Syria, Persia, and Parthia. It would have been the mother-tongue of Jews living in the Holy Land. Not all the crowd knows Hebrew and, if Paul were to address them in Greek, it would be a serious insult given their concerns that Paul is much too friendly with Gentiles.

Paul's Address to the Crowd in Jerusalem (22:1–21)

This is the second of three accounts of Paul's conversion in the book of Acts.

Only the new features supplementing what is said before will be commented on (see comments on 9:1–31; see also 26:1–23). The setting of this address before a hostile crowd of Jews in Jerusalem needs to be carefully considered in the reading of what Paul says. He tailors his comments appropriately to communicate the reality of his conversion to this group. Paul's address is effective in communicating the events surrounding his conversion, but it does not have the desired impact on this crowd. Rather than hundreds turning their hearts to Christ, they are enraged and want him flogged.

In Aramaic (22:2). See comments on 21:40. The fact that this nonnative Palestinian who is well known for his preaching among the Greeks can speak Aramaic causes the crowd to take note.

Brought up in this city (22:3). This expression (*anatethrammenos*) is key for understanding Paul's formative years. Although Paul was born in Tarsus and lived the first few years of his life there, he apparently spent most of his school-days in Jerusalem. We do not know if his parents moved here when he was young[445] or if they sent Paul here for the purpose of his education. We know from 23:16 that he has a family connection with Jerusalem. Exactly how old he is when he first starts his education in Jerusalem is not known. It would not be suprising if he began schooling there as early as ten or twelve years of age after some elementary-level education in Tarsus in a Jewish context.[446] Paul probably learned Greek as his native tongue and later acquired Aramaic and Hebrew. As a Roman citizen, he may also have learned some Latin.[447] It is improbable that the young Paul has received any formal training in Greek rhetoric and literature in Tarsus. He never hints at receiving a Greek education (*paideia*) that was so widely valued by well-educated Jews (e.g., Philo and Aristeas).[448]

Gamaliel (22:3). Paul studied with this famous teacher of Israel who represented the school of Hillel. Paul's method of interpreting the Old Testament as seen in his letters bears the mark of Hillel influence (see comments on 5:34).

Thoroughly trained in the law of our fathers (22:3). Before his conversion to Christ, Paul knew the Old Testament extraordinarily well. Not only that, he became familiar with the traditions of the Pharisees. This means he would have known all of the purity laws, regulations regarding the Sabbath, procedures regarding the sacrifices and the festivals, and many other rules regulating every part of daily life. Above all, he would have gained a commitment to the Torah (the first five books of the Old Testament) and the temple as central to Jewish life. He would also have acquired an attitude toward the Gentiles as impure, idolatrous people.

There is no doubt that Paul's training in the Law was thorough, but the wording of the text indicates that he received a *strict* training. His instruction was rigorous, meticulous, and accurately reflected the venerable traditions of the Pharisees.

Zealous for God (22:3). Paul clearly displayed a passion for God, but "zeal" implies more than this in a Jewish context. "Zeal" is identified with a willingness to use violence to defend the Torah. In recent Jewish history, the most revered examples of this were the high priest

Mattathias and his sons who rebelled against the blasphemous and impure Gentile rulers and eventually led Israel to a successful war of independence known as the Maccabean revolt (in the second century B.C.). The members of the Jewish movement of Paul's day that were seeking independence from Rome referred to themselves as "Zealots." When he wrote his letter to the Romans (prior to this occasion), Paul expressed his heart's desire to see the salvation of the Jews: "For I can testify about them that they are zealous for God, but their zeal is not based on knowledge" (Rom. 10:2). They are missing Christ.

I persecuted the followers of this Way to their death (22:4). Paul acknowledges he was responsible for the murder of Christians. It is little wonder that he could say, "For I am the least of the apostles and do not even deserve to be called an apostle, because I persecuted the church of God" (1 Cor. 15:9). Paul never forgot his misdirected zeal and his murderous past. It did not paralyze him, however, but gave him a profound appreciation of the mercy and grace of God and moved him to fulfill his commission from Christ with all of his strength until the end of his days.

All the Council can testify (22:5). The entire Sanhedrin is aware of the persecuting activity of Paul. Indeed, together with the high priest, they authorized the persecution.

Suddenly a bright light (22:6). The account of Paul's encounter with Christ is basically the same as Luke previously records (see comments on 9:3–9).

Jesus of Nazareth (22:8). Literally, "Jesus the Nazarene." This is the only one of the three accounts where Jesus refers to himself as "the Nazarene."

Saw the light, but they did not understand the voice of him who was speaking (22:9). In the earlier account, the men traveling with Paul "heard the sound but did not see anyone" (9:7). Some take this as an apparent discrepancy between the two versions of the conversion, mainly because the Greek text literally reads, "but they did not *hear* the voice." The answer lies in the fact that they did not hear the voice with comprehension—as an audible revelation of the resurrected Messiah. They probably heard the voice, but could not make out the words, only sensing it as noise.[449]

A devout observer of the law and highly respected by all the Jews living there (22:12). It is significant that Paul describes Ananias to this crowd of Jews assembled in Jerusalem in this way. It may impress the Jews, but the real difference is that Ananias has already embraced Jesus as the Messiah. This is a significantly abbreviated account of the role of Ananias when compared to the earlier version (see comments on 9:10–19).

The God of our fathers (22:14). Paul's reference to God in this way serves to underline the fact that he has not turned to a false god, but understands himself as maintaining his fidelity to the one true God, but now with a new knowledge.

The Righteous One (22:14). For Paul, Jesus is not only the Messiah, but "the Righteous One" (see comments on 3:14).

Be baptized (22:16). The rite served as a sign of Paul's cleansing from sin. This was all accomplished in the name of the Lord Jesus Christ. Jesus is the agent of God for procuring Paul's salvation and for all people who will call on his name. He has become the present and dominant influence in Paul's life from this point forward.

When I returned to Jerusalem (22:17). Paul's return to Jerusalem does not occur until three years later when he goes for a two-week period to become acquainted with Peter. This follows a period of ministry in Damascus and in Arabia (Nabatea).

Praying at the temple, I fell into a trance (22:17). This is now the third recorded vision that Paul has had since his trip to Damascus. The first is the actual appearance of Christ to him on the Damascus road and the second is the vision that he receives of Ananias's coming to him (9:12). Visions as a means of divine guidance play a crucial role in Paul's Christian experience (see also 16:9; 2 Cor. 12:1–6). Note how the vision comes to him while he is earnestly seeking God in prayer.

Saw the Lord speaking . . . he said to me (22:18). The Lord himself commands Paul to leave Jerusalem because the Jews will not accept his testimony. Paul objects by suggesting that his testimony will be all the more powerful and compelling because he had formerly been one with them in opposition to the Jesus movement, even in the killing of Stephen. How could they not be convinced? The Lord does not argue with Paul, but merely tells him that he will send him far away to proclaim the gospel to the Gentiles. Paul yields to his wise and all-knowing Lord.

The Crowd Reacts Violently (22:22–29)

Once Paul mentions the word "Gentile" and his alleged instructions from God to take salvation to the Gentiles, the crowd becomes enraged. This only confirms in their minds the allegation that he has taken a Gentile into the inner courts of the temple. Paul's address thus comes to an abrupt end whereupon he is taken in for an inquisition by flogging. At this point, he reveals his Roman citizenship to the centurion and averts the terrible ordeal he is about to face.

Throwing off their cloaks and flinging dust into the air (22:23). The crowd becomes so angry and frantic that they begin throwing whatever is available. Just as Paul shakes off the dust of his feet as a symbol of protest against those who oppose the gospel at Pisidian Antioch and shakes out his clothes against the opposition at Corinth (13:51; 18:6), so these Jews symbolically portray their opposition to all that Paul is saying and stands for.

He directed that he be flogged (22:24). The Roman flog (Greek = *mastix*; Latin = *flagrum*) is an instrument designed to inflict a great deal of pain and physical damage to the back. One scholar describes the instruments well and their potential for affliction: "While it sometimes consisted of a handle on which were fixed leather straps, it was often an instrument of brutal innovation. The lashes could be knotted cords or wire having bristled ends or be strung with knucklebones and lead pellets. This method of interrogation, though never overtly construed as punitive, could nevertheless result in crippling or even death before the truth had been arrived at."[450]

Is it legal for you to flog a Roman citizen? (22:25) The Porcian and Julian laws prohibited such a flogging (see comments on 16:37).

Tell me, are you a Roman citizen? (22:27). Roman citizens were given a document *diploma civitas Romanae* recording their citizenship for purposes of identification. It was a hinged wooden tablet with two leaves (a *diptych*). It is not known whether Paul carried this document with him verifying his claim of Roman citizenship; yet, if he was found making a false claim, he could be punished by death.[451]

I had to pay a big price for my citizenship (22:28). Roman citizenships were not sold on the open market. Claudius Lysias is here admitting that he paid a great deal of money to bribe a Roman official to put his name on a list of candidates.[452] The Roman historian Dio Cassius gives evidence that this was a widespread problem during the reign of the emperor Claudius:

> For inasmuch as Romans had the advantage over foreigners in practically all respects, many sought the franchise by personal application to the emperor, and many bought it from Massalina and the imperial freedmen. For this reason, though the privilege was at first sold only for large sums, it became so cheapened by the facility with which it could be obtained that it came to be a common saying, that a man could become a citizen by giving the right person some bits of broken glass.[453]

It appears that Lysias bought his citizenship early in the reign of Claudius. He then took on the Roman *nomen* Claudius, as was the custom of those receiving citizenship during his reign.[454]

I was born a citizen (22:28). There are two plausible theories on how Paul's family came to acquire Roman citizenship, although both are admittedly speculative. The first view suggests that Paul's ancestors settled in Tarsus at some time during the Seleucid era (2d cent. B.C.) as colonists from Israel. Roman citizenship may be bestowed on Paul's father or grandfather by one of the Roman generals—Pompey, Julius Caesar, or Mark Antony—who, successively, were in control of the province of Cilicia in the first century B.C. and engaged in wars. If Paul's father or grandfather rendered an outstanding service to the Roman cause (such as providing tents to the Roman forces in Tarsus or by serving in the mercenary forces), then, as an expression of gratitude, either of the Roman generals may have bestowed citizenship on the family.[455]

The second view is that Paul's grandparents received citizenship after being emancipated from slavery. Under this reconstruction, Paul's ancestors became prisoners and were subsequently enslaved by the Roman general Pompey when he invaded Israel, took control of the country for Rome, and sacked the temple. After a generation or so, the family was emancipated by their Roman owners and extended citizenship, a practice well attested in the Roman era. Sometimes this freedom was purchased by relatives and friends—a lucrative practice for the Roman master.[456]

Ordered the chief priests and all the Sanhedrin to assemble (22:30). Claudius Lysias is not handing the case over to the Sanhedrin. Because of his Roman citizenship, Paul will need to stand trial before the Roman procurator Felix. Lysias orders the Sanhedrin (see comments on 4:13) to meet because he does not understand the nature of the charges against Paul and wants the Jewish leaders to gather the relevant facts for this case.

▶ Paul's Roman Citizenship

Paul possessed the high-status privilege of being a Roman citizen.[A-134] His name was written on a register in Rome and recorded on the citizen registry in Tarsus.[A-135] As a citizen, he was accorded the right of a Roman trial, exemption from certain forms of degrading punishments (such as being beat with a *flagrum*), protection from summary execution, and the right of appeal. Among the responsibilities coming with citizenship were voting rights (*suffragium*), eligibility for Roman offices (depending on wealth status), potential liability for military service, and financial obligation to one's municipality.

It was not always necessary for Roman citizens to show their devotion to the emperor by engaging in emperor worship, worship of the goddess Roma, or by participating in the worship of any of the official Roman cults. Philo reports that the majority of Jews living in Rome were Roman citizens and yet were not compelled to compromise their ancestral laws.[A-136] Even Philo himself, as a wealthy Roman citizen living in Egypt, was never forced to worship the emperor or other gods.

Paul Appears Before the Sanhedrin (23:1–11)

In Paul's hearing before the Sanhedrin, disorder reigns and the facts of the case are never discussed. Part of the blame lies at the feet of Paul, who adeptly changes the focus from himself to the issue of bodily resurrection. Paul's driving concern is not to find some means of being released from custody, but in bearing witness to all of the principal leaders of the Jews.

In all good conscience to this day (23:1). Paul is probably not reflecting back as far as his pre-Christian days—when he rejected Jesus and persecuted the church (although in his conscience at that time, he was convinced he was serving God with zeal). He is here probably thinking of his preaching in the synagogues of Asia Minor, Macedonia, and Achaia that elicited violent opposition, his presentation of the gospel to Gentiles, and the way he explained to them their obligations before God in terms of the law.

God will strike you (23:3). This is not a curse, but rather a simple statement of assurance that God will deal with this injustice (e.g., Ps. 94:23). In some instances, this judgment came rapidly

(Acts 5:9–10; 13:11). Ananias was struck dead by assailants some nine years later.

You whitewashed wall (23:3). Paul is here using a prophetic image from the book of Ezekiel. The intent of the figure is to portray something fundamentally weak, poorly constructed, and unstable yet appearing as new, appealing, and strong. Ezekiel says: "When a flimsy wall is built, they cover it with whitewash, therefore tell those who cover it with whitewash that it is going to fall. . . . I will tear down the wall you have covered with whitewash and will level it to the ground so that its foundation will be laid bare. When it falls, you will be destroyed in it; and you will know that I am the LORD" (Ezek. 36:10–16; see also CD

◄

WHITEWASHED WALLS

Buildings on the island of Mykonos.

▶ The High Priest Ananias

This high priest is not to be confused with the earlier high priest Annas, father-in-law of Caiaphas (see Acts 4:6). This is Ananias, son of Nebedeus, who served as high priest from A.D. 47–59.[A-137]

Josephus portrays Ananias as popular with the people, but corrupt, engorging himself with wealth. At one point he sent his servants to the threshing floors demanding the workers to pay the tithes that belonged to the priests. Any who refused to surrender their money, the servants

beat. Some of the older priests who depended on these tithes for support actually starved to death.[A-138]

Ananias was also well known as a collaborator with Rome much to the vexation of the Pharisees and Jewish revolutionaries. At the outbreak of the Jewish war, Ananias went into hiding in Jerusalem near an aqueduct. The Jewish revolutionaries found him and his brother, Hezekiah, and killed them both.[A-139]

Select List of Jewish High Priests		
Name	**Date**	**New Testament Event**
Annas	A.D. 6–15	• High Priest during Jesus' early life
Joseph Caiaphas	A.D. 18–37	• High Priest during Jesus' earthly ministry, his trial, death, resurrection, and ascension • He was also in office during the early years of the church: Pentecost, the arrest of Peter and John, and the conversion of Paul • High Priest when Saul was persecuting the church
Ananias, Son of Nebedeus	A.D. 47–59	• In office during the Jerusalem Council • Paul's arrest at Jerusalem and hearing before the Sanhedrin
Ishmael ben Phiabi	A.D. 59–61	• High Priest when Festus assumed the procuratorship of Judea
Mattathias, son of Theophilus	A.D. 65–67	• High Priest at the outbreak of the Jewish war
Pinḥas of Ḥabtam	A.D. 67–70	• High Priest during the destruction of Jerusalem and the temple • The last High Priest

8:12). Perhaps Paul's statement is more than an emotional response to being struck; it may be a prophetic announcement of the weakness and instability of Israel's leadership and God's impending judgment.

Violate the law by commanding that I be struck (23:3). Paul may have in mind here Leviticus 19:15, which reads, "Do not pervert justice; do not show partiality to the poor or favoritism to the great, but judge your neighbor fairly."

I did not realize that he was the high priest (23:5). For nearly the past twenty-five years, Paul has been away from Jerusalem. He is not nearly as concerned as he once was about who the influential people were in the city. He has probably never seen Ananias before.

Do not speak evil about the ruler of your people (23:5). This is a direct quotation

of Exodus 22:27. Paul genuinely feels regret about having violated this instruction from the law in spite of how he was wrongly treated. Yet Paul's statement is correct and still may serve as an unwitting prophetic warning by Paul to the assembled Sanhedrin.

I am a Pharisee (23:6). Most noteworthy about this declaration is that Paul does not say, "I *once was* a Pharisee." Paul continues to regard himself as a Pharisee, but one who has rightly recognized Jesus as the Messiah sent from God. By implication, this means that Paul continues to value much of the Pharisaic doctrine he received, their respect for the Scripture, and their zeal for God, as well as many other key features of Pharisaism.

The son of a Pharisee (23:6). Literally, "the son of Pharisees." Apparently, Paul's father and grandfather were also Pharisees. This helps explain his family's commitment to get him to Jerusalem at an early age for training in the law and subsequently to become a disciple of Gamaliel.

I stand on trial because of my hope in the resurrection of the dead (23:6). Although it is to some degree true that Paul is employing a "divide and conquer" approach in his provocative remarks to the Sanhedrin, it is of paramount importance to recognize that this is the central issue for which he is being persecuted and tried.

The Sadducees say that there is no resurrection (23:8). The Sadducees viewed only the Torah as Scripture; none of the other writings, including the Prophets, were binding. Since there is no explicit reference to a bodily resurrection in the Torah, the Sadducees denied this teaching and presumably viewed it as a later, unbiblical, development. Their disbelief in the resurrection is attested by Josephus although he described it for his Greek readers as denying a belief in the immortal soul.[457] Jesus also debated with them over this point (Luke 20:27–40).

There are allusions to the resurrection in a variety of Old Testament passages, but Daniel 12:2–3 is the most explicit: "Multitudes who sleep in the dust of the earth will awake: some to everlasting life, others to shame and everlasting contempt. Those who are wise will shine like the brightness of the heavens, and those who lead many to righteousness, like the stars for ever and ever."[458] Much of Judaism in the time leading up to Christ anticipated a bodily resurrection. This is illustrated well in the story about the Jewish mother and her seven sons who were martyred by the executioners of Antiochus IV Epiphanes.[459] Their belief in the resurrection of the dead enabled

them to face martyrdom with noble spirits. When the second brother was ready to die, he exclaimed to Antiochus: "You accursed wretch, you dismiss us from this present life, but the King of the universe will raise us up to an everlasting renewal of life, because we have died for his laws" (2 Macc. 7:9). The rabbis who put together the Mishnah, the heirs of the Pharisaic school, left no doubt about an importance of a belief in the resurrection: "And these are they that have no share in the world to come: he that says that there is no resurrection of the dead."[460]

There are neither angels nor spirits (23:8). The Sadducees' disbelief in the realm of angels and spirits is surprising given their commitment to the Torah where references to angels abound, such as the angel who appeared to Hagar (Gen. 16:7–11), the two angels at Sodom (Gen. 19:1, 15), the angel of the Lord who kept Abraham from slaying Isaac (Gen. 22:11–15), Jacob's vision of a ladder to heaven with angels ascending and descending on it (Gen. 28:12), the angel who led the Israelites through the desert (Ex. 23:20), as well as references to demons (Deut. 32:17). Luke is the only ancient writer who records this feature of their belief. This may not have been an absolute denial of the existence of angels and spirits, which is more a product of our time than theirs, but a reticence to accept a belief in the multitudinous hierarchies of spirits that some Jewish teachers of their day postulated (such as evidenced in *1 Enoch*, *Jubilees*, and some of the Dead Sea Scrolls).[461]

We find nothing wrong with this man (23:9). The focus of the debate has remain centered on the issue of the reality of a future bodily resurrection, not on whether Jesus of Nazareth has risen from the tomb.

What if a spirit or an angel has spoken to him (23:9). The Pharisees agreed with Paul to a large extent—belief in a bodily resurrection and the possibility that a divine being could impart information to someone. Yet, as one writer puts it, their agreement "falls far short of recognizing the key point, which is the reality of the resurrection in Paul's experience of Jesus as Lord."[462] It was not an angelic mediator who spoke to Paul on the Damascus road; it was the resurrected and exalted Jesus of Nazareth.

The Lord stood near Paul (23:11). Luke does not say whether Jesus appears to Paul in bodily form or in a dream-vision, but this is certainly a timely appearing. Paul is probably on the throes of discouragement wondering if he will survive, and, if he does, will he be released and be able to fulfill his ambition of going to Rome and on to Spain? Jesus not only previously appears to Paul on the Damascus road, but also at a discouraging point in his ministry in Corinth (see 18:9).

So you must also testify in Rome (23:11). The Lord's comments reassure Paul that he will survive and proclaim the

REFLECTIONS

AFTER JESUS ASCENDED TO HEAVEN and took his place at the right hand of God, he did not cease to be actively involved with his people. He continues to be intimately concerned with the extension and well-being of his church. As "head" of the church, he continues to provide encouragement, direction, guidance, and counsel. Are we hearing him today?

gospel in Rome. What the Lord does not reveal at this time is that it will be two years before he arrives there, that he will be shipwrecked at sea, and that he will testify in Rome bound in chains.

A Plot to Kill Paul Is Discovered (23:12–22)

The Jews formed a conspiracy (23:12). Luke clarifies in the next verse that it is not the Jewish people as a whole who now represent the enemies of the faith, but a zealous group of forty men with a design on Paul's life.

An oath not to eat or drink until they had killed Paul (23:12). This kind of zeal for the law is well illustrated in the Mishnah: "He who stole a sacred vessel of the cult (Num. 4:7), and he who curses using the name of an idol, and he who has sexual relations with an Aramaean woman—zealots beat him up on the spot (Num. 25:8, 11). A priest who performed the rite in a state of uncleanness—his brothers, the priests, do not bring him to court. But the young priests take him outside the courtyard and break his head with clubs" (*m. Sanh.* 9:6).

The expression translated by "oath" here (*anathema*) is used in the Greek Old

Testament to translate the Hebrew term *ḥērem*. It designates something hostile to God and therefore under a ban and to be destroyed. Thus, the idolatrous cities of the Canaanites became *ḥērem* (or *anathema*) and were to be utterly destroyed (see Deut. 13:16; 20:17).

We are ready to kill him before he gets here (23:15). The meeting place of the Sanhedrin was in the center of the city at the *liškat haggazît* (the "Chamber of Hewn Stone"), just west of the southwestern portion of the temple wall. Josephus calls this place the *Xystos*.[463] It was approximately a quarter-mile from the Antonia Fortress. The group of forty have planned to ambush Paul at some strategic point between the two locations. This was a bold plan since Paul would be escorted by Roman soldiers. The conspirators are obviously prepared to kill one or more of the soldiers to get to Paul.

The son of Paul's sister (23:16). This is a rare and fascinating insight into Paul's family. We do not know whether Paul's sister and her family have taken up residence in Jerusalem or whether the nephew has come to Jerusalem, as Paul had, for his education. Neither do we know if Paul's nephew is a believer. It is clear, however, that he possesses a family affection for Paul and wants to save his life.

He went into the barracks and told Paul (23:16). In his Jerusalem custody, Paul is not kept in a dark inner cell and chained to the floor by leg irons as he had been in Philippi. This is a more honorable custody since the *chiliarch* knows that Paul is a Roman citizen. Apparently, Paul is able to receive visitors.

Take this young man to the commander (23:17). Paul asks the centurion to take

his nephew to the *chiliarch* so he can reveal the conspiracy. The *chiliarch* listens sympathetically to the boy and enjoins him to silence about the plot.

Paul Is Sent to Caesarea (23:23–35)

The plot is not only a serious threat to Paul—a Roman citizen whom Claudius Lysias now has responsibility to protect—but also to Roman soldiers protecting him. Lysias probably also recognizes that there is a risk that this situation might escalate into a much greater problem. The *chiliarch* thus makes the decision to send Paul to Caesarea immediately under a heavy guard and the cover of night.

Get ready a detachment of two hundred soldiers (23:23). The total number of Roman soldiers escorting Paul to Caesarea is 470. Although this seems like an enormous number for protecting one man on his journey, Claudius Lysias rightly recognizes the volatile nature of this situation at a time when Jewish antipathy against Rome has nearly reached a boiling point. The size of this detachment functions as an adequate deterrent to forestall any attack by the forty men and any others they may have pulled into their planned ambush.

Go to Caesarea (23:23). Caesarea, not Jerusalem, was the seat of the Roman proconsul as well as the administrative and judicial center for Judea (see 10:1).

He wrote a letter as follows (23:25). In Greek, this is a technical expression (*typos*) indicating that Luke has available to him the exact text of the letter.[464]

Claudius Lysias (23:26). This is the first reference to the *chiliarch's* name. His *nomen* "Claudius" likely reflects that fact that he received his citizenship under the principate of the emperor Claudius.

To His Excellency (23:26). This is the NIV's translation of the Greek word *kratistos*, the same expression that is used of Theophilus, the recipient of Luke's two-volume work (Luke 1:3). *Kratistos* is a title of respect for Roman citizens of the aristocratic equestrian order and for those who hold high office (usually held by men of the equestrian order).465

For I had learned that he is a Roman citizen (23:27). Lysias is guilty of twisting the facts to some degree perhaps in an effort to portray his actions in the best possible light. In reality, he learned that Paul is a Roman citizen *after* he rescued him from the murderous mob. He also failed to mention that he had Paul stretched out and ready to be flogged.

No charge against him that deserved death or imprisonment (23:29). In spite of the earlier false testimony that Paul had taken Trophimus into the inner courts of the temple, a capital crime, this was never mentioned in the Sanhedrin hearing.

As far as Antipatris (23:31). Antipatris was a city about thirty-five miles northwest of Jerusalem on the main road leading to the port city of Caesarea via Lydda.466 It was less than ten miles from the coast and situated in the plain of Sharon near the Judean hills at the headwaters of the Yarkon river. The city had

▶ **COIN MINTED UNDER ANTONIUS FELIX**

▶ **Felix**

Felix was the Roman procurator of Judea for roughly eight years (A.D. 52–59) and had ruled for five years when Paul was taken into custody.A-140 He did not come from a background of wealth and status, but was actually a freed slave. Both he and his brother Pallas had been the slaves of Antonia, the mother of Claudius. This was the first time that a Roman procuratorship had ever been held by a freedman.

His reign over Judea, Samaria, Galilee, and Perea did much to stimulate further unrest among the Jews, which eventually led to the war against Rome. The Roman historian Tacitus sums up his leadership with this remark: "Practicing every kind of cruelty and lust, he wielded royal power with the instincts of a slave."A-141 Elsewhere, Tacitus says that Felix "stimulated outbreaks [of Jewish unrest] by injudicious disciplinary measures."A-142 According to Josephus, Felix had his soldiers track down and catch Jewish zealots virtually every day and immediately executed them, many of them by crucifixion. One of his most heinous crimes was conspiring to put to death the Jewish high priest Jonathan.A-143

He was ousted from his office by the emperor Nero in A.D. 59 after his inept handling of an uprising in the city of Caesarea. A dispute had arisen between the Jewish population of the city and the Syrian inhabitants' citizenship status in the city. The conflict led to rioting and street fighting. "One day the Jews were victorious, and Felix came into the market-place and ordered them with threats to retire. When they refused, he sent his soldiers against them and killed a large number, whose property was promptly plundered."A-144 This happened while Paul was in Roman custody in Caesarea.

Selected List of the Roman Procurators of Judea		
Name	Date	NT Event
Coponius	A.D. 6–10	• The first Roman procurator of Judea after the deposition of Herod Archelaus
Valerius Gratus	A.D. 15–26	• Procurator during much of Jesus' life prior to the beginning of his ministry
Pontius Pilate	A.D. 26–36	• Procurator during Jesus' ministry • Jesus is crucified during his administration • Peter and John arrested during his rule
NO PROCURATOR		
Herod Agrippa I	A.D. 41–44	• Herod Agrippa I is made king over Judea, Samaria, and Galilee
Ventidius Cumanus	A.D. 48–52	• Procurator during the time of the Jerusalem Council
Felix	A.D. 52–59	• Paul is tried before him (Acts 24)
Festus	A.D. 60–62	• Paul is tried before him (Acts 25)
Albinus	A.D. 62–64	
Gessius Florus	A.D. 64–66	• Last procurator before the destruction of Jerusalem
Sextus Vettulenus Cerialis	A.D. 70–72	• First procurator after the destruction of Jerusalem

a long history as the ancient Aphek (see Josh. 12:18). Herod the Great renamed the city after his father Antipater: "In memory of his father he founded a city, choosing a site in the loveliest plain in his kingdom with an abundance of rivers and trees, and naming it Antipatris."[467] The distance for the next day's journey to Caesarea was about twenty-seven miles.

They let the cavalry go on with him, while they returned to the barracks (23:32). Now that they are in lands populated predominately by Gentiles and presumably safer from the threat of an ambush by Jewish zealots, the four hundred soldiers are ordered to return to Jerusalem.

Asked what province he was from (23:34). Felix asks this question not out

of personal interest, but in an attempt to establish if the case is within his jurisdiction. Since the Roman province of Cilicia falls under the authority of the Roman legate of Syria—to whom Felix

ANTIPATRIS

The site of Antipatris (Aphek) with a seventeenth-century Turkish fortress in the background.
▼

reports—he is therefore responsible for handling the case.[468]

Kept under guard in Herod's palace (23:35). The literal reference is to Herod's *praitōrion*, which is best understood as his palace. Not only has Herod built a remarkable port at Caesarea, but he "adorned it with the most splendid palace."[469] After Herod passed off the scene, the Roman procurators made their residence at the palace. The fact that Paul is held in the palace does not mean that he spends two years living in opulence.

Similar to the Antonia Fortress in Jerusalem, this facility would have had rooms for those kept under light custody.

Paul's Trial Before the Roman Procurator Felix (24:1–21)

Five days after Paul's arrival in Caesarea, a trial is convened. The Roman procurator Felix properly serves as judge of the trial and hears the cases of both the plaintiffs and the defendant. Luke gives a précis of both presentations. The trial is adjourned without a decision so Felix can

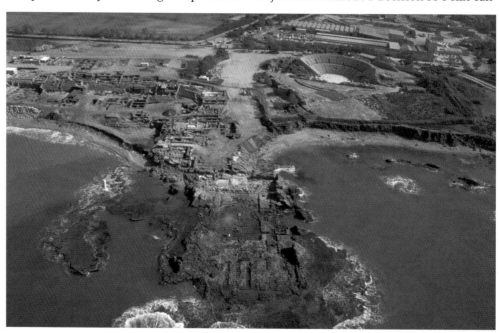

► **HEROD'S PALACE IN CAESAREA**

The foreground represents the foundations of Herod's palace by the sea.

► Herod's Palace By the Sea

In 1976, Ehed Netzer of Hebrew University of Jerusalem began excavating a site on a rocky promontory of Caesarea. Renewed excavations of this site in 1992 by Netzer and members of an American team led by Kathryn Gleason and Barbara Burell of the University of Pennsylvania have led to a provisional identification of this site as Herod's *praitōrion*—his seaside palace. [A-145]

A striking feature of the "promontory palace" is

a pool measuring 115 feet long and 59 feet wide in the center of the complex. Water channels leading to it suggest that it would have been filled with fresh water. Surrounding the pool on all four sides are the foundations of a large structure with rooms for a range of purposes. The discovery of a variety of Herodian era artifacts—including pottery and lamps—suggest that the palace was built sometime between 22–10 B.C.

await the testimony of the Roman commander of forces in Jerusalem.

The high priest Ananias went down (24:1). The presence of the high priest—the highest authority of the Jewish nation—and some of the Jerusalem elders at this trial underline its importance and significance to the Jewish leaders.

A lawyer named Tertullus (24:1). Nothing is known of this man outside of this passage. He is a *rhētor*, that is, he is a professional attorney. As such, he has knowledge of Roman law and proper court procedure as well as training in the art of rhetoric. Since it is not required for the plaintiff to have a legal advocate, their hiring of Tertullus reveals their determination to win a conviction.

Tertullus presented his case (24:2). Before Tertullus gets to the heart of his case, he gives a laudatory introduction in which he heaps lavish (and, in this case, undeserved) praise on Felix. This type of beginning to a case, known as a *captatio benevolentiae*, was common in the courtroom and often effective in winning the respect and favor of the judge.[470]

A long period of peace under you (24:2). Tertullus begins his case with an empty line of flattery. The only way Felix endeavored to bring peace was by having his soldiers hunt down and kill extremist Jewish freedom fighters (*sicarii*) (see "Felix" at 23:23). In reality, Felix did more than any other governor to disrupt any semblance of peace there might have been in the Holy Land.

Your foresight (24:2). The Greek word *pronoia* ("foresight") was often used of

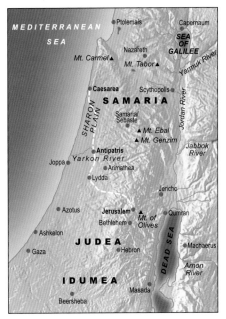

the providence of God in Hellenistic Judaism (e.g., *3 Macc.* 4:21; 5:30). It could also be used of Hellenistic rulers who exercised excellent insight in the management of public affairs, as it was used of the Syrian ruler Seleucus IV: "For he [the high priest] saw that without the king's attention [*pronoia*] public affairs could not again reach a peaceful settlement, and that Simon would not stop his folly" (2 Macc. 4:6).

A troublemaker (24:5). "Troublemaker" (*loimos*) is a word that in its literal sense means a "plague" or a "pestilence." It came to be used as a metaphor for a dangerous person—like someone who carries a deadly disease and infects other people. Using a different term but the same image, the emperor Claudius in a letter refers to certain activities of the Jews as "stirring up a universal plague [*nosos*] throughout the world."[471] The "plague" image is used frequently in the Greek Old Testament. *Loimos* refers to the "wicked man" of Psalm 1:1 and the "mocker" in many of the Proverbs.[472] Eli's sons were "troublemakers" because "they had no regard for the Lord" (1 Sam. 2:12).

Stirring up riots among the Jews all over the world (24:5). The Greek word *stasis* is the counterpart to the Latin *seditio* and similar in meaning to our word "sedition." The charge of *stasis* was serious among the Roman authorities who were seeking to maintain peace in the empire—especially in a province where outbreaks of hostility were increasingly commonplace. There is clearly some truth to Tertullus's charge when one considers the reaction to Paul's preaching in synagogues in Pisidian Antioch, Iconium, Lystra, Thessalonica, Berea, and Corinth.

CAESAREA

▼

A ringleader of the Nazarene sect (24:5). This is the earliest use of "Nazarenes" as a description of the Christian movement. The origin of this name is rooted in the description of Jesus as from Nazareth (Jesus the *Nazōraios*, see 2:22; 3:6).

Tertullus characterizes this movement as a *hairesis*, the term from which is derived the English word "heresy." The term itself does not necessarily have the kind of negative connotations implied by "heresy." Josephus used the term to distinguish the various schools of thought within Judaism—the Pharisees, Sadducees, and the Essenes.[473] But the term took on pejorative overtones (see 24:14; 28:22); that is how Tertullus seems to use it.[474] Christianity is thus presented by him as an illegitimate or deviant form of Judaism.

Tried to desecrate the temple (24:6). The implication is that Paul brought Trophimus into the inner courts with the intent of desecrating the temple. This was a serious charge for which, if proven, Paul could receive the death penalty. Without the alleged witnesses—Jewish pilgrims from Asia Minor—the charge was without substance.

So we seized him (24:6). Tertullus gives the impression that the temple police apprehended Paul in an orderly fashion. He says nothing about the mob scene. It is possible that he is implying that Lysias exceeded his jurisdiction by taking Paul out of their hands. This is the interpretation of the Western tradition of the text (verse 7 in certain versions), which adds, "but the commander, Lysias, came and with the use of much force snatched him from our hands." Thus, Felix should hand Paul over to the Sanhedrin, who would try him and, if guilty, hand him back over to the Romans for execution.[475]

Paul replied (24:10). After Tertullus finishes, Paul is given the chance to respond to the accusations. This account is given in verses 10–21. As with the case presented by Tertullus, Luke only gives us a summary of the salient points, but possibly bases it on actual court documents.[476] Like Tertullus, Paul properly and politely begins with a *captatio benevolentiae*, but not by bending the truth to endear himself to Felix.

Twelve days ago (24:11). This expression in the original is best interpreted to mean that Paul was only in Jerusalem a total of twelve days.[477] Now having been in Caesarea for five days (24:1), it has only been seventeen days since his arrival in Jerusalem. An extraordinary amount has happened in that brief span of time:

- Day 1: Paul arrives in Jerusalem (21:18).
- Day 2: Paul meets with the leaders of the Jerusalem church (21:18).
- Days 3–9: Paul observes a seven-day ritual of purification (21:27).
- Day 9: Paul is arrested (21:33).
- Day 10: Paul appears before the Sanhedrin (22:30).
- Day 11: The plot against Paul's life is uncovered (23:12).
- Day 12: Paul is taken to Caesarea.
- Days 13–17: Paul awaits trial in Caesarea.

The Way (24:14). See comments on 9:2.

I believe everything that agrees with the Law and that is written in the Prophets (24:14). Paul represents himself as a faithful and observant Jew. He continues to regard himself as a Pharisee (23:6). The difference, of course, is that he sees the hope of Judaism fulfilled in Jesus of Nazareth. In upholding the law, Paul does not necessarily agree with all of the Pharisaic traditions that surround the law and he also reinterprets the meaning and significance of certain key parts of the law (e.g., the law governing circumcision; see Rom. 2:29).

I have the same hope in God (24:15). As an outcome of embracing all that is written in the prophets, Paul claims to share the same future hope as nearly all Jews (with the exception of the Sadducees). At the heart of this is a belief in the coming descendant of David who will be the end-time deliverer for Israel. It also encompasses a belief in the resurrection of the dead (Dan. 12:2).

A resurrection of ... the wicked (24:15). Many texts in the Judaism of the time of Christ affirm a belief in a general resurrection, developing the teaching of Daniel 12:2. For example, the *Testament of Benjamin* 10:6–10 teaches that all will be resurrected and God will judge the nations for all of the wrongs they have committed. Similarly, *4 Ezra* (2 Esdras) 7:32–35 speaks of a day when "the earth shall give up those who are asleep in it" and the Most High will judge all people according to their deeds.[478] According to the Gospel of John, Jesus also affirms this belief in a general resurrection (John 5:28–29). In his letters, Paul never explicitly develops this teaching (though cf. 1 Cor. 15:12–13), but he emphasizes that all people must appear before the judgment seat of Christ (see 2 Cor. 5:10).

After an absence of several years (24:17). Paul's most recent visit was about five years earlier when he briefly visited the Jerusalem church following his Corinthian ministry and prior to his trip to Ephesus (18:22). Prior to that was his trip to Jerusalem for the so-called Apostolic Council in A.D. 49 (Acts 15).

I came to Jerusalem to bring my people gifts for the poor (24:17). This is Luke's only explicit reference to the collection of money Paul has gathered for the impoverished Jewish Christians in Jerusalem (see comments on 21:18). This was the second time that Paul brought relief to the city. The first time was roughly twelve years earlier when he came to Jerusalem as a delegate from the church at Antioch (11:27–30; 12:25). At that time, James, Peter, and John asked Paul to continue to "remember the poor" (Gal. 2:10). Paul was faithful to this request and gathered a substantial relief offering from the churches of Asia Minor, Macedonia, and Achaia "for the poor among the saints in Jerusalem" (Rom. 15:26). The gift was not only motivated by the desire to help those in need, but also expressed thanks from the Gentiles because they now share in the spiritual blessings of the Jews (Rom. 15:27). One can have a glimpse into how Paul gathered this collection from the Macedonian and Achaian churches in 2 Corinthians 8:1–9:15.

And to present offerings (24:17). These offerings must be seen as distinct from the gifts for the poor. This term (*prosphoras*) refers to sacrificial offerings. Paul paid the expenses for four men to purchase animals, bread, grain, and liquid as sacrificial offerings in fulfillment of their Nazirite vows (see comments on 21:22–23). Beyond this, there is no evidence that Paul presented any other offerings as part of the temple worship.

I was ceremonially clean (24:18). Paul had undertaken the seven-day Jewish ritual of purification (see comments on 21:24).

Who ought to be here before you (24:19). A group of Jewish pilgrims from Asia Minor (presumably Ephesus) instigated the disturbance in the temple courts by falsely accusing Paul. Yet they are not present at the proceedings before Felix. Why none of them is present is somewhat perplexing, especially in light of how important this case is to the high priest and members of the Sanhedrin who have accompanied him. Do the Asian Jews know that their testimony will not stand up under close scrutiny? Or are they simply pressed by time to return home to their jobs and their families? Whatever the reason, their absence greatly damages the case of the Jewish leaders. As one expert on Roman law notes, "The Roman law was very strong against accusers who abandoned their charges."[479]

Paul's Caesarean Imprisonment (24:22–27)

Paul remains in Roman custody in Caesarea for two full years (A.D. 57–59) awaiting the resumption of his trial. He is afforded an occasional opportunity to talk with the Roman procurator and his wife, which he takes advantage of for the presentation of the gospel.

Felix, who was well acquainted with the Way (24:22). With the thousands who have become Christians in Jerusalem and the many Christian communities that have developed in Caesarea and throughout Palestine, it is not surprising that this Roman governor is acquainted with the movement. The precise wording here suggests that he is either "well acquainted" with the Jesus movement or "better acquainted" with it than the Jerusalem leaders (it is a comparative adjective). What kind of information he has received about Christianity is unknown. As the Roman procurator of this volatile region, surely his chief concern is to know what kind of security risk this movement posed. He is sufficiently familiar with them to know that they are not insurrectionists or rioters.

When Lysias the commander comes (24:22). Felix formally adjourns the trial until he can obtain further information from the *chiliarch*. Presumably Lysias does come at some point and the trial is resumed, although Luke says nothing about this. If he does, Felix does not find enough information to release Paul or proceed with a conviction.

Give him some freedom and permit his friends to take care of his needs (24:23). Felix orders Paul to be kept in a lightened form of military custody. This does not mean that Paul is unchained; he is probably manacled or chained to his centurion or other military personnel. He is most likely kept in a secure room of Herod's palace (see "Herod's Palace By the Sea" at 23:35). Since the Romans do not take responsibility for providing food and clothing to someone in custody, Paul's friends are given access to him for taking care of his needs. [480] These friends are probably members of the Christian community at Caesarea as well as Luke and any of the other delegates from the churches who may have remained with him for a time. One wonders if Cornelius and members of his household (see Acts 10) might have been among the people who care for Paul during this time.

His wife Drusilla, who was a Jewess (24:24). Drusilla was one of three daughters of Herod Agrippa I, the king of Palestine who died suddenly in Caesarea after appearing to people as a god (see 12:19–

23). Drusilla was six years old when her father died in A.D. 44, which means that she was only fourteen years old when she married Felix and nineteen years old at this juncture. [481]

Drusilla was Felix's third wife. One of his previous wives was the granddaughter of Anthony and Cleopatra—a marriage that made Felix a relative of the emperor Claudius. The circumstances of Drusilla's marriage to Felix reveal something of his sordid character. Drusilla had recently been married to Azizus, king of Emesa (a small territory in Syria). When Felix subsequently met Drusilla, he was overcome with desire for her. Josephus says that "she did indeed exceed all other women in beauty." [482] Longing to make this woman his own wife, Felix secured the services of a magician from Cyprus and made every effort to take her away from Azizus. Enticed by the many promises of Felix to make her a happy woman, she was persuaded to leave her husband and become Felix's wife. [483]

He spoke about faith in Christ Jesus (24:24). When Paul is given the opportunity to speak to Felix and Drusilla, he clearly presents his conviction that Jesus is the fulfillment of the messianic hope of Israel. This would have involved an explanation of why he had to suffer and die as

REFLECTIONS

TO SPEAK OF THE COMING JUDGMENT HAS BECOME unfashionable in the evangelistic sharing or preaching of many Christians. We are afraid of turning people off by appearing extremist. The apostle Paul regularly speaks about a time of impending accountability before God in his preaching. Less concerned about how people feel, he is overcome by his feeling of responsibility for clearly informing people that God indeed will call people to account one day.

well as rise from the dead. Paul exhorts them to put their faith in this Jesus.

Paul discoursed on righteousness ... and the judgment to come (24:25). Jesus taught that when the Spirit came, he would "convict the world of guilt in regard to sin and righteousness and judgment" (John 16:8). Paul continues his presentation of the gospel to Felix and Drusilla by focusing on these themes in concert with the work of the Spirit.

Self-control (24:25). Sandwiched between Paul's themes of righteousness and the coming judgment is the topic of self-control. The term *enkrateia* never appears in the Greek Old Testament (except *4 Macc.* 5:34), but Paul presents it as a virtue that the Spirit produces in the life of a believer (Gal. 5:23). The roots of the use of this term in ethical contexts probably go back to Plato, who emphasizes the cultivation of *enkrateia*, that is, mastery over oneself, especially over sensual desires and pleasures.[484] Socrates, Aristotle, and the Stoics regard self-control as a cardinal virtue. Similarly, the Hellenistic Jew Philo repeatedly stresses the importance of developing self-control.[485] Paul's discourse on self-control, together with his teaching on righteousness and the judgment, is probably intended to help Felix and Drusilla recognize their guilt before God as a means of pointing them to their need for the forgiveness that comes from putting their faith in Christ Jesus.

Hoping that Paul would offer him a bribe (24:26). Felix does not recognize his own lack of self-control with regard to his lust for money. He invites Paul to meet with him periodically not to discuss the problem in his own soul, but to provide Paul with ample opportunity to offer him a bribe. Apparently Felix has the impression that Paul has access to considerable wealth. This probably stems from Felix's awareness that Paul has come to Jerusalem with a sizeable amount of money. Although it was illegal for Felix to accept a bribe, this law was frequently overlooked in the governance of the provinces.

When two years had passed (24:27). Paul remains in Roman custody in Caesarea for two full years. Some think that Paul may have written his letter to the church at Philippi during this imprisonment (see the introduction to Philippians). Luke apparently stays in Caesarea while Paul is in custody; he is with Paul when Festus determines that Paul should be sent to Rome (Acts 27:1). This extended stay in Caesarea would have been invaluable to Luke as he continued to gather information for his Gospel and the book of Acts.

Felix was succeeded (24:27). Felix is recalled because of his inept handling of a flareup of violence between Jews and Greeks in the city of Caesarea (see "Felix" at 23:23). Josephus says that under normal circumstances, Felix would have faced a much greater punishment for this misdeed:

When Porcius Festus was sent by Nero as successor to Felix, the leaders of the Jewish community of Caesarea went up to Rome to accuse Felix. He undoubtedly would have paid the penalty for his misdeeds against the Jews had not Nero yielded to the urgent entreaty of Felix's brother Pallas, whom at that time he held in the highest honour.[486]

Because Felix wanted to grant a favor to the Jews, he left Paul in prison (24:27). Felix is in a precarious position with the

Jews. His killing of many of the insurrectionists (*sicarii*) and his insensitive treatment of many other affairs has embroiled Jewish opinion against him. To release Paul would have inflamed the Jewish leaders even more. Yet to extradite Paul to the Sanhedrin for trial would surely have resulted in the apostle's death. He does not want to face the political implications from Rome for the death of a Roman citizen. The most expedient course for Felix is the continuous postponement of the trial.[487]

Paul Stands Trial Before Festus (25:1–12)

With the change of procurators comes a resumption of Paul's trial. Any hope of a dismissal under Felix evaporates with his recall by the emperor. As soon as Festus arrives on the scene (A.D. 59), the Jerusalem leaders exploit the situation to seek an extradition of Paul to Jerusalem. This does not work and a hearing is convened in Caesarea.

Festus went up from Caesarea to Jerusalem (25:1). Shortly after assuming his new position, Festus travels to the principal city of his domain to become acquainted with the religious and political leaders. As an outsider, he has much to learn about this volatile region.

The chief priests and Jewish leaders appeared before him (25:2). "Chief priests" refers to the current high priest, former high priests, and the priestly group from whom the high priests are chosen. The high priest is now Ishmael ben Phiabi. After he takes office, a terrible schism arises between the ruling elite and the chief priests, resulting in violence.[488] The two groups are united, however, in their opposition to Paul and the Jesus movement. The fact that Paul's case is one of the first items they discuss with the new Roman procurator demonstrates the importance of the case to them.

◀

PORCIUS FESTUS COIN

▶ Porcius Festus

Nero appointed Festus as the replacement for Felix in A.D. 59 and he governed until his premature death in A.D. 62. In the only portrayal of Festus outside of the New Testament, Josephus represents him as an honorable and capable leader, but facing a set of insurmountable crises.[A-146]

Nothing is known about his background. Upon coming to Judea he was immediately faced with the ongoing strife between the Jews and Greeks in Caesarea, the *sicarii* setting villages on fire and plundering them, a messianic pretender leading people into the desert, and a dispute over a high wall that the temple officials erected that obstructed Agrippa and Festus from observing the inner courts of the temple from the palace. All of these events further contributed to the massive unrest in the country that led to the Jewish war four years after the death of Festus.

Festus was succeeded by Albinus (A.D. 62–64). Josephus says that, "Albinus, who followed him, acted very differently, being guilty of every possible misdemeanor."[A-147]

As a favor to them (25:3). The Jewish leaders quickly attempt to take advantage of the new procurator's natural tendency to ingratiate himself to them. For maintaining security in this region, Festus would certainly want to achieve their goodwill. This is especially important in the aftermath of the Jew-Gentile rioting in Caesarea that led to the demise of his predecessor Felix.[489] The case of Paul—a person with whom he has no prior familiarity—would be a matter of indifference to him. Although it is his duty to uphold Roman law, the rulers of the eastern provinces frequently bent the law to obtain their desired political aims.

They were preparing an ambush (25:3). Luke does not state specifically who is preparing the ambush. Presumably, the forty men who previously took the vow would still want to carry it out (23:13–14). Others also may have joined them in their strategy to rid the Holy Land of the outspoken man they consider to be perverting the law. The plan now is to ambush Paul somewhere on the road from Caesarea to Jerusalem. As with the previous strategy, they would not be able to accomplish their aim without some Roman casualties.

He convened the court (25:6). Festus reopens Paul's case by inviting leaders from Jerusalem to travel to Caesarea and present their charges against him. This time there is no mention of a hired rhetorician/lawyer to represent the Jerusalem side. They apparently raise the same charges, accusing Paul of abandoning the Jewish law and defiling the temple.

I have done nothing wrong . . . against Caesar (25:8). In his defense, Paul implies that the Jewish leaders are accusing him of sedition. In a Roman context, this was a serious charge, which could lead to death. It may be an expansion of Tertullus's charge that Paul was a "troublemaker" (see 24:15). The charge may be based on reports that the priests have heard from Diaspora Jews in places such as Thessalonica (17:6–7), where Paul had run-ins with the Roman authorities.

Festus, wishing to do the Jews a favor (25:9). Luke recognizes that politics has now entered into the trial and that any notion of fair and just proceedings is hopeless.

Are you willing to go to Jerusalem and stand trial (25:9). Festus now changes his mind and reveals an openness to change the venue of the trial to Jerusalem. It may seem odd to us that a Roman ruler would ask his prisoner about his willingness to stand trial in a different city, but as a Roman citizen, Paul has the right to insist on a Roman trial.[490] It is unclear what Festus has in mind: Is he proposing that Paul stand trial in the Sanhedrin and he would be present and merely approve the outcome of their deliberations? Or is he planning to hold the trial in the Antonia Fortress in the presence of the Jerusalem leaders?

I appeal to Caesar (25:11). As a Roman citizen, Paul has the right to make an appeal to have his case heard in Rome by the emperor. There were varied forms of this provision giving citizens the right to appeal at any point during the course of legal action or after a verdict had been rendered.[491] Paul's case has been in limbo for two years and now seems to be moving in a disadvantageous direction. To prevent his case from being moved to Jerusalem, Paul asserts his right of appeal (*provocatio*) at this time. Why he had not done so previously can only be explained on the basis that he assumed the charges against him would eventually be dismissed, whereupon he could travel to Rome (according to his plans) as a free man.

Paul has seen enough to convince him that he will not receive a fair trial in Jerusalem. Because of his nephew's previous warning and the antipathy of the Jewish leaders against him, perhaps he is also suspicious of the very thing that they are plotting against him. The apostle is clearly not fearful of suffering for the sake of Christ—even to the point of death. Yet the overriding concerns of the gospel drive him to use the means available to him to forestall an extradition to Jerusalem so he can travel to Rome and present his case to the emperor himself. The appeal will give him an unprecedented opportunity for presenting the gospel at the highest seat of Roman power. Perhaps Paul now sees his right of appeal as the way the Lord has given him for getting to Rome to testify before the authorities (see 23:11).

Paul will be making his appeal to appear before Nero, who has been emperor for five years by A.D. 59. At this point in Nero's principate, he showed a fair amount of stability as he was still under the influence of his tutor, Seneca (the Stoic philosopher) and Sextus Afrianus Burrus. The horrible atrocities

◄

AERIAL VIEW OF CAESAREA

The theater is visible in the top right. The remains of the hippodrome are in the foreground.

against Christians will take place five years hence after the burning of Rome (A.D. 64).

After Festus had conferred with his council (25:12). Festus has the power to deny Paul's request if it is not reasonable or falls within a list of exceptions.[492] Of course, he has the option of dismissing the charges altogether, though the latter course of action is not in the interest of maintaining order among the Jews. To help him make a decision, Festus meets with his own council—a panel of eight to twenty local Roman citizens, military men, and civil servants who function as an advisory group on judicial matters.[493]

Paul Appears Before Agrippa (25:13–27)

After Paul makes his appeal to the emperor, he must wait for the procurator to write an accompanying report about the case. During this time, the client-king from the northern territories (which includes a portion of the area of modern Lebanon) comes to welcome the new procurator. This king is the grandson of Herod the Great, a valued friend of Rome, knowledgeable about the affairs of the Jews, curator of the temple, and someone in charge of appointing high priests in Jerusalem. If anyone could legally lay claim to the title "king of the Jews," it is Agrippa. For Festus, his arrival presents a fortuitous opportunity to gain additional perspective on the case. Since Agrippa possesses no legal jurisdiction in Judea, the hearing should be regarded as merely an informal inquiry into Paul's case.

Bernice (25:13). Bernice was the younger sister—not the wife—of Agrippa.[494] Yet suspicions abounded that there was an inappropriate relationship between the two.[495] At the time of this hearing with Paul, she and her brother would have been thirty-one and thirty-two years of age.

Bernice was previously married to Marcus Julius Alexander (in A.D. 41), who died shortly afterward, and to her uncle, Herod of Chalcis (whose kingdom Agrippa inherited), who died in A.D. 48. She and her two children from Herod lived with Agrippa for the next fifteen years. It was during this time that rumors circulated that she was having an incestuous relationship with her brother. To thwart the evil gossip, she married King Polemon of Cilicia in A.D. 64 (about five years after the hearing with Paul), but this marriage did not last and she returned to her brother. She later fell in love with Titus, the Roman general who destroyed Jerusalem, and became his mistress. She went to Rome in A.D. 75 and lived with him on the Palatine, but popular sentiment forced Titus to terminate this liason.

She was in Jerusalem at the outbreak of the Jewish war and interceded on behalf of the Jews to the Roman procurator, Gessius Florus (A.D. 64–66), with substantial risk to her own life. She and her brother also made repeated efforts to

The Lineage of Herod the Great

dissuade the Jewish revolutionaries, but were not successful.

To pay their respects to Festus (25:13). The couple comes to Caesarea to meet the new procurator of Judea. They have a vested interest in Judea and certainly want to secure the new procurator's goodwill.

Festus discussed Paul's case with the king (25:14). This is the perfect opportunity for Festus to discuss Paul's case with someone far more knowledgeable about Jewish affairs than he is. In the next eight verses, Luke summarizes Festus's presentation of the case to Agrippa. How Luke knows what is said in this private discussion is difficult to discern unless he has access to informants who

were present and heard what was said.[496] It is also possible that Luke is merely inferring what is said based on what is widely known about the case.[497]

Before he has faced his accusers (25:16). It was an established Roman custom acknowledged as law that the plaintiffs had to make their accusations before a judge in the presence of the defendant: "This is the law by which we abide: No

◀

COIN WITH THE IMAGE OF HEROD AGRIPPA II

▶ Marcus Julius Agrippa (Herod Agrippa II)

Marcus Julius Agrippa was the eldest of four children and only son born to Agrippa I, who died in A.D. 44 in Caesarea when an angel of the Lord struck him down (see Acts 12:23).[A-148] The younger Agrippa was in Rome at the time of his father's death. Emperor Claudius wanted to immediately make Agrippa II the successor to his father's throne, but the emperor's counselors convincingly dissuaded him because the boy was only seventeen years of age. The rule of Judea was once again returned to a procuratorship, and Cuspius Fadus (A.D. 44–46) was appointed.

Six years later (A.D. 50), Claudius bestowed on Agrippa the kingdom of Chalcis (part of present-day Lebanon). Over the next few years, Claudius extended Agrippa's domain to include other territories in the north in addition to important portions of Galilee and Perea while Judea remained under Roman governorship. Claudius also gave him the influential and powerful right to appoint the high priests.[A-149]

Coins and inscriptions demonstrate that Agrippa preferred the title "king" and was often referred to as "the great king" (*megas basileus*).[A-150] Agrippa's loyalties were more stongly aligned with Rome than with the Jewish cause. Nevertheless, he attempted to create goodwill with the Jews. He went so far as to have the city of Jerusalem paved with white marble, in part so that the building workers would not be unemployed.[A-151] When the Jewish war broke out, however, Agrippa did all he could to dissuade the Jewish aggressors while he remained solidly on the side of the Romans.

Because of his loyalty to Rome, Vespasian confirmed him in the rulership of his kingdom after the war and even increased the extent of his reign. The historian Josephus corresponded with Agrippa about the history of the Jewish war he was engaged in writing.[A-152] The precise date of his death is unknown, but he probably lived until the 90s. He apparently never married or fathered any children.

one may be condemned in his [the plaintiff's] absence, nor can equity tolerate that anyone be condemned without his case being heard."[498] Similarly, Appian states, "The law requires, members of the council, that a man who is on trial should hear the accusation and speak in his own defense before judgment is passed on him."[499]

About their own religion (25:19). This is not the common Greek word for "religion," but a term (*deisidaimonia*) often translated "superstition" and can mean "a terrible fear of the gods" or "dread of demons." Although it could be used in a positive sense ("reverence for the gods," as in 17:22), Festus is here being derogatory in his comments about Christianity.

A dead man named Jesus who Paul claimed was alive (25:19). Previously, in his hearing before Felix, Luke records Paul as stating that he is on trial because of his belief in the resurrection of the dead (24:21). Now we know that Paul specifically relates his belief in the resurrection to one particular person whom he believes God has already raised—Jesus of Nazareth.

For the Emperor's decision (25:21). The term here used for emperor is *Sebastos*, the Greek equivalent of the Latin *Augustus*. The word itself means "revered" or "worthy of reverence." It is a title that the Roman Senate first conferred on Gaius Octavius (Caesar Augustus) and was subsequently used for his successors.

Agrippa and Bernice came with great pomp (25:23). "Pomp" is the NIV's translation of the Greek word *phantasia*, a word used in Aristotle for the faculty of the imagination.[500] Here it refers to an ostentatious display that sometimes accompanies the arrival and procession of a king.

With the high ranking officers and leading men of the city (25:23). The high ranking officers are literally, *chiliarchos*, the commanders of the cohorts in the city (the same rank as Claudius Lysias in Jerusalem). According to Josephus, five cohorts were stationed at Caesarea.[501] In addition to the military officers, all the leading civic officials were also present. The apostle Paul would have the chance to address an elite gathering. This continues to fulfill the words of Jesus, who predicted regarding his witnesses: "They will lay hands on you and persecute you. They will deliver you to synagogues and prisons, and you will be brought before kings and governors, and all on account of my name" (Luke 22:12).

The whole Jewish community has petitioned me (25:24). This does not refer to every Jew living in Judea, but rather the

REFLECTIONS

THE RESURRECTION OF JESUS IS central and decisive for Paul's preaching and the witness of the early Christians. Paul tells the Corinthians, "If Christ has not been raised, our preaching is useless and so is your faith" (1 Cor. 15:14). When we share the gospel today, it is essential that we not only explain that Jesus died for our sins, but that he also rose from the dead. If Jesus remained in the grave, then we would still be dead in our sins and without hope. But the truth is this: "He is alive!"

legal representatives of the nation, namely, the Sanhedrin and the chief priests.

His Majesty (25:26). Literally, "my Lord [*kyrios*]." The Roman emperors were also referred to by the title "Lord." This was especially true in the eastern Mediterranean region. Egyptian papyri have been discovered where the title *kyrios* is applied to Augustus (P.Oxy. 1143.4), Claudius (P.Oxy. 37.6), and Nero (P.Oxy. 246.30, 34, 37). As one scholar puts it: "The title denoted the status and power that the *Princeps* enjoyed in the Roman world."502

As a result of this investigation I may have something to write (25:26). Festus is still at a loss on how to present Paul's case to the emperor. Convinced that Paul is not guilty of sedition against the emperor, he is hopeful that this informal hearing will clarify the issues so that he can write a competent report. Roman law required such a report from Festus: "After an appeal has been made, records must be provided by the one with whom the appeal has been filed to the person who will adjudicate the appeal."503

Paul's Explains His Conversion to Agrippa (26:1–23)

This is now the third occasion where Luke chooses to include a recounting of Paul's conversion experience (see 9:1–30; 22:3–21). In this instance, he summarizes the essence of what Paul says as he stands before King Agrippa. This is not a formal court defense, but is rather more of an opportunity for the curious Agrippa to find out firsthand what Paul is proclaiming that is stirring up so much trouble. As in Paul's previous presentation, it is important to consider the distinctive

audience and setting, since Paul adapts them to the unique demands of each occasion. Here Paul appeals particularly to Agrippa, who knows better than Festus the traditions and culture of the Jews.

I consider myself fortunate (26:2). Paul begins his address to Agrippa by respectfully expressing his appreciation for the opportunity and by commending Agrippa's grasp of Jewish customs and manners. Paul politely urges him to carefully listen to his entire case.

The Jews all know the way I have lived (26:4). Paul's first line of argument is to demonstrate that he was and remains utterly Jewish in all that he proclaims. He has not broken away from the ancestral faith and embraced something entirely new.

My hope in what God has promised our fathers (26:6). Paul still bases his faith entirely on the Torah, the Writings, and the Prophets (what we now call the Old Testament). The difference is that he has come to believe that the promises throughout the Scriptures have been fulfilled in Jesus the Messiah. On this basis, he then attempts to establish for Agrippa that the central issue is one of interpretation of the Old Testament hope. Has it or has it not been fulfilled in the person of Jesus?

Why should any of you consider it incredible that God raises the dead? (26:8) Paul immediately goes to the key stumbling block for many Jews in accepting what he has to say about Jesus—the issue of his resurrection. There is no Christian faith without the resurrection. Paul previously told the Corinthians, "if Christ has not been raised, our preaching is useless and so is your faith" (1 Cor. 15:14). Paul asks rhetorically why it is so incredible to believe in the resurrection. This is particularly true for Pharisees who, in principle, affirmed a belief in end-time resurrection.

All that was possible to oppose the name of Jesus (26:9). Paul now admits to his own previous unwillingness to recognize Jesus as Messiah and how that resulted in his fervor to persecute Christians. Here he indicates that he had a part in putting many saints to death. We know of Stephen, but history is silent about the names and stories of the others. Paul saw the Jesus movement as "a cancer attacking the vitals of Israel's life; it must be uprooted."[504] This is understandable from the vantage point of the Jew since Christianity called into question the traditional role of the temple, the law, the sacrifices, and the purity regulations.

I cast my vote against them (26:10). When Paul says that he cast his vote against those he was persecuting (26:10), this simply means that he approved of their death,[505] not that he was a member of the Jewish ruling council (the Sanhedrin). He was too young at this point in his life to be a member of the Sanhedrin.

I went from one synagogue to another to have them punished (26:11). Paul gave vent to his zeal by traveling to a number of synagogues throughout Judea and then on the frontiers of Israel to oppose the spread of Christianity. The synagogues each had their own ruling body that could administer punishments to its members (such as the thirty-nine lashes), but in certain cases Paul sought extradition to Jerusalem. Once in Jerusalem, the

accused were imprisoned and some were found guilty of a capital offence and put to death.

Tried to force them to blaspheme (26:11). One of the methods Paul used when he interrogated the believers was to compel them to repudiate Christ. This apparently met with little success since these believers preferred synagogal punishments, imprisonment in Jerusalem, and even death over denying their precious Lord.

On one of these journeys I was going to Damascus (26:12). Paul goes on to tell of his dramatic encounter with the risen Christ on the road to Damascus. It is told in almost precisely the same terms as it was narrated twice previously in the book of Acts.

In Aramaic (26:14). Paul now makes it explicit that the Lord Jesus speaks to him in Aramaic. But this is previously intimated by the Aramaic form of Paul's name (*Saoul*).

It is hard for you to kick against the goads (26:14). A goad is a long stick with a sharpened, pointed end. It was used by the keepers of livestock, particularly oxen, to prod the animal when it was yoked up to a wagon or farm implement. The animal, of course, did not like being jabbed with the stick and would kick at the object. The kicking was obviously useless and the animal soon learned it was better to submit to the farmer's direction rather than to kick against the goad. This expression came to be used figuratively in a variety of literary contexts. It became proverbial in classical Greek writers to express the futility of struggling against one's destiny. Euripides, for instance, has Dionysus say to Pentheus: "I would control my rage and sacrifice to him if I were you, rather than kick against the goad."[506] The writer of Ecclesiastes says that "the words of the wise are like goads" (Eccl. 12:14). Here the message the Lord was conveying to Paul was that it would be useless for him to persist on the wrong path of resisting what God had accomplished in Christ and what he was now accomplishing through the church.

Appoint you as a servant (26:16). Paul now gives us more details of what the Lord said to him on this occasion than either of the other two accounts. Jesus announced that he was appointing Paul as a "servant." This is a rich expression pointing back to Isaiah's prophecy of the coming "Servant of the Lord," who would be a light to the Gentiles (Isa. 42:1–7). Jesus came in direct fulfillment of this prophecy, constantly referring to himself and his ministry in terms of the language and imagery of "the servant" in Isaiah. The Lord was now commissioning Paul *to continue* the ministry of the Lord Jesus in the world as his agent.

I will rescue you (26:17). The Lord promised Paul protection as he fulfilled his ministry. This does not mean that Paul would be free from suffering; on the contrary, the Lord told him he would face suffering. It did mean that the Lord would protect him sufficiently to carry out his divinely intended mission.

Turn them from darkness to light, and from the power of Satan to God (26:18). Jesus promised to work through Paul to reach many Gentiles with the message of the cross. This redemptive message would save them, fulfilling the terms of Isaiah

42:6–7: "[You will be] a light for the Gentiles, to open eyes that are blind, to free captives from prison and to release from the dungeon those who sit in darkness." This would not be just a simple task, but a real spiritual battle. People had been deceived and were held in bondage by the power of sin and the power of a living, intelligent being opposed to God and his kingdom program.

Forgiveness of sins and a place among those who are sanctified by faith in me (26:18). Two great benefits result from this message of redemption. Both forgiveness and sanctification become key themes in Paul's preaching to the Gentiles. Paul later reflected the language of this passage well when he wrote to the Colossians: "For he has rescued us from the dominion of darkness and brought us into the kingdom of the Son he loves, in whom we have redemption, the forgiveness of sins" (Col. 1:13–14).

I was not disobedient (26:19). Having told Agrippa of his encounter with the risen Christ, Paul now defends his course of actions by insisting that he could not possibly disobey instructions given to him directly by God.

I preached that they should repent (26:20). The essence of what he has been proclaiming to the Gentiles is a message of repentance. This includes a sorrow for sin, but also a reorientation of the whole of one's life around the kingdom of God and the work of the Messiah. True repentance can be seen in a changed lifestyle.

I have had God's help to this very day (26:22). In spite of the many dangers he faced and the threats to his life, not least of which was the Jewish mob that apprehended him in the temple and tried to kill him, Paul has continued fulfilling his commission because of the daily help God provides. Throughout his ministry, he draws on the enabling power of God. A few years later he remarked, "I labor, struggling with all his energy, which so powerfully works in me" (Col. 1:29).

I am saying nothing beyond what the prophets and Moses said would happen (26:22). Summing up his defence to Agrippa, Paul insists that the heart of his message is nothing other than what was announced in the Old Testament: The Messiah would suffer, die, and rise from the dead and this message would bring saving light to both Jews and Gentiles.

The Response of Agrippa and Festus (26:24–32)

Paul is not able to finish his presentation before he is interrupted by Festus, who has now concluded that Paul is no threat; he is simply an educated nut. This opens up a period of dialogue between Festus, Agrippa, and Paul. The apostle does his best to seize this opportunity to clearly communicate the gospel to these men, particularly Agrippa, whom he sees as more open. Spiritually, there is no positive response to Paul's message. Legally, the procurator and the king both recognize Paul's innocence of all charges. It is significant that both of these officials find nothing illegal about Christianity.

Your great learning is driving you insane (26:24). Festus interrupts Paul's monologue at the point where he is proclaiming the death and resurrection of Christ. Both aspects of this teaching about the Messiah would have been incomprehensible to Festus. First, before coming to Palestine, Festus would no doubt have been briefed about the Jewish expectation of a messiah figure who would come and lead his people in revolt. Surely he has also heard of the many false messiahs who have already surfaced and led uprisings. These are a significant security risk to Roman rule. But now Festus hears an eloquent discourse on how the Messiah must suffer and die—a notion he has never heard from a Jew. Second, for a Roman, the idea of the resurrection of the body after death was ludicrous. The afterlife was a time when the person would finally be free from the bondage of material existence. It is little wonder that Festus concludes that Paul is raving mad.

True and reasonable (26:25). Paul immediately and courteously denies the accusation and asserts the essential truthfulness of what he is saying. For Paul, it is not merely a matter of perspective or personal belief; rather, the gospel is objectively true. But the gospel is also reasonable (*sōphrosynē*)—the precise opposite of madness (*mania*). This characterization of the gospel message was particularly apt for a Gentile since *sōphrosynē* expressed an ideal of philosophy. It had to do with a knowledge of deity and the relationship of oneself to deity.[507]

The king is familiar with these things (26:26). Agrippa possesses a knowledge of the Law and the Prophets as well as the prevailing Jewish understanding of these texts. He is also aware of the Jesus movement and the kinds of things that have been asserted about Jesus.

Not done in a corner (26:26). This is a proverbial expression in Greek philosophy.[508] Paul is stressing that the central events of what he proclaims—namely, the public ministry, death, and resurrection of Jesus of Nazareth—did not take place in some faraway land or even in a set of private visionary experiences. They happened in Jerusalem itself and involved the principal Jewish and Roman leaders of the nation. As such, these events are open for analysis and verification.

Do you believe the prophets? (26:27). For someone who already believes the message of the prophets, Paul can quickly and convincingly demonstrate the fact that the Messiah must suffer and die, that this death would be an atonement for sin, that there is hope of a bodily resurrection, and that the Messiah would rise from the dead. Paul prepares to explain this to Agrippa, but he is abruptly interrupted by the king.

Do you think that in such a short time you can persuade me to be a Christian? (26:28) Without hearing the tone of Agrippa's remark, it is difficult to know if he poses this question sarcastically or with some degree of sincerity. The king knows the direction Paul is headed and clearly does not want to hear him continue on at this point.

I pray God that not only you but all who are listening to me today may become what I am (26:29). In a straightforward

---

REFLECTIONS

IN SPITE OF PAUL'S ELOQUENT proclamation of the gospel in this august gathering, there was no response. It does not appear that even one of the persons present turned his or her heart to Christ on that day. Like Paul, we will face times when our sharing falls on deaf ears. It is our job to be faithful and to take advantage of the opportunities that God gives us for communicating the gospel.

---

manner, Paul affirms that it truly is his desire that everyone in this hearing—the procurator, the king, the queen, the military commanders, and the civic leaders of Caesarea—will all become Christians.

Except for these chains (26:29). At this point, Paul may have held up his chains as a dramatic gesture to the audience.

This man is not doing anything that deserves death or imprisonment (26:31). After an informal time of discussion, Festus and Agrippa jointly conclude that Paul has committed no capital offense or even anything worthy of imprisonment.

This man could have been set free (26:32). After declaring Paul's innocence of the charges, Agrippa observes that it is too late to dismiss the charges because of Paul's appeal to the emperor. Strictly speaking, it would not have been illegal to free Paul, but Festus would have risked offending the emperor. An expert on Roman law notes, "No sensible man with hopes of promotion would dream of short-circuiting the appeal to Caesar unless he had specific authority to do so."[509]

The Voyage to Rome and Shipwreck (27:1–44)

Throughout this chapter and part of the next, Luke tells the story of Paul's harrowing voyage to Rome. While Paul's boat skirted the south shore of Crete, it is caught suddenly by a violent northeast wind and driven out to sea. After two weeks of an unrelenting storm and when all on board have lost hope, the boat is shipwrecked on the island of Malta.

Luke relates the account in significant detail and in an engaging way that keeps the reader in constant suspense. Because of the divine promise that Paul will appear before Caesar, the question in the minds of the readers is not *if* Paul will make it to Rome, but *how* he will do so given the overwhelming odds against him. How will the divine plan be fulfilled when it seems that everything is working against it?[510]

Paul and some other prisoners (27:1). No indication is given as to how many prisoners there are or the nature of the crimes for which they are incarcerated. Paul is included with them as just another prisoner.

The Imperial Regiment (27:1). The literal reading here is "the *Sebastos* [or *Augustus*] cohort." Archaeologists have discovered two inscriptions, one in Latin and one in Greek, that refer to a cohort of this title in the Roman army stationed at Syria (including Judea) in the first century.[511] Nothing more is known about Julius than what is in this text.

We boarded a ship from Adramyttium (27:2). There were no cruise ships or passenger vessels in the first century. It was common for people to travel on cargo vessels. This particular ship comes from a city on the west coast of Asia Minor, about thirty-five miles north of Pergamum and thirty-seven miles due east of Assos (see the map on Acts 20). This is a small privately owned cargo vessel presumably on its way back to its home port. The centurion's intent is to book passage on a vessel that will take them to one of the major ports of south Asia Minor, where they can board a larger grain vessel heading to Rome.

Aristarchus, a Macedonian from Thessalonica (27:2). On Aristarchus, see comments on 20:4. He was among the delegates accompanying Paul with the collection for the Jerusalem believers. Apparently he is the only one of the group who remains with Paul in Caesarea for the two years of his imprisonment and will continue to minister to Paul through his own Roman imprisonment. The text does not say that Aristarchus is also a prisoner at this time, but for some unknown reason (but probably related to his commitment to the gospel) he will be imprisoned in Rome (Col. 4:10).

We landed at Sidon (27:3). Sidon was one of the principal cities of Phoenicia, but now part of the province of Syria under Roman rule. It was located about seventy miles north of Caesarea.

SIDON

In kindness to Paul (27:3). Literally, Julius shows *philanthrōpia* to Paul. This is the word from which is derived the English "philanthropy," but here simply means "benevolence" or "kindness." This was an esteemed virtue in the Hellenistic world; the word refers frequently in moral exhortation to "civilized" behavior.[512]

Allowed him to go to his friends (27:3). These "friends" are Christians in the city. Some from the first wave of Jewish-Christian missionaries scattered by the persecution in Jerusalem came to Phoenicia and planted churches (11:19). Paul may have already met many of these believers as he passed through the city on one of his trips to Jerusalem (11:30; 12:25; 15:3).[513]

Passed to the lee of Cyprus (27:4). This refers to the side of Cyprus where ships were most protected from the autumnal prevailing winds. Because Luke mentions passing by the coast of Cilicia and Pamphylia, the boat probably traveled north of Cyprus. This was the opposite side of Cyprus Paul passed when he traveled from Miletus to Jerusalem (21:3).

We landed at Myra in Lycia (27:5). Myra was one of the key cities of the territory of Lycia in southern Asia Minor. It was about forty miles east of the other Lycian city, Patara, where Paul had docked in his voyage from Miletus to Jerusalem with the collection (21:1). The city of Myra was actually three and a half miles inland on a plateau.[514] It was served by a port called Andriace, where the boat would have docked. Myra has yet to be excavated, but many Roman ruins are still visible, including the eleven thousand-seat theater and an immense granary built during the reign of Hadrian (A.D. 117–38). Myra was due north of Alexandria, Egypt, and a key stopping point for the grain vessels that traveled on to Rome.

Depending on the precise route the Adramyttium vessel took, the boat covered a distance of 450 to 500 miles from Sidon to Myra. According to a tradition preserved in the western form of the text, the voyage took a total of fifteen days.

bottom left

MYRA IN LYCIA

The theater.

PORT CITY OF ANDRIACE

▼

▶ **"Santa Claus": Saint Nicholas of Myra**

Myra is perhaps best known for a Christian leader who lived there in the late third and early fourth century: St. Nicholas. In the Netherlands, this saint was venerated as "Sante Klaas" and in America became known as "Santa Claus."[A-153] He was probably martyred during the Diocletian persecutions.

Little accurate historical information is known about his life and ministry in Myra, but numerous legends surfaced and he became popular throught the Middle Ages. The principal legend known in America is based on a story involving his concern over the fate of three daughters of a poor man in his city. Lacking enough money for dowries, the father allegedly planned to sell the girls into slavery to a brothel. Learning of the father's decision, Nicholas secretly tried to enter their house late one night to leave three bags of gold. Finding the doors and windows locked, he dropped the three bags down the chimney. They miraculously fell into the stockings that the girls had hung up to dry.

An Alexandrian ship sailing for Italy (27:6). The centurion is able to locate an Alexandrian grain vessel heading for Rome without any difficulty. With a population of over a million people, Rome was greatly dependent on the regular shipment of grain from Egypt.

Arriving off Cnidus (27:7). The port of Cnidus lay at the tip of a long peninsula at the southwestern portion of Asia Minor (in the territory of Caria) that extended between the islands of Cos and Rhodes. This was about a 150-mile trip from Myra. In his voyage to Jerusalem from Miletus, Paul's boat would have passed within visual distance of this city (see 21:1). The ancient geographer Strabo provides a helpful description of this port city:

> Then to Cnidus, with two harbours, one of which can be closed, can receive triremes, and is a naval station for twenty ships. Off it lies an island which is appoximately seven stadia in circuit, rises high, is theatre-like, is connected by moles with the mainland, and in a way makes Cnidus a double city, for a large part of its people live on the island, which shelters both harbors.[515]

When the wind did not allow us to hold our course (27:7). A westward voyage on a sailboat in the Mediterranean took considerably longer than the same trip eastward because of adverse winds through the entire trip. An eastward voyage that might take ten days could take between fifty and seventy days when traveling

MODEL OF AN EGYPTIAN MERCHANT VESSEL
▼

westward. The difficulty and length was compounded all the more when traveling in the winter.[516]

We sailed to the lee of Crete, opposite Salmone (27:7). The boat journeys southwest toward the island of Crete, where the crew attempts to round the eastern cape. Salmone is a promontory on the easternmost side of the island (today it is called Cape Sideros). Because of the strong northwest winds, the crew of the boat seeks protection by sailing along the southern side of the island. Interestingly, the name "Salmone" is of Phoenician origin and describes a refuge from exposure to the wind.[517]

Fair Havens, near the town of Lasea (27:8). This small port was roughly halfway around the island east of Cape Littinos. The ancient village of Lasea has also been identified. It lay about five miles east of Fair Havens.

Sailing had already become dangerous (27:9). According to ancient sources, sea travel was particularly risky in the fall from September 14 to November 11 and considered extremely dangerous from November 11 to March 10.[518] Visibility (mists and fogs) as well as the constant threat of severe winter storms rendered this period an inadvisable time to travel by sea.

It is not suprising, however, to find a grain vessel traveling during this dangerous period. Suetonius notes that because of regular shortages of grain in Rome, the emperor Claudius "took all possible steps to import grain, even during the winter months—insuring merchants against the loss of their ships in stormy weather (which guaranteed them a good return on their ventures)."[519]

PAUL'S VOYAGE FROM CAESAREA TO CRETE

▼

▶**Crete**

This island is the fifth largest in the Mediterranean (after Cyprus, Sicily, Sardinia, and Corsica).[A-154] It measures 162 miles from east to west and ranges between nine and thirty-seven miles north to south. At the center of the island, Mount Ida reaches an elevation of 8,058 feet. The principal cities of the island were Cnossus, Gortyn, and Lyttus. During the first century, Crete was part of a Roman province with Cyrene (north Africa). There is literary and archaeological evidence of a Jewish presence on the island. The island was evangelized at some point early in the first century. After his Roman imprisonment, Paul returned to the island and left Titus there to give leadership and assistance to the churches.

By now it was after the Fast (27:9). This is another way of referring to the Jewish Day of Atonement (*Yom Kippur*). A number of passages in Jewish literature connect the day with fasting. The Mishnah, for example, stipulates, "On the Day of Atonement, eating, drinking . . . are forbidden."[520] The date of this festival was on Tishri 10 on the Jewish lunar calendar. In A.D. 59, the observance would have fallen on October 5.[521] The Jewish Feast of Tabernacles (Booths or *Succoth*) fell shortly after this on Tishri 15. Since Luke does not mention the Festival of Tabernacles, it is likely then that the boat arrives in Fair Havens sometime in the five-day period of October 10–15, A.D. 59.[522]

Men, I can see that our voyage is going to be disastrous (27:10). Paul asserts this warning not as a prophetic insight from the Spirit, but as a common-sense observation based on his personal experience at sea (2 Cor. 11:25–26) and his knowledge that sea travel is typically avoided from this time on because of the inherent dangers. Because of the Lord's providential care, there will be no loss of life, as Paul assumes.

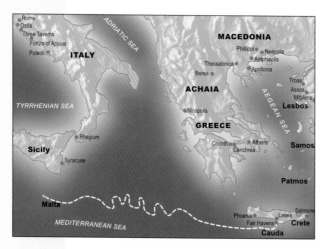

The pilot and . . . the owner of the ship (27:11). The *kybernētēs* is the "steersman"—essentially, the captain of the ship. The *nauklēros* may be the owner of the ship but may also be a representative of the owner and thus concerned about the financial interest of the voyage.[523] The grain vessels are privately owned and the shipowners are free agents. They take advantage of "a healthy private enterprise system conferring great rewards on speculators and adventurous transporters."[524] Both of these men disagree with Paul and decide to press further on.

Hoping to reach Phoenix and winter there (27:12). The owner and the captain of the ship apparently consult others about whether to seek a better port in Cyprus to spend the winter. The group decision is not to take the risk to travel on to Rome, but simply to coast westward along the southern shore of Crete another fifty miles or so to a better harbor. The precise location of this harbor in Crete remains uncertain. Most scholars think it was near the modern coastal village of Loutro.

A wind of hurricane force, called the "northeaster" (27:14). The conditions are fine for reaching Phoenix as long as the northeast), *euroaquilo* (northeast wind), *vulturnus, eurus* (east wind), etc.[526]

Today this wind is called a "Gregale" and can approach hurricane force and endanger shipping. In 1555 it is reported to have caused waves that drowned six hundred persons in the city of Valletta, the principal port city of the island of Malta.[527]

A small island called Cauda (27:16). Caught by the violent wind, the ship is driven south. This island of Cauda is located about twenty-three miles south of Phoenix. Today it is called Gaudos and is the most southerly Greek island. The ancient island did possess a city and a harbor, but there is little chance of this vessel making it.

Make the lifeboat secure (27:16). The lifeboat was normally towed behind the ship. Since towing a boat is dangerous in a storm, the sailors pull the rope and bring the little boat on board. The difficulty in doing so is probably caused by the dinghy taking on water.[528]

They passed ropes under the ship itself to hold it together (27:17). There are a

gentle wind blows from the south, but this abruptly changes. A violent wind from the northeast blows across the island, down from Mount Ida, and howls from the shore south out to the sea. Luke describes this wind as *typhōnikos*, a Greek word from which is derived our English "typhoon." Ancient sailors named this dangerous wind *Euraquilo*, a name with which Luke shows his familiarity. *Euraquilo* is actually a bilingual compound formed from a shortened form of the Greek *euronotos* (east wind) and the Latin *Aquila* (north wind).

Although at one time critical scholars claimed that this hybrid word is found nowhere else and took it as a sign of Luke's literary creativity, the term has been discovered on a Latin inscription found in the city of Thugga in proconsular Africa.[525] It appears on a wind-rose inscribed on a pavement that bears the names of the wind in each direction. Beginning with the north and moving clockwise it reads: *septentrio* (north wind), *aquilo* (north wind; apparently slightly

◀ *left*

STONE ANCHOR

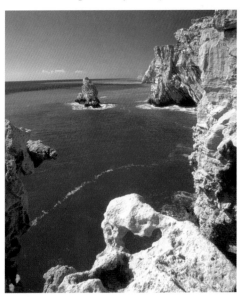

◀

ISLAND OF CAUDA

Modern Gavdos.

variety of views as to what this bracing procedure involves, but the most likely explanation is a practice called "frapping." Heavy ropes or cables were passed under the bow of the ship and secured transversely on either side. The object of this procedure was to keep the planks of the ship tight against the "ribs" (the inner wooden beams that formed the skeleton of the boat). This gave the ship extra protection in the fury of the storm.[529]

The sandbars of Syrtis (27:17). These are "the notoriously dangerous shoals and shallows of the Libyan continental shelf of North Africa from Cyrenaica through Tripolitania to Tunisia: the Greater Syrtis to the southeast and the Lesser off Gabés to the southwest."[530] The Syrtes are 375 miles away from the island of Cauda. Sailors' fears of Syrtis are well summed up by Dio Chrysostom: "Those who have once sailed into it find egress impossible; for shoals, cross-currents, and long sandbars extending a great distance out make the sea utterly impassable or troublesome."[531] Luke's mention of their fear of these treacherous shoals at this point demonstrates that the crew knows it is in for a long, harrowing voyage.

Lowered the sea anchor (27:17). Luke literally says that they lower the "vessel" (*skeuos*). The NIV interprets this to be an anchor, but it probably refers to the sails (the same word was used for the sheet lowered from heaven in 10:11).[532] All the sails are taken down and only a storm-sail is kept up, which is necessary to keep the boat steady.[533]

Finally gave up all hope of being saved (27:20). With the storm showing no sign of diminishing, the sailors and passengers begin fearing the worst possible outcome. They think they may have missed Sicily and will never make it to the North African (Tunisian) coast alive.

The men had gone a long time without food (27:21). In such a storm, anxiety and seasickness would surely eliminate any appetite.

An angel of the God whose I am and whom I serve stood beside me (27:23). After days of being tossed around at sea and at the point when all on board are at the point of despair, God intervenes not to stop the storm, but to communicate a message of encouragement and hope to

Paul through a divine emissary. The angel specifically tells Paul that the ship will be destroyed, but not one person will die. In communicating the content of this appearance to the passengers, Paul tailors his remarks to be understood by a group of people not familiar with Christianity or Judaism. Greeks and Romans believed in divine intermediaries, however, and would probably not have been skeptical about what Paul was saying. Paul makes it clear that it is not a messenger of Zeus (or any other deity from the pantheon of Gentile gods), but the God he serves.

You must stand trial before Caesar (27:24). This is a new revelation to Paul. When Jesus spoke to him previously in Jerusalem, he simply assured him that he would survive to testify about him in Rome (23:11).

On the fourteenth night (27:27). In a detailed and careful study done over a hundred years ago about this voyage on the basis of interviews with experienced Mediterranean sailors, J. Smith calculated that in a gale such as this, the boat would have averaged about one-and-a-half miles per hour. Given the distance of 476 miles from Cauda to Malta on the course the storm-driven boat would likely have taken, Paul's boat would have been within a few miles of the island on the fourteenth night.[534]

The Adriatic Sea (27:27). Literally, "the sea of Adria." Today the Adriatic Sea refers specifically to the long narrow body of water that extends between Italy and the Balkan Peninsula. In the Roman period that was distinguished as the Gulf of Adria whereas the Sea of Adria extended much further south and from Crete to Sicily.[535]

They took soundings (27:28). It must be remembered that there were no sonar or acoustical instruments available to ancient sailors. The "sounding" referred to here was a depth measurement taken by a hand line. A series of lead weights were attached to the end of the line separated by measured intervals. Archaeologists have discovered some of these weights. The bottom of the weight was hollowed out so that it could be filled with tallow or grease. When lowered and drug on the floor of the sea, the grease would pick up rocks and debris.[536] The use of this kind of line is well illustrated by a passage from Herodotus:

> The nature of the land of Egypt is such that when a ship is approaching it and is yet one day's sail from the shore, if a man try the sounding, he will bring up mud even at a depth of eleven fathoms. This shows that the outpouring of land goes that far.[537]

REFLECTIONS

THERE WAS ANOTHER OCCASION when followers of Jesus were on a boat that was threatened by a tempestuous storm. Just as the boat was ready to be swamped by the waves, Jesus "rebuked the wind and the raging waters; the storm subsided, and all was calm" (Luke 8:24). Jesus could easily have calmed this storm, yet he allowed the storm to rage. In the midst of the storm, however, God gave a sign of his awareness of their plight and a special promise of his protection. In a similar way, God allows us to weather many storms throughout our lifetimes, but he is present with us and extends his protection to us until it is our appointed time to die.

They dropped four anchors from the stern (27:29). The four anchors would have slowed the speed of the ship enough to keep it from careening perilously onto the rocks of the shore. Normally a ship was anchored from the bow. Anchoring it from the stern (the rear) would enable it to continue its forward progress until it reached shore.[538]

An attempt to escape from the ship (27:30). Knowing the extreme danger of being on board a vessel speeding toward the rock shore in ferocious winds and high, choppy surf, the crew decides to abandon ship and take their chances on board the dinghy. The apostle Paul, however, foils their plans by informing the Roman military personnel. The action of the soldiers in cutting the lines holding the dinghy would certainly have occasioned a great deal of tension and bitter emotions of the crew toward the soldiers and Paul.

Just before dawn Paul urged them all to eat (27:33). Paul's appeal would surely help to restore some measure of calm to the passengers, who are waiting impatiently for dawn and the impending prospect of making it to shore.

Not one of you will lose a single hair from his head (27:34). Paul reiterates here the assurance given to him by the angel of God (27:22) by means of a Jewish/Old Testament idiom. The expression is illustrated in the remarks made by Saul to his men regarding Jonathan: "As surely as the LORD lives, not a hair of his head will fall to the ground."[539] This is a way of stressing the certainty that no person would die.

Gave thanks to God in front of them all (27:35). Paul boldly prays and gives thanks to the one true God in the presence of worshipers of numerous other deities. It was typical Jewish custom to give thanks to God before a meal. In spite of some of the language of this passage ("took some bread . . . broke it"), this is not a celebration of the Eucharist or the

---

▶ The *Isis:* An Immense Alexandrian Grain Vessel

Underwater archaeologists have not yet recovered an Alexandrian grain vessel, but there is an important literary account by Lucian that describes one of these ships, the *Isis:*

> What a huge ship! 180 feet long, the ship-wright said, and well over a quarter as wide [over 45 feet wide], and from deck to bottom, where it is deepest, in the bilge, 44 feet. Then, what a tall mast, what a yard to carry! What a forestay to hold it up! How gently the poop curves up, with a little golden goose below! And correspondingly at the opposite end, the prow juts right out in front, with figures of the goddess, Isis, after whom the ship is named, on either side. And the other decorations, the paintings and the topsail blazing like

fire, anchors in front of them, and capstans, and windlasses, and the cabins on the poop—all very wonderful to me. You could put the number of sailors at an army of soldiers. She was said to carry corn enough to feed Attica for a year.[A-155]

Other ancient writers attest to ships of immense size. A grain ship called the *Syracusia* (3d c. B.C.) may have had a capacity of nearly two thousand tons according to Athenaeus. The first-writer Pliny speaks about a boat constructed during the reign of Caligula that carried a monument weighing approximately thirteen hundred tons.[A-156] A Roman vessel was recently discovered at Caesarea Maritima that has been tentatively dated to the first century A.D. and measures 147 feet in length.[A-157]

Lord's Supper. Paul is encouraging everyone on board (273 non-Christians) to eat for nourishment and strength; this is not a time of Christian community reflecting on the death of Christ.

276 of us on board (27:37). This is by no means an unrealistic number of people to be aboard an Alexandrian grain vessel. Josephus claims that there were six hundred people aboard a ship he was on that was shipwrecked in the Sea of Adria.[540]

Throwing the grain into the sea (27:38). The explicit mention of grain as the cargo here confirms the impression that this was indeed an Alexandrian grain vessel. Their intent would have been that by lightening the ship, the vessel would travel farther up the beach before it grounded. This would enhance their chances of making it safely to shore. The grain would have been stored in the hull in sacks, not poured in loosely.[541]

They saw a bay with a sandy beach (27:39). A sandy beach, as opposed to a rocky set of cliffs, is the perfect place to land the boat. The crew now does everything they can to reach the beach.

Untied the ropes that held the rudders (27:40). Two large paddles were attached on each side of the stern in ancient ships. When it was necessary to anchor the boat from the stern, these paddles were lifted out of the water and secured by ropes.[542]

Struck a sandbar (27:41). "Sandbar" is an interpretation of the Greek word *dithalassos*, which literally means, "between two seas" or "where two seas meet." That this is a sandy shoal is probably the correct interpretation. Some have suggested

that this wording points to a precise identification of the location on Malta where the ship went aground, namely, in a place that is today known as "St. Paul's Bay." This bay is located on the northwestern portion of the island. A small island called Salmonetta is only a hundred yards off the mainland. The channel separating the mainland from the island may have been the place "between two seas."[543] Because of the proximity of Salmonetta to the mainland, it is conceivable that the sailors think the island is simply a promontory from the mainland. By the time they realize there is a narrow and shallow waterway separating the two, it is too late to change directions.

Archaeologists undertaking surveys of the waters around Malta have discovered eight shipwrecks of Roman era boats.[544] In recent years, a British expedition has been searching for Paul's ship.[545]

The soldiers planned to kill the prisoners (27:42). According to the Code of Justinian, a Roman guard who allowed a prisoner to escape could face the same penalty awaiting the accused prisoner.[546] Most of the soldiers do not want to take any risk with the prisoners they are responsible for. Some of these prisoners may have been accused of capital offenses. In the panic of the moment, little thought apparently seems to be given to the potential punishment a soldier might face for killing a Roman citizen.

Paul Spends the Winter in Malta (28:1–10)

The suspense continues in this next section. No sooner has Paul made it safely to shore than he is bitten by a poisonous snake and expected to die. God continues to protect Paul, however, and not only does he survive a venomous snakebite, but he is able to engage in a significant and dramatic ministry on this island during the winter months.

Malta (28:1). Malta, or *Melitē* as it is called in Greek, is a Mediterranean island lying fifty-eight miles south of the island of Sicily and 180 miles north of Libya. It measures about seventeen miles at its longest distance from southeast to northwest and about nine miles at its widest distance from east to west. The island became part of the Roman empire in 218 B.C. and was part of the Roman province of Sicily.

The islanders (28:2). The word translated "islanders" is the Greek word *barbaros*, which is often translated "barbarian." This was the word Greek-speakers used to refer to people who did not know Greek as their native tongue. The term implies that the foreign language sounded like a meaningless set of syllables—such as "bar- bar- bar-"; thus the word was onomatopoetic. The ancestors of the islanders were Phoenician, and they continued to speak a Phoenician dialect. A number of Punic inscriptions have been found on Malta (Punic was a Phoenician dialect spoken in Carthage, North Africa).[547] Luke's characterization of the islanders as *barbaroi* may reflect some of the voyagers' initial frustration in not being able to communicate with the people. Because of the island's contact with Rome, some would have known Greek or Latin and were able to converse with those coming off the boat.

They built a fire (28:2). It is difficult to imagine what could feel better to 276 cold and wet people on this late October day than a blazing hot fire.

A viper (28:3). The Greek word *echidna* points to a poisonous snake and typically refers to a viper.[548] Jesus uses the word metaphorically to speak of the danger posed by the Pharisees: "You snakes! You brood of vipers! How will you escape being condemned to hell?" (Matt. 23:33). Although there are no poisonous snakes on the island of Malta today, the population may have progressively rid the small island of this danger over the next two thousand years.

Justice has not allowed him to live (28:4). The islanders are referring to the goddess *Dikē* ("Justice"). *Dikē*, the daughter of Zeus, was believed to watch over human affairs and report all wrongdoings to Zeus so the guilty persons could pay for their crimes. In the first century, she was viewed as a goddess of punishment and revenge who would execute judgment from her place in the underworld. In this instance, the islanders interpret the snakebite to reflect the judgment of *Dikē* on Paul for a crime that has gone undetected or unpunished by human authorities.[549]

They changed their minds and said he was a god (28:6). The islanders have seen this type of snake bite people before and know what to expect. When Paul is unaffected by the bite, they assume he must be a god. Luke's abbreviated account changes topics here, but we can assume that Paul once again takes advantage of the situation to deny that he is a god and to proclaim to them the living and true God (cf. what he did in Lystra, recorded in 14:8–20).

Publius, the chief official of the island (28:7). Although nothing else is known of Publius, archaeologists have discovered a Greek inscription on Miletus dating to the first century that refers to the chief official of the island with precisely the same expression that Luke uses here: "*prōtos* of the island."[550]

He welcomed us to his home (28:7). It is difficult to imagine that his home is large enough to accommodate 276 people. Perhaps Luke means that he, Aristarchus, Paul, and Julius are invited to stay at this exquisite estate. This kind of preferential treatment is not surprising since the people of the island have just acclaimed Paul as a god.

After prayer, placed his hands on him and healed him (28:8). Jesus often laid his hands on people when he healed them, and the people sometimes expected him to put his hands on them as part of the process.[551] This is the way Paul's eyes were healed when Ananias ministered to him after he lost his sight on the Damascus road (9:12, 17).

The rest of the sick on the island came and were cured (28:9). God uses Paul in a mighty way on this island to bring healing to numerous people. Assuredly, Paul also shares the gospel with them and at least some people are saved, although Luke does not tell us this part of the story in his highly condensed account.

They honored us in many ways (28:10). The "honor" that Luke speaks of here is probably best understood in the sense of financial support and many gifts, which Luke elaborates in the remainder of the verse. "The grateful inhabitants of the island saw to it that the Christian travelers should not be in need during the rest of their journey."[552]

Paul Arrives in Rome (28:11–31)

Paul arrives safely in Rome after a tranquil voyage from Malta. After fellowshiping with believers in the port city of Puteoli, Paul is met by Christians from Rome on his way to the capital city. Luke does not focus on Paul's ministry to the believers in Rome for the concluding chapter of Acts, but rather describes the apostle's efforts to evangelize the unbelieving Jewish community in Rome.

The book of Acts ends somewhat anticlimactically with no verdict from the Roman court and emperor. Yet, for Luke, the important part of his story has been told. Paul has reached Rome and is there proclaiming the kingdom of God. The full story still remains untold. The church continues to proclaim the gospel as it awaits the return of Christ.

After three months (28:11). All 276 remain on the island for the winter months, probably November and December of A.D. 59 and January of A.D. 60.

An Alexandrian ship (28:11). They are able to book passage on another Alexandrian grain vessel that made it safely into port before the severe *Euraquilo* storm hit. This vessel, its crew, and passengers have also spent the winter on the island with the boat safely docked at the principal port of the island, known as Valletta today. Although it is still early and risky to sail, the captain of the Alexandrian vessel thinks the conditions are favorable for making it the relatively short distance to Sicily and then to Italy.

With the figurehead of the twin gods Castor and Pollux (28:11). This Alexandrian freighter sails under the ensign of the *Dioskouroi*, the twin sons of Zeus and brothers of Helen.[553] They are known by name as Castor and Polydeuces (Latinized

as Pollux). The vessel has been dedicated to the appropriate deities, given the fact that the twins were revered as gods who rescue sailors in their distress. They were also worshiped as the third sign of the Zodiac—Gemini.[554]

Syracuse (28:12). The first port the boat reaches is on the southeast coast of the island of Sicily, about ninety miles north of Malta.[555] Syracuse was the center of government for the Roman province (that included the island of Malta). The city was served by two ports, a large one on the mainland and another smaller one on a diminutive island (Ortygia) closely adjacent to the mainland. Still visible today are the remains of a sixth-century B.C. temple of Apollo (also dedicated to Artemis), a fifth-century Greek theater with a semicircular auditorium hewn from the rock, and a large Roman amphitheater.

Arrived at Rhegium (28:13). After the three-day stop in Syracuse, the boat sails another seventy miles to the southwest coast (at the "toe") of Italy and the port at the city of Rhegium. Rhegium was a strategic Roman city that governed the Strait of Messina, a seven-mile-wide waterway separating Sicily and Italy.

▶ Puteoli

Throughout the first half of the first century A.D., Puteoli was Rome's principal shipping port. The bulk of the enormous shipments of grain from Alexandria and north Africa were unloaded at Puteoli.[A-158] This was a likely destination, then, for the Alexandrian grain vessel, although the emperor Claudius had improved the port of Ostia at the mouth of the Tiber for handling more cargo vessels and had created an additional port (Portus) two miles north of Ostia.

Puteoli, known also by its Greek name *Dikearchia,* was located in the Roman district of Campania on the north shore of what is today called the Gulf of Naples. The same gulf was also served by another port city, Neapolis (modern Naples), about seven and a half miles south of Puteoli. Campania had yet another port, Cumae, which was located about ten miles northwest of Neapolis. Of the three ports, Puteoli was by far the largest and of greatest significance for trade in the first century.

Puteoli's harbor was greatly enhanced in the first century with the construction of a breakwater.[A-159] This mole was nearly a quarter mile in length. It carried fifteen masonry piers with arches (with at least one triumphal arch), columns with statues, and a lighthouse. The total amount of shoreline for docking and warehouses (the *emporium*) extended about one and a quarter miles.

The city itself was large. Some have estimated a population of as much as a hundred thousand people in the first century. The beautiful location made it a popular place with the Roman élite who owned villas there. It was also home to many immigrants from the Eastern provinces of the empire, including Asia Minor, Syria, and Egypt. There is evidence of a sizeable Jewish population in the city.[A-160]

There were two navigational hazards fifteen miles to the north of Rhegium and identified with two sisters in Greek mythology—Scylla and Charybdis. Scylla was a large rocky cliff on the Italian side of the strait and Charybdis was a treacherous whirlpool in a narrow channel of the sea on the Sicilian side.[556]

We reached Puteoli (28:13). With the aid of a southerly wind, the large grain vessel makes the 180-mile trip to Puteoli in just two days.

There we found some brothers (28:14). Paul, Luke, and Aristarchus discover a community of believers in this city. This is not surprising given the volume of travel from the East into Puteoli. The church most likely started from within the Jewish community. These Jews may have been reached by Christian Jews from Rome or just as easily by believers arriving from Ephesus, Alexandria, or elsewhere.

Invited us to spend a week with them (28:14). Since they are making the rest of the journey to Rome on foot, they do not need to stay in the city to wait for the unloading of the boat or to book passage on a different vessel. The Christians in the city graciously open up their homes and extend warm hospitality to the trio as well as to Paul's guard, Julius. The offer of free lodging and meals by these kind people probably incline Julius to accept their hospitality. One certainly wonders what is in Julius' mind after being with the apostle for nearly four months—seeing the miracles, hearing him in prayer and worship, listening to the apostle's discussions with Luke and Aristarchus, and now experiencing Christian hospitality.

And so we came to Rome (28:14). Against all odds—a harrowing voyage lost at sea, shipwreck, and snakebite—Paul arrives at Rome. At this point, he is still on the outskirts, but now it is simply a five- or six-day 130-mile trip up the Via Appia to Rome.

The brothers there (28:15). Believers in the city of Rome—both Jews and Gentiles—have heard about Paul's arrival at the port of Puteoli. Perhaps someone from the church at Puteoli has made a quick journey to Rome to inform the fellow Christians there. Paul had written to the believers in Rome several years earlier with his long letter, informing them of his desire to come to the city. The extensive greetings in Romans 16 demonstrate that Paul already knows many Christians in the city.

▶ **The City of Rome**
IMPORTANT FACTS:

- Population: about 1,000,000
- Multi-Ethnic Cosmopolitan City: Italians from various districts as well as peoples from Greece, Asia Minor, Syria, Judea, Persia, Egypt, North Africa, Spain, Gaul, Germany, Brittania, and elsewhere
- Religion: the entire pantheon of Roman gods, numerous Greek deities, some Asian, Persian and Egyptian deities, the goddess *Roma*, and the ruler cult
- Ports: Ostia, Portus, Puteoli
- Position: Seat of the Roman Government for the empire and Residence of the Emperor

---

▶ **Rome**

Rome was the political, economic, and military center of the enormous Roman empire.[A-161] It was the wealthiest and most powerful city in the world in the first century.

The city was fifteen miles inland from the Tyrrhenian Sea and situated along the banks of the Tiber river. It was divided into fourteen different regions, the most well known being the Circus Maximus and the Forum Romanum. The perimeter of the city measured just over thirteen miles.

The forum was the hub of the political, religious, and economic life of Rome. Here the Senate building was located as well as the Mamertime prison, where prisoners were kept prior to their executions. The Colosseum had not yet been built (it was completed in A.D. 80). Throughout the city were numerous temples dedicated to many deities and to the deified Caesars. The palaces of the Caesars were located in the Circus Maximus and crowned the Palatine Hill.

Only a small percentage of people in Rome enjoyed its great wealth. Many slaves and poor people lived in Rome, dwelling in large blocks of apartment buildings (*insulae*) that ranged from three to five stories in size. Some scholars have estimated that as many as two hundred thousand people relied on a government welfare system that provided free grain to the unemployed masses of the city.

Four years after Paul's arrival in the city, ten of the fourteen districts of Rome burned to the ground (A.D. 64). Nero found the Christians in the city an easy target for blame and began a horrible persecution of these believers, which Tacitus recounts.[A-162]

clockwise from top

ROME

Interior view of the Colosseum.

The Arch of Constantine, which he built to commemorate his military victory in A.D. 312.

The Church of St. Peter in Montorio, west of the Tiber, commemorating the area where he was said to have been crucified upside-down.

Outside view of the Colosseum.

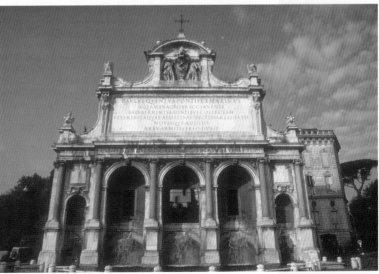

It is reasonable to assume that the nucleus of this church had its start shortly after Pentecost when some Jewish pilgrims filled with the Spirit and embracing Jesus as Messiah returned from Jerusalem and shared their new beliefs and experience in the synagogues (cf. 2:10). If not at this earliest stage, then either Jewish Christians from Palestine or the Diaspora went to Rome and shared the gospel or Jewish pilgrims from Rome encountered the gospel on subsequent visits to Jerusalem.[557] Since the early 30s, the church had presumably grown in numbers, especially with more and more Gentiles coming to faith in Christ. The church faced a major upheaval in A.D. 49 when Claudius ordered all Jews to leave the city (a proscription that would have included all Christian Jews as well; cf. comments on 18:2). According to Suetonius, there had been much consternation and debate in the synagogues about Christ leading up to this edict from the emperor.[558] When

Nero became emperor five years later (A.D. 54), it is safe to assume that many Jews (again, including Christian Jews) began trickling back into the city.

The Forum of Appius (28:15). The delegation of Christians from Rome come to meet Paul and his companions at a small market town in Latium about forty miles south of the city on the Appian Way. The forum was located at the juncture of where a canal came close to the main highway. Taking a boat pulled by a mule while the passengers slept made a nighttime journey possible (Strabo, *Geography* 5.3.6). The famous Roman writer Horace complains about the boatmen and "stingy tavern-keepers" at the Forum of Appius, as well as the poor drinking water (which made him ill), the gnats, and the frogs.[559]

The Three Taverns (28:15). Another group of Christians came as far as *Tres Tabernai* to meet Paul—a distance of

ROME

thirty miles south of Rome on the Appian Way. "Tavern" (*tabernus* in Latin) does not have the same connotation in English as it did in Latin. The *tabernai* were probably "a group of inns where travelers could rest, eat, and spend the night."[560]

Paul thanked God and was encouraged (28:15). Three years earlier Paul wrote, "I have been longing for many years to see you. . . . Pray that I may be rescued from the unbelievers in Judea and that my service in Jerusalem may be acceptable to the saints there, so that by God's

will I may come to you with joy and together with you be refreshed" (Rom. 15:23, 31–32). Although his circumstances in coming to Rome are significantly different than what he had anticipated, he has finally arrived and is grateful to God for the opportunity to be with these dear believers. Their prayers have been answered.

Paul was allowed to live by himself (28:16). When Paul enters Rome, the centurion Julius would have taken him to a prisoner reception facility most likely

---

▶ Jews in Rome in the First Century

Life was not easy for Jews in Rome in the first century. There was a great deal of anti-Jewish sentiment, which reached boiling points when the emperor Tiberius expelled the Jews from the city in A.D. 19, and then Claudius carried out the same measure in A.D. 49. It is difficult to know if Claudius's eviction extended to literally all Jews in the city, the majority, or a large number of perceived troublemakers. Claudius's edict was issued just eight years before Paul wrote his letter to the Romans and eleven years before he arrived in the city. By the time Paul came to Rome in A.D. 60, there was clearly a substantial number of Jews living in the city again. Because of these vicissitudes, it is impossible to know precisely what the Jewish population in the city would have been at this time. A rough estimate would be twenty to thirty thousand (although some scholars have suggested more).[A-163]

Although there is evidence of a Jewish presence in Rome as early as the second century B.C., the Jewish population swelled significantly after Pompey conquered Judea and Jerusalem in 63 B.C. The general brought back with him thousands of Jewish prisoners, who were sold as slaves. Many of these people were manumitted during their lifetimes and granted Roman citizenship.[A-164] Most of the Jews lived in a Jewish ghetto in the fourteenth district of

Rome across the Tiber River—a section called the *Trastevere*.

Philo provides us with the most detailed information about this community:

> He [the emperor Augustus] was aware that the great section of Rome on the other side of the Tiber is occupied and inhabited by Jews, most of whom were Roman citizens emancipated. For having been brought as captives to Italy they were liberated by their owners and were not forced to violate any of their native institutions. He knew therefore that they have houses of prayer (*proseuchai* = synagogues) and meet together in them, particularly on the sacred Sabbaths when they receive as a body a training in their ancestral philosophy. He knew too that they collect money for sacred purposes from their first-fruits and send them to Jerusalem by persons who would offer the sacrifices.[A-165]

Numerous Jewish inscriptions (mainly epitaphs) discovered in the city give evidence of at least ten different synagogues by name, although it is difficult to know how many of these date back to the first century.[A-166] These inscriptions also point to the fact that some Jews had moved from the Trastevere district to other parts of the city, such as Subura, Porta Capena, and the Campus Martius.

located at the military camp in the northeast part of the city (the *Campus Cohortium Praetoriarum*). There it is decided to grant Paul a lightened form of military custody. Rather than confining him to custody in a Roman prison, Paul is given the freedom to rent an apartment and live by himself.

[**The centurion delivered the prisoners to the *stratopedarch,* and Paul was allowed to live by himself outside the barracks] (28:16).** The manuscripts of the Western form of the text (which, in turn, influenced the Byzantine family of manuscripts and is thus present in the KJV) inserts this historical information. Most scholars, while denying that this insertion was written by Luke, nevertheless believe it contains some valuable historical traditions and regard it as an accurate commentary on the text. The *stratopedarch* is most likely to be identified as the chief administrator of the Praetorian Guard (the *princeps castrorum* or the *princeps praetorii*).[561] The passage also suggests that Paul's apartment would have been located near the Praetorian barracks near the Porta Viminalis in the northeast part

of the city. Paul may have been required to reside close to the military camp, which may explain why he did not move into the home of a Roman Christian somewhere else in the city.

With a soldier to guard him (28:16). Paul is no longer assigned a centurion to guard him—only an ordinary soldier. In spite of his lightened form of military custody, he is still bound to this soldier by a chain attached to his wrist (see 28:20).[562] Why Paul is granted this form of light custody may have to do with the fact that, upon reviewing the charges and speaking with Julius, the *stratopedarch* determines that Paul is neither a dangerous criminal nor a flight risk. It may also have to do with the weakness of the case against him—both Festus and Agrippa think that the charges against Paul should be dismissed.

He called together the leaders of the Jews (28:17). Apparently Paul is unable to travel to the synagogues to present his case for Jesus of Nazareth as the Messiah and hope of Israel. Thus he takes the bold step of inviting the Jewish leaders—pre-

ARCH OF TITUS

(bottom left)
Built by Domitian to celebrate his brother's military victory over Jerusalem and Judea.

(bottom right)
The Via Sacra from near the Colosseum with Titus's Arch in the background.
▼

sumably the rulers of the synagogues and the elders—to come and dialogue with him. There is no evidence of a centralized organizational structure to the Jewish community in Rome such as the Sanhedrin that functioned in Jerusalem or the *gerousia* in Alexandria. Rather, the Jewish community is structured as a loosely networked set of religious associations.[563]

When they had assembled, Paul said to them (28:17). Luke provides us with a concise summary of Paul's address to them, which summarizes the events surrounding his arrest, trial, and appeal. Paul emphatically denies that he has done anything contrary to the core convictions of Judaism.

It is because of the hope of Israel that I am bound with this chain (28:20). Once again, Paul emphasizes that the central issue in his dispute with the Jerusalem authorities is over "the hope of Israel," which, for Paul, is a belief that Jesus of Nazareth is the fulfillment of Israel's messianic hope. Bound up closely with this is the belief that Jesus rose from the dead and that there will be a future resurrection (see 23:6; 24:15; 26:6).

We have not received any letters from Judea concerning you (28:21). It would be surprising if the Jerusalem authorities never made contact with the leaders of the Jewish community in Rome about Paul, especially given the effort they expended to do away with Paul while he was in Palestine. It was probably only a matter of time until they received a letter from Jerusalem. It is yet another question as to whether the Jewish leaders would want to go to the expense and trouble of prosecuting their case against Paul before the emperor in Rome, espe-cially knowing the weakness of the case with respect to Roman law.

People everywhere are talking against this sect (28:22). The Roman Jewish community has already debated intensely over whether Jesus was "the Christ," which led to violent confrontations and rioting—apparently the final straw leading to Claudius's expulsion of the Jews from the city.[564] Evidently, the Jewish community in Rome continued to hear reports from Jews scattered throughout the empire about how disruptive this messianic sect had been in their own communities.

They arranged to meet Paul on a certain day (28:23). In spite of their initial prejudice against Christianity (based on their own experience with Jewish Christians in Rome and the reports they have heard elsewhere), the Jewish leaders show an interest in hearing Paul and debating with him. They probably also have an innate curiosity about why this formerly prominent Pharisee would join such a sect and become an important leader of the movement.

Came in even larger numbers to the place where he was staying (28:23). The meeting attracts far more people than Paul anticipates. If Paul's rented lodging is near the Praetorium barracks, most of the Jews must travel from across the river on the opposite side of the city to get there. Assuming that Paul rents a room on the third- (fourth- or fifth-) story of a tenement house, the available space for such a meeting would have been rather limited.

From morning till evening he explained and declared to them the kingdom of God (28:23). The theme of the kingdom of God is larger and more expansive than a simple proclamation of the gospel (the *kerygma*). Paul explains the gospel in light of the whole of God's unfolding plan. Not only would Paul have spent considerable time expounding the plan of God from the Hebrew Scriptures (perhaps by using the LXX), but he would have recited the teaching of Jesus about the kingdom.

Tried to convince them about Jesus from the Law of Moses and from the Prophets (28:23). Specifically, Paul wants to convince these Jewish leaders that Jesus of Nazareth fulfills the meaning and the promises of the Law and the Prophets. Reciting the relevant passages from Genesis to Malachi, which Paul would have known by heart, he explains how they are uniquely fulfilled in Jesus. As one scholar speculates: "Paul on this occasion must have exerted all his powerful qualities of mind and heart as he endeavored to persuade the leading Jews of Rome of the truth of the gospel. . . . The debate must have been keen and impassioned."565

Some were convinced . . . others would not believe (28:24). This response is typical of Paul's proclamation of Christ in the Diaspora synagogues.566 The difference this time is that these Jewish leaders have

already become exposed to the gospel and are already unfavorably inclined toward the message when they begin listening to Paul. The positive response of some is greatly encouraging to Paul and to the Christian community in Rome.

The Holy Spirit spoke (28:25). This introduction to the passage from Isaiah reveals Paul's belief in the divine inspiration of the Scriptures.

You will be ever hearing but never understanding. . . . For this people's heart has become calloused (28:26–27). When they begin to leave, Paul makes one final statement to the Jewish leaders who remain unconvinced that Jesus is the Messiah of Israel. He recites a passage from Isaiah 6:9–10, which speaks of the unresponsiveness of God's people to divine revelation because of the callousness of their hearts. One can only wonder about the emotion in Paul's voice as he utters this. In applying this passage to the unresponsive hearers, Paul follows the example of Jesus, who also pronounced these words to Palestinian Jews hostile to his message.567 When Paul wrote to the Roman Christians a few years earlier, he attributed the unresponsiveness of many Jews to their hardened hearts (Rom. 11:7–8).

God's salvation has been sent to the Gentiles (28:28). This does not imply a final rejection of the Jews in favor of the Gentiles. Paul anticipates a time when there will be a massive turning of Jews to Jesus the Messiah (see Rom. 11:25–32). This may represent a departure from his principle of "to the Jews first" and a statement that his priority from henceforth will be to reach Gentiles with the gospel. "Luke may well be presenting

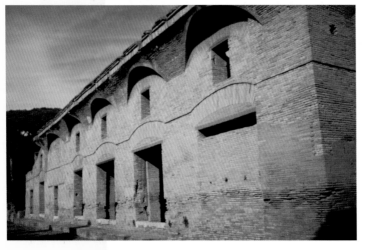

him as an example for the church generally to follow."[568]

For two whole years (28:30). Arriving in Rome in early A.D. 60 (perhaps March), this means that Paul is in custody at least until early in A.D. 62. Probably during this time Luke writes his second volume. At the conclusion of his writing, Paul still has not faced his trial. Had Paul already been released, it is difficult to explain why Luke would not have recorded the outcome of the trial (unless he was planning to do so in a third volume—a work never completed). Paul has been in custody four years, and his readers await the anticipated acquittal by the emperor. It would have made a better ending to the Gospel and Acts to portray Paul as free from chains and proclaiming the gospel to Gentiles in regions beyond Rome.

One of the activities Paul engages in during this time is letter writing. From his Roman apartment chained to a soldier, he writes Philippians (if it was not written while he was in prison in Caesarea, or even earlier during his Ephesian ministry), Colossians, Philemon, and Ephesians. Philippians may plausibly be explained as having been written just before Paul's trial at the end of the two years since it reflects an approaching crisis that could end in life or death for the apostle (Phil. 1:19–26).[569]

In his own rented house (28:30). It is inappropriate for us to think a single story two-bedroom home on a nice suburban street. Paul rents space on an upper floor of a Roman *insula*—a block apartment in a densely populated urban area. Housing prices were extraordinarily expensive in ancient Rome. Paul's apartment is probably modest—what we may even call a "slum dwelling."

How he is able to afford this is a matter of speculation. It is doubtful that he is able to work at his tentmaking business since he is chained by the wrist to a soldier.[570] It is possible that Paul may be drawing on an inheritance (this is highly speculative), but far more likely his source of income comes from contributions from fellow believers.

Boldly and without hindrance he preached (28:31). When Paul writes to the Ephesians (probably during this imprisonment), he asks these believers to pray that he will be enabled to proclaim the gospel boldly while he is "in chains" (Eph. 6:19–20). Perhaps he faces the threat of discouragement or intimidation from a variety of quarters. Luke, however, represents Paul as proclaiming the kingdom with great boldness.

The Roman authorities and the soldier chained to Paul could have used a variety of means to silence his proclamation of the gospel. Luke claims that the Roman authorities are tolerant of Paul's ministry and message during this period of time.

REFLECTIONS

PAUL WAS NOT IN IDEAL CIRCUM-stances for sharing the gospel. He was confined to his apartment, chained to a Roman soldier, and suffered from some physical limitation (his "thorn in the flesh"). Nevertheless, God strengthened and enabled him to shine brightly in Rome. Do you suffer a physical handicap? Do you feel limited by your circumstances? God delights in empowering the weak to be his witnesses!

ANNOTATED BIBLIOGRAPHY

Commentaries

Bruce, F. F. *The Book of the Acts* (*revised*). NICNT. Grand Rapids: Eerdmans, 1988.

This has been a longstanding classic on the book of Acts. F. F. Bruce had an eye for bringing out helpful historical background information to illuminate the text.

Larkin, William J. *Acts*. IVPNTC. Downers Grove, Ill.: InterVarsity, 1995.

This is an exceptional commentary that properly highlights the strong emphasis on mission throughout Acts. The reader will find valuable insights (especially on cultural issues) and helpful explanations of the text, combined with discussion of practical and contemporary significance.

Marshall, I. Howard. *The Acts of the Apostles*. TNTC. Grand Rapids: Eerdmans, 1980.

This is an outstanding paperback commentary that provides background information, but gives a greater amount of attention to the theological issues and themes. Marshall has long been appreciated for his lucid writing style.

Williams, David J. *Acts*. NIBC. Peabody, Mass.: Hendrickson, 1985.

This is well written and contains many excellent historical and theological insights.

Witherington, Ben, III. *The Acts of the Apostles: A Socio-Rhetorical Commentary*. Grand Rapids: Eerdmans, 1998.

This 874-page volume is perhaps now the best all-around commentary on the book of Acts. It is well written and gives extensive insight into the social and cultural background of each of the passages. Witherington is conversant with the recent scholarship on Acts and makes good use of it for illuminating the meaning of the text.

Special Studies

The Book of Acts in Its First Century Setting. Grand Rapids: Eerdmans, 1993–1996.

The Tyndale Fellowship in Cambridge, England, has sponsored the publication of a massive historical study of the book of Acts that has appeared in five volumes. These are indispensible for anyone wanting to gain a firm and up-to-date treatment of the historical background of Acts. The series consists of the following titles:

1. Bruce D. Winter and Andrew D. Clark, eds. *The Book of Acts in its Ancient Literary Setting* (1993).
2. David W. J. Gill and Conrad Gempf, eds. *The Book of Acts in its Graeco-Roman Setting* (1994).
3. Brian Rapske. *The Book of Acts and Paul in Roman Custody* (1994).
4. Richard Bauckham, ed. *The Book of Acts in its Palestinian Setting* (1995).
5. Irina Levinskaya. *The Book of Acts in its Diaspora Setting* (1996).

Hengel, Martin, and Anna Maria Schwemer. *Paul: Between Damascus and Antioch*. Louisville, Ky.: Westminster John Knox, 1997.

This is a landmark historical study of Acts 6–15, covering the years A.D. 33–49.

Riesner, Rainer. *Paul's Early Period: Chronology, Mission Strategy, Theology*. Grand Rapids: Eerdmans, 1998.

This is an invaluable historical study of the historical events and chronology of the events surrounding Paul's life from his conversion to the writing of 1 Thessalonians.

Main Text Notes

1. Irenaeus, *Against Heresies* 3.1.1.
2. Ibid., 3.14.1.
3. This is also known as an "Anti-Marcionite prologue." Cited from J. A. Fitzmyer, *The Gospel According to Luke* (New York: Doubleday, 1981), 1:38.
4. Eusebius, *Eccl. Hist.* 3.4; Jerome, *De Viris Illustribus* 7.
5. Col. 4:14; 2 Tim. 4:11; Philem. 24.
6. F. G. B. Millar and G. P. Burton, "*Equites*," *OCD*[3], 551.
7. R. F. O'Toole, "Theophilus," *ABD*, 6.511.
8. C. J. Hemer, *The Book of Acts in the Setting of Hellenistic History* (WUNT 49; Tübingen: Mohr-Siebeck, 1989; rpt. Winona Lake, Ind.: Eisenbrauns, 1990), 362.
9. I. H. Marshall, *The Acts of the Apostles* (TNTC; Grand Rapids: Eerdmans, 1980), 21. This conclusion is reaffirmed by D. Peterson, "Luke's Theological Enterprise," in *Witness to the Gospel: The Theology of Acts*, eds. I. H. Marshall and D. Peterson (Grand Rapids: Eerdmans, 1998), 534.
10. J. T. Squires, "The Plan of God," in *Witness to the Gospel*, 19–39, esp. 37–39.
11. D. Peterson, "The Motif of Fulfillment," in *Witness to the Gospel*, 100–101.
12. J. T. Squires, *The Plan of God in Luke-Acts* (SNTSMS 76; Cambridge: Cambridge University Press, 1993), 192–94; Peterson, "Luke's Theological Enterprise," 540.
13. Peterson, "Luke's Theological Enterprise," 540–44.
14. So also Hemer, *Book of Acts*, 365–410, 414.
15. For further discussion and references, see H. J. Cadbury, "Appendix C: Commentary on the Preface of Luke," in *The Beginnings of Christianity. Part I: The Acts of the Apostles*, eds. F. J. Foakes-Jackson and K. Lake (Grand Rapids: Baker, 1979; orig. 1932), 4:491.
16. Josephus, *Ag. Ap.* 2.1 §1
17. See, for example, *Pss. Sol.* 8:15.
18. See N. Avigad, *The Herodian Quarter in Jerusalem* (Jerusalem: Keter Publishing House, n.d.); B. Blue, "Acts and the House Church," in *The Book of Acts in Its Graeco-Roman Setting*, eds. D. W. J. Gill and C. Gempf (BAFCS 2; Grand Rapids: Eerdmans, 1994), 130–38, 140–44.
19. *m. Sanh.* 1:6.
20. See Marshall, *Acts*, 64–65; D. J. Williams, "Judas Iscariot," *DJG*, 408.
21. L. & K. Ritmeyer, "Akeldama: Potter's Field or High Priest's Tomb?" *BAR* 20.6 (Nov./Dec. 1994): 22–35, 76. Their conclu-

sions are also supported by G. Avni and Z. Greenhut, "Akeldama: Resting Place of the Rich and Famous," *BAR* 20.6 (November/December 1994): 36–46.
22. See Luke 10:1; Eusebius, *Eccl. Hist.* 1.12.
23. Lake and Cadbury, *Beginnings of Christianity*, 4:15.
24. W. Reinhardt, "The Population Size of Jerusalem and the Numerical Growth of the City," in *Acts in its Palestinian Setting*, 262–63.
25. J. Jeremias, *Jerusalem in the Time of Jesus* (Philadelphia: Fortress, 1969), 61.
26. Josephus, *Ant.* 7.15.3 §393.
27. Ibid., 16.7.1 §§179–82.
28. See D. Tarler and J. M. Cahill, "David, City Of," *ABD*, 2.64.
29. See H. Shanks, "Is This King David's Tomb?" *BAR* 21.1 (Jan./Feb. 1995): 62–67.
30. See BAGD, s.v.
31. M. Broshi, "The Archaeology of Palestine 63 B.C.E.—CE 70," in *CHJ*[3], 10.
32. 1QS 6:13–25.
33. See Blue, "Acts and the House Church," *Graeco-Roman Setting*, 140–44.
34. Josephus, *Ant.* 14.4.3 §65.
35. *m. Tamid* 7:3.
36. Jeremias, *Jerusalem*, 116–17.
37. Josephus, *J.W.* Trans. G. A. Williamson (New York: Viking Penguin, 1970), 5.5.3 §201.
38. Ibid., 5.5.2 §§190–92.
39. See, for example, Pss. 22, 69; Jer. 11:19; Dan. 9:26; Zech. 13:7.
40. *m. Sotah* 7:7–8; *m. Tamid* 7:3.
41. Josephus, *J.W.* 2.20.4 §566.
42. Ibid., 2.8.14 §165.
43. Josephus, *Ant.* 18.1.4 §16. On the Sadducees, see Schürer, *HJP*[2], 2:391.
44. G. Bornkamm, "πρέσβυς," *TDNT*, 6:659.
45. Ibid., 18.4.3 §95.
46. As cited in P. W. van der Horst, *Ancient Jewish Epitaphs: An Introductory Survey of a Millennium of Jewish Funerary Epigraphy (300 B.C.E–700 C.E.)* (Kampen: Kok Pharos Publishing House, 1991), 141.
47. Str-B, 1:876.
48. J. Fitzmyer, *The Acts of the Apostles* (AB 31; New York: Doubleday, 1998), 301.
49. *T. Sol.* 22:7.
50. Plato, *Apology of Socrates* 29D.
51. E.g. Josh. 10:24; 1 Kings 5:3; Ps. 8:6; 110:1.
52. Matt. 22:44; 1 Cor. 15:25–26; Eph. 1:22; Heb. 2:8.
53. Clement of Alexandria, *Stromata* 2.20.112.
54. C. K. Barrett, *The Acts of the Apostles*, 2 vols., (ICC; Edinburgh: T. & T. Clark, 1993–98), 1:259; B. Witherington III, *The Acts of the*

Apostles: A Socio-Rhetorical Commentary (Grand Rapids: Eerdmans, 1998), 209.

55. This is the view of J. Duncan M. Derrett, "Ananias, Sapphira, and the Right of Property," in *Studies in the New Testament*, vol. 1 (Leiden: Brill, 1977), 197–98.

56. Derrett, "Ananias, Sapphira," 198.

57. See Johannes P. Louw and Eugene A. Nida, *Greek-English Lexicon of the New Testament Based on Semantic Domains*, 2d ed. (New York: United Bible Societies, 1989) §11.32, 78.

58. See also Deut. 4:10; 23:2, 3, 4, 9; Judg. 20:2; 1 Kings 8:14; Ps. 22:22; et al.

59. Marshall, *Acts*, 115.

60. Cicero, *Tusc.* 3:12, 26. See P. W. van der Horst, "Shadow," *ABD*, 5.1148–50.

61. Ps.-Aristotle, *De mirabilibus auscultationibus* 145 (157) as reported in P. W. van der Horst, "Peter's Shadow: The Religio-Historical Background of Acts v. 15," *NTS* 23 (1976–77): 208.

62. *m. ʿAbod. Zar.* 3:8.

63. *m. ʾOhal.* 2:1–2.

64. Tobit 6:7.

65. *T. Benj.* 5:2.

66. See Luke 4:33, 36; 6:18; 8:29; 9:42; 11:24.

67. K. Lake, "Localities In and Near Jerusalem Mentioned in Acts," in *Beginnings*, 5:478.

68. Gen. 22:11; Judg. 6:11, 12, 21; 1 Kings 19:7; 2 Kings 19:35; Isa. 37:6.

69. See, for instance, Duane Garrett, *Angels and the New Spirituality* (Nashville: Broadman & Holman, 1995), 19–23.

70. Barrett, *Acts*, 1:284.

71. Ibid., 1:289.

72. Deut. 26:7; 1 Chron. 29:18; 2 Chron. 20:6; Ezra 7:27.

73. Josephus, *Ant.* 13.10.6 §297.

74. Hemer, *Book of Acts*, 162, suggests that Josephus rather than Luke may be wrong on the dating of Theudas.

75. Josephus, *J.W.* 2.8.1 §118.

76. Josephus, *Ant.* 18.1.1, 6 §§1–10, 23–25.

77. *m. ʾAbot* 4:11.

78. Josephus, *Ant.* 4.8.21 §238.

79. See M. Wilkins, "Disciples," *DJG*, 176–82.

80. See, for example, Plato, *Meno* 82b; Aeschines, *Or.* 3.172. For additional texts, see Barrett, *Acts*, 1:308.

81. Chrysostom, *Hom. Act.* 21.1; Migne, *PG*, 60:164 (as reported in Hengel, "Between Jesus and Paul," 6).

82. See M. O. Wise, "Languages of Palestine," *DJG*, 434–44.

83. See Witherington, "A Closer Look—The Hellenists," *Acts*, 240–47.

84. J. J. Scott, "The Church's Progress to the Council of Jerusalem According to the Book of Acts," *BBR* 7 (1997): 209–11.

85. See the evidence in M. Hengel, "Between Jesus and Paul," in *Between Jesus and Paul: Studies in the Earliest History of Christianity* (Philadelphia: Fortress, 1983), 16 and n. 109 on p. 147.

86. Jeremias, *Jerusalem*, 131. He cites *m. Peʾah* 8:7 and a variety of texts from the Talmuds.

87. Such a suggestion occurs as early as Irenaeus (*Haer.* 1.26.3; 3.12.10; 4.15.1).

88. Barrett, *Acts*, 1:304.

89. Josephus, *J.W.* 2.20.5 §571.

90. Josephus, *Ant.* 4.8.14 §214.

91. For references, see Barrett, *Acts*, 1:312 and Str-B, 2:641.

92. Irenaeus, *Adv. Haer.* 1.26.3 and Eusebius, *Eccl. Hist.* 3.29.1–3.

93. Ex. 29:10, 15, 19; Lev. 1:4; 3:2, 8, 13; 4:15.

94. For the texts, see Str-B, 2:647–61.

95. Jeremias, *Jerusalem*, 204.

96. See R. Riesner, "Excursus I: An Essene Quarter in Jerusalem?," in *Acts in its Palestinian Setting*, 190–92.

97. Philo, *Embassy* 155.

98. Tacitus, *Ann.* 2.85.

99. M. Hengel, *The "Hellenization" of Judea in the First Century after Christ* (Philadelphia: Trinity Press, 1989), 13.

100. W. Schrage, "συναγωγή," *TDNT*, 7:837.

101. *t. Meg.* 3.6; cf. also *y. Meg.* 73d.

102. See Str-B, 2.661–65; Schürer, *HJP²*, 2:76, 445; *b. Meg.* 26b.

103. N. Avigad, "A Depository of Inscribed Ossuaries in the Kidron Valley," *IEJ* 12 (1962): 1–12 (cited in Fitzmyer, *Acts*, 358).

104. *Gos. Thom.* 71.

105. Witherington, *Acts*, 260.

106. See W. A. van Gemeren, "Shekinah," *ISBE*, 4.466–68.

107. Josephus, *Ant.* 12.3.3 §136.

108. On "glory," see C. C. Newman, "Glory," *DLNT*, 394–400.

109. Josephus, *Ant.* 2.8.2 §199.

110. Ibid., 2.9.7 §236.

111. J. Jeremias, "Μωϋσῆς," *TDNT*, 4:851.

112. Marshall, *Acts*, 141.

113. *m. ʾAbot* 2:7.

114. See M. Stohl, "Sakkuth," *DDD²*, 722–23; idem, "Kaiwan," *DDD²*, 478.

115. G. C. Heider, "Molech," *DDD²*, 585.

116. 2 Kings 21:62; 2 Chron. 28:3.

117. See R. K. Harrison, "Molech," *ISBE*, 3:401–2; 2 Kings 17:17; 21:6; Ps. 106:38; Ezek. 16:21.

118. Fitzmyer, *Acts*, 383; Bruce, *Acts*, 147 (note 78).

119. Fitzmyer, *Acts*, 384.

120. Witherington, *Acts*, 273.

121. 2 Chron. 24:20–21; Neh. 9:26; Jer. 2:30; 26:20–24.

122. Justin Martyr, *Dialogue With Trypho* 120.5; Tertullian, *De patientia* 14; *Scorpiace* 8.

123. See also Ps. 68:17; Josephus, *Ant.* 15.5.3 §136.

124. For the texts, see Str-B, 3:554–56.

125. See R. Riesner, *Paul's Early Period: Chronology, Mission Strategy, Theology* (Grand Rapids: Eerdmans, 1998), 59–63.

126. Ps. 37:12; see also Lam. 2:16; Ps. 112:10.

127. See also Eph. 1:20; 1 Peter 3:22.

128. See Dan. 7:13; *1 En.* 46–53.

129. Acts 13:21; Rom. 11:1; Phil. 3:5.

130. Based on the use of the word in Philo, *Cherubim* 32 (§114) and Diogenes Laertius 8.10.

131. See Fitzmyer, *Acts*, 394.

132. *m. Sanh.* 6.6.

133. For the references, see Lake and Cadbury, *Beginnings*, 4.88.

134. See F. S. Spencer, "Philip the Evangelist," *DLNT*, 929–31.

135. Eusebius, *Eccl. Hist.* 3.39.9–10.

136. Hengel, "Luke the Historian," 115.

137. Josephus, *Ant.* 13.10.2–3 §§275–83; *J.W.* 1.2.7 §§64–65.

138. Josephus, *Ant.* 14.5.3 §88; *J.W.* 1.8.4 §166. On Herod renaming the restored city, see *Ant.* 15.8.5 §392; *J.W.* 1.21.2 §403.

139. See Irenaeus, *Against Heresies* 1.23.1–4; Origen, *Cont. Cel.* 6.11; Tertullian, *de Anima* 34; *Against All Heresies* 1; Eusebius, *Eccl. Hist.* 2.13–14.

140. See E. M. Yamauchi, "Gnosis, Gnosticism," *DPL* 350–54.

141. See C. E. Arnold, "Magical Papyri," *DNTB*, 666–70.

142. E. Lane, *Corpus Monumentorum Religionis Dei Menis*, part 1 (EPRO 19; Leiden: Brill, 1971), 45–46 (no. 69).

143. So also Witherington, *Acts*, 289; Bruce, *Acts*, 170.

144. Barrett, *Acts*, 1:413.

145. Ibid., 1:416–17.

146. Homer, *Odyssey* 1.22–23.

147. See also Strabo, *Geog* 1.1.6; Philostratus, *Vit. Apoll.* 6.1; Herodotus, *Hist.* 3.114.

148. Josephus, *Ant.* 14.5.3 §§86–88.

149. F. L. Horton and J. A. Blakely, "'Behold, Water!' Tell el-Hesi and the Baptism of the Ethiopian Eunuch (Acts 8:26–40)," *RB* 107 (2000): 56–71.

150. On Ethiopia, see R. G. Morkot, "Ethiopia," *OCD*[3], 558; "Nubia," *OCD*[3], 1052; R. H. Smith, "Ethiopia," *ABD*, 2:665.

151. BAGD, s.v.

152. Schürer, *HJP*[2], 3.1.57–59.

153. *CPJ*, II.432.57–61 (AD 113).

154. A. Segal, *Rebecca's Children: Judaism and Christianity in the Roman World* (Cambridge, Mass.: Harvard University Press, 1986), 93.

155. Spencer, *Portrait of Philip*, 178–80; Barrett, *Acts*, 1:431.

156. See also Barrett, *Acts*, 1:434.

157. Irenaeus, *Haer.* 3.12.8; see also Eusebius, *Eccl. Hist.* 2.1.13.

158. On Azotus, see M. Dothan, "Ashdod," *ABD*, 1:477–82; idem, "Ashdod," *NEAE*, 1:93–102.

159. Hengel & Schwemer, *Paul*, 131; Riesner, *Paul's Early Period*, 87.

160. See McRay, *Archaeology*, 233–34; idem, "Damascus (The Greco-Roman Period)," *ABD*, 2:8.

161. 2 Sam. 7:14; see also Ps. 89:26–27; Ps. 2:7.

162. See Hengel & Schwemer, *Paul*, 106–26.

163. Ibid., *Paul*, 132.

164. See Acts 9:11; 21:39; 22:3.

165. Hengel & Schwemer, *Paul*, 174.

166. See Ezra 2:33; Neh. 7:37; 11:35.

167. Josephus, *J.W.* 32.3.5 §§54–58.

168. Ibid., 2.19.1 §513.

169. See J. Kaplan, "Lod," *NEAE*, 3:917; W. Ewing & R. K. Harrison, "Lod," *ISBE*, 3:150–51.

170. On Joppa, see J. Kaplan & H. Ritter-Kaplan, "Jaffa," *NEAE*, 2:655–59; idem, "Joppa," *ABD*, 3:946–49.

171. Josephus, *J.W.* 3.9.3 §§419–27.

172. Schürer, *HJP*[2], 2:110–14.

173. *m. Šabb.* 23.5.

174. *b. Pesaḥ* 65a.

175. See Jeremias, *Jerusalem*, 309–10.

176. On Caesarea, see R. L. Hohlfelder, "Caesarea," *ABD*, 1:798–803; K. G. Holum, A. Raban, A. Negev, A. Frova, M. Avi-Yonah, L. I. Levine, and E. Netzer, "Caesarea," *NEAE*, 1:271–91; K. G. Holum, R. L. Hohlfelder, R.J. Bull, and A. Raban, *King Herod's Dream: Caesarea on the Sea* (New York: Norton, 1988).

177. Josephus, *J.W.* 1.21.7 §414, ed. Williamson.

178. Ibid., 2.18.1 §457.

179. Appian, *Civil War* 1.100.

180. H. M. D. Parker and G. R. Watson, "Centurio," *OCD*[3], 310.

181. D. Kennedy, "Roman Army," *ABD*, 5:791.

182. Polybius, *Histories* 6.24.9 (as cited in W. J. Larkin, *Acts* [IVPNTC; Downer's Grove, Ill.: InterVarsity Press, 1995], 153).

183. M. J. Olson, "Italian Cohort," *ABD*, 3:578–79; T. R. S. Broughton, "The Roman Army," in *Beginnings*, 5:441–43.

184. Broughton, "Roman Army," 442.

185. See Acts 5:19; 8:26; 12:7; 27:23.

186. BAGD, s.v.

187. W. Hauck, "κοινός," *TDNT*, 3:790.

188. Midrash on Psalm 146 as cited in Barrett, *Acts*, 1:509.

189. Fitzmyer, *Acts*, 457.

190. *m. ʾOhal.* 18:7.

191. BAGD, s.v.

192. See the discussion in Schürer, *HJP²*, 2:81–83.

193. J. J. Scott, "The Cornelius Incident in the Light of its Jewish Setting," *JETS* 34 (1991): 482.

194. Witherington, *Acts*, 356.

195. C. W. Stenschke, *Luke's Portrait of Gentiles Prior to Their Coming to Faith* (WUNT 2/108; Tübingen: Mohr Siebeck, 1999), 153.

196. See R. F. Youngblood, "Peace," *ISBE*, 3:731–33.

197. Barrett, *Acts*, 1:527.

198. On the Roman *familia*, see F. Dupont, *Daily Life in Ancient Rome* (Oxford: Blackwell, 1992), 103–6.

199. Schürer, *HJP²*, 3:1:15.

200. Philo, *Embassy* 36 (281–82).

201. BAGD, s.v.

202. Hengel & Schwemer, *Paul*, 205–24.

203. *Didache* 11:7–12; Hermas, *Mandate* 11:1–21.

204. Hermas, *Mandate* 11:3, 17.

205. The best discussion of these famines and the impact they had on Judea is in Riesner, *Paul's Early Period*, 125–36.

206. Winter, "Acts and Food Shortages," in *Graeco-Roman Setting*, 61–62.

207. Dio Cassius, *Hist.* 59.17.2, 60.11.1–4; Suetonius, *Gaius* 39.1; P. Michigan 123, 127; see Riesner, *Paul's Early Period*, 129.

208. Orosius, *Adv. Pag.* 7.6.12.

209. Josephus, *Ant.* 12.8.3, 4, 6 §§272, 274, 284.

210. Suetonius, *Claud.* 2.

211. 1 Cor. 6:1–4; 2 Cor. 8–9.

212. For further support of the view that the visit of Acts 11:30 and 12:25 = the visit of Gal. 2:1–10, see: Witherington, *Acts*, 375 and Appendix 1, 817–20; Bruce, *Acts*, 231; Hemer, *Book of Acts*, chaps. 6–7.

213. On Herod Agrippa I, see Josephus, *Ant.* 18–19. See also D. R. Schwartz, *Agrippa I: The Last King of Judaea* (TSAJ 23; Tübingen: Mohr Siebeck, 1990); Schürer, *HJP²*, 1:442–54; D. C. Braund, "Agrippa," *ABD*, 1:98–100; H. W. Hoehner, "Herod," *ISBE*, 2:696–97.

214. Josephus, *Ant.* 19.7.3 §331.

215. See Eusebius, *Eccl. Hist.* 3.1, 20, 23–24.

216. Ibid., 2.1, 9; 3.5.

217. See *m. Sanhedrin* 7:3, 9:3.

218. Riesner, *Paul's Early Period*, 119.

219. On the feast of Unleavened Bread, see: B. M. Bokser, "Unleavened Bread and Passover, Feasts Of," *ABD*, 6:755–65; M. O. Wise, "Feasts," *DJG*, 234–41.

220. As cited in H. Conzelmann, *Acts of the Apostles* (Hermeneia; Philadelphia: Fortress, 1987), 93; Vegetius, *On Military Affairs* 3.8.

221. See B. Rapske, *Paul in Roman Custody* (BAFCS 3; Grand Rapids: Eerdmans, 1994), 206–207; Lucian, *Tox.* 29.

222. Barrett, *Acts*, 1:583.

223. See Blue, "Acts and the House Church," 135–36.

224. Hemer, *Book of Acts*, 227.

225. See also Barrett, *Acts*, 1:584.

226. See M. Noll, *Angels of Light, Powers of Darkness* (Downer's Grove, Ill.: InterVarsity Press, 1998), 170–72.

227. Acts 15:13; Gal. 1:19; 2:9, 12.

228. Josephus, *Ant.* 20.9.1 §200.

229. R. Bauckham, "James and the Jerusalem Church," in *Palestinian Setting*, 434–35.

230. *Code of Justinian* 9.4.4.

231. Ibid., 19.8.2 §351.

232. J. D. G. Dunn, *The Acts of the Apostles* (NC; Philadelphia: Trinity Press, 1996), 173.

233. On Seleucia, see A. H. M. Jones, H. Seyrig, & S. Sherwin-White, "Seleucia in Pieria," *OCD³*, 1380; L. J. Hoppe, "Seleucia," *ABD*, 5:1075–76; W. S. LaSor, "Seleucia," *ISBE*, 4:384–85.

234. H. W. Catling, "Salamis," *OCD³*, 1347; E. Meyer, "Salamis," *Der Kleine Pauly*, 4:1505–1506; C. Gempf, "Salamis," *ABD*, 5:904–905.

235. Barrett, *Acts*, 1:612.

236. See Gill, "Cyprus," 220–23, for a discussion of Paul's likely route.

237. H. W. Catling, "Paphos," *OCD³*, 1108; E. Meyer, "Paphos," *Der Kleine Pauly*, 4:484–87.

238. H. J. Klauck, *Magie und Heidentum in der Apostelgeschichte des Lukas* (SBS 167; Stuttgart: Verlag Katholisches Bibelwerk, 1996), 61.

239. See C. E. Arnold, *Powers of Darkness: Principalities and Powers in Paul's Letters* (Downer's Grove, Ill.: InterVarsity Press, 1992), 71–74; Klauck, *Magie und Heidentum*, 62.

240. Josephus, *Ant.* 20.7.2 §142.

241. Suetonius, *Aug.* 94–98.

242. See G. J. Toomer, "Claudius Thrasyllus," *OCD³*, 343. See also A. D. Nock, "Paul and the Magus," in *Beginnings*, 5:183–84; Suetonius, *Tiberius* 14, 62; *Gaius* 19.

243. Suetonius, *Nero* 36, 40.

244. Pliny, *Nat. Hist.* 30.17; Suetonius, *Nero* 56.

245. CIL, 6.31543.

246. On this inscription, now see Nobbs, "Cyprus," in *Graeco-Roman Setting*, 279–89 and Mitchell, *Anatolia*, 2:6–7.

247. W. Ramsay, *The Bearing of Recent Discovery on the Trustworthiness of the New Testament* (Grand Rapids: Baker, 1953 [rep. of 1915 ed.]), 151.

248. Mitchell, *Anatolia*, 2:6.

249. Ibid., 2:6; Nobbs, "Cyprus," 287; S. Mitchell and M. Waelkens, *Pisidian Antioch: The Site and its Monuments* (London: Duckworth, 1998), 12.

250. See Hemer, *Book of Acts*, 227–28.

251. LSJ, s.v.

252. F. F. Bruce, *Paul: Apostle of the Heart Set Free* (Grand Rapids: Eerdmans, 1977), 37–40; idem, *New Testament History* (New York: Doubleday, 1972), 234–35.

253. Riesner, *Paul's Early Period*, 151–54.

254. On Perga, see E. A. Judge, "Perga," *ISBE*, 3:767–68; W. W. Gasque, "Perga," *ABD*, 5:228; G. E. Bean & S. Mitchell, "Perge," *OCD*[3], 1139.

255. On Pisidia, see W. H. C. Frend, "Pisidia," *ISBE* 3.873–74; S. Mitchell, "Pisidia," *OCD*[3], 1186; W. W. Gasque, "Pisidia," *ABD*, 5:374–75.

256. Mitchell, *Anatolia*, 2.4.

257. Schürer, *HJP*[2], 2:441–43.

258. Ibid., 2:447–48.

259. See Schürer, *HJP*[2], 2:456–59; Num. 15:37–41; Deut. 6:4–9; 11:13–21; *m. Meg.* 4:3.

260. Philo, *Spec. Laws* 2.62 (Yonge trans.).

261. Witherington, *Acts*, 406–407.

262. *b. Ketub.* 96a.

263. Barrett, *Acts*, 1:658.

264. See also Ps. 69:28; Rev. 13:8; 17:8; 20:12–15; 21:27.

265. Mitchell, "Antioch of Pisidia," 265; Mitchell and Waelkens, *Pisidian Antioch*, 12.

266. Str-B, 1:571.

267. See C. Kruse, "Apostle, Apostleship," *DLNTD*, 76–82.

268. A. H. M. Jones and S. Mitchell, "Lycaonia," *OCD*[3], 894; F. F. Bruce, "Lycaonia," *ABD*, 4:420–22.

269. C. Breytenbach, "Zeus und der lebendige Gott: Anmerkungen zu Apostelgeschichte 14.11–17," *NTS* 39 (1993): 399; Mitchell, *Anatolia*, 1:173.

270. Mitchell, *Anatolia*, 1:173.

271. Ovid, *Metamorphoses* 8.618–724.

272. See Mitchell, *Anatolia*, 1:24.

273. Iamblichus, *De misteriis* 1.1.

274. See Hemer, *Book of Acts*, 195–96.

275. See L. H. Martin, "Hermes," *DDD*[2], 409; F. Graf, "Zeus," *DDD*[2], 939.

276. See Herodotus, *Hist.* 7.197.2.

277. See "Grief," *DBI*, 351–52.

278. Num. 14:6; 2 Kings 18:37; 19:1; 22:11; Ezra 4:1.

279. *m. Sanhedrin* 7:5.

280. Bar. 6:17 (LXX = v. 15), see the extended polemic in vv. 3–72; see also Deut. 4:28; Ps. 115:4–8; Isa. 44:9–20; Wis. 15:15–19.

281. *Letter of Aristeas* 135.

282. See also 1 Sam. 17:36; 2 Kings 19:4, 16; Ps. 42:2; 84:2.

283. *Bel and the Dragon* 4–5.

284. See Ps. 146:6; 4Q521 5.ii.2.

285. *m. Ber.* 9:2.

286. Breytenbach, "Zeus und der lebendige Gott," 399–400.

287. Foakes-Jackson and Lake, *Beginnings*, 4:162.

288. Barrett, *Acts*, 1:688.

289. Ex. 29:36; 30:10; Lev. 16:30; Isa. 53:10.

290. See Ex. 15:22–27; Num. 14:22.

291. *m. ʾAbot* 3.5.

292. Barrett, *Acts*, 2:721.

293. CD 7:16; 4QFlor 1:12–13.

294. See, for example, Isa. 45:20–23; Jer. 12:15–16; Zech. 8:22.

295. *Vita Greg. Thaumaturg.* 46:944, as cited in Witherington, *Acts*, 462.

296. See, for example, Sir. 23:23; *T. Reu.* 3:3; 4:6; 5:3.

297. See 1 Cor. 6:18; 7:2; Gal. 5:19; Eph. 5:3; Heb. 13:4.

298. Wis. 14:23–27; see also 1 Cor. 10:7–8; Rev. 2:14, 20.

299. See A. J. M. Wedderburn, "The 'Apostolic Decree': Tradition and Redaction," *NovT* 35 (1993): 384–89.

300. Origen, *Against Celsus* 8.30.

301. *Comm. on Isaiah* 236 on 10:11 as cited in Wedderburn, "Apostolic Decree," 385.

302. For a full presentation of this view, see Wedderburn, "Apostolic Decree," 362–89.

303. Philo, *Spec. Laws* 2.15 (§ 62).

304. 2 Cor. 1:19; 1 Thess. 1:1; 2 Thess. 1:1.

305. For example, Witherington, *Acts*, 468; Barrett, *Acts*, 2.741.

306. Deut. 29:28; Jer. 32:37.

307. Str-B, 2:741.

308. See *m. Qidd.* 3:12.

309. C. J. Hemer, "The Adjective Phrygia," *JTS* 27 (1976): 122–26; idem, "Phrygia: A Further Note," *JTS* 28 (1977): 99–101.

310. Mitchell, *Anatolia*, 2:3.

311. See, for example, Fitzmyer, *Acts*, 578.

312. Mitchell, *Anatolia*, 2:3.

313. On Bithynia, see T. R. S. Broughton & S. Mitchell, "Bithynia," *OCD*[3], 244–45; and A. Sheppard, "Bithynia," *ABD*, 1:750–53.

314. Eusebius, *Eccl. Hist.* 3.4.

315. Witherington, *Acts*, 485.

316. C. Gempf, "Neapolis," *ABD*, 4:1052.

317. On Roman colonization, see A. N. Sherwin-White and B. M. Levick, "Colonization, Roman," *OCD*[3], 364.

318. C. Koukouli-Chrysantaki, "Colonia Iulia Augusta Philippensis," in Bakirtzis and Koester, *Philippi*, 21.

319. See Schürer, *HJP*[2], 2:439–41; 3:1:65; Str-B, 2:742; W. Schrage, "συναγωγή," *TDNT*, 7:814; H. Greeven, "προσευχή," *TDNT*, 2:808. For further arguments for this conclusion, see D. L. Matson, *Household Conversion Narratives in Acts* (JSNTSup 123; Sheffield: University Press, 1996), 145–46.

320. Koukouli-Chrysantaki, "Philippensis," 28–35.

321. *m. Meg.* 1:4; 4:3.

322. Hemer, *Book of Acts*, 114.

323. Homer, *Iliad* 4.141–42.

324. Pliny, *Nat. Hist.* 7.56.195.

325. For references, see C. J. Hemer, "Lydia and the Purple Trade," in *New Documents*, 3:54.

326. *IG* 10:2:1:291.

327. Koukouli-Chrysantaki, "Philippensis," 26.

328. Van der Horst, *Ancient Jewish Epitaphs*, 136.

329. See L. Maurizio, "Anthropology and Spirit Possession: A Consideration of the Pythia's Role at Delphi," *JHS* 115 (1995): 69–86, esp. 83–86.

330. On the Python, see J. W. van Henten, "Python," *DDD²*, 669–71. See also C. Arnold, *Powers of Darkness*, 32–33; Plutarch, *De Defectu Oraculorum* 9 (414e).

331. See 2 Kings 22:14; Ps. 54(57):3; 77(78):35, 56.

332. See C. Breytenbach, "Hypsistos," *DDD²*, 439–43; Trebilco, "Paul and Silas—'Servants of the Most High God' (Acts 16:16–18)," *JSNT* 36 (1989): 51–73.

333. *m. Sanh.* 7:7.

334. Origen, *De Principiis* 3.4.5.

335. *Clementine Homilies* 9.16.

336. H. Koester, "Paul and Philippi: The Evidence from Early Christian Literature," in *Philippi*, 52.

337. For the many references, see Schürer, *HJP²*, 3.1.150–56.

338. Tacitus, *Histories* 5.5.

339. As cited in Fitzmyer, *Acts*, 587; Cicero, *De legibus* 2.8.19.

340. Rapske, *Roman Custody*, 126.

341. Ibid., 127.

342. Acts 13:52; Gal. 5:22.

343. Barrett, *Acts*, 2:800.

344. As cited in Rapske, *Roman Custody*, 49; Livy 10.9.4; see also, Cicero, *De Republica* 2.31.

345. Ulpian in *Digesta* 48.6.7.

346. Strabo, *Geog.* 7.7.4; 7. Frag. 24.

347. For more information about Thessalonica, see Gill, "Macedonia," 414–15; H. L. Hendrix, "Thessalonica," *ABD*, 6:523–27.

348. I. Levinskaya, *The Book of Acts in Its Diaspora Setting* (BAFCS 5; Grand Rapids: Eerdmans, 1996), 155.

349. See F. M. Gillman, "Jason," *ABD*, 3:649.

350. Dio Cassius, *Roman History* 56.25.5–6.

351. E. A. Judge, "The Decrees of Caesar at Thessalonica," *RTR* 30 (1971): 3–4; Dio Cassius, *Roman History* 57.15.8.

352. Judge, "Decrees of Caesar," 6.

353. See McRay, *Archaeology*, 295–97.

354. See Gill, "Macedonia," 415–17.

355. See Levinskaya, *Diaspora Setting*, 158–62.

356. See McRay, *Archaeology*, 302–8.

357. For a good description of the characteristics and beliefs of these two philosophical schools, see E. Ferguson, *Backgrounds of Early Christianity*, 2d ed. (Grand Rapids: Eerdmans, 1993), 333–56; T. Schmeller, "Stoics, Stoicism," *ABD*, 6:210–14; E. Asmis, "Epicureanism," *ABD*, 2:559–61.

358. Cited in W. Meeks, *The Moral World of the First Christians* (LEC; Philadelphia: Westminster, 1986), 59; *Epistle to Menoeceus* = Diogenes Laertius 10.13f.

359. See Hemer, *Book of Acts*, 117.

360. On the Areopagus, see H. M. Martin, "Areopagus," *ABD*, 1.370–72; T. J. Cadoux, "Areopagus," *OCD²*, 102–103.

361. C. Hemer, "Paul at Athens: A Topographical Note," *NTS* 20 (1974): 341–50, contends that Paul appeared before a formal session of the court in the agora in the immediate neighborhood of the Stoa Basileios.

362. Thucydides, *History of the Peloponnesian War* 2.38.5 (as cited by Bruce, *Acts*, 332).

363. For an outstanding concise treatment of this speech, see C. Gempf, "Athens, Paul at," *DPL*, 51–54.

364. Williams, *Acts*, 297.

365. *Description of Greece* 1:1:14.

366. *Life of Apollonius of Tyana* 6:3:5.

367. *Lives of Philosophers* 1:110.

368. Quoted in Bruce, *Acts*, 339.

369. Ibid.

370. Eusebius, *Eccl. Hist.* 4.23.3.

371. On the city of Corinth, see J. Murphy-O'Connor, "Corinth," *ABD*, 1:1134–39; idem, *St. Paul's Corinth: Texts and Archaeology* (GNS 6; Wilmington, Del.: Liturgical Press, 1983); idem, "The Corinth That Paul Saw," *BA* 47 (1984): 147–59; J. Wiseman, "Corinth and Rome I: 228 B.C.–A.D. 267," *ANRW*, II.7.1 (1979), 438–548; V. P. Furnish, "Corinth in Paul's Time: What Can Archaeology Tell Us?" *BAR* 14 (1988): 14–27.

372. Strabo, *Geog.* 8.6.20.

373. McRay, *Archaeology*, 315–17, has made a good case supporting the credibility of Strabo's account and the extensive sexual immorality in the city.

374. Bruce, *Acts*, 346 n. 4.

375. See P. Lampe, "Prisca," *ABD*, 5:467–68; idem, "Aquila," *ABD*, 1:319–20.

376. Philo, *Embassy* 159–61; Suetonius, *Tib.* 36.

377. Dio Cassius, *Roman History* 60:6 (as cited in Bruce, *History*, 295).

378. Suetonius, *Claud.* 25.4.

379. See P. W. Barnett, "Tentmaking," *DPL*, 925–27.

380. P. Lampe, "Paulus—Zeltmacher," *BZ* 31 (1987): 256–61.

381. Murphy-O'Connor, "Corinth," 149.

382. *Pirqe ʾAbot* 2.12 (as cited in Barnett, "Tentmaking," *DPL*, 927).

383. See Levinskaya, *Diaspora Setting*, 162–66.

384. On Gallio, see K. Haacker, "Gallio," *ABD*, 2:901–903; see also B. W. Winter, "Gallio's Ruling on the Legal Status of Early Christianity (Acts 18:14–15)," *TynBul* 50 (1999): 213–24.

385. The entire Greek text is given in Foakes-Jackson and Lake, *Beginnings*, 5:460–64. An English translation of the text can be found in C. K. Barrett, *The New Testament Background: Selected Documents*, rev. and exp. ed. (San Francisco: Harper, 1989), 51–52.

386. The translation is from Barrett, *Background*, 51–52. The brackets indicate places where the text has been restored. In the original, the text is broken away at these points.

387. Winter, "Gallio's Ruling," 222.

388. Ibid., 221.

389. Jewish traditions about the Nazirite vow are contained in the tractate "Nazir" in the Mishnah (see the English translation by H. Danby, *The Mishnah* [Oxford: Oxford University Press, 1933], 280–93).

390. On Apollos, see B. B. Blue, "Apollos," *DPL*, 37–39 and L. D. Hurst, "Apollos," *ABD*, 1:301.

391. For more information about Ephesus, see Trebilco, "Asia," 302–57; R. Oster, "Ephesus," *ABD*, 2:542–49; and C. E. Arnold, "Ephesus," *DPL*, 249–53. Serious students will also want to consult, Helmut Koester, ed., *Ephesus: Metropolis of Asia* (HTS 41; Valley Forge, Penn.: Trinity Press, 1995).

392. Strabo, *Geog.* 14.1.24.

393. Aelius Aristides, *Orat.* 23.24.

394. Marshall, *Acts*, 306; Witherington, *Acts*, 570.

395. S. M. Baugh, "Paul and Ephesus: The Apostle Among His Contemporaries," Unpublished Ph.D. Dissertation (Irvine, Calif.: University of California Press, 1990): 81–82.

396. Levinskaya, *Diaspora Setting*, 146; *Inschriften von Ephesos* 1251.

397. This was granted by Antiochus II Theos (287–246 B.C.); Josephus, *Ant.* 12.4.10 §225.

398. For a discussion of Jews in Ephesus, see Levinskaya, *Diaspora Setting*, 143–48.

399. *Inschriften von Ephesos* 1676, 1677; D. Knibbe and B. Iplikcioglu, "Neue Inschriften aus Ephesos IX," *JOAIW* 55, Hauptblatt 107 no. 4101 (1984). See the discussion in Baugh, "Paul and Ephesus," 82–86.

400. Baugh, "Paul in Ephesus," 99.

401. Trebilco, "Asia," 312–14.

402. This translation is from: H. D. Betz, ed., *The Greek Magical Papyri in Translation* (Chicago: University of Chicago Press, 1986), 96; *Papyrus Graecae Magicae* 4:3007–3025.

403. See Acts 24:17; Rom. 15:25–31; 1 Cor. 16:1–4; 2 Cor. 8–9.

404. The key study on this theme has been written by R. Oster, "The Ephesian Artemis as an Opponent of Early Christianity," *JAC* 19 (1976): 24–44.

405. See R. A. Kearsley, "Asiarch," in *ABD*, 1:495–97; Baugh, "Paul in Ephesus," 132–64.

406. Cited in Trebilco, "Asia," 347; Dio Chrysostom, *Orationes* 34.33.

407. Bruce, *Acts*, 381.

408. See Riesner, *Paul's Early Period*, 316.

409. See N. Purcell, "Houses, Italian," OCD^3, 731–32.

410. Bruce, *Acts*, 387.

411. See the chart in Witherington, *Acts*, 610.

412. See Witherington, *Acts*, 616; Mark 10:41–45; Rom. 12:16; 2 Cor. 10:1; Phil. 2:3.

413. Ezek. 33:2–5; see also Ezek. 3:18–21.

414. Homer, *Odyssey* 8163.

415. H. Beyer, "ἐπίσκοπος," *TDNT*, 2:610; Plato, *Leges* 8.849a.

416. G. A. Deissmann, *Bible Studies* (Edinburgh: T. & T. Clark, 1923), 230–31; MM, 244–45.

417. Philo, *Heir* 30.

418. 1 Tim. 1:19–20; 4:1–3; 2 Tim. 2:17–18; 3:1–9.

419. 1 Cor. 9:12–15; 2 Cor. 11:7–11; 1 Thess. 2:9.

420. For references, see Barrett, *Acts*, 2:983.

421. Witherington, *Acts*, 626.

422. On Cos, see W. A. Laidlay and S. Sherwin-White, "Cos," OCD^3, 403–4.

423. Hemer, *Book of Acts*, 125.

424. Barrett, *Acts*, 2:990–91, reaches a similar conclusion.

425. On Ptolemais, see M. Dothan & Z. Goldmann, "Acco," *NEAE*, 1:16–17; M. Dothan, "Acco," *ABD*, 1:50–53; Schürer, HJP^2, 2:121–25.

426. Josephus, *J.W.* 3.3.1 §35.

427. Ibid., 2.18.5 §477.

428. Eusebius, *Eccl. Hist.* 3.31; 5.24; see also 3.39.

429. Isa. 20:2–4; see also 1 Kings 11:29–39; Jer. 27:1–22; Ezek. 4–5.

430. Lake and Cadbury, *Beginnings*, 4:269.

431. Xenophon, *Hellenica* 5.3.1.

432. On Mnason, see J. Paulien, "Mnason," *ABD*, 4:881–82.

433. Barrett, *Acts*, 2:1003.

434. For example, Bruce, *Acts*, 404–405.

435. See Acts 24:17; Rom. 15:25–27, 31; Gal. 2:10; 1 Cor. 16:1–4; 2 Cor. 8:1–7; 9:1–5.

436. Josephus, *Ant.* 19.6.1 §§293–294.

437. Fitzmyer, *Acts*, 694; *m. ʾOhal.* 2.3.

438. Jeremias, *Jerusalem*, 210.

439. Josephus, *J.W.* 5.5.8 §244.

440. Ibid., 5.5.8 §243.

441. Rapske, *Roman Custody*, 140.

442. See Rapske, *Roman Custody*, 141–42.

443. Philostratus, *Life of Apollonius* 6.34.

444. G. H. R. Horsley, "The Fiction of 'Jewish Greek,'" in *New Documents*, 5:23.

445. This is the conclusion of W. C. van Unnik, *Tarsus or Jerusalem: The City of Paul's Youth* (London: Epworth Press, 1962), 52.

446. See Hengel, *Pre-Christian Paul*, 18–39.

447. H. W. Tajra, *The Trial of St. Paul* (WUNT 2/35; Tübingen: Mohr Siebeck, 1989), 86.

448. Barclay, *Diaspora*, 383.

449. Marshall, *Acts*, 355.

450. Rapske, *Roman Custody*, 139.

451. Suetonius, *Claudius* 25; Epictetus, *Disc.* 3.24.41.

452. Sherwin-White, *Roman Law*, 154–55.

453. Dio Cassius 60.17.5–7.

454. Tajra, *Trial*, 75.

455. W. M. Ramsay, *St. Paul the Traveler and Roman Citizen* (New York: G. P. Putnam's Sons, 1896), 30–32; Bruce, *Paul*, 37–40; idem, *New Testament History*, 234–35; C. J. Hemer, "The Name of Paul," *TynBul* 36 (1986): 183; Tajra, *Trial*, 83.

456. Hengel, *Pre-Christian Paul*, 11–14.

457. Ibid., 2.8.14 §165.

458. E.g. Ps. 49:15; Isa. 26:19; Hos. 6:1–3; 13:14.

459. See 2 Macc. 7:9, 11, 14, 22–23, 29; see also 2 Macc. 12:43–44; 14:46.

460. *m. Sanh.* 10.1.

461. Dunn, *Acts*, 304, takes a similar position.

462. Johnson, *Acts*, 399.

463. See Schürer, *HJP²*, 2:223–25; A. J. Saldarini, "Sanhedrin," *ABD*, 5:977–78.

464. E. A. Judge in *New Documents*, 1:78.

465. LSJ, s.v.

466. On Antipatris, see Murphy-O'Connor, *Holy Land*, 161–63; Schürer, *HJP²*, 2:167–68; M. Kochavi, "Antipatris," *ABD*, 1:273–74.

467. Josephus, *Ant.* 1.21.9 §417.

468. Rapske, *Roman Custody*, 155.

469. Josephus, *J.W.* 1.21.5 §408.

470. See Tajra, *Trial*, 120. See also B. Winter, "The Importance of the *captatio benevolentiae* in the Speeches of Tertullus and Paul in Acts 24:1–21," *JTS* 42 (1991): 505–31.

471. Cited in Sherwin-White, *Roman Law*, 51.

472. E.g. Prov. 19:25; 21:24; 22:10.

473. Josephus, *J.W.* 13.5.9 §171.

474. Tajra, *Trial*, 122; Fitzmyer, *Acts*, 734.

475. Tajra, *Trial*, 124.

476. B. Winter, "Official Proceedings and the Forensic Speeches in Acts 24–26," in *The Book of Acts in Its Ancient Literary Setting* (BAFCS 1; Grand Rapids: Eerdmans, 1993), 334.

477. E. Haenchen, *The Acts of the Apostles* (Oxford: Basil Blackwell, 1971), 654, n. 2 (based on an explanation by Adolf Schlatter). See now also Witherington, *Acts*, 654; Hemer, *Book of Acts*, 192.

478. For a discussion of the many Jewish texts that teach a general resurrection, see Str-B, 4:2:1166–98.

479. Sherwin-White, *Roman Law*, 52.

480. Rapske, *Roman Custody*, 172.

481. Josephus, *Ant.* 19.9.1 §354; Schürer, *HJP²*, 1:461.

482. Ibid., 20.7.2 §142.

483. Ibid., 20.7.1 §§139–43.

484. Plato, *Republic* 390b; 430c.

485. For the many references, see W. Grundmann, "ἐγκράτεια," *TDNT*, 2:340–41.

486. Josephus, *Ant.* 20.8.9 §182 [Loeb edition].

487. See Tajra, *Trial*, 134.

488. Josephus, *Ant.* 20.8.8 §179.

489. Tajra, *Trial*, 135.

490. Ibid., 140.

491. Rapske, *Roman Custody*, 186–89; Tajra, *Trial*, 145–46.

492. Rapske, *Roman Custody*, 188.

493. Tajra, *Trial*, 148.

494. On Bernice, see D. C. Braund, "Bernice," *ABD*, 1:677–78; Schürer, *HJP²*, 1:474–79.

495. Josephus, *Ant.* 20.7.3 §145.

496. This is the view of Larkin, *Acts*, 349.

497. Hemer, *Book of Acts*, 348–49.

498. As cited in Fitzmyer, *Acts*, 750; Ulpian, *Digest* 48.17.1.

499. As cited in Bruce, *Acts*, 457, n. 28; Appian, *Civil War* 3.54.

500. LSJ, 1915–16.

501. Josephus, *Ant.* 19.9.2 §365.

502. Fitzmyer, *Acts*, 752.

503. Ulpian, *Digest* 49.6.1.

504. Bruce, *Acts*, 464.

505. Williams, *Acts*, 417.

506. Euripides, *Bacchae* 795.

507. For a discussion and numerous references in Greek literature, see U. Luck, "σώφρων κτλ.," *TDNT*, 7:1098–1100.

508. Epictetus, *Discourses* 2.12.17; Plato, *Gorgias* 485D; Plutarch, *Moralia* 777B.

509. Sherwin-White, *Roman Law*, 65.

510. C. J. Thornton, *Der Zeuge des Zeugens: Lukas als Historiker der Paulusreisen* (WUNT 56; Tübingen: Mohr Siebeck, 1991), 366.

511. *ILS* 2683 (= *CIL* 3.6687) and *IGRR* 3.1136 (=*OGIS* 421). For a discussion of these texts, see Broughton, "Roman Army," 443–44; Hemer, *Book of Acts*, 132–33, n. 96.

512. See the references in Barrett, *Acts*, 2:1183; Johnson, *Acts*, 445.

513. Witherington, *Acts*, 761.

514. On Myra, see S. Mitchell, "Myra," *OCD³*, 1016; E. M. Yamauchi, "Myra," *ABD*, 4:939–40.

515. Strabo, *Geog.* 14.2.15.

516. Hemer, *Book of Acts*, 135, note 102 (summarizing the study of L. Casson).

517. Ibid., 135–36.

518. Rapske, "Acts, Travel and Shipwreck," 22; Vegetius, *De re militari* 4:39; Pliny, *Nat. Hist.* 2.47.122.

519. Suetonius, *Claudius* 18.

520. See also Josephus, *Ant.* 17.6.4 §165; Philo, *Moses* 2.23; *Spec. Laws* 1:186; 2:193; *m. Yoma* 8:1.

521. Rapske, "Acts, Travel and Shipwreck," 23–24; Hemer, *Book of Acts*, 137–38.

522. Riesner, *Paul's Early Period*, 224–24; Hemer, *Book of Acts*, 137–38.

523. Barrett, *Acts*, 2:1190.

524. Rapske, "Acts, Travel, and Shipwreck," 28.

525. *CIL* 8.26652.

526. See Hemer, *Book of Acts*, 141–42; idem, "Euraquilo and Melita," *JTS* 26 (1975): 100–11.

527. "Gregale," *Encyclopædia Britannica Online.* http://www.eb.com:180/bol/topic?idxref=38 6818 [Accessed 1 January 2001].

528. Lake and Cadbury, *Beginnings*, 4:332.

529. For a description of the various views, see H. J. Cadbury, "Note XXVIII. Ὑποζώματα," in *Beginnings*, 5:345–54. Taking the view presented here is Hemer, *Book of Acts*, 143, n. 120.

530. N. Purcell, "Syrtes," *OCD*[3], 1466.

531. Dio Chrysostom, *Orationes* 5.8–9.

532. This is the view of Barrett, *Acts*, 2:1197.

533. Hemer, *Book of Acts*, 143.

534. J. Smith, *The Voyage and Shipwreck of St. Paul*, 4th ed. (Grand Rapids: Baker, 1978), 126–28. His calculations are accepted by most commentators.

535. M. Cary and W. M. Murray, "Adriatic Sea," *OCD*[3], 14; Hemer, *Book of Acts*, 145–46.

536. Hemer, *Book of Acts*, 147 (in reliance on a study by L. Casson).

537. Herodotus, *History* 2.5.

538. On the various anchors used on Greek and Roman vessels, see D. Haldane, "Anchors of Antiquity," *BA* 53.1 (1990): 19–24.

539. 1 Sam. 14:45; see also 2 Sam. 14:11; 1 Kings 1:52.

540. Josephus, *Vita* 3 §15.

541. Hirschfeld, "Ship," 28.

542. Smith, *Voyage*, 141, n. 2.

543. Bruce, *Acts*, 494; Hemer, *Book of Acts*, 150; Smith, *Voyage*, 143.

544. E. A. Yamauchi, "On the Road With Paul: The Ease—and Dangers—of Travel in the Ancient World," *CH* 14.3 (1995): 19.

545. J. M. Gilchrist, "The Historicity of Paul's Shipwreck," *JSNT* 61 (1996): 29.

546. *Code of Justinian* 9.4.4.

547. Hemer, *Book of Acts*, 152; Bruce, *Acts*, 497.

548. BAGD, s.v.

549. P. W. van der Horst, "Dike," *DDD*[2], 251–52.

550. *IGRR* 1.512 = *IG* 14.601; see C. J. Hemer, "First Person Narrative in Acts 27–28," *TynBul* 36 (1985): 100.

551. Mark 6:5; 8:23, 25; Luke 4:40; 13:13; Mark 5:23.

552. Barrett, *Acts*, 2:1226.

553. On these gods, see K. Dowden, "Dioskouroi," *DDD*[2], 258–59; R. C. T. Parker, "Dioscuri," *OCD*[3], 484.

554. See G. J. Toomer, "Constellations and Named Stars," *OCD*[3], 382.

555. On Syracuse, see A. Betz, "Syracuse," *ABD*, 6:270–71.

556. Homer, *Odyssey* 12.101–102; Horace, *Carmina* 1.27.19.

557. R. Brändle and E. W. Stegemann, "Die Entstehung der Ersten 'Christliche Gemeinde' Roms im Kontext der Jüdischen Gemeinden," *NTS* 42 (1996): 10–11.

558. Suetonius, *Claud.* 25.

559. Horace, *Satirae* 1.5.3–6.

560. J. D. Wineland, "Three Taverns," *ABD*, 6:544.

561. Sherwin-White, *Roman Society*, 110; Rapske, *Roman Custody*, 176–77; Tajra, *Trial*, 179.

562. Rapske, *Roman Custody*, 181.

563. Schürer, *HJP*[2], 3:1:95–96.

564. Suetonius, *Claud.* 25; see comments on Acts 18:2.

565. Bruce, *Acts*, 507.

566. See Acts 13:43; 14:1–2; 17:4–5, 12.

567. See Matt. 13:13; Mark 4:12; Luke 8:10; John 12:39–40.

568. Marshall, *Acts*, 425.

569. So also Hemer, *Book of Acts*, 190.

570. Rapske, *Roman Custody*, 325–26.

Sidebar and Chart Notes

A-1. See J. Murphy-O'Connor, "The Cenacle—Topographical Setting for Acts 2:44–45," in *The Book of Acts in Its Palestinian Setting*, ed. R. Bauckham (BAFCS 4; Grand Rapids: Eerdmans, 1995), 303–21.

A-2. Epiphanius, *De mensuris et ponderibus* 14 (as cited in J. Murphy-O'Connor, "The Cenacle," 307).

A-3. See M. Broshi, "Excavations in the House of Caiaphas, Mount Zion," in *Jerusalem Revealed: Archaeology in the Holy City 1968–1974* (New Haven, Conn.: Yale University Press, 1976), 57–60.

A-4. For additional information about the "Cenacle," see "Cenaculum," *ODCC*[3], 313, and J. Finegan, *The Archaeology of the New Testament: The Life of Jesus and the Beginning of the Early Church* (Princeton, N.J.: Princeton University Press, 1969), 147–52; J. Murphy-O'Connor, *The Holy Land*, 4th ed. Rev. and expanded, *OAG* (Oxford: University Press, 1998), 105–6.

A-5. See J. Huehnergard, "Languages (Introductory)," *ABD*, 4.155-70.

A-6. See the discussion of evidence for Jewish presence in most of these countries in Schürer, *HJP²*, 3.1-86; Jeremias, *Jerusalem*, 58-73.

A-7. On the languages of Asia Minor, see S. Mitchell, *Anatolia. Land, Men, and Gods in Asia Minor*, 2 vols. (Oxford: Clarendon Press, 1993), 1.173-76.

A-8. Philo, *Embassy* 282.

A-9. F. Millar, *The Roman Near East: 31* B.C.–A.D. (Cambridge, Mass.: Harvard University Press, 1993), 401-2.

A-10. Schürer, *HJP²*, 3:16-17; Millar, *Roman Near East*, 404-5; M. Hengel & A. M. Schwemer, *Paul: Between Damascus and Antioch. The Unknown Years* (Louisville, Ky.: Westminster John Knox Press, 1997), 110-26.

A-11. Josephus, *Ant.* 18.2.33–35 §37.

A-12. Josephus, *J.W.* 5.4.2 §144.

A-13. *b. Yoma* 25a (as cited in Schürer, *HJP³*, 2:224).

A-14. Finegan, *Archaeology*, 132.

A-15. Str-B, 2:637.

A-16. *m. Soṭah* 9:15.

A-17. Josephus, *Ant.* 20.5.1 §97–99.

A-18. *m. Mak.* 3:12–14.

A-19. For discussion, see R. Riesner, "Synagogues in Jerusalem," *The Book of Acts in Its Palestinian Setting* (BAFCS 4; Grand Rapids: Eerdmans, 1996), 192–200; P. W. van der Horst, "Was the Synagogue a Place of Sabbath Worship Before 70 CE?" in *Jews, Christians, and Polytheists in the Ancient Synagogue: Cultural Interaction During the Graeco-Roman Period*, ed. S. Fine (BSHJ; New York: Routledge, 1999), 18–43; Hengel, "Between Jesus and Paul," 17–18.

A-20. *Corpus Inscription Judaicarum*, 2:333 (no. 1404). Translation from Riesner, "Synagogues," 193.

A-21. Riesner, "Synagogues," 197–98.

A-22. M. Hengel, *The Pre-Christian Paul* (Philadelphia: Trinity Press, 1991), 68–69; Riesner, "Synagogues," 205; Hemer, *Book of Acts*, 176.

A-23. F. F. Bruce, *The Book of Acts*, rev. ed. (NICNT; Grand Rapids: Eerdmans, 1988), 134.

A-24. Philo, *Moses* 1.5 (§20–24) (de Jonge edition).

A-25. On the Samaritans, see Schürer, *HJP²*, 2.15–20; Jeremias, *Jerusalem*, 352–58; R. T. Anderson, "Samaritans," *ABD*, 5.940–47; H. G. M. Williamson, "Samaritans," *DJG*, 724–28; K. Haacker, "Samaritan," *NIDNTT*, 3.449–67.

A-26. See also Josephus, *Ant.* 9.14.3 §288.

A-27. Josephus, *Ant.* 12.5.5 §§258–61.

A-28. Sir. 50:25–26.

A-29. Jeremias, *Jerusalem*, 354; *Pirqe R. Eliezer* 38.

A-30. Justin, *First Apology* 26.

A-31. See J. Scheid, "Semo Sancus Dius Fidius," *OCD³*, 1383.

A-32. P. Lond 121.560–71 (= *PGM*, VII.560–71).

A-33. On eunuchs, see the excellent discussion in F. S. Spencer, *The Portrait of Philip in Acts: A Study of Roles and Relations* (JSNTSup 67; Sheffield: JSOT Press, 1992), 166–72.

A-34. Herodotus, *Hist.* 8.104–106; Lucian, *The Eunuch* 6.

A-35. Josephus, *Ant.* 4.8.40 §§290–91.

A-36. This is adapted from Ajith Fernando, *Acts* (NIVAC; Grand Rapids: Zondervan, 1998), 287–91.

A-37. On Damascus, see Hengel, *Paul*, 55–61; J. McRay, *Archaeology & the New Testament* (Grand Rapids: Baker, 1991), 232–34.

A-38. Schürer, *HJP²*, 2.36.

A-39. Josephus, *J.W.* 2.20.2 §561; 7.6.7 §368.

A-40. On Tarsus, see W. W. Gasque, "Tarsus," *ABD*, 6.333–34; Hengel & Schwemer, *Paul*, 151–77; Hengel, *Pre-Christian Paul*, 1–6; Hemer, "Tarsus," *ISBE*, 4:734–36.

A-41. Strabo, *Geog.* 14.5.13.

A-42. McRay, *Archaeology*, 235.

A-43. S. Mitchell, "Archaeology in Asia Minor 1990–1998," *AR* 45 (1999): 190.

A-44. See Holum, et al., "Caesarea," *NEAE*, 1:271–91.

A-45. R. L. Hohlfelder, "Herod the Great's City on the Sea," *National Geographic* 171/72 (1987): 260–79. The video was featured on National Geographic's "Explorer," but, unfortunately, is not available for purchase from the society.

A-46. See http://digcaesarea.org/ [Accessed 1 January 2001].

A-47. Josephus, *J.W.* 1.21.5–8 §§408–15.

A-48. On Antioch of Syria, see: F. W. Norris, "Antioch," *ABD*, 1:269; J. M. McRay, "Antioch on the Orontes," *DPL*, 23–25; R. E. Brown and J. P. Meier, *Antioch and Rome* (New York: Paulist Press, 1983); G. Downey, *A History of Antioch in Syria from Seleucus to the Arab Conquest* (Princeton, N. J.: Princeton University Press, 1961); W. A. Meeks and R. L. Wilken, *Jews and Christians in Antioch in the First Four Centuries of the Common Era* (SBS 13; Missoula, Mont.: Scholar's Press, 1978).

A-49. Strabo, *Geog.* 16,2:5; cf. Diodorus Siculus 17:52 and Pliny *Nat. Hist.* 6:122. See Hengel & Schwemer, *Paul*, 186.

A-50. Hengel & Schwemer, *Paul*, 196.

A-51. Ibid.,184; Riesner, *Paul's Early Period*, 113–14 (the ancient account is in the *Chronicle of Malalas*).

A-52. Hengel & Schwemer, *Paul*, 205, argue for a much longer period of ministry in Antioch and Syria. Witherington, *Acts*, 83 and F. F. Bruce, "Paul the Apostle," *ISBE*, 3:709, suggest a much longer time in Tarsus and a shorter time in Antioch and Syria.

A-53. For the entire account, see Philo, *Flaccus*; see also Schürer, *HJP²*, 1:389–98.

A-54. See Josephus, *Ant.* 18.8.1–9 §§257–309.

A-55. This account of hostilities in Antioch is only recorded in the *Chronicle* of Malalas (10:315). See the discussion in Hengel & Schwemer, *Paul*, 184–86.

A-56. Suetonius, *Claud.* 18.

A-57. Josephus, *Ant.* 20.2.5 §§51–53.

A-58. Eusebius, *Eccl. Hist.* 6.14.

A-59. Ibid., 3.39.

A-60. Ibid., 2.16.

A-61. On Mark and Egyptian Christianity, see B. Pearson, "Christianity in Egypt," *ABD*, 1:954–60.

A-62. See also Hemer, *Book of Acts*, 359–62.

A-63. Eusebius, *Eccl. Hist.* 2.25.

A-64. Josephus, *Ant.* 19.8.2 §§343–50.

A-65. On Cyprus, see J. McRay, "Cyprus," *ABD*, 1:1228–30; H. W. Catling, "Cyprus," *OCD³*, 419–20; A. Nobbs, "Cyprus," in *Graeco-Roman Setting*, 279–89; D. W. J. Gill, "Paul's Travels Through Cyprus (Acts 13:4–12)," *TB* 46 (1995): 219–28.

A-66. See 1 Macc. 15:23; 2 Macc. 12:2; Philo, *Embassy* 282.

A-67. Schürer, *HJP²*, 2:68–69; Dio Cassius 68.32.1–3 .

A-68. *PGM*, IV:930–55.

A-69. On Roman names, see H. Solin, "Names, Personal, Roman," *OCD³*, 1024-26.

A-70. On Antioch near Pisidia, see Mitchell and Waelkens, *Pisidian Antioch*; S. Mitchell, "Antioch of Pisidia," *ABD*, 1:264–65; idem, "Antioch," *OCD³*, 107; idem, *Anatolia*, 2:7–8; B. van Elderen, "Antioch (Pisidian)," *ISBE*, 1:142.

A-71. A. N. Sherwin-White and B. M. Levick, "Colonization, Roman," *OCD³*, 364.

A-72. Mitchell, "Antioch of Pisidia," 264.

A-73. Josephus, *Ant.* 12.3.4 §§145–53.

A-74. Mitchell, *Anatolia*, 2:10.

A-75. Mitchell & Waelkens, *Pisidian Antioch*, 32–33.

A-76. Schürer, *HJP²*, 2:433–37; 3:92–103; *New Documents*, 4:213–20 (§113).

A-77. On Iconium, see W. W. Gasque, "Iconium," *ABD*, 3:357–58; D. A. Hagner, "Iconium," *ISBE*, 2:792–93.

A-78. Bruce, *Acts*, 272.

A-79. D. H. French, "Acts and the Roman Roads of Asia Minor," *Graeco-Roman Setting*, 52, 55.

A-80. C. Breytenbach, *Paulus und Barnabas in der Provinz Galatien. Studien zu Apostelgeschichte 13f.; 16,6; 18,23 und den Adressaten des Galaterbriefes* (AGJU 38; Leiden: Brill, 1996), 162–63.

A-81. Breytenbach, *Provinz Galatien*, 163–64.

A-82. On Lystra, see D. S. Potter, "Lystra," *ABD*, 4:426–27; D. A. Hagner, "Lystra," *ISBE*, 3:192–93.

A-83. Breytenbach, *Provinz Galatien*, 165.

A-84. See B. van Elderen, "Some Archaeological Observations on Paul's First Missionary Journey," in *Apostolic History and the Gospel: Biblical and Historical Essays Presented to F. F. Bruce on his 60th Birthday*, eds. W. W. Gasque and R. P. Martin (Grand Rapids: Eerdmans, 1970), 156–61.

A-85. *Jubilees* 15:26.

A-86. Josephus, *Ant.* 13.9.1 §254.

A-87. Judith 14:10; see also Est. 8:17 in the LXX version.

A-88. R. G. Hall, "Circumcision," *ABD*, 1:1027; Martial, *Epigrams* 7.35, 82.

A-89. 1 Macc. 1:48, 60–61; 2 Macc. 6:10; *4 Macc.* 4:25.

A-90. See the discussion in J. M. G. Barclay, *Jews in the Mediterranean Diaspora: From Alexander to Trajan, 323 BCE–117 CE* (Edinburgh: T. & T. Clark, 1996), 438–39; Philo, *Spec. Laws* 1.2.

A-91. Barclay, *Jews*, 1027.

A-92. For more extensive discussion, see the following sources: Advocates of the view that Acts 15 = Gal. 2:1–10 (the "North Galatia" view): Barrett, *Acts*, 2:xxxvi-xli; Fitzmyer, *Acts*, 538–39; Dunn, *Acts*, 195–97; D. J. Williams, *Acts* (GNC; San Francisco: Harper, 1985), 246–50. Advocates of the view that Acts 11:27–30 and 12:25 = Gal. 2:1–10 (the "South Galatia" view): Mitchell, *Anatolia*, 2:5; Witherington, *Acts*, 440–45; Bruce, *Acts*, 283–85; Hemer, *Book of Acts*, 277–307; Riesner, *Paul's Early Period*, 286–91; Marshall, *Acts*, 244–47.

A-93. On Troas, see C. J. Hemer, "Alexandria Troas," *TynBul* 26 (1975): 79–112; E. M. Yamauchi, "Troas," *ABD*, 6:666–667; Trebilco, "Asia," in *Graeco-Roman Setting*, 357–59.

A-94. Strabo, *Geog.* 13.1.26.

A-95. Mitchell, "Archaeology in Asia Minor," 138–39.

A-96. On Macedonia, see D. W. J. Gill, "Macedonia," in *Graeco-Roman Setting*, 397–417; F. Papazoglou, "Macedonia Under the Romans," in *Macedonia: 4000 Years of Greek History and Civilization*, ed. M. M. Sakellariou (Athens: Ekdotike Athenon S. A., 1983), 192–221.

A-97. Papazoglou, "Macedonia Under the Romans," 204–7.

A-98. On Philippi, see H. L. Hendrix, "Philippi," *ABD*, 5:313–17; McRay, *Archaeology*, 283–88; and, especially, C. Bakirtzis and H. Koester, eds., *Philippi at the Time of Paul and After His Death* (Harrisburg, Penn.: Trinity Press International, 1998).

A-99. As cited in Rapske, *Roman Custody*, 125 n. 55; Cicero, *In Verrem* 2.5.142.

A-100. An outstanding article has been written on this topic: see K. P. Donfried, "The Cults of Thessalonica and the Thessalonian Correspondence," *NTS* 31 (1985): 336–56.

A-101. On this term, see G. H. R. Horsley, "The Politarchs," in *Graeco-Roman Setting*, 419–31; idem, "Politarchs," *ABD*, 5:384–89.

A-102. O. Broneer, "Athens: 'City of Idol Worship'," *BA* 21 (1958): 1–28.

A-103. Seneca, *Ad Marciam* 26.6 (as cited in N. C. Croy, "Hellenistic Philosophies and the Preaching of the Resurrection [Acts 17:18, 32]," *NovT* 39 [1997]: 34).

A-104. Lucretius, *De rerum Natura* 3.624–33 (as cited in Croy, "Hellenistic Philosophies," 30).

A-105. Epicurus in the Sovereign Maxims (in Diogenes Laertius, 10.139) as cited in Croy, "Hellenistic Philosophies," 30.

A-106. D. W. J. Gill, "In Search of the Social Élite in the Corinthian Church," *TynBul* 44 (1993): 333–34.

A-107. Wiseman, "Corinth and Rome," 516.

A-108. Described in a presentation made by Dr. James Wiseman on Nov. 21, 1999 in Boston, Mass. at the annual meeting of the Society of Biblical Literature.

A-109. On Alexandria, see A. K. Bowman, "Egypt," in *The Cambridge Ancient History*, vol. 10: *The Augustan Empire, 43 B.C.–A.D. 69*, 2d ed. (Cambridge: Cambridge University Press, 1996), 699–701; B. A. Pearson, "Alexandria," *ABD* 1.152–57 and D. W. Rathbone, "Alexandria," *OCD*³, 61–62.

A-110. The entire account is written up by Philo in his *Flaccus*.

A-111. The journal is *Jahreshefte des Österreichischen Archäologischen Instituts in Wien*.

A-112. H. Engelmann, D. Knibbe, and R. Merkelbach, eds., *Die Inschriften von Ephesos*, Inschriften Griechischer Städte aus Kleinasien (Bonn: Rudolf Habelt, 1980–84).

A-113. There is an extensive bibliography on Jewish magic in antiquity. See especially, P. S. Alexander, "Incantations and Books of Magic," in Schürer, *HJP*², 3:1:342–79; idem, "Jewish Elements in Gnosticism and Magic c. CE 70–CE 270," *CHJ*³, 1052–78;

A-114. M. Simon, *Verus Israel* (Oxford: Oxford University Press, 1986).

A-114. Josephus, *Ant.* 8.2.5 §§41–49.

A-115. For an English translation of the *Testament of Solomon*, see D. C. Duling, "Testament of Solomon," in *The Old Testament Pseudepigrapha*, vol. 1 (Garden City, N.Y.: Doubleday, 1983), 935–87.

A-116. For additional discussion, see C. E. Arnold, *Power and Magic* (Grand Rapids: Baker, 1997), 14–20.

A-117. Plutarch, *Quaestiones Convivales* 7.5.

A-118. M. Meyer and R. Smith, *Ancient Christian Magic* (San Francisco: Harper, 1994).

A-119. Pausanias, *Description of Greece* 4.31.8.

A-120. Numerous pictures of the extant cultic images of the Ephesian Artemis have been collected and published by R. Fleischer in two publications: *Artemis von Ephesus und verwandte Kultstatuen aus Anatolien und Syrien* (Leiden: Brill, 1973) and in "Artemis Ephesia," in *Lexicon Iconographicum Mythologiae Classicae*, vol. 2, Parts 1 & 2 (Zürich & München: Artemis, 1984).

A-121. For an extended discussion of this inscription, see *New Documents* 4:7–11; *Inschriften von Ephesos*, 6:2212.

A-122. *Inschriften von Ephesos*, 2:547.

A-123. As cited in Baugh, "Paul in Ephesus," 114; *Inschriften von Ephesos*, 2:585.

A-124. On Miletus, see E. Yamauchi, *The Archaeology of New Testament Cities in Western Asia Minor* (Grand Rapids: Baker, 1980), 115–27; Trebilco, "Asia," 360–62.

A-125. Josephus, *Ant.* 14.10.21 §§ 244–46.

A-126. Trebilco, *Jewish Communities*, 159–62.

A-127. Josephus, *J.W.* 2.12.2 §§229–30.

A-128. Josephus, *J.W.* 5.5.2 §§193–94.

A-129. An English translation is given and discussed in Barrett, *Background*, 53 (no. 50). See also the discussions in D. R. Edwards, "Gentiles, Court of the," *ABD*, 2:963; Schürer, *HJP*², 2:222.

A-130. Josephus, *J.W.* 2.13.5 §§261–63; see also *Ant.* 20.8.6 §171.

A-131. Fitzmyer, *Acts*, 700.

A-132. On the Sicarii, see Schürer, *HJP*², 1:463–64.

A-133. Josephus, *J.W.* 2.13.3 §§254–57.

A-134. On Roman citizenship, see A. N. Sherwin-White, *The Roman Citizenship*, 2d ed. (Oxford: Oxford University Press, 1974); idem, *Roman Law and Roman Society* (Grand Rapids: Baker, 1992), 144–62; Hengel, *Pre-Christian Paul*, 6–15; Rapske, *Roman Custody*, 83–90.

A-135. Sherwin-White, *Roman Law*, 147; Tajra, *Trial*, 83.

A-136. Philo, *Embassy* 155–57.

A-137. Josephus, *Ant.* 20.5.2 §103.

A-138. Ibid., 20.9.2 §§206–207.

A-139. Josephus, *J.W.* 2.17.9 §441.

A-140. On Felix, see Schürer, *HJP*², 1:460–66.

A-141. As cited in Schürer, *HJP*², 1:461; Tacitus, *Historiae* 5.9.

A-142. Tacitus, *Ann.* 12.54.

A-143. Josephus, *Ant.* 20.8.5 §160–65.

A-144. Josephus, *J.W.* 2.13.7 §270.

A-145. See B. Burrell, K. Gleason, and E. Netzer, "Uncovering Herod's Seaside Palace," *BAR* 19.3 (May/June 1993): 50–57, 96; L. I. Levine and E. Netzer, "Caesarea (Excavations West of the Theater: The Promontory Palace)," *NEAE*, 1:280–82.

A-146. Josephus, *Ant.* 20.8.9–11 §§182–96; *J.W.* 2.14.1 §271; on Festus, see Schürer, *HJP*², 1:467–68; J. B. Green, "Festus, Porcius," *ABD*, 2:794–95.

A-147. Josephus, *J.W.* 2.14.1 §272.

A-148. On Agrippa II, see Schürer, *HJP*², 1:471–83; D. C. Braund, "Agrippa," *ABD*, 1:99–100.

A-149. Josephus, *Ant.* 20.5.2 §104.

A-150. See Schürer, *HJP*², 1:475, for references.

A-151. Josephus, *Ant.* 20.9.7 §§219–22.

A-152. Josephus, *Life* 65 §§362–67.

A-153. See "Nicholas, St.," *ODCC*³, 1148.

A-154. On Crete, see W. A. Laidlaw, L. F. Nixon, & S. R. F. Price, "Crete, Greek and Roman," *OCD*³, 408–9 and F. W. Bush, "Crete," *ISBE*, 1:813–15.

A-155. Lucian, *Navigium (The Ship or the Wishes)* 5; I have altered the translation of K. Kilburn (*Lucian* [LCL 6; Cambridge, Mass.: Harvard University Press, 1968], 435–36) slightly by changing cubits (which I reckoned as 18 inches) to feet.

A-156. See N. Hirschfeld, "The Ship of Saint Paul: Historical Background (Part I)," *BA* 53.1 (March, 1990): 27–28. See also M. Fitzgerald, "The Ship of Saint Paul: Comparative Archaeology," *BA* 53.1 (March, 1990): 31–39.

A-157. Fitzgerald, "Ship," 36; idem, "The Ship," in *The Harbours of Caesarea Maritima: Results of the Caesarea Ancient Excavation Project, 1980–1985*, ed J. P. Oleson (BAR International Series 491, 594; Center for Maritime Studies, University of Haifa, 3, 5; Oxford: Tempus Reparatum, 1989).

A-158. On Puteoli, see H. K. Lomas, "Puteoli," *OCD*³, 1280–81; S. T. Carroll, "Puteoli," *ABD*, 5:560–61; G. H. Allen and A. F. Harris, "Puteoli," *ISBE*, 3:1059–60; see Seneca, *Epistulae* 77.1–2.

A-159. Strabo, *Geog.* 5.4.6.

A-160. Josephus, *Ant.* 17.12.1 §§23–25; *J.W.* 2.7.1 §§101–105.

A-161. On Rome, see J. F. Hall, "Rome," *ABD*, 5:830–34; M. Reasoner, "Rome and Roman Christianity," *DPL*, 850–55; H. F. Vos, "Rome," *ISBE*, 4:228–36.

A-162. Tacitus, *Ann.* 15.44.

A-163. Brändle and Stegemann, "Die Christliche Gemeinde in Rom," 4.

A-164. Schürer, *HJP*², 3:1:73–75.

A-165. Philo, *Embassy* 23 §155–56.

A-166. Ibid., 3:1:95–98.

CREDITS FOR PHOTOS AND MAPS

Arnold, Clinton E. . . . . pp. 4, 373, 384, 390, 402, 407,
415(3), 416, 417(2), 418, 457

Bredow, Dennis . . . . pp. 291, 318, 371, 379, 387, 397, 405, 452, 484

Claycombe, Hugh . . . . pp. 31, 184–185, 240

Dunn, Cheryl (for Talbot Bible Lands) . . . . pp. 100, 142, 321, 343, 350,
365(2), 369, 420, 422(2)

Franz, Gordon . . . . pp. 40, 288, 335(2), 348, 373, 388, 474, 478, 488

Haradine, Jane (public domain photos) . . . . pp. 17, 125, 226, 308(3), 426, 465

Isachar, Hanan . . . . pp. 2–3, 20, 21, 49, 64, 107, 193

King, Jay . . . . pp. 158, 180, 287, 377, 437

Kohlenberger, John R. III . . . . pp. 13, 21, 28, 39, 42, 63, 107, 115, 191, 226,
232, 251, 267, 278, 284, 289, 290, 296, 298,
300, 302, 316, 317, 330, 334, 340, 347, 353,
354, 364, 366, 367, 379, 382, 394, 401, 403(2),
404, 413, 419, 421, 428, 451, 471, 472

Konstas, Ioannis . . . . pp. 372, 383, 392, 399, 423, 473

McRay, John . . . . pp. 297, 369, 381, 382, 395, 427, 480

Radovan, Zev . . . . pp. 16, 18, 24, 26, 27, 29, 32, 42, 50, 54, 65, 66, 68, 69,
79, 98, 111, 116, 120, 122, 125, 127, 128, 134, 165,
170, 172, 173(2), 174, 177, 178, 181, 187, 190, 230,
239(2), 247, 250, 254, 257, 261, 264, 270, 274, 283,
287, 303, 306, 307, 322, 325, 337, 349, 356, 357, 371,
372, 384, 389, 398(2), 430, 435, 448, 450, 461, 468, 470, 473

Rigsby, Richard . . . . pp. 428, 472

Ritmeyer, Leen . . . . pp. 29, 55, 93, 144, 164, 223, 241, 243, 326, 436

Tabernacle . . . . pp. 7, 10, 272

University of Michigan . . . . pp. 220, 362, 411

Wilson, Mark . . . . pp. 267, 298, 338, 342, 344, 345, 469

Zondervan Image Archive (Neal Bierling) . . . . . . pp. 4, 8, 15, 22, 30, 43(2), 47, 54,
61, 71(2), 80, 93, 104, 109(2), 122, 123(2), 135,
143, 151, 156, 163, 169, 175, 182, 186, 192, 193, 218–219,
224, 227, 228, 229, 242, 253, 260(2), 269, 271, 279(2), 283, 285,
292, 293, 296, 298, 301, 304(3), 307, 309, 310(2), 313(2), 315,
321, 331, 336(2), 340(2), 349, 353, 356, 361, 370, 374(2), 376(2),
380, 384(2), 385, 386, 390, 396(3), 400, 425, 429, 431, 438,
443, 446, 449, 458, 459, 469, 480, 483(4), 486(2)